C48

D0154365

# THE COLLECTED WORKS OF JEREMY BENTHAM

*General Editor*

J. R. Dinwiddy

# CONSTITUTIONAL LAW

Jeremy Bentham's massive, unfinished *Constitutional Code* (1822–32) is the major work of his last years and contains the most important statement of the theory of constitutional democracy which emerges after his well-known 'conversion' to political radicalism in 1809–10. Bentham develops here in a final form the theory and institutions of an ideal representative democracy addressed to 'all nations and all governments professing liberal opinions'. In the course of drafting the *Code* he was also stimulated by serious prospects of seeing it adopted in Portugal, Greece, and several Latin American countries.

The first volume is based on the only volume Bentham himself published in 1830 and covers chapters I to IX on the territory of the state, electorate, public opinion, legislature, prime minister, and administration. The new edition supersedes the Bowring text of 1841, edited by Richard Doane, but incorporates collations of Bowring, the original 1830 version, and various extracts published by Bentham in his lifetime. The fully annotated text clarifies and develops the historical allusions and explains the numerous obscure passages which Bentham himself failed to correct. An especially detailed subject index provides the scholar with easy access to material which otherwise is difficult to find in this complex legal document. The editors' introduction explores the evolution of the *Code*, Bentham's efforts at having his work accepted by leaders of the new states of his day, and his vision of a complete code of laws, which he latterly called the *Pannomion*.

Frederick Rosen is Lecturer in Government, London School of Economics and Political Science, University of London.
James H. Burns is Professor of the History of Political Thought, University College London.

### The Collected Works of Jeremy Bentham

The new critical edition of the works and correspondence of Jeremy Bentham (1748–1832) is being prepared and published under the supervision of the Bentham Committee of University College London. In spite of his importance as jurist, philosopher, social scientist, and leader of the Utilitarian reformers, the only previous edition of his works was a poorly edited and incomplete one brought out within a decade or so of his death. Eight volumes of the new *Collected Works*, five of correspondence and three of writings on jurisprudence, have appeared since 1968, published by the Athlone Press. Further volumes in the series are to be published by Oxford University Press. The over-all plan and principles of the edition are set out in the General Preface to *The Correspondence of Jeremy Bentham* vol. I, which was the first volume of the *Collected Works* to be published.

# CONSTITUTIONAL CODE

## VOL. I

edited by
**F. ROSEN**
and
**J. H. BURNS**

CLARENDON PRESS · OXFORD

K
3240.4
B36
1938

EE

Oxford University Press, Walton Street, Oxford OX2 6DP
London New York Toronto
Delhi Bombay Calcutta Madras Karachi
Kuala Lumpur Singapore Hong Kong Tokyo
Nairobi Dar es Salaam Cape Town
Melbourne Auckland
and associated companies in
Beirut Berlin Ibadan Mexico City Nicosia

Oxford is a trade mark of Oxford University Press

Published in the United States
by Oxford University Press, New York

© Oxford University Press, 1983

Reprinted in 1984

All rights reserved. No part of this publication may be
reproduced, stored in a retrieval system, or transmitted,
in any form or by any means, electronic, mechanical,
photocopying, recording, or otherwise, without the prior
permission of Oxford University Press

British Library Cataloguing in Publication Data
Bentham, Jeremy
Constitutional code. —(The Collected works
of Jeremy Bentham)
Vol. 1
1. Democracy
I. Title    II. Rosen, F.    III. Burns, J. H.
IV. Series
321.8'01    JC423
ISBN 0-19-822608-X

Library of Congress Cataloging in Publication Data
Bentham, Jeremy, 1748–1832.
Constitutional code.
"New edition supersedes the Bowring text of 1841,
edited by Richard Doane, but incorporates collations
of Bowring, the original 1830 version, and various
extracts published by Bentham in his lifetime"—
No more published.
Includes indexes.
1. Constitutional law.   I. Rosen, F.   II. Burns, J. H.
(James Henderson)   III. Title.   IV. Series: Bentham,
Jeremy, 1748–1832.   Works.   1983.
K3240.4.B46   1983        342'.001       82-18793
ISBN 0-19-822608-X      342.201

Typeset by Joshua Associates, Oxford
Printed in Great Britain
at the University Press, Oxford
by David Stanford
Printer to the University

3 - 5 - 85

# ACKNOWLEDGEMENTS

The thanks of the Bentham Committee are due to the following bodies for financial assistance towards the cost of editorial work on this volume: The British Academy, The Social Science Research Council, University College London, and University of London Central Research Fund. The Committee is also indebted to the Twenty-Seven Foundation and the Isobel Thornley Bequest, which have supplied grants to assist the publication of the volume. The Committee also wishes to thank the following for access to books and manuscripts, permission to quote from manuscripts and other assistance: The Librarian of University College London and his staff; the Trustees of the British Library; the Librarian of the British Library of Political and Economic Science; Director, Bibliothèque Publique et Universitaire, Geneva; Director, General State Archives, Athens; and Director, National Library, Athens.

Both the editors are indebted to a number of research assistants who worked on various parts of the *Constitutional Code* on a full or part time basis: Dr G. Feaver, Mr N. Pilling, Dr J. Micklewright, Dr M. Woodcock, Dr R. Morse, Dr W. McKercher, Dr Ellen Kennedy, Dr J. Cotton, Mr J. Annette, Dr M. Smith, and Dr S. Conway. Dr Morse was especially helpful in the early work on the collations, and Dr Smith provided invaluable assistance in the final preparation of the introduction, notes, collations, and indices. Dr Conway helped with the proofs and prepared the name index. The staff of the Bentham Project over the years have been unfailingly helpful and special thanks are due to Miss Claire Gobbi. The General Editor, Dr J. R. Dinwiddy, has provided useful criticism of the introduction and notes for which we are especially grateful. Dr L. J. Hume has generously placed at our disposal his notes and writings on the *Constitutional Code*, and Dr Pedro Schwartz has been of assistance in providing information about Bentham's activities in Spain and Latin America. A number of colleagues have assisted the editors in elucidating difficult and obscure references in the text: Dr I. S. Asquith, Dr A. Goldworth, Mr J. R. Ketchum, Mrs L. Droulia, and Dr V. Wright.

The editors gratefully acknowledge the typing assistance of Mrs Elsie Banham who typed most of the collations and subject index, Mrs E. M. Simpson, and Mrs Paula da Gama Pinto who typed the introduction.
F.R.
J.H.B.

# CONTENTS

ABBREVIATIONS                                                          x

EDITORIAL INTRODUCTION                                                xi

PREFACE                                                                3

I   TERRITORY OF THIS STATE, NAME, SITUATION,
    BOUNDARIES, DIVISIONS                                            11

II  ENDS AND MEANS                                                   18

III SOVEREIGNTY, IN WHOM                                             25

IV  AUTHORITIES                                                      26

V   CONSTITUTIVE AUTHORITY                                           29
    1. Constitutive what——in whom                                   29
    2. Powers                                                        29
    3. Powers exercised, how                                        32
    4. Public Opinion Tribunal:——Composition                       35
    5. Public Opinion Tribunal:——Functions                         36
    6. Securities against Legislative, and Judiciary                39

VI  LEGISLATURE                                                      41
    1. Powers:——and Duties                                          41
    2. Responsibility                                                45
    3. Powers as to Sublegislatures                                 47
    4. Seats and Districts                                          48
    5. Electors who                                                 48
    6. Eligible who                                                 48
    7. Election Offices                                             48
    8. Election Apparatus                                           48
    9. Recommendation of proposed Members——how promulgated         48
    10. Voters' Titles, how preestablished                          48
    11. Election, how                                               48
    12. Election Districts and Voting Districts, how marked out     48
    13. Vote-making Habitations, how defined                        48
    14. Term of Service                                             48
    15. Vacancies, how supplied                                     48
    16. Security of the Assembly against Disturbance by Members     48
    17. Indisposition of Presidents, how obviated                   48
    18. Attendance                                                  48
    19. Remuneration                                                49
    20. Attendance and Remuneration——how connected                 49

# CONTENTS

21. Sittings public and secret     56
22. Term of Service——Continuation     57
23. Self-suppletive function     59
24. Continuation Committee     67
25. Relocable who     72
26. Wrongful exclusion obviated     92
27. Legislation Enquiry Judicatory     93
28. Legislation Penal Judicatory     111
29. Members' Motions     114
30. Dislocable how     117
31. Securities for appropriate aptitude     117

VII   LEGISLATOR'S INAUGURAL DECLARATION     133
1. Authentication, how     133
2.    I. Ends aimed at     136
3.    II. Appetites guarded against     137
4.    III. Economy and Uncorruption promised     138
5.    IV. Notoriety of Law to all promised     140
6.    V. Justice accessible to all promised     141
7.    VI. Impartiality in Elections promised     142
8.   VII. In International Dealings, Justice and Beneficence promised     142
9. VIII. Impartiality in the general exercise of power promised     144
10.    IX. Assiduity promised     144
11.    X. Subordination to the Constitutive Authority promised     145
12.    XI. Encroachment on subordinate Authorities abjured     145
13.   XII. Insincerity abjured     145
14. XIII. Arrogance abjured     146

VIII   PRIME MINISTER     147
1. Fields of Service     147
2. Functions     149
3. Relation to the Legislature     152
4. Self-suppletive function     154
5. Term of Service     156
6. Remuneration     156
7. Locable who     157
8. Located how     157
9. Dislocable how     159
10. Registration System     159
11. Publication System     162
12. Securities for appropriate aptitude     168

IX   MINISTERS COLLECTIVELY     170
1. Ends in view     170
2. Ministers and Subdepartments     171
3. Number in an Office     174
4. Functions in all     186
5. Subordination-grades     202
6. Self-suppletive function     215

# CONTENTS

| | |
|---|---|
| 7. Statistic function | 218 |
| Bis-section the First. All Books together | 218 |
| Bis-section the Second. Original Outset Books | 226 |
| Bis-section the Third. Journal Books | 239 |
| Bis-section the Fourth. Loss Books | 250 |
| Bis-section the Fifth. Subsidiary Books | 262 |
| Bis-section the Sixth. Abbreviations | 263 |
| 8. Requisitive function | 268 |
| 9. Inspective function | 276 |
| 10. Officially informative function | 283 |
| 11. Information-elicitative function | 290 |
| 12. Melioration-suggestive function | 293 |
| 13. Term of service | 295 |
| 14. Attendance | 296 |
| 15. Remuneration | 297 |
| 16. Locable who | 310 |
| Supplement to § 16. Locable who | 329 |
| 17. Located how | 337 |
| Supplement to § 17. Located how | 346 |
| Concluding Instruction to the Public Opinion Tribunal | 362 |
| 18. Dislocable how | 364 |
| 19. Subordinates | 366 |
| 20. Insubordination obviated | 383 |
| 21. Oppression obviated | 389 |
| 22. Extortion obviated | 410 |
| 23. Peculation obviated | 412 |
| 24. Legislation-regarding functions | 417 |
| 25. Securities for appropriate aptitude | 419 |
| 26. Architectural arrangements | 438 |

## COLLATIONS

| | |
|---|---|
| A. 1830 Collation | 461 |
| B. Bowring Collation | 480 |
| C. Bentham on Humphreys' Code Collations | 517 |
| D. Official Aptitude Maximized, Expense Minimized Collations | 520 |

| | |
|---|---|
| INDEX OF SUBJECTS | 529 |
| INDEX OF NAMES | 609 |

# ABBREVIATIONS

Apart from standard abbreviations the following should be noted:

| | |
|---|---|
| Bowring | *The Works of Jeremy Bentham*, published under the superintendence of . . . John Bowring, 11 vols., Edinburgh, 1838–43. |
| 1830 | *Constitutional Code; for the use of All Nations and All Governments professing Liberal Opinions*, Vol. i, London, 1830. |
| P.C.D. | *Parliamentary Candidate's proposed Declaration of Principles: or say, A Test proposed for Parliamentary Candidates*, London, 1831. |
| WR | 'Bentham on Humphreys' Property Code', *Westminster Review*, vi (1826), 446–507. |
| 1827 pamphlet | *Article Eight of the Westminster Review No. XII. for October 1826, on Mr. Humphreys' Observations on the English Law of Real Property, with the Outline of a Code, etc. By Jeremy Bentham, Esq.*, London, 1827. |
| 1826 *Extract* | *Extract from the Proposed Constitutional Code, Entitled Official Aptitude Maximized, Expense Minimized*, London, 1826. |
| 1830 *Off. Apt. Max.* | *Official Aptitude Maximized; Expense Minized, as shewn in the several papers comprised in this volume*, London, 1830. |
| UC | Bentham papers in the Library of University College London (Roman numerals refer to boxes, Arabic to leaves). |
| BL Add. MS | British Library Additional Manuscript |
| *CW* | *The Collected Works of Jeremy Bentham*, London, 1968– |
| Colls | Journal of John Flowerdew Colls, 1821–5, BL Add. MS 33,563. |
| *Iberian* | *The Iberian Correspondence of Jeremy Bentham*, ed. Pedro Schwartz, 2 vols., London–Madrid, 1979. |

All references to books and articles in this list are to works written by Bentham.

# EDITORIAL INTRODUCTION

Jeremy Bentham's *Constitutional Code* represents the culmination of his long career as an advocate of reform and codification. Begun in 1822 when Bentham was already 74 years old and unfinished at the time of his death in 1832, it formed the major part of the last of several attempts to realize his vision of a complete code of laws which in his later years he called the *Pannomion*. The present work corresponds to the only volume of the *Code* actually published by Bentham in 1830.[1] It constitutes little more than a quarter of the massive ninth volume of the *Works of Jeremy Bentham*, edited by John Bowring, which bears the title 'The Constitutional Code'.[2] Although the Bowring volume was skilfully edited by Bentham's former secretary, Richard Doane, it failed to follow Bentham's own plan of a three-volume work, and Doane's lengthy 'Book I', constructed from a variety of manuscripts, obscured the structure of Bentham's own conception.[3] The present work follows Bentham's plan (see Table 1) and is the first of a three-volume edition of the *Constitutional Code*. It is intended that manuscripts and published writings related to the *Code*, which in extent surpass the text of the *Code* itself, should appear in a series of supplementary volumes.

## HISTORY OF THE WORK

Bentham was most probably prompted to start the *Constitutional Code* by the invitation he received from the Portuguese Cortes in April 1822 in response to his offer of November 1821 to draft penal, civil, and constitutional codes.[4] Bentham admitted in his offer for Portugal that the codes had not yet been written. To write them he required the prior acceptance of his offer. 'At the age of three-and-

[1] *Constitutional Code; for the use of All Nations and All Governments professing Liberal Opinions. By Jeremy Bentham*, vol. i, London, 1830.

[2] *The Works of Jeremy Bentham*, published under the superintendence of . . . John Bowring, 11 vols., Edinburgh, 1838-43. Sir John Bowring (1792-1872), first editor of the *Westminster Review*, minor diplomat, and Bentham's literary executor.

[3] For 'Book I' see Bowring, ix. 1-145. Doane discusses this addition in ibid. ix, p. iv.

[4] Bentham to the Portuguese Cortes, 7 Nov. 1821; Felgueiras to Bentham, 3 Dec. 1821, ibid. iv. 575-6. See also Doane's comment in ibid. ix, p. iii.

xi

seventy, the current of blood runs slow: something is wanting, something from without to quicken it.'[1] Bentham had been stimulated by political events in Spain and Portugal at this time and the emergence of new states in Latin America. 'You never knew Bentham in better health, or more animated, than he is now', wrote James Mill to Étienne Dumont in June 1821.[2] Mill was referring to Bentham's extensive correspondence with political leaders in Spain and Portugal and his attempts to secure the engagement of his services as legislator. Mill was somewhat sceptical of Bentham's efforts and reported a remark of John Herbert Koe, Bentham's former secretary and friend, that 'an invitation, from any government, to make a code, if it should ever come, would put an end to all thought of a code forever—that although he thinks an invitation would give him courage, it would do the reverse; and that he would immediately shrink from the task'.[3] Mill and Koe were mistaken. On the basis of the acceptance of his offer by the Portuguese Cortes, Bentham began, though he did not complete, the major work of his last years.

The offer was the most promising Bentham had received during his involvement with the liberal regimes in Spain and Portugal.[4] But even at this period of considerable optimism, Bentham found little actual success as a legislator. Although he was well known in intellectual circles, largely through the wide circulation of Dumont's versions of his works and his extensive correspondence, the construction of a complete legal code and its actual adoption by a state were, both intellectually and politically, much more difficult. Perhaps the recognition of this difficulty led Bentham to write in 1822 his *Codification Proposal* addressed like the *Constitutional Code* not merely to Spain or Portugal but to 'All Nations Professing Liberal Opinions'.[5] *Codification Proposal* contained a series of letters or testimonials from people in countries such as England, Switzerland, Spain, Portugal, Italy, France, the United States, and South America, and followed

---

[1] Bentham to the Portuguese Cortes, 7 Nov. 1821, ibid. iv. 576.

[2] Mill to Dumont, 8 June 1821, Dumont MSS, Bibliothèque Publique et Universitaire, Geneva, MS 76, fo. 21, published in *The Iberian Correspondence of Jeremy Bentham*, ed. P. Schwartz, 2 vols., London–Madrid, 1979, i. 539. James Mill (1773-1836), utilitarian philosopher and associate of Bentham since 1808; Pierre Étienne Louis Dumont (1759-1829) Swiss political writer and editor of several of Bentham's works.

[3] Ibid., fo. 22. John Herbert Koe (1783-1860), Q.C. 1842, county court judge 1847-60.

[4] See the correspondence in Bowring, iv. 570-6.

[5] *Codification Proposal addressed . . . to All Nations Professing Liberal Opinions*, London, 1822 (Bowring, iv. 535-94). Supplements to *Codification Proposal* were added in 1827 and 1830.

in form the earlier *Papers relative to Codification and Public Instruction.*[1] These testimonials did not give a parochial cast to the proposal. Instead, they were used to justify Bentham's claim to legislate for any state which would accept his offer.[2] Once Bentham had begun his *Constitutional Code*, disappointment with Spain, Portugal, and later with Greece, would not bring his efforts to a halt. In looking beyond the horizons of particular states to all states based on liberal principles, Bentham's reference to the *Code* as a 'utopian' work can be most clearly understood.[3]

## 1822 MANUSCRIPTS

The first manuscripts consistently headed 'Constitutional Code' were written in April 1822 and a vast quantity of material was accumulated by the end of the summer. These first writings took the form of lengthy essays on a number of themes such as 'Securities', 'First Principles', 'Rule—Good and Bad', 'Factitious Dignity', 'Supreme Operative', 'Corruption', and 'Public Opinion Tribunal'.[4] Although the writing began in earnest in April, it became especially intensive in July and August. Bentham also drew on unpublished material from earlier manuscripts written for other works. These included manuscripts headed 'Emancipation Spanish' and 'Rid Yourselves of Ultramaria' which were written originally for Spain, the former between 1818 and 1820 and the latter between 1820 and 1822; 'First Lines' written in April–June 1821; and manuscripts omitted from the published *Codification Proposal*.[5] But most of the manuscripts were written specially for the *Code*. Bentham eventually discarded all of

---

[1] London, 1817 (Bowring, iv. 451–533).

[2] In April–June 1821, Bentham also wrote a lengthy manuscript entitled 'First Lines of a Proposed Code of Law for every nation compleat and rationalized'. See UC xxxvii. 7 (3 Apr. 1821).

[3] See Bowring, v. 278. This passage appears in the 'Introductory View' to Bentham's 1826 *Extract* from the *Constitutional Code*. See p. xxxix below.

[4] On 'Securities' see UC xxxviii, xliv, cviii, cxiii, cxiv, clx; on 'First Principles' see UC xxxvi, xxxviii, clviii; on 'Rule—Good and Bad' see UC xxxvi, xxxviii, cvi, cxiii, clx and esp. xxxiv. 12 (30 July 1822); on 'Factitious Dignity' see UC xxxviii, clx, clxii; on 'Supreme Operative' see UC xxxvi, xxxvii, xxxviii, lxxxiv and esp. xxxiv. 15 (16 Aug. 1822); on 'Corruption' see UC xxxviii, cvi, clxiv, clxvii, clxxii and esp. xxxiv. 14 (7 Aug. 1822); on 'Public Opinion Tribunal' see UC xxxviii, clx. See generally UC xxxiv. 12 (30 July 1822).

[5] For MSS headed 'Emancipation Spanish' and 'Rid Yourselves of Ultramaria', see UC clxii, clxiv, clxxii; MSS on 'First Lines' are in UC xxxvi, xxxvii; for examples of MSS from *Codification Proposal* later used in the *Constitutional Code* see UC lxxxiv.

this material both from the volume published in 1830 and from the 1830 three-volume plan. Nevertheless, in the Preface to the 1830 volume, he referred to an 'introductory dissertation' he had planned to append to this first volume of the *Code* concerned with 'the various forms of which the supreme authority in a state is susceptible'.[1] He noted that the material for such a dissertation on the different forms of government was already in existence and had been so for a long time, but that he had not arranged it properly. Bentham also stated that the want of such an arrangement was a factor responsible for the delay in the appearance of the 1830 volume, but, as will be shown, this does not appear to have been the case. Doane, however, attempted to fulfil Bentham's hopes in creating the 'Book I' of the Bowring edition based largely on the 1822 manuscripts.

Among the manuscripts on which Doane drew was a lengthy essay, or series of essays, entitled 'Supreme Operative' which explored the weakness and inaptitude of monarchy and aristocracy and the virtues of representative democracy. This material seems closest to what Bentham had in mind and a small part of it was used by Doane in his 'Book I'.[2] A portion of this manuscript was written directly for the *Code* between the end of June and mid-July 1822; another substantial portion was taken from manuscripts originally written for *Codification Proposal* between December 1821 and February 1822.[3] These manuscripts, represented by 372 marginal entries, were then arranged on 6 August 1822 into a plan of 19 'Sub-Heads'.[4] Bentham never returned to this material and only the Doane extract has ever appeared in print.

The material on the 'Supreme Operative' formed, as we have noted, only one of the general essays developed at this time for the *Code*. Let us examine several other examples. One heading for a lengthy essay was 'Corruptive Influence' or 'Corruption'. On 5 and 7 August 1822 Bentham arranged a body of manuscripts partly written for the *Code* in 1822 and partly taken from manuscripts headed 'Emancipation Spanish' and 'Rid Yourselves of Ultramaria' written in June-August 1820 and March 1821.[5] A small portion of this material also appeared in the Doane 'Book I'.[6] Another series of manuscripts was

---

[1] Cf. p. 3, below.          [2] Bowring, ix. 127-45.

[3] For 'Supreme Operative' MSS written specially for the *Code*, see UC xxxviii. 123-39 (1-16 July 1822), xxxvi. 102-43, 156-63 (June, July 1822), xxxvii. 71-6 (4 July 1822), and xxxvi. 101-76 (June, July 1822); for MSS excluded from *Codification Proposal*, see UC xxxviii. 13-20, 108-22 (Aug., Dec. 1821, Jan., Feb. 1822), lxxxiv. 16-19, 19-22, 28-35, 74-6, 78-83, 93, 96, 98-105, 107-8, 109-10, 114-15, 117-24, 144-51, 153-8, 168-77 (Dec. 1821, Jan., Feb. 1822).

[4] UC xxxiv. 15.      [5] UC xxxiv. 14.      [6] Bowring, ix. 64-76.

written on the subject of 'Securities'. This material seems to have evolved from writings on parliamentary reform and particularly on the theme of 'economy in office'. Some of the manuscripts were written in 1818 and headed 'Official Economy'.[1] In April, May, and June 1822, Bentham wrote a long manuscript under the heading of 'Economy as to Office'.[2] This carefully-arranged work of 159 sheets was concerned with 'securities' and especially with 'securities for moral aptitude', an important theme of the *Constitutional Code*. In a letter to Dumont, Bentham referred to it as 'a forerunner and in part of my *Constitutional Code*'.[3] Some portions of this manuscript were eventually headed 'Constitutional Code' but the manuscript was never included in the *Code*.[4]

By early August Bentham had written and organized a considerable body of *Code* material. Nevertheless, he continued through the month of August to draft further essays. As a first chapter to the *Code*, he wrote and collected some manuscripts entitled 'First Principles'.[5] But by mid-August this effort seems to have been abandoned. He also wrote during August a series of essays on 'Rule— Good and Bad' which dealt with forms of misrule such as corruption, delusion, and the use of fictions.[6] But after August 1822 Bentham seemed to turn away from these lengthy, general, and introductory essays.

During the autumn of 1822 Bentham became involved with Hassuna D'Ghies, the young ambassador from Tripoli, who became for a period Bentham's 'disciple and adopted son'.[7] D'Ghies seems to have visited Bentham first in July 1822 and was a frequent visitor until early 1823.[8] To his brother, Samuel, Bentham happily wrote that 'you would be as jealous as a Dragon if you knew half the esteem and affection I have for this young man'.[9] D'Ghies was only 31

---

[1] See, for example, UC clx. 6-27 (Nov. 1818).

[2] UC cxiii. 1-159.

[3] Bentham to Dumont, 26 May 1822, Dumont MSS, MS 33/v, fo. 25.

[4] See, for example, UC clx. 56, 58 (28, 30 Apr. 1822), 76 (21 May 1822).

[5] Cf. p. xiii n. 4 above.                                               [6] Ibid.

[7] Bentham to D'Argenson, 1 Jan. 1823, BL Add. MS 33,545, fos. 609-14. See also L. J. Hume, 'Preparations for Civil War in Tripoli in the 1820s: Ali Karamanli, Hassuna D'Ghies and Jeremy Bentham', *Journal of African History*, xxi (1980), 311-22.

[8] A journal kept between 1821 and 1825 by John Colls, Bentham's secretary, records numerous visits from a variety of people including D'Ghies, important correspondence and the publication of works. See BL Add. MS 33,563, fos. 63-136. For the visits by D'Ghies, see ibid. fos. 106-17.

[9] Bentham to Samuel Bentham, 16 Jan. 1823, BL Add. MS 33,545, fo. 615. Sir Samuel Bentham (1757-1831), naval architect and engineer, Inspector General of Naval Works, 1796-1807, Civil Architect and Engineer to the Navy Board, 1808-12.

years old when he met Bentham. His father was Secretary of State for Foreign Affairs in Tripoli. D'Ghies had spent the previous eight years travelling in Europe and was obviously in Bentham's eyes both a charming and cultivated young man. Bentham could see in his new acquaintance a chance to influence the constitutional development of the Barbary states and D'Ghies seems to have enlisted his support for this purpose. The major writing that Bentham produced was the work, 'Securities against Misrule', where he attempted to develop and adapt his conception of 'securities for appropriate aptitude' to a state ruled by a Muhammadan prince.[1] Bentham went so far as to draft a letter to his friend John Quincy Adams (1767-1848), the future President of the United States, to suggest on the authority of D'Ghies that Tripoli would be ripe for revolution and that such a revolution, if supported by the United States, would rid it of the annoyance of the Barbary powers.[2] However, none of the projects with D'Ghies came to fruition and D'Ghies left London in 1823. Although Bentham's involvement with D'Ghies might be seen as a distraction from his work on the *Code*, the major manuscript, 'Securities against Misrule', displayed a systematic treatment of 'securities' within an institutional context which Bentham had not developed previously and which would be a feature (though in a different form) of the *Constitutional Code*.[3] Furthermore, Bentham's relationship with D'Ghies provided another example of the way he believed that his own activities as an author of constitutions could be married to revolutionary politics. Finally, through D'Ghies, Bentham established one more link with the Mediterranean where he would find the greatest stimulus for the development of the *Code*.


## CONSTITUTIONAL CODE FOR GREECE

Although Bentham had been aware of the Greek war of independence since 1821, his involvement in Greek affairs began in the spring of 1823. Edward Blaquière (1779-c.1832), naval officer, ardent liberal, disciple of Bentham since 1813 and an assistant in his codification ventures in Spain and Portugal, brought the Greek agent, Andreas

---

[1] The MSS are in UC xxiv. Bentham did not publish the work but part of it was printed in the Bowring edition. See Bowring, viii. 555-600.

[2] Bentham to Quincy Adams (draft), 10-13 Jan. 1823, UC xxiv. 378-86. For Bentham's relationship with John Quincy Adams, see Bentham to Quincy Adams, 19 June 1826, Bowring, x. 554-5, and Bentham to Jackson, June 1830, Nicholas P. Trist MSS, Library of Congress, Washington D.C., printed in Bowring, xi. 39-40, incorrectly dated 26 Apr. 1830.

[3] See esp. Bowring, viii. 583-92.

Louriottis, to London to raise money for the war.[1] Through Blaquière and Bowring, who served as Secretary of the London Greek Committee, Louriottis soon visited Bentham and eventually Bentham made contact with the leading figures of the revolution.[2] On 9 February 1823 Bentham began to draft an essay which commented on particular articles of the Greek Constitution of 1822.[3] He completed his 'Observations' in time for Blaquière's departure for Greece in early March. During this period his hopes for playing a role in the constitutional development of Greece were high, but he was already aware that he faced formidable obstacles. The absence of Greek editions of his writings was a constant problem. Although at this stage he believed that translations of his works might be made in Greece, he was soon to learn that this was not possible.[4] He also tried unsuccessfully to enlist the help of Dr Samuel Parr (1747-1825), 'the Whig Dr Johnson', with whom he had maintained friendly contact over the years, in obtaining a Greek translation of the 'Observations'.[5] A second obstacle Bentham faced was his apprehension that works based on republican principles, though highly regarded by the Greeks themselves, could not be seen to be favourably received, because the Greeks needed to enlist the support of the European powers against the Turks. For this reason, Bentham asked Blaquière to have the material translated and published at his own expense so that the work would not appear as the responsibility of the constituted authorities.[6]

Bentham's 'Observations' was well-received in Greece where it was presented to the Legislative Council by Blaquière and Louriottis. Bentham received warm testimonials from Alexander Mavrocordato, then Secretary of the Provisional Government and eventually the

[1] William St. Clair, *That Greece Might Still Be Free*, London, 1972, p. 207. On Blaquière, see Bowring, x. 474-5 and C. Gobbi, 'Edward Blaquière: agente del liberalismo', *Cuadernos Hispano-americanos*, 350 (1979), 306-25.

[2] Colls's journal, fo. 119, records visits from Louriottis on 19 Feb. and Blaquière, for dinner, on 20 Feb. 1823.

[3] Bentham based his 'Observations' on the edition of the Greek constitution appearing in C. D. Raffenel, *Histoire des événements de la Grèce*, Paris, 1822. The manuscript, which Blaquière took to Greece on 3 Mar., was written between 26 Feb. and 2 Mar. See UC cvi. 327-83; earlier material may be found at UC xxi. 180-92, 209. See also UC xxi. 271-89.

[4] Bentham seems to suggest to Dr Samuel Parr that his published works were already being translated in Greece by his 'disciples'. See Bentham to Parr, 17 Feb. 1823, Bowring, x. 535, printed in *The Works of Samuel Parr*, ed. J. Johnstone, 8 vols., London, 1828, viii. 6-10.

[5] Ibid.; and Parr to Bentham, 20 Feb. 1823, Bowring x. 536-7.

[6] Bentham to Blaquière, 2 Mar. 1823, UC xii. 103: 'It bears so strongly on Monarchies in general and in particular, that it would scarcely be consistent with prudence on their part to appear to regard it with a favorable eye.'

main leader of the Greek government, and from the Legislative Council.[1] From the Legislative Council came the announcement that a person 'skilled in the English language' had been assigned to translate his 'Observations' into Greek, a proposal which, though contrary to Bentham's instruction to Blaquière, was most welcome.[2] However, there is no evidence that such a translation was completed.

In the meantime Bentham proceeded to draft the *Constitutional Code*. 'These were days of boundless happiness to Bentham' wrote Bowring referring to the events of 1823, 'when, from every side, testimonials of respect and affection were flowing towards him, and when all events seemed concurring in advancing the great interest to which he was devoted.'[3] Bentham's *Code* writings in early 1823 still reflected the general character of the essays of 1822. In April and May Bentham drafted yet another introductory chapter entitled 'Ruling Principles' which would have no place in the final version of the *Code*.[4] Furthermore, he was also drafting the 'rationale' for some of the early chapters on subjects such as sovereignty and legislative authority. This material, also in the form of lengthy essays, was similarly excluded from the *Code* but some was utilized by Doane for his 'Book I'.[5] At this stage Bentham conceived of the *Code* as consisting of three parts: the 'enactive' (the enacted provisions), the 'expositive' (explaining terms, etc.), and the 'ratiocinative' (giving reasons). He later added two more, the 'exemplificational' (providing examples) and the 'instructional' (giving instructions to the legislator). Bentham drafted each part of the *Code* separately and had not yet decided to combine the different parts within the various chapters and sections.

In the summer and autumn of 1823, the nature of Bentham's writing changed considerably. The *Code* started to take the form which Bentham would adopt in the published version. He began to discard the earlier 1822 material from the text. At the same time he published his brief work, *Leading Principles of a Constitutional Code For Any State*, first in *The Pamphleteer* and then as a separate work.[6]

---

[1] Mavrocordato to Bentham, 22 June/4 July 1823, UC xii. 127, printed in Bowring, iv. 580-1. Prince Alexander Mavrocordato (1791-1865), president of the first Greek National Assembly, 1822; leader of the 'Anglophile' party, and Prime Minister 1831, 1841, 1844, 1854-5.

[2] Orlandos and Scandalides to Bentham, 12 May 1823, Bowring, iv. 581.

[3] Ibid. x. 539.          [4] See UC xxxiv. 19-24 and xxxvi. 216-74.

[5] See, for example, UC xxxvii; see also Bowring, ix. 95-127.

[6] *The Pamphleteer*, xxii (1823), 475-86 (Bowring, ii. 267-74). Colls's journal indicates that Bentham received 250 copies of *Leading Principles* on 23 Aug. In the next few days (as well as over succeeding months), he distributed a number of copies. For example, fifty copies were sent to Bowring of which six were sent on to Greece.

Although *Leading Principles* was written as an introductory work, it bore the marks of Bentham's considerable efforts at compressing and consolidating his text. Bentham defined the principal ends sought and the means for achieving them briefly and succinctly. *Leading Principles* was never incorporated into the published *Code*, but the even more limited treatments of ends and means developed in the latter reflect this earlier discussion.[1]

Bentham attempted to complete a draft of the *Code* to accompany Leicester Stanhope on his journey to Greece as one of the representatives (with Lord Byron) of the London Greek Committee. Stanhope, later fifth Earl of Harrington (1784-1862), had had a distinguished career in India serving as private secretary to the Marquis of Hastings and then became an ardent Philhellene and disciple of Bentham.[2] Stanhope and Blaquière in Greece and Bowring in London served Bentham well in his attempts to become the legislator of Greece. Stanhope apparently began visiting Bentham in May 1823, several months after the formation of the London Greek Committee.[3] He was one of the first to receive a copy of *Leading Principles* and on 23 September he received a number of Bentham's books and pamphlets for transport to Greece.[4] On 26 September Colls's journal recorded the delivery to Stanhope of part of the *Code*:[5]

R.D. to Col. Stanhope with the Text of Chapters 1.2.3.4.5.6.8.9. & s.2 of ch. 10 of Constitutional Code with the Marginals of these on four column paper as also of Chapters 11, 12, 13 & Ch. [14?] on the Quasi Jury—another copy of the Marginals of the five first chapters on a sheet of Bank post columnwise, occupying half the sheet—Col. Stanhope requested to add to the title of Rad. Ref Bill—the following words—Adapted to the purpose of constituting the Election Code, being chapter (       ) for the accompanying Constitutional Code.

Stanhope then departed for Greece and two further instalments of the *Code* were sent to him by post. On 10 October the journal recorded:[6]

To Foreign Post with Chapters 10, 11, and 12 of Constitutional Code, for Col. Stanhope. . . .

[1] Cf. Chs. II and VII, pp. 18-19 and 136-7 below. There is only one reference to *Leading Principles* in the *Code* at Ch. IX. § 17. Art 53 and n., p. 352 and n. 2, below.
[2] Bentham to Say, 9 Sept. 1828, Bibliothèque National, Paris, partly printed in Bowring, xi. 2-3.
[3] Colls's journal, fo. 122, records a visit for dinner on 19 May.
[4] Ibid., fos. 125 and 126.
[5] Ibid., fo. 126, 'R.D.' stands for Richard Doane. The square brackets and question mark in the reference to Ch. 14 is in the original.
[6] Ibid., fo. 126.

And the entry for 14 October:[1]

To Foreign post, with S.5. *Term of service of Ch. VIII of the Prime Minister*—
to be substituted to the section sent on a former occasion; . . .

The parcel of books and manuscripts which Stanhope took to
Greece arrived safely with him. Stanhope unexpectedly found the
Greek government 'almost in a state of anarchy'.[2] Besides trying to
reconcile the various factions he planned to establish several printing
presses which would counter the spirit of monarchy and aristocracy
which he found widespread. On these presses, he hoped to publish
extracts from Bentham's works. Of the two parcels posted to Stanhope after his departure, the first, containing chapters X, XI, and
XII, was lost in the post and never reached Stanhope in Ancona. Bentham sent a second copy soon afterwards with William Parry, who
was leaving for Greece to serve under Lord Byron.[3]

Although a reconstruction of the text of this version of the *Code*
from Bentham's extant manuscripts is not possible, and the full draft
sent to Greece has not been recovered, it is possible to see the way
Bentham conceived of the *Code* at this time and its state of development in relation to Bentham's final plan. One general plan, UC xxxviii.
9–10, seems to have been drafted and revised over the 1823–4 period
when Bentham sent the *Code* to Greece, and it forms the basis of this
discussion. The plan itself is not dated, although three dates, 17 February, 30 March, and 3 April 1824 appear on material clearly added
to the original text. The original is in a copyist's hand (probably
Colls's) and the later additions are by Bentham himself with some
headings of later chapters on the judiciary added by Doane. From
this plan, it is possible to obtain, first, a sketch of what Bentham sent
to Greece in 1823; second, his conception of the *Code* in March
1824 in the table sent to Stanhope; and finally, revisions made after
that date which incorporated further developments.

The parcel which Bentham sent to Greece with Stanhope contained, as we have seen, the texts of chapters I–VI, VIII–IX, and section 2 of chapter X. Chapter VII was sent later in March 1824 and
on the general plan it is not yet broken down into sections, providing
evidence that it had not yet been fully drafted. Chapters I–IV are
similar to those in the final 1830 text except that the title of chapter

---

[1] Colls's journal, fo. 126.

[2] Stanhope to Bentham, 1 Dec. 1823, UC xii. 160.

[3] Colls's journal, fo. 127, records Colls taking the parcel with these chapters
to Bowring for transmission by Parry on 4 Nov. On the loss of the original parcel,
see Stanhope to Bentham, 1 Dec. 1823, UC xii. 160. William Parry (fl. 1824–5),
a major in Byron's brigade, assisted in preparing the defence of Missolonghi in
1824. He published *The Last Days of Lord Byron*, London, 1825, which contained criticisms of Stanhope and an absurd description of Bentham.

II, Object of this Constitution, was replaced by 1825 with the title it now bears, Ends and Means.[1] Chapter V, Constitutive Authority, was conceived at this time in eleven sections. This was reduced by 1825 to six sections mostly by consolidating a series of separate sections on the relationship between the electorate and the Legislature, Prime Minister, Ministers, the Justice Minister, other judicial functionaries and the Sublegislatures within the statement of the general powers of the Constitutive Authority in section 2.[2]

Chapter VI on the Legislature contained seventeen sections and was shorter than the 1830 version, because Bentham had not yet incorporated the sections concerned with the Election Code.[3] Furthermore, Bentham's conception of this chapter had not yet matured. For example, he originally devoted three separate sections to the subject of contracts between the Legislature and citizens, foreigners, and foreign governments respectively.[4] This subject was important to him because the 'omnicompetent' Legislature had the power to nullify contracts made by previous legislatures, and this power might be conceived to threaten security of property, another value on which Bentham placed great emphasis. In the end, Bentham dealt with the problem of government contracts briefly in a general section on 'Responsibility'.[5] Several other sections were eventually covered by the incorporation of the Election Code. One section, entitled, 'Number that gives validity' was eventually dropped from the *Code* in 1826.[6] As for the length of the legislative term, Bentham proposed two sections: providing either for a term of one year or for a two-year term with re-eligibility limited to service in the Continuation Committee. It is not clear if Bentham left open the possibility that the one-year term could be extended by re-election.[7] In the 1830 *Code*, Bentham did not fix the legislative term but proposed that it should be as brief as possible; he also proposed that no sitting deputy could be re-elected for a specified period.

A number of sections on the Legislature, which were later added to the *Code*, did not appear in this early version for Greece. The provision of substitutes or deputes (the self-suppletive function) was not at this stage extended to the Legislature.[8] Bentham did not yet introduce the Legislation Enquiry Judicatory which was linked to his

---

[1] UC xxxviii. 220 (3 Feb. 1825).                                        [2] Ibid.

[3] This became Ch. VI. §§ 4–17 in the 1830 version. On the Election Code, see pp. xxv–xxvi and p. 48, below.

[4] §§ 3–5.            [5] See Ch. VI. § 2. Arts. 3–11, pp. 45–7, below.

[6] UC xxxviii. 223 (10 July 1826).

[7] In Jan. 1825 he sent to Greece a revised version of this material. Bentham to Provisional Government of Greece, 28 Jan. 1825. Bowring, iv. 588.

[8] It was added early in 1826. See Ch. VI. § 25. Art. 53n, p. 90 n. a, below.

work on evidence and procedure; nor the section on 'Members' Motions' concerned with amendments to the *Pannomion*.[1] Both of these awaited further developments in his conception of the *Pannomion*. Finally, in 1823/4 Bentham referred to restrictions on the power of all officials as 'checks' and did not employ the phrase 'securities for appropriate aptitude' in this context until 1825/6.[2]

Chapter VIII on the Prime Minister also contained fewer sections than the final 1830 version. Bentham had not yet developed and extended the notion of 'fields of service' to the Prime Minister.[3] The section on the self-suppletive function was added during this period but does not seem part of the *Code* originally sent to Greece. Also omitted was a section dealing with the relationship between the Prime Minister and the Legislature which, in the final version, displayed Bentham's growing sympathy towards the institutions of the Presidency of the United States.[4] Finally, at this point Bentham did not envisage the two sections on the registration and publication systems dealing with the use of manifold writing and with the maximization of publicity in government.[5] All of these sections were added by 1825.

Chapter IX, Ministers Collectively, was to become one of the longest and most complex in the *Code*. The version sent to Greece covered much less ground than the finished version and contained fourteen rather than the twenty-six sections.[6] At this stage the chapter consisted of two major elements. The first was the various functions of the administration discussed either collectively or individually. Nearly half the sections of this early version were devoted to the elaboration of

---

[1] See Ch. VI. § § 27 and 29, pp. 93–111 and 114–17, below.

[2] Cf. UC xxxviii. 220 (3 Feb. 1825) with 221–2 (1825) and 223 (10 July 1826). Note the continued use of 'checks' in Ch. VI. § 1. Art. 1, p. 42, below. The phrase 'securities for appropriate aptitude' had been used often by Bentham for many years but not in this context.

[3] See UC xxxviii. 9 and 10, where 'fields of service' is included in chapters on judicial officers but not in Ch. VIII, Prime Minister.

[4] See Ch. VIII. § 3, pp. 152–4, below.

[5] Ch. VIII. § § 10–11, pp. 159–68, below. See UC xxxviii. 221.

[6] UC xxxviii. 9: § 1, Sub-ministers and Sub Departments; § 2, Union and Separation; § 3, Functions, belonging to all the Subdepartments; § 4, Suppletive function; § 5, Procurative function; § 6, Eliminative function; § 7, Statistic function; § 8, Melioration suggestive function; § 9, By whom locable; § 10, Out of whom located; § 11, Term of Service; § 12, How dislocable; § 13, Pay; § 14, Checks. Bentham then revised this order and the terminology, changed a section and added a section to read: § 1, Ministers and Subdepartments; § 2, Union and Separation; § 3, Power of Deputation; § 4, Functions, belonging to all the Subdepartments; § 5, Procurative function; § 6, Reparative [function]; § 7, Eliminative function; § 8, Statistic function; § 9, Melioration suggestive function; § 10, Term of Service; § 11, Remuneration; § 11 [*sic*], Locable, who; § 12, Located, by whom; § 13, Dislocable, how; § 14, Checks.

these functions. The second consisted of Bentham's conception of the system of education, competitive examination, and remuneration for members of the administration. Although these remained the major constituents of the chapter, Bentham consolidated the discussion of functions and made important additions to these themes in later versions.

Bentham had not created the chapter on the Defensive Force which eventually became chapter X. The chapter on the individual Ministers was at this point chapter X, and section 2, which Bentham included in Stanhope's parcel, dealt with the Legislation Minister. His role was especially important in drafting legislation and maintaining the coherence and symmetry of the *Pannomion*.[1] Bentham's plan for this chapter included eleven Ministers.[2]

Colls wrote in his journal that in addition to the marginal summaries for the chapters enclosed, marginals were also sent for 'Chapters 11, 12, 13 and Ch. [14?] on Quasi Jury'.[3] From the materials available it is not clear which chapters were meant by the reference. Colls may have made a mistake and meant chapters X, XI, and XII (the chapters which were about to follow by post on Ministers Severally, Judiciary Collectively, and Justice Minister) plus the chapter on the Quasi Jury. Alternatively, he may have referred to another ordering, chapter XI, Judiciary Collectively, chapter XII, Judges Immediate, and chapter XIII, Judges Immediate Depute Permanent, but this seems to have been a later arrangement.[4]

In the first of the parcels posted to Stanhope after his departure Bentham enclosed a version of chapters X-XII.[5] Of these, chapter XI (later to become chapter XII), Judiciary Collectively, created the greatest difficulties. As we shall see, in examining the functions of the Judiciary he found it necessary to make substantial excursions into the realms of judicial procedure and evidence which would become major obstacles to the completion of the *Code*. The version sent to Greece contained twenty-four sections, but Bentham was soon at work forming the chapter on Judges Immediate out of the last eight sections. By 30 March 1824 he had recast the chapter into

[1] See Bowring, ix. 428-37.

[2] Election, Legislation, Army, Navy, Interior Communication, Preventive Service, Indigence Relief, Education, Domain, Foreign Relation, and Finance. In 1825, the Health Minister was added and in 1826 the Trade Minister. See UC xxxviii. 220 and xlii. 94-6.

[3] As noted before, the brackets and question mark appear in the original. In a summary of the entries relating to Greece taken from Colls's journal and most likely prepared for Bowring, these references to marginals are omitted. London Greek Committee MSS, National Library, Athens.

[4] See UC xxxviii. 9-10.                    [5] See UC xxxviii. 9.

a series of twenty-four sections as opposed to the thirty-six envisaged in the Table accompanying the 1830 volume (Table 1).

Bentham's chapter on the Justice Minister underwent only minor changes between this period and the 1830 Table.[1] The most important was the shift, just after the manuscript was sent to Greece, in the order of the chapters in which the chapter on the Justice Minister was placed after rather than before all other chapters on the Judiciary, thus becoming chapter XXII.

The final parcel sent to Stanhope contained a revised version of chapter VIII, section 5 on the term of service of the Prime Minister.[2] Bentham's thoughts on this theme were obviously still developing as appears from the fact that he wrote two alternative sections for the same subject in the chapter on the Legislature. Bentham's new version proposed a one-year term with re-eligibility limited to periods of one and two years until a sufficient number of equally experienced candidates were available for re-election.[3]

Although Bentham was able to send to Greece in September–October 1823 eleven of the first twelve chapters of the *Code*, the work was, as he recognized, far from complete.[4] Bentham was at this time bothered by a chronic eye complaint, but this would not have been the only reason for the state of the manuscript. He began work on this draft of the *Code* in the early summer, and it was unlikely that so ambitious a project could have been finished by late September. Furthermore, although Bentham completed the 'enactive' parts of the *Code* (at least as much of it as he sent), he was unable to finish and send the 'expositive' and 'ratiocinative' parts. The development of these parts of the *Code* presented no small problem. Although the 'enactive' articles were in one sense the most important in that they contained the legal provisions of the *Code*, on their own they constituted a bare skeleton of the system. Bentham was especially anxious to prevent the rise of a body of 'judge-made' law which interpreted

[1] As with the Prime Minister, he added a section on Fields of Service, but this was not done until 1826.

[2] Of the manuscripts sent to Greece, only this parcel has been recovered. See F. Rosen, 'Bentham's Letters and Manuscripts in Greece', *The Bentham Newsletter*, v (1981), 56.

[3] In the 1830 *Code* the Prime Minister has a proposed four year term though restrictions on re-eligibility are also applied.

[4] The titles of the twelve chapters were: Ch. I, Territory of this State, name, situation, boundaries, divisions; Ch. II, Object of this Constitution; Ch. III, The sovereignty, in whom; Ch. IV, Authorities in this State; Ch. V, Of the Constitutive authority; Ch. VI, Of the Legislative Authority; Ch. VII, Legislator's Inaugural Declaration; Ch. VIII, Prime Minister; Ch. IX, Of the Sub Ministers collectively; Ch. X, Of the Sub-Ministers severally; Ch. XI, Of the Judiciary collectively; Ch. XII, Justice Minister. UC xxxviii. 9.

and developed these basic provisions, as was the case with the Common Law in England and the United States. Thus, he sought to make the reasons for the various enactments and the definitions of terms so explicit and clear that problems of interpretation could be reduced to a minimum. Eventually, for the part of the *Code* he published in 1830, he used and combined five headings (enactive, expositive, ratiocinative, instructional, exemplificational). But for Greece he had only the 'enactive' articles to send. In a letter to Stanhope he referred to the expositive and ratiocinative parts as 'ultimately indispensable accompaniments' of the enactive provisions. 'In some measure', he continued, 'I hope the Enactive part will speak for itself and convey its own exposition and its own Reasons; but as to a deplorably large proportion, I can entertain no such hope.'[1] He hoped to send the ratiocinative material to Greece as soon as he completed it, and, in the revised section on the 'Term of Service' of the Prime Minister which he sent out on 14 October, a brief series of 'enactive' articles was followed by a lengthy rationale where he justified his provisions.

Bentham's failure to send the expositive and ratiocinative parts of the *Code* to Greece may have had an important and perhaps unintended consequence for the development of the *Code*. At this time he began to set aside a considerable amount of material written as 'rationale' for the 1823 *Code* and seemed to concentrate on developing the whole *Code* from the enactive articles.[2] This may represent the first steps towards the combination of enactive, expositive, and ratiocinative material in the *Code*. If he had completed the *Code* as originally conceived in the three separate parts, this important development might not have taken place.

A final note on the *Code* sent to Greece contains Bentham's instructions to Stanhope to transform the *Radical Reform Bill* into the Election Code.[3] The *Radical Reform Bill* was originally published in 1819 and may be regarded as the earliest writing which actually formed part of the *Code*. It was written to advance the cause of parliamentary reform, but as it took the form of a parliamentary bill, Bentham hoped that it could be adapted as an Election Code covering the machinery of elections and qualifications for suffrage. In writing it, Bentham followed the practice he had adopted earlier of separating the 'enactive' from the 'ratiocinative' material and while his 'reasons' were closely linked to English constitutional practice, he may have thought that the 'enactive' material could on its own form

---

[1] Bentham to Stanhope, 21 Oct. 1823, UC xii. 140.

[2] Some of this material appeared in Doane's 'Book I'. Bowring, ix. 95–127.

[3] *Bentham's Radical Reform Bill, with Extracts from the Reasons*, London, 1819 (Bowring, iii. 558–97).

an Election Code for any state including Greece. The transformation of the *Radical Reform Bill* into an Election Code presented more problems than Bentham was prepared to admit in his brief instruction to Stanhope, and he never managed to prepare a satisfactory Election Code to form part of the *Constitutional Code*.[1]

While Bentham continued to work on the *Code*, in February and March 1824 he turned again to Greek affairs. He was drawn into the negotiations and politics of the Greek loan of 1824 and became a kind of father-figure to the Greek Deputies, John Orlandos (c. 1800-52) and Louriottis.[2] Stimulated by these events, Bentham sent two packets of writings to Stanhope who was still in Greece.[3] In the various drafts of letters and notes accompanying this material, a good deal can be learned about the state of the *Code*. Bentham noted in a letter to Stanhope that he had been revising the *Radical Reform Bill* to form a better Election Code having found in it some puzzles and absurdities.[4] If the work had already been printed in Greece, he proposed to add a sheet of 'Corrigenda' to it. Bentham's revisions to the *Radical Reform Bill* have not been found and were never incorporated into the published version of the *Code*. It seems that Bentham himself was well aware that the *Radical Reform Bill* did not make a good Election Code, but he was not willing to take the time to draft a new one.

As for the text of the *Constitutional Code*, Bentham first noted that although in the previous autumn he had sent to Stanhope the long chapter on the Judiciary, he had still not completed the other material on the various judicial officers. Now he was sending only the titles of chapters and sections covering the whole judiciary and a brief manuscript on Sublegislatures.[5] He apologized for not sending the remainder of the actual text explaining that he was prevented from doing so 'partly by one indispensable fiddle faddle or another, partly by the necessity I found myself under of making an excursion into the region of Judicial procedure'.[6] Bentham's 'excursion'

[1] Bentham's incorporation of the Election Code into the *Constitutional Code*, Ch. VI. §§ 4-17, p. 48, below, did not resolve these difficulties.

[2] Some of the extensive correspondence between Bentham and Orlandos and Louriottis at this time has been published in Eugène Dalleggio, *Les Philhellènes et la Guerre de l'Independance*, Athens, 1949, pp. 157-75. Further unpublished material is in UC xii, the Louriottis MSS, Centre for Neohellenic Research, Athens, the General State Archives, Athens, and the National Library, Athens.

[3] According to Colls's journal, fo. 130, these were sent on 17 and 27 Mar.

[4] Bentham to Stanhope, 19-21 Feb. 1824, Stanhope Archive K 121/39, General State Archives, Athens.

[5] See Colls's journal, fo. 130, and Bentham to Stanhope, 19-21 Feb. 1824, Stanhope Archive K 121/39, General State Archives, Athens.

[6] Bentham to Stanhope, 19-21 Feb. 1824, Stanhope Archive K 121/39, General State Archives, Athens.

eventually became a lengthy manuscript on judicial procedure which was never completed in his lifetime, but was edited by Doane for the Bowring edition.[1] However, it was also becoming clear that Bentham would have difficulty completing the *Constitutional Code*. Perhaps he felt that without settling the rules of judicial procedure the *Constitutional Code* could not be completed, because satisfactory judicial institutions could not be created. Nevertheless, he remained optimistic about his great project. The chapter on the Sublegislatures was to be the last, and there remained for the 'enactive' portion only the additional chapters on the Judiciary. A series of instructions to the legislator together with the 'expository' and 'rationale' parts were 'in a state of considerable forwardness'.[2] Bentham even speculated as to who was going to hold various offices and tentatively proposed Mavrocordato for Prime Minister and Orlandos as a possible Justice Minister.

If he was prevented from completing the *Constitutional Code* Bentham hoped that he might be able to find a person who would be 'capable as well as willing, to put in tolerable order, the mass, not a small one, already got together, though not completed'.[3] Bentham's hope was not an unreaonable one. He was surrounded by numerous friends and disciples who assisted him in the composition, completion or translation of his work. Dumont is the obvious example but there were many more. At this time John Stuart Mill was undertaking the completion from the manuscripts of the massive *Rationale of Judicial Evidence*.[4] His father, James Mill, had assisted Bentham on a number of projects. Richard Smith was to produce the English translation of Dumont's *Théorie des peines et des récompenses* in *The Rationale of Reward* and *The Rationale of Punishment*.[5] Peregrine Bingham's edition of the *Book of Fallacies* appeared in 1824.[6]

[1] *Principles of Judicial Procedure with the Outlines of a Procedure Code* (Bowring, ii. 1-188).

[2] Bentham to Stanhope, 19-21 Feb. 1824, Stanhope Archive K 121/39, General State Archives, Athens.

[3] Ibid.

[4] *Rationale of Judicial Evidence, specially applied to English Practice*, ed. John Stuart Mill, 5 vols., London, 1827 (Bowring, vi. 189-585, vii. 1-600). John Stuart Mill (1806-73), utilitarian philosopher and MP for Westminster, 1865-8.

[5] *Théorie des peines et des récompenses*, ed. E. Dumont, Paris, 1811; *The Rationale of Reward*, London, 1825 (Bowring, ii. 189-266) and *The Rationale of Punishment*, London, 1830 (Bowring, i. 388-525). Richard Smith was a collector of stagecoach duties at the Stamp and Taxes Office. He also edited thirteen works for the Bowring edition. Bowring, x. 548 n.

[6] *The Book of Fallacies*, London, 1824 (Bowring, ii. 375-487). Peregrine Bingham (1788-1864), barrister and legal writer, subsequently a police magistrate in London.

Francis Place assisted with the publication of *Not Paul, but Jesus* and George Grote edited the *Analysis of the Influence of Natural Religion*.[1] Bentham could reasonably expect that further assistance might be forthcoming from his followers as he plunged more deeply into the problems of the various Codes. T. Perronet Thompson, together with Stanhope and James Young, eventually assisted Bentham in the completion of the chapter of the *Code* on the Defensive Force.[2] John Neal, the American lawyer who lived with Bentham during 1826, provided useful information on American practice for both the Penal and Constitutional Codes.[3] George Bentham, Jeremy's nephew, lived with Bentham from 1826, and besides having produced a French translation of part of Bentham's *Chrestomathia* in 1823, he assisted with work on the Penal and Procedure Codes.[4] Edwin Chadwick also lived with Bentham for a period at this time and worked on the *Constitutional Code*.[5] Bentham was especially well served by his secretaries. Although John Colls eventually turned against Bentham, he

---

[1] *Not Paul, but Jesus. By Gamaliel Smith, Esq.*, London, 1823; *Analysis of the Influence of Natural Religion on the Temporal Happiness of Mankind, By Philip Beauchamp*. London, 1822. Francis Place (1771–1854), radical reformer, master tailor, and associate of Bentham since 1812; George Grote (1794–1871), MP for the City of London, 1832–41, historian of Greece, and subsequently treasurer and president of University College London.

[2] Bowring, ix. 333–428. See also p. xlii and n. 2, below. For James Young, see p. 319 n., below. Thomas Perronet Thompson (1783–1869), radical politician and army officer who became proprietor of the *Westminster Review* in 1829. Subsequently an MP.

[3] John Neal (1793–1876) published at New York and Boston in 1830 *Principles of Legislation: from the manuscripts of Jeremy Bentham.* . . . This was the first version to appear in English of Dumont's *Traités de législation civile et pénale*. Neal had spent a considerable period with Bentham in 1826–7. See also Bowring, x. 555–6 and p. 55 n. 1, below. For an example of Neal's assistance, see UC lxiv. 178–297. Bentham also received assistance from Richard Rush, John Quincy Adams and Adams's nephew, John Adams Smith, when attached to the American diplomatic service in London. See Bentham to Jackson, June 1830, Nicholas P. Trist MSS, Library of Congress, Washington D.C., printed in Bowring, xi. 39–40, incorrectly dated 26 Apr. 1830.

[4] George Bentham (1800–84), the son of Bentham's brother, Samuel, became a notable nineteenth-century botanist. In his late twenties, while living with Bentham, he read for the bar and assisted him in his work. MSS copied by George Bentham are often headed 'GB'. See, for example, UC lxiv. 20, 46, 49, 51–76 (for the Penal Code), and liia. 64–74, 76–83 (for the Procedure Code). It is worth noting that, unlike Bentham, George Bentham dated sheets of 'marginals' apparently from the dates on the MSS, as the dates on 'marginals' differ from the dates in the watermarks in the paper.

[5] S. E. Finer, *The Life and Times of Sir Edwin Chadwick*, London, 1952, p. 32. Sir Edwin Chadwick (1800–90), sanitary reformer, secretary of the Poor Law Commission, 1834–46, and a commissioner of the Board of Health, 1848–54.

was responsible for most of the transcriptions of the *Code* manuscripts.[1] Richard Doane assisted with the *Code* but more importantly, he provided posthumous service to Bentham in finishing both the Constitutional and Procedure Codes for the Bowring edition.

In a further letter to Stanhope, Bentham expressed the hope of enlisting the support of Orlandos and Louriottis in obtaining a commission for a full set of codes: the Penal and Civil as well as the Constitutional.[2] At the minimum, he hoped to consult them about the *Constitutional Code* when it was finished. Bentham also sent to Stanhope a recently completed draft of the Legislator's Inaugural Declaration (Ch. VII) with which he remained somewhat dissatisfied. He reported to Stanhope that upon writing it, he felt that it was too long and sent it to James Mill for comment. Mill seems to have agreed with Bentham as to its length and proposed that it should not be actually pronounced in front of the electors, but simply assented to in a few words. Bentham does not appear to have adopted Mill's suggestion, and, in the final version, Bentham proposes that the entire document be read by the representative in front of his constituents.[3] Nevertheless, Bentham left the text (which in section headings resembled the final text) in Stanhope's hands to use as he thought best.[4]

By March 1824 Bentham had worked out, as the table of chapters and sections sent to Stanhope indicated, a *Constitutional Code* of twenty-three chapters.[5] In his letters to Stanhope at this time, he grew increasingly confident. On 27 March, Bentham noted that the work was 'so near to its conclusion: a week I think from this day will suffice'.[6] His attention now turned to having the *Code* translated

[1] John Flowerdew Colls (1801–78), Bentham's amanuensis for almost a decade until 1829, author of *Utilitarianism Unmasked*, London, 1844, and rector of Laindon, Hertfordshire, 1853–78.

[2] Bentham to Stanhope, 14 Mar. 1824, UC xii. 219–20.

[3] See Ch. VII, § 1, Art. 1, pp. 133–4, below.

[4] Bentham to Stanhope, 16 Mar. 1824, UC xxxix. 26; UC xxxix. 27 (7 Mar. 1824).

[5] The titles of the twenty-three chapters were: Ch. I, Territory of this State, name, situation, boundaries, divisions; Ch. II, Object of this Constitution; Ch. III, Sovereignty, in whom; Ch. IV, Authorities in this State; Ch. V, Constitutive authority; Ch. VI, Legislative Authority; Ch. VII, Legislator's Inaugural Declaration; Ch. VIII, Prime Minister; Ch. IX, Of the Ministers collectively; Ch. X, Of the Sub-Ministers severally; Ch. XI, Judiciary collectively; Ch. XII, Judges Immediate; Ch. XIII, Judges Immediate Depute permanent; Ch. XIV, Judges Immediate Depute occasional; Ch. XV, Quasi Jury; Ch. XVI, Judicial Visitors; Ch. XVII, Immediate Pursuer Generals; Ch. XVIII, Immediate Defender Generals; Ch. XIX, Immediate Registrars; Ch. XX, Professional Lawyers; Ch. XXI, Judges Appellate; Ch. XXII, Justice Minister; Ch. XXIII, Sub-Legislatures. UC xxxviii. 9–10.

[6] Bentham to Stanhope, 27 Mar. 1824, UC xii. 268.

into Greek. In spite of the favourable reception given to his various works and manuscripts, Bentham had heard little from Greece about actual translations. Through Bowring, Bentham now hoped that a translation with the Greek and English printed in parallel columns might be made in Paris under the supervision of Adamantios Korais (1748-1833), the celebrated classical scholar, who had lived in Paris for many years.[1] Korais, originally from Greece, had apparently written to Bowring agreeing to this arrangement, but when Bentham wrote to Korais in August 1824, he said that while the *Code* was 'now at length in a state in which I would venture to commit it to the press', the manuscript had to be transcribed into a more legible hand before it could be sent. In its place Bentham enclosed the revised version of the *Radical Reform Bill*, apologizing for the cumbersome detail, but suggesting that it might be translated at this time in place of the *Code*.[2] Although it is unlikely that the *Constitutional Code* was in such an advanced state as to be ready for translation, a note to the Bowring edition suggests that Korais's ill-health led to the frustration of the plan.[3]

Another opportunity in Greece arose with the receipt by Bentham of a letter from Theodore Negris (1790-1824), the Minister of Justice, who was at the time drafting a civil code and who sought Bentham's assistance.[4] Stanhope had originally suggested that Negris write to Bentham, and Bentham replied enthusiastically.[5] Bentham even suggested that Negris might hold the office of Justice Minister under his new *Constitutional Code*.[6] Unfortunately, Negris died soon after he wrote to Bentham, and their joint project never developed.

These contacts with Greece provided considerable stimulus for Bentham. But he was aware of the enormous political obstacles to the adoption of his codes. He recognized that Greece suffered even more than the new states of Latin America from the absence of a settled government and a developed habit of obedience among the people.[7] He was told of the reluctance of Greek leaders to subscribe to republican principles and of their leaning towards monarchy which

---

[1] On 17 Feb. 1823 Bentham reported to Parr that Korais (called 'Corai' or 'Coray' by Bentham) had recommended to his fellow-countrymen that Bentham's works should be translated into Greek in preference to those of anyone else who had written on the subject of legislation. Bowring, x. 535.

[2] Bentham to Korais, 12 Aug. 1824, UC xii. 304-5. See Colls's journal, fo. 132.

[3] Bowring, iv. 586n.

[4] Negris to Bentham, 6 May 1824, UC xii. 283, printed in Bowring, iv. 585-6.

[5] Bentham to Negris, 12 July 1824, UC xii. 293-4, printed in Bowring, iv. 586-7. See also Stanhope to Bentham, 4 May 1824, UC xii. 279.

[6] Bentham to Negris, 12 July 1824, UC xii. 294.

[7] UC xxi. 210-11 (28 Feb. 1824).

was the result of the pressures of the European powers. He was a first-hand observer of the disarray and sinister activity among the Greek leadership in the negotiations for the first Greek loan. It was highly unlikely that the *Code* would ever be adopted. Bentham's manuscripts were received by the Greek legislature 'with expressions of deep-felt gratitude', but it was doubtful that Bentham's writings would find a translator or be published in Greece.[1] The few items of Bentham which appeared in print (none was longer than a few paragraphs) were the result of the efforts of Stanhope and J. J. Meyer, the Swiss editor of Ἑλληνικα Χρονικα, utilizing printing presses brought from England.[2] There were neither people sufficiently educated to translate nor the facilities required to publish a work like the *Constitutional Code*.

### THE CONSTITUTIONAL CODE: 1825-1827

By the end of 1824 Bentham could write of the *Constitutional Code* as being 'at the point of completion'.[3] To Dumont in December he urged: 'Have a little patience you shall have the Const. Code and the Procedure Code into the bargain.'[4] But his hopes for success with the *Code* in Greece were beginning to fade, and his attentions now turned to Latin America. This was not a new interest. Through his involvement with Spain and Portugal and directly with the emerging new states in Latin America, Bentham developed numerous contacts throughout the Spanish- and Portuguese-speaking world.[5] Dumont's *Traités de Legislation* was translated into Spanish in 1821-2 by Ramon Salas, a Professor at the University of Salamanca, and this edition was read widely throughout Latin America.[6] Bentham had

---

[1] Stanhope to Bentham, 4 May 1824, UC xii. 279.

[2] See Rosen, op. cit. 55; Meyer to Bentham, 12/23 May 1824, UC xii. 285; Bentham to Meyer, 21-2 Sept. 1824, UC xii. 312-18; St. Clair, op. cit. pp. 186-7, 242. Johann Jakob Meyer (1798-1826), Swiss pharmacist and philhellene, killed at the fall of Missolonghi.

[3] Bentham to Burdett, 23 Sept. 1824, Bodleian Library, MS Eng. Lett. d. 97, fo. 5, printed in Bowring, x. 543-4.

[4] Bentham to Dumont, 14 Dec. 1824, Dumont MSS, MS 74, fo. 48; see also Dumont to Bentham, 3 Feb. 1825, UC x. 143.

[5] See P. Schwartz, 'Bentham's Influence in Spain, Portugal and Latin America', *The Bentham Newsletter*, i (1978), 34-5; Alamira de Avila-Martel, 'The Influence of Bentham on the Teaching of Penal Law in Chile', Theodora L. McKennan, 'Benthamism in Santander's Colombia', Antonio-Enrique Pérez Luño, 'Jeremy Bentham and Legal Education in the University of Salamanca during the Nineteenth Century', ibid. v (1981); M. Williford, *Bentham on Spanish America*, Baton Rouge, 1980.

[6] *Tratados de legislación civil y penal*, 5 vols., Madrid, 1821-2.

known Bernardino Rivadavia (1780–1845), the President of Argentina 1826–7, since 1818.[1] Rivadavia made a Spanish translation of Dumont's *Tactique des Assemblées législatives* which was used in the assembly of Buenos Aires.[2] José del Valle of Guatemala (d. 1834) was another disciple of Bentham who turned to him for assistance in constructing a civil code.[3] Bentham had an important disciple in Francisco de Paula Santander (1792–1840), Vice-President of Colombia from 1821 to 1828 and President from 1832 to 1837, but his relationship with Simon Bolivar (1783–1830), President of Colombia 1821–30, was more problematic. Although Bolivar and Bentham corresponded for some years, Bolivar eventually banished Bentham's works from Colombian educational institutions in 1828.[4]

In a letter to Bolivar, written in August 1825, and in a table of chapters and sections prepared at the same time, Bentham provides a useful summary of the state of the *Code*.[5] The *Code* was now extended from twenty-three chapters in March 1824 to twenty-nine and looked more like the final version.[6] The most important addition was the lengthy chapter X on the Defensive Force. In late 1824 Bentham had planned or written a very long section on the Army Minister which he then transformed into the separate chapter which constituted a major addition to the *Code* on the subject of military organization.[7] Bentham also added four chapters to follow the hitherto final chapter on the Sublegislatures. Two, entitled Local Headmen and Local Registrars, were concerned with the two main officers at the local level. The third was entitled Judicial Prehensors and referred to judicial officers whose main function was to take physical possession of persons or things as directed by a

---

[1] See Bentham to Rivadavia, 18 Aug. 1818, BL Add. MS 33,545, fos. 310–11; Rivadavia to Bentham, 25 Aug. 1818, ibid., fos. 312–13. Bentham to Rivadavia, 3, 12 Oct. 1818, ibid., fos. 325–8, printed in *Iberian*, i. 89–102.

[2] Schwartz, op. cit. 34.

[3] Del Valle to Bentham, n.d., Bowring, iv. 593.

[4] See *Iberian*, i. 397–401, ii. 777–8, 805–9, 824–60, 900–16, 943–4, for correspondence between Bolivar and Bentham between 1820 and 1827. See also McKennan, op. cit. 29–43.

[5] Bentham to Bolivar, 13 Aug. 1825, Casa Natal del Libertador, Caracas, O'Leary, vol. 12, pt. 1, fos. 237–48, printed in *Iberian*, ii. 900–16. A draft of the letter dated 14, 16, 17, 25 July 1825 is at UC xii. 335–44. The table is at UC xxxviii. 221–2.

[6] With the addition of Ch. X Defensive Force, the chapter, Judiciary Collectively, should have become Ch. XII. Bentham's failure to renumber resulted in the incorrect total of twenty-eight rather than twenty-nine chapters in UC xxxviii. 221–2.

[7] See UC xliia. 3 (20 May 1824); xl. 27–8 (27 Sept. 1823, 8 July 1824); see also the table at UC xxxviii. 220 (3 Feb. 1825).

judge.[1] The final chapter was devoted to assessing the strengths and weaknesses of a 'simple' versus a 'federative' form of government. In revising his chapters on the various judicial officers Bentham divided the chapter, Immediate Pursuer Generals, to form two chapters, Government Advocates, and Government Advocate General. He also changed the title of Immediate Defender Generals to Advocates of the Helpless.

In the earlier chapters of the *Code*, the 1825 version displayed some important advances. The first five chapters appeared in the form they would take in the final version. Chapter VI on the Legislature now fully incorporated the *Radical Reform Bill* as the Election Code and, except for sections on the term of service, relocation, and wrongful exclusion, was fully formed. These sections were added by July 1826.[2] The Legislator's Inaugural Declaration (VII) was fully developed except for the introductory section, and the chapter on the Prime Minister (VIII) was in its final form. Of the first volume of the *Code* (i.e. the present volume) only the lengthy chapter IX, Ministers Collectively, though now expanded to twenty-two sections, was not fully developed. This version contained a number of sections which Bentham would remove from the final version or consolidate into other sections. In 1825 he planned separate sections on the procurative, reparative, venditive, and eliminative functions concerned with the purchase, use, and disposal of things.[3] This material was later placed in the section on the functions generally and in a new section entitled Requisitive Function.[4] Bentham also consolidated the material in the section on the union and separation of the various subdepartments within the earlier section headed Ministers and Subdepartments.

It is likely that a copy of this table or one very close to it accompanied Bentham's letter to Bolivar. Bentham was also at this time anxious to distribute his more recent work and especially the *Constitutional Code* in Spanish translations. He was dissatisfied with an earlier translation into Spanish of the *Codification Proposal*,[5] but he was now utilizing the skills of Dr Antoni Puigblanch (1775-1840), a Spanish refugee living in London who was formerly Professor of Hebrew and Civil Law at Alcalá.[6] Puigblanch translated *Leading*

---

[1] See Bowring, ix. 637-9. Bentham intended to deal more generally with the notion of Prehension in the Procedure Code. See UC xxxviii. 222 and Bowring, ii. 116-17.

[2] See UC xxxviii. 223 (10 July 1826).

[3] Ch. IX, §§ 5-8 in UC xxxviii. 221.

[4] Ch. IX, §§ 4 and 8, pp. 186-202, and 268-76, below.

[5] *Propuesta de Código dirigida por J.B. a todas las naciones que profesan opiniones liberales*, London, 1822.

[6] Bentham to Bolivar, 13 Aug. 1825, op. cit. See also Bowring, iv. 584n.

*Principles*, and Bentham enclosed six copies for Bolivar.[1] As for the *Code* itself, Bentham sent with this letter a translation made by Puigblanch of chapter VII, Legislator's Inaugural Declaration.[2] He also enclosed material from chapter IX on remuneration, education, and competitive examinations for the administration and planned to send six copies 'if I can get the translation made and printed in time for the present conveyances if not, a copy in manuscript'.[3] In addition, he planned to send Bolivar the table of chapters and sections in English with Spanish translation 'if I can get one time enough'.[4]

Bentham also noted in this letter that the entire *Constitutional Code* would have been finished the previous year but for the need to complete the Procedure Code. The latter, he claimed, was so far advanced that it could be completed before Bolivar's return letter arrived in England. Bentham then noted that the Penal and Civil Codes, to which the Procedure Code gave 'execution and effect', should also be drafted. As for the Penal Code, Bentham did not think that this should take him much longer to write than one of the longer chapters of the *Constitutional Code*. Although he recognized that the Civil Code would be more difficult, he saw no great obstacle to writing it.

Between 1825 and 1827 Bentham continued to develop the *Constitutional Code*. Besides a brief introductory section, entitled Ends in view, important additions, such as section 3, Number in an Office; section 5, Subordination grades; section 10, Officially informative function; section 11, Information-Elicitative function; section 20, Insubordination obviated; section 22, Extortion obviated; section 23, Peculation obviated; and section 26, Architectural arrangements; were made to chapter IX during this period. Reasons for Bentham's omission of these sections in 1825 can be offered in some cases. As we have noted, the inclusion of the material on extortion and peculation

---

[1] *Principios que deben servir de guía en la formación de un código constitucional para un estado*, London, 1824.

[2] *Declaración ó Protesta de Todo individuo del cuerpo Legislativo al tomar posesión de su destino* . . . London, 1825. Bentham correctly refers to the original Ch. VII (in English) as not 'as yet printed'.

[3] For the publication of this material as an extract from the *Code*, see p. xxxix below.

[4] According to Dr Pedro Schwartz, none of the excerpts from the *Code* sent to Bolivar has been recovered. However, Dr Schwartz has reported seeing printed versions of both the Legislator's Inaugural Declaration and the *Constitutional Code* in the remnants of José Cecilio del Valle's library at the house of Mr and Mrs Asturias, Guatemala City. Bentham himself refers to the translation of the *Code* being made by Puigblanch in May 1827 (Bowring, iv. 584n). This would not, of course, have been included in the letter to Bolivar.

probably accompanied the development of the Penal Code. The material in the sections on subordination grades and insubordination may have been stimulated by his writing on the military for chapter X. The material in the sections on information may have evolved from his work on evidence and procedure. Nevertheless, all of these sections were fully developed between 1825 and 1827. The over-all length and size of the *Code* continued to increase. In 1826 Bentham added the chapter on Appellate Judiciary Registrars to his plan.[1] Some titles were also altered at this time. The chapter, Judicial Visitors, became Judicial Inspectors, and Advocates for the Helpless became finally Eleemosynary Advocates.[2]

By February 1827 when the first volume was ready for the press, Bentham's conception of the whole of the *Constitutional Code* was reaching maturity. The last three sections were now added to chapter X on the Defensive Force.[3] The chapter, Judiciary Collectively, had increased to thirty-one sections.[4] Eventually, the whole *Code* was extended to thirty-two chapters with the inclusion of Judiciary Messengers and Sublegislation Ministers. These were most likely late additions, and they were not broken down into sections for the Table accompanying the 1830 volume.[5]

## THE EVOLUTION OF THE *PANNOMION*: 1825–1830

By 1825 Bentham, as we have seen, had begun to regard the *Constitutional Code* as being closely related to the three other Codes of the *Pannomion*: Procedure, Penal, and Civil. When writing to John Quincy Adams in June 1826 to congratulate him on his election as President of the United States, he could proclaim that 'in a Constitutional Code, a Penal Code, and a Procedure Code, I have already made such progress as would enable any one of several persons I have in mind to complete them from my papers, in case of my death before completion'.[6]

The Procedure Code was the first of the Codes to which Bentham turned in the course of drafting the *Constitutional Code*. Although judicial procedure was a subject on which he had written for many years, the Procedure Code, which developed in the 1820s, grew out of both manuscripts and problems associated with the *Constitutional*

---

[1] UC iv. 353 (8 Nov. 1826).   [2] Ibid.

[3] UC xcvii. 203 (20 Feb. 1827).

[4] Ibid. See also UC xcvii. 204 (21 May 1827).

[5] See Table 1. A more detailed discussion of the evolution of Chs. X–XXXII will accompany the later volumes of this edition of the *Constitutional Code*.

[6] Bentham to Quincy Adams, 19 June 1826, Bowring, x. 555.

*Code*.[1] Bentham began to draft it in August 1823; the early manuscripts were often originally written for the *Constitutional Code* and then replaced with the heading 'Procedure'.[2] We have seen that by February 1824 Bentham had realized that the chapters on the judiciary in the *Constitutional Code* had to be based on principles of judicial procedure. But in beginning the Procedure Code it was clear that the completion of the *Constitutional Code* would be delayed. Between 1824 and 1827 Bentham wrote extensively on judical procedure.[3] By the end of 1825 the Procedure Code was well developed.[4] In November 1824 and March 1825 Bentham toyed with various ideas of separate publication of the Procedure Code though he emphasized its close link with the *Constitutional Code*.[5] In March and May of 1827 Bentham returned to the Procedure Code.[6] With Volume I of the *Constitutional Code* committed to the press, he may have envisaged its rapid completion.[7] Nevertheless, Bentham did not prepare it for the press. Three years later in the Preface to the published volume of the *Constitutional Code* Bentham noted that he was ready to attach a Procedure Code Table to the *Equity Dispatch Court Bill* on which he was then working.[8] Bentham did not complete this work and there is no evidence that he prepared the Procedure Code Table for it.[9]

Work on the Procedure Code itself began to fade after 1827. Bentham's interest may have declined with the publication of the *Rationale of Judicial Evidence* in 1827.[10] He saw a close connection between evidence and procedure and with the publication of the work on evidence, the completion of his writing on procedure may have become less urgent. Furthermore, after 1827, Bentham became increasingly interested in the possibilities of legal reform in England through his association and correspondence with Sir Robert Peel, Henry Brougham, and Daniel O'Connell and the formation of the Law Reform Association. Extensive correspondence with, in Bentham's view, reluctant reformers such as Peel and Brougham also led

---

[1] See Ch. V, § 5, Art. 6n, p. 38 n. 1, below.

[2] See, for example, UC xliia. 29–42, 44–52, 163–8; xliib. 450–1, 507–22; liii. 9, 10, 12, 15–16.

[3] See UC liia, liib, liii, lv, lvi, lvii, lxi.

[4] See, for example, UC liii.  [5] UC lvii. 241–2.

[6] See UC liii. 117–18, 120–2.

[7] See the advanced stage of the MS in UC lv. 23–37 (May 1827). The fullest table of parts and chapters was developed at this time (UC lvii. 47).

[8] See p. 5, below.

[9] p. 5 n. 3, below. See also Bowring, iii. 297–317 for the text of the *Equity Dispatch Court Bill*.

[10] See p. xxvii n. 4, above.

to major pamphlets.[1] O'Connell was to carry the standard of law reform as a disciple.[2] Bentham expended considerable energy in forming the Law Reform Association which was designed to attract leading men to press for law reform generally as opposed to the more controversial constitutional reform. A number of distinguished figures joined the association, but it never achieved much success and was soon abandoned.[3] These considerable efforts by Bentham after 1827 were in one sense closely linked to his work on judicial procedure, but they may have led him to abandon the arduous task of completing the Procedure Code.

Although Bentham was interested in penal law and its reform from his earliest writings, his attempt to formulate a Penal Code as an integral part of the *Pannomion* began comparatively late.[4] From March 1826 and especially in July of that year he began in earnest to draft and arrange the Penal Code. He worked on it intensively the following year. In January 1827 a draft of the 'Table of Contents' was written, and in July, the Table, as it appears here as Table 2, seems to have been completed and printed.[5]

In late 1827 and throughout 1828, Bentham continued to work on the Penal Code and there is evidence of his working on it as late as March 1831.[6] Although the Penal Code was not completed, Bentham did not apparently run into any great difficulty in drafting it, and he left a considerable body of manuscript.[7] He was covering familiar ground, and the problems connected with its integration into the *Pannomion* were fairly peripheral. For example, to discuss offences against property Bentham had to develop a conception of

---

[1] See *Lord Brougham Displayed*, London, 1832 (Bowring, v. 549-612). This work contains two brief extracts from vol. iii of the *Constitutional Code*: Ch. XII, §§ 5 and 32, Bowring, ix. 470-3, 535-7. See the correspondence with Brougham in Bowring, x. 574-6, 588-9, and the Brougham MSS, University College London. See also the correspondence with Peel in UC xib and BL Add. MSS 40,391, 40,393, and 40,400.

[2] See the correspondence with O'Connell in Bowring, x. 594-605, xi. 24-30, the National Library of Ireland, and University College Dublin. See also *Justice and Codification Petitions*, London, 1829 (Bowring, v. 437-538).

[3] Bowring, xi. 30.          [4] Ch. V, § 6, Art. 2n, p. 39 n. 1, below.

[5] Cf. UC lxviii. 83 (Jan. 1827), which is an early draft. In an extensively annotated copy of the printed table (UC xcvii. 184), with the annotations dated 25 July 1827, Bentham proposed extensive further developments in his Table of Contents. The material in Part I was developed more extensively with the addition of sections under the various chapter headings and with some development of the chapters. Similar additions were made in Part II where (for example, in Ch. XII) the chapters had not yet been divided into sections. See also UC lxviii. 80.

[6] See UC lxiv. 20, 51-76, 298-9; lxvii. 236-47; lxviii. 97-100.

[7] See UC lxiv, lxv, lxvii, lxviii.

property which could be employed in the Civil Code and in the section on the statistic function in the *Constitutional Code*.[1] Similarly, material on public offences (see especially Part II, chapter XX) was connected with chapter X on the Defensive Force in the *Constitutional Code*.[2] Furthermore, the late addition of sections 22 and 23 on peculation and extortion to chapter IX of the *Constitutional Code* probably reflected the influence of Bentham's drafting of the Penal Code.[3] Nevertheless, difficulties and developments such as these would not have held up the completion of the Penal Code. It is more likely that Bentham did not have an overwhelming reason for completing it.

Of the four main pillars of the *Pannomion* the Civil Code was the one for which Bentham wrote the least. Most of what was written was either sketchy or introductory.[4] In April 1830 when the first volume of the *Constitutional Code* was published, Bentham attempted a brief sketch of a Civil Code and a definition of its relationship to the rest of the *Pannomion*.[5] This writing on the Civil Code is related to the Preface to the present work, also drafted in 1830, where considerable emphasis is placed on stating some leading features of the Civil Code in place of the Table which Bentham had originally hoped to append.[6] Bentham's failure to develop the Civil Code should not be taken to represent neglect by him of the civil law in the *Pannomion*. In the midst of the material on the Civil Code is a lengthy manuscript of approximately 300 sheets on Blackstone which was used as an occasion to develop a general critique of the terminology of jurisprudence and to lay the theoretical foundations for the *Pannomion*.[7] Furthermore, Bentham wrote a lengthy manuscript on the law of real property, an important part of the civil law, on the occasion of the publication of James Humphreys's proposals.[8] He also developed a major critique of the Equity Courts, and some Civil Code manuscripts bear alternative titles such as 'Real Property

---

[1] UC lxv. 108-10.      [2] UC lxviii. 83 (Jan. 1827) and Table 2.

[3] These sections were not envisaged in 1825 as forming part of the Code. See UC xxxviii. 220 (3 Feb. 1825), 322 (15 July 1826), 340 (13 Mar. 1827).

[4] See, for example, UC xxx. 2-6 (Nov. 1824), 8-12 (Jan. 1826), 13-23 (Aug. 1824), 26-32 (Jan., Aug. 1827), 33-40 (Sept.-Oct. 1828), 41-59 (Oct. 1827-Feb. 1828).      [5] UC xxxi. 276-8, 280-2, xxx. 165-79.

[6] See p. 5 ff., below.      [7] UC xxx. 60-164; xxxi. 1-220 written in 1828-9.

[8] James Humphreys, *Observations on the Actual State of the English Laws of Real Property*, London, 1826. Bentham wrote 'A Commentary on Mr. Humphreys' Real Property Code', first for the *Westminster Review*, vi (1826), 446-507, and then separately as a pamphlet. See Bowring, v. 387-435. Bentham's MSS on this topic are considerable. See UC lxxvii and lxxviii. James Humphreys (d. 1830), barrister and legal writer. He was a liberal in politics, and delivered a course of lectures on law at University College London.

Commission' and 'Equity Dispatch Court'.[1] Perhaps Bentham was distracted from drafting the Civil Code, a more complex and difficult work than any other part of the *Pannomion* except for the *Constitutional Code*, by these opportunities to engage in public debate over issues within the field of civil law. At the same time he was becoming increasingly aware of the need for an over-all conception of the *Pannomion* within which the Civil Code would fit. This latter concern was exemplified in the Blackstone manuscript and in the later material on the *Pannomion* generally.[2] Bentham may have attempted to look through the Civil Code to a vision of the whole *Pannomion*.

## CONSTITUTIONAL CODE VOLUME I: 1827–1830

As the first volume of the *Code* moved towards completion, Bentham published two extracts from it. The first was the *Extract from the Proposed Constitutional Code, Entitled Official Aptitude Maximized, Expense Minimized* which, though wrongly dated 1816, seems to have been printed by July 1826.[3] The 1826 *Extract* (as it will be called) contained the material from chapter IX (sections 15–17 and some articles from an early version of section 18) dealing with Bentham's plans for an educated civil service based on competitive examinations and 'pecuniary competition'. Similar material was sent earlier in 1825 both to Greece and to Bolivar in Latin America, but these excerpts were probably in manuscript form.[4] The 1826 *Extract* was later reprinted in a large volume of collected essays entitled *Official Aptitude Maximized; Expense Minimized.*[5] Bentham referred to this work as his 'pasticcio' as it contained a variety of previously published pieces which were loosely connected to the theme of enhancing ability in public office while, at the same time, minimizing public expense.[6] Both for this volume and the 1830 *Code*, Bentham added the Supplements to sections 16 and 17 and dropped the 1826 version

[1] UC lxxvi. 6-7, 9, 11-12 (Aug. 1830). For Bentham's writings on the Equity Courts, see *Equity Dispatch Court Proposal*, London, 1830 (Bowring, iii. 297-317) and the unfinished *Equity Dispatch Court Bill* (Bowring, iii. 319-431). See also UC lxxxi. 94-167; lxxxvi; cxiv. 221-92.

[2] Some of which was published as *Pannomial Fragments* (Bowring, iii. 211-30).

[3] London, 1826. See Bentham to Dumont, 26 July 1826, Urquhart MSS, Balliol College, Oxford.

[4] For the extract sent to Greece, see Bentham to Provisional Government of Greece, 28 Jan. 1825, Bowring, iv. 587. For the extract for Bolivar, see p. xxxiv, above.

[5] London, 1830 (Bowring, v. 263-386). Bowring omits the extract from his version, as it was also printed in the *Code* (Bowring, ix. 266-94).

[6] Bentham to Peel, 7 Apr. 1827, BL Add. MS 40,393, fo. 148.

of section 18. Bentham believed that the two volumes were closely connected, joined by the theme and injunction, 'maximize aptitude, minimize expense', and it is somewhat curious that both might have been published in 1827 but did not appear until 1830. The second extract was concerned with Bentham's system of registering copies of documents made by the manifold writing system, an invention of which he had been an ardent supporter for many years.[1] This brief extract appeared as part of 'Bentham on Humphreys' Property Code' in the *Westminster Review* of October 1826.[2]

By April 1827 the first volume of the *Code* (the present work) was in the press.[3] At this stage, however, Bentham still conceived the *Code* in two volumes with the second beginning with the major chapter XII on the Judiciary.[4] By September 1828, largely as a result of the development and expansion of chapter X, Defensive Force, he began to conceive of the *Code* in three volumes.[5] Throughout this period Bentham was sending unbound copies of chapters I-IX (the present work) to a number of people whom he thought likely to be interested in the work. Bentham's correspondence records copies sent to Henry Brougham, Col. James Young, and King Ludwig I of Bavaria; and copies were offered to King William I of the Netherlands and the Duke of Wellington.[6] To the two monarchs Bentham explained that, although drafted for the republican states of Latin America and written on the assumption that representative democracy was the best form of government for these states, there was a good deal in the *Code* on subjects such as the judiciary and administration which would be of interest to reigning monarchs. 'Though, as a whole', wrote Bentham, 'it would be incompatible with Monarchy, several parts are alike suitable to every form of Government.'[7]

At the beginning of April 1830 Bentham announced the publication of the first of his three-volume *Constitutional Code*.[8] The

---

[1] See Ch. VIII, § 10, pp. 59–62, below.

[2] See p. 159 n. 1, below.

[3] Bentham to Peel, 7 Apr. 1827, BL Add. MS 40,393, fo. 148.

[4] Bentham to Say, Jan. 1827, UC xii. 375.

[5] Bentham to Say, 9 Sept. 1828, Bibliothèque Nationale, Paris, partly printed in Bowring, xi. 2–3.

[6] Bentham to Brougham, 2 Nov. 1827, UC Brougham MSS 26,007; Bentham to King Ludwig I of Bavaria, 20 Dec. 1827, Bowring, x. 579; Bentham to Young, 16 Feb. 1828, UC ix. 130–1; Bentham to King William I of the Netherlands, 6 Feb. 1827, BL Add. MS 33,546, fo. 126; Bentham to Wellington, 29 Nov. 1828, BL Add. MS 33,546, fos. 256–7. Ludwig I (1786–1868), King of Bavaria 1825–48; William I (1772–1844), King of the Netherlands 1814–40.

[7] Bentham to King William I of the Netherlands, 6 Feb. 1827, BL Add. MS 33,546, fo. 126.

[8] Bentham to Herries, 31 Mar.–9 Apr. 1830, UC x. 233.

'pasticcio', *Official Aptitude Maximized; Expense Minimized*, was still in the press but would appear shortly. What led Bentham to publish his *Code* three years after it was in print is not clear. If he was waiting in 1827 for the completion of the work before publishing, he was not much closer to completion in 1830. Although the new chapter on the Defensive Force was about to be printed (but not published), the remainder of the text had not progressed to the stage where publication was possible.

It is probable that Bentham's Preface to the volume was hastily drafted in March–April 1830.[1] He had delayed writing the Preface earlier as he was awaiting the completion of the later volumes.[2] In the Preface he anticipated that the *Code* would be useful primarily in Latin America, but possibly in the future in the British empire as well.[3] We have already discussed Bentham's involvement with leading figures in Latin America, and his continuing involvement with men like Del Valle and Santander in 1830 may have led to the decision to publish. His reference to the British Empire might have been more narrowly directed to India. Bentham had long hoped through James Mill to influence the development of the legal system in India and he corresponded to this end with Lord William Bentinck and Rammohun Roy.[4]

At some point Bentham had intended to write a full Introduction to the volume, but this could easily have been a major work on its own. Although in the Preface he looked back to his earlier writings on forms of government as the basis for an Introduction, he devoted much more time in the actual Preface to his conception of the *Pannomion*. Bentham's late writings on 'Nomography' and on the *Pannomion* generally, where he attempted to see the *Pannomion* as a whole and approach the problem of constructing the major Codes in a systematic manner, may be seen as the kind of material he would have used had he written a full Introduction to the *Code* in 1830.[5]

---

[1] UC cxii. 69 (23 Mar. 1830).

[2] Bentham to Young, 16 Feb. 1828, UC ix. 130.          [3] See pp. 3–4, below.

[4] See Bowring, x. 450; Bentham to Young, 28 Dec. 1827, ibid. 576–7; Bentham to Bentinck, 19–20 Nov. 1829, UC x. 179–85; Young to Bentham, 30 Sept. 1828, Bowring, xi. 7–9; Young to Bentham, 14 Nov. 1830 in J. Bowring, *Memoirs of Jeremy Bentham*, BL shelf-mark c61.c15, and inserted at p. 82, and printed in Bowring, xi. 59–60. Cf. Eric Stokes, *The English Utilitarians and India*, Oxford, 1959, esp. pp. 51–2. Lord William Cavendish Bentinck (1774–1839), MP for various constituencies between 1796 and 1839; Governor-General of Bengal, 1827–33, and of India, 1833–5. Rajah Rammohun Roy (*c.*1774–1833), Indian Brahmin and intellectual, converted from Hinduism to Christianity. He opposed the practice of suttee, and worked for various liberal causes in India.

[5] *Nomography; or the Art of Inditing Laws* (Bowring, iii. 231–95); *Pannomial Fragments* (Bowring, iii. 211–30).

The publication of the first volume of the *Code* and *Official Aptitude Maximized; Expense Minimized* was a relatively small affair. According to some financial accounts Bentham received from Robert Heward, the publisher, fifty copies of the *Code* were boarded and sewn in 1830 with three copies reported sold in 1830 and ten in 1831.[1] Ninety-seven copies of *Official Aptitude Maximized; Expense Minimized* were boarded and sewn with five sold in 1830 and eight in 1831. The printed version of chapter X, Defensive Force, is even rarer. Although Bentham distributed a number of these, as he did with the first *Code* volume in 1827, only one copy is known to have survived.[2]

## TEXT

The *Constitutional Code* will be published according to Bentham's three-volume plan which accompanied the text of the 1830 volume and is reprinted here as Table 1. The present work, volume one, corresponds to Bentham's 1830 printed text. Bentham customarily destroyed the final manuscript when a text was printed. Little manuscript directly related to this volume has survived, and it possesses no authority over the printed text. In spelling, punctuation, the use of italics and other devices the present volume has attempted to follow the 1830 volume as closely as possible. Although Bentham himself sent the first volume of the *Code* to the press and for a number of years had the opportunity to correct it, the text as published contained a large number of errors. For example, Bentham seldom revised the numerous cross-references to correspond to the succession of changes in the structure of various chapters and sections. Similarly, errors in the numbering of articles were left uncorrected. Many of these errors were corrected by Doane for the Bowring edition, but his corrections were not recorded. In the present text all variations from Bentham's original 1830 text are recorded in the 1830 Collation.[3] That these variants, though often minor, total more than seven hundred testifies to the extent of Bentham's failure to correct the

[1] BL Add. MS 33,553, fos. 301-2, 309-10. It is not clear if these accounts record, as copies 'sold', those distributed by Bentham at his own expense.

[2] This copy is now in the Library of Congress, Washington D.C. See D. Baumgardt, 'A Lost Volume of Bentham's Constitutional Code', *The Library of Congress Quarterly Journal of Current Acquisitions*, i (1944), 40-1; Bentham to Tyrell, 3 June, 13 July 1830, BL Add. MS 34,661, fos. 4-5. See also Bentham's list of books sent to Del Valle and Herrera, 21 Jan. 1831, UC iv. 383, printed in *Iberian*, ii. 1031; Bentham to Graham, 14 Dec. 1830, BL Add. MS 33,546, fo. 471.

[3] pp. 461 ff., below.

text. Where variations from the 1830 text are substantial, these also appear in the present text in square brackets and often with explanatory textual footnotes.

The Bowring version is superior to the 1830 volume in so far as numerous errors have been corrected. However, Doane missed a number of errors and made, perhaps inevitably in a work of such complexity, a few additional ones. Unfortunately, Doane also attempted to improve the sense of Bentham's prose by revising the existing punctuation. At some points the effect is misleading; at others, Doane's version renders the passage more cumbersome than it need be. Wherever possible, the present editors have returned to the phrasing and punctuation of the 1830 text. Nevertheless, as the Bowring version is familiar to most scholars and it will be of interest to see how that version differs from the present one, all differences between the two texts are recorded in the Bowring Collation.[1] Although Doane's text possesses no authority, many of his corrections have been followed. One important revision concerns the supplements to sections 16 and 17 of chapter IX. Doane placed these in their correct positions to follow their respective sections and then placed the 'Concluding Instruction to the Public Opinion Tribunal' after the Supplement to section 17. As sections 15–17 and the 'Concluding Instruction' were already in print when Bentham wrote the two Supplements, he merely added the Supplements to the published text so that the Supplement to section 16 followed the text of section 17 and the 'Concluding Instruction'. Bentham clearly would have wished them placed properly in a new edition.

There are four main collations which are placed after the main text of the volume. These enable the reader to reconstruct the 1830 and Bowring texts, as well as a number of extracts, and contain all of the variations from the present text which appear in those works. Variants not covered by the collations are listed in the introductory notes and especially the notes to the 1830 and Bowring Collations.[2] The Collations are intended to cover all *Code* material which was printed or published either before or at the same time as the original publication in 1830. Material extracted from the *Code* and republished after 1830 has not been included in the collations. For example, the text of the *Parliamentary Candidate's Proposed Declaration of Principles* of 1831 is based on chapter VII, Legislator's Inaugural Declaration.[3] Although a textual note explores the main differences between the two texts, no collation is provided. It is hoped that a fully edited text will appear in a later volume.

---

[1] pp. 480 ff., below.     [2] pp. 461 and 480, below.
[3] See Ch. VII, p. 133 n. 1, below.

The present editors had originally planned to incorporate all or part of Bentham's Election Code as an appendix to the present volume. For reasons which have already been discussed, it is not practical to extract a basic Election Code from the considerable material which links the *Radical Reform Bill* to English practice. To include all of the text, properly annotated, as an appendix to the present volume would make this volume inordinately lengthy. With some reluctance the editors felt it was necessary to assign the Election Code to a later volume.

Throughout the *Code* there are numerous cross-references to the Penal and Procedure Codes.[1] As we have seen, Bentham wrote extensively on these Codes at the time he was drafting the *Constitutional Code* and felt that the various Codes were closely linked. However, because neither Code was completed, Bentham's references to them raise several problems, as the references cannot be assigned to specific texts. The references to the Penal Code have been directed to the Table of Contents to the Penal Code which was affixed to the 1830 volume and is reproduced here as Table 2. References to the Procedure Code, where possible, are made to the version appearing in the Bowring edition. However, Bentham's references do not always correspond to this material. For example, Bentham's references to the Procedure Code would require a more extensive chapter on evidence than appears in the Bowring version.[2] In the present volume, therefore, Bentham's cross-references to the Procedure Code are connected either to the Bowring version or to other works by Bentham on evidence and procedure.

Bentham's Table of the *Constitutional Code* which sets out the chapters and sections of the whole work, and appears here as Table 1, is reprinted as it appeared in the 1830 volume without the reference omitted by mistake from chapter VIII to '§ 12, *Securities for appropriate aptitude*'. Although the headings of the various sections of Volume I do not correspond exactly with those actually employed by Bentham, they are so close that no revision has been thought necessary.

After the publication of the 1830 text Bentham continued to write material which might have been incorporated in some further version of it. For example, he wrote between March and May 1830 a draft of a proposed supplement to chapter IX, section 15 on the relationship between remuneration and duty.[3] It is difficult to ascertain Bentham's intentions for writings such as this and the editors

---

[1] See Ch. V, § 5, Art. 6n, p. 38 n. 1, and § 6, Art. 2n, p. 39 n. 1, below.
[2] See, for example, Ch. VI, § 27, Art. 20n, p. 99 n. 1, below.
[3] See BL Add. MS 33,549, fos. 143–55; see also ibid. fo. 184.

have concluded that the inclusion of such material as part of the actual *Code* would not be warranted. Despite its length and complexity, the *Code* is a highly compressed work and much material written for it, especially essays which discuss general principles and provide the rationale for particular provisions, was eventually excluded by Bentham himself from the final version. A number of these manuscripts remain of considerable interest and will form part of the supplementary volumes of *Code* material.

More appropriate to this volume, however, are a series of notes in Bentham's hand in a printed version of the 1830 volume located in the Library of University College London.[1] These notes refer to various events and people and where possible they have been discussed and annotated in footnotes to the text.

The text of this volume corresponds as closely as possible with the style and conventions of the 1830 text. Some minor variations, such as replacing double with single inverted commas in quotations are listed in the introductory note to the 1830 Collation.[2] Bentham's footnotes are indicated by suprascript letters, editorial footnotes by suprascript numerals. Editorial apparatus is kept to a bare minimum and confined to the use of square brackets to indicate editorially inserted words.

---

[1] UC Bentham Collection shelf-mark 2 c.19.
[2] p. 461, below.

# CONSTITUTIONAL CODE;

FOR THE USE OF

## ALL NATIONS

AND

## ALL GOVERNMENTS

PROFESSING

## LIBERAL OPINIONS.

BY

## JEREMY BENTHAM.

## VOL. I.

## LONDON:

PRINTED FOR THE AUTHOR,

AND

## PUBLISHED BY ROBERT HEWARD,

AT THE OFFICE OF THE WESTMINSTER REVIEW,

2 WELLINGTON STREET, STRAND

## 1830.

# PREFACE

OF the three Volumes of which the proposed Constitutional Code will consist, the first makes thus its appearance by itself, without waiting for the two others. To their completion, however, very little is now wanting; they are, both of them, in such a state of forwardness, that, were the Author to drop into his last sleep while occupied in the tracing of these lines, able hands are not wanting, from which the task of laying the work before the public would receive its completion.

Of the various concurrent causes of the retardation,——one has been ——the desire of the Author to attach to this First Volume an Introductory Dissertation, having for its *subject-matter* the various forms of which the supreme authority in a state is susceptible; and for its *object*, by bringing to view the advantages and disadvantages of each, to exhibit their respective degrees of eligibility; meaning always by eligibility, conduciveness to the maximum of the aggregate of happiness. Taking, for the source of distinction and partition, the relative numbers of the ruling and influential one or few, on the one part, and the subject-many on the other,——are therein brought to view—— in the first place, the three simple forms of government——Monarchy, Aristocracy, and Democracy; in the next place, the several compounds, actual and possible, capable of being formed by their admixture.

For this discussion, *matter*——in quantity adequate, or little short of it——has, this long time, been in existence: but, as to *form*, that which presented itself as the best adapted, has not yet been given to it.

Under these circumstances, it seems to me, that for the chance of giving to the work, at a point of time not likely ever to arrive, the degree of supposed perfection, the phantasmagoric image of which has, like a *New Jerusalem*, been always in view,——good economy could not now advise the foregoing the advantage of making application of this same matter, to such measures, as are already on the carpet, placed thereon by the authority of Government itself. On this consideration it is, that this first Volume makes its appearance, without waiting for either of the two next.

The political communities, whose benefit this foremost part of my *all-comprehensive Code* (or say, in one word, of my *Pannomion*) has had principally in view——these communities have been for the time

[1] See the Introduction, p. xli.

3

*present*, those, more particularly, which have grown out of the wreck of the Spanish monarchy (not to speak as yet of the Portuguese) in the American hemisphere. To time future—whether before the present generation has passed away or not till a length of time after, and what length, I cannot take upon me to pronounce—was all along referred the applicability of the work to the use of the British Empire.[1]

In saying *the work*, I meant the whole of it, considered as a *whole*: for, as to *parts* of it, in no small quantity, if applicable to any one form of government, so are they to every other; and this, without any diminution of the proportions of power at present possessed by the several constituted authorities.

As to this part, and some others, of the fruits of my unremitted labours,—the cause of their thus meeting the public eye in an un-matured state, is this:—What occurs to me at this moment is—that, if so it be, that they afford any promise of being in any way or degree beneficial to mankind,—it behoves me to make the most of the short remainder of my life, for the purpose of causing them to be brought into the world under my own eye. On this consideration accordingly it is, that I have added to this volume a sort of skeleton of the contents of the two others, in the form of a Table of the *titles*, of the chapters and their several sections.

Continuing the preference thus given to real usefulness over appearances, to this Volume or a subsequent one, I have or shall have added similar skeletons, of such of the parts of my proposed Pannomion as regard what, in contradistinction to *international*, may be designated by the appellation of *internal* law. These are:—1. The *Right-conferring*, commonly called the *Civil*, Code:—2. The *Wrong-repressing*, commonly called the *Penal*, Code: both belonging to what I call the *substantive* branch of law:—3. The *Procedure* Code, constituting what I call the *adjective* branch: growing—the whole of it together,—and in my view of the matter, without need of distinction,—out of those two sub-branches of the substantive branch.[2]

To a student in the art of legislation, it might be a sort of pastime —taking in hand any one of these same skeletons, to guess all along

---

[1] For discussions of Bentham's conception of the *Pannomion* and the specific nations for which the *Constitutional Code* was written, see the Introduction, pp. xi and xxxv.

[2] The Tables for the *Constitutional Code* itself, and for the Penal Code, are reproduced in this edition as Tables 1 and 2. No Table for the Civil Code or for the Procedure Code was published in Bentham's lifetime: see further p. 5 and n. 3.

——what may be the composition, of the flesh and blood——the muscular and vascular system——destined to be attached to it: as, from the protuberances in the cranium, *phrenologists* undertake to determine the moral and intellectual contents of the cerebrum and cerebellum:——a sort of puzzle, not calling for more labour than does a game of chess, and assuredly standing somewhat above it in the scale of usefulness.[1]

When what is above was sent to press I was in expectation of being able to add, to the two *Constitutional Code* and *Penal Code* Tables subjoined to this volume, a third; namely, the *Civil Code* Table. But, by ulterior consideration has been produced——the apprehension of such a portion of ulterior delay, as would amount to an infringement, too great to admit of apology, of the undertaking, by which, in an advertisement, the promise had been afforded, of the appearance of this Volume on the first of this present month of April.[2]

To some ulterior opportunity must, therefore, of necessity, be referred——the appearance of this same *Civil Code* Table:——which opportunity will not, I hope, be far distant; probably not more so than the appearance of the *Dispatch Court Bill*, to which a Procedure Code Table is in readiness to be annexed.[3]

In the meantime, an arrangement presents itself, by which, to any expectations which may have been raised by the announcement in question, some little satisfaction may, it is hoped, be provisionally afforded. It consists——in the giving, in this place, insertion to a simple and short indication, of a few *leading and distinctive features*, by the aggregate of which, the method pursued in the proposed Civil Code, will be seen to have been rendered decidedly, manifestly, widely, and,

[1] The remainder of this 1830 Preface was not reprinted in Bowring. As the beginning of the next paragraph indicates, the first part of the preface (1830, pp. v–viii) was printed before the remainder was written.

[2] No such advertisements can be found in the most likely papers, the *Morning Chronicle* and the *Globe and Traveller*, between 1 January and 1 April 1830; nor does there seem to have been any advance announcement in the *Westminster Review*. That the first volume of the *Constitutional Code* was indeed published at the beginning of April 1830 is evident from a letter dated 3 April 1830 in which Bentham says that the volume 'is just this instant published' (UC x. 233: Bentham to J. C. Herries).

[3] *Equity Dispatch Court Proposal; containing a plan for the speedy and unexpensive termination of the suits now depending in Equity Courts*, London, 1830 (Bowring, iii. 297–317). The related *Equity Dispatch Court Bill; being a Bill for the institution of an experimental judicatory under the name of the Court of Dispatch* (Bowring, iii. 319–431), was not published until it appeared in the Bowring edition, where it is described as the last work upon which Bentham was engaged before his death, and as having been 'written at different periods in 1829, 1830, and 1831'. No Civil Code or Procedure Code Table in fact appeared with either work.

it is hoped, not disadvantageously, different from every method that has ever been pursued in any authoritative Civil Code, which, in any political community, has ever as yet made its appearance.

I. *Distinctive feature the first.*——Antecedently to all articles of the *enactive* kind, as exemplified throughout in the text of the proposed Constitutional Code,——an adequate allotment of articles of the *expositive* kind, presenting an exposition of the import of the several all-comprehensive terms, which will come to be employed in and by the thereinafter ensuing articles of the enactive kind.

Take, for example, on the one part, the words *obligation, burthen;* on the other part, the words *right, power, exemption, benefit, trust;* which last is *power*, but charged with the obligation of not making use of it but for the benefit of another person. These may be termed names of so many *fictitious entities*, in contradistinction to the words *things immoveable, things moveable*, and *persons;* under one or other of which three denominations, all names of *truly existing entities* may be ranged. These may be stated as so many words belonging to the vocabulary of *universal jurisprudence*. So likewise, in the hereunto annexed Constitutional and Penal Code Tables, all that are not in familiar use.

By proceeding in this way, and accordingly by this method, clear ideas will, it is hoped, be found associated with these same simple terms, by the use and application of which, expression will be given to the several enactments, by which, throughout the whole text of the work, they are followed. *Rule*, thus observed, this:——antecedently to names of *complex* ideas, bring to view, and render as extensively as possible clear and intelligible, the names of the *simple* ideas of which they are respectively composed.

On the occasion of all hitherto existing Codes,——of these same terms of universal jurisprudence, the *import* has been tacitly assumed to be no less *clear*, than the *terms* themselves are *familiar*. But, unhappily, by whosoever will take the trouble of examining into this matter, the truth of the case will be found to be widely different.

In regard to *ideas*, familiarity is no more a proof of *clearness*, than, in regard to *opinions*, it is of *correctness*.

II. *Distinctive feature the second.*——From each portion of the *Civil* Code, reference made to a correspondent portion of the *Penal* Code: each will thus be rendered, as mathematicians say, the *complement*, to the correspondent one. *Given* the method pursued in and by the *Penal*, given is thus the method, pursued in and by this same about-to-be-presented *Civil* Code.

In no hitherto existing Civil Code, authoritative or proposed,——between the method therein pursued, and the method pursued in a Penal

Code, *of* or proposed *for*, the same political community,——is any such connection and correspondence held up to view, or exemplified: they are mutually, (these same portions of the one and the other Code) as a logician would say, *disparate;* as a mathematician would say, *incommensurable*.

III. *Distinctive feature the third.*——On the occasion of the Civil Code, as well as on the occasion of the Penal Code,——keeping steadily and undeviatingly in view that quality of cognoscibility or (to derive the word from an English root) say *knowableness*, on which every good effect, capable of being derived from any portion whatever of the matter of law, is so essentially and absolutely dependant.

To this end I keep in view the fable of the *bundle of sticks*, conjunctively unmanageable and inapplicable to use, separately manageable and applicable. In looking over the catalogue of the different sorts of *things*, which require respectively to be taken for subjects of enactment,——I look out, at the same time, for the different classes of *persons*, who in one way or other have respectively an *interest* in these same sorts of *things:* this, to the intent that each individual person may have it in his power to make himself acquainted, with all the several ordinances made by the legislature, with which, on pain of being rendered a sufferer by his want of knowledge, it is incumbent on him to be at all times apprized of, without being obliged to incumber his mind by lodging in it the matter of any such laws, from his unacquaintance with which no such unpleasant consequence will ensue.

Thus it is——that, for example, by every *sort* of *things*, with which, in the capacity of *manufacturers*, or in that of *vendors*, all persons belonging to either of the above classes of *persons* are conversant,—— a demand will be produced for a separate article in the list of *particular codes*, as effectually as by every different *profession* exercised by a class of *persons* at large, in and by every *sort* of *situation, occupied* by a class of persons belonging to the *Official Establishment*.

Thus, in the case of *things immoveable:* of which class of things *buildings* are one modification. These being subject-matters of possession, and naturally of fabrication,——from the enactments made in relation to *these things*, will a demand be created for two correspondent *Particular Codes:* namely, the *Builder's* Code, and the *Householder's* Code; whereupon, he who is a *builder* and not a *householder* will have need of having present to his *mind*, and accordingly on his *shelves*, the matter of the *Builder's* Code, without incumbering it or them with the matter of the *Householder's* Code; while he, who is a *householder*, and not a *builder*, will have need of having present to *his* mind, and accordingly on his shelves, the matter of the *Householder's*

Code, without need of incumbering it or them with the matter of the *Builder's* Code.

Moreover, on this occasion, a consideration which presents itself to view, is——that in regard to *possession*, whatever string of topics may require to be touched upon under the head of any *one* species of *valuable thing* in the Pannomion and Civil Code of any one political community,——the same string may require to have place in the Pannomion and Civil Code of every other such community. As for example, whatever the *thing* be——whether a *house* or a *horse*——if it be *in the man's possession*, (whether in the *physical* or in the *legal* sense of the word *possession*), an *efficient cause* there will have been of the *commencement* of it being in such his possession——as also, unless he be immortal, sooner or later, *some one* efficient cause (not to speak of others) of its *ceasing* so to be.

Now then, for an extensively applicable, and practically useful definition. Of each and every subject-matter of possession, be it what it may,——that person is, at every assignable point of time, *in possession*, in whose favour an *efficient cause of commencement* of possession in regard to it, having taken place, no *efficient cause of the cessation* of such possession has taken place.

Here then may be seen, under the head of every imaginable subject-matter of possession, in relation to which any portion of law peculiar to that same subject-matter has place,——the need of two divisions of the matter of the Civil Code, headed respectively, *Efficient cause of commencement of possession*, and *Efficient cause of cessation of possession*. Not that, in relation to every species of *thing* which can be in a man's possession, or every species of *personal service*, the right to which can be in a man's possession,——it will be needful or proper, that the *matter* of the Code should be in the same terms, or to the same effect; of the identity in question, all that is either needful or universally admissible, is——identity as between head and head.

In this mode of arrangement may be seen an instrument of abbreviation, and a security against inconsistency and conflict between one expression of will and another in the same Pannomion. In whatsoever instances, in regard to any two sorts of *things*, the matter of the arrangement made by the law is in import intended to be the same,——insertion being given to it under the head of one of these two sorts of things, in the appropriate part of the law,——instead of re-exhibiting this same matter in that part of the Code which has for its subject the *other* sort of thing, simple *reference* will be the instrument employed for the purpose of designation: simple *reference*, instead of *repetition* by *reimpression*.

Now for the practical usefulness of these same instruments of elucidation. In regard to anything that you call your own, is it your wish to know whether it be really and assuredly your own? Well then: what you must stand assured of is,—in the first place, that in your favour, in regard to it, *some one* article, belonging to the list of *efficient causes of commencement* in regard to legal possession had had place; in the next place, that in your disfavour, no one article belonging to the list of *efficient causes of cessation* (meaning *final* cessation) of such possession has taken place.

In no existing Civil Code is this instrument of elucidation, or any token of it, to be found.

The case is—that every such Civil Code is a *chaos*, and every such chaos a different one. In every one of them to make out the list of the instances in which application is made of these two efficient causes, what you would have to do is,—to dig into every part of this chaos and pick them out of it.

IV. *Distinctive feature the fourth.*—Under each head, from the matter included under that head, *reference* made to every *other* portion of matter, in which,—in any other part of the Code or the Pannomion,—provision, bearing upon this same subject-matter of enactment, has place. Good effects, produced by this feature, and which will be seen to be the same in this case as in the last foregoing, these—

1. Consistency. 2. Conciseness, by avoidance of repetition.

V. *Distinctive feature the fifth.*—Use made, throughout, of the distinction between the five species of matter, the demand for which may have place in the text of a code of law, on the occasion of one and the same arrangement: 1. The Enactive. 2. The Expositive. 3. The Instructional. 4. The Ratiocinative. 5. The Exemplificative.

# STATE OF &#123;      &#125;
# ITS CONSTITUTIONAL CODE[a]

## CHAPTER I

## TERRITORY OF THIS STATE, NAME, SITUATION, BOUNDARIES, DIVISIONS

*Enactive*

ARTICLE 1. &#123;    &#125; is the denomination of this state. Its constitution is that which stands expressed in this present Code.

*Enactive*

ART. 2. The territory appertaining to it is as follows. &#123;   &#125;
☞ Here insert its situation on the globe, in latitude and longitude, with a designation of its boundaries, natural and conventional.

*Enactive*

ART. 3. The whole territory is divided into Districts. Each District is an Election District (as to which see Ch. vi. LEGISLATURE) sending one Deputy to serve as a member of the Legislature. Subject to alteration by the Legislature, by union or division of entire Districts, each District is moreover the territory of a Sublegislature, as per Ch. [xxx.] SUBLEGISLATURES. Also, subject, in like manner, to alteration, it is the territory of an Appellate Judicatory, as per Ch. xii. JUDICIARY, and Ch. xxii. APPELLATE JUDICATORIES. Of these Districts the denominations are as follows. ☞ Here insert the list.

---

[a] (Constitutional Code.) Of the whole *Pannomion*, the first part in the order of importance, thence in the order of appearance, is this Code: in the order of importance, because on the end herein declared, as per §3,[1] and the means here employed in the first instance for the attainment of it, will depend the several subordinate ends pursued, and the several correspondent sets of means, employed in all the several other Codes. *Pannomion* is, in Greek, the *whole* body of the *laws*.

---

[1] It is not clear what Bentham intended by this cross-reference. 'Ends and Means' are discussed in Ch. II: see especially Art. 1 for the 'all comprehensive ... end in view'.

11

*Enactive*

ART. 4. Each District is divided into Subdistricts. Each Subdistrict is, as per Election Code, (see Ch. vi. LEGISLATURE §4,) a *Vote receiving*, or say *Voting District*.[1] Each Voting District sends one Deputy to the Sublegislature of the District. Subject to union and division, as above, each Subdistrict is the territory of an Immediate Judicatory, as per Ch. xii. JUDICIARY, and Ch. xiii. JUDGES IM-MEDIATE. Of these Subdistricts, the denominations are as follows.
        ☞ Here insert the list.

*Enactive*

ART. 5. Each Subdistrict is divided into Bis-subdistricts. Each Bis-subdistrict is the territory of a Local Headman, as to whom see Ch. [xxvi]. In case of need,——for example, by change in populousness or condition in other respects,——Bis-subdistricts may come to be united or divided, as above. Of a Bis-subdistrict, if divided, the Sections will be Tris-subdistricts, and so on.

*Enactive. Instructional*

ART. 6. In this scheme of territorial division, the Legislature will, at all times, make any such alteration as in its judgment the exigencies or convenience of the time shall have required. Of the Districts ori-ginally marked out, it will make any two or more into one: it will divide any one or more, each of them into two or more, reserving to each the name and attributes of a District. So likewise as to Sub-districts and Bis-subdistricts. But, seeing the complication and confu-sion that might ensue,——it will not, but in a case of urgency, at any of these three stages in the course of division, proceed upon any plan, which shall not be, as above, *commensurable* with the one originally employed.

INSTRUCTIONAL DISSERTATION

The several portions of territory, for the denomination of which the above-mentioned appellations are respectively employed, are the sup-posed results of so many supposed sectional operations, having for their subject matter the *entire* or *aggregate* of the dominions of the state in question, whatever it be; distant dependencies not being taken into account: so many of these denominations, so many *grades* or *stages* in the process of division:——a process, the effect of which is

[1] See Ch. VI, § 4n, p. 48n.

12

to multiply the subject matter of the division, by a number equal to that of the *divisor* employed. Thus, for simplicity of conception, suppose the same divisor 20 employed at each operation: divide the whole territory of the state by 20, you have 20 of the portions above denominated *Districts:* divide the districts each by 20, you have in each District 20 *Subdistricts;* in the whole territory, 400 Subdistricts: divide the Subdistricts each by 20, you have in each Subdistrict 20 *Bis-subdistricts*, in each District, 400 Bis-subdistricts; in the whole state, 8000 Bis-subdistricts: divide the Bis-subdistricts each by 20, you have in each Bis-subdistrict 20 *Tris-subdistricts;* in each Subdistrict 400 Tris-subdistricts; in each District 8000 Tris-subdistricts: in the whole state, 160,000 Tris-subdistricts.

For any such divisional operation, it appears not that any practical use can be assigned, other than that of its being employed in furnishing stations for functionaries; for functionaries of some sort or other, one or more, in the several sections of territory which, taken together, exhibit the result of it.

If, in any state, application be made of the principles of the present proposed Code, the number of the sectional operations performed, and thence of the *stages*, or say *grades*, of division produced and employed, as above, will naturally be influenced by the magnitude of the aggregate territory of such state, combined with that of the population. It will not however increase in any regular proportion: for, after a certain number of these grades or stages, every good effect contemplated by addition to the aggregate number, may be produced by augmenting the divisor, and thence the number of the sections of territory at one or more stages; thus avoiding the production of the bad effect, to wit, the *complication*, which would be the necessary result of every addition made to the number of these same stages.

On the above grounds, and others, which will appear presently, the number of stages represented by the denomination *Tris-subdistricts*, is the number here regarded as the greatest number, for which, in the most extensive state, there can be any use: while, on the other hand, as, for example, in a *Swiss Canton*, the smallness of the aggregate territory may have the effect of reducing the number of these stages or grades to *one*, or even rendering any such divisional operation, with its results, altogether needless.

In Ch. xxvi of this proposed Code, the existence is assumed of a demand for a public functionary, in every portion of territory, which, according to the above explanation, comes under the denomination of *a Bis-subdistrict*——a portion of territory resulting from the division of the above-explained portion called *Subdistrict*, as that

13

does from the division of the portion styled *a District*, as above explained: both of them susceptible of different denominations, according to the different purposes to which they are respectively made applicable. This same least portion of territory is the portion employed as the seat or station of a sort of functionary who, in Ch. xxvi, will be found designated by the appellation of a *Local Headman:* a functionary of whose situation and proposed functions, some conception, though very rough and subject to great amendment, particularly in the way of addition, may be conveyed by the word *Maire*, in the sense in which it is universally employed in France; the word *Mayor*, in the sense in which it is in some instances employed in England; and the word *Alcalde*, in the sense in which it is employed in Spain, and the dominions still or of late belonging to Spain, in America and elsewhere.

A further, though tacitly made, assumption is, that, in each territory belonging to an *Immediate* Judicatory (so called in contradistinction to an *Appellate* Judicatory), there will be a demand for *Local Headmen*, (number indetermined, because on the present occasion, impossible to be determined,) each with his appropriate territory—constituting his *local field of service*.

A state of things, which might perhaps come to be found exemplified, is—that, in which, in the instance of this or that territory of an Immediate Judicatory, territory and population considered together, the extent might be so small, that a single *Local Headman's* station, having for its limits the same as those of the territory of the Judicatory, would be found sufficient. But, by this circumstance, no demand would be produced for any change, in the arrangement, here grounded on the supposition of an indefinite number of *Local Headmen's territories*, included in every *Immediate Judge's territory*.

Of a demand for a sort of territory of a still inferior grade—of a sort of territory which would come under the denomination of a *Tris-subdistrict*, the notion may naturally enough be presented in English by the word *parish*, in the several other European languages, by the several words derived in those languages respectively from the same root: that is to say, the Greek word, which signifies a cluster of neighbouring habitations, and which, in Latin characters is expressed by the word paroecia, or in Greek παροικία. But, supposing the existence of a peremptory demand for a class of territories, of a grade so low as the one expressed by this same word *Tris-subdistrict*,—no sufficient reason will, it is believed, be found for the allotment of any thing more than an extremely limited *logical* field of action to the corresponding functionary: no reason for any such field of action, comparable in extent to that which will here be seen allotted to the *Local Headman* in his territory.

Only, as above observed, for simplicity of conception,—has the same [divisor],[1] to wit, 20, been assumed, on the instance of every stage or grade brought to view. In practice, the diversities incident to magnitude of territory and population considered, together with the ever-variable magnitude of population in each territory, whatsoever be the state in question,—divisions of very different magnitudes, in the several grades or stages compared with one another, will be found requisite; and, by means of all these diversities taken together, the same number of stages or grades will be found applicable to different states, the aggregate portions of which are of the most widely differing magnitudes.

What is plain is—that to no state whatsoever can application be made of this Code, without its finding such state already subjected to some all-comprehensive scheme or other of territorial division, as above explained. But, by no such existing scheme will any naturally insuperable impediment be opposed to the scheme here proposed, in so far as, by the adoption of it, a promise may be thought to be afforded, of any specific and assignable advantageous effects. By separation or aggregation, or both together, the existing portions of territorial divisions, whatsoever they may be, and howsoever denominated, may be made applicable to all the several purposes which will here be seen proposed: and thus may they be made the seats of functionaries, invested with the functions herein respectively defined.

As to the *names* herein given to the results of the several successive divisional operations, some conception of the peculiar use of them can scarcely fail to have presented itself to view. For, thus it is that the order, of which the numeration table gives the expression, may be given to any scheme of division established or proposed, which otherwise, by the total want of all indication of the relation between one elementary part and another—in a word, by the perfect *arbitrariness* of the import of every denomination employed, must impose so heavy and needless a task on the conception and memory of every person, to whose cognizance it comes to be presented.[a]

To the forming of an adequate idea of the disadvantages attendant on the existing system of denomination for this class of objects, and

[a] In this scheme may be seen exhibited a portion of universal language applicable to the subject with equal advantage and facility to the several different languages of all civilized nations: the language of the numeration table being alike needed by all, and accordingly alike employed by all: and thus far, the language of each may be understood by the natives of every other, and to incomparably greater perfection than at present the language of any one is understood by the natives of that one.

---

[1] 1830 and Bowring, 'division'; but Bentham is clearly referring to the divisor.

thence of the advantage producible by the adoption of the here-proposed one,——it would be necessary to look over the list of them, as they stand exemplified in some one or more political state: and that of the British dominions, compared and contrasted with those of France, will perhaps be deemed sufficient. In the case of France, as regenerated by the Revolution, simplicity and uniformity will be found observable; natural expressiveness, not: in the case of England, Scotland, and Ireland, natural expressiveness equally wanting; and, instead of simplicity and uniformity, a chaos.[a]

In France, the whole kingdom, distant dependencies out of the question, is divided into *départements*; each department, into *arrondissements*; each *arrondissement*, into *Justices de paix*;[1] each *Justice de paix*, into *communes*. Of *paroisses*, (in English, *parishes*,) no mention is made.

In the here proposed plan of nomenclature, they would be thus denominated:

1. Départements——districts.
2. Arrondissements——subdistricts.
3. Justices de paix——bis-subdistricts.
4. Communes——tris-subdistricts.

From the example of England, no instruction,——equivalent to the time, space, and labour requisite for the extraction and communication of it,——could be obtained: so great the diversification, so thick

---

[a] If, in the present instance, this same principle of denomination is, in its nature, applicable with more or less advantage, so it will, it is believed, be found to be in a great variety of other instances: if to any natural and material whole, so to any ideal or other factitious aggregate——say, for example, to any of those aggregates which form the subject matter of natural history: and in particular, if classed by divisional operations, performed in the dichotomous mode, as exhibited table-wise in Dr Dumeril's admirable French work on Zoology.[2] But, ere it had proceeded far, this mode of designation would probably be found too unwieldy for use, at any rate unless figures could be substitutes for words.

---

[1] Bowring, here and below, '*Cantons*'. This is of course strictly correct, the *canton* being the intermediate administrative area between the *arrondissement* and the *commune* in the scheme introduced in France after the Revolution of 1789. The *justice de paix* was the court, or the area of that court's jurisdiction, presided over by a *juge de paix*, as provided in the scheme of judicial organisation established in August 1790. The jurisdiction of a *juge de paix* coincided with the boundaries of the *canton*, so that Bentham's error is terminological rather than substantive.

[2] André Marie Constant Dumeril (1774-1860), trained as a physician, became Professor of Anatomy and subsequently of Zoology at Paris. Bentham's reference here is probably to Dumeril's *Zoologie Analytique, ou méthode naturelle de classification des animaux rendue plus facile à l'aide de tableaux synoptiques*, Paris, 1806.

the complication and confusion, in which it is involved. If a *county* be taken as corresponding to *district*, the number of grades of division is, in some counties, different from what it is in others: and, in two counties in which the number of these stages is the same, the denominations given to .the results, are different.[1] See Mr Rickman's highly instructive preface, prefixed to the Population Returns made to the English House of Commons, and printed.[2]

For different purposes, two schemes of division have place:——the one, called *civil* or *temporal*, instituted for the purpose of security against adversaries, internal and external; the other, called *ecclesiastical* or *spiritual*, instituted in a dark age by a foreign potentate—— foreign, with reference to the British Isles——for the purpose of extracting money, on pretence of saving souls.[3]

On the *temporal* plan, the result of the division, made in the ultimate grade, is called a *township, village*, or *hamlet*: in the spiritual, a *parish*; in some instances, the two results are coincident; in others, not. For a multitude of important purposes, in particular for *taxation* and *registration*, the *spiritual* plan has, in the case of this ultimate result, been adopted into the *temporal*; and by this adoption, vast and various is the confusion and mischief that has been produced. See Ch. xxvii. LOCAL REGISTRARS.

In a political state, the territory of which, (distant dependencies out of the question,) were not much different from that of France, England, Scotland, or even Ireland,——the result of the ultimate sectional operation might, perhaps, be of a magnitude between that of the French *arrondissement*, and that of the French *commune*. With a view to the present purpose, all these integers of territory are put upon a level: for, great as is the difference between the largest of

---

[1] Bentham presumably had in mind the counties of Yorkshire and Lincolnshire. Both were divided administratively into three areas, but whereas the divisions of Yorkshire were known as 'Ridings', those of Lincolnshire were known as the Parts of Holland, the Parts of Kesteven, and the Parts of Lindsey.

[2] John Rickman (1771-1840), a noted statistician, had been private secretary to Bentham's stepbrother Charles Abbot (1757-1829), later 1st Baron Colchester, when the latter was Speaker of the House of Commons. Abbot was active in the introduction of a regular census in Britain, and Rickman, who was a Clerk Assistant in the House of Commons from 1814 until his death, prepared the census reports and 'Preliminary Observations' in 1801, 1811, 1821, and 1831.

[3] The original division of England into parishes is usually attributed to Theodore of Tarsus, Archbishop of Canterbury from 669 until his death in 690, who was also responsible for substantial modifications in the division of the country into dioceses. The parish system was further developed in the reign of Edgar (973-5), but seems not to have been complete before the reign of Edward III in the fourteenth century. The original parishes commonly corresponded to the earlier township or village.

them and the smallest—between France and Scotland—still, it is not (it is believed) so great, as not to be capable of being made up for, by a difference in number; that is to say, by giving, to a country resembling France in magnitude, a greater number—to a country resembling Scotland, a lesser number, of these same *atoms* of territory, if such they may be called: for *atom* is from the correspondent Greek word, which means that which is not susceptible of ulterior division, or at least has not been subjected to it.

Note here as to economy, and the effect produced in relation to it, by the number of grades of territorial divisions. On one account, the greater this number, the greater the aggregate mass of expense: on another account, the greater this same number, the less the mass of expense. The circumstance by which the increase is effected in the expense is this—that, by each grade of divisional operation, are produced a set of sub-territories, each of them with a set of officers and official residences to be provided for. The circumstance by which diminution is effected in the expense is—that in proportion to the increase in the number of those same sets of officers, and official residences, is the diminution in the magnitude of each such sub-territory: and thence, (supposing them rendered as equal as may be in magnitude,) the less is their magnitude, and the less the journeys which those inhabitants whose habitations are at the greatest distance from the seat of business—the official residence—will have to make in passing to and from it, with the intervening demurrage. Too apt to be overlooked, but not the less real and important, is this latter *item* of expense. In the case of the vast majority, expense in time is expense in money. The expense in officers' pay and official residences is borne proportionably by the opulent few and the unopulent many: the expense in time employed, as above, in journeys, is borne almost exclusively by the unopulent many: by those to whom their time affords no profit, no loss is sustained from the unprofitable expenditure of it.

## CHAPTER II

### ENDS AND MEANS

*Enactive. Instructional*

ART. 1. Of this constitution, the all-comprehensive object, or end in view, is, from first to last, the greatest happiness of the greatest number; namely, of the individuals, of whom, the political community, or state, of which it is the constitution, is composed; strict regard

being all along had to what is due to every other—as to which, see
Ch. vii. LEGISLATOR'S INAUGURAL DECLARATION.

Correspondent fundamental principle: the *greatest happiness principle*.

Correspondent all-comprehensive and all-directing rule—*Maximize happiness*.

### Enactive. Instructional

ART. 2. Means employed, two—aptitude maximized; expense minimized.

Correspondent principles—1. The official-aptitude-maximization-principle. 2. The expense-minimization-principle.

Correspondent rules. Rule 1. Maximize appropriate official aptitude.

Rule 2. Minimize official expense.

For the manner in which these rules second one another, see Ch. ix. MINISTERS COLLECTIVELY. §15, *Remuneration*. §16, *Locable who*. §17, *Located how*.

### Expositive

ART. 3. Included in the matter of *expenditure* is the matter of *punishment*, as well as the matter of *reward*.

### Expositive

ART. 4. The matter of punishment is evil applied to a particular purpose.

### Expositive

ART. 5. The matter of evil is composed of pain and loss of pleasure.

### Expositive

ART. 6. The matter of reward is the matter of good applied to a particular purpose.

### Expositive

ART. 7. The matter of good is composed of pleasure and exemption from pain.

### Enactive. Instructional

ART. 8. Consistently with the *greatest happiness principle*, evil cannot be employed otherwise than as a *means*: as a means of producing, in the character of punishment, or otherwise, more than equivalent pleasure, or excluding more than equivalent pain, or producing the one, as well as excluding the other.

### Enactive. Instructional

ART. 9. Employed in the character of punishment, it cannot, according to the greatest happiness principle, be employed otherwise than as an *instrument of coercion:* coercion, by *fear* of future punishment in case of future delinquency: coercion, for the production, as above, of more than equivalent good.

### Instructional

ART. 10. According to this same principle, pleasure is at once *an end* and *a means:* as *an end*, aimed at on every occasion: as *a means*, employed on particular occasions, to wit, when the matter of it is employed as the matter of reward.

### Enactive. Instructional

ART. 11. Employed as the matter of *reward*, the matter of *good* cannot, according to the greatest happiness principle, be employed otherwise than as *an instrument of inducement.*

### Instructional

ART. 12. Of the matter of reward necessary to be employed as an instrument, or say a means of *government*, it is but in small proportion that it can be obtained, otherwise than by the help of *evil* employed in the way of punishment, and other ways as a means: witness, taxation: hence, under the greatest happiness principle, the necessity of minimizing expenditure, in the case of reward, as well as in the case of punishment.

### Instructional

ART. 13. To render the conduct of *rulers* conducive to the maximization of happiness, it is not less necessary to employ, in their case, the instrument of *coercion*, than in the case of *rulees*. But, the instrument of *coercion* being composed of the matter of *evil*, and the instrument of *inducement* of the matter of *good*——rulers are by the unalterable constitution of human nature, disposed to maximize the application of the matter of good to *themselves*, of the matter of evil to *rulees*.

### Instructional

ART. 14. Appropriate aptitude may be considered as having place in the case of *rulees*, as well as in the case of *rulers:* in both cases, according to the greatest happiness principle, it is aptitude for the maximization of happiness. But, in the case of *rulers*, it has a more particular signification: it is aptitude for the maximization of happiness in a particular way; namely, by a system of operations performed on *rulees*.

### Expositive

ART. 15. Of appropriate official aptitude, *elements*, or say, *branches*, three——moral, intellectual, and active; of intellectual, again, two—— cognitional and judicial; knowledge and judgment.

### Ratiocinative. Enactive. Instructional

ART. 16. Rules for maximization of appropriate moral aptitude.

Rule I. The sovereign power give to those, whose interest it is that happiness be maximized.

Rule II. Of the possessors of subordinate power, maximize the responsibility——namely, as towards the aforesaid possessors of the sovereign power.

Note that, only by expectation of eventual *evil* (*punishment* included) can responsibility be established: neither by *expectation* of *eventual* good, nor by the *possession* of *good* (*reward* included) can it be established.[a]

[a] (*Responsibility.*) Partly with, partly without design, the ideas, attached to the word *responsibility*, and its conjugate *responsible*, have come to us enveloped in a thick cloud: and from this cloud has flowed, it will soon be seen, practical evil——evil in the shape of waste, depredation, and corruption, covering the whole field of government. In a word, by it has been promoted, and in no small degree, the success of those designs, by which, instead of being, as it ought to be, *minimized*, official expense has, under so many governments, though under no other in so high a degree as under the English, been *maximized*. The time for the employment of this important word having here arrived, the operation of clearing it from the delusion of which it has been made the instrument, could not any longer be delayed.

The laws being, by the supposition, apt (for on no other supposition can they be either made or continued)——the object of the Legislator must, on every occasion, be——to maximize compliance with them: to maximize it on the part of all *persons*, and in particular, as on the present occasion, on the part of all *functionaries*. To maximize *compliance* with the laws, is, in other words, to maximize the *execution* and *effect* given to them. But, at the hands of no person, can any such execution and effect be depended upon, except in so far as, to this purpose the quality called *responsibility* has on his part place: responsibility, and *that* responsibility *effective*.

For the creation and preservation of this effective responsibility, punishment, it will be seen,——*punishment* (by means of the *fear* of it) is the only instrument which, as in other, so in official situations, can be employed. For engaging a man to take upon himself the obligations attached to the situation, *reward*, in some shape or other, is indeed an instrument, and, generally speaking, the only apt instrument that can be employed: but, to the purpose of ensuring the regular

ART. 17. For official aptitude, cognitional, judicial, and active, joined
to minimization of expense, principles employed are three.

Principle I. Probation, or say public-examination-principle.

and apt fulfilment of those same obligations, punishment is the only instrument
which, the nature of man being such as it is, can be made applicable with effect.

Say then for shortness,

1. For constituting effective responsibility, punitional responsibility is indispensable.

2. By reward——by remuneration——no effective responsibility can be constituted. *Remuneratory responsibility* may be spoken of, but can neither be realized,
nor so much as conceived.

Give a man the matter of reward, and afterwards, in case of misconduct on
his part, take it away again, thus, it is true, may responsibility, and in a proportionable degree, be effected. But it is by the taking it away, not by the giving it,
that the effect is produced: and the taking it away is not reward but punishment.
Suppose money taken from him, the same quantity of money would have had
the same effect on him, had he had it from any other quarter under any other
name, instead of having it from the Legislator, under the name of *reward*.

To functionaries, however, as to other persons, reward is more acceptable
than punishment. Accordingly, while, for the establishment of this same effective responsibility, they have, in the instance of *other* persons, imployed *punishment*, and that in no small abundance,——with correspondent abundance, for the
production of the same desirable effect, in their *own* instance they have every
where employed *reward*. With this instrument thus employed, not only have
they represented themselves as having, in their own instance, established *responsibility*——responsibility under that very name, and that responsibility *effective*——
but the degree of its efficiency they have represented as rising in exact proportion to the quantity of the acceptable matter thus employed. In no imaginable
shape have they omitted thus to employ it: but the matter of opulence being the
only sort of acceptable matter capable of being applied, on every occasion and
to every person, let *pecuniary*, or the degree considered, let *opulential*, be the
name of the sort of *responsibility* thus professed to be established.

Seldom has profession been more hollow. The pretended species of responsibility thus described——it is not in the nature of it to be *effective*.

Not that for the speaking of it as such, a pretence is wanting; a pretence——nor
that an unplausible one: a pretence not only for the employing of this acceptable matter, but for maximizing it: for maximizing it in quantity and value——
maximizing it in all imaginable shapes——pretence is always ready at hand. That
where punishment is employed, its degree of certainty being given, the efficiency
of it——to wit, to the purpose of effective responsibility——will be as its magnitude, cannot but be admitted. Well then (says the distributer of good things) if
this is true of *punishment*, is it not so of *reward?* Answer. Not it indeed. When,
towards the production of effective responsibility, any thing is done by means of
the matter of reward, it is not by rewarding that the effect is produced, but by
punishing:——not by any thing that has been given to a man, but by that, whatever it be, which is taken from him; and, as to his having on a former occasion
received it under the name of reward, *that*, as above shown, makes not, to this
purpose, any the smallest difference.

True it is——the more you give to a man the more there is that, upon occasion,
you can take from him again; provided always that, at the time in question, you

Principle II. Pecuniary-competition-principle.

Principle III. Responsible-location-principle——location of subordinate by effectually responsible superordinate.

Inseparable is the connexion between all three principles. See Ch. ix. MINISTERS COLLECTIVELY. §[15], *Remuneration.* §[16], *Locable who.* §[17, Located] how. Ch. xii. JUDICIARY. §[28], *Locable who.*

## *Enactive*

ART. 18. For the functions exercised by the several functionaries, in the exercise of their several powers, and the fulfilment of their respective trusts, see the indication given in the chapters headed by the denomination of the several classes of functionaries: as per table of chapters and sections hereunto annexed.

## *Enactive. Instructional*

ART. 19. In relation to every official situation, a recapitulatory indication will be found given, of the securities herein provided for the maximization of appropriate aptitude, in all its above-mentioned branches, on the part of the functionary, by whom it is filled. See, in

find him in possession of it, and that you can manage so as to get at it. But, whether to effective responsibility any very advantageous addition can be made by giving a man money, for no more than a chance, more or less considerable, of being able to get that same money, or a part of it, back again from him,——may be left to be imagined.

By no quantity of the matter of reward, be it ever so great, can any the smallest addition be ever made to the degree of effective responsibility producible without it——producible by punishment alone. By punishment without reward, you can make a man suffer as much pain as man's nature is capable of suffering; and, by all the matter of reward you can give him or take from him, you cannot make him suffer any more.

What is more——by the pretended responsibility produced by the gift of money ——effective responsibility, so far from being increased, is, as has been seen, diminished; diminished, and *that* in a degree proportionate to the opulence produced by the money.

The short reason is——that, as the opulence increases, the value and efficiency of any quantity of punishment professed, or even endeavoured, to be employed in the production of punitional responsibility, is diminished: diminished, because, as opulence increases, so does the [facility] of obtaining accessaries before and after the fact——of obtaining accomplices and supporters.

As in the shape of *opulence*, thus is it with the matter of reward in all its several other shapes: *power, factitious dignity, reputation, ease* in so far as compatible with the enjoyment of power——in an official situation, ease at the expense of duty——and *vengeance* at the expense of justice. The more in all these shapes taken together a man has of it, the more is his effective responsibility—— his responsibility to the effect of his being made to suffer in proportion to his misconduct, diminished.

the several chapters, the several sections intituled *Securities for appropriate aptitude.*

## Expositive

ART. 20. Considered in respect of its immediate *effects*, responsibility is distinguishable into *punitional, satisfactional,* and *dislocational;* in respect of its *source*, into *legal* and *moral*,——legal, produced by the *legal sanction;* moral, by the *moral sanction*, as applied by the Public Opinion Tribunal, as per Ch. v. CONSTITUTIVE. §4, *Public Opinion Tribunal——Composition.* Of the satisfactional mode, the only generally applicable submode is the *pecuniarily-compensational*——say, for shortness, the *compensational.*

## Instructional

ART. 21. *Compensational responsibility* has the effect of *punitional*, in the ratio of the sum parted with, to the remainder left. By it, wounds inflicted by the wrong are curable: it is on this account, preferable, as far as it goes, to simply *punitional*, by which, though employed for the hope of preventing greater future evil, pain is the only effect produced with certainty.

## Expositive. Instructional

ART. 22. *Legal* responsibility is distinguishable into *judicial* and *administrational:* judicial, where, in the shape of punishment, the effect is produced by the judicial authority, on the ground of *moral inaptitude;* administrational, where, by superordinate authority, dislocation is applied on the ground of inaptitude, *intellectual* or *active*, pure of moral. By [dislocation],[1] evil from the like inaptitude on the part of the dislocatee is prevented with certainty; of punishment, except in the singular case of physically disabilitative punishment in the instance of the individual offender, the preventive effect is clouded in uncertainty.

## Instructional

ART. 23. To pecuniary compensation, pecuniary *responsibility* to a corresponding extent is necessary. But, beyond that extent, in proportion to its extent, obstruction is afforded by it to its own efficiency, as well as to that of *punitional* and *dislocational.* In other words, up to the amount of his debts, a man's responsibility to the purpose of his being made to afford compensation in a pecuniary shape is, indeed, in the direct ratio of his opulence; but, when a man's

---

[1] 1830 and Bowring, 'dislocational'; but the substantive rather than the adjective seems to be required by the context.

opulence exceeds the amount of his debts, this effective responsibility is rather in the *inverse* than in the *direct* ratio of it: this, even under a system, legislative and judicial, which has for its end the maximization of the happiness of the maximum number; much more, under a system by which, to the happiness of the ruling one, in conjunction with that of the ruling and otherwise influential few, that of the subject many, is in intention and effect constantly sacrificed. In the monarch, in whose situation opulential responsibility is maximized, effective responsibility, punitional, satisfactional, and dislocational, is *nihilized*.

## Instructional

ART. 24. As to moral responsibility, imperfect as it is, this species of security against misconduct is the more necessary to be brought to view, inasmuch as, in monarchies in general, were it not for this, there would be no responsibility at all: and, in other words, the monarch would be altogether without motives for compliance with the laws, even with those of his own making, which are, at all times, such as, and no other than, it is agreeable to him to make. It is by this source of restraint alone, that the English form of government——a mixture, composed of monarchico-aristocratical despotism with a spice of anarchy——has been preserved from passing through the condition of France, Russia, and Austria, into that of Spain and Portugal. Even without the assistance of a posse of his own creatures, acting under the name of a parliament——he may kill any person he pleases, violate any woman he pleases; take to himself or destroy any thing he pleases. Every person who resists him while in any such way occupied, is, by law, killable, and every person who so much as tells of it, is punishable. Yet, without the form of an act of parliament, he does nothing of all this. Why? Because by the power of the Public Opinion Tribunal, though he could not be either punished or effectually resisted, he might be, and would be, more or less annoyed.

## CHAPTER III

## SOVEREIGNTY, IN WHOM

### Enactive

ART. 1. The sovereignty is in *the people*. It is reserved by and to them. It is exercised, by the exercise of the Constitutive authority, as per Ch. iv.

# CHAPTER IV

## AUTHORITIES

*Enactive*

ART. 1. The Authorities, which have place in this State are these—
1. The Constitutive.
2. The Legislative.
3. The Administrative.
4. The Judiciary.
Their relations to one another are as follows.

*Enactive*

ART. 2. To the *Constitutive* Authority it belongs, amongst other things, to depute and *locate*, as per Ch. vi. LEGISLATURE, the members composing the Legislative; and eventually, as per Ch. v. CONSTITUTIVE, §[§]2,3, to dislocate them: but not to give direction, either *individual* or *specific*, to their measures, nor therefore to *reward* or *punish* them: except in so far as *relocation* may operate as reward, and *dislocation* as punishment; or, in so far as, at the instance of the Constitutive, punishment may come to be eventually applied to them, by the hands of succeeding Legislatures, as per Ch. v. CONSTITUTIVE, §[§]2,3, Ch. vi. LEGISLATURE, §28, *Legislation penal judicatory.*

*Enactive*

ART. 3. To the *Legislative* it belongs, amongst other things, to *locate* the *Chiefs* of the two other departments; and eventually to dislocate them: to give—not general only, but upon occasion, *individual direction* to their conduct, as well as to that of all the several functionaries respectively *subordinate* to them; eventually also to punish them, in case of non-compliance with its directions.

*Enactive*

ART. 4. To the *Administrative* it belongs, amongst other things, to give execution and effect to the ordinances of the Legislative, in so far as regards the persons and things placed under its special direction, by the Legislative: to wit, in so far as litis-contestation has not place.

*Enactive*

ART. 5. To the *Judiciary* it belongs, amongst other things, to give execution and effect to the ordinances of the Legislative, in so far as litis-contestation has place: to wit, either as to the question of *law*, or as to the question of *fact*.

### Enactive. Expositive

ART. 6. Taken together, the *Legislative* and the *Administrative* compose the *Government;* the *Administrative* and the *Judiciary*, the *Executive;* the *Legislative* and the *Executive*, what may be termed the *Operative*, as contra-distinguished from the *Constitutive*.

### Expositive

ART. 7. Note, as to the word *supreme*. If attached any where to the name of any authority,—to no other authority than those in the same department, can it be understood to bear reference. Thus may be spoken of a *Supreme Administrative*, and a *Supreme Judiciary;* although, with reference to Supreme Legislature, they are both of them subordinate, as is the Legislative itself to the Constitutive.

### Enactive

ART. 8. So many of these supreme *authorities*, the Constitutive included, which is supreme over all the others, so many *Departments:* to each *authority*, a *department*.

### Enactive

ART. 9. The Legislature has under it as many *Sub-legislatures*, as in the territory of the state here are *Districts:* to each District, a Sub-legislature.

### Enactive

ART. 10. Within the Administrative Department are *Sub-departments*, thirteen in number. For their appellations see Ch. ix. §2.

### Enactive. Instructional

ART. 11. In the case of the Legislative Department, the source of distinction and division is, as will be seen, furnished partly by the *local*, partly by the *logical*, field of service: in the case of the Supreme Legislature, both fields being without limit; in the case of the Sub-legislatures, both of them limited, as per Ch. [xxx.] SUBLEGISLATURES: in the case of the Administrative Department, this same source is furnished by the *logical* field alone: as for instance, *Election, Legislation, Army*, &c. as per Ch. xi. MINISTERS SEVERALLY: in each of the Subdepartments, so denominated, the authority of the head functionary extends over the whole territory of the state.

## Enactive. Expositive

ART. 12. In the Legislative Department and Subdepartments, the official situation is necessarily *many-seated:* the power accordingly *fractionized:* in the Legislature, *seats* as many as in the territory there are Districts: in each Sublegislature, seats as many as in the District there are Subdistricts.

## Enactive

ART. 13. In both the other Departments, the official situation is in every instance *single-seated.* Prime Minister, one; for each Administrative Subdepartment, or union of Subdepartments, Minister, one. In each Immediate and each Appellate Judicatory, Judge, but one. Over all these Judicatories, Justice Minister, one. In each District, immediately under its Sublegislature, Sub-prime Minister, one. In each Subdepartment of the District, under the Sublegislature and the Sub-prime Minister, Minister, one. In each ultimate section of the territory of the state, Headman, one.

## Enactive. Ratiocinative

ART. 14. In each of these situations,—with and under each principal functionary, serve as many auxiliaries as he finds it necessary to depute: as to which, in the several chapters headed by the names of the several functionaries, see the section intituled *Self-suppletive function.* Thus, at all times, whatsoever be the quantity of business to be done, there are hands for it in sufficient number without need of retardation; and thus is promptitude maximized. Nor yet is any door thus opened to abuse. For, for no such effect are adequate causes—adequate motives—to be found. For the conduct of these his instruments, the principal is effectually *responsible:* and thus, in their instance, (remuneration having place in no other shape than that of power in possession,—with the power, dignity, and pay, of their respective principals, in expectancy only), frugality is not, by the establishment of those suppletive situations, or any of them, diminished.

# CHAPTER V

## CONSTITUTIVE AUTHORITY

### SECTION 1

#### CONSTITUTIVE WHAT—IN WHOM

*Expositive*

ART. 1. The constitutive authority is that, by which at all times the holders of the several other authorities in this state, are what they are: by it, immediately or interventionally, they have been in such their situations located, and therefrom are eventually dislocable.

*Enactive*

ART. 2. The Constitutive authority is in the whole body of Electors belonging to this state: that is to say, in the whole body of the inhabitants, who, on the several days respectively appointed for the several Elections, and the operations thereunto preparatory, are resident on the territory of the state, deduction made of certain classes—mode of exercise, as per Election Code hereunto annexed:[1] as to which, see Ch. vi. LEGISLATURE, §[§]4 to 13.

*Enactive*

ART. 3. Classes thus deducted, are—1. Females; 2. Males, non-adult: that is to say, who have not attained the age of {21} years. 3. Non-readers: that is to say, those who have not, as per Ch. vi. LEGISLATURE, §[5], *Electors who*, by reading, given proof of appropriate aptitude. 4. Passengers.

### SECTION 2

#### POWERS

*Enactive*

ART. 1. Subordinate to the Constitutive authority, as per §1, are all other authorities, and thereby all other public functionaries belonging to the state.

Those whom it cannot dislocate in an immediate, it can in an un-immediate or say interventional way; to wit, by dislocating those

[1] See Ch. VI, § 4n, p. 48n.

who, having the power, have failed to dislocate them, in conformity
to its sufficiently understood desire.

### Enactive. Expositive

ART. 2. Exercisible by the Constitutive, in relation to them respectively, are the several functions following, with the power therein
essentially included. These are——

I. *Locative function:* exercised by locating, in the official situation
in question, the individual in question.

II. *Dislocative function:* exercised by dislocating, out of the situation in question, the functionary therein located.

III. *Punifactive function:* exercised by putting, at the time of dislocation, in a way to be punished, but by a different authority, the
functionary so dislocated.

### Enactive

ART. 3. I. *Locative function.* Functionaries, in relation to whom this
function is exercised by the members of the Constitutive authority,
are as follows——

[1]. Their *Deputies*, deputed by them to the legislature, to act as
Members of the Supreme Legislature, styled collectively *the Legislature*. In relation to all these, this power is exercised by the members
of the whole Constitutive body, as divided into the bodies belonging
to the several Election Districts; in each District, the Members of the
Constitutive electing for that District a member of the Legislature.[a]

[a] *Ratiocinative*, or say *Rationale*.

(*Deputy*.) Question. Why *Deputy* rather than *Representative*?

Answer. Reason 1. Because by the word *Deputy*, a plain matter of fact is indicated, and *that* the appropriate one.

2. Because the word *Representative* is less apposite, and not exclusively
characteristic. In the concerns of individuals, for example, in the field of private
right, many are the cases in which it is necessary that one person should act on
behalf of another, without having been appointed by him for that purpose: witness Guardians of Orphans, Administrators of property of Intestates, and the like.

3. Under favour of this ambiguous and indeterminate use of the word *Representative* in preference to *Deputy*, it is——that, in the case of the English form of
Government, the fictitious and fallacious security for the people against the
Monarch and the Aristocracy, has been imposed upon the people, in the character of a real one. To the Members who, in effect, are located——some, by the
located and at pleasure dislocable instruments of the Monarch, others by individuals possessing an interest opposite to theirs——the appellation of *Representative*
is habitually applied:——applied, and by many whom shame might deter from
styling them *Deputies*——Deputies of the people, belonging to the Districts for
which they respectively sit. Styled *Deputies*, they would be immediately recog-
nised as Impostors; obtainers of a share in supreme power on false pretences.

Styled as they are *Representatives*, the colours of imposture are not altogether

*Enactive*

ART. 4. [2]. The members of the several Sub-Legislatures. In relation to each sublegislative body, this power is exercised by the members of the Constitutive body, belonging to its District, as divided into the bodies belonging to the several Subdistricts therein contained; the body belonging to each such Subdistrict electing a member of the Sublegislature.

*Enactive*

ART. 5. II. *Dislocative function.* Functionaries, in relation to whom this function may upon occasion be exercised, are the following—

    1. The several Members of the Legislature.

    2. The Prime Minister.

    3. The several Ministers belonging to the Administrative Department: as per Ch. ix. §2.

so glaring upon the face of this their common name: and, as to their being *Members*, Members of the body in question, it is a truth but too incontrovertible: as such, they are admitted to act, nor would any others be admitted in their places: any thing of course they would rather style themselves, than what to the knowledge of every body they are not, to wit, *Deputies.*

Question 2. Why, rather than *Depute?* Answer. By the word *Depute*, the matter of fact would indeed be expressed; and in a manner equally *apposite:* not, however, in a manner equally, because not exclusively, *appropriate.* Of the word *Depute*, continual need, as will be seen, has place, for the designation of functionaries in little less than all the several subordinate grades: of functionaries— located, each of them, by no more than a single principal, and with functions wanting little of being altogether identical with his.

The Deputy of the Prime Minister will thus be seen to be styled the *Prime Minister Depute:* the Depute of a Minister, the *Minister Depute.* The Election Minister, for example, the *Election Minister Depute:* and so on in the case of the *Justice Minister* and the several Judges, and other judiciary functionaries.

In all these instances, the word *Depute* is in the adjective form: as in the case of the functionary, who, in Scottish Law, is styled *Sheriff Depute.*[1]

To no functionary other than those deputed by the Electors of the Election Districts to the Legislature, and of the Election Subdistricts to the several Sublegislatures,—is the term *Deputy*, in the substantive form, applied in this Code: and, by this means, the idea of the highest sort of functionary, styled a *Deputy*, and that of the subordinate sort of functionary styled a *Depute*, are preserved from being confounded.

---

[1] In Scotland the office of the Sheriff was hereditary, and he was authorised, as early as 1357, to appoint a depute, latterly chosen from the legal profession, who performed the duties of the office and for whom the Sheriff was responsible. After 1747, the appointment of both the Sheriff and the Sheriff-Depute was vested in the Crown, but no Sheriffs were in fact appointed: the Sheriff-Depute came to be popularly styled simply 'the Sheriff'. See *Encyclopaedia of the Laws of Scotland*, 18 vols., Edinburgh, 1926-51, xiii. 517-35.

4. The Justice Minister.

5. In each Judicatory, Appellate as well as Immediate, the Judge and the several other Magisterial functionaries, as per Ch. xii. JUDI-CIARY COLLECTIVELY. § 3, *Judiciary functionaries.*

6. In every such situation, as above, every Depute.

7. The several Local Headmen and Local Registrars.

8. The several Members of the several Sublegislative bodies.

*Enactive*

ART. 6. Exercisible, upon occasion, in like manner, by the Constitutive authority belonging to each District, is the dislocative function, in relation to the several functionaries following—

1. The several Members of the Legislative body belonging to that same District.

2. The several District *Prime Ministers*, or say *Premiers*, serving under the several Sublegislatures.

3. The several District Ministers, serving under the several Sublegislatures and their several District Prime Ministers.


SECTION 3

POWERS EXERCISED, HOW

*Enactive*

ART. 1. I. *Locative function.* Exercised, in relation to the several members of the Legislative body, is the locative function of the Constitutive, in the several Election Districts and Subdistricts, in the hereunto-annexed Election Code,[1] as per Ch. vi. LEGISLATURE, §[§]4 to 13.

*Enactive*

ART. 2. Exercised is this same function, in relation to the several members of the several Sublegislative bodies,—in the same manner as there delineated, with reference to the several members of the Legislature.

*Enactive. Instructional*

ART. 3. In each Subdistrict, immediately after he has voted for a Deputy to act as a member of the Legislature for the District, each member of the Constitutive body will, at the same place, and in the same manner, vote for another Deputy to act as a member of the Sublegislature of that same District. The arrangements of detail,—

[1] See Ch. VI, § 4n, p. 48n.

necessary to adapt, upon the same principles, the mode of ascertaining the election of a member of the Legislature, to the case of a member of a Sublegislature,—are, upon the face of the Election Code, obvious: they will be settled *in terminis* by the Legislature.

### Enactive

ART. 4. II. *Dislocative function*, 1.—How exercised by the entire Constitutive. On the receipt of a requisition, signed by {one fourth?} of the whole number of the Electors of any Election District, requiring the dislocation of any functionary in §2, *Powers*, Art. [5], the hereinafter-mentioned Election Minister will appoint a day or days, as near as may be,—on which, in the several Districts, the Electors shall meet at the several Voting Offices of the several Subdistricts therein respectively contained, in the same manner as on the occasion of an Election. The Voting Cards of those who are *for* the proposed dislocation, will, on the concealed surface, as per Ch. vi. LEGISLATURE, §[8], *Election apparatus*, Art. 4,[1] bear the words '*Dislocate him:*' of those who are *against* the proposed dislocation, the words '*Retain him.*' In each District, the votation finished, the Voting-box will, by the Vote Clerk, be forthwith transmitted to the Election Minister's Office. By the Election Minister, as soon as all are received, or the time for receiving them is elapsed, they will, in concert with the Legislation Minister, be opened in the Legislation Chamber, at the next sitting of the Legislature. The numbers will thereupon be immediately cast up, and the result declared. In case of dislocation, the vacancy produced on this extraordinary occasion will thereupon be forthwith filled up, in the same manner as on any ordinary one.

### Enactive

ART. 5. 2.—How by the Constitutive of a District.

Proportion, of the requisitionists, the same in this case as in that of the entire Constitutive, as above. Voting Boxes transmitted to the Election Clerk of the District. As soon as all have been received, or the time for receiving them has elapsed, he, at the next sitting of the Sublegislature, opens them, in concert with the Legislation Minister of the *District*, in the Sublegislation Chamber; casts them up, and declares the result, as above. The vacancy, if any, is thereupon filled up, as above.

### Instructional

ART. 6. By such requisitionists, as per Art[s]. 4, 5, will be seen the propriety of making the ground of the requisition as particular and

---

[1] See *Bentham's Radical Reform Bill, with Extracts from the Reasons*, London, 1819 (Bowring, iii. 558–97), Bowring, iii. 572–3; and Ch. VI, § 4n, p. 48n.

determinate, as well as concise, as the nature of the case will admit: that is to say, the description of the alledged misconduct, with the intimation of the manner in which it has diminished, or tended to diminish, the aggregate happiness of the greatest number; referring to written evidence, if any such there be, but not repeating it or commenting on it, much less employing appellatives, dyslogistic or eulogistic, or addresses to the passions in any other shape, or fallacies in any shape. As to which, see *The Book of Fallacies*.[1] The less their regard for these cautions, the less (they will understand) will be the probability, that their requisition will be productive of the effect desired by it.

*Enactive*

ART. 7. III. *Punifactive function*—how exercised. If, in addition to *dislocation*, in the case mentioned in Art. 4, *punifaction* be required, —in this case, together with the pair of Voting Cards, bearing respectively the words *Dislocate him* and *Retain him*, will be delivered by the Vote Clerk, another pair, bearing in like manner the words *Accuse him* and *Absolve him*. Thereupon, in regard to accusation and absolution, the result will be ascertained and declared, in the same manner, as in regard to dislocation and retention, as above.

*Enactive*

ART. 8. If the majority be, as above, in favour of accusation, the Election Minister will, as per Art. 4, make declaration to that effect: in which case, by that same declaration, the function and duty of conducting legal pursuit to that effect, devolves at the instant upon the hereinafter-mentioned Government Advocate General, as to whom, see Ch. xix. GOVERNMENT ADVOCATE GENERAL.

*Enactive*

ART. 9. The judicatory, in which such pursuit will be carried on, will be the Legislation Penal Judicatory, as per Ch. vi. LEGISLATURE, §28, *[Legislation] Penal Judicatory.*

*Enactive*

ART. 10. But, should it ever happen, that the functionary, in whose instance, in addition to dislocation, punishment is required, is at that same time a member of the Legislature,—in such case, for avoidance of partiality and the imputation of partiality on the part of the

---

[1] *The Book of Fallacies: from Unfinished Papers of Jeremy Bentham. Edited by a friend* [Peregrine Bingham], London, 1824 (Bowring, ii. 375-487).

Legislature,—the requisitioners may take their choice as between that year and the {three} several years next ensuing.

## SECTION 4

### PUBLIC OPINION TRIBUNAL:—COMPOSITION

#### Enactive. Expositive. Ratiocinative

ART. 1. This constitution recognises the *Public Opinion Tribunal*, as an authority essentially belonging to it. Its power is judicial. A functionary belonging to the Judiciary, exercises his functions by express location—by commission. A member of the Public Opinion Tribunal exercises his functions without commission; he needs none. Dislocability and puniability of members excepted, the Public Opinion Tribunal is to the Supreme Constitutive, what the Judiciary is to the Supreme Legislative.

#### Enactive. Expositive

ART. 2. Of the following members may this Judicatory be considered as being composed.

1. All individuals, of whom the Constitutive body of this state is composed.

2. All those classes, which, under §1, Art. 3, stand excluded from all participation in such supreme power.

3. Of all other political communities, all such members, to whom it happens to take cognizance of the question, whatever it may be.

#### Enactive. Expositive

ART. 3. Of this Judicatory, different classes or assemblages of persons may be considered as constituting so many Committees or Subcommittees. Examples are as follows—

1. The auditory, at the several sittings of the Supreme Legislature.

2. The auditory, at the several sittings of the several Sublegislatures.

3. The auditory, at the several sittings of the several Judicatories. See Ch. xii. JUDICIARY COLLECTIVELY, §2, *Actors [on] the judicial theatre.*

4. Persons having business with the several functionaries belonging to the *Administrative* department; such business excepted as, for special reasons, shall by law have been consigned to temporary secrecy.

5. At meetings, publicly held for the consideration of any political question, the several individuals present.

6. The auditory, at any dramatic entertainment, at which objects of a political or moral nature are brought upon the stage.

7. All persons, taking, for the subject of their speeches, writings, or reflections, any act or discourse of any public functionary, or body of public functionaries belonging to this state.

### Instructional

ART. 4. Public Opinion may be considered as a system of law, emanating from the body of the people. If there be no individually assignable form of words in and by which it stands expressed, it is but upon a par in this particular with that rule of action which, emanating as it does from lawyers, official and professional, and not sanctioned by the Legislative authority otherwise than by tacit sufferance, is in England designated by the appellation of *Common Law.* To the pernicious exercise of the power of government it is the only check; to the beneficial, an indispensable supplement. Able rulers lead it; prudent rulers lead or follow it; foolish rulers disregard it. Even at the present stage in the career of civilization, its dictates coincide, on most points, with those of the *greatest happiness principle;* on some, however, it still deviates from them: but, as its deviations have all along been less and less numerous, and less wide, sooner or later they will cease to be discernible; aberration will vanish, coincidence will be complete.


## SECTION 5

### [PUBLIC OPINION TRIBUNAL:—] FUNCTIONS

### Enactive. Expositive

ART. 1. To the several members of the Public Opinion Tribunal, as such, belong the distinguishable functions following; namely—
*Statistic* or say *Evidence-furnishing function.* Exercise is given to it, in so far as indication is afforded of facts, of a nature to operate, as grounds for judgment, of approbation or disapprobation, in relation to any public institution, ordinance, arrangement, proceeding or measure, past, present, or supposed future contingent, or to any mode of conduct, on the part of any person, functionary or nonfunctionary, by which the interests of the public at large may be affected.

### Expositive

ART. 2. *Censorial function.* Exercise is given to it, in so far as expression is given to any judgment of approbation or disapprobation, in relation to any such object as above.

*Expositive*

ART. 3. *Executive function.* Exercise is given to it, in so far as, by the performing or withholding of good offices, such as a man is by law warranted in withholding, or by the performing of evil offices, such as a man is by law allowed to perform, addition,—whether in consequence of such indication, as above, or otherwise,—is made to, or defalcation made from, the happiness of the person in question, as above; and as by the thus withholding of good offices the effect of punishment, so by the rendering of them may the effect of reward, be produced.

*Expositive*

ART. 4. *Melioration-suggestive function.* Exercise is given to it, in so far as, from the observation of what is amiss, or wanting, a conception of something better, having been formed, has as such been held up to the view of those whom it may concern, to the end that, if approved, it may be brought into practice.

*Enactive. Ratiocinative*

ART. 5. On *functionaries*, the exercise of the statistic function is not only *morally* but *legally* obligatory: for the rendering of this service, the mass of benefit which, in whatever shape, pay included, stands attached to their respective offices, is their reward. On *non-functionaries, morally* only: *factitious* reward, none is provided for them, none is needed for them; *natural*, appropriate, and exactly proportionate reward, in proportion as his service is known, and the nature of it understood, each man will receive, in and by means of the esteem, produced by the contemplation of it.

*Expositive. Instructional*

ART. 6. Of the heads, to which imperfections, ascribed to the law, by amendments, may be referrible, examples are as follows:—

I. As to *matter.* Want of conduciveness to the general *end.* The arrangement, as supposed, not so conformable to the greatest happiness principle as it might be.

II. For examples of want of *compleatness* as to *matter*, see any of the lists of *exceptions* in this Code, and suppose any one of those same exceptions omitted.

III. For examples of want of *compleatness* as to *form*, in any one of the lists of *examples*, suppose this or that example not inserted.

IV. As to *form.* Want of *clearness:* to wit, in such or such a clause or assemblage of clauses; as to the effect, obscurity or ambiguity:

37

as to the cause, that is to say the words,——redundancy, deficiency, inappositeness, or miscollocation.

V. As to *matter* or *form*, want of *compleatness:* this or that case, as supposed, not being provided for: because, as supposed, not contemplated.

VI. In the *Adjective Code* in particular; or say the *Procedure Code*,[1] on the part of this or that arrangement, want of conduciveness to the general end: to wit, by reason of want of conduciveness to this or that one of the ends of justice, direct and collateral: the direct end, being the giving execution and effect to the correspondent portion of the Substantive Code; the collateral end, the keeping the practice clear of needless delay, vexation and expense——evils correspondent and opposite to so many specific collateral ends of justice.

Note, that in speaking of ends, instead of *one*, the number of direct ends may be stated as being *two:* in which case [the opposite evils][2] will be *misdecision* and *non-decision:* for by non-decision may be produced the effect of misdecision; to wit, in disfavour of the pursuer's side.

## *Enactive*

ART. 7. When a supposed amendment, as above, is suggested, the two forms, in either of which, for the preservation of symmetry, it

---

[1] Bentham wrote on the subject of Judicial Procedure for more than thirty years, but between 1823 and 1828 he attempted to draft a Procedure Code which would accompany the Constitutional and other Codes in making up the Pannomion. He wrote a vast amount of manuscript (see UC lii-lvii), but the work was never completed. Richard Doane, the main editor of the *Constitutional Code*, also undertook to edit the treatise on procedure from the manuscripts for the Bowring edition. See *Principles of Judicial Procedure, with the Outlines of a Procedure Code* (Bowring, ii. 3-188), and especially Doane's note (Bowring, ii. 4). In the present volume of the *Constitutional Code*, there are approximately twenty references to a Procedure Code. Many of these do not correspond definitely to a particular discussion in Doane's edition. Some, however, refer to points developed by Bentham in other writings which are partly concerned with Judicial Procedure, such as the *Equity Dispatch Court Bill* (Bowring, iii. 319-431) or the *Rationale of Judicial Evidence, specially applied to English Practice*, ed. John Stuart Mill, 5 vols., London, 1827 (Bowring, vi. 189-585, vii. 1-600). At other times, Bentham seems to be referring more generally to a Procedure Code which should accompany the *Constitutional Code* in a state where it is adopted. On the particular reference here, see further, *Principles of Judicial Procedure*, Ch. III (Bowring, ii. 15-22). A fuller understanding of the relationship between the Constitutional and Procedure Codes must necessarily await new editions of Bentham's various writings on evidence and procedure during this period. On the relationship of the Procedure Code to other Codes which make up the *Pannomion*, see also pp. xxxv-xxxvii. On Bentham's intention to append a Procedure Code Table to the *Equity Dispatch Court Bill*, see p. 5 and n.

[2] 1830, 'they'. This was changed in Bowring to 'the opposite evils' to clarify the passage.

may be expressed, may be seen in Ch. vi. LEGISLATURE, §29, *Members' Motions*. Of the non-preservation of symmetry, the consequences may be seen in Ch. xi. §2, *Legislation Minister*.

### Instructional

ART. 8. In support of his amendment, the proposer will do well to subjoin, under the following heads, concise indications of the reasons, by the consideration of which, he was induced to propose it. These will be,

I. Evil effects, regarded as flowing from the law as it stands: or,

II. Good effects expected to result from the proposed amendment, if adopted.

The more condensed and compact his reasons, the greater will be their chance of being attended to: by every attempt to move the passions it will be lessened.

### Instructional

ART. 9. On the tutelary influence of the Public Opinion Tribunal, this Constitution relies, in a more especial manner, for the efficiency of the securities which it provides, for good conduct, on the part of the several functionaries, belonging to the Judiciary Department. See in the several Chapters the several Sections headed by the words *Securities for appropriate aptitude*.

### SECTION 6

#### SECURITIES AGAINST LEGISLATIVE, AND JUDICIARY

### Enactive

ART. 1. To every person, elector, inhabitant, or foreigner,——to every individual of the human species, belongs the right of exercising, in relation to the condition of every department of this government, and the conduct of every functionary thereto belonging, the *statistic*, *executive*, and *melioration-suggestive* functions above-mentioned.

### Enactive. Ratiocinative

ART. 2. So likewise the *Censorial:* how strong soever the terms, in which the approbation or disapprobation stands expressed. Vituperation, if indecorous, will receive its proportionate punishment at the hands of the Public Opinion Tribunal: defamation, if mendacious or temeracious, at the hands of the Penal Code.[1] Defamation there is

---

[1] The definition and codification of penal law was a major interest of Bentham from his earliest writings. The most substantial work on the subject is the

none, without intimation given of some illegal or immoral act;—intimation individually, or at least specifically, determinate. If, being false, the intimation is temeracious only, and not mendacious, the official situation, of the party defamed, is a ground—not of aggravation, but of extenuation. The military functionary is paid for being shot at. The civil functionary is paid for being spoken and written at. The soldier, who will not face musquetry, is one sort of coward. The civilian who will not endure obloquy, is another. Better he be defamed, though it be ever so unjustly, than that, by a breach of official duty, any sinister profit sought should be reaped. To him who has power, opulence, or reputation, self-defence is, in proportion to his power, opulence, or reputation, more easy than if he had none: defenders cannot be wanting to him, so long as he has patrons, colleagues, or dependents.

*Enactive*

ART. 3. By prohibition, restriction or taxation, to throw obstruction in the way of production or diffusion of political tracts, especially newspapers and other periodical ones, would, on the part of the Legislature, be a breach of trust, a violation of its duty to the Constitutive; an act of insubordination, obstructing their constitutional superordinates in the exercise of their authority, by depriving them of the means of forming correct judgments: an act of partiality and

*Principles of Penal Law* (Bowring, i. 365–580), which is a combination of translations from Dumont's *Traités de législation civile et pénale*, 3 vols., Paris, 1802, and *Théorie des peines et des récompenses*, 2 vols., London, 1811, with material from other works and manuscripts. Richard Smith, who had published two translations from the *Théorie des peines et des récompenses*—*The Rationale of Reward*, London, 1825, and *The Rationale of Punishment*, London, 1830—also prepared the *Principles of Penal Law* for the Bowring edition. However, the Penal Code to which Bentham refers here and throughout the *Constitutional Code* was never finally drafted. Bentham wrote at length for this purpose in the late 1770s, and from approximately 1818 till his death. During the period when the *Constitutional Code* was being written, he again wrote a considerable amount of material for his projected Penal Code (see especially UC lxi and lxiv–lxviii, most of which has never been published). He also prepared a Table of Contents for the Penal Code, which was inserted at the end of the 1830 volume of the *Constitutional Code*, and appears here as Table 2. In the reference here, Bentham probably had in mind Pt. II, Ch. VI, 'Offences affecting Reputation', § 1. 'Wrongful defamation'. The references to the Penal Code in the text of the *Constitutional Code* at times, as here, seem to be connected with the proposed Code for which the Table of Contents was prepared; but at other points Bentham seems to speak more generally of a Penal Code which should accompany the *Constitutional Code* in a state where it is adopted. On the relationship of the Penal Code to the other Codes which make up Bentham's *Pannomion*, see pp. xxxvii–xxxviii.

oppression, withholding from one class of men, documents not withholden from another: withholding, from *the many*, benefits, not
withholden from the more wealthy *few:* withholding instruction
from those, by whom it is most needed. It would be an anti-constitutional act: as such, it would call for marks of disapprobation, at the
hands of the members of the Supreme Constitutive; namely, as well
in their character of Electors, as in their character of Members of the
Public Opinion Tribunal.

### Enactive. Expositive

ART. 4. No such act of insubordination is committed, by punishment judicially inflicted, or demanded, for defamation, when effected
or endeavoured at by falsehood, accompanied by criminal *evil-
consciousness*, or culpable *temerity of assertion*, as to which see the
Penal Code.[1]

### Instructional

ART. 5. Every act, whereby, in the above or any other way, a man
seeks to weaken the effective power of the Public Opinion Tribunal,
or by falsehood, or (what comes to the same thing) by suppression of
truth, to misdirect it, is evidence, of hostility on his part to the greatest
happiness of the greatest number: evidence of the worst intentions,
generated by the worst motives: evidence which, though but tacit and
circumstantial, and though it be ever so unwilling, is not the less conclusive. Every act, whereby a man seeks to diminish the circulation of
opinions opposite to those which he professes, is evidence of his consciousness of the rectitude of those which he is combating, and thereby
of the insincerity, hypocrisy, tyrannicalness, and selfishness which have
taken possession of his mind. Sincere or insincere, he may, without fear
of injustice, be numbered among the enemies of the human species.


# CHAPTER VI
## LEGISLATURE


## SECTION 1
### POWERS:——AND DUTIES

### Enactive

ART. 1. The Supreme Legislature is omnicompetent. Coextensive
with the territory of the state is its local field of service; coextensive

[1] See p. 39, n. 1.

with the field of human action is its logical field of service.——To its power, there are no limits. In place of limits, it has checks. These checks are applied, by the securities, provided for good conduct on the part of the several members, individually operated upon; as per § 31, *Securities for appropriate aptitude.*

### Enactive. Ratiocinative

ART. 2. The power thus unlimited is that of the Legislature *for the time being.* To no anterior Legislature belongs any power, otherwise than by confirmation given to it by the Legislature for the time being. Dead men can neither fine, nor imprison, nor banish living ones.

### Enactive

ART. 3. But, in so far as nothing appears to the contrary, confirmation, of the acts of all anterior Legislatures, and of all authorities subordinate to them, takes place of course.

### Enactive

ART. 4. For the means employed for preserving Government engagements against violation. See § 2, *Responsibility.*

### Enactive

ART. 5. The Supreme Legislative Authority has, for its immediate instrument, the Supreme *Executive*, composed of the *administrative* and the *judiciary*, acting within their respective spheres. On the will of the Supreme Constitutive, the Supreme Legislative is dependent, as per Ch. v. § 2, *Powers.* Absolute and all-comprehensive is this dependence. So also on the will of the Legislature, the will of the Executive, and the wills of the Sublegislatures.

### Enactive

ART. 6. Only by unalterable physical impotence, is the Supreme Legislature prevented from being its own Executive, or from being the sole Legislature. The Supreme Legislature will not, to the neglect of its own duties, take upon itself any of those functions, for the apt exercise of which, when taken in the aggregate, those subordinate authorities alone, can, in respect of disposable time, appropriate knowledge, judgment, and active aptitude, have been provided with sufficient means. But, in case of non-performance, or unapt performance, or well-grounded apprehension of either,——to the exercise of no function of the Executive or the Sublegislative authority can the Supreme Legislature be incompetent. Unfaithfulness, yes: but to the

Supreme Legislature, neither can usurpation nor encroachment, be imputed.

### Enactive. Expositive

ART. 7. To those functions which belong exclusively to itself, the Legislature accordingly adds, in case of necessity, those which belong respectively to all those its several subordinates, as per the several ensuing Chapters.

### Enactive. Expositive

ART. 8. In those same Chapters may moreover be seen, so many exemplifications, of the subjects, to which the attention and proceedings of the Legislature will, constantly or occasionally, be directed.

### Enactive

ART. 9. Separately or collectively, the Constituents of a Member of the Legislature will, at all times, as such, make to such their deputy what communication they think fit: to his cognitive faculty, to his judicative faculty, or even to his will, it may be addressed. But, in so far as the good of the community taken in the aggregate is the paramount object of his care, no obedience will he pay to any such particular will, to the detriment of what appears to him the universal interest. Paramount to his duty to a part is, on every occasion, his duty to the whole. An engagement, exacted of him by a part, would be an act of insubordination as towards the whole. It belongs not to him to judge, until he has seen or heard. His will is commanded by his judgment, not his judgment by his will. Such contrariety may have place, without detriment to moral aptitude on either side. They may have good reason for dislocating him; he for exposing himself to be so dislocated.

### Instructional. Ratiocinative

ART. 10. If, on this or that particular occasion, in the opinion of Constituents, or in the opinion of their Deputy, a conflict should have place between their particular aggregate interest and the national interest, he will not be considered as violating his duty to the public, by giving his vote in favour of that same particular interest. For, the national interest being nothing more than an aggregate of the several particular interests, if against that which has been regarded as being the national interest, there be a majority, this result will prove, that, in the so declared opinion of that same majority, that, which had been spoken of as if it were the national interest, was not so: and if, in support of that which, by a *majority* of his *Constituents*, is regarded as being their interest, there be *not* a *majority* in the *Legislature*, his vote will be of no effect; and, to the national interest, no evil will have been done by it. On the other hand, a practice, which in every case is evil, is *insincerity:* and in this case, by the supposition no good at all, therefore no preponderant good would be produced by it.

### Instructional. Ratiocinative

ART. 11. Accordingly, if so it should happen, that, after *speaking* in *support* of an arrangement, which, in the opinion of his Constituents, is contrary to their particular interest, he gives his vote *against* that same arrangement,—in such conduct there is not any real inconsistency. By his *speech*, his duty to the *public* is fulfilled; by his *vote*, his duty to his Constituents.

### Instructional. Ratiocinative

ART. 12. Moreover, what, on an occasion of this sort, may very well happen, is—that an arrangement which, in the eyes of Constituents, is detrimental to their interest, is not so: and *vice versâ*: and, in this case, his speech in support of the opposite arrangement may have the effect of working a change in their opinion; and, on a succeeding occasion, causing them to concur with the arrangement supported by him, instead of opposing it.

### Enactive. Ratiocinative

ART. 13. Variable at all times,—variable at the pleasure of the Legislature for the time being,—is every article in this and every other Code. For every moment of its duration, on its reasonableness, first in the eyes of the Legislative, then in the eyes of the Constitutive, is its sole dependence. Not to speak of *years*, if, for any one day, error could prudently be exempted from correction, so might it for every other. If the wisdom of to-day is superior to that of to-morrow, so may it be to that of every day, to the end of time. Blinded by prejudice must that man be, who, assured that he is wiser to-day than he was yesterday, holds himself not equally assured that to-morrow he may be wiser than to-day. Blinded by vanity or selfishness must that man be, who, assured that in knowledge and judgment he is beyond those who are gone before him, holds not himself equally assured, that, in those same endowments, those who come after him may be beyond *him.* By individual responsibility, as per §2, *Responsibility*, sufficient is the security afforded against inconsiderate and groundless changes: a degree of security far superior to any which can be afforded, by any Constitution, by which correction of error is inhibited to or by the Legislature.

44

## SECTION 2

### RESPONSIBILITY

#### *Enactive*

ART. 1. Of the Constitutive Authority, the constant will, (for such it cannot but be presumed to be,) is that the national felicity—the happiness of the greatest number—be maximized: to this will, on each occasion, it is the duty of the Supreme Legislature, according to the measure of its ability, to give execution and effect.

#### *Enactive*

ART. 2. If, on any occasion, any ordinance, which to some shall appear repugnant to the principles of this Constitution, shall come to have been enacted by the Legislature, such ordinance is not on that account to be, by any judge, treated or spoken of, as being null and void: not even although its tendency, intended as well as actual, were to appear to him to be, to diminish the mass of power hereby reserved to the Constitutive Authority. But if, of any such act, the tendency be anti-constitutional, as above, it may form an apt ground for an exercise to be given by the Electors, to their incidental dislocative, and punifactive functions, applying them respectively to such members of the Legislature, by whom motion, speech, or vote shall have been given in favour of the supposed anti-constitutional arrangement; and, in any Judicatory, such, by the Judge principal, may any such act, on its coming regularly before him, be in his opinion declared to be.

#### *Enactive. Ratiocinative*

ART. 3. To the Constitutive Authority, and *that* alone, it belongs to enforce the observance, of contracts entered into by the Legislature; and in one word, to afford such redress as can be afforded to misdeeds in whatever shape, perseveringly committed by the Legislature. A law, ordaining that, in no case, a contract entered into by the Legislature, shall remain in any part unperformed by it, would be alike inefficient to good purposes, efficient to bad ones.

#### *Ratiocinative*

ART. 4. A contract, if fit to be performed, was made for increase of felicity, not for lessening it. Be the contract what it may, prove that by non-observance of it, more felicity, all items taken into account, would be produced, than by observance, you prove that it ought not to be observed. If all contracts were to be observed, all misdeeds

45

would be to be committed: for there is no misdeed, the committal of which may not be made the subject of a contract; and to establish in favour of themselves, or of any other person or persons an absolute despotism, a set of Legislators would have no more to do, than to enter into an engagement, say with a foreign despot, say with a member of their own community, for that purpose. A Monarch, that he may persevere in a course of depredation and oppression with the less disturbance, binds himself (suppose) to perpetuate it. An instrument has been contrived for this purpose. It is called *an oath*—a coronation oath. Propose to him to assuage the misrule, 'Alas! my oath!' (he cries) 'my oath!' and all who share or look to share in the profit of the misrule, join with him in chorus.

*Enactive*

ART. 5. In the case of a contract entered into by the Government with any person or persons belonging to this state, it will rest with the Judiciary to take cognizance of it, as in a case between individual and individual. Yet, to a decision pronounced thereupon by the competent judicial authority, should the Legislature, by any ordinance, act in declared repugnance, such ordinance is not, on that account, to be regarded as *null and void*.

*Enactive*

ART. 6. So, in the case of a contract with the government of any foreign state.

*Enactive*

ART. 7. So, in the case of a contract with a subject of any foreign state.

*Enactive*

ART. 8. But, in all three cases, apt grounds may have place for the exercise of the incidental dislocative function, on the part of the Constitutive Authority, as per Ch. v. CONSTITUTIVE, §2, *Powers*, at the charge of the Members, who have concurred in the breach of public faith: the dislocative function, with or without the punifactive.

*Enactive*

ART. 9. For wrong, in any shape, alledged to have been done to any foreign Government, whether by breach of contract or otherwise, such Government may have judicial remedy, by suit in the immediate Judicatory of the Metropolis of the state; Defendant, the Government Advocate General of this state.

*Enactive*

ART. 10. Yet, on any such occasion, should any ordinance have been issued, by the Legislature, in relation to the matter of such suit after the commencement thereof, it belongs not to any Judge to omit giving execution and effect to that same ordinance.

*Enactive*

ART. 11. But, here, likewise, apt grounds may have place, for the exercise of the remedial functions of the Constitutive Authority, as above.

## SECTION 3

### POWERS AS TO SUBLEGISLATURES

*Enactive*

ART. 1. In relation to the hereinafter-mentioned Sublegislatures, the Supreme Legislature exercises the several functions, *directive, corrective, arbitrative.*

*Enactive*

ART. 2. I. *Directive function.* In the exercise of this function, it gives, as often as it sees convenient, antecedent and preparatory direction to their several proceedings.

*Enactive*

ART. 3. II. *Corrective function.* In the exercise of this function, it in like manner abolishes, reverses, amends, or causes to be amended, any of their ordinances, or other proceedings.

*Enactive*

ART. 4. III. *Arbitrative function.* In the exercise of this function, as often as, between one Sublegislature and another, contestation has place, it gives termination thereto by an appropriate arrangement.

*Instructional*

ART. 5. In the case of a federal Government, here may be the place for appropriate alteration. The Sublegislatures would be the Legislatures of the several States.

§4. *Seats and Districts.* See *Election Code,* §1.[1]

§5. *Electors who.* See *Election Code,* §2.

§6. *Eligible who.* See *Election Code,* §3, and below, [ §25. *Relocable* ] *who.*

§7. *Election Offices.* See *Election Code,* §4.

§8. *Election Apparatus.* See *Election Code,* §5.

§9. *Recommendation of proposed Members—how promulgated.* See *Election Code,* §6.

§10. *Voters' Titles, how preestablished.* See *Election Code,* §7.

§11. *Election, how.* See *Election Code,* §8.

§12. *Election Districts and Voting Districts, how marked out.* See *Election Code,* §9.

§13. *Vote-making Habitations, how defined.* See *Election Code,* §10.

§14. *Term of Service.* See *Election Code,* §11, *Members' Continuance*; and in this Ch. §22, *Term of Service—Continuation.*

§15. *Vacancies, how supplied.* See *Election Code,* §12.

§16. *Security of the Assembly against Disturbance by Members.* See *Election Code,* §13.

§17. *Indisposition of Presidents, how obviated.* See *Election Code,* §[14].


## SECTION 18

### ATTENDANCE

### *Enactive*

ART. 1. Exceptions excepted, the Legislature sits every day in the year. Exceptions are Vacation days. Vacation days are every seventh

---

[1] *Bentham's Radical Reform Bill, with Extracts from the Reasons* (Bowring, iii. 558-97) is a detailed parliamentary bill for instituting universal suffrage, annual parliaments, and election by secret ballot. Bentham intended the publication to serve as the Election Code to which he refers here and elsewhere in the *Constitutional Code.* Either because of its length or because its terminology was more directed at English practice and would require extensive revision, Bentham never actually incorporated the Election Code into the *Constitutional Code.* In a note to the Table of Contents of the 1830 volume, he stated that it was still in print and presumably available for use in conjunction with the *Constitutional Code.* Although some of the terms differ between the two works, the titles and sections to which Bentham refers follow closely those of the *Radical Reform Bill.* See also the Introduction, pp. xxv-xxvi.

day; that is to say, every day of general rest. But urgency declared, sittings have place in Vacation days.

### Ratiocinative

ART. 2. A domestic servant is a servant of one: a Legislator is a servant of all. No domestic servant absents himself at pleasure, and without leave. The masters of the Legislator give no such leave. From non-attendance of a domestic servant, the evil is upon a domestic scale: of a Legislator, on a national scale. A Legislator is a physician of the body politic. No physician receives pay but in proportion to attendance. The physician has no vacation days.[1]

## SECTION 19

### REMUNERATION

### Enactive

ART. 1. Of a Member of the Legislature the pecuniary remuneration is {          } per day. Added to this are the power and dignity inseparable from the office. Of ulterior emolument, receipt, if from unwilling hands, is *extortion;* if from willing ones, *corruption:* as to which, see Penal Code.[2] For principles as to Official Remuneration, see Ch. ix. MINISTERS COLLECTIVELY. §15, *Remuneration.*

## SECTION 20

### ATTENDANCE AND REMUNERATION—HOW CONNECTED

### Enactive

ART. 1. Into the Assembly Chamber there is but one entrance. The retiring rooms are behind and above. Committee rooms have other entrances.

[1] Though inserted at the end of the single article constituting §19, this seems a more appropriate point for the following MS note by Bentham in the annotated copy of the 1830 volume referred to in the Introduction, p. xlv: 'For the multitude of Non-Attendance see Vote 16 March 1831.' This can be elucidated by reference to the *Commons Journals* for 16 March 1831, lxxxvi (1831), 388, when the Speaker reported to the House the names of those MPs who had not appeared on the previous day when their names were called during the balloting for select committees to deal with disputed elections. Eighty members, whose excuses for non-attendance were not accepted, were ordered to attend the ballots on 17 March; and a further five to attend on Tuesday 22 March.

[2] Extortion appears in the Table of Contents of the Penal Code in Pt. II, Ch. III, §11. Corruption, though its substance is covered under other headings, is not listed as a separate offence. See Table 2. On the Penal Code generally, see Ch. V, §6, Art. 2n, p. 39n.

*Enactive*

ART. 2. Each day, on entrance into the Assembly Chamber, each member receives that day's pay at the hands of the Doorkeeper. In his view, and in that of the company in the Assembly Chamber, is a clock. On delivery of the pay, the Doorkeeper stamps, in the *Entrance and Departure Book*, on the page of that day, the member's name, adding the hour and minute.

*Enactive*

ART. 3. No member departs without leave of the President, who, on a sign made by the departer, rings, by a string within his reach, a bell hanging near the Doorkeeper, who, after stamping in the Entrance and Departure Book, on the page of that day, the member's name, with the hour and minute, lets him out. (A retiring place, opening only into the Chamber, is of course supposed.)

*Enactive*

ART. 4. Sick or well, for no day, on which he does not attend, vacation days excepted, does any *Legislator* receive his pay.

*Enactive*

ART. 5. Under the direction of the hereinafter-mentioned *Legislation Minister*, is kept the *Non-attendance*, or say *Absentation Book*. In it, from the *Entrance and Departure Book*, entry is made of the days, on which the several absenting members have respectively absented themselves: and for the information of their respective constituents, he causes the result to be published in the Government newspaper on the next day, as also at the beginning of each month; and at the time when the Election Minister issues his mandates for the General Election, a summary of all the absentations of the last preceding Session under the names of the several absentees.

*Enactive*

ART. 6. If, by sickness, a member has been prevented from attending, he, on the first day of his re-attendance, presents to the Doorkeeper a *sickness ticket*, on which are marked the day or days of non-attendance, with an intimation of the nature of the sickness, authenticated by his name in his own hand-writing, and the attestation of a physician.

*Enactive*

ART. 7. To clear a member from the suspicion of employing sickness as a pretence for avoiding to give his vote or speech, questions may be put to him and others, in the face of the Assembly, and observations made. For ulterior securities against non-attendance, see §23, *Self-suppletive function.*

### Ratiocinative

ART. 8. A soldier, if he fails in his attendance, is punished as a deserter: punished with corporal punishment: in England, with flogging or perhaps with death. Under this code, or any that is in consonance with it, in the case of no man, military or non-military, will punishment in either of those shapes be employed: for in neither is it needed. But, in this case, as in every other, whatever is needed, why should it not be applied? and what can be milder than the simple withholding of reward in proportion as the service remains unperformed?

### Ratiocinative

ART. 9. If, how severe soever, such means, as are regarded as efficacious and necessary, are employed for securing the service, exacted, whether with or without his previous consent to the engagement, from a common soldier, in what higher situation, were they ever so severe, should measures equally efficacious, supposing them necessary, be grudged? And should not they be the less grudged, the higher the duties of the situation in the scale of importance?

### Ratiocinative

ART. 10. As between individual and individual, where it is by the quantity of time employed in service that the quantum of remuneration is measured——payment being made by the day, as in the case of a common labourer or artizan, or by the hour, as in the case of a professional instructor——in what case, unless on the score of pure charity, does any person think of paying or asking payment for any quantity of time, during which no service has been performed? Why then as between an individual and the public?

### Ratiocinative. Instructional

ART. 11. By usage, intermission of Legislative business has hitherto been every where established. But, by such usage, were it ever so many more times as extensive as it is, the need of uninterrupted attendance would not be disproved. Whatsoever is, any where, the proportion of attendance actually given, the presumption indeed is, of course, that it is sufficient——sufficient for all purposes. But, for this presumption there exists not, any where, any the smallest ground. From the bare consideration of the nature of the case, the assurance may be entire, that, in the state in question, whatsoever it

51

be, evil effects of the most serious kind have been continually taking place: and, in almost any proportion, such effects may have had place, without its being possible to trace them, or at any rate without their having in general been traced, to their cause.

### Instructional

ART. 12. In political states other than the Anglo-American states—that is to say in all mixed monarchies, non-attendance has had, for its obvious cause, the sinister interest of rulers.

### Instructional

ART. 13. These rulers are 1, the Monarch, with his more especial dependents—2, his junior partners in the concern—the members of the aristocracy, and in particular those who have seats in any Legislative Chamber.

### Instructional

ART. 14. By the Monarch and his dependents more especially it is, that those vast gaps have been made, which have had place between session and session, and which have for their efficient cause, the operations called *prorogation* and *adjournment: prorogation*, avowedly the act of the Monarch himself; adjournment that of the Monarch, by the hands of those his agents.

### Instructional

ART. 15. In England, for example, by the act of the Monarch alone, about the half of the year is habitually taken from the public service: in this case, the act is called *a prorogation*, and to this defalcation is added *that* of a month or more taken at various times by the House of Commons: not to speak of the House of Lords: in this case, the act is called *an adjournment*.[1]

### Instructional

ART. 16. The original object was, of course, as history shows, to extinguish the existence of these troublesome concurrents and sharers

---

[1] A prorogation of Parliament, a prerogative act of the Crown, brings a session to an end. An adjournment, resolved upon by each House for itself, is an interruption of proceedings during a session. See *Erskine May's Treatise on the Law, Privileges, Proceedings and Usage of Parliament*, ed. Sir Barnett Cocks, 18th edn., London, 1971, pp. 255–6. Bentham's point at the end of Art. 14 is presumably that a government in command of majorities in both Houses could in practice secure an adjournment when it so wished. So far as Art. 15 is concerned, at the time when Bentham was writing and for a large part of the following hundred years it was comparatively unusual, for much of the time extremely rare, for Parliament to be in session between August and February.

in the sweets of Government: *that* being found impracticable, the next object, of wish and endeavour, was, is, and will be, to minimize their action. Of the whole quantity of the time employed by them, a certain portion must of necessity, for the purpose and under the direction of the Monarch, be employed in going through the forms necessary to the extraction of money, and in such other business, as the conjunct interest of the Monarch and the Aristocracy requires to be performed. For this purpose, whatsoever quantity of time is necessary, is by law always at his command. Upon all measures whatsoever coming from any other quarter, and in particular all measures tending to the melioration of the constitution, an exclusion is put, of course, in whatever way may be most commodious; and the most commodious, because the least exposed to observation, is the making such disposal of the time as shall either prevent any thing troublesome from being brought on the carpet, or, when on, from being finished—as to this, see *Parliamentary Reform Catechism. Introduction.*[1]

## Instructional

ART. 17. In addition to *power*, which, together with *ease*, is thus obtained in the wholesale way, comes the ease, which is obtained in the retail way by non-attendance, at business times, on the part of particular individuals. Hence comes the curious phenomenon. In the principal House for business, seats 658: number necessary to be filled to give validity to the proceedings, 40: every session, several times does it happen, that, for want of this necessary number, the day is lost to the public service. The President excepted, by whom (under the name of *speaker,*) the business must be directed,—[in] no session by any one member, has attendance, on every day, perhaps been ever paid: out of the 658, not one by whom, under this head, *that* has been done, which ought to have been done by every one. In addition to those, who are paid by the over-paid offices, by which they are kept in a state of corruption,—chance having of late produced an individual by whom the public service, for which he was engaged, has for years been made his principal and gratuitous occupation; at the observation of such a phenomenon, every body continues lost in amazement.[2] But *power without obligation* is the very definition of

[1] *Plan of Parliamentary Reform, in the form of a Catechism, with reasons for each article; with an Introduction, showing the necessity of radical, and the inadequacy of moderate, reform*, London, 1817, 2nd edn., 1818 (Bowring, iii. 433-557). The passage here referred to by Bentham is in Bowring, iii. 501-2.

[2] This probably refers to Joseph Hume (1777-1855). After a few months in Parliament in 1812, he was converted to radicalism by Francis Place, and, re-entering the Commons in 1818, remained a member almost continuously until

despotism: *slavery*, the condition of those who are subject to it. Here, then, is a form of government, under which, by those who should be servants, those, who should be masters, are kept in a state which is *by law* a state of slavery: howsoever by the healing hand of Public Opinion, the rigour of the despotism may be softened.

### Instructional

ART. 18. In the Anglo-American United States, although power is not eased of obligation, still, in this same form, is breach of constitutional duty suffered to have place. Of each year, on an average, not so much as two-fifths are occupied in fulfilment.[1] Of this neglect, what can be the cause? Answer—unreflecting imitation: imitation, too, of an original, the general inaptitude of which affords, to those who have rid themselves of it, matter of such just and unceasing self-congratulation. True it is that, in the copy, the individual and retail idleness is not, because for various reasons it cannot be, any thing near so flagrant as in the original: but the aggregate and wholesale idleness is little less enormous.

### Ratiocinative. Instructional

ART. 19. When, in all situations in which the business is of subordinate importance, the attendance is so unintermitted,—why should it be less so, in those in which the business is all-comprehensive, and the importance of it supreme?

### Instructional

ART. 20. Every year, in a tone of exultation, assuredly by no means ungrounded, the President, in his Message to Congress, reminds the people of the good done in the course of the last.[2] One day may perhaps produce the opposite account: the amount of the good, which, by blindness and idleness, has thus been left undone. But, by the phrase *good left undone*, much too favourable is the representation given of the effect. Of the good left undone, one portion—and *that* by far the most important—is composed of the exclusion that should have been put upon the evil—the extensive and positive afflictions which have thus been suffered to take place.

his death. In 1821 Bentham described Hume as 'the only Member of Parliament who thoroughly deserves that name' (UC viii. 130).

[1] Sessions during the first thirteen Congresses of the United States lasted on average between two and three months, though some were as short as one month, others as long as seven or eight months.

[2] The constitutional provision (Article II, Section 3) that 'The President shall from time to time give to the Congress Information of the State of the Union' had given rise to an annual Message at the beginning of the Congressional session.

*Instructional*

ART. 21. Amongst the accounts, thus given by authority, let there be one, for example, of the misery produced by tardiness, on the occasion of the adjustment of the state of the Insolvency laws, as between the central government and the several states: a matter which, to this day, 24th Jan. 1826, remains, after all, unadjusted.[1]

*Instructional*

ART. 22. For the inefficiency here mentioned, two more causes are visible: one is, *that* which belongs to the present head—the suffering so much to be unemployed: the other is, the suffering so much to be wasted in the commencement of businesses, the time employed in which is by the conclusion of the session turned to waste, for want of their being handed [over][2] by the outgoing to the incoming Legislature. As to this, see §24, *Continuation Committee.*

*Instructional*

ART. 23. As to the subsidiary obligations above provided, the more efficient, the less favourably, of course, will these chains be thought of and spoken of, by those for whose wear they are designed. But, at no less price can the effect be accomplished.

*Instructional*

ART. 24. On architecture good Government has more dependence than men have hitherto seemed to be aware of. Those who wish not for absentation or untimely departure, from any *seat of business,*

---

[1] John Neal (1793–1876), an American lawyer, author and, for a time, disciple of Bentham, resided at Queen's Square Place in 1826. He provided information for Bentham about United States government and politics, and was Bentham's source regarding the insolvency laws. See the Bowring Collation, p. 515. Though Congress was empowered by the Constitution (Article I, Section 8) to enact bankruptcy legislation, it had failed to do so, and State insolvency laws provided for the relief of debtors. The incident to which Bentham refers followed the Supreme Court decision in *Sturges v. Crowninshield* (1819) which declared a State insolvency law invalid as impairing the obligation of contracts. The uncertainty created by the Supreme Court decision invalidating the State laws continued until 1827 when the Court reversed its decision. Federal bankruptcy legislation was not enacted until 1841. Bentham, relying on Neal's information, is somewhat misleading in suggesting that the cause of the delay was the short legislative session rather than the political opposition to the legislation which was thought to favour the mercantile classes. See Charles Warren, *Bankruptcy in United States History*, Cambridge, Massachusetts, 1935.

[2] 1830, 'even', which Bowring changes to 'over' as more appropriate in the context.

55

must not admit of multiplied or unobserved entrances and exits. Those who wish to exclude abuse from *prisons*, must not have a space in which either the behaviour of any prisoner, or the treatment he experiences, is not continually exposed to every desiring eye.[1] Those Judges, whose wish it is to exclude inspectors from the seat of judicature, (and such of course, have ever been all English Judges) know well how powerless every other *veto* is, in comparison of that which the Architect alone can issue, and secure completely against non-observance.

## Instructional

ART. 25. *Non-attendance* is not the only cause of frustration and re-tardation in the provision for public exigencies. *Another* is the want of a supply for the *involuntary* deficiency created by death or sick-ness. For remedy, see §23, *Self-suppletive function*. A *third* may be seen in the improvidence, or sinister providence, by which each suc-cessive Legislature is deprived of the benefit of all former work, com-menced and left unfinished by its predecessor. For remedy, see §24, *Continuation Committee*.[2]

## SECTION 21

### SITTINGS PUBLIC AND SECRET

#### Enactive

ART. 1. Special cause to the contrary excepted, the sittings of this Assembly are, at all times, public. The auditory is a committee of the Public Opinion Tribunal, hearing and reporting for the information of the Constitutive.

#### Enactive

ART. 2. So far as is consistent with convenience in respect of health, sight, hearing, minutation, and necessary intercommunication be-tween actor and actor on the Legislation theatre, together with

---

[1] This was of course the essential principle of Bentham's Panopticon, on which see further pp. 444–5 and nn.

[2] For further discussion, see also Ch. VI, § 25, Arts. 54–5, p. 91. In the copy of the 1830 volume referred to in the Introduction, p. xlv, Bentham has the fol-lowing MS note at this point: 'For the evils of discontinued Attendance, see Debates of Commons 1831 Dec^r 6.' This refers to the King's Speech at the open-ing of the new session of Parliament, which announced that the Reform Bill was to be reintroduced. The Bill had passed all its stages in the House of Commons during the previous session, but had been defeated on second reading in the Lords on 6 October 1831. It was reintroduced in the Commons on 12 December.

lodgment for requisite and appropriate furniture, this Constitution requires that the number of the members of the Public Opinion Tribunal, to whom access and appropriate accommodation is given, be maximized.

### Enactive

ART. 3. To the hereinafter-mentioned Legislation Minister it belongs, to keep a *secret sitting book*. In it, in the case of a secret sitting, are entries made as follows:——
1. Year, month, and day of the motion for secrecy.
2. Names of movers, voters, and speakers for and against the secrecy.
3. Names, or initials, in their own hand-writings respectively.
4. Alledged cause of the demand for secrecy.

### Enactive

ART. 4. If divulgation has not already had place, cognizance is taken, of course, by the next succeeding Legislature, of the truth and sufficiency of the allegations: if either be wanting, censure is passed on the members, by whom the secrecy was voted.

### Enactive

ART. 5. Then is the regular time for divulgation. But if the cause for secrecy subsists, divulgation may be referred to the same Legislature on some succeeding day of that year, or to the next succeeding Legislature: and so on from Legislature to Legislature.

### Enactive

ART. 6. For other cases for secrecy as to the operation of public functionaries, see Ch. viii. PRIME MINISTER. §11, *Publication system*.

## SECTION 22

### TERM OF SERVICE—CONTINUATION

### Ratiocinative. Instructional

ART. 1. Exceptions excepted, the shorter the term of service in the Legislative Assembly, consistently with the avoidance of precipitation and [with the performance of][1] duty, can be rendered, the better. For reasons see §23, *Self-suppletive function*, §24, *Continuation Committee*, and §25, *Relocable who*.

[1] 1830, 'with the avoidance of precipitation and duty'; Bowring, 'with the avoidance of precipitation and performance of duty': the further emendation above seems necessary to clarify the point completely.

## Instructional

ART. 2. Exception may be, if in any part of the territory of the State there be Districts, one or more, so situated, in respect of remoteness from the seat of legislation, and difficulty of travelling taken together, that, by the time consumed in the journey, too great a difference would be made between those Districts and the others, in respect of means of giving information to, and support to their interests in, the Legislative Assembly.

## Instructional

ART. 3. Note that, on this occasion, the time necessarily expended in the giving and receiving information, as between the Legislature and the constituted Authorities and individuals residing in the remote Districts, in relation to exigencies peculiar to these Districts, is the only time which, in the nature of the case, needs, to this purpose, to be taken into account. For, as to the regular time of election, if as per § 25, *Relocable who*, the Members who have sitten [in] any year are excluded from relocability in the next, the day of universal vacancy being always foreseen and predetermined, the first of the days occupied in the election process may, without difficulty, be appointed to be as many days anterior to that same day, as shall be necessary, including the time occupied in the journey from the District to the seat of Legislature, to secure the timely arrival of the elected Deputy at the seat of Legislature.[1] Thus much as to the regularly recurring vacancies: as to the accidental vacancies, caused by death, resignation, or dislocation, replenishment will be seen effectually secured by § 23, *Self-suppletive function*.

## Instructional

ART. 4. Supposing these arrangements thus settled,——Elections may just as well take place, in virtue of a pre-established and continued general regulation, as in virtue of a special mandate offered by an individual functionary, such as the *Election Minister*, as per Election Code,[2] and Ch. xi. MINISTERS SEVERALLY. § 1, *Election Minister*. Indeed much better: for when the performance of a process or operation is made, or left, dependent upon the act of a public functionary,

---

[1] For the 1830 and Bowring texts of the latter part of this sentence, from 'as many days' to the end, see the Collations, pp. 463 and 487 below. The text above follows 1830 but deletes the seemingly redundant phrase 'as shall be sufficient' following the first reference to 'the seat of Legislature'.

[2] In *Bentham's Radical Reform Bill* (Bowring, iii. 558-97), the Election Minister is called the Election-Master-General. See Ch. VI, § 4n, p. 48n.

or, in a word, on the act of any person whatever, it is left liable to
be prevented by any one of a variety of accidents, as also by sinister
design on the part of that same functionary, with or without concert
with others.

### Instructional

ART. 5. In Monarchies it was that the *Representative*, or say the
*Deputation system*, originated. Of course, under such a form of
government, no such process as that of deputation to a common assembly could be commenced, otherwise than in consequence of, and
in conformity to, the will of the Monarch, as promulgated on some
particular day, by a known servant of his, appointed for this purpose.
Hence the need of *Election authorizing-and-commencing mandates.*

### Instructional

ART. 6. In no one of the several Anglo-American United States, is
the term of service in the Legislative Assembly more than one year.
In one of them, *Connecticut*, it is, or was, no more than half a year.[1]
In the General Congress, it is *two* years. The difference has for its
obvious cause the consideration of distance. Had the considerations
mentioned, and expedients referred to, in Art. 3, occurred, would or
would not the length of the *term of service* have in that case been
thus doubled?


## SECTION 23

### SELF-SUPPLETIVE FUNCTION

#### Enactive. Expositive

ART. 1. *Self-suppletive function.* To every Deputy is communicated,
by the act of Election, the power, of locating and keeping located,
upon and for every occasion, some person of his own choice, to act
in all things in his stead, at what time soever he is incapable of acting,
for himself, or does not act. To every Deputy accordingly belongs
this power, together with the obligation of keeping it in exercise.[2]

---

[1] See the Constitution of Connecticut, 1818, Article III, Sections 2 and 5, in
C. K. Kettleborough, *The State Constitutions*, Indianapolis, 1918, pp. 238–9. No
other state seems to have followed this example.

[2] In Bentham's annotated copy of the 1830 volume, referred to in the Introduction, p. xlv, the following MS note appears at this point; there is no indicator
and it may be meant to refer to Art. 1 or to Art. 2 or to the section as a whole:
'Resolution of the Committee of the whole House (of Commons). Date of Order
for printing 10 May 1830. "3dly That by Letters Patent under the Great Seal
of Ireland, bearing date the 23d of May 1797 Doctor Barrington, now Sir

### Enactive

ART. 2. Compensationally, punitionally, and dislocationally responsible, is the Deputy for the acts of this his substitute.

### Enactive. Ratiocinative

ART. 3. Exceptions excepted, locable as a Deputy's Substitute is every person who is locable as Deputy.

Exception 1. Another member of the same Legislature. For, to a person so situated, though the power of giving a vote, over and above his own, might be communicated,—the power of making a speech over and above his own, or a motion over and above his own, could not.

### Enactive

ART. 4. By the Legislation Minister will be kept a set of blank *Substitution instruments*. On each occasion, one of these instruments, filled up and signed by the Deputy, and signed by the Substitute, is, on his entrance into the Assembly Chamber, delivered by him to the Doorkeeper: as to whom, see § 20, *Attendance and Remuneration, &c.*

### Enactive

ART. 5. To provide against casual inability on the part of the Deputy, as to the locating a Substitute in time for the occasion,—every Deputy, previously to his taking his seat in the Assembly Chamber, lodges, in the office of the Legislation Minister, a *Substitution instrument*, in favour of some person, appointed to act as his permanent Substitute; the instrument being filled up and signed by himself, and signed by the Substitute, who thereby engages to keep himself within reach, in readiness to attend on requisition. But, to such *permanent Substitute*, may, on each occasion, as above, be substituted an *occasional* Substitute.

### Enactive

ART. 6. On timely information received, that, on the then next, or any succeeding sitting day, the Deputy in question will certainly or

Jonah Barrington, was appointed to the said office of Judge of the High Court of Admiralty in Ireland, [with power to depute and surrogate in his place] one or more deputy or deputies, as often as he should think fit".' The words in square brackets, representing a line in the MS note trimmed off in binding or rebinding, have been supplied from the *Commons Journals*, lxxxv (1830), 398. The passage comes, not from a resolution, but from a Report received by the Commons from a Committee of the Whole House.

probably not be able to pay attendance,——the Legislation Minister will cause to be summoned the above-mentioned Substitute: or the information may be given to the Substitute immediately, with or without its being given to the Legislation Minister: if dated and signed by the person giving it, it may be given either by the Deputy himself or by any other Member of the Legislature, or by any other person sufficiently known to the Deputy.

### Ratiocinative

ART. 7. *Question* 1. Why thus make provision of a Substitute to each Deputy?

*Answer. Reasons.* I. Whatsoever need or use there is for a Deputy, to act as member of the body in question, on any one day of the session,——the same there will be, for any thing that can be known to the contrary, on every other.

### Ratiocinative

ART. 8. II. Whatsoever arrangements can, as above, be taken, as per §20, *Attendance, &c.*, for securing plenitude of attendance on the part of the Deputy,——to render them completely effectual, without provision made of an eventual substitute, is not possible. Witness *definitive vacancy* by death, incurable infirmity, resignation, or dislocation: witness *occasional vacancy*, or say *non-attendance*——involuntary, through sickness, voluntary, through any one of an inscrutable multitude of causes. By the arrangements proposed in this Section, this plenitude would be rendered complete and never-failing: every seat having daily a member duly authorized to fill it.

### Ratiocinative. Expositive

ART. 9. III. For want of this desirable plenitude, a mode of corruption has at all times been carried on to an indefinite extent: corruption, effectually safe, not only as against punishment at the hands of legal tribunals, but against scrutiny and censure at the hands of the Public Opinion Tribunal. A man whom, had he been in attendance, the apprehension of that censure would have engaged to vote on the right side,——absents himself and thereby, though he does not give to the wrong side the whole benefit of his vote, deprives the right side of it, and this, without any check to hinder him,——gives thus, on every occasion, to the wrong side half the benefit of a vote given in favour of that same wrong side. Corruption, where the purpose of it is thus executed, may be distinguished by the name of *semi-corruption* or say *absentation corruption*. Happily though in this form it cannot with certainty be *punished*,——yet, what is much better, it may, in the way that will be seen, be, with adequate certainty, *prevented.*

### Ratiocinative

ART. 10. IV. *Prevention of fluctuation.* In Legislative and other bodies, instances are not uncommon, where the same measure has, by one and the same body, without any change in the number or sentiments of the Members, been alternately adopted and rejected: those who are in a majority one day finding themselves in a minority another day: hence, confusion and uncertainty, in the minds and actions of all persons whose interests are thus disposed of. Where attendance is optional, there are no assignable limits to the magnitude of the evil thus produced, nor to the frequency of its recurrence. By the plenitude here secured, evil in this shape would altogether be excluded.

### Ratiocinative

ART. 11. V. Saving of *solicitations of attendance:*——solicitations, with the accompanying *vexation, consumption* of individual's *time,* and sometimes even *delay* to public measures.

### Ratiocinative

ART. 12. VI. Thus, and for the first time, will the aggregate *will actually* expressed, be rendered constantly identical with the aggregate *will* which, on the occasion of all Elections of Deputies, to a Legislative or other representative assembly, is not only *intended* to be expressed, [but also]¹ almost as generally, howsoever erroneously, *regarded* as being actually expressed. Thus will an undesirable and reproachful distinction be obliterated: an imperfection, hitherto submitted to as if it were inherent in the constitution of a body of the sort in question, cleared away.

### Ratiocinative

ART. 13. VII. For want of this remedy,——questions, to the number and importance of which no limit can be assigned, must for their decision, have been dependent on *accident:* on accident in an unlimited variety of shapes, of which *sickness*, though a principal one, is but *one.* Apply this security, the power of accident over this case is at an end.

---

¹ 1830 and Bowring, 'and'.

*Ratiocinative*

ART. 14. *Question* 2. Why give the suppletive power to the Deputy, instead of reserving it to his Constituents?

*Answer. Reasons.* I. If the Constituents are the only persons to whom the power of providing the supply is given, the supply cannot ever be adequate; and the mode of making it cannot but be productive of divers evil effects; whereas, if the power be given to the Deputy, the supply may be rendered surely adequate, no such evil effects will be produced, and divers positive good effects will be produced.

*Ratiocinative*

ART. 15. II. In this way, the adequacy of the supply may be, and by the here proposed arrangements, naturally will be, made perfectly sure. The Deputy, in case of his non-attendance, is made responsible for the attendance of a Substitute. This he may be without difficulty. The seat of the Legislature being naturally the metropolis of the State,—its sittings, as per §18, *Attendance*, unintermitted, and the metropolis the principal seat of business in the State,—the influx into it, on one account or other, from all the districts, naturally abundant and constant,—and in particular the influx of men who, in respect of condition in life, will be among the most apt for the situation in question—and these very arrangements furnishing an additional inducement for such influx,—all these things considered, any want of apt persons, ready, for the sake of the benefit, to take upon themselves the burthen, seems not in any degree to be apprehended.

*Ratiocinative*

ART. 16. III. On the part of the eventual Substitute, if located by the Deputy, the attendance, in case of temporary non-attendance on the part of the Deputy, is more effectually secure, than if he were located by the Constituents in an immediate way, as above, it could be. The Substitute, being resident on the spot, will on every occasion be within call of the Deputy; and, the Deputy being bound for attendance on that same occasion,—thus, between the one and the other, adequate motives are accompanied by adequate means.

*Ratiocinative*

ART. 17. IV. Suppose the Substitute located by the Constituents,—no such assurance of constancy in the supply can be obtained. By whatsoever causes, as above, non-attendance on the part of the Deputy is producible, by these same so is it on the part of the Substitute. Substitutes, more than one, could not be proposed to be sent

63

along with the Deputy: and whatsoever greater number could be proposed to be so sent, still the assurance could not be entire. True it is, that the above-mentioned course—of taking for the Substitute a person resident at the seat of service, would be open to their choice. But, it would not be likely to be uniformly adopted: for, if permanently resident at that same seat of service, he would not be known to them: and if, in the case of this or that District, there were any such known person,—in the case of this or that other there would not be. At the best, the number that could be thus located—located to serve throughout the session—would be thus limited: whereas, to the number that could be located, one after another, as occasion called, by the Deputy, there are no limits.

## Ratiocinative

ART. 18. V. Suppose, however, an eventual Substitute located by the constituents. In the case of a vacancy, on the part of either Deputy or Substitute, here would be a demand for a fresh election. But, while the process of election was going on,—here would be but one of the two on the spot, and during that time there would be the same danger of want of attendance, as if no such provision of an eventual Substitute had been made.

## Ratiocinative

ART. 19. VI. On this supposition, too, comes the vexation and expense of the Election: loss of time on the part of all who attend: expense of journey to and fro and demurrage, on the part of many: and, from all this loss, no assignable advantage in any shape obtained.

## Ratiocinative

ART. 20. VII. Antecedent to the close of the Session, which, under the here proposed annuality of Election, is the same thing with the death of the Legislature,—there would be a certain number of days occupied by the Election process: during this time, the vacancy would of necessity remain unsupplied.

## Ratiocinative

ART. 21. VIII. So likewise, a greater number of days, during which a still longer vacancy would be produced by another cause. The utmost service that could be looked for at the hands of a new Member or Substitute, in the course of so short a time, would be regarded as not capable of compensating for the vexation and expense of the Election process, as above.

*Ratiocinative*

ART. 22. IX. If the provision of a Substitute be made by the Electors, it must be at an expense charged upon the public: if by the Deputy himself, it may be made without expense: in the metropolis, for as many days in the year as can present the demand, sufficiently apt men in sufficient number, able and willing to serve, for so many different portions of so short a length of time, in so high a situation, without pecuniary retribution,—and taken together for the whole of it, one after another,—never can be wanting. Then, as to pay,—suppose the Substitute paid, and paid by the public, his pay will require to be at least equal to that of his Principal. It will, in truth, require to be greater; for, to that same Principal belongs the whole of the power; to the Substitute no part at all, except such, if any, as the Principal feels the desire, or lies under the necessity, of imparting to him: which is what can no otherwise be done, than by forbearing himself to exercise it. This being the case, if a *Substitute*, engaging for constancy of attendance, can be had *gratis*, much more can the *Principal*—the *Deputy;* and whatsoever pay, if any be necessary, suffices for the Substitute, still less will suffice for that same Principal.

*Ratiocinative*

ART. 23. X. Positive good effects that afford a promise of being produced by this arrangement are as follows:—

1. Increase given to appropriate aptitude in all its branches, by admission given to persons who otherwise would have stood excluded. A person who, though in respect of such his aptitude, is the object of universal confidence, would, through old age or infirmity, have been incapacitated from, or disinclined to, the subjecting himself to any such constancy of attendance as is as above required under the notion of its being indispensable,—may, by the here proposed relief, be disposed to take upon himself the trust.

*Ratiocinative*

ART. 24. XI. [2.] So, in like manner, a person who, though recommended to the notice and favour of the Electors by preeminent pecuniary responsibility, would otherwise, by the indolence naturally attendant on opulence, be deterred. In this case, as in the former, the natural subject of the proposed Deputy's choice would be some person, by whose appropriate aptitude, in the situation of Substitute, honour would, in the opinion of the [Deputy],[1] be done to that same choice.

---

[1] 1830 and Bowring, 'Depute'; but Bentham seems to be referring to the opinion of the Deputy.

## *Ratiocinative*

ART. 25. XII. In both these cases, an opening is made for new men, in whose instance a special promise of appropriate aptitude is afforded; afforded, and, by means and motives, beyond such as are likely to have place on the part of a majority of the Electors.

## *Ratiocinative*

ART. 26. XIII. Attached to the situation of Deputy, here, in both these cases, would be *patronage:* and from this patronage, the value of the situation would, in the eyes of candidates and competitors, receive increase. True it is, that, in other cases, patronage is a source and instrument of corruption: not so in this case. In no shape is any advantage given, which is not altogether dependent upon the free will of the people in the quality of Electors. In the case of the approved and respected patron, may be seen a promise of *moral*, in that of the *opulent patron*, of *pecuniary responsibility;* in that of the subject of their choice, a promise of appropriate *intellectual* and *active aptitude*.

## *Instructional*

ART. 27. What is above considered, it may be worth further consideration, whether it might not, with advantage and safety, be left at the option of every Deputy, whether to attend in his own person or by such his Substitute: attendance, on the part either of the one or the other, being unremittingly enforced. As to the public, it has been seen that it would be likely to be a gainer by this indulgence: and, it does not appear, whence suffering or danger in any shape can come: as to the individuals in question, the advantage, in various shapes, to them is obvious and out of dispute.

## *Instructional. Ratiocinative*

ART. 28. For distinction sake, that is to say, for pointing, in a more particular manner, the eyes of the people upon the conduct of the Substitutes, and in this point of view upon that of their respective locators,——might it not be of use that they should wear some conspicuous habiliment? for example, across the shoulders a broad ribbon, on which are marked, in universally conspicuous letters, their official denominations?

## *Instructional*

ART. 29. So also, in the case of the Members of the proposed *Continuation Committee;* as to whom, see §24, *Continuation Committee*.

*Enactive*

ART. 30. On every day, on which the seat of any Member in the Assembly shall have remained vacant, neither the Deputy, nor any Substitute of his being on service,——notice of such absentation will, by the Registrar, be entered in the register of the assembly; and *placards* in sufficient number forthwith transmitted to the *Election Clerk* of the District, by whom they will be posted up on the outside of his official edifice, in conspicuous situations appropriated to the purpose.[1]

*Enactive*

ART. 31. If, within {7} days after such day of default, no *Excuse paper*, stating the inevitable cause of such vacancy, shall have been delivered in to the Registrar,——information of such further default will be transmitted by him to the Election Clerk in his District; and, at the same time, to the Election Minister, at the seat of the Assembly. On the receipt thereof, the Minister will forthwith transmit to the Election Clerk his mandate, ordering for the district in question, a fresh election. For the *excuses*, allowable on different occasions, for failure of attendance and other compliances where and when due, see the Procedure Code.[2]

*Enactive*

ART. 32. If an *Excuse paper*, as above, be delivered in,——the Assembly will, in the first place, pronounce as to the sufficiency or insufficiency of the excuse. In case of its insufficiency, the Legislature will give orders for a fresh election, as above; and as to the *Substitute*, who likewise will, in this case have made default, it will either content itself with rendering the default universally known by appropriate publication, or in case of need proceed to punishment, as per §28, *[Legislation] Penal Judicatory*.


SECTION 24

CONTINUATION COMMITTEE

*Enactive. Ratiocinative. Instructional*

ART. 1. Lest, by the exit of Members, by whom introduction or support has been given to useful arrangements, any such arrangement

---

[1] See also Ch. VI, § 20, Art. 5, p. 50.

[2] On excuses, see *Equity Dispatch Court Bill* (Bowring, iii. 319–431), Bowring, iii. 420n. On the Procedure Code, see Ch. V, § 5, Art. 6n, p. 38n.

should, after proposal and acceptance, be lost or deteriorated,——as also lest the appropriate intellectual and active aptitude produced by experience should, by such secession, be rendered less than, without prejudice to appropriate moral aptitude,——to wit, to length of exposure to corruption from the Executive,——it may thus be made to be, ——each Legislature, antecedently to its outgoing, will elect a Committee, the Members of which,——to the number of from {seven} to {twenty-one,} or more,——will, under the name of the *Continuation Committee*, under the direction of the Legislature, apply their endeavours, collectively or individually, in the next succeeding Legislature, to the carrying on of the designs and proceedings of the then next preceding Legislature, in an unbroken thread.

### *Enactive*

ART. 2. Locable in the Continuation Committee is, in each year, not only every Member of the outgoing Legislature, but every Member of the Continuation Committee, serving in that same Legislature. Thus may any person serve as a Continuation Committee man for any number of successive years.

### *Enactive. Ratiocinative*

ART. 3. A Continuation Committee man has, for the above purpose, on every occasion, right of argumentation and initiation, or say of speech and motion: but, not having been elected by the people, he has not a vote.

### *Enactive*

ART. 4. Subject to any such alteration as the Legislature may at any time think fit to make, the pay of a Continuation Committee man is the same as that of a Deputy.

### *Ratiocinative*

ART. 5. *Question* 1. Why make provision for the continuation of proceedings, which, having been commenced under one Legislature, would otherwise have been dropped, for want of being continued under the next?

*Answer. Reasons.* I. If for this purpose, no provision were made, useful arrangements, to the importance, extent, or number of which no limits can be assigned, may experience a delay, to which also no limits can be assigned. Say *Time lost.*

### *Ratiocinative*

ART. 6. II. Others, of which at the time the need may in any degree have been, or even may continue urgent, may, by some temporary accident, be prevented from even being so much as proposed. Say *Good measures lost.*

### Ratiocinative

ART. 7. III. In whatever instance, in the hope of consummation, proceedings, having been instituted, have by the extinction of the Legislature been left unfinished,—here is so much of the time employed in them consumed in waste. Say *Functionaries' time wasted.*

### Ratiocinative

ART. 8. IV. True it is—that, in this case, though the legislative arrangements, with a view to which the proceedings were commenced, have not taken place,—yet, in the course of these same proceedings, *information* more or less valuable will commonly have been obtained. But, on the other hand, in so far as information, elicited on behalf of a proposed arrangement, has not been accompanied with such information as, in case of completion, would have been elicited in opposition to it—here comes a proportionable danger, that the information thus obtained will be more or less delusive. Say *Delusive information probabilized.*

### Ratiocinative

ART. 9. V. Arrangements, to the extent, number, and importance of which no limit can be assigned, may,—in consideration of the length of time that would be necessary to the bringing to maturity the body of information necessary to constitute an adequate ground,—be precluded from being ever initiated, proposed, or so much as mentioned. The more extensive and important the arrangements, the more protracted the preparation will naturally be conceived to be: and the more protracted it is conceived to be, the more perfectly will all prospect of consummation be excluded. Say *Improvement prevented from being so much as conceived.*

### Ratiocinative

ART. 10. VI. The shorter the life of the legislative body, the greater the evil in its above several shapes. Under the present proposed Code, this life is limited to a single year; or, in case of necessity, produced by *distance* of some parts of the territory from the seat of legislation, to, at the utmost, two years; and, the greater this distance, the greater will naturally be the length of time necessary to give completeness to the information.

*Ratiocinative*

ART. 11. VII. As the same Continuation Committee man may be re-located by successive Legislatures in any number, there will be no limit but that of his life to the quantity of *experience* thus placed at their command.

*Ratiocinative*

ART. 12. VIII. True it is——that, in the practice of nations, no instance of any such provision is adducible. But, the absence of it may, without difficulty, be accounted for by other suppositions than that of its needlessness: to wit, by the *vis inertiæ* of government, by the natural blind continuance in the course continued in by predecessors, and by sinister interest, and interest-begotten prejudice, on the part of rulers.

*Ratiocinative*

ART. 13. IX. In the earliest ages, *printing* being unknown, *writing*—— a jewel in the hands of the extremely few, *travelling* moreover unsafe and tedious, means of eliciting any such extensive body of information in a permanent shape were unattainable: in succeeding ages, when bodies having a sort of momentary and precarious share in legislation, were brought together, it was under the spur of temporary necessity for some one or two limited purposes:——commonly for no other but the obtaining a pecuniary supply: their convener, a Monarch, who, when once the purpose was accomplished, felt no motives for continuing, but the most irresistible ones for dismissing, as quickly as possible, such troublesome associates.

*Ratiocinative*

ART. 14. *Question* 2. Why not give to the Members of these Committees the right of voting?

*Answer. Reasons.* I. To the purpose for which the institution is proposed, that right is neither necessary nor subservient: Servants, not fellow Masters, these functionaries stand in this respect on the same footing with *Ministers*, to whom speech and motion without vote is given, as per Ch. ix. MINISTERS COLLECTIVELY. §24, *Legislation regarding functions.*

*Ratiocinative*

ART. 15. II. Though, for the year during which they serve as Deputies with votes, they will have been chosen by their proper Constituents,——they will not have been chosen, by those same or any other

Electors, for any one of the succeeding years, during which the need of their services, in the character of *Continuation Committee men*, may come to have place.

### Ratiocinative

ART. 16. III. For as much as, to the purpose in question, it may be necessary that the number of them should not be fixed,——the consequence is——that if they had votes, the power of keeping the number of the Members of the Legislature in continued fluctuation would be, in case of such non-fixation, possessed by whatsoever authority they were located by.

### Ratiocinative

ART. 17. IV. Supposing, as above, the right of voting not imparted to them,——they may, without difficulty or ground of objection, be located by their own colleagues, who, on this supposition, are, as will be seen, their only apt locators.

### Ratiocinative

ART. 18. *Question* 3. Why thus give to their colleagues the location of these functionaries?

*Answer. Reasons.* I. In the possession of these their colleagues will be the best evidence, whereon to pass judgment on their appropriate aptitude in all its branches: and in particular in the intellectual and the active, being those which, in their instance, are principally in demand: while, by their non-possession of the right of voting, will be obviated all danger and objection, on the score of any such deficiencies of appropriate moral aptitude, as might otherwise be the result of their length of continuance in office: a length which, after this precaution, may without danger be maximized. Influence of will on will, none: influence of understanding on understanding will be their sole influence.

### Ratiocinative

ART. 19. II. In the possession of these their colleagues alone, will moreover be the evidence, whereon to judge of the nature and probable quantity, of the business for which their assistance will be needed, and thence of the number of them which that business may require.

### Ratiocinative

ART. 20. III. The choice of Committee men out of their own associates has, by universal need, been rendered the universal practice, on the part of the legislative and other numerous bodies.

*Ratiocinative*

ART. 21. IV. Take here for emblem Sisyphus and his stone.[1] Sinister policy joins with ignorance and heedlessness in perpetuating the useless torment. The *Continuation Committee system* applies to the stone a *board*, which detains it at its maximum of elevation, and the next impulse given to it lodges it on the desired eminence.

## SECTION 25

### RELOCABLE WHO

*Enactive*

ART. 1. No person who, for any District, has sitten as a Member of the Legislature, can, for that or any other District, be, in that situation, relocated, unless, and thence until, of the persons who have served as Members, there exists at the time, a number thrice (or twice?) as great as that of the whole number of the Members, of whom the Legislative Body is composed.

*Enactive*

ART. 2. For the ascertaining, on each occasion, the existence of this necessary number, it will be among the functions of the Legislation Minister, having before him the list of the Members of the Legislature, to keep account, and for the several years to mark off, as the occurrences take place, the several quondam Members, who, by death or otherwise, have become *definitively* unrelocable.

*Enactive*

ART. 3. For *reasons* for Art. [1], and for the locability of a Member in the Continuation Committee of the next year, see §24, *Continuation Committee.*

*Ratiocinative. Instructional*

ART. 4. A position, upon which the here-proposed arrangement is grounded, is—that, without non-relocability—and *that* for a term sufficient to present to the Electors two sets at least of competitors, the number of whom, when added together, shall be little or nothing less than the double of that of the situations to be filled,—any supposed opening, for improvement or correction of abuse, will be but illusory: for that, unless it be in a number insufficient to produce

---

[1] In Greek mythology Sisyphus was eternally punished by having to push a heavy stone to the top of a hill only to see it roll back to the bottom.

72

any effect, the set of men located at the first Election will, to every
practical purpose, continue in place, on all subsequent Elections; just
as they would have done had there never been any Elections by which
they could be dislocated.

### Ratiocinative. Instructional

ART. 5. If the number of persons capable of being competitors be
short of this,—all the effect, produced by the elimination and election process, will be,—the adding to the original number of the
acting managers, a certain number of dormant ones, who will be all
along sharers in the latent profits of the power, without being sharers
in the responsibility attached to the open exercise of it.

### Expositive. Instructional

ART. 6. Joint proprietors of a fund, for whatever purpose established,
suppose, an indefinite and ever-changing number, having for its limits
the original number of the transferable shares. Number of original
managers during the first year of the institution, say, for example,
24: of these, 18 stay in, without re-election; 6 only go out, and that
of course, the first year, giving place, consequently, to 6 new ones,
and so in every succeeding year. Of this arrangement, what is the
result? Answer. Every year after the first,—total number, instead of
24, 30: whereof 24 in possession: 6 others in expectancy only, but
that expectancy sure. Thus is the election no more than an empty
show: no proprietor, besides the six managers in expectancy, seeing
any the least chance of his being elected, should he offer himself:
accordingly, no such offer is ever made: whole number—30—revolve
in a cycle, consisting of a short arithmetical *repetend* in the form of
a *circulate*.

### Exemplificational. Instructional

ART. 7. In every instance in which the sort of arrangement in question has place, the truth of this theory stands demonstrated by experience. Witness the case of the *East India* Company: witness that
of the *Bank of England* Company: witness that of the several *minor*
companies, too numerous for enumeration, which have been organized upon the model of those two gigantic ones.[1]

---

[1] In the case of the East India Company the mode of election to which Bentham refers was established by the Regulating Act of 1773 and lasted until 1853.
C. H. Philips, *The East India Company 1784–1834*, Manchester, 1940, p. 4 & n,
mentions that the six Directors 'out of rotation' were 'expected to dine with the
Court from time to time'. In the case of the Bank of England the original by-laws
of 1694 were amended in accordance with an Act of Parliament passed in 1697,

## Exemplificational. Instructional

ART. 8. In the case of the City of London, and its governing body the *Common Council*, it stands exemplified, and receives a still stronger confirmation: in that case, the seats——not merely in a small proportion, as above, but the whole number, are at all Election times open, and the Elections have place in every year: yet in the whole number rarely indeed, except by death or resignation, does any change take place.[1] Of this stagnation, what is the consequence? *Answer*. What it cannot fail to be any where: imbecility, corruption ——inaptitude in a word in every shape, comparison laid with the aptitude which might securely be substituted to it, by the here proposed all comprehensive temporary non-relocability system: and assuredly not at any less price.

## Instructional

ART. 9. For proof or disproof of this same position, the case of the Anglo-American United Congress, with its *House of Representatives and Senate*, presents another obvious and proper object of reference. But, in that case, circumstances occur, which would render the examination tedious, and the result undecisive. The case is *there* a complicated one, complicated with that of the general system of government and state of society in other particulars: and, where simple cases are sufficiently decisive, it would be lost labour to dwell on complicated ones: it would not have been mentioned, but to show that it has not been overlooked.[2]

---

to provide that not more than two-thirds of the twenty-four Directors were to be re-elected at any annual election. See W. Marston Acres, *The Bank of England from Within 1694-1900*, London, 1931, pp. 38, 40, 79-80. The list of Directors printed by Acres (pp. 613-30) seems to indicate that re-election after the required year's interruption was so common as to justify Bentham's claim. The 1697 system lasted until 1872.

[1] Bentham's statement here is confirmed by Alexander Pulling, *A Practical Treatise on the Laws, Customs, and Regulations of the City and Port of London*, London, 1842, p. 58, where he says that every year the City's Common Council of over 200 members was re-elected 'with scarcely an exception'. The Webbs make the point that because the city's twenty-six wards were divided into no fewer than 169 precincts, each Common Councillor must have been personally acquainted with all his constituents. Sidney and Beatrice Webb, *English Local Government: the Manor and the Borough*, 2 vols., London, 1924, ii. 685-6.

[2] The Constitution of the United States provides (Article I, Section 2) that the whole of the House of Representatives shall be elected in every second year, and (Article I, Section 3) that one-third of the Senate shall be elected biennially.

### Instructional

ART. 10. For the same reason, nothing more is here said of the French Chamber of Deputies, under the Charter, with its provision for the annual elimination of one fifth.[1]

### Instructional

ART. 11. The same reason will serve for similar silence, on the present occasion, as to the case of the English House of Commons.

### Instructional

ART. 12. In conclusion, where for each situation, there are not at least two candidates, standing upon tolerably equal ground, all appearance of choice is, in a greater or less degree, illusory.

### Instructional

ART. 13. The contrivance has for its model that of the Juggler. Holding up a pack of cards with the faces to the company,—'*young gentleman*,' (says he to one of them) '*fix upon which you please*,' care being all the while taken that one and one alone shall be in such sort visible, as to give determination to choice.

### Ratiocinative

ART. 14. *Question* 1. Why, during the time proposed, or for so much as any one session, exclude all persons who have served as Deputies, from serving again?

*Answer. Reasons.* I. Because from undiscontinued relocability, evil effects naturally flow, as will be seen, in all shapes.

### Ratiocinative

ART. 15. II. To the public, whatever good could be expected from undiscontinued relocability, ·and undiscontinued relocatedness in consequence, is ensured, with addition and without any evil, by the *Continuation Committee* institution, as above.

### Ratiocinative

ART. 16. III. As to individual Deputies, no evil in any shape would be produced—no pain of privation—no disappointment: since no sooner did any one of them look to the situation, than the limits to his continuance in it would meet his eyes. True it is, that, in the case of a person whom the commencement of the authority of this Code

---

[1] This provision was made in Article 37 of the *Charte constitutionnelle* of 1814, under which France was governed until the Revolution of 1830.

might find in the possession of the situation in question, the exemption from uneasiness would not have place: and from this circumstance a proportionable obstruction to such commencement could not but reasonably be expected.

### Ratiocinative

ART. 17. IV. As to the evil effects from undiscontinued relocability, they have for their immediate cause the probabilization of relative inaptitude in all shapes, on the part of the relocated functionary.

### Ratiocinative

ART. 18. V. First, as to the inaptitude correspondent and opposite to appropriate aptitude in all shapes taken together. Under the circumstances in question, the undiscontinued relocability wants very little, scarce any thing at all in effect and practice, of being tantamount to location for life: in the eyes of Electors in general, as well as their Deputies, *non-reelection* will have the effect of *dislocation*. The Deputy who has served his one year, has, at the Election of the second year, possession to plead, and his services that have been performed in the course of that same first year. Be those services ever so slender, no equal plea can be put in by a competitor, who, not having served at all, has not had the possibility of rendering any such services.

### Ratiocinative

ART. 19. VI. Next, as to *moral* inaptitude in particular. In the natural course of things, this disqualification, so far as it is constituted by corruptedness, will be universal. *Corruptees*, these same relocated Members: *corruptors*, with or without design, in the superior regions, the two great givers of good gifts—the *Prime Minister* and the *Justice Minister:* in the inferior regions, the leading men among each Deputy's Electors.

### Ratiocinative

ART. 20. VII. *Matter of corruption*, the aggregate of these same good gifts, attached to the several official situations, as to which they are locators: elements of this aggregate—contents of this *cornucopia*, money, money's worth, power, (power of *patronage* included) and reputation, comprising whatsoever *dignity*, or say *distinction* stands inseparably attached to these same situations: the two other ingredients in the official *cornucopia* of a Monarchy—to wit, *ease* at the expense of *duty*, and *vengeance* at the expense of *justice* being, it is hoped, excluded pretty effectually from that of the present proposed

Constitution, by various appropriate arrangements, pervading the whole texture of it.

## Ratiocinative

ART. 21. VIII. *Efficient cause* of corruption in this case, expectation of the eventual receipt of some portion or portions of that same matter, in case of compliance with the several wills, declared or presumed, of the corruptors. Here, as elsewhere, let it never be out of mind—it is not so much by the actual receipt of these objects of desire that the corruptedness is produced, as by the eventual expectation of them: for, by the receipt in one instance, it is not produced any otherwise than in so far as receipt is necessary to engender and keep alive expectation in other instances.

## Ratiocinative

ART. 22. IX. Corrupt*ees, per contrà*, those same corrupt*ors* above-mentioned. Elements of the matter of corruption in their situations —1, increase of power—2, diminution of responsibility—*restrictive*, or say *refrenative* responsibility.

## Ratiocinative

ART. 23. X. Thus in the *superior* regions: in the *inferior* regions, Corrupt*ors* the *leading* men among the Electors: matter of corruption, the benefit of their influence with those their colleagues. Corrupt*ees per contrà*, those same leading men. Elements of the matter of corruption in their situation, 1, such portions of the matter of corruption as are of too little value to be objects of concupiscence to the Deputies for themselves or their connections: 2, gratification, from courtesy and flattery received and expected from their Deputies, in consideration of the support received or expected: 3, benefit to the particular local interest or supposed interest, of the District they belong to, at the expense of the general interest of the State.

## Ratiocinative

ART. 24. XI. Correspondent *per contrà* corrupt*ees* in this case, these same corrupt*ors*. Matter of corruption in this case, 1, at the hands of the eventually re-elected Deputy, expectation of good things of minor value, not good enough to be worth the acceptance of Deputies or their connections, and thus obtainable from the favour of the above-mentioned Arch-corruptors:—2, expectation of courtesy and flattery, at the hands of these same Deputies, in return for the favours looked for by them, as above. As to the good things just mentioned, the original source from which they will in great part, perhaps in most part, be looked for, is the favour of the *Arch-corruptor[s]* above-mentioned: the channel through which they will be regarded as flowing, being the favour of the several also above-mentioned *Sub-corruptors*.

### Ratiocinative

ART. 25. XII. Under the influence of this corruption, the greater number of the members will naturally be found belonging to one or other of two classes: those who have nothing but *votes* to sell, and those who, besides votes, have *talents* to sell. As to comparative *prices;* of the *vote-seller*, the price will not deviate much from uniformity: of the *talent-seller*, the price will not only rise above that of the *vote-seller*, but swell to an amount, to which no determinate limit can be assigned: no limit, other than that which bounds the aggregate value of all that the above-mentioned *arch-givers* of good gifts have to bestow, and *that* which, for himself and his connections of all sorts, the Deputy in question is capable of receiving. As to the *talents*, they may be distinguished into talents for *speaking*, and talents for *management*. As between these, the highest price will, in general, be obtained by the talents for speaking, these being at once the more rare, and by much the more conspicuous.

### Expositive. Instructional

ART. 26. Thus, on this part of the *moral* world, is the *attraction of corruption* not less universal than the *attraction of gravity* in the *physical* world: and, in the present case, every year, the cohesion, of which the matter of corruption is the cement, will be closer than in all former years.

### Expositive. Instructional

ART. 27. As is the blood of man to the tiger who has once tasted of it, so are the sweets of office to the functionary who has once tasted of them. Seldom by any thing but hopelessness of re-enjoyment will the appetite be extinguished.

### Instructional

ART. 28. But, though the power of the matter of corruption is naturally thus efficient, some length of time, different according to idiosyncrasy and other circumstances, will be necessary to the production of the effect: for, though, for the formation of the virtual contract, converse and particular explanations between the parties may be unnecessary,—not so such means of acquaintance with one another's dispositions, as are requisite to form a ground for practice; and, for

the obtainment of this information, a certain length of time is generally necessary. Hence, in the antiseptic regimen, one general rule. In
the case of every two functionaries whose situations operate upon
each other with a corruptive influence, *minimize the time of contact*.
But for this resource, all endeavours to obviate the contagion might
be hopeless: but, this resource being at command, the case is by no
means desperate.

### Expositive. Instructional

ART. 29. Emblem, the *red hot roller*, under which, for smoothing, a
stuff is passed without injury. Allow to the time of contact a certain
increase, the stuff is in a flame.

### Instructional

ART. 30. Of the principle here in question, ulterior application will
be seen made, in so far as the nature of the case admits; and in particular in the Judiciary department. See Ch. xii. JUDICIARY COL-
LECTIVELY, §17, *Migration*.

### Instructional

ART. 31. Though, to the extent to which it is applicable with advantage, the principle has not perhaps been applied in any country,—
there is not perhaps any in which more or less application has not
been made of it.

### Instructional

ART. 32. Of the sole reason for the undiscontinued relocability system, on the ground of *utility*, the essence is contained in the word
*experience*. But, on the occasion here in question, the idea commonly
attached to this word wants much of being clear or sufficiently comprehensive.—*Experience* is applicable to two different situations—
1, to that of the Deputies—2, to that of the Electors. On this occasion, that of the Deputies seems to have been the only one commonly
thought of. Moreover, on the occasion of the application thus made
of it, the idea attached to it seems to have been vague and indeterminate. To fix it, the expression must be changed, and to the indeterminate expression *experience*, the so thoroughly determined expression
*appropriate aptitude* substituted. Now, to the most important branch
of appropriate aptitude, namely, the *moral*, the system in question
has just been shown to be not only not favourable, but positively and
highly adverse. Remain the two other branches of the aptitude,
namely, the *intellectual* and the *active*. True it is then, that, considered apart from the moral, to these it cannot but be acknowledged

to be, generally speaking, favourable: but, in the *moral* branch suppose a deficiency, any increase in these two branches, so far from raising the degree of aptitude, taken in the aggregate, may, as has been seen, lower it.

### Instructional

ART. 33. Here, then, comes in one great use of the *Continuation Committee:* to the Members as such, the right of speech and that of *motion* being alone given, that of *voting* being discarded. Thus it is —that, by means of this engine, a supply of intellectual and active aptitude may be kept up, without any the least diminution of moral aptitude; a supply, and *that* susceptible of increase, as long continued as any which, by undiscontinued relocability and relocation, could have been provided, at the expense of moral aptitude.

### Instructional

ART. 34. After all, where, on this occasion, *experience* is ascribed to the situation of the functionary in question, of what qualification, on his part, under that name, can there be any reasonable assurance? From his merely filling the situation, if *that* be all, nothing can be inferred; and, unless this or that individual be in view, this is all that can, on any sufficient grounds, be affirmed. Upon the *attention*, bestowed upon the business to which his situation puts it in his power to apply his mind,—will depend whatever aptitude he may possess in either of the two branches; take away the attention, the experience amounts to very little: that is to say to the present purpose: for another there is, as will be seen with reference to which this *little* will be considerably better than nothing.

### Exemplificational. Instructional

ART. 35. For an example look to the *English* Legislative Assemblies, and in particular to the *House of Lords*. Here you may see beyond all doubt possession of the situation, possession on the part of hundreds, and on the part of each unit, whatsoever *experience* the possession cannot fail to give. Look at this experience, and then see what, in the case of the vast majority, is the produce, in the shape of any one of the branches of appropriate aptitude.

### Instructional

ART. 36. Remains now the *experience* considered as desirable in the situation of the *Electors:* experience as to comparative aptitude, as between Candidate and Candidate. As to this, see the next Article.

*Ratiocinative*

ART. 37. *Question* [2]. Why not render the *non-relocability per-petual?*

*Answer. Reason.* That, for the choice of the Electors of each Dis-trict, there may be, in a state capable of being, and not unlikely to be, competitors with each other, two persons at least,——of whose comparative appropriate aptitude in future as to the situation in question, the Electors have had the means of judging, from observa-tions made of their respective degrees of appropriate aptitude, in and for that same situation, as therein already manifested; which men may accordingly, relation had to that same situation, be termed *tried men:* and, in respect of the interest which the observers have had in the accuracy of the observation, the conduct of their Deputies being thus the concern of the Electors,——the Electors may thus, in the words of the common phrase, be said to have had *experience* of it. Suppose the relocability to have place from the first,——they would, as above, (vacancies by death, resignation, or the extremely rare case of dislocation excepted,) seldom have any to choose out of but the original stock; in which case, the Election process would be of little or no use: suppose no relocability to have place at any time, they would have no *tried men*——in the above sense of the word *tried*[——] to choose out of.

*Instructional*

ART. 38. In the instance of each Deputy, after one year of service in that situation, for how many years shall his non-relocability therein continue? The choice seems to be between *two* years and *three* years. The country not being *a given quantity*, materials constituting a sufficient ground for a decisive answer are not, it should seem, to be found. The following considerations will present to view the diffi-culty, and at the same time a circumstance which lessens it.

*Instructional*

ART. 39. Make the interval of non-relocability too long, the danger is——1, that the chance or even the assurance, of repossessing the situation, will not be sufficiently attractive: the minds of those who would otherwise have been competitors, will have been turned off to other pursuits; 2, moreover, the State will, for so long, have remained debarred, from the benefit looked for, from the giving to the Electors the choice as between men called *tried men*, as above. Note, however, that, supposing no failure in the number of these peculiarly apt com-petitors,——this effect extends not beyond the *preparation period:*——

81

the first year, reckoning from the day of the adoption of the Constitution here proposed.

### Instructional

ART. 40. As to the circumstance[1] by which the difficulty is *lessened*, it consists in the multitude of situations, which, in the instance of each such temporarily dislocated Deputy, will, under this Constitution, be open to his desires.

### Instructional

ART. 41. 1. In this one Supreme Legislature, there will be seen, as per Ch. v. CONSTITUTIVE, §2, *Powers*, a multitude of *Sublegislatures*, exercising, each of them, though to less local extent, most of the functions of that one. In the Supreme Legislature suppose, by the Deputy in question, no more than a moderate share of appropriate aptitude manifested, and *that* for no more than one year——such manifestation made in such a place, cannot but be expected by him, and with reason, to operate as a powerful recommendation: particularly, that body of appropriate *information* considered, which, even though no outward manifestation of his having received it shall have happened to be given, cannot fail to have presented itself to his notice.

2. Ministerial situations, immediately under the Supreme Legislature, and thence under the Prime Minister. True it is——that, in these, the openings will be so few,——and the qualifications which will be found necessary, so rare,——that the number, by whom, for the present purpose, their situations can be looked to as a resource, will be proportionably small. Though the number of those same situations is thirteen,——whether for the filling them so large a number of persons will be necessary, will depend on local circumstances: and, in these same situations, instead of *temporary non-relocability*, the nature of the case will be seen to require *perpetual continuance*, saving special causes of dislocation. As to these Ministers, see Ch. xi. MINISTERS SEVERALLY.

3. Under each Sublegislature, a set of Subministerial situations, wanting little of being equal in number to the above-mentioned *Ministerial* ones.

4. Situations in the *Judiciary*. In each *Immediate Judicatory*, four situations,——no one of them, with reference to the ex-functionaries in question, beneath acceptance. So likewise the same number in each *Appellate Judicatory*. True it is——that it will not be till a

[1] 1830 and Bowring, 'circumstances'; but the singular is clearly required. See the end of Art. 38.

considerable time after the commencement of the Constitution, that
this resource will be open to them: nor then, except on the supposition of their having passed through the appropriate *probationary
period*, and thereupon migrated for the time from the Judiciary into
this transitory situation. As to this, see Ch. xii. JUDICIARY COL-
LECTIVELY. §28, *Locable who.*

## Instructional

ART. 42. On the first establishment of a Constitution, which is as
much as to say on the first formation of a new State,—the people
find themselves under a dilemma. *Experience* of the character of
public men, with a view to their location in the several efficient situations, is at the same time preeminently desirable, and necessarily
deficient; accordingly, *that* is the state of things, wherein arrangements, for stocking the establishment with such appropriate experience, are most needful. But, at that same period, men, in any tolerable
degree possessed of appropriate aptitude will be most rare: and, at
the same time, the need of appropriate aptitude for these same situations the most pressing. In this state of things, if on the part of the
set of men first located, a degree of appropriate aptitude should
chance to be possessed, sufficient for carrying on in any way the
business of government,—the higher the degree of that aptitude, the
greater may be the risk incurred, by the substituting, to the men by
whom such appropriate experience has been had, other men *by*
whom, and *of* whom, no appropriate experience at all has been had.

## Instructional

ART. 43. Exception made of the case of the new Republican States,
sprung peaceably, as if in the way of childbirth, out of already established parent states, under the Anglo-American Confederacy,[1]—new
Republics will not have been seen formed, otherwise than by the
complete subversion or dismemberment of Monarchical, Aristocratical, or Monarchico-Aristocratical Governments. But, it is only in
consequence of an excessive degree of palpable misgovernment, that
of England over its emancipated Colonies excepted, that any such
revolution has ever yet taken place:[2] and, of such bad government,

[1] By the time Bentham was writing eleven new states had been added to the
original thirteen colonies; but perhaps only the three earliest additions—Vermont, Tennessee, and Kentucky—correspond at all closely to the pattern he
indicates. Otherwise the new states were established largely in new territory
acquired by cession by Britain and Spain or by the Louisiana Purchase of 1803,
and as a result of the rapid westward expansion of the area of settlement.

[2] Bentham is presumably here contrasting the then recent break between
Spain and Portugal on the one hand and their colonies in Latin America, with

one never-failing effect has been—the rendering the people, in a degree proportioned to the badness of it, unapt for the business of government. When the power has come into their hands, appropriate aptitude, intellectual and active, sufficient for the throwing off the yoke of the old bad government, and for the formation of a new government, has indeed had place among them, by the supposition. But, in conjunction with this necessary existing *minimum* of *intellectual* and *active* aptitude, slight indeed is the degree of appropriate *moral* aptitude which, as above, cannot but have had existence. As to *that* which consists in the being desirous of giving to the people at large the benefit of such degree of appropriate intellectual and active aptitude as the individual in question possesses, instead of giving that benefit exclusively to himself and his own particular connexions,—the total absence of it may not be inconsistent with a degree of intellectual and active aptitude, sufficient for the institution, and even for the continuance, of a government in the hands of the set of functionaries first located.

## *Instructional*

ART. 44. Of this state of things, exemplifications are but too abundant; and too notorious to need specifying.

## *Instructional*

ART. 45. Of this same state of things, one consequence is, that, in regard to the points here in question, scarcely can any arrangement be proposed, which does not lie open to objections,—and such objections as,—if considered by themselves, and without regard to the objections to which every arrangement differing from it stands exposed,—might not unreasonably be regarded as decisive.

## *Instructional. Ratiocinative*

ART. 46. Under these circumstances, of the two opposite risks, one or other of which cannot but be incurred, *that* incurred by *undiscontinued relocability* presents itself as the greatest; *that* by *temporarily discontinued locability*, as the least. Under undiscontinued locability, relocation of by far the greater number has been seen to be highly probable. Thus would it be, at the very next Election after that by which they were seated for the first time: and, whatsoever were the degree of their firmness in their several seats on the first re-election, at the time of every fresh election it will have received increase. But, in every situation, with length of possession, the appetite for power,

the case of Britain and her North American colonies, where, he suggests, there had not been 'an excessive degree of palpable misgovernment'.

far from experiencing diminution, experiences increase; and, in the situation here in question, while the appetite is thus receiving increase, so is the facility of gratifying it: to wit, from the strength, so necessarily given by habitual intercourse, to the connexion of those Members of the Supreme Legislative Assembly, with the unavoidably so constituted arch corruptors—the givers of good gifts—the respective heads of the *Administrative* and the *Judiciary* Departments, more especially of the *Administrative.* The consequence, if not absolutely certain, at any rate but too highly probable, is—a gradual but regular progression from a Representative Democracy to a Monarchico-Aristocratical form of Government, working by fear and corruption, and thence to a despotic Monarchy, with its standing army, working by fear alone, without need of corruption: every thing going on from comparatively good to bad, and from bad to worse, till the maximum of what is bad is reached, and, bating the chance of a violent revolution, perpetuated.

### Instructional

ART. 47. Such, for example, was the course, in which, at the time of the English Civil Wars, the Parliament, in conclusion called the *Rump Parliament*, had, at the time of its forced dissolution, been running, in consequence of the perpetual non-dislocability, which,—with intentions probably at the outset as patriotic at least as any which in any such situation were ever entertained,—the original members had succeeded in obtaining for themselves.[1]

### Instructional

ART. 48. On the other hand, under the *temporarily discontinued relocability system*, if with a Legislature composed, each year, of an entire new set of Members for three or even two years, the Government can but maintain itself in existence,—appropriate experience, on the part of Deputies and Electors, will go on increasing: *corruption*, to an extent capable of producing evil in a tangible shape, will, by means of the *securities* here provided against it, be excluded; and what change there is will be from good to better and better. For, by this change in the composition of the Supreme Legislature, no change

---

[1] The Rump was the remnant of fifty-three members left after 'Pride's Purge' in December 1648, when the Presbyterian majority of the House of Commons in the Long Parliament of 1640-60 was expelled to ensure support for the policy of bringing Charles I to trial. The 'forced dissolution' to which Bentham refers took place in April 1653. The Rump was summoned again in 1659, after Cromwell's death and his son Richard's withdrawal as Lord Protector; and the Presbyterian members were subsequently readmitted.

as to the individual at the head of the *Executive* will be necessitated or so much as probabilized; and in him will be the powers of *location* and *dislocation*, as to all the other official situations, in which the business of Government is carried on.

## Instructional

ART. 49. As to the just mentioned *securities*——those which apply to the situation of the head of the Administrative Department——the *Prime Minister*,——in this way will be seen to operate——not only those which are placed in the Chapter denominated from that high functionary, but those also which are placed in the Chapter headed MINISTERS COLLECTIVELY; namely, in §15, *Remuneration,* §16, *Locable who,* §17, *Located how,* §[25], *Securities,* &c. For although, in a more direct and manifest way, they will be seen bearing upon the situations of those his several locatees, immediate subordinates, and dislocables,——yet, by the *limits* they apply to his choice when filling those several situations, and the *checks* they apply to the powers exercised by these his instruments, those securities, the application of which may, to a first glance, appear confined to *those* situations, may be seen moreover to apply, all of them, in effect, to *his.* But, neither do these, nor any others which could be added, bear upon the situation of Deputy, commissioned by the Electors to act in their behalf in that Supreme Legislative situation, which, as per Ch. iv. AUTHORITIES, is [part of] the Supreme *Operative.*[1] All *locators* subordinate to the Members of the Legislature,——and at the head of them the head of the Administrative Department,——are responsible, *legally* as well as *morally,* as for all other exercises of their authority, so for every *choice* it falls in their way to make. Upon the situation of the *Deputies of the people*, no *legal* responsibility can attach, other than that which is constituted by the extraordinary and difficultly applicable, though indispensable, remedy, applied, should it ever be applied, by *dislocation* exercised at their charge by their respective *Electors:* upon the situation of the Electors *themselves*, neither can any *legal*, nor so much as any *moral* responsibility attach, consistently with the altogether indispensable freedom of their choice.

## Instructional

ART. 50. Meantime, in every situation, *moral* aptitude will depend upon the influence exercised by the Public Opinion Tribunal, as will the efficiency of that influence upon the degree of liberty possessed

[1] Bentham here mistakenly equates the Legislative authority with the Supreme Operative, which he defines earlier as comprising not only the Legislative but also the Administrative and Judiciary authorities. See Ch. IV, Art. 6, p. 27.

by the press; and, under the best possible form of government, the sufficiency of that liberty will be in a lamentable degree dependent upon the particular structure of the minds of those in whose hands the reins of Government happen, at the outset, to be placed. The *Anglo-American States*, now so happily confirmed in the possession of a form of Government, the only as yet fully settled one, which, in an enlightened age, deserves the name of a Government—were for years within an ace of losing it. From 1798 to 1802, a law was in force, having for its object the saving the rulers, wherever they were, from the mortification of seeing any disapprobation of their conduct, expressed in terms, other than such as they themselves would approve of; and, by those who afterwards had the magnanimity to expose themselves to it, a trial, the severest, perhaps, that a man in power is capable of undergoing, was submitted to.[1]

## *Instructional*

ART. 51. In England, by a mixture of magnanimity and weakness— in what proportion cannot as yet be known—the example, to a degree not less astonishing than laudable, has been for some time copied.[2] In this, as in all cases in which tyranny has been relaxed, the danger is—lest, by gratitude, the people should be betrayed into a greater degree of confidence, than, even under the best possible form of Government, can find a sufficient warrant.

[1] By the Sedition Act of 1798, passed by a Congress in which the Federalist party had a majority, publishing or printing 'false, scandalous, or malicious writings' intended to bring the government, the Congress, or the President into contempt or disrepute, or to excite popular hostility to them, or to incite resistance to the laws of the United States, or to encourage hostile designs against the United States, was declared punishable as a misdemeanour. A Congressman belonging to the Jeffersonian Republican party was fined and imprisoned under the Act, and several well-known journalists were also prosecuted. With the electoral victory of the Republicans in 1800, the life of this and other associated acts passed in 1798 was cut short. Bentham is mistaken in the second date he gives, for, despite a Federalist attempt in January to extend it, the Sedition Act ceased to be operative on 3 March 1801.

[2] Bentham seems to have in mind the change in government attitudes which is reflected in the number of state prosecutions for seditious, blasphemous, and defamatory libel during the fifteen years between the end of the Napoleonic wars and the publication of the 1830 *Code* volume. These reached a peak of approximately 63 cases in 1819, and the total was in double figures in every year but two from 1817 to 1824 inclusive. Between 1825 and 1830, on the other hand, only seven such cases appear to have occurred. See W. H. Wickwar, *The Struggle for the Freedom of the Press 1819–1832*, London, 1928, p. 315.

*Ratiocinative*

ART. 52. Objections to the temporary non-relocability system, with answers.

| I. *Objections* | II. *Answers* |
|---|---|
| 1. By the non-relocability system, temporary as it is, freedom of choice is, for the time, taken away. | 1. Of no use is freedom of choice, otherwise than as a security for appropriate aptitude on the part of the object of the choice. But, until the proposed term of non-relocability is expired, freedom of choice is not, (it has been shown,) conducive in any degree to the location of appropriate aptitude: it is, on the contrary, in a high degree, conducive to the location of inaptitude; of inaptitude, as to every branch of appropriate aptitude. When the non-relocability ceases to operate as a bar to aptitude, it is here removed. |
| 2. To every irreproachable Member, dislocation from his situation——dislocation, and for so long a term, and without so much as any imputation of misbehaviour, will be productive of suffering, and *that* unmerited. | 2. Productive of suffering? Yes, if unexpected, and thence he unprepared for it: to wit, pain of disappointment. But, every one being completely prepared for it, no such suffering can have place. As his location cannot be effected without his own consent,——if upon the whole the enjoyment were not expected by him to be preponderant over all suffering, he could not be in the situation in which, by the supposition, he is. |
| 3. Power, so small in respect of its duration, no person, endowed with adequate appropriate aptitude in all its several branches, would vouchsafe to accept. | 3. Yes: persons in abundance. Even supposing the situation of Member of the Legislature led to nothing else, instances of situations which, though much less desirable, are objects of extensive |

competition, may be seen in every state. But, over and above the facility for obtaining, at the hands of Ministers, desirable situations for his friends, an advantage, the complete prevention of which, how desirable soever, is impossible, is—that the seat in the Legislature is a stepping-stone into divers other seats: to wit, 1, in the Continuation Committee, 2, in the next Sublegislature, 3, at the expiry of the non-relocability term, a seat in the Legislature, and thence again into a Continuation Committee.

## Instructional. Ratiocinative

ART. 53. Comparative view of the undiscontinued locability and the temporary non-relocability system. Upon the whole, as between the temporary non-relocability system, coupled with the Continuation Committee Institution on the one part, and the undiscontinued relocability system on the other, the points of comparison may be summed up as follows.

I. Temporary non-relocability and Continuation Committee System.

1. By the prospect of a situation in the Committee,—it secures, on the part of all apt Members, together with the desire of that situation, prospect of competition; thence exertion, and by exertion, maximization of appropriate aptitude in all its branches.

2. The term of non-relocability expired,—it secures, in a number proportioned to the length of the term, *tried men*, out of whom, on the election of Members of the Legislature, the Electors will have their choice: and at the same

II. Undiscontinued relocability System.

1. No such prospect, no such motive for exertion: for the being re-elected, the negative merit of not having given offence to individuals will, on the part of a great majority, suffice.

2. On no occasion, unless by accident, and *that* not likely to be frequent, does it admit of the non-relocation of the person once elected, howsoever unapt: nor accordingly does it lay open the choice.

time opens the door to men as yet untried, who, under the other system, would have regarded it as shut.

3. It keeps on foot a select body of appropriate political *watchmen* without-doors, engaged by interest in their quality of leading Members of the Public Opinion Tribunal, to keep watch on the conduct of their rivals and future competitors—the Members of the Legislature in the several years.

3. It provides no such security for appropriate aptitude, in any shape, on the part of the Members of the Legislature.

4. It secures for the Sublegislatures a supply of appropriate aptitude, such as they could not, by any other means, be provided with.

4. It affords no such supply.

5. It thereby affords to the Legislature a probable supply, more or less extensive, of functionaries, who, to the stock of national knowledge and judgment, acquired in the Legislature, have added a stock of local knowledge and judgment, acquired in Sublegislatures.

5. No such supply.[a]

[a] Conceptions, to a considerable extent opposite to those which gave birth to the here-proposed arrangements, may be seen in a published letter of the author's to the then existing Portuguese Cortes, Ann. 1821.[1] Supposing *those* conceptions, and not *these*, erroneous,—a principal cause of the error may be seen in the want of an idea sufficiently clear, associated at that time with the word *experience:* a deficiency which, it is hoped, will on the present occasion be found supplied. Another cause is—that the idea of the *Continuation Committee* had not, at that time, as yet presented itself; any more than *that* of extending, to the situation of Deputy to the Legislature, the principle of *self-supply*, which, having been originally suggested by the circumstances of the *Judicial department*, has been since extended to the Administrative, and now, last of all, that is to say, as late as the commencement of the year 1826, to the Legislative Department.

[1] This 'Letter to the Portuguese Nation, on antiquated Constitutions . . .' was published, with an 'Advertisement' dated 1 July 1821, as the third of Bentham's *Three Tracts relative to Spanish and Portuguese Affairs; with a continual eye to English ones*, London, 1821 (Bowring, viii. 463-86). See Bowring, viii. 482-6, where the question of 'non-reeligibility' is discussed at pp. 483-5, and where an editorial note (p. 485n) draws attention, as Bentham does here, to the subsequent change in his view of the matter.

*Ratiocinative*

ART. 54. *Question* [1]. Why, to the security provided, in §20, *Attendance and Remuneration*, for each day's attendance, by forfeiture of that day's pay, add the further securities in this present section provided?

*Answer. Reasons.* Against non-attendance on particular days, not only the mere loss of those days' pay, but even the utmost penal security applicable in a pecuniary shape, would necessarily be insufficient: inadequate would be not only the mere withdrawal of remuneration, but any positive *fixt mulct* that could be applied. To men of a certain elevation in the scale of opulence, a pecuniary *punishment* that might generally even appear excessive, would even operate as a *licence:* to some even as an object of mockery. In this case, therefore, as in every other for securing compliance, no instrument other than *punishment*, in such amount as to be sure of operating in that character, and in such sort as to outweigh the utmost profit by the offence, could have been sufficient. Applied to the *Principal* alone, or the *Substitute* alone, even this sort of security could not be sufficient: by allegations, the falsity of which could not be sufficiently made manifest, either would be able to shift off the blame from himself, and fasten it either upon the other, or upon *accident*.

*Ratiocinative*

ART. 55. *Question* 2. Intending to provide additional securities so much more efficient, and of themselves so sufficient, why commence with a security, the effect of which is thus precarious?

*Answer. Reasons.* I. As far as it goes, pecuniary punishment, in this mildest of all forms, is the most secure of execution that the nature of the case admits of; and, to a considerable extent, efficiency would not be wanting to it.

II. In the case of the several subordinate situations, it appeared indispensable: and to have withholden the application of it to this, would have been contributing to the propagation of mischievous delusion, by attributing to all men, to whom it shall have happened to be located in this situation, a needless and delusive character of peculiar dignity, independent of good desert.

## SECTION 26

### WRONGFUL EXCLUSION OBVIATED

*Instructional*

ART. 1. The case of partial exclusion by force or fraud, or extra-ordinary accident excepted,—against deficiency in respect of *plenitude of attendance*, and thence risk of *fluctuation*, in legislative arrangements, provision, such as appeared sufficient, has been made, in and by former sections: viz. §18, *Attendance*—§19, *Remuneration*—§20, *Attendance and Remuneration*—§23, *Self-suppletive function*—§24, *Continuation Committee*—§25, *Relocable who* —remains, as a case calling for provision, *that* of a temporary deficiency, produced by one or other of the three just mentioned causes.

*Enactive*

ART. 2. On each occasion, the authority belongs to the majority, of the Members then present, at the appropriate place of meeting.

*Enactive*

ART. 3. If, by force, artifice or accident, any Member or Members, who would otherwise have been present, have been prevented from being so, the proceeding is not, by any such impediment, rendered null and void. But, supposing the fact of such impediment established, and the case such, that the number so excluded would, had it been present, have composed, with the addition of that of the others, a majority on the other side,—a declaration to that effect will naturally be passed; and things will be placed, as near as may be, on the same footing, as if the Members, so excluded, had been present.

*Enactive*

ART. 4. If the exclusion has had force or artifice for its cause, all persons, Members and others, intentionally concerned in the production of it, will, at the discretion of the majority, be compensationally, as well as punitionally and dislocationally responsible. As to this, see §28, *Legislation Penal Judicatory.*

*Enactive*

ART. 5. If, in the bringing about any such fraudulent exclusion, any Member, or other functionary, dislocable by the *Constitutive* Authority, has been purposely concerned, here will be another occasion for the exercise of its incidental dislocative, as per Ch. v. CONSTITUTIVE, §2.

## SECTION 27

### LEGISLATION ENQUIRY JUDICATORY[1]

*Expositive*

ART. 1. *By a Legislation Enquiry Judicatory*, understand a Judicatory, by which, on any particular occasion, by the hands or the authority of the Legislature, for the purpose of constituting a ground for its ulterior proceedings, and in particular for the enactment of a new law, *evidence* is elicited. To no other purpose does this Judicatory act. By this circumstance it stands distinguished from a *Judicatory* ordinarily so called: and by this circumstance alone are the powers and mode of proceeding distinguished from those, by which, in an ordinary Judicatory, a ground is made for definitive judication: as to these, see Art[s]. 16, 18, 19, 29, 30.[2]

*Enactive. Instructional*

ART. 2. By its own or by other hands, the Supreme Legislature will give exercise to this branch of its power, according to the nature of each individual case.

*Expositive*

ART. 3. By whichsoever hands exercised, the sort of function, exercised by exercise given to these powers, is termed the *evidence-elicitative function;* or, for shortness, the *elicitative function.*

*Expositive*

ART. 4. *Principal*, or say *effective*, call the *purpose*, to which the *imperative*, (including the *enactive*,) function of the Legislature is exercised; *preparatory* or *preparative*, *that* to which the *elicitative* is exercised.

*Instructional*

ART. 5. Correspondent to the *imperative* function in the exercise of *Legislative*, is that same function when performed in the exercise of *judicial* authority. In the one situation as in the other, on every occasion, it were, (as will be seen in Art. 17,)[3] desirable, were it practicable, that of both functions—the *principal* and the *preparatory*—

---

[1] See Ch. IX, § 10, Art. 9n, p. 285.

[2] Bentham's reason for choosing these particular articles for further reference is not clear, since there are others which deal more explicitly with the distinction between the Legislation Enquiry Judicatory and an ordinary judicatory.

[3] The point of Bentham's reference to Art. 17 is not clear.

93

the exercise were the work of the same hands. But, of this desirable purpose, the accomplishment will, in the one situation as in the other, to a more or less considerable extent, be found impracticable. What remains is—to maximize the accomplishment of it, in so far as may be without the introduction of preponderant evil from other sources.

### Instructional

ART. 6. Whether, without preponderant evil in other shapes, this preparatory function can be exercised by the hands of the Legislature itself, will depend—partly upon the quantity of its applicable *time*, partly upon the importance of the *occasion* and the *purpose*. On the occasion of each individual enquiry, it will depend—partly upon the presumable *importance* of the *result*, partly upon the quantity of *time* requisite for an adequate exercise of the *elicitative* function, partly upon the quantity of applicable time which, at the moment, the Legislature has at its disposal, and not called for by *other purposes* of superior importance. But rare in the extreme are, as may have been seen, the cases, in which, for this subordinate purpose, any of the Legislature's applicable time can be spared. See §[1], *Powers and Duties*.

### Instructional. Expositive

ART. 7. Evidence *ready elicited*, evidence requiring to be elicited, or in one word say *elicitable*. Under one or other of these denominations will come whatsoever evidence can, on any occasion, need to be under the eye of the Legislature. Under the appellation of *evidence ready elicited* comes the whole stock, of that which, for all occasions together, for judicial and legislational purposes together, has been elicited and preserved. In consideration of this distinction, it has been characterized by the denomination of *preappointed* evidence.[a]

### Expositive, Instructional

ART. 8. Of preappointed evidence, examples are as follow—1, The aggregate mass of *scriptitiously* expressed evidence, (as to which, see Art. 11,)[1] composed of *exemplars*, of the several documents emanating from, or recorded in, the Register Books, belonging to the several

---

[a] See the Author's Work on *Evidence*.[2]

---

[1] The reference required here may be to Arts. 10 and 12 below.

[2] *Rationale of Judicial Evidence, specially applied to English Practice*, ed. John Stuart Mill, 5 vols., London, 1827 (Bowring, vi. 189-585, vii. 1-600). For the discussion there of 'preappointed' evidence, see Bowring, vi. 508-85.

offices contained in the official establishment of the State. These documents constitute the subject matter of the *Universal Registration System*, as to which see Ch. viii. PRIME MINISTER, §10, *Universal Registration System.*[1]

### Expositive. Instructional

ART. 9. 2.—In particular, the statements made and recorded under the care of *Local Registrars*, as per Ch. xxvii. LOCAL REGISTRARS, [§5, *Death-recording.* §6, *Marriage-recording.* §7, *Birth-recording.* §8, *Maturity-recording.* §10, *Post-obit-administration-granting.* §11, *Property-transfer-recording.* §12, *Contract-recording.* §13, *Extra-judicial-evidence-recording.* §14, *Subjudiciary topographical function*].[2]

### Expositive

ART. 10. *Oral* or *epistolary*——in one or other of these two modes or forms, will be elicited, whatsoever *evidence*, on the occasion and for the sort of purpose in question, requires to be elicited in the form of *discourse:*——*oral* the mode, where the signs employed are of the *evanescent*, and unless in the extraordinary case of muteness or deafness, of the *audible* kind: *epistolary*, where expressed by signs of the *permanent* kind made by the operation called *writing*, or the operations substituted to it——say, in one word, by *scriptitious* signs.

### Expositive

ART. 11. Note, that as to *elicitation*, it may, on the part of the [*elicitor*], or say *elicitator*, be either *passive* or *active:* passive, in so far as the discourse brought into existence is delivered spontaneously, by him whose discourse it is: the elicitee being occupied with it in no other way than by *receiving* it: *active*, in so far as extracted from him by the elicitor, by means of questions, or say interrogatories, actual or virtual: in which last case the *elicitor* is [*interrogator*], or say *examiner;* the person, to whom a question is addressed, *interrogatee*, or say *examinee.*[a]

---

[a] In English practice, *the examinee* is, in some cases, preposterously styled *the examinant.*

---

[1] Bentham's heading for Ch. VIII, § 10 is in fact simply 'Registration System': see p. 159. But here and elsewhere he refers to his system generally, and to that section, as the 'Universal Registration System'. See Ch. IX, § 6, Art. 5, p. 215; and Ch. IX, § 26, Art. 43, p. 454.

[2] In the 1830 text the section numbers and some of the titles are confused here and do not correspond to Bentham's own plan in the Table of Contents. The mistakes are corrected in Bowring: for details see the 1830 Collation, p. 464.

For the elementary functions comprised in the *Evidence-elicitative function*, see title *Evidence* in the *Procedure Code*.[1]

### Expositive. Instructional

ART. 12. Considered in respect of its *source*, the evidence to be elicited may be distinguished into *personal* and *real: personal*, in so far as it consists of a portion of discourse, uttered, as above, by some *person: real*, in so far as it is afforded by the condition or appearance of some *thing* or assemblage of *things*, or by a *person* otherwise than by means of human action or *discourse*, as in the case of a wound or bruise sustained. Evidence, in the *scriptitious* form, is, in respect of the *things signified, personal;* in respect of the *signs, real.* So far as the evidence is, as above, *personal,*—he, whose discourse it is, may be termed a *testifier*, or say *testificant:* so far as it is *real*, the thing or *things* which are the *sources* of it, whether they belong to the class of *moveable* or to that of *immoveable* objects, will commonly be in the *custody* of some *person.* Spoken of with reference to the source of evidence so possessed by him, this person will be an *Evidence-holder.* To a person in either of those characters, or in both, may an authoritative mandate, issued for the obtainment of evidence—say an *evidence-requiring mandate*—be to be addressed.

### Instructions. Expositive

ART. 13. In so far as it is by hands other than those of the whole Legislature, that the evidence sought by it is elicited, or endeavoured to be elicited,—the hands by which it is thus elicited or endeavoured to be elicited, may be said to be those of a *Committee*, say an *Evidence-elicitation Committee:* as to which, see Art[s]. 23 to 26.

### Instructional

ART. 14. 1. With what *powers;*—2, of what person or *persons* consisting;—3, at what time or *times;*—4, in what place or *places;* and [5,] under what *checks*, may the operations of this same Legislation Enquiry Judicatory be most aptly carried on?

Correspondent to the unlimitedness of the demand, must be the extent and variety of the provision, made under these several heads, for the satisfaction of it.

---

[1] Although general principles concerning evidence are discussed in Ch. XI, 'Evidence', of the *Principles of Judicial Procedure* (Bowring, ii. 3–188), as edited by Richard Doane, Bowring, ii. 57–62, the evidence-elicitative function is not specifically analysed. See, however, the discussion in the *Equity Dispatch Court Bill* (Bowring, iii. 319–431), Bowring, iii. 421–3. On the Procedure Code generally, see p. 38n.

### *Enactive. Instructional. Expositive*

ART. 15. *Powers.* For procuring and securing attendance, whether at the seat of Legislation or elsewhere, for the purpose of oral examination,—the Legislature will, of course, possess, and upon occasion exercise, all those which, by this Code and the Procedure Code[1] connected with it, are given to ordinary Judges: and to these it will add all such, if any, as, being necessary to no other purpose than that of Legislation, will not have been instituted for the purpose of Judicature: as, for instance, the giving, on this occasion and to this purpose, unlimited exercise, to the function of eliciting information through the hands of *Government Envoys* to foreign Governments, or Government *Agents*[2] of all classes, *resident* in the dominions of foreign Governments: so, of functionaries belonging to the *Army* and *Navy* Subdepartments, and serving at the time in distant local fields of service.

### *Instructional*

ART. 16. In relation to *power* considered as applied, for the purpose of Legislation, to the extraction of *evidence*, or say *appropriate information,*—note here a *disadvantage*, under which *Legislation* lies, as compared with *Judicature*. The sort of *negative* information which is capable of being afforded by *silence*, in return for interrogation actual or virtual, being, to a comparatively inconsiderable, if any, extent, capable of being made subservient to the purpose of Legislation; —hence it is, that the Legislator finds himself destitute of the faculty of obtaining appropriate and requisite information, in cases in which, to a large extent, and with no small advantage, it is obtainable by the *Judge*. For, as in domestic, so in legal procedure, as in a non-penal so in a penal case, highly instructive, as in domestic procedure no person can have failed to experience, is the information capable of being furnished by silence in the character of *self-condemning evidence*.

### *Instructional. Ratiocinative*

ART. 17. Though in no case for the *exclusion* of *deception*,—yet in all cases for the exclusion of *delay*, *vexation*, and *expense*, where *preponderant* over the evil of [definite ][3] misjudication or non-judication,

---

[1] See p. 38n.

[2] 1830 and Bowring, 'Government. *Agents*': the full stop is evidently a misprint.

[3] 1830 reads 'definitive', which Bowring changes to 'definite' to clarify the passage.

does the *Procedure Code*,[1] connected with this present Code, inter-
dict the extraction of evidence. To the extraction of evidence for a
*Legislative* purpose, the limit, thus applied to the extraction of it for
a judicial purpose, will not of necessity apply. For, by the choice
which the Legislator has of places, times, and hands,—delay to the
public service, and vexation and expense to individuals, may, on each
occasion, be minimized. On the other hand, to the evil producible by
*misjudication* or *non-judication*, there are limits;—and, by the
authority of the Legislature, those limits, are rendered narrow ones:
to the evil producible by *mislegislation* or *non-legislation*, none.

### Expositive. Instructional

ART. 18. Clearness, correctness, impartiality, all-comprehensiveness,
non-redundance—thence instructiveness and *non-deceptiveness*—
under one or other of these heads may be placed, it is supposed, whatsoever properties are desirable in the entire of a body of evidence elicited to form a ground for a proposed measure: *clearness*, that is to say,
exemptness, as well from *ambiguity* as from *obscurity*: *impartiality*,
that is to say, comprehensiveness, or say exemption from deficiency,
as well as from incorrectness, in so far as those imperfections would
respectively be productive of undue assistance to either side; all-
comprehensiveness, for the sake of sufficiency of information and
avoidance of deceptiousness, on the part of the effect: to wit, the effect
produced on men's judgments by the whole body of the evidence: non-
redundance, for the sake of *clearness*, and for saving of useless delay,
vexation and expense, on the part of all persons interested.

### Instructional. Ratiocinative

ART. 19. In the case of the Procedure Code connected with the
present Code, and for the purposes of judicature, the application
made of the two following securities against deception by falsehood,
is maximized. These are—

I. For the security of testimonial evidence scriptitiously expressed,
wheresoever delivered, and whether spontaneously or responsively,
—against falsehood, as well *temeracious* as *mendacious*, responsibility, *satisfactional* as well as *punitional*, in the same manner as if
the evidence had been delivered in the *Justice Chamber*, in the shape
of responsion in the *oral* mode to interrogation in that same mode.

### Enactive. Instructional

ART. 20. II. In explanation, confirmation, or invalidation of any
such scriptitiously delivered evidence,—the testifier, at all times, in

---

[1] See p. 38n.

case of need, subject to examination in the *oral* mode. See Procedure Code, title *Evidence.* [1]——See also in this present Code, Ch. xxi. IMME-DIATE JUDICIARY REGISTRARS, §5, *Minutation how.* From neither of these securities will the Legislature fail to derive such benefit as, in each case, the nature of the case affords.

### Ratiocinative

ART. 21. For, seldom can the sufficiency of the securities afforded against deception,——whether by evidence, or *for want* of evidence, ——be maximized, without the benefit of instant answers or silence in return to questions arising instantly out of preceding answers or silence, and the interpretation thereupon capable of being afforded ——by tone, countenance, gesture, and deportment.

### Enactive. Instructional

ART. 22. On each occasion, the Legislature will constitute or distri-bute the Enquiry, in such manner as the exigency or convenience of the occasion shall be deemed to require. It will conduct the whole by its own hand, or the whole by other hands; or part by its own, other parts in any number by so many different hands or sets of hands.

### Instructional. Ratiocinative

ART. 23. The hands which, to the purpose here in question, the Legislature acts by, may, when any other than its own, be spoken of as being the hands of a *Committee*. Such Committee is capable of being made to consist either of a single person, or of persons in any number: but to every even, it will prefer any odd, number: for, otherwise, by the want of a casting voice, the whole operation or any part of it, may at any time be stopped, and the Enquiry frustrated.

### Expositive. Instructional

ART. 24. By the appellation *Legislation-evidence Elicitor*, or, for shortness, *Legislation Elicitor*, or say *Legislational Inquest man*, un-derstand a Committee man thus employed. In English practice, *The Grand Inquest of the Nation* is an appellation, by which the House of Commons has, on this occasion, been designated.[2] *Inquisitor* would

[1] Oral versus written evidence is not discussed in Ch. XI, 'Evidence', of the *Principles of Judicial Procedure* (Bowring, ii. 3–188), Bowring, ii. 57–62; but see the *Equity Dispatch Court Bill* (Bowring, iii. 319–431), Bowring, iii. 421–3, and the extended discussion in the *Rationale of Judicial Evidence* (Bowring, vi. 189–585, vii. 1–600), Book III, Bowring, vi. 383–507. On the Procedure Code gener-ally, see p. 38n.

[2] The phrase——perhaps more commonly 'grand inquest of the realm'——had been current in application to the House of Commons since at least the latter

have been more commodious, but for the odious idea so indissolubly associated with it.

### Enactive. Expositive

ART. 25. A Legislational Elicitor, or say Inquest man, may be either a *Deputy*, or a person other than a Deputy: if a person other than a Deputy, either a person at large, or, according to a common phrase, say a person from *without doors*, or else a *Continuation Committee man;* he being, as such, though not a Deputy, yet, as per §24, *Continuation Committee*, a Member of the Assembly.

### Instructional

ART. 26. An apt *Legislation-evidence Elicitor* may be any Judge Ordinary, Immediate or Appellative; and in both cases the Judge *Principal* or a Judge *Depute*, as to whom, see Ch. xiv. [JUDGE] IMMEDIATE [DEPUTES] PERMANENT: Ch. [xv.][JUDGE]IMMEDIATE [DEPUTES] OCCASIONAL.

### Enactive. Instructional. Ratiocinative

ART. 27. If the [Elicitor][1] be a Deputy,—the *elicitation process* will not be carrying on, at any time of the day, at which the Legislature is sitting on Legislation business. Incompatible with the indispensable plenitude of attendence, as per §[§]18, 20, and [23], would such exterior occupation be: during the whole of the time so occupied, the Deputy's Constituents in particular, and the State in general, would be deprived of the benefit of his service, on that part of the business, which is of intrinsic and superior importance. Thus, whether it were without or with his consent, that the occupation were allotted to him. Moreover, if without his consent, the power of location so applied might, in that case, be employed as an instrument of virtual expulsion for any length of time, and thereby as an engine of oppression and tyrannical dominion. And so in the case of a *Continuation Committee man.*

### Instructional. Ratiocinative

ART. 28. For obviating delay to the detriment of the public interest, and vexation and expense to individuals, by journeys to and fro, and

---

part of the seventeenth century (see *OED*, s.v. 'inquest'). One context in which Bentham would certainly have met it was Blackstone's *Commentaries on the Laws of England*, where it occurs in the account of the process of impeachment. See William Blackstone, *Commentaries on the Laws of England*, 4 vols., Oxford, 1765-9, iv. 256.

[1] 1830 and Bowring, 'Elector'; but the context evidently requires 'Elicitor'.

demurrage for the purpose of oral examination,—the Legislature will have at its option the carrying on the enquiry into *different facts* or classes of facts by any number of *Elicitation Committees*, at any number of *places* at the same time.

### Instructional

ART. 29. On this occasion, for the maximization of *publicity*, it will feel itself at liberty, in the choice of an *edifice* for this purpose, to exercise powers such as might not belong to a Judge; as for example, taking any public or even, in the case of necessity, any private edifice.

### Instructional

ART. 30. Only in so far as *confrontation* is necessary—necessary, to wit, to the discovery of relevant and relatively material truth, will persons more than one be convened from mutually remote places, to the seat of Legislature or elsewhither, to be orally examined at the same time.

### Expositive

ART. 31. *Purposes*, for which *confrontation* may be requisite, are *explanation, contradiction, counter-evidence*. By *counter-evidence* understand such evidence of an opposite tendency as may be delivered without contradiction opposed to anterior assertions.

### Instructional

ART. 32. In a case, in which conflict has place between divers particular interests,—an arrangement, desirable in so far as practicable, is—that the Elicitation Judicatory should consist either of a single person, approved by all parties interested,—or of divers persons, in number the same as that of the conflicting interests, and approved respectively by those several interests; with the addition of a Chairman, approved alike by all interests.

### Instructional. Ratiocinative

ART. 33. In the case of such conflict, it will commonly be found conducive to justice to allow to each interest it's professional Advocate: care being taken to prevent such needless addition as might otherwise be made, by causing one and the same interest to be split in appearance into divers interests.

### Instructional. Ratiocinative

ART. 34. So, in case of a conflict between the public and this or that particular interest: care being taken that such allowance be not employed as an instrument of needless delay.

*Enactive. Instructional. Ratiocinative*

ART. 35. Exceptions excepted, as per §21, *Sittings public and secret*, as in an ordinary so in a Legislative Enquiry, publicity will be maximized.

*Instructional. Ratiocinative*

ART. 36. The situation of *Judge* being *that* in which men will be in use to make due and appropriate distinction between ordinary cases, and the few extraordinary ones, in which the purposes of justice are best served by secrecy, so it be but temporary,—the Legislature will, on this consideration, incline to employ, as *Legislational Elicitor*, if acting singly, a Judge in preference to a person at large.

*Instructional. Ratiocinative*

ART. 37. Cases, however, may occur, in which, where the obligation of secrecy is deemed necessary to be imposed, reason may be found for employing, for this purpose, a *many-seated* Judicatory, say a Judicatory of *three*, in preference to a *single-seated* Judicatory, filled by a Judge. For, against the temptation to apply to purposes of depredation or oppression, the power afforded by secrecy,—the greater number will afford a security not afforded by the lesser: each member, of the secret tribunal, thus formed, being capable of giving eventual information against every other: and, any suspicion which might otherwise be entertained by the Public Opinion Tribunal, of sinister design, on the part of a majority in the Legislature,—may thus, by means of the greater number, be more effectually obviated.

*Instructional*

ART. 38. To the conduct of the Legislature and the instruments employed by it in this business, as above,—will be seen applying the same *checks* as those which apply to it on the occasion of the exercise given by it to its peculiar Legislative function, as per §31, *Securities for appropriate aptitude*. To the possessors of the *Constitutive* Authority, in their character of Members of the *Public Opinion Tribunal*, it will belong—to keep an ever watchful eye on the conduct of these their servants, in such sort as to give maximization to the efficiency of those several securities.

*Instructional. Expositive*

ART. 39. *Legislation Enquiry Report*, or for shortness say *Legislation Report. Methodization, condensation, application*—by these terms may denomination be given to functions, by the exercise of which, after completion given to the exercise of the *Elicitation* function, an instrument of the sort thus denominated is framed: *methodization*, that is to say, placing one after another, in the order best adapted to *correctness*, *completeness*, and *clearness* of conception, the facts respectively *sought* in the character of *conclusions* from the aggregate body of the evidentiary matter elicited: and, in relation to each such conclusion, the propositions expressive of the evidentiary facts, or assemblages of evidentiary facts, regarded as constituting respectively a *ground* for these several conclusions: *condensation*, that is to say, collecting, and expressing by one general proposition, the propositions respectively expressive of a group of relatively particular facts: *application*, that is to say, pointing out in what manner the above-mentioned propositions, general and particular, contribute to the affording of the information sought by the whole enquiry.

A *Report* is the appellation by which, in *English* practice, a written instrument, occupied in the exercise of these functions, is denominated. In the present instance, a Report, thus occupied, may be termed, as above, a *Legislation Enquiry Report*, or, for shortness, a *Legislation Report*.

### Instructional

ART. 40. The need of *consistency* and *symmetry* considered,—seldom can such a Report be aptly penned, unless in the original concoction of it, it has been the work of no more than a *single* hand. Such, accordingly, is commonly the English practice. But, on any occasion, when once the instrument has been framed by some single hand, others in any number may be occupied with advantage in the making or proposing of amendments. And, on the supposition of a case, in which, between two or more portions, of the subject matter of an enquiry made for a given single purpose, no other connection has place,—for despatch or alleviation of labour, the drawing up of the Report may, of course, without prejudice to the design, be committed to that same number of different hands.

### Instructional. Expositive

ART. 41. Under this head, not inconsiderable is the light, derivable, by any other nation, from English practice.

[*Regularly*] *elicited*, and *occasionally*, or say *incidentally elicited*, or about to be elicited—to one or other of these heads may be referred whatsoever mass of evidence, applicable to Legislative purposes, is employable at any given point of time: *regularly* elicited, those masses which are furnished by the occurrences and state of things registered of course in the several offices: *occasionally elicited*, those which, for the purpose of some particular Legislative measure, have from time to time been respectively elicited, by the act of so many Elicitation Judicatories, on the several *occasions* constituted.

### Instructional. Exemplificational

ART. 42. In English practice, locators, on this occasion, have been each one of the three branches of the Sovereign authority—*King, Lords,* and *Commons:* such is the order in which the three authorities are, in general, mentioned. But, on the present occasion, it requires to be reversed. Authority the most *frequently* thus exercised, that of the House of Commons: next most frequently, that of the House of Lords: lastly, that of the Monarch.

### Instructional. Ratiocinative

ART. 43. First, as to the House of Commons: and, in this case, first as to the *quality* of the particular object endeavoured at: next as to the *mode* in which the endeavour is carried on.

As to the *quality* of the object in view, it may reasonably be regarded, for the most part, as being beneficial. For, the whole compages of Government having been and being in so large a proportion still composed of the rubbish of the dark ages, and thence so palpably ill adapted to its professed end—the maximization of public happiness,—need of reform and improvement has always been, and continues to be, visible throughout the whole texture of it. But, seldom, if ever, otherwise than with the help of an enquiry of this sort, can any adequate ground for any considerable reform or improvement be, on any occasion, made.

### Instructional. Exemplificational

ART. 44. Next, as to the *mode* of carrying on the enquiry. This is still more uniformly well-adapted to the purpose, whatever it be, than the purpose itself is beneficial. Properties desirable in a mass of evidence, for whichever purpose, judicial or legislative, elicited—*appositeness, clearness, correctness, impartiality, all-comprehensiveness, non-redundance*—thence, *instructiveness* and *non-deceptiveness:* these are the *properties* with which the rules here laid down aim at investing all such masses of evidence, as shall have been elicited in conformity to them:—these same are the rules, which, with such exceptions as will be mentioned, appear to have been conformed to as far as powers sufficed, in and by the mode in use in the House of Commons.

*Instructional*

ART. 45. In the way of contrast, the usefulness of these rules may be seen receiving additional illustration and confirmation, from a comparison with rules, devised and employed in this same process, by the Judicial Establishment: of these rules, an exposition in detail may be seen in a Work on *Evidence*, by the Author of this Code.[1]

*Instructional*

ART. 46. Of this contrast, the efficient cause will not be found exposed to doubt: it will be seen in the difference between the interests which have been in operation in the two different situations. On the sort of occasion in question, the interest of the House of Commons, including that of its Elicitation Committees, has, generally speaking, been in alliance with that of the great majority of the people: and, on this same occasion, by no other means could they have given support to that common interest, so effectually, as by pursuing rules, conducive to appropriate instruction, as above: while, by no set of rules, subservient to deception and misinstruction, could they have given equal support to that same rightly directed and directing interest.

*Instructional. Exemplificational*

ART. 47. Diametrically opposite to that same exclusively rightly directed and rightly directing interest has, at all times, been the particular and thence sinister interest of those ruling Members of the Judiciary Establishment, by whom,—on pretence of *declaring* it, as if already made by *others*,—the *rule of action* has, over so vast a portion of the field of legislation, and in particular over the department of *evidence*, been *made:* made, that is to say, in that undelineable crooked and ever-shaking form, in which alone it could ever have been made by hands so situated. Creatures of the Monarch— and, till comparatively of late years, arbitrarily dislocable creatures —instruments of the *Monarch*, and, by the act of their location, constituted members of the *aristocracy*—invested with powers, to which there have never been any other legal limits than those which have been applied by the power of those their confederates,—they have at all times found themselves in a condition to give effect to their own particular and sinister interest: and this, not only to an unbounded extent at the expense of the universal interest, but, to a considerable extent, even at the expense of the interests of those their partners. Deriving remuneration from taxes imposed and levied

[1] See p. 94, n. 2.

105

by themselves to their own use upon suitors,—they have thereby given to themselves an irresistible interest in the maximizing the *number* of those useless proceedings, on which these taxes have been assessed: and, at the same time in maximizing *uncertainty*, by maximizing the encouragement given to delinquent suitors on both sides, to persevere in the track of injustice and maleficence: at the same time, giving to all who can come up to their price, the faculty of gaining their ends, to an extent more or less considerable, at the expense of their adversaries, by means of the pecuniary burthen thus imposed: thus, uniting *sale* to *denial* of justice, and effectuation of injustice.

### Instructional. Exemplificational

ART. 48. For the maintenance of the thus profitable system of uncertainty, they accordingly laid down those *[exclusionary] rules*, by the enforcement or relaxation of which they could *admit* or *reject* evidence, and thus give success to the one or the other side at pleasure: while, by their diversified modes of *ill-adapted elicitation*, they maximized the *expense*, and with it their own *profit* out of the expense; and, by holding out *success* to *mendacity*, maximized the quantity of it, and thereby the number of *evil deeds* and *evil-doers*. Thus far, by their oppositeness, the system of rules pursued by these functionaries, serve[s] in a direct way for throwing light upon the system exemplified and recommended, as above.[1] As to the all-pervading practice of *mendacity*, and in particular in a *written* state, in their *own persons* in their several situations,—and that of forcibly injecting the poison into the mouths or pens of all suitors, by refusing all assistance to all who should refuse to taint themselves with it —these practices, with so many more of like complexion that might be mentioned, belong to the present purpose no otherwise than by serving to characterize the *source*, from which the system opposite to the one here recommended, has derived itself.

### Instructional. Exemplificational

ART. 49. As to the House of Commons, and the observations whereby it has so frequently been necessary to bring to view the corruptedness, which, in such abundance, has place in that part of the Government,—between those general ones and the more particular ones which have just been seen, no real inconsistency will be found to

---

[1] 1830, 'system of rules . . . serve . . . systems exemplified . . .'; Bowring changes to 'systems of rules . . . serve . . . system exemplified . . .'. It is clear, however, from the end of the article that Bentham is contrasting one system with another.

have place. Of all forms of Government that ever were in existence, till *that* of the Anglo-American United States became visible,—*that* of England, with all its corruptions, was, beyond comparison, the least adverse to the only defensible end of Government: and in no other source than the power and practice of the House of Commons, could any part of whatever is good in the form of the Government, have originated. It is owing to what is good in the House of Commons —in particular, it is owing to the power of the Public Opinion Tribunal—that power, which has been hatched under the wings of the House of Commons—that *that*, as well as the other authorities in the state, may at length be thus spoken of without fear or danger: in particular, the Judicial Establishment, the practice of which, had it not been for the door left open to complaint in the House of Commons, would not, in respect of the support given by it to arbitrary power, have been surpassed by that of the Spanish Inquisition: for, not more hostile to the tutelary power of the Public Opinion Tribunal can the mind of a Spanish Inquisitor ever have been, than that which, even yet, continues from time to time to be manifested by the most influential of the English Judges.

### *Instructional. Exemplificational*

ART. 50. Thus far the *good:* comes now the *evil:* call it, in one word, *impotence*. It consists in a *deficiency*, under which the House of Commons labours, in respect of the appropriate *powers* necessary to the giving adequate exercise to this its *evidence-elicitation* function.

Neither for securing *verity* in responsion; nor for securing *responsion* itself; nor so much as for securing *attendance* for the purpose of responsion, does the House of Commons, in the exercise of its share in the Supreme Legislative authority, possess a power equal to that which is exercised by Judges, on the occasion of the most trivial contestation between individual and individual, in their professedly subordinate sphere. With relation to no one of these purposes, does *time* oppose any limit to the power of Judges: to that of the House of Commons, it opposes limits which, as long as the life of the House continues, grow every day narrower and narrower, till at last, before that life is extinct, this power is gone. Before seven years are at an end, this body suffers that predestinated, which may be termed its *natural*, death,—and before that time it commonly dies a violent one. As to *verity* in particular,—in so far as punishment for *mendacity* operates as a security for it, the Judges, (by means of a ceremony called an *oath*, and the word *perjury* employed in connection with it—a ceremony which they have contrived shall be performed where the performing of it,—withholden, where the withholding of it best suits their sinister interest)——subject a man to banishment, with forced labour, for as many as seven years, or even to still more severe inflictions.[1] The utmost suffering, to which, in any case, for any one of the above-mentioned *three* purposes, this of *security for verity* not excepted, an individual can be subjected is——*that* of simple imprisonment; and *that*, for a time, which, as above, depends——not on the demand for punishment, but on the age of the House of Commons: and may find itself limited to less than as many days, or hours, as that which the Judges have at command will last years. Upon the whole, a considerable time before the end of the seven years, this power amounts to nothing: for, by keeping out of the way, in the first place, of *summonition*, in the next place of *prehension*, a man may set it at defiance: and, from the weakness of this power, suffers, of course, every measure of reform or improvement, to the initiation of which, the *evidence-elicitation* process is a necessary preliminary.[2]

*Instructional*

ART. 51. So much as to the House of *Commons*. Now as to the House of *Lords*. As to every purpose, but that of giving support to its own particular and sinister interest, in addition to that of the Monarch, with which it stands associated,——this branch of the actually existing Supreme Authority of the State being so much worse than useless,——if, with reference to the purpose here in question, not to speak of other purposes, it were afflicted with the same debility as that which has just been seen in the case of the House of Commons,——the people, if not the better, would at any rate be little the worse. As to shortness of life, except that it stands assured of resurrection in the same persons, its case is the same as that of the House of Commons. Not so, however, as to the power of punishing for mendacity, under the name of *perjury*, and with the punishment attached to that name: for, that command over the Almighty which, as above,——by the magic words '*So help you God*,' and the kiss given to a book,——King, Lords, and Commons have concurred in giving to

[1] Transportation for seven years as a penalty for perjury was provided for by the statute of 1729, 2 Geo. II c. 25, which further made it a felony without benefit of clergy to escape or to return to the realm within the seven years.

[2] Bentham's meaning in this passage is somewhat obscure and he may not have represented the position accurately. By the Septennial Act of 1716 the life of a Parliament was indeed limited to seven years, and this seems to have been in Bentham's mind. But the power of the House of Commons to imprison offenders against its privileges was in fact limited to the duration of the parliamentary *session*. The House of Lords, on the other hand, could impose indefinite imprisonment in such cases. Bentham may have intended this contrast.

Judges, the House of Lords, while it sees the House of Commons destitute of it, exercises by its own hands without reserve: in a word, the House of Commons is *not* in the practice of administering an *oath:* the House of Lords *is.*[1]

### Instructional

ART. 52. On each occasion, whether an enquiry of the sort in question shall be entered upon by the body so highly superior in the scale of factitious dignity,—it belongs to *accident* to determine: and this accident consists sometimes of an expectation of amusement in the breast of the Member by whom the motion is made; sometimes in the recurrence of the notion, that, lest the inutility of such a body to every interest but its own and that of the Monarch should become too manifest, a show of activity should from time to time be kept up.

### Instructional

ART. 53. Lastly, as to the *Monarch*. When, by his authority, an *Evidence-elicitation Judicatory* is instituted, *Commission* not *Committee* is the word.

I. As to the *object* in view. Instituted by the House of Commons, seldom can the *Committee* have had any other than the *promotion*, —seldom the *Commission* any other than the *exclusion*, of reform or improvement.

### Instructional. Ratiocinative

ART. 54. II. As to *appropriate powers*. By the instruments of the Monarch, neither could comprehensiveness nor impartiality be secured to the body of evidence elicited by them, if such were really their desire. By law, neither for *responsion*, for *veracity*, nor so much as for *attendance*, do they possess any such power as that possessed by the Judges, or even as that possessed, as above, by the House of Commons. *Consequence*,—the only persons, at whose hands, for any one of these purposes, compliance is at their command, are their own dislocable subordinates, together with any such other person to whom it happens to stand subjected to their will by corruptive influence:—*Quality of the information*, such as may be expected from packed witnesses speaking to packed Judges.[2]

[1] The House of Lords had always had the power to swear witnesses, though its committees received the same power only in 1858. Neither the House of Commons nor any of its committees had power to administer an oath until 1871.

[2] Although Royal Commissions were by their warrants of appointment given powers to compel the attendance of persons and the production of papers, these powers were inoperative in practice because not enforceable at law. Essentially this was because the Act of 1641 abolishing the Court of Star Chamber, 16 Chas. I

### Instructional

ART.55. [III.] As to *composition*. According to circumstances, the
Commission is given to number *one*, or to a greater: number *one* is,
by reason of the comparative secrecy of the measure, and the un-
ostentatiousness of the expense, best suited to the purposes of *inspection visits* to *distant* dependencies. A *many-seated* sham Judicatory
of this kind is the resource,——when, on complaint made of some
more than ordinarily scandalous system of abuse,——Ministers are prevented by shame from refusing enquiry, and by fear from trusting to
the House of Commons. By fear:——for, the corruption which would
with certainty, suffice to engage the *House* in a *body*, to acquiesce
in this or any other desired imposture,——would not suffice to secure
the excluding from a *Committee* every Member who would not concur in such suppression of evidence as the purpose might require. In
the case of a *distant inspection visit*, forecast is exemplified: and the
object is——to forestall and avert all such sincere enquiries, as are yet
in no other than a future-contingent state: in the case of the *many-
seated* Elicitation Judicatory, acting at the *seat of Government*,——
the object is——to make a pretence for refusing some enquiry actually
called for in the House of Commons. When, for example, under the
eye of King, Lords, and Commons,——Judges, and other judicial functionaries of all classes, have been in the notorious habit of practising
extortion on false pretences,——thereupon, on pretence of paving the
way for reform, comes a *Commission*, under which the population of
the judgment seat, as well as that of the witness's box, is composed
of accomplices; with the *principal* for *Locator*. From a Commission
of this sort, a collateral benefit is naturally and commonly, if not
constantly, derived: what is called a *job* is effected: and, in place of
punishment, criminals receive remuneration for their crimes.[1]

c. 10, prohibited the Crown from establishing any jurisdiction of this kind by
use of the prerogative. See R. M. Jackson, 'Royal Commissions and Committees
of Inquiry', the *Listener*, lv (1956), 388; T. J. Cartwright, *Royal Commissions
and Departmental Committees in Britain*, London, 1975, p. 142.

[1] The commission Bentham criticises here was appointed in April 1824 to
enquire into the proceedings of the Court of Chancery. It was headed by Lord
Eldon, the Lord Chancellor, and the other members included the Master of the
Rolls, the Vice-Chancellor, the Solicitor-General, and a number of Masters in
Chancery and barristers. Evidence was taken from fifty-three witnesses between
June 1824 and December 1825, and the report of the Commission was ordered
to be printed on 9 March 1826. On this and other aspects of the discussion of
Chancery and related procedures in the period from 1810 onwards, see C. P.
Cooper, *A Brief Account of some of the most important Proceedings in Parlia-
ment relative to the Defects in the Administration of Justice in the Court of
Chancery*, London, 1828.

*Instructional*

ART. 56. One feature, familiar to, if not constant in, English practice, requires here to be laid open to view. It belongs to the *form* of the *Reports:* it consists in the suppression of the interrogatories, by which the responses have been elicited; and, still more frequently of the names of the several Interrogators. Of this suppression, so far as regards the *interrogatories*, a natural and not unfrequent consequence is—obscurity or misconceivedness; so far as regards the power-clad Interrogator,—consequence and final cause, subtraction of his conduct from that scrutiny of the Public Opinion Tribunal to which he has been subjecting the Interrogatee. The practice may be set down among the natural fruits of aristocratical oppression: presumptive evidence of intentional abuse of power, on the part of as many as give into it.

## SECTION 28

### LEGISLATION PENAL JUDICATORY

*Enactive. Instructional*

ART. 1. To any of the following chief functionaries should misconduct be imputed, for the punishment of which, dislocation, with extra publicity, shall not be deemed sufficient,—it rests with the Legislature to form an occasional Special Judicatory for the trial of them.

Functionaries thus triable are—

I. Any Member of the then present Legislature.

II. Any Member of any anterior Legislature.

III. The Prime Minister of the then present, or any preceding time.

IV. The Justice Minister of the then present, or any preceding time.

*Enactive*

ART. 2. Number of Members of this Judicatory, three or five.

*Enactive*

ART. 3. Judges, either all of them Members of the then present Legislature, or persons, who,—at the time when the decree for the prosecution is pronounced,—are not, any of them, Members—either of the Legislature, or of any part of the Official Establishment.

*Enactive*

ART. 4. Mode of location, secret suffrage.

### Enactive

ART. 5. The Legislature will at the same time appoint persons, one or more, to officiate as Pursuers.

### Instructional

ART. 6. I. In relation to this extraordinary judicial function,—the Legislature will, on each occasion, judge, whether its time will admit of its taking upon itself this extra charge.

### Enactive. Instructional. Ratiocinative

ART. 7. II. If *all* the Members do not, neither should *any:* for, it should not be in the power, either of an individual or of the whole body, in this or any other way, to produce, during the whole or any part, of the time occupied in the Enquiry, a virtual vacancy in the particular seats in question, as to the exercise of the legislational function; thus depriving constituents of the service of their agents, as to the principal and peculiar part of their duty.

### Ratiocinative

ART. 8. III. Though,—more especially in the case of a Member,— nothing that can be done, can exclude altogether so inevitable an imputation as that of partiality—still, the transference of this temporary function to other hands, will, in no small degree, lessen the ground of the imputation, if men of generally acknowledged aptitude, moral as well as intellectual, are the persons located. In the case where the Prime Minister, or the Minister of Justice—located, both of them, by the Legislature—being parties accused, are guilty,—much less difficulty will a man who has not, than a man who has, contributed to their location, find, in contributing to their punishment.

### Enactive

ART. 9. Neither in non-penal nor in penal cases, does the Legislature act, on any occasion, as an Appellate Judicatory: in that field of service, it trusts altogether to the appropriate subordinate authorities. Only in case of punishable criminality, as practised by them in the exercise of their functions, does it take cognizance of the course taken in and by that exercise.

### Enactive. Ratiocinative

ART. 10. But, for as much as of necessity,—in so far as the propriety of the conduct of any such judicial functionary, on the occasion of a non-penal suit comes in question,—that which should, on that occasion, have been done, cannot but come, though, as it were, in a preliminary or collateral way, under the cognizance of the Legislature,—any error which, on that same occasion, shall, in the eyes of the Legislature have manifested itself, will not be left unredressed.

### Ratiocinative

ART. 11. For, knowingly and wilfully to leave a wrong in any shape unredressed, would,—on the part of those, who, without preponderant evil, have full power to redress it,—be an open profession of injustice, tending to the destruction of public confidence.

### Enactive. Instructional. Ratiocinative

ART. 12. On every such occasion, the Legislature will, at the same time, be upon its guard,—lest, by this means, it should insensibly be led to constitute itself into an ordinarily officiating Appellate Judicatory: an office, as to the functions of which it is essentially incompetent; to wit, as well, in respect of the multitude of the Members of which it is composed, as in respect of the vacancy, which would thereby be created in the exercise of its appropriate and peculiar functions.

### Enactive. Instructional

ART. 13. Accordingly, if, on the face of the application, no criminality in any shape be imputed to the functionary whose conduct is the subject of complaint,—the Legislature will uniformly refuse to take cognizance of it. In a case, in which such imputation is made,— if no sufficient reason for imputing criminality is found, the Legislature may accordingly make declaration to that effect, forbearing to accompany such declaration of acquittal with any decree, imperative or opiniative, in relation to any such alledged wrong, as above.

### Enactive. Instructional

ART. 14. On every such occasion,—if, in the eyes of the Legislature, the accusation has been not only insufficiently grounded or altogether ungrounded, but accompanied with evil consciousness or temerity,—it will, if it see sufficient reason,—on the same evidence, and without the formality of a separate suit,—proceed,—as in the case where compensation is given in the name of *costs*,—to punish the wrongful accuser with such punishment as the case shall appear to demand.

### Instructional

ART. 15. Note, that, only in case of a *decision*,—or, where *decision* is due, *non-decision* by an *Appellate Judicatory*,—or by the *Justice*

*Minister*, in the extraordinary and narrow field of the judicial service allotted to him, as per Ch. xxv. §4, *Judicative function*,—can any such *non-penal*, under the guise of a *penal* suit, as above, be apprehended: for as much as, for redress, of wrong done by an Immediate Judicatory, the correspondent Appellate Judicatory is constituted, and its doors kept wide open,—while, as above, those of the Legislature are against all such applications, shut.

### Instructional

ART. 16. Note also that, for prevention of wrong otherwise about to be done, or redress of wrong done, by a Judge, without deficiency on his part in respect of appropriate *moral* aptitude,—facilities may be seen afforded, in and by Ch. xii. JUDICIARY COLLECTIVELY: §19, *Judges' contested interpretation reporting function*—§20, *Judges' eventually emendative function*, and §21, *Judges' sistitive, or say execution-staying function:* and moreover by the general facility for amendment, afforded by the *melioration-suggestive function* allotted by this Code throughout, to individuals as well as to judiciary and other functionaries.

## SECTION 29

### MEMBERS' MOTIONS

### Instructional. Expositive

ART. 1. In proposing an ordinance, a Member will do well to consider, whether in the law as it then stands, there be any Article, to the matter of which, such his ordinance would, if adopted, be repugnant, in such sort, that if that Article were thereafter to receive its execution, the so proposed ordinance would thereby in some way or other, be contravened. In case of non-repugnancy, his new proposed ordinance is independent and *non-emendative:* in the case of repugnancy, it is, to the extent of the repugnance, *emendative*.

### Instructional. Ratiocinative

ART. 2. If thus it be *emendative* in effect, he will do well to render it declaredly so: for, thus only can the *Pannomion*[a] be kept clear, of that needless and useless voluminousness, with obscurity, confusedness and incomprehensibility for its effects, by which, in the nature of the case, it cannot otherwise escape being more or less vitiated.

---

[a] (*Pannomion.*)[1] From the Greek:—the whole body of the laws.

[1] See the discussion of the *Pannomion* in the Introduction, pp. xxxv ff.

### Instructional. Expositive

ART. 3. *Declaredly emendative*, an ordinance may be, in either of two modes—the *directive* or the *reeditive*. In the *directive* mode, the Draughtsman will proceed in the manner of an author, in directing corrections to be made, in and by a list of *Emendanda* or *Corrigenda*. Taking for the subject of his reference the *Pannomion* as it stands— 'In such an Article,' (he will say) referring to Code, Chapter, Section and Article, 'omit so and so;' or, 'between such and such words, insert so and so;' or, 'to such and such, substitute such or such words;' or, taking the Article entire, 'omit such or such an Article;' or, 'between such and such an Article, insert such or such an Article or Articles;' or, 'to such or such an Article or Articles, substitute the following.'

### Instructional. Enactive

ART. 4. Follows a formulary for the introduction of an amendment. 'By the Legislature,' {Year, Month, and Day}. 'In' {referring, as above, Art. 3, to the portion of the *Pannomion*} 'the following amendments are this day made.' {Hereupon follows the direction as above.} Attestator, the *Legislation Minister*. Each amendment, if adopted, being the work of the Legislature,—the proposer will not, in penning his proposal, scruple thus to speak in the name of the Legislature.

### Instructional. Enactive

ART. 5. In the *reeditive* mode, the proposer proceeds, in the manner of an author, who is publishing a new edition of his work. Introductive formulary as follows:—'By the Legislature'—{Year, Month and Day, and place in the *Pannomion*, as above.} 'It is ordained as follows.' Thereupon, comes the new matter. If, in this ordinance, there be any thing which is in repugnance to any part of the *Pannomion*, as above,—to minimize doubt and needless quantity of matter, he will proceed in manner following. '*Repealed* on this occasion are'—then will follow the indication of the several Articles. On this occasion, no alteration will he direct to be made in any Article. Instead of giving any such direction, he will repeal the entire Article, and substitute a new one.

### Instructional. Enactive

ART. 6. In an *emendative* ordinance expressed in the *reeditive* mode, indications will be given as follows:—

    I. Indication made,—by appropriate types and other means,—of words, omitted, added, or substituted, as above: in such sort that, in the new edition, if possible, by a single glance, the eye may be able to distinguish the new matter from the old.

II. Indication made,—of the proposer, his seconder, his other supporters, and his opposers. Thus, to all persons concerned will it, in all times, be made known,—in what particulars, at what times, by what ordinances, at whose instance, and under whose opposition,—effect, good or bad, on the interest of the community, has been produced.[1]

### Enactive

ART. 7. To every Member, it belongs, of right, to make whatsoever motion he thinks fit, in whatsoever terms he thinks fit, in relation to any matter he thinks fit: on its being seconded by any other Member, —any such motion becomes a subject of discussion, and is eventually capable of being converted into an ordinance of the Legislature.

### Instructional

ART. 8. In case of need, should it happen to the Legislature to find its time wasted by ill-considered motions, it will, for remedy, instead of one such preliminary adopter, require two or more.

### Instructional. Ratiocinative

ART. 9. To obviate, however, the voluminousness and confusion, liable to ensue, from laws made, at different times, on the motion of different persons,—on principles in respect of *form* as well as *matter*, disparate or adverse,—a Member, antecedently to any motion tending to the enactment of a new ordinance, will do well to consider, to the province of which of the several *Ministers*, if any, the matter belongs: thereupon, to communicate on the subject with such Minister or Ministers,—and, in so far as they and he agree, to consult with the *Legislation Minister* as to the bearings of the proposed ordinance on those already in existence, and thence, as to the *form* in which, on its introduction, the proposed ordinance may most conveniently stand expressed: and, in particular, whether in the *independent* and *non-emendative* form, as per Art. 1, or in the *emendative:* and, if in the *emendative*, whether in the *directive*, or in the *reeditive*, as per Art[s]. 3, 4, 5, 6.

### Instructional

ART. 10. If, to any such Minister, such communication shall have been omitted to be made,—*reasons* for the omission will be expected to be given: so, in case of non-concurrence on the Minister's part,

---

[1] See Ch. IX, § 25, Art. 1n, p. 419n.

reasons for and against such non-concurrence. No such Minister is bound to concur in any such motion: but to him the mover is expected to communicate it; he, to receive it and to attend to it: and so throughout its progress, until it is either adopted or rejected.

## SECTION 30
### DISLOCABLE HOW
#### *Enactive*

ART. 1. From the situation of Member of the Legislative Assembly, causes of dislocatedness are these—
1. Resignation.
2. Acceptance, of any other office belonging to the Official Establishment of this State.
3. Acceptance, of any office belonging to the Official Establishment of any Foreign State.
4. Acceptance, of factitious honour or dignity, in any shape, at the hands of any Foreign Government.
5. Mental derangement.
6. Disturbance, of Legislative proceedings, as per §16, *Security for the Assembly against disturbance, &c.*
7. Criminal delinquency, pronounced by the sentence of a [Judicatory], located for this purpose by the Legislature, as per §28, *Legislation Penal Judicatory.*
8. Dislocation, by his constituents, in virtue of their *incidental dislocative*, as per Ch. v. CONSTITUTIVE, §2, *Powers.*

## SECTION 31
### SECURITIES FOR APPROPRIATE APTITUDE[1]
#### *Instructional*

ART. 1. The assemblage of securities, here proposed with reference to the highest department, the Legislature, forms the commencement of an all-pervading system of the like securities, covering the whole field of the Official establishment, and applying to all public functionaries in every department and subdepartment. The same endeavour will accordingly be seen successively applying itself to the situation of Prime Minister,—to the situations of the several Ministers,—to the several Sublegislatures, their Members, and Subordinates,—and with

---

[1] See Ch. IX, § 25, Art. 1n, p. 419n.

more especial solicitude to that of the several Members of the Judiciary establishment; and lastly to the bis-subdepartment occupied by the Local Headmen and Local Registrars, whose logical fields of service, in their respective smallest local fields of action, lie in subordination to the directing functionaries of the Administrative and Judiciary departments; and are composed accordingly of portions of the logical fields of service of both.

Security against abuse of power composes one branch of the system of securities here provided: one branch, but not the only one: for, security against abuse of power is but one branch, though the principal one, of security for appropriate *moral* aptitude: and to this are added security for appropriate *intellectual* and security for appropriate *active* aptitude.

### Instructional

ART. 2. For this purpose, and on these several occasions, confidence (it cannot be denied) may with truth be said to be minimized: *distrust* and *suspicion* maximized. Principle acted upon, say for shortness, the *confidence-minimization principle:* whence, as to practical deductions, the *controul-maximization principle.*

### Instructional

ART. 3. Corresponding *rules* are the following.—I. To no official situation, attach any more power than is necessary to enable the functionaries to exercise the functions of it with the most effectual subserviency to the dictates of the *greatest-happiness principle.*

### Instructional

ART. 4. II. To every such situation, apply such instrumentary arrangements as, by means of appropriate *selection, restraint* and *constraint* shall afford the efficient security for appropriate aptitude in all its branches.

### Instructional

ART. 5. III. The arrangements for *restraint* are those which promise to afford the most effectual security against abuse of power: to wit, of the several powers respectively instituted and conferred.

### Instructional

ART. 6. These principles and rules have for their bases certain *axioms*, or say *assumptions*. These are expressive of certain supposed matters of fact: the existence of certain propensities in all human minds.

*Instructional*

ART. 7. I. In all human minds, in howsoever widely different proportions,——*self-regard,* and *sympathy* for others or say *extra-regard,*
have place.

*Instructional*

ART. 8. II. But, in self-regard even sympathy has its root: and if, in
the general tenour of human conduct, self-regard were not prevalent
over sympathy,——even over sympathy for all others put together,——
no such species as the human could have existence.

*Instructional. Expositive*

ART. 9. Take any two persons, A and B, and suppose them the only
persons in existence:——call them, for example, *Adam* and *Eve. Adam*
has no regard for himself: the whole of his regard has for its object
*Eve. Eve* in like manner has no regard for herself: the whole of her
regard has for its object *Adam.* Follow this supposition up: introduce
the occurrences, which, sooner or later, are sure to happen, and you
will see that, at the end of an assignable length of time, greater or less
according to accident, but in no case so much as a twelvemonth,
both will unavoidably have perished.

*Instructional*

ART. 10. To give increase to the influence of sympathy at the expense of that of self-regard, and of sympathy for the greater number
at the expense of sympathy for the lesser number,——is the constant
and arduous task, as of every moralist, so of every legislator who
deserves to be so. But, in regard to sympathy, the less the proportion
of it is, the natural and actual existence of which he assumes as and
for the basis of his arrangements, the greater will be the success of
whatever endeavours he uses to give increase to it.

*Instructional*

ART. 11. A consequence is——that whatsoever evil it is possible for
man to do for the advancement of his own private and personal interest (or what comes to the same thing, what to him appears such)
at the expense of the public interest,——that evil, sooner or later, he
will do, unless by some means or other, intentional or otherwise,
prevented from doing it.

*Instructional*

ART. 12. To the above rule suppose there is this or that exception:
still, with a view to practice, there might as well be none: forasmuch

as by no criterion will it be possible, to distinguish the individuals in whose instance the exception has place, from those in whose instance the general rule has place: more especially when, as in the case of all Legislative arrangements of a general nature, the individuals in question are unassigned and unassignable.

### Instructional

ART. 13. Neither to the public service is it in the nature of the precautions in question to be hurtful; nor yet so much as to the reputation or the feelings of the individuals to whom they apply.

Not to the public service? Yes, indeed, if of the care thus taken to avoid giving to functionaries *more* power than, as above, is needful, the effect were—to withhold from them any part of that which is needful. But, in proportion to the attention with which the arrangements in question are looked into by him, and compared with others, will be every man's assurance,—that in no existing Code is the scope given to the power of ruling functionaries so ample as in the present proposed Code.

### Instructional

ART. 14. Not even to the reputation or the feelings of any individual functionary or non-functionary are these precautions hurtful. Yes, if [they] applied to him to the exclusion of others, or in a more particular manner than to others. But, no: for, without any exception, they apply to all persons alike.

### Instructional

ART. 15. To say—they ought not to apply to me, is as much as to say—*I am not of the human species:* or at the least with the Pharisee, *'I am not as other men are.'*[1]

### Instructional

ART. 16. As little can these precautions be said to be needless. For, wheresoever no obstacle—no bar to evil doing is opposed, and motives inciting to evil doing are at work, evil doing will, by the prevalence of self-regard over sympathy, be sure to be let in. Suppose the probability of evil doing ever so faint, still ought the obstacles in question to be opposed to it, considering that by their being opposed to it, evil may be excluded, while, as above shown, from their being so opposed, in no shape can evil, public or private, be introduced.

---

[1] Luke 18: 11.

*Instructional*

ART. 17. Accordingly, on this supposition, in respect of the treatment given by them to the *subject many*, proceed, on every occasion, the ruling *one* and the ruling or sub-ruling *few*. No evil, how atrociously and extensively mischievous soever, do they speak of or deal by as too mischievous to be likely to be exercised: no mischievous act,[1] in so far as the subject many are regarded as capable of being the actors, and these rulers themselves as liable to be sufferers by it, do they leave unnoticed, or by force of restraint and punishment, omit to use their endeavours for the prevention of it.

*Instructional*

ART. 18. In the estimates acted on by rulers, the degree of propensity to evil in the minds of the subject many is commonly carried rather beyond than short of the truth. In particular, such is the estimate acted upon by all Legislators: such is the estimate acted upon by all Judges, especially by all Judges, who, as in England, are suffered to act, and act accordingly, as Legislators: except always in so far as the persons acted upon belong to those classes which are linked with theirs by a community of particular and sinister interest.

*Instructional*

ART. 19. Widely different, not to say opposite, in relation to propensity to evil on their part, is the estimate by these confederates acted upon. Is it the *ruling one* that is in question? His estimate of himself, as expressed in his own language, is—*I am not as other men are: they are of the species composed of miserable sinners. I am of the species between God and man.* Thereupon, from the lips and pens of those to whom he is an object of hope or fear, comes the response in chorus—*O yes, sir, so you are!*

*Instructional*

ART. 20. Are they the *ruling few?* Of the like complexion here too, is the estimate acted upon,—and a certain theory, on which it is grounded. *Motives* (says this theory,) *are of two sorts, impure* and *pure*. With few or no exceptions, the motives which give determination to the conduct of all, whose situation in the conjunct scales of power and opulence is beneath a certain level, are *impure* or *pure*, as it may happen: in all situations *above* that same level, at all times

[1] 1830, 'in regard to no mischievous act': the first three words are evidently redundant, and are omitted in Bowring, as above.

supremely and invariably pure:[a] to suppose that, on any occasion, they do or can fail of being so, is an affront and a gross injury: an injury to which, either at the hands of justice, or at those of the party injured, condign punishment is due.

### Instructional

ART. 21. Not that in this theory about *purity* and *impurity*, there is any thing better than stark nonsense: not that any one who utters it, knows what it is he means by it. But, if the theory wants so much, the practical conclusions from it want not any thing of being sufficiently intelligible:—*Reserve all restraints for those others: none are needful, all are injurious, if applied to ourselves.*

### Instructional. Exemplificational

ART. 22. In point of fact—unquestionable fact—how stands relative behaviour in correspondence with the condition of the two situations? [In the position] supposed[1] as above? No: but exactly the reverse. The more dependent a man is for the comforts of life on his good behaviour to others, the better is his behaviour to them: the less dependent, the worse. The greater a man's power, the stronger his propensity in all possible ways to abuse it. Of this fact, all history is one continued proof. Ye, who, for examples, fear to look near home,—send your regards to a safe distance. Look to the twelve

---

[a] Prototype and model of this theory, that of the origin of *metals*, as delivered in the old English Law Book, Plowden's Commentaries,—case, styled *Fogassa's Case:*—father and mother of all metals, mercury and sulphur: in a pure state, they beget the precious, in an impure, the base metals.[2]

For a supposed all-comprehensive and unsophisticated, if preferred to a sophisticated account of motives, see *Springs of Action Table*, by the Author of this Code; and for elucidation of it, *Introduction to the Principles of Morals and Legislation.*[3]

---

[1] 1830, 'Of that supposed'; Bowring emends to 'In the position supposed' to clarify the passage.

[2] Bentham's reference here seems to be mistaken in several respects. The case he cites should properly be Fogossa's case, that is, *Reniger v. Fogossa*, for which see *The Commentaries or Reports of Edmund Plowden* (first published in 1571), 2 vols., London, 1816, i. 1-20. But the case intended seems to be that of *The Queen v. the Earl of Northumberland*, ibid. i. 310-39, where (at p. 339) reference is made to the work of Encelius—that is, Christoph Entzelt (1517-83)—*De re metallica . . . libri III*, published at Frankfurt in 1551 and again in 1557.

[3] *A Table of the Springs of Action . . . with Explanatory Notes and Observations*, London, 1815 and 1817 (Bowring, i. 195-219); *An Introduction to the Principles of Morals and Legislation*, London, 1789 (Bowring, i. 1-154). Motives form the subject of Ch. X. of *An Introduction to the Principles of Morals and Legislation (CW)*, pp. 96-124.

Cæsars:[1] there you have distance in time: look to all oriental despots: there you may have distance in time and space.

### Instructional. Ratiocinative

ART. 23. But, if such were not the effect of power in all lesser masses, neither could it have been so in those greatest possible masses. Not in the inverse but in the direct ratio of the quantity of power possessed is the degree of propensity to do evil in every shape: the degree of the propensity, and therefore the quantum of the demand for securities against the existence and the effects of it. If to any one it appears, that in any part of the scale, this proportion fails to hold good, let him say in what, and wherefore.

But, in this respect, suppose high and low upon a par;—suppose even, that, in the high situations, the evil propensity is less strong than in the low ones;—still, so long as, in the case of the mind in question, the existence of it is in any degree admitted,—the demand for the securities in question must be allowed to be indispensable.

### Instructional

ART. [24]. If so it be, that these securities for appropriate aptitude are thus incontestably beneficial and needful,—the sort of reception a man gives to them when proposed, may serve as a test of his own appropriate aptitude, moral and intellectual. Regarding them as beneficial and needful, does he contest their being so? judge thence of his sincerity and probity: regards he them as not beneficial, or as not useful? judge thence of his understanding.

### Instructional

ART. [25]. Different will naturally be the reception experienced by these securities, at the hands of rulers, in different governments: most favourable, in a pure representative democracy: less favourable, in a pure and absolute monarchy: most completely unfavourable, in a mixed monarchy, composed of a mixture of monarchy and aristocracy, with or without a tinge of representative democracy.

### Instructional

ART. [26]. I. Look first to a pure representative democracy. Why in this case most favourable? *Answer.* The reason is almost too obvious to bear mentioning. Every man is a gainer by the efficiency of these securities: no man can entertain a hope of being a gainer from their absence, or their inefficiency.

[1] The first twelve Roman Emperors (reckoning Julius Caesar as the first) are the subject of *De vita Caesarum*, written in the second quarter of the second century by Gaius Suetonius Tranquillus.

### Instructional

ART. [27]. One class, and that the only one, by which an unfavourable reception will naturally be given to it, is the *Lawyer* class: and, even in their case, not to the whole system,—but only to that part of it, which applies to the Judicial Department.

### Instructional. Exemplificational

ART. [28]. For exemplification and instruction, look to the Anglo-American United States. In that seat of good government,—by that class, and by that alone, is a system of authorized depredation kept in exercise at the expense of all the other classes: accordingly, for no system of securities, the tendency of which is to lessen the amount of evil from *that* source, can any favourable reception be reasonably expected at such hands.

### Instructional. Exemplificational

ART. [29]. Of the ascendancy of this class the cause is—that when the people cast off the other parts of the English yoke,—neither time, nor the state of appropriate intellectual aptitude on the part of leading men, admitted of their casting off, except in here and there an easily detached fragment, that part, which, under the name of *Common Law*, had, by those of the King's creatures and instruments, by whom were occupied the chief judicial situations, been gradually imposed upon the rest of the community,—for their own benefit, in subserviency to and in conjunction with that of the Monarch,—by whom they had been located, and were at every moment dislocable. In this same *Common Law*, with its essential and most elaborately organized uncertainty, its factitious delay, vexation, and expense, did they behold an instrument which, with more or less effect, would, in all such hands as could obtain a share in the use of it, be applicable to the purposes, for which, as above, it had been originally framed.

### Instructional

ART. [30]. True it is—that, in that same fortunate region, by the *official* class of lawyers, no such share is reaped in the plunderage as by the professional class: nor, in the professional class, are the largest lots nearly equal to those which are reaped by the same class in the mother country: the magnitude being kept comparatively small by the multiplicity of the competitors: but by this very multiplicity will their appetite for the golden fruit, and their fear of losing any part of it, be sharpened, and their horror of every thing that threatens to lessen it, augmented: and, misrepresentation being the grand instrument of their trade,—the use of it, in a case of such vital importance cannot reasonably be expected to be spared.

## Instructional

ART. [31]. II. Look next to a pure and absolute Monarchy. So as the power of depredation and oppression, to the use of himself and such instruments and favourites as, from time to time, it may please him to let in for a participation in the benefit of that same power, remains unchanged,—security against abuse of power[1] by all other functionaries, so far from being to the Monarch a sure object of displeasure, will naturally enough be an object and source of satisfaction in his eyes. Depredation committed by them to their own profit, will be to him so much loss: for, the greater the spoil taken by them, the less remains for him: and, as to oppression as well as depredation,—by whatsoever is committed by them in gratification of their own appetites, discontent is produced and secret enmity, from which he has never any thing to hope, and always more or less to apprehend: considering, as he cannot but now and then consider, that his life is at the mercy of every man who will risk his own life for the hope of destroying that of the supposed author of his sufferings.

## Instructional

ART. [32]. In this case, the misfortune is—that, of the aggregate mass of securities against abuse of power in functionaries, the greatest part, as has been, and will be further seen, unavoidably depends upon the power of the Public Opinion Tribunal: and a Monarch will always be fully sensible, to the difficulty which there cannot but be—in [allowing] that authority [to oppose][2] its force to abuse of power, in the shapes in which it appears to him that he would be a sufferer by it,—without seeing and feeling that same force acting against that same abuse, in the shapes in which the whole or the greatest part of the profit from it is reaped by himself.

## Instructional

ART. [33]. To come to particulars. Security against abuse of power on the part of the Legislative authority,—no such Monarch can, of course, be naturally expected to endure: for his is the Legislative authority. Not so as to his subordinates, all or any, in the Administration

---

[1] 1830, 'abuse of its power'; Bowring, as above, correctly omits 'its' as redundant.

[2] 1830, 'in preventing that authority from opposing'; Bowring, 'in allowing that authority to oppose'. The emendation seems required by the sense of the passage.

Department: not so, as to his subordinates even in the Judiciary Department: for, of appropriate aptitude in both those departments, his absolute power enables him to reap for himself the full benefit: while, on every occasion on which, in his view of the matter, it threatens to oppose obstacles to his will,——he can extinguish it, or completely guard himself against the effects of it. Not altogether without reason, therefore, may he be expected to give acceptance—— if not to all securities against abuse of power in those departments, ——at least, to all such securities as can be employed, without giving, to the Public Opinion Tribunal, an influence, capable, in his eyes, of opposing obstacles to any such depredation and oppression as it may happen to him to feel disposed to see committed.

## Instructional

ART. [34]. III. Look now to pure aristocracy. Look, in a word, to British India: for, though a controuling power is in the hands of the mixed monarchy to which the members of that same aristocracy are subject,——yet it is by themselves that all the details of Government in the way of legislation are carried on. Securities against abuse of power on the part of the Legislative authority, they cannot reasonably be expected to endure; for they themselves are Legislators. So neither against abuse of power on the part of occupants of situations in the Administrative department: for, by themselves, or by those in providing for whom they provide for themselves, are those same situations occupied: accordingly, ruin is the universally expected and most effectually denounced lot, of all who should presume to bring to light, or hold up to view, within the field of their power, any instance of such abuse: all this under the eye and to the perfect satisfaction of the superior authority——the King's Board of Controul—— whose care it is, to whatsoever else they apply this same controul, not to apply it to depredation, to oppression, or to that power by which complaint is stifled, and misery thus maximized.[1]

## Instructional

ART. [35]. Thus irremediably adverse are they naturally rendered, to the application of all such securities to the legislative and administrative departments. Not altogether so in regard to the judicial depart-

---

[1] The Board of Control (strictly, the Board of Commissioners for the Affairs of India) was established by Pitt's India Act of 1784 to supervise the government of India. The Commissioners were appointed by the Crown, and their powers, which effectually superseded those of the Directors of the East India Company, were in practice exercised by the President of the Board of Control, a member of the British ministry.

ment. For, to such a degree, on the part of their subjects, for want of appropriate civil law judicature and procedure, does security for property remain deficient,—that by the deficiency the quantity of the matter of wealth capable of being extracted from them, is manifestly diminished. The consequence is—that, supposing appropriate legislation and judicature capable of being established, with such effect as to give increase to the quantity of wealth so extractible, and at the same time without giving to the Public Opinion Tribunal any such power as would oppose a sensible check to the profitable and indispensable abuse of power in the other departments,—a system, of good judicature and correspondent legislation, might, not altogether without reason, be expected to find, at least among the most enlightened of that same body, its advocates.

A circumstance that contributes to render such a result the less improbable is—that, as to those situations, in which, in cases regarded as the most important, judicial power is exercised,—the power of location is in the hands—not of these same aristocrats, but of the Monarch; and, by the depredation exercised to so vast an amount by those creatures of their superior, the sub-aristocratical creatures of the aristocratical rulers are sufferers without being gainers.

### Instructional

ART. [ 36 ]. IV. Look lastly to mixed Monarchy: composed, as above, of a mixture of Monarchy and Aristocracy: the one and the few sharing between them the absolute power: but, in proportions at all times variable; because, at all times, depending upon and varying with the degree of vigour in the Monarch's mind, and the direction taken by it. In this case, the horror of all such securities is naturally, not to say necessarily, universal on the part of both: into no one department of Government will the idea of any application made of them be endurable. The Monarch cannot abuse his power to his own benefit, without their concurrence; nor therefore without suffering, and even, upon occasion, helping, them to make abuse of power to their benefit: they cannot abuse their power to their own benefit without his concurrence, as above. The ruling *one* cannot keep his subjects under a system of regulated plunderage, without letting in the sub-ruling or co-ruling *few* for a proportion of the plunder: they cannot get in that same share, but either through his hands or with his concurrence. He cannot extort a million a year for the gratification of his own appetites, without keeping the official establishment filled with overpaid offices, needless offices, and sinecures, to the amount of ulterior millions shared by them among themselves. He cannot keep up a vast and needless permanent military force on both elements, without sharing among them the offices, military and civil, belonging to it.

## Instructional

ART. [37]. On the other hand, legislative assemblies, the proceedings of which cannot be carried on without a certain degree of publicity, being of the essence of this form of Government, it cannot——easily, if at all, be carried on, without suffering the Public Opinion Tribunal to be in existence, and to exercise, with more or less effect, and with much more than under a pure Monarchy, its abuse-restraining and tutelary power. For, in every such assembly, there will of course be at all times two parties, contending against one another, for such parts of the plunderage as are at the disposal of the Monarch, and for all such other power as is open to competition: and their sole means of contending with one another is, on all occasions, a virtual appeal, more or less explicit, to the will and undefinable power of the people, say——to the Public Opinion Tribunal, by which that same saving power is exercised.

## Instructional

ART. [38]. Think now——whether, under any such form of government, for any efficient system of Securities for appropriate aptitude on the part of the Members of the Official Establishment, in the several departments, Legislative, Administrative, and Judicial, and in particular for that moral aptitude by which, in proportion as it has place, needless expense is excluded,——any thing like a favourable reception can on any reasonable grounds be expected. Can it in the Legislative Department? No: for, between the Monarch and the Aristocracy, all legislative power is shared. Can it in the Administrative Department? No: for, there likewise, through the same channels, afforded by overpaid places, needless places, sinecure places, pensions for retreat, and pensions without even that pretence, whatsoever portion of the matter of wealth can be extorted from those by whose labour it is produced, is shared among these same self-styled pure, and too indisputably exalted, hands.

## Instructional

ART. [39]. Can it in the Judiciary? No: for, without any the least trouble or odium,——by the hands of their necessary and dependent instruments——the higher class of Judges,——the three superior classes of functionaries——King, Lords, and Commons——can carry on, and reap the profit of, abuse of power, in cases to an indefinite extent, in which, by so operose a machine as that of Parliament, fear of shame, of public discontent, of resistance, of the trouble of getting through the forms,—would concur in preventing their carrying it on with their own hands. In a chamber called a *Court of Justice*,—half a minute,—in some cases, of four men's, in others of one man's time, —not only can do, but is habitually employed in doing, that which, in the two chambers called *Houses of Parliament*, if in those places it could be done at all, would cost months, not to say years, to do, in those forms, without which validity might be questionable, and disobedience not improbable. So much for *time:* then, as to *words*,— issued from a bush of artificial hair, a word or two, such as *conspiracy, Christianity, blasphemy, libel, hurt to feelings, bonos mores*,— can convert innoxious acts into crimes, punish men at pleasure and without warning, banish security from property, substitute secret judicature to public, stifle all complaint, bar out all redress, take children out of the hands of fathers, engage booksellers to cheat printers, extinguish literary property in a book without looking at it. Banish security from property? Yes: and, not only from all property, but from whatever else possesses value: for, wherever by the name of *Common Law, Judge-made law* reigns,—security is an empty name.

### Instructional

ART. [40]. Add to this the service rendered to Legislators in their individual capacity, by the impunity secured to them in the character of Magistrates:—conferred there by and established by Common Law, behold accordingly a power of oppression, too enormous to be assumed and established by Statute Law.

### Instructional

ART. [41]. Under this form of government,—thus conveniently assistant, not to say necessary, to abuse of power in the Legislative and Administrative, is an unrestrained and correspondent abuse of power in the Judiciary department: in this state of things, whether in or for any one of the three departments any efficient securities against such abuse have, under this same form of government, any much better chance of finding acceptance than in or for any other, must be left to experience to declare.[a]

[a] The course of experience here alluded to, is it not sufficient? Add then one fact more, with the *volumes*, as the phrase is, *spoken* by it. In a work, now for upwards of a twelvemonth past published, and repeatedly advertised,* a knot of

* *Indications respecting Lord Eldon.*[1]

[1] *Indications respecting Lord Eldon, including History of the pending Judges'-Salary-Raising Measure*, London, 1825, first appeared in *The Pamphleteer*, xxv (1825), 405–43, as 'Observations on Mr Secretary Peel's House of Commons

## *Instructional*

ART. [42]. Securities here provided, for appropriate aptitude in the situation of members of the Legislative Body, are these—

English Judges, under the immediate authority, and to the vast profit of the heads of the law,—that is to say, of all the Judges,—and in conjunction with a set of professional lawyers, whom, as is shown, they have even forced into the confederacy,—have been proved to be in the constant and long-continued practice of a crime—'obtainment of money by false pretences'—for which, by an Act of the Legislature,* expressed in these very words, men at large have, for near a century past, been consigned to imprisonment, transportation, or the pillory, at the option of another set of Judges belonging to the same Judiciary. Of the establishment of this demonstration, what has been the consequence? Prosecution of the accused? No. Prosecution of the accuser? No: for by such prosecution, the accused, with their guilt upon their heads, would be dragged into the broadest day-light: and, though there is but one accuser, yet it is from published works of other persons in considerable number, that the facts constitutive of the matter of accusation are derived: what was done by the accusation being an indication given of the bearing of the law upon those same facts. Meantime, by all Parliament men, by all Judges, by all professional lawyers of all classes,— it is either read or heard of: it is known to be true, and, as if by universal consent,—regarded, or turned aside from, in the most perfectly uninterrupted silence.

All this while, the more deeply and more manifestly the members of this section of the *ruling few*, are plunged in the habit of those transgressions, a single act of which suffices to consign any one of the *subject many* to punishment and infamy,—the louder are they in that chorus of protestations, and self-eulogies, and mutual certificates of impeccability, in which, if there were any approach to the truth, all security against deficiency in appropriate *moral* aptitude, not to speak of *intellectual* and *active*, would be needlessly and uselessly vexatious.

Never, till the people have opened their eyes wide, never till they have lifted up *their* voices likewise in full chorus—giving at once support, confidence, and ulterior impulse to whatsoever men in power their good fortune may have listed in their service,—no, never will the plague of lawyers be stayed. Pruning? Yes, that they will peradventure consent to; but, by appropriate pruning, this poison tree, like any other tree, is not destroyed, but fructified and preserved.

Folly alone can expect criminality in high places to take flight, so long as it continues not only unpunished but respected: respected, and even, in forms prescribed by itself, worshipped.

*30 G. II, Ch. 24, §1.[1]

---

Speech, 21st. March, 1825, introducing his Police Magistrates Salary Raising Bill . . . the announced Judges' Salary Raising Bill, and the pending County Courts Bill'. It appeared again as item VIII in *Official Aptitude Maximized; Expense Minimized: as shown in the several papers comprised in this volume*, London, 1830 (Bowring, v. 263-386), Bowring, v. 348-82. Sir John Scott (1751-1838), 1st Earl of Eldon, was Lord Chancellor almost continuously from 1801 until 1827, and Sir Robert Peel (1788-1850) was Home Secretary from 1822 to 1827. Extensive MS material for the *Indications* pamphlet is in UC xix.

[1] 'An Act for the more effectual Punishment of Persons, who shall attain, or attempt to attain, Possession of Goods or Money, by false or untrue Pretences;

I. For appropriate aptitude in all its branches taken together—

1. *Locators*, those whose interest it is that the happiness of the greatest number be maximized: as per Ch. ii. ENDS and MEANS: Ch. iii. SOVEREIGNTY, IN WHOM: Ch. vi. §[§]4 to 13 inclusive: condition and number of the locating Electors.

2. General responsibility, as per §2, *Responsibility*.

3. Shortness of term of service in each [Member]:[1] namely, no more than one year, as per §14, with the accidental addition of the fragment of another, as per §22, *Term of service* [—*Continuation*].[2]

4. Non-relocability, till after the lapse of two or three years, reckoned from the expiration of the last preceding term of service, as per §25, *Relocable who:* §26, *Wrongful exclusion obviated:* that choice of persons, who have had experience, and of whom experience has been had, may never be wanting.

5. General responsibility of the whole body, and its several members, as per §2, *Responsibility*, and §23, *Self-suppletive function*, and Ch. v. CONSTITUTIVE, §6, *Securities against [Legislative]*, &c.

6. Special causes of temporary secrecy excepted,—publicity of legislational sittings, as per §21, *Sittings, public and secret*.

7. Publicity, permanent as well as immediate, given—to the part taken by the several members, on the occasion of each motion, as per §29, *Members' Motions*, Art. 6.

8. Securities for appropriate aptitude, on the part of all subordinate functionaries,—in the several other departments, administrational and judiciary,—without whose concurrence scarcely can any considerable evil be produced by the ordaining body. See the sections intituled *Securities, &c.* in the chapters, headed Ch. [viii.] PRIME MINISTER—Ch. ix. MINISTERS COLLECTIVELY—Ch. xii. JUDICIARY COLLECTIVELY—Ch. xxvi. LOCAL HEADMEN—Ch. xxvii. LOCAL REGISTRARS.

### Instructional

ART. 43. II. Securities, applying more particularly to *moral* aptitude.

1. Provision made, against corruption in every shape, as per §[19], *Remuneration;* and, by constancy of appropriate occupation, to the

for preventing the unlawful Pawning of Goods; for the easy Redemption of Goods pawned; and for preventing Gaming in Publick Houses by Journeymen Labourers Servants and Apprentices' (1757).

[1] 1830 and Bowring, 'Elector'; but the passage evidently refers to the member of the Legislature.

[2] See the Collations for the 1830 and Bowring versions of this cross-reference: the text above restores the actual title of § 22 as it stands in both editions.

exclusion of time for corruptive intercourse, as per §18, *Attendance;* §20, *Attendance and Remuneration.*

2. In case of delinquency, punibility at the hands of succeeding Legislatures, as per §28, *Legislation Penal Judicatory.*

3. Special security provided against mutual disturbance to members, during Legislational Sittings; as per §16.

4. All-comprehensive subjection to the tutelary power of the *Public Opinion Tribunal*, through the instrumentality of the LEGISLATOR'S INAUGURAL DECLARATION, as per Ch. vii.

### Instructional

ART. 44. III. Securities, applying more particularly to *intellectual* aptitude.

1. Exceptions excepted, original locability of all persons without distinction by the respective Electoral Bodies.

2. After the expiration of the preparation period, as in the case of Ministers and other functionaries belonging to the Administrative Department, as per Ch. ix. MINISTERS COLLECTIVELY, §16, *Locable who,*—sole persons locable, those by whom proof of appropriate aptitude has been given; namely, by means of the *Examination Judicatory* thereby organized.[1]

3. Provision made, for all comprehensiveness of appropriate information, as per Ch. viii. PRIME MINISTER, §10, *Registration System*, and §11, *Publication System;* Ch. ix. MINISTERS COLLECTIVELY, §7, *Statistic function;* Ch. xii. JUDICIARY COLLECTIVELY, §14, *Publicity, recordation, publication;* Ch. xxi. IMMEDIATE JUDICIARY REGISTRARS; Ch. xxvii. LOCAL REGISTRARS; Ch. vi. LEGISLATURE, §27, *Legislation Enquiry Judicatory.*

4. Provision made, for giving to fresh enactments, on their introduction, the most apt form, in respect of the conjunct qualities of correctness, comprehensiveness, clearness, conciseness, or say succinctness, and methodicalness,—and without diminution of appropriate power,—as per §29, *Members' Motions:* and on the responsibility of a subordinate Minister, located for this purpose; as per Ch. xi. MINISTERS [SEVERALLY], §2, *Legislation Minister.*

---

[1] Bentham seems to suggest here that potential members of the Legislature must pass the examinations required for entry into the Administrative department in the system outlined in Ch. IX, § 16, pp. 310–37. This proposal does not appear to be discussed elsewhere either in the *Constitutional Code* or in the Election Code. See F. Rosen, 'Jeremy Bentham and Democratic Theory', *The Bentham Newsletter*, iii (1979), 46–61, where (at pp. 56–7 and nn.) this article and relevant MS material are discussed.

5. Provision made, in respect of those same qualities, by needful legislative interpretation and special amendment, according as the need is brought to view in the course of *Judicature:* as per Ch. xii. JUDICIARY COLLECTIVELY, §19, *Judges' contested-interpretation function.* §20, *Judges' eventually emendative function.* §[22], *Judges' preinterpretation function.*

### Instructional

ART. 45. IV. Securities, applying more particularly to appropriate active aptitude.

1. Provision made, for the uninterrupted sittings of the Legislative body: as per §[1], *Powers and duties;* and §18, *Attendance.*

2. Provision made, for the uninterrupted attendance of each Member, as per §18, *Attendance,* and §20, *Attendance and Remuneration;* or, in case of accident, by a Depute of his choice, and for whom he is responsible: as per §23, *Self-suppletive function.*

# CHAPTER VII[1]

## LEGISLATOR'S INAUGURAL DECLARATION[a]

### SECTION 1

#### AUTHENTICATION, HOW

### Enactive

ART. 1. In the front of the Election District Office, in face of the assembled multitude, immediately after the notification made by the Election Clerk of the person in whose favour a majority of the votes

---

[a] Of a formulary of this sort, the chief use is to keep the Legislative and other constituted authorities in the more effectual subjection to the Constitutive: to

---

[1] Most of the material in this chapter was reprinted in *Parliamentary Candidate's proposed Declaration of Principles: or say, A Test proposed for Parliamentary Candidates,* London, 1831, subsequently referred to as *P.C.D.* As this pamphlet was published after the *Constitutional Code,* no collation is provided here, although some major variations will be noted. The main changes introduced in the pamphlet are: (a) the use of the note to Ch. VII as the basis of the Introduction; (b) the omission of §1. Art. 5; (c) the inclusion of a lengthy new section on the diffusion of knowledge and the press entitled 'Useful Knowledge to all promised'; (d) the omission of §§11 and 12; and (e) the addition of text regarding the use of the Table of Fallacies in §13. As a result of these changes the sections of the *P.C.D.* are numbered differently. For a discussion of the Legislator's Inaugural Declaration, see the Introduction, p. xxix.

has been declared,——the person so elected will, in token of assent, read aloud with his name thereto subscribed, the *Legislator's Inaugural Declaration*, in all the several words in and by which it stands expressed in the sections hereinafter following.

wit, by means of the power of the moral sanction, as exercised by the Public Opinion Tribunal.

The points here enumerated are in general such, that, in relation to them,—— more especially in the case of persons in the situation in question,——the force of the legal sanction cannot, in the nature of the case, be brought to bear, in such sort, as to subject men to punishment under the name of *punishment*, for aberration, in any direction, from the assumed line of rectitude. But, in the exercise given to its power, the *Public Opinion Tribunal* neither is, nor ought to be, nor can be, fettered, by those formalities, by which the exercise of the power of the legal sanction ought every where to be, and to a certain degree is every where restricted.

Under the sort of law established and enforced by the power of the moral sanction,——the penalty, for transgression in whatsoever shape, is forfeiture of a correspondent degree of popularity: and no formality of trial is necessary to the giving execution and effect to this forfeiture.

Take here an example. For the purpose of an indisputably necessary branch of service,——the Legislature allots (suppose,) a somewhat larger sum than could have been necessary:——for no such impropriety of conduct, without preponderant evil in the shape of [dissension] and danger of civil war, could those who joined in the allotment be subjected to legal punishment, as per § 28, *Legislation Penal Judicatory*, at the hands of their successors. But, in the case of a general habit of profuseness, an excess of this sort would, by the public mind, be carried to account, and contribute to the formation of a body of displeasure, by the aggregate weight of which, the popularity and influence, of the persons in question, might at length be sunk.

So, in the case of unfriendly deportment, in this or that particular instance, towards this or that foreign power. Of misconduct in this shape, the natural tendency would be——to produce, in the first instance, an interruption of intercourse in the commercial and other mutually useful shapes, and ultimately perhaps war.[1] Other examples more impressive might not improbably be found; but, for the explanation of the general design, these (it is believed) will be found sufficient.

Upon the whole, the instrument may be considered as a sort of *Moral Code*, adapted to the situation of Legislators; and as containing a sort of map of the field of legislation.

A moral disease, with the seeds of which, most if not all opinion-professing instruments in use have hitherto been tainted, and contributed to inoculate is—— *insincerity;* and, besides the bad effect thereby produced on the whole moral frame,——this vice, in so far as, on the occasion here in question, it has place, fails of producing the particular effect, for the production of which it was designed.

For this reason it is, that, in the Code, as above, care is taken to allow each individual, on taking the Declaration, to give equal publicity to a notification of

---

[1] 1830 and Bowring, 'perhaps of war'; but 'of' is evidently redundant, since it would imply that the misconduct leads to an *interruption of war*, rather than to *war*, as the context requires.

## Enactive

ART. 2. In case of unavoidable absence on his part, by reason of sickness or other accidental cause,—as also to provide for the case, in which, without his knowledge, or without his consent, he has been proposed to be elected as if he had been a candidate,—any person, —acting on his behalf, with his consent, and in proof thereof, producing an exemplar thereof, signed by the proposed member, as above,—will, upon declaring, on his responsibility, the cause of such absentation, be admitted to read the Inaugural Declaration in his stead: saying, immediately before the commencement of such his reading—'I, (mentioning his name,) at the desire of A. M. (mentioning the member's name,) read this his Inaugural Declaration in his stead: and it is his desire, that the words of it be considered as his as effectually as if it had been by himself that they were read.'

## Enactive. Ratiocinative

ART. 3. For prevention of insincerity, and that it may be left without excuse,—any person so elected may, in manner following, subjoin to the so attested exemplar of his Declaration, any such exceptions, or say expressions of partial dissent, and any such supposed amendments, and explanations, as he thinks fit.

## Enactive. Instructional

ART. 4. In this case, whatsoever be the words or clauses from which he means to state himself as dissenting,—or to which he is desirous of seeing any proposed amendment made or explanation given,—he will give indication of them, by enclosing them respectively in brackets, with a numerical figure, letter, or other mark of reference, which will accordingly be [repeated] at the commencement of such his statement.

his dissent as to any article or articles at pleasure:—for which purpose, he will also, if so minded, have made known, antecedently to the Election, any such dissent, proposed amendment, or explanation, to Electors, to enable them to give their votes accordingly. For want of such openly declared reservation, declarations of this sort are apt to be regarded as no better than empty forms: and the matter, instead of being mended, is but made worse, by giving to the declaration the denomination of an *oath*.

Note as to structure of sentences. In contrariety to the general rule, as prescribed by general utility by which lengthiness in sentences is, on the score of obscurity, interdicted,—in the present instance, the ratiocinative matter is imbedded in, or interwoven with, the enactive and instructional: use, purpose, and reason,—the rendering it manifest and undeniable, that this same ratiocinative matter has been actually present to the mind, of him whose approbation of it has been declared.

At the same time, and in the same way, he will, if so minded, declare the considerations, which, in the character of *reasons*, have been the causes, by which such his dissent, or indication of supposed amendment, or requisite explanation, has been produced. But, (to prevent confusion,) in the exemplar in which such his reasons are written, he will not be at liberty to write more than {          } lines in any one page, referring the overplus, if any, to a separate paper: which paper, if published, will be published by himself, and at his own expense.

### Instructional

ART. 5. Lest, by any such exceptions, amendments, or explanations, dissent to the essence of the declaration should, under pretence of assent, be virtually expressed,——any other member of the Legislative Body may, at the time that such supposed virtually dissenting member is taking his seat, move that he may be considered as virtually refusing to officiate as member thereof: whereupon, if such be the judgment of the Assembly, his election will be declared of no avail, and the appropriate arrangements will be taken for the election of another deputy in his stead.


## SECTION 2

### I. ENDS AIMED AT

I, A. L. in testimony of my attachment to the principles of the Constitution, do hereby make the solemn declaration following.

1. I recognise, as the *all-comprehensive*, and only right and proper end of Government, the greatest happiness of the greatest number of the members of the community: of all without exception, in so far as possible: of the greatest number, on every occasion on which the nature of the case renders it impossible by rendering it matter of necessity, to make sacrifice of a portion of the happiness of a few, to the greater happiness of the rest.

2. I acknowledge, as and for the *specific* and *direct* ends of Government, these which follow:——

I. Positive ends——maximization of subsistence, abundance, security against evil in every shape: against evil from every source: against physical calamity, against human hostility; against hostility from external, against hostility from internal adversaries; against hostility from internal resistible adversaries; against hostility from internal irresistible adversaries: for such, so long as they rule, and in proportion as they rule ill, are evil rulers: such,——unless by apt arrangements debarred from all hope of sinister success,——are and ever will be all rulers everywhere.

II. The all-comprehensive negative and *collateral* end of Government I acknowledge to be——avoidance or minimization of expense in every shape: in the shape of money; in the shape of unintended hardship; in the shape of intended hardship, intended for the purpose of punishment: minimization of expense,——as in the shape of punishment, so in the shape of reward and the matter of reward: seeing that, without certain hardship and eventual punishment, the matter of reward cannot be extracted from the grasp of individuals, and placed at the disposal of Government.

I acknowledge,——that, of all these indispensable ends, no one can be compassed, but by and in proportion to appropriate aptitude, on the part of the several functionaries of Government: more particularly on the part of those of the people's upper servants, of whom I am one: appropriate aptitude in all its several shapes, moral, intellectual, and active: appropriate intellectual aptitude in its two several shapes——knowledge and judgment. Appropriate *moral* aptitude, I acknowledge, it will be my own fault if, on any occasion, I fail to invest myself with: namely, by taking for the guides of my conduct the several above-mentioned ends: appropriate *intellectual* and *active* aptitude it shall be my diligent endeavour to invest myself with, according to the measure of my faculties.

These same uncontrovertible ends of all good government, I once more acknowledge accordingly, and in these few words bring together and recapitulate:——*Greatest happiness of greatest number maximized; national subsistence, abundance, security, and equality maximized;*[1] *official aptitude maximized: expense, in all shapes, minimized.*

## SECTION 3

### II. APPETITES GUARDED AGAINST

On my guard I will accordingly, on every occasion, keep myself, against the power of all those appetites, to the sinister influence of

---

[1] Although Bentham mentions 'equality maximized' in this recapitulation, he has not in fact discussed it in the passage above. Also, in the annotated copy of the 1830 volume referred to in the Introduction, p. xlv, which incorporates some MS notes and corrections by Bentham, and in *P.C.D.*, he has in this passage deleted the words '*of greatest number*' following '*Greatest happiness*'. This is of some interest in view of Bentham's known hesitation over the formulation of the fundamental principle of his system. See Robert Shackleton, 'The Greatest Happiness of the Greatest Number: the history of Bentham's phrase', *Studies on Voltaire and the Eighteenth Century*, xc (1972), 1480-1; and see Bowring, ix. 6 for material written in 1822 and used by Doane in the 'Book I' of the *Constitutional Code*.

which, the inalterable nature of my situation keeps me so constantly and perilously exposed: appetite for power, appetite for money, appetite for factitious honor and dignity, appetite for vengeance at the expense of opponents, appetite for ease at the expense of duty.

Constant, in particular, will be my endeavours, to keep extinguished in my breast, all appetite for respect in every shape in which it is factitious. To preeminent respect at the hands of the community at large, I acknowledge no other title, than what is constituted by preeminent service:——service, proved and made universally manifest, by appropriate evidence. In the mass of those *honours*, or, as they are also called, *dignities*, which are factitious,——I behold an instrument of unmerited triumph in the hands of those who share in them, of unjust depression on the part of all besides: the work of imposture, on the part of him by whom the draught for respect is drawn; of folly, on the part of him by whom it is paid.


## SECTION 4

### III. ECONOMY AND UNCORRUPTION PROMISED

Unremitted shall, on every occasion, be my care, and my exertions, to keep the official establishment clear of all those drains, by which, in exorbitant excess, the substance of the people is drawn into the coffers of self-seated rulers, or unfaithful stewards: clear of all needless offices, of all useless offices, of all overpay of overpaid offices, of all dutiless offices, of all accumulation of offices in one hand: numbering among dutiless offices every case, in which, not serving in fact, a man serves in words, by deputy: the deputy being thus the working functionary, the principal an impostor, by whom money is obtained on a false pretence; nor moreover will I forget, that he who accepts a second office, holding at the same time one, for the exercise of which, the whole of his disposable time may eventually be requisite, manifests thereby his intention of neglecting the duties of one or both.

On the subject of official pay,——never will I cease to remember, that all pay, given to him who would serve equally well without pay, is given in waste: that the less a man is content to receive, for taking upon himself the duties of an office, the more conclusive is the evidence given, of his relish for the functions of it: that if, instead of receiving, he would be content to give, money for the occupation, the evidence would be still more conclusive: the more so, the more he would be content to give for it: that the higher the pay of an office is, the greater the probability is, that the functions of it may be the object of his abhorrence, and every occasion embraced for avoiding the pain of exercising them: that, the higher the pay, the stronger the temptation to substitute,—and the more surely adequate the means, of substituting,—as far as possible, to the services due to the public, any such private occupations as to the individual are most agreeable: that, of the quantum of pay that will be satisfactory to a man, no other man can be so good a judge as he: that, if a comparatively indigent man is exposed to the temptation of breaking his trust for money,—so is the comparatively opulent man;—who moreover with more expensive habits, has proportionably augmented means of engaging accomplices and protectors: and that, as universal experience demonstrates, the most extravagantly paid of all functionaries have, everywhere, and at all times, been the most extravagant of prodigals, and the most rapacious of depredators.

Bearing in mind, that no desirable office, and in particular, that no lucrative office, can have place any where, without being a source of corruption;—of corruptingness in him by whom it is conferrible, of corruptedness in him by whom it is receivable;—bearing this in mind, —I will, were it only for this reason, keep my attention steadily bent, on the means of minimizing—as well the number, as the pay, of all such offices: never ceasing to remember, that, as waste produces corruption, so does corruption waste; till thus, by depredation, oppression, and dissipation, the body politic is exhausted, debilitated, destroyed.

In particular,—in no act of waste, in no act of corruption, will I ever participate, under any such cloak, as that of *a pension of retreat:* never ceasing to remember, on how widely different a footing stands every such grant from that of the compensation, granted to military men, for disablement incurred in military service: knowing, and duly considering, that no such pay without service is ever received or looked for, by him whose means of subsistence, are composed of the retribution received by individuals for services rendered to individuals: remembering, that no physician has any pension of retreat from his patients, handicraft from his employers, or shopkeeper from his customers: nor yet is there any want of physicians, handicrafts, or shopkeepers.

As little, under any such notion as that of affording *honour* to the nation, *dignity* to its functionaries, encouragement to piety, to learning, to arts, to sciences, and in particular to fine arts, or merely curious sciences or literary pursuits,—as little, under any such delusive pretence, will I concur in laying burthens on the comparatively indigent many, for the amusement of the comparatively opulent few: at their own expense will I leave them to pursue the gratification of their own tastes.

In the application made of punishments, never will I concur, in afflicting with factitious affliction, a fellow-citizen, for no other cause than that of his differing from myself, or from others, on a matter of opinion, or on a matter of taste. No such privilege will I arrogate to myself as that of deciding what things he shall or shall not believe, or by what things he shall or shall not be pleased. By no such means will I ever seek to constitute my opinion the standard of other men's opinions, my taste the standard of other men's tastes.

Never, on the occasion of the treatment to be given to delinquents, —never will I suffer myself to be guided by any other wish or rule, than that by which a surgeon is guided in the treatment given to his patients. No more will I be guided by anger in the one case, than he is in the other. Never will I concur in administering, to any such patient of mine, pain, in any quantity, exceeding the least, that, in my eyes, is sufficient, for preserving the whole community, himself included, from pain in some greater quantity.

In my endeavours for the maximization of official appropriate aptitude, on the part of the several functionaries of the state in their several situations,—I will not forget the keeping all candidates for office, subjected, in the most public and universally satisfactory manner, to the most demonstrative tests, which, in the case of each Department, and each function of that Department, the nature of the duty admits of: nor, on the occasion of whatever provision may be made for their appropriate instruction, will I be unmindful of the incontestible truths—that the only effectual security for appropriate aptitude with relation to any office, is the rendering such demonstration of it an indispensable condition to the attainment of that same office,—and that, in proportion as, in addition to adequate means, adequate inducement for the attainment of such aptitude are found by individuals at their own expense, all provision for that purpose, at the expense of the public, is probable corruption, as well as certain waste.


## SECTION 5

### IV. NOTORIETY OF LAW TO ALL PROMISED

Mindful, that a portion of law, in relation to which, in proportion as it is known, it is known that execution will not be given to it, is no better than a dead letter; and that a law, in relation to which, while by some it is known, by others it is not known, that execution will be given to it, is so much worse than a dead letter as to be a cruel snare,—my sincere endeavours shall at all times be directed, to the keeping the field of Government clear of all such snares.

To this end, my anxious attention shall, at all times, be applied,—— not only to the securing, to the text of the law, at all times, an extent corresponding and equal, to that of the whole aggregate of the obligations to which the people stand subjected,——but also to the keeping the whole mass of the law itself in such sort methodised and divided into parts, as that each individual may have in hand every portion of law in which he has a special interest in any shape, clear as possible of all matter in which he has not any such interest: the whole, in a form as clear, correct, complete, concise, and compact as possible: those parts of it, in which all persons have an immediate interest, being, under all the variations which it may happen to them to undergo, kept in such a state, as that they may, without difficulty, form the matter of the earliest instruction administered in schools.

## SECTION 6

### V. JUSTICE ACCESSIBLE TO ALL PROMISED

Mindful I shall ever be——that the services of Judicial functionaries, are the only instruments, by which execution can be given to the law, and security or redress to the citizen, against injury in any shape at the hands of internal adversaries.

Mindful, that upon this as upon any other sort of instruments to impose a tax, is to deny the use of it to all who cannot pay the tax, and in this case to sell to all who can and will pay it, the power of employing the instrument in the destruction of those who cannot.

Mindful, that the effect of this denial is the same, whatever be the pocket that receives the produce of the tax.

Mindful, that to impose any such injury-promoting and security-denying prohibition, is to sell to the rich the means of irresistible and unpunishable aggression,——to deny to the poor the possibility of self-defence,——to establish oppression, to join in depredation, and to produce by law the evils of anarchy.

Mindful, that every particle of needless delay and vexation,—— introduced or left by the Legislator or the Judge, in the proceedings, ——produces the afflictive and prohibitive effect of a tax, without the profit of it.

Mindful, that where no intention of injury has place, on either side, the effect of every such tax, and of every such neglect, is to heap affliction upon affliction on both sides.

Sensible I am, that a Legislator is accessory to every injury, against which he withholds protection, as well as to every injury to which he gives or leaves facility:——sensible, that he is the accomplice of every

141

oppressor and every depredator, into whose hands he thus puts an instrument of injury, or in whose power he places a victim, by keeping the means of redress out of his reach.

Bearing all these things in mind,——I promise and declare, that, on no occasion shall my diligent endeavours be wanting, to the keeping at all times excluded from the system of Judicature, not only every particle of expense purposely imposed, but every particle of needless delay and vexation, which, for want of such attention, may be liable to have place.

## SECTION 7

### VI. IMPARTIALITY IN ELECTIONS PROMISED

On the Election of the several Ministers, in the filling of whose situations a Member of the Legislature has a vote,——namely, the Prime Minister, the Justice Minister, and the Legislation Minister,——I will, on each occasion, after the fullest and most impartial enquiry and consideration in my power,——with scrupulous fidelity, give my vote, in favour of that individual, in whom, in my judgment, the aggregate of appropriate aptitude, in all its several branches, has place in the highest degree; and who accordingly is, in the corresponding degree, able and willing to give execution and effect to the ordinances of the Legislature, in so far as guided by the principles in this my Declaration manifested.

## SECTION 8

### VII. IN INTERNATIONAL DEALINGS, JUSTICE AND BENEFICENCE PROMISED

On the occasion of the dealings of this our State with any other States,——sincerely and constantly shall my endeavours be directed to the observance of the same strict justice and impartiality, as on the occasion of the dealings of the Legislature with its Constituents, and other its fellow-countrymen, of this our State.

Never will I seek to add, to the opulence or power of this our State, at the expense of the opulence or power of any other State, any otherwise than, in the competition between individual and individual, each may, without injury, seek to advance his own prosperity in preference to that of the other.

All profit, by conquest in every shape, I acknowledge to be no other than robbery: robbery, having murder for its instrument; both operating upon the largest possible scale: robbery, committed by the ruling few in the conquering nation, on the subject many in both nations: robbery, of which, by the expense of armament, the people of the conquering nation are the first victims: robbery and murder, the guilt of which, as much exceeds the guilt of the crimes commonly called by those names, as the quantity of suffering produced in the one case exceeds the quantity produced in the other.

Seeing, that in all war, it is only through the sides of the unoffending many that the guilty few can ever receive a wound,—never will I, for any other purpose than that of national self-defence, or receipt of compensation for pecuniary damage actually sustained, consent to make war on any other State: nor yet for pecuniary damage, till all endeavours for the obtainment of compensation, in the way of arbitration or other means less destructive than general war, are hopeless: nor unless, if not prevented by war, future injury from the same source as the past, is actually apprehended by me.

Never will I consent to the receiving, under the dominion of this our State,—even though it were at the desire of the inhabitants,— any portion of territory, situate at any such distance from the territory of this State, as to prevent any of the wants, of the inhabitants of such other territory, from receiving, at the hands of the Supreme Legislature of this our State, relief as effectual, as that which they could receive, were their places of habitation situated within the pristine limits of the territory of this our State: regarding, as I do, all such dominion, as no better than an instrument, and device, for the accumulation of patronage and oppressive power, in the hands of the ruling few in the dominating State, at the expense, and by the sacrifice, of the interest and felicity, of the subject many, in both States.

No recognition of superiority, on the part of this our State, in relation to any other State, will I ever seek to procure, or consent to receive: no factitious honour or dignity will I seek to procure, or consent to receive, for this my own State, or any of its citizens, at the hands of any other State.

I acknowledge all honour to be false honour, all glory to be false glory, all dignity false dignity,—which is sought to be advanced, or maintained, at the expense of justice, probity, self-regarding prudence, or effective benevolence: I acknowledge all such words to be words of delusion, employed by rulers, for the purpose of engaging subject citizens to consent, or submit, to be led, for the purpose of depredation, to the commission of murder upon the largest scale: words, which, as often as they are employed, will, in proportion as the eyes of men are open to their true interests, reflect dishonour, more and more intense and extensive, on all those by whom they are thus employed.

On every favourable occasion,——my endeavours shall be employed to the rendering, to the subjects, and for their sake to the constituted Authorities, of every foreign State, all such positive good offices, as can be rendered thereto, without its being at the expense of some other State or States, or against the rightly presumable inclination, as well as at the expense, of the majority of my fellow-countrymen, in this our State.

Never, by force or intimidation, never by prohibition or obstruction, will I use any endeavour to prevent my fellow-countrymen, or any of them, from seeking to better their condition in any other part, inhabited or uninhabited, of this globe. In the territory of this State, I behold an asylum to all: a prison to none.

## SECTION 9

### VIII. IMPARTIALITY IN THE GENERAL EXERCISE OF POWER PROMISED

On every occasion, in the exercise of this my vocation, sincere and anxious shall be my endeavour, to keep my mind as clear as may be, of undue partiality in every sense: of partiality in favour of any class or individual, to the injury of any other: of partiality, through self-regarding interest: of partiality, through interest inspired by sympathy: of partiality, through interest inspired by antipathy: more particularly will I be on my guard against partiality in favour of superiors, to the prejudice of inferiors: of superiors, in whatsoever scale of comparison: opulence, power, reputation, talent, natural or acquired.

In my conduct towards my fellow-countrymen,——I will, on every occasion, in this my situation, apply my closest attention to the observance of the same strict rules, as if it were that of a Judge. Acting as a Legislator, I acknowledge myself to be acting as a Judge; bound, to the observance of the same inflexible impartiality in this case as in that: bound——but by ties, as much stronger, as the number of the persons, whose happiness is at stake, is greater.

## SECTION 10

### IX. ASSIDUITY PROMISED

Mindful, that by absentation, half the effect of a vote on the wrong side is produced, I will not, on any occasion, by plea of sickness or other excuse, seek to exempt myself from the obligation of attendance.

## SECTION 11

### X. SUBORDINATION TO THE CONSTITUTIVE AUTHORITY PROMISED

Never, except for the avoidance of determinate and clearly preponderant evil,——nor for that purpose but during the absolutely necessary time,——never will I concur, in withdrawing the proceedings of the Legislature, from the view and scrutiny of the people: the people its Constitutional superiors: the people——the only legitimate source of power: the people, by whose authority, for whose sake, and at whose expense, all power, conferred by this our Constitution, has been created.

## SECTION 12

### XI. ENCROACHMENT ON SUBORDINATE AUTHORITIES ABJURED

Sensible, that, if duly fulfilled, the duties specially attached to the situation of Member of the Supreme Legislative, never will or can cease to be sufficient to occupy the whole of a public man's disposable time,——and that nothing but disobedience, tardiness, inaptitude, or casual and momentary want of time, on the part of Subordinates, can create, on the part of the Supreme Legislative, any such necessity as that of assuming to itself, in the whole or in part, business belonging to any one of their several departments:——strictly and constantly will I keep myself on my guard against every such temptation as that of acting, without necessity, in any part of the field of service belonging to any one of those several subordinate authorities; sensible, how prone, for want of such due caution, man in authority is to afford, in this way, to the appetite for patronage and oppressive power, an irregular and mischievous gratification. Saying this, I have in mind, in a particular and distinct manner, the functions and branches of business belonging to the several Departments subordinate to the Legislature; namely, the Administrative, the Judicial, and the Sublegislative.

## SECTION 13

### XII. INSINCERITY ABJURED

Never, by deception or delusion in any shape,——never will I seek, to compass any point, either in the framing of Legislative ordinances or other authoritative instruments, or in debate. In all such discourses, my endeavours shall be constantly directed to the giving to them the greatest degree of *transparency*, and thence of simplicity, possible.

On every occasion, it shall be among the objects of my endeavours, to keep my own discourse, and, as far as depends upon myself, the discourse of others, as pure as may be from the taint of fallacy: of fallacy in every shape; and in particular, in those shapes in which it is delineated in the Table of Fallacies, which, to this purpose, is kept hung up, to serve as a perpetual memento, for the use of all hearers, as well as of all speakers: of all persons judging, as well as of all functionaries judged.[1]

## SECTION 14

### XIII. ARROGANCE ABJURED

Acknowledging that I am but an Agent, chosen by my Constituents, to bear a part in the managing of such of their concerns, as the nature of the case places them under an incapacity of managing for themselves,—I arrogate not to myself any superiority over them, or any one of them, on that score.

Of no power or influence attached to my situation, will I ever avail myself, to any such personal and sinister purpose, as that of creating dependence, or exacting or receiving homage. To avoid wounding, by hautiness of demeanour, the sensibility of such of my fellow-citizens, whose business brings them into communication with me, shall be among my sincere and constant cares.

---

[1] Despite this reference, Bentham did not prepare in a final form a Table of Fallacies either for the *Constitutional Code* or for *The Book of Fallacies* (Bowring, ii. 375–487). However, there are references in the manuscripts for *The Book of Fallacies* to such a Table being 'hung up'. See especially UC civ. 35–9. Furthermore, Bentham's 'Table of Contents' for *The Book of Fallacies* printed in Bowring, x. 519–21 might conceivably be used as such a Table. In *P.C.D.*, p. 17, Bentham revises this passage as follows: 'Table of Fallacies, which to this purpose, I could wish to see kept hung up, in every place of meeting in which any of the representatives of the people, or of their constituents, meet as such —to serve as a perpetual memento, for the use of all hearers, as well as of all speakers—of all persons judging, as well as of all functionaries judged—subject to such amendments, as future experience, observation, and reflection, may from time to time have suggested.'

# CHAPTER VIII

## PRIME MINISTER

### SECTION 1

#### FIELDS OF SERVICE

*[Enactive]*

ART. 1. Co-extensive with that of the Legislative is the Prime Minister's *local* field of service.

*Enactive*

ART. 2. Under the Legislature, to the Prime Minister's *logical* field of service belongs, as per Ch. iv. Art[s]. 4 and 5, whatsoever portion of the *Legislature's* logical field of service does *not* belong to the *Judiciary* Department, headed by the *Justice Minister*. For the particulars of the Prime Minister's service in this field, see §[§]2, 3, 4.

*Expositive*

ART. 3. By the Prime Minister's logical field of service, understand that ideal space, within which is to be found the aggregate of the several *persons* and *things* constituting the subject matter of the *operations* performed, and correspondent functions exercised, by him,—together with the aggregate of the *operations*, which he is *empowered* to exercise, in relation to those same *persons* and those same *things*.

*Expositive*

ART. 4. So also in the case of the several Ministers: as per Ch. ix. MINISTERS COLLECTIVELY, §[2], *Ministers and Subdepartments*.

*Ratiocinative*

ART. 5. *Question. Prime Minister* why thus denominated?

*Answer. Reasons.* Because by this denomination, his situation is more appositely designated than by any other: and, by incorrect ideas,—if associated with the denomination, of the functionary occupying so important a situation,—evil results in practice would, to no inconsiderable amount, be liable to be produced.

*Ratiocinative*

ART. 6. *Minister* is from the Latin, and means *servant*. All functionaries belonging to the Administrative are, as such, *servants*—

147

located and dislocable servants—of the *Legislature:* so much for the word *Minister*. In this same Department, of all other functionaries belonging to it, this functionary is the *superordinate:* so much for the adjunct *Prime*. He is, to those immediate servants of the *Constitutive*, what, in a Monarchy, the functionary of this same name is to the Monarch. Thus it is, that, with reference to one of those different authorities, his is subordinate; with reference to the other, superordinate.

### Ratiocinative

ART. 7. For significance and adequacy, no other denomination can compete with this. By the Spanish denomination *Gefe Politico* (Political Chief), employed in some cases, *superordination* only is presented to view: *subordination*, not.

### Ratiocinative

ART. 8. So as to the denomination *President:* a denomination which, from the *precedent* set in the Anglo-American United States, has been but too extensively adopted. To this denomination, that same objection of *inadequateness*, that is to say of *incompleteness*, from whence comes *incorrectness*, applies with equal force.

### Ratiocinative

ART. 9. In the case of these same United States,—it is, on another account, inapposite. To *preside*—from the Latin *præ* and *sedeo*—is to *sit before*, or *above*, a number of other persons, who, in the same place, are sitting at the same time. Now, this is what the President of the United States never does, nor ever can do. He is on purpose, and to a very wise purpose, placed at a perpetual distance from Congress, the body with which he communicates, and from which he receives mandates. By *'Message'* only—*that* is the word—are communications to them made by him. Thence comes the good consequence that, never taking part in their Debates, never does he expose himself to those angry feelings and imputations of sinister conduct, from which, consistently with the nature of man, and the nature of the case, debates, especially when on political subjects, can seldom be altogether free.[1]

---

[1] Although the Constitution of the United States does not expressly provide for it, the concept of the 'separation of powers' was largely taken for granted in its framing and certainly determined its interpretation. The result has been much as Bentham describes; and it may be further noted that, when he wrote, and for long afterwards, it was not the practice even for presidential 'Messages' to be delivered personally by the President in a speech to the Congress.

*Instructional*

ART. 10. The conception, naturally presented by the name *President*, to foreigners, is *that* of a person sitting in Congress, *presiding* over the proceedings of its two Assemblies, or one of them, just as the sort of functionary, called in English the *Chairman*, does in all formal meetings, private and non-official, as well as public and official. By men of the United States, this misconception has every now and then been noted as a mark of relative ignorance on the part of the thus misled foreigners. But the error, such as it is, lies, (it has been seen,) at the door—not of the foreigners, but of the natives. The *foreigners* take the word of the *natives*, and by this confidence it is that they are led into the mistake. The natives, at the same time, lose the credit of the arrangement, and the foreigners the benefit of the instruction derivable from it: they even receive misinstruction instead of it.

## SECTION 2

### FUNCTIONS

*Enactive*

ART. 1. To the Prime Minister, exercisable within his logical field of service, belong the functions following: namely,

I. *Executive* function. Exercise is given to it, in so far as, within that same field, he gives execution and effect, to any ordinances, emanating, whether immediately or unimmediately, from the Legislature: thus giving corresponding execution and effect to the rightly presumed will of the Constitutive.

*Enactive*

ART. 2. [II.] *Directive* function. In the exercise of this function,— by him, is the business of the Administrative Department conducted: by him, with the assistance of the several Ministers and their respective subordinates, performed. Under his direction they all are. In their functions may be seen his functions. For theirs, see Ch. ix, §4, and Ch. xi. in the several sections headed by the names of their respective officers.

*Enactive*

ART. 3. [III.] *Locative function.* In the exercise of this function, by him are the Ministers, all of them, located.

*Enactive*

ART. 4. *Promotion* is *location:* location to wit, in a situation higher than that which, before such promotion, the person so promoted occupied.

*Enactive*

ART. 5. [IV.] *Dislocative function.* In the exercise of this function, —by him are the Ministers, all of them, eventually dislocable:—provided that in the room of each one dislocated, a successor is, by the same act, lest the service of the Subdepartment should be at a stand, located: provided also, that any person who is then officiating, or has officiated, in the situation of Depute in that same office, as per §4, may be so located, in such sort, that his *term of service*, as per §5, in the situation of Minister Principal, shall continue, until the operations preliminary to location, as per Ch. ix. MINISTERS COLLECTIVELY, §16, *Locable who*, and §17, *Located how*, have been gone through, and no longer.

*Enactive*

ART. 6. So likewise their respective subordinates of every grade.

*Expositive*

ART. 7. *Suspension* is *temporary dislocation.*

*Enactive*

ART. 8. [V.] *Imperative* function. In the exercise of this function, to him belongs the command in chief of the whole *Land Defensive force.* For its constituent parts, see Art[s. 10, 11], and Ch. x. DEFENSIVE FORCE.

*Enactive*

ART. 9. So, of the whole of the *Sea Defensive* force. As to this, see Ch. x. §16, *Sea [Defensive] force.* As to the other functions, see §3, *Relation to Legislature*, and §4, *Self-suppletive function.*

*Enactive*

ART. 10. Power in relation to grades. As to those in the *Radical* or say *Non-stipendiary* Land force, or in one word *Militia*, see Ch. x. §3.

*Enactive*

ART. 11. As to those in the *Engrafted*, or say *Stipendiary* Land Defensive force, or in a word the *Stipendiary* branch of the *Army*,—

150

of every functionary thereto belonging, the grade is at all times at his entire disposal. Private or officer, he may at any time either locate, or to any superior situation, without exception, promote. So also, to any co-equal situation, transfer. So also suspend, or, subject to appeal as per Art. [16], dislocate.[a]

### Instructional

ART. 12. To be an apt possessor of this function, it is not necessary that the functionary should be a military man. In the United States' Constitutional Code, these same offices are given to the President: and, since Washington's time, no military man has borne that office: the object is—to place the force, in case of necessity, at his disposal.[1] On any such occasion he would act, of course, by professional advice.

### Enactive

ART. 13. So, as to the Stipendiary Sea Defensive force: or in one word *Stipendiary Navy.*

### Enactive

ART. 14. Except it be in the actual presence of an enemy,—every such act of location, promotion, transference, dislocation, and suspension, must, to be valid, be evidenced by an instrument, authenticated by his signature; or, if in the presence of an enemy, as soon afterwards as may be.

---

[a] Still more unlimited, according to the construction, put upon the clause in question, (namely, United States' Constitution, Article II, Section II, Clause I,) is, I have been assured by distinguished functionaries, the power understood to belong to the President in relation to the whole defensive force of the Union, including Army and Navy of the Union, and Militia of the several States 'when called into the actual service of the United States.' Yet, for this construction, the only support I can find is that afforded by the words '*Commander in chief.*' Edition of 1811. Bookseller, Jonathan Forbes. Place, Winchester. Say *more unlimited* the power, because, in that case, there is no such Appeal clause as in the present case, by Art. [16].[2]

---

[1] Bentham's statement was correct when Volume I of the *Constitutional Code* was printed in 1827, but had ceased to be so by the time the volume was published in 1830; for in 1828 Andrew Jackson (1767-1845), after a notable military career, had been elected for the first of his two terms as President.

[2] Article II, Section 2 of the Constitution provides that 'The President shall be Commander-in-Chief of the Army and Navy of the United States, and of the Militia of the several States, when called into the actual Service of the United States.' Historically this provision was to be an important factor in the growth of presidential power.

*Enactive*

ART. 15. Of every such instrument, exemplars[a] will, in the way of *manifold writing*, as per § [ 10 ], be written and disposed of as follows:

1. Kept in the Prime Minister's Office, one.
2. Kept by the Prime Minister himself, one.
3. Delivered with all practicable promptitude to the functionary so located, promoted, transferred, dislocated, or suspended, one.
4. Transmitted to the Registrar,—of the Office, into, in, or from, which the location, promotion, dislocation, or suspension has been made,—one.
5. In case of promotion,—transmitted to the Registrar of the Office, from which the promotion has been made,—one.
6. Transmitted to the Legislation Minister's Office, one.

*Enactive*

ART. 16. Any person,—who, by any such act of location, promotion, transference, dislocation, or suspension, regards himself as aggrieved,—may, for redress, or clearance of his character, apply as per Ch. ix. MINISTERS COLLECTIVELY, § [ 21 ], *Oppression obviated*. But, how completely soever cleared, by no decree of the Judicatory so constituted will he be relocated. Whether to relocate or not, the Prime Minister, on perusal of the evidence, will, on his responsibility, determine.

SECTION 3

RELATION TO THE LEGISLATURE

*Enactive*

ART. 1. Exceptions excepted, no otherwise than by epistolary discourse, to wit, by Message, does the Prime Minister address the Legislature. For reasons, see § 1, *Fields of service*, Art. [ 9 ]. No place has he in the Legislation Chamber. For the places which the several Ministers have therein, see Ch. ix. MINISTERS COLLECTIVELY, § 24, *Legislation-regarding functions*.

*Enactive*

ART. 2. Exception is—if, on some extraordinary occasion, for the purpose of explanation, he has been invited or ordered by the Legislature to a personal conference.

---

[a] (*Exemplars.*) Not copies, nor transcripts: they being all alike originals.

*Enactive*

ART. 3. On the occasion of a Message sent by him to the Legislature, functions exercisible by him are the following:

I. The *Informative:* to wit, when an occasion occurs, on which the Legislature has need of information concerning a state of things, the particulars of which would not otherwise be so clearly, correctly, comprehensively, and trust-worthily learnt from any other quarter.

*Enactive*

ART. 4. Examples are—

1. A state of things resulting from a negotiation with an Agent of any foreign power.

2. Facts indicative of need of melioration, in the constitution of any part of the Official establishment, or in the conduct of any functionary thereto belonging.

*Enactive*

ART. 5. II. The *Indicative* or *Suggestive* function. In the exercise of this function, he proposes, in *general* terms, subject-matters for the consideration of the Legislature.

*Enactive*

ART. 6. III. The *Initiative* function. In the exercise of this function, he proposes, *in terminis*, the tenor of any proposed ordinance or order, which, with or without amendment, appears to him to be in its purport, fit to receive the sanction of the Legislature.[a]

*Enactive*

ART. 7. Of the exercise of this function, the effect may be produced by the Prime Minister, either by Message in his own name,—or through the instrumentality of a Minister,—in the name of the Minister,—or through the instrumentality of a Deputy, in the name of the Deputy.

*Enactive*

ART. 8. For any definite and serious evil, which can be shown to have had place, or to be in imminent danger of taking place, for want

[a] In the Anglo-American United States, such is the practice.[1]

---

[1] Article II, Section 3 of the Constitution provides that 'The President shall from time to time give to the Congress Information of the State of the Union, and recommend to their Consideration such Measures as he shall judge necessary and expedient.'

of his having given exercise to any one of the above functions, he is responsible.

### Instructional

ART. 9. Except where, for release from this responsibility, it may be advisable for him to communicate, by Message,—communication by the instrumentality of a Minister, in the name of the Minister, if consenting and approving, will be the more eligible course: to wit, in respect of its leaving the freedom of the Assembly less exposed to disturbance.

### Enactive. Instructional

ART. 10. IV. The *Statistic function*. In the exercise of this function, at the commencement of every year,—the Prime Minister will, in the form of a Message, lay before the Legislative Assembly, the general condition of the State, according to his view of it, pointing their attention, in general terms, to any measures which present themselves as conducing to the conservation or the melioration of it.

## SECTION 4

### SELF-SUPPLETIVE FUNCTION

### Enactive

ART. 1. Lest the business of his office should be at any time at a stand,—to the Prime Minister belongs the power of *self-supply;* with the obligation of keeping it in exercise. It is exercised by the location of an at all times dislocable *Depute.*

### Expositive

ART. 2. By a *Depute*, understand in this case a functionary, who, being thus located and dislocable, exercises, on the occasions, on which the business would otherwise be at a stand, the functions belonging to the office; location of subordinates excepted.

### Enactive

ART. 3. These occasions are—
  1. Inaptitude of the Principal, by reason of infirmity, whether of body or mind.
  2. Vacancy of the office.

### Enactive

ART. 4. Exception excepted, as per Art. 2, to every branch of the service of the Principal, does the power of the Depute extend.

### Enactive. Ratiocinative

ART. 5. Punitionally, as well as compensationally and dislocationally, for the acts of the Depute, is the Principal responsible. By acceptance of the office,—not simply for performance, but for apt and complete performance, of the functions, does he contract: irresponsible, he might safely commit any breach of trust, in any shape, by the instrumentality of any person consenting to subject himself to the risk.

### Expositive

ART. 6. *Punitionally:* that is to say, to the purpose of being subjected to punishment,—suffering under the name of *punishment, over and above* the suffering produced by the exaction of *compensation:* or, *in lieu* of it, in those cases in which compensation cannot have place: for example, where there is no individual specially wronged. *Compensationally:* that is to say, to the purpose of being compelled to yield compensation. *Dislocationally:* that is to say, to the effect of being dislocated.

### [*Enactive*]

ART. 7. Within {          } days after his own location, a Prime Minister is expected to locate such his Depute: and thereafter, immediately upon the dislocation of a preceding, a succeeding one.

### Enactive

ART. 8. The instrument of location, with the year, month, and day of the month, will be signed by the principal, and in token of acceptance, by the Depute. Exemplars three: disposed of as per §[2,] Art. [15], No[s]. 1, 2, 3.

### Enactive

ART. 9. The Principal and the Depute will not officiate at the same time. The power of this office must not, without necessity, be shifted from hand to hand. If, on any day, an instrument has been signed by the Principal, an instrument signed on that same day by the Depute is of no validity; unless on the sudden incapacity or death of the principal: in either of which events, in case of urgency, an instrument, signed by the Depute, stating the event and declaring the urgency, may be valid. But, in this case, the Principal cannot act on the same day as that on which, by the act of his Depute, he has, as above, been declared incapable.

*Enactive*

ART. 10. On the decease of the Principal, the functions of the office, the locative excepted, as per Art. 2, are exercised by the Depute, until a successor has been located; to wit, as per §[8], by the Legislature.

*Enactive*

ART. 11. Dislocable at any time is the Prime Minister Depute by the Principal: as likewise by either of the authorities by which the Principal is dislocable.

## SECTION 5

### TERM OF SERVICE

*Enactive*

ART. 1. Of a Prime Minister, the term of service is {four} years.

*Enactive*

ART. 2. No Prime Minister is re-eligible, until there are in existence, at the same time, out of whom choice may be made {two or three} quondam Prime Ministers, he being one.

*Enactive* ·

ART. 3. {      } Days before the cessation of a Prime Minister's term of service, the election is performed: as to which, see §8.

*Enactive*

ART. 4. If, antecedently to the expiration of a Prime Minister's term of service, the Legislature has omitted to make a fresh Election, the omission is, on the part of all by whose default it has had place, an anti-constitutional offence, tending to substitute [for] a Representative Democracy, Monarchy, or Aristocracy; and, punitionally, as per Ch. vi. §28, as well as dislocationally, every offender is responsible.

## SECTION 6

### REMUNERATION

*Enactive. Ratiocinative. Instructional*

ART. 1. The Prime Minister's pay is {        } a year, paid quarterly in advance. From *unwilling* hands, receipt of ulterior emolument is *extortion:* from *willing, corruption.*

*Instructional*

ART. 2. As to this possessor of the supreme single-seated situation, note, that though he is at all times subordinate to the majority of the Members of the Legislature in their aggregate capacity, yet is his power incomparably greater than that of any one, taken apart: inferior, in respect of his dislocability,—he is *superior* even to the *whole* Legislature, in respect of the agreeable and desirable nature of one part, to wit the *locative* part, of the power exercised by him,— the *extent* to which, and *frequency* with which, the exercise of it is called forth,—and the longer *duration*, as per §5, of his *term of service*.

## SECTION 7

### LOCABLE WHO

*Enactive*

ART. 1. Exceptions excepted,—in this office, any person, who, in the judgment of the Legislative authority, is, in respect of all points of appropriate aptitude taken together, most apt, is locable.

*Enactive*

ART. 2. Excepted are,
   I. All Monarchs, and every person, connected by any known tie of consanguinity, or affinity, with any Monarch.

*Enactive*

ART. 3. II. Every person, who has not, either in a resident or migratory state, passed at least {         } years, in some part or other of the territory of this State.

## SECTION 8

### LOCATED HOW

*Enactive*

ART. 1. Located is this functionary, by those, to whose will it belongs to him to give execution and effect. He is located by the Legislature.

*Enactive*

ART. 2. Next after pronouncing respectively the Inaugural Declaration, as per Ch. vii. or their adhesion thereunto,—the Members of

the Legislature proceed to vote for the Election of the Prime Minister.[1] The votes are given—first in the secret mode, as per Election
Code, §8, *Election how:*[2] then immediately in the open mode.

### Enactive

ART. 3. Given in the secret mode, the votes are not counted, looked
at, or in any other manner, any of them, known,—till after the result
of the votation in the open mode has been declared.

### Enactive

ART. 4. If, of the two different modes, the results be in favour of different persons, he who has the majority in the open mode is located.

### Enactive

ART. 5. If he who, in the open mode, has the *comparative* majority,
has not the *absolute* majority,—he, and the person whose number of
votes comes next to his, are thereupon voted for, without the others.
On this latter occasion, in case of equal numbers, lot decides. For the
mode, see Ch. ix. MINISTERS COLLECTIVELY, §16, [*Locable
who*].[3]

### Instructional

ART. 6. For the sake of instruction by experience, is this double
mode of election here proposed. Neither in the shape of delay, vexation, or expense, nor in any other shape, does *evil* present itself, as
likely to be produced; at any rate, in quantity, capable of outweigh-
ing the *good*, attached to whatsoever *instruction* may be the result.
Of this instruction, the particular nature seems not, however, very
easy to be anticipated. By the *open* mode, each man's vote is subjected, at the same time, to the *seductive* influence of his *Co-Deputies*,
and of the several *Candidates*, for the situation to be filled: on the
other hand, so is it to the *tutelary* influence of the *Public Opinion
Tribunal*,—organ of the Constitutive authority. By the *secret* mode,
it is exempted from both these antagonizing influences: on the other
hand, it is subjected to the *seductive* influence of the personal interests, and affections, sympathetic and antipathetic, of each individual
voter. After a certain length of experience,—the Legislature for the
time being, under the guidance of the public voice, will be in a condi-

---

[1] Bentham seems to imply here that the Legislator's Inaugural Declaration is
to be recited twice, since the first reading takes place, in front of the electors,
before the Legislature meets: see Ch. VIII, § 1, Art. 1, pp. 133-4.

[2] On the Election Code generally, see Ch. VI, § 4n, p. 48n.

[3] See especially the supplement to § 16, Arts. 61-78.

tion to pronounce, on the ground of experience, between the *three* competing modes: to wit, the two simple ones, and the compound, composed of both.

From the application of the same course of experiment to the *Prime Ministers* of the several Sublegislatures, the instruction obtainable from this source will, in the proportion of their number, receive diversification and increase.


## SECTION 9

### DISLOCABLE HOW

*Enactive. Ratiocinative*

ART. 1. Dislocable is this functionary at any time, by that authority, for the giving execution and effect to whose will, he has been located. He is dislocable by the Legislature.

*Enactive. Ratiocinative*

ART. 2. So, by the Constitutive authority, as per Ch. v. §2.

*Enactive*

ART. 3. Other efficient causes of dislocatedness in this case, are the same as in the case of a Member of the Legislature, as per Ch. vi. [LEGISLATURE,] §30, *Dislocable how*, No[s]. 1, 2, 3, 4, 5, 7.


## SECTION 10

### REGISTRATION SYSTEM.[1]

*Enactive. Ratiocinative*

ART. 1. For the more commodious, correct, prompt, uniform, and all-comprehensive performance of the process and function of

---

[1] When Bentham was preparing Volume I of the *Constitutional Code* for the press, he published this section as a 'passage of an about-to-be published proposed Constitutional Code' in an article, 'Bentham on Humphreys' Property Code' in the *Westminster Review*, vi (1826), 446–507. The article was subsequently printed as a pamphlet, *Article Eight of the Westminster Review No. XII. for October 1826, on Mr. Humphreys' Observations on the English Law of Real Property, with the Outline of a Code, etc. By Jeremy Bentham, Esq.*, London, 1827, where the extract from the *Constitutional Code* appears at pp. 42–4. The article and extract are reprinted in Bowring, v. 387–416; the extract is at pp. 406–7. For the differences between these earlier versions and the later text of the section, see the Collations, pp. 517 ff. Most of the variants are minor, and those of interest have been noted in the text here.

Registration in all the several departments and subdepartments,—as likewise on the part of the Prime Minister, for the correspondent receipt by him of all documents, the receipt, and, as occasion calls, the perusal of which may be necessary to the most apt exercise of the several functions belonging to his own office,—he will, as soon as may be, cause to be established and employed in practice in the several offices of the several departments and their subdepartments, the Sublegislative included, the mode of writing styled the *Manifold* mode.[a]

[a] *Manifold Writing. 1. Mode of execution.*[1]
In the *manifold way*, the mode of writing is as follows:—
Instead of a pen, a style, of the hardest and strongest metal, without ink, is employed. Under the style, as under a pen, are laid, one under another, in number the same as that of the exemplars required, sheets of appropriate thin *paper*, alternating with the correspondent number of thin sheets of *silk*, into each of which has been worked all over, some of the black matter used in printing, and called *printer's ink*. In this way, by one and the same course taken at one and the same time, by the style, may exemplars be produced, in any number not exceeding twelve, with not much more expense of time and labour, than is commonly employed in the production of a single exemplar, by pen and ink. Eight exemplars at once, all of them perfectly legible, have thus been habitually produced. In London, this mode of writing has for about twenty years been regularly applied, to the purpose of conveying simultaneous information to a number of newspapers. To other purposes it has also been employed, under the eye of the author of this work.
For the performance of the operation, the stronger the hand the better.
To perform in perfection requires some practice, in addition to that which has been applied to the art of writing with pen and ink.
If there be a difference in the exemplars, that which is furthest from the style, not that which is the nearest, gives the most perfect and clearest impression.
*Silk*, when a good deal worn, answers much better than when new.
Supposing this mode of writing employed to any considerable extent, the silk would require to be smoothed by some appropriate means: for example, by being passed through rollers.
The *thinner* the silk the better. That which has been mostly employed is that which, in English, is called sarsenet. As to the paper, that which is at present employed is called fine single crown tissue paper: price 19s. 6d. per bundle, containing two reams.
In strength, by reason of its thinness it cannot be expected to be altogether equal to what is most commonly in use in England: nor in whiteness, nor thence, in respect of beauty and legibility, are all the exemplars, by reason of the oil, which is an indispensable ingredient. They are nevertheless perfectly apt for these its intended purposes. No more than half the number wanted need be or ought to be taken on the oiled paper: to wit, every other one. The paper of the others will remain in primitive whiteness, except a slight extravasation of the oil

[1] Bowring, ix. 209 omits this note here because it had appeared in an earlier volume of the edition (v. 406): see the discussion of earlier versions of this section, p. 159.

*Ratiocinative. Instructional*

ART. 2. Particular uses of the manifold mode of writing are as follows—

By the multitude of exemplars, produced at an expense, which, with the exception of that of the paper, is less than the expense of two in the ordinary mode, it affords means for furnishing, at that small expense, to parties on both sides, for themselves and assistants, all such documents as they can stand in need of.

*Ratiocinative. Instructional*

ART. 3. Every exemplar being, to an iota, exactly and necessarily the same as every other,—the expense of revision by skill and labour[1] is thereby saved, as well as *unintentional aberration* rendered impossible.

*Ratiocinative. Instructional*

ART. 4. An examplar, kept in the Registrar's Office, will serve as a standard, whereby a security will be afforded against all *intentional* falsification, on the part of the possessor of any other exemplar.

*Ratiocinative. Instructional*

ART. 5. By the reduction thus effected, in the expense of all judicial writings, emaning from the Judicatory,—the protection, afforded by Judicature[2] in its best form, to wit, that which has for its ground orally elicited and immediately minuted evidence, will be brought within the reach of a vast proportion of the whole number of the people, to whom it could not otherwise be afforded.

of the ink round the edges of the letters. The effect might even be produced by a single oiled paper: to wit, the one to which the style is immediately applied. But in this case the labour necessary to produce the effect will be greater.[3]

---

[1] So 1830 and Bowring; *WR*, 1827 pamphlet and Bowring, v, 'skilled labour'.

[2] So 1830 and Bowring; *WR*, 1827 pamphlet and Bowring, v, 'judication'. The latter reading fits the context better, but Bentham's meaning is clear.

[3] The inventor of manifold writing was Ralph Wedgwood (1766-1837). After an unsuccessful career as a potter, Wedgwood came to London with his new invention in 1805. Following a brief period of poverty, he soon became prosperous. Bentham was an early enthusiast: writing to Samuel Bentham on 23 September 1808, using Wedgwood's invention, he declared: 'I find it performs with great facility' (BL Add. MS 33,544, fos. 388-9). See also Bowring, vi. 576n.

*Ratiocinative. Instructional*

ART. 6. A collateral benefit—a degree of security hitherto un-exampled, against *destruction* of judicial documents, by *calamity* or *delinquency*, may thus be afforded, by the lodging of exemplars, in divers offices in which they would be requisite for other purposes: exemplars of documents from the Immediate Judicatories being, at the Appellate Judicatory, requisite for the exercise of its judicial functions; and, in the office of Justice Minister, for the exercise of his inspective and melioration-suggestive functions. So also in the other Departments.

*Instructional*

ART. 7. To save the expense of custody, and prevent the useful from being drowned in the mass of useless matter,—the Legislature will make arrangements for the periodical destruction or elimination of such as shall appear useless: care being at all times taken for the pre-servation of all such as can continue to be of use, either eventually for a judicial purpose, or for the exercise of the statistic and meliora-tive-suggestive functions, as per Ch. ix. MINISTERS COLLEC-TIVELY, §[§7], 12; Ch. xi. MINISTERS SEVERALLY, §[2], *Legislation Minister;* and Ch. xii. JUDICIARY COLLECTIVELY, §[§]19, 20, 21, 22.[1]

## SECTION 11

### PUBLICATION SYSTEM

*Expositive*

ART. 1. By the *publication system*, understand that, by which the several matters of fact, acquaintance wherewith is in any wise ma-terial to the business of the Subdepartment or Department in ques-tion, are rendered, or endeavoured to be rendered, at all times, present, to the mind of every person in whose instance such presence is likely to be in any way of use. The greater the *number* of the per-sons, to whose minds, at any given point of time, it is actually made present, the greater the *extent* given to the *publication*—to the *pub-licity* thus effected.

*Enactive. Instructional*

ART. 2. Exceptions excepted,—in every Subdepartment and Depart-ment, and in every Office belonging to each Subdepartment and Department, publicity will at all times be maximized.

---

[1] *WR*, 1827 pamphlet and Bowring, v, add '§ 23' to this cross-reference.

*Instructional*

ART. 3. Exception 1. The evil, produced by the unavoidable *expense*, preponderant over the good produced by the extent proposed to be given in the instance in question to the publicity. Antagonize thus one with another the two principles, and the rules respectively prescribed by them.

Rule 1. *Maximize publicity.*

Rule 2. *Maximize frugality.*

Rule 3. By every deduction made from the amount of the expense, the *extent* given to publicity may, with clear advantage, be increased. Hence, one advantage of the *manifold writing mode*, as per §10, Registration System.

*Instructional*

ART. 4. The *good* produced by publicity is of two sorts: to wit, 1, the *general;* 2, the *particular.* The *general* consists in the efficiency it gives to the force of the law, and to that of the Public Opinion Tribunal: to wit, in the character of an instrument of security for appropriate aptitude on the part of all public functionaries: the *particular* consists in the particular use derivable from the information, afforded concerning each particular matter of fact, to the several individuals, whose happiness may be promoted, or their conduct beneficially influenced by it.

*Instructional*

ART. 5. Exception 2. Where, in this or that particular case, in addition to the evil of *expense*, if any, the evil of the publicity would, in the instance of this or that particular person or class of persons, be preponderant over the good.

*Instructional*

ART. 6. Of the Subdepartments in which this preponderance is most apt to have place, examples are the following:

1. The *Constitutive Department:* to wit, in respect of the evil that would result from its being known which way the several voters, or any of them, gave their votes. For the reasons for which the evil of publicity would, in this instance, be destructive of the Constitution, and not accompanied by good in any shape, see ELECTION CODE, *Preliminary Explanations.*[1] The thing requisite is—that, of each

---

[1] See *Bentham's Radical Reform Bill* (Bowring, iii. 558-97), Bowring, iii. 558-63. The Preliminary Explanations contain a justification of secrecy in suffrage. On the Election Code generally, see Ch. VI, § 4n, p. 48n.

voter, the *inward* wish be expressed by his vote: to wit, on the presumption, that, in so far as, by the direction given to it, he sees no probability of advancing his own at the expense of the general interest, he will give to it such direction as, according to what he thinks or has heard, will be most for the advantage of the general interest. But, in so far as this direction were known, and he apprized of its being so, the wish expressed by his vote would be——the wish of whatever person he had most to fear or hope from: and, as the number of the persons, who have most to fear or hope from a man, will be in the conjunct proportion of his legal power and his opulence,——hence, supposing votes public, a constitution, democratical in *appearance*, may be aristocratical in *effect:* and the happiness provided for——not that of the *many*, but, at the expense of the many, that of the *few.*

2. The *Army Bis-subdepartment:* to wit, by making known to the enemy of the State the strong and the weak points of its means of defence.

3. The *Navy Bis-subdepartment:* the two together constituting the *Defensive Force Subdepartment:* to wit, by information given as above.[1]

4. The *Preventive Service Subdepartment:* to wit, in respect of the like information given to delinquents.

[5]. The *Health Subdepartment:* to wit, in respect of any such evil as may be liable to result from its being known who the persons are who have been labouring under any disease to which disrepute is attached.

6. The *Foreign Relation Subdepartment:* to wit, by information given, to those, who at any time are *liable* to become *enemies*, and who are at all times, *in one way or other, rivals.*

7. Add the *Judiciary Department*, as to which, see Ch. xii. JUDICIARY COLLECTIVELY, §14, *Publicity, &c.*

### Instructional. Ratiocinative

ART. 7. In each several case, in so far as secrecy is provided for, the assumption is——that, in that case, publicity would be liable to become subservient to hostile purposes:——to the support of this or that

---

[1] Bentham generally reserves the term 'subdepartment' for the thirteen subdepartments listed in Ch. IX, §2, Arts. 1-2, pp. 171-2. 'Department' is used mostly to designate the four supreme authorities listed in Ch. IV, Art. 1, p. 26: see 'Judiciary Department' in no. 7 of the present article. 'Bis-subdepartment' is rarely used. Occasionally Bentham deviates from this arrangement by referring to subdepartments either as departments or as bis-subdepartments. Here he considers the whole Defensive Force administration as a single subdepartment and accordingly refers to what are normally called the Army and Navy subdepartments as bis-subdepartments.

interest, in hostility with the interest of the greatest number in this State. In the case of the *Defensive Force* and *Preventive Service Subdepartments*, the effect of the publicity might, if extended to certain persons, be the giving aid to hostile designs already entertained, and endeavoured to be carried into effect: in the case of the *Foreign Relation Subdepartment*, it might be—either the giving aid to such designs, if already entertained, or even the giving birth to the like designs.

### Instructional. Ratiocinative

ART. 8. In each such case,—a point of *time* will however be assignable, after which the evil at first producible by publicity, will have ceased to be thus producible. But, at no time can the good produced by publicity cease to exist or to operate. For, at no time can the operation of the tutelary power of the Public Opinion Tribunal— that judicial power to which the publicity furnishes its necessary evidence—cease to be needed. If it be known, that, upon the cessation of the particular demand for the secrecy, it will cease,—the obstruction afforded by it to the operation of the legal as well as Public Opinion Tribunals, and the evil produced by it, will be minimized, and the quantity much reduced.

### Instructional

ART. 9. Thus it is—that, under this system, to the extent of the *publicity* thus requisite and thus ordained,—and thence to the correspondent and necessarily previous *registration*,—there are no limits, other than those which are set to it by one or other of two considerations: the one is—the *expense* necessitated by the operation; a consideration which applies to all cases: the other is—the demand for temporary *secrecy:*—a demand, the nature and extent of which are produced and regulated by various special causes, depending on the nature of the business of the department or subdepartment.

### Ratiocinative. Instructional

ART. 10. As there are not any limits other than as above, to the extent of the demand for publication, so neither are there to that of the good derivable from it. As to this, see the sections intituled *Securities, &c.* in Ch. vi. [LEGISLATURE]; Ch. viii. PRIME MINISTER (this present chapter); Ch. ix. MINISTERS COLLECTIVELY; and Ch. xii. JUDICIARY COLLECTIVELY; Ch. xxvi. LOCAL HEADMEN; Ch. xxvii. LOCAL REGISTRARS. For particulars, in the case of the Administrative Department, see Ch. ix. MINISTERS COLLECTIVELY: §7, *Statistic function.*

## Expositive

ART. 11. Considered in respect of its *extent*, publication may be distinguished into *internal* and *external*.

Understand by *internal* or say *special*, that mode of publication, the operation of which is confined to the particular official situation, or the particular Subdepartment, in the course of the business of which the facts in question came into existence; by *external*, that produced by the conveyance of the information, to persons other than those belonging to, or having business with, that same Office, Department, or Subdepartment: of external publicity the benefit therefore is not confined to any other limits than those which apply to the numbers of mankind at the time in question and all succeeding ones.

## Expositive. Instructional

ART. 12. Of internal publication, the appropriate *instrument* will be the *manifold writing apparatus*, as per §10; of external, *the printing press*, by which to the degree that has been seen, the expense is diminished.

## Instructional

ART. 13. To both these modes and degrees of publication, the *Registration System* is not only subservient but necessary; and in this subserviency may be seen its only uses, over and above those which consist in the information, which, in the case of each official situation, is afforded, to the functionary, by whom, at the time in question, it is occupied.

## Instructional

ART. 14. Rules for limitation of the exceptive rules, by which secrecy is prescribed.

Rule 1. The exemption from publication should not go beyond the reason for it: the concealment, beyond the demand for concealment: that is to say, beyond the extent of the evil liable to be produced by divulgation.

Rule 2. The evil from divulgation depends partly upon the situation of the *persons*, by whom the information is received; partly upon the *time* at which it is received.

Rule 3. Limitation as to *persons*. In the case of a Department or Subdepartment, the business of which may present a demand for secrecy,——the exclusion from information should not extend to any functionary, in whose instance information is necessary to the due performance of his official service: especially if at [his] hands no communication is likely to be made to any person, who is likely to employ it in giving rise or existence to the evil apprehended.

Rule 4. But, as every addition, made to the number of the persons possessed of the information, adds to the probability of promiscuous or otherwise mischievous communication,—by no person should the communication be suffered to be received, other than him or them, in whose instance the receipt of it is necessary to the due performance of the services in question, as above.

### Instructional

ART. 15. Limitation as to *time*.

Certain Subdepartments there are, in which the nature of the business seems scarcely to admit of any limitation to the time during which the good of the service may require the secrecy to be observed. These are—1. The Defensive Force Subdepartment 2. The Foreign Relation Subdepartment. In these instances, for preventing the concealment from being continued longer than the good of the service requires, two arrangements present themselves.

I. Let it be part of the business of the *Prime Minister* from time to time—say at the beginning of each year,—to make a *Report* to the Legislature, stating the instances, in which, in these several Subdepartments, the demand for secrecy has, in his opinion, ceased, that divulgation may be made accordingly.

### Instructional

ART. 16. II. In like manner, and on the same principle, let the Legislature annually appoint a *Committee* for the same purpose: that its *Report* may serve as a check to the Prime Minister's Report: for which purpose, it should make known all instances, if any, in which continuance is given by him to any concealment, which, in their opinion, is not necessary.

### Instructional

ART. 17. On both occasions,—instead of, or along with, the instances, in which the concealment requires to be *continued*, the *Report* may have for its subject matter, those in which it may, without prejudice to the service, be *discontinued*, and divulgation substituted. In every instance in which such *continuance* is recommended, such mode of *designation* will, of course, be employed, as shall suffice for preventing all such disclosure as is not intended.

167

*Instructional*

ART. 18. Note, that the greater the proportion of new members is in each successive Legislature, the less the probability is, that concealment will be continued beyond the duration of the exigency.

## SECTION 12

### SECURITIES FOR APPROPRIATE APTITUDE

*[Enactive]*

ART. 1. For maximization of appropriate aptitude on the part of the Prime Minister, securities here provided are as follows:

1. The *Registration* system, as per §10; whereby, as in the case of Members of the Legislature, his several official acts——including all those of his subordinates, which, by his authorization or acquiescence, are rendered his——are, at the pleasure of his superordinates: to wit, the *Legislative* authority, and the *Constitutive*,——submitted to their cognizance.

2. The *Publication* system, as per §11; whereby, with no exceptions,——other than those respectively made, by the consideration of the *expense*, and by the demand presented by *special cause* for *temporary secrecy*,——those same acts will be promptly, regularly, constantly, and effectually, presented to the cognizance of those same superordinate authorities.

3. *Dislocability* by the *Legislature* as per §9, Art. 1.

4. *Dislocability* by the *Constitutive* authority as per §9, Art. 2.

5. *Responsibility*, for insufficiency in the exercise of his several functions, *informative*, *indicative*, and *initiative*, as per §3, *Relation to Legislature*.

6. *Dislocability*, by *acceptance* or *retention*, of any other *office* belonging to the Official Establishment of this State: as in the case of a Member of the Legislature, as per Ch. vi. §[30, *Dislocable how*, Art. 1].

7. So, by acceptance or retention, of any *office, gift,* or *factitious honour or dignity*, at the hands of any foreign government, as in that same case, as per Ch. vi. §[30, Art. 1], or at the hands of any individual foreigner, for favour received of the Prime Minister, or expected to be done by him, in the exercise of any function belonging to his office.

8. Obligation, to keep in exercise, a *Depute* or Deputes; coupled with responsibility for their aptitude, as per §4, *Self-suppletive function*.

9. *Responsibility*, for the aptitude of his immediate *subordinates*, as per Art[s]. 2, 3, 4, here ensuing.

10. *Securities* applying to the several situations of these his *subordinates* and instruments, as per Ch. ix. MINISTERS COLLECTIVELY, §25, *Securities.*

11. In particular, checks to arbitrariness, in his choice of subordinates,——by means of the evidence of appropriate aptitude necessitated on the part of all persons locable in the Administrative Department, as per Ch. ix. MINISTERS COLLECTIVELY, §16, *Locable who*, and the pecuniary competition, necessitated, as per §17, *Located how.*

12. Functions, *statistic, censorial,* and *melioration-suggestive*, exercisible by all persons, as Members of the *Public Opinion Tribunal*, in relation to his situation and his conduct therein, as in the case of the Legislature and its Members, as per Ch. v, CONSTITUTIVE, §5, *Function[s] of the Public Opinion Tribunal.*

13. Dislocability, and responsibility, punitional and compensational, for criminal delinquency, as in the case of a Member of the Legislature, as per Ch. vi. §28, *[Legislation] Penal Judicatory.*

### Enactive

ART. 2. If, from any person, offering adequate security for eventual responsibility, information has, publicly or privately, been received by him, by[1] indication of misconduct, or inaptitude, in any shape, on the part of any Minister, as manifested by any individual occurrence,——to the Prime Minister it thereupon belongs, forthwith to take remedial measures, by enquiry instituted.

### Enactive

ART. 3. At the requisition of any such indicator, his name and personality may be, and at his desire ought to be, provisionally kept secret: subject nevertheless to disclosure, for the purpose of judicial pursuit or public exposure, in case of mendacity, insincerity, or falsehood, accompanied with temerity, in respect of the indication so afforded.

### Enactive. Ratiocinative

ART. 4. To the case of all existing Ministers located by any predecessor of his, this responsibility of the Prime Minister extends, as well as to the case of those located by himself: if originally unapt, the functionary ought not to have been located: if become unapt, he ought not to have been continued.

---

[1] Bowring, 'of'. Neither reading seems entirely satisfactory.

*Enactive*

ART. 5. To the Prime Minister accordingly with relation to those his immediate subordinates, apply the several securities established in those instances in relation to the several subordinates: as per Ch. ix. MINISTERS COLLECTIVELY, §[25], *Securities, etc.* Art[s]. [26, 27, 28, 29].

# CHAPTER IX

## MINISTERS COLLECTIVELY

### SECTION 1

#### ENDS IN VIEW

*Instructional*

ART. 1. ENDS IN VIEW—as in every other Department of the Official Establishment, so in this, are—1, maximization of appropriate good: 2, minimization of correspondent evil. Under these two heads may, on this occasion, be comprised the two all-comprehensive branches of the main universal end—the greatest happiness of the greatest number.

*Expositive*

ART. 2. By *the appropriate good*, understand, on this occasion, the due and successful performance of the several operations, by the performance of which the functions belonging to the several functionaries employed in the Administration Department are exercised, and the business of their several offices carried on: by *the correspondent evil*, evil in its several shapes—to wit, delay, vexation, and expense to functionaries and *suitors:* main end, maximization of the good: collateral end or ends, minimization of the evil.[a]

[a] In the case of the logical division thus made, the *condivident parts* (it may perhaps be observed), in some places, contrary to rule, run one into another: *good*, meaning pleasure or exemption from pain, or an efficient cause of the one or the other: *evil*, pain, or loss of pleasure, or an efficient cause, as above. But, as language has been framed, the entanglement, such as it is, was unavoidable; and, at any rate, in the first-mentioned of these ends, the *good* will be seen to be most *preeminent;* in the last-mentioned, the *evil.*

Of the matter of good, the component elementary parts, or say *species*, are frequently styled *benefits;* of the matter of evil, *burthens:* two corresponding

## Instructional

ART. 3. In these may be beheld two landmarks, set up for the guidance of the legislator in his course. The collateral end, considered in these its several branches, has the more need to be here noted, the more apt it is to be overlooked: in particular, so far as regards *suitors*. See this distinction further developed in §7, *Statistic function*.

## Expositive

ART. 4. By a *suitor*, as in the case of the Judiciary Department, (as per Ch. xii. JUDICIARY COLLECTIVELY,) so in this, understand any person considered as having business to transact with any functionary belonging to this Department, and acting or applied to in such his capacity.

For the arrangements having more particularly in view this same collateral end, see §21, *Oppression obviated*, and §25, *Securities, &c.*

## SECTION 2

### MINISTERS AND SUBDEPARTMENTS

## Enactive

ART. 1. Under the Prime Minister are the Ministers following: namely,

1. The Election Minister; as to whose functions, see §4, *Functions in all*, and Ch. xi. §1.

2. The Legislation Minister; as to whose functions, see §4, and Ch. xi. §2.

3. The Army Minister; as to whose functions, see §4, and Ch. xi, §3.

4. The Navy Minister; as to whose functions, see §4, and Ch. xi. §4.

[5]. The Preventive Service Minister; as to whose functions, for the prevention of delinquency and calamity, see §4, and Ch. xi. §[5].

[6]. The Interior Communication Minister; as to whose functions, see §4, and Ch. xi. §[6].

7. The Indigence Relief Minister; as to whose functions, see §4, and Ch. xi. §7.

and as it were correlative denominations, for the employment of which the demand will, under every system of law, be of continual occurrence.

By a *benefit*, is meant a portion of the matter of *good*;—by a *burthen*, a portion of the matter of *evil:*—considered as experienced by some person from the operation of some particular cause.

8. The Education Minister; as to whose functions, see §4, and Ch. xi. §8.

9. The Domain Minister; as to whose functions, see §4, and Ch. xi. §9.

10. The Health Minister; as to whose functions, see §4, and Ch. xi. §10.

11. The Foreign Relation Minister; as to whose functions, see §4, and Ch. xi. §[11].

12. The Trade Minister; as to whose functions, see §4, and Ch. xi. §12.

13. The Finance Minister; as to whose functions, see §4, and Ch. xi. §13.

*Enactive*

ART. 2. To each Minister belongs a Subdepartment of the corresponding denomination; but, under the authority of one and the same Minister there may, upon occasion, be any number of these same Subdepartments.

*Expositive*

ART. 3. Collectively taken, the functionaries, who, under the Prime Minister, are respectively at the head of these Subdepartments, are denominated *Ministers:* severally, they are denominated from the names of the respective Subdepartments: as thus—*Election Minister, Legislation Minister*, and so on.

*Expositive*

ART. 4. But, though of each Minister the *logical field of service* is styled *a Subdepartment*, his official name is—not *Subminister*, but simply *Minister.*

*Expositive*

ART. 5. Accordingly, as often as, in this Code, the word *Ministers* occurs, understand by that denomination—not the *Prime Minister*, but only these same Ministers.

*Enactive. Expositive*

ART. 6. *Sub-Minister* is the official name, of a functionary who, to a Sublegislature, bears the same relation as the above-mentioned Ministers bear to the Legislature.

*Enactive. Expositive*

ART. 7. In like manner, *Sub-Prime Minister* is the official name, of the functionary, who, to a Sublegislature, bears the same relation as the Prime Minister bears to the Legislature.

### Enactive. Instructional

ART. 8. At the commencement of the authority of this Code, and so on during the preparation period, as per §16, *Locable who*, the Prime Minister, under the direction of the Legislature, will allot to each Minister one or more of the above-mentioned Subdepartments. On this occasion, he will have regard——on the one hand, to the avoidance of the *waste* and *corruption* produced by the paying of *divers* functionaries where *one* would suffice,——on the other, to the quantity of *time* requisite for the conduct of the several businesses, and the faculty of finding individuals, in whose instance the several branches of appropriate aptitude, with relation to the respective businesses, will be found united.

### Enactive. Ratiocinative

ART. 9. Where two or more Subdepartments have been allotted to one and the same Minister, it belongs not to the Prime Minister, without the concurrence of the Legislature, so to separate them as to add to the number of the Ministers; for, by so doing, scarcely could he avoid giving increase to the expense; and thus, whether to or for his own benefit or not, imposing upon the people a correspondent tax.

### Expositive. Instructional

ART. 10. Examples of unions, which, antecedently to experience, seem most likely to be effectible without detriment to the service, are the following:

I. The Army, Navy, and Preventive Service Subdepartments.[a]
II. The Interior-communication and Domain Subdepartments.
III. The Indigence Relief and Education Subdepartments.
IV. The Trade and Finance Subdepartments.


## SECTION 3

### NUMBER IN AN OFFICE

### Enactive

ART. 1. In each official situation, functionaries no more than one.

---

[a] In the Army and Navy Subdepartments, Courts Martial belong, in one point of view, to the Judiciary Establishment.

*Ratiocinative*

ART. 2. Short reason, here as elsewhere, *official aptitude maximized; expense minimized*. Reasons in detail, the following——See, moreover, §15, *Remuneration;* §16, *Locable who;* §17, *Located how.*

*Ratiocinative*

ART. 3. I. APPROPRIATE MORAL APTITUDE.

I. The state of the law being given,——for every practical purpose, appropriate *moral* aptitude must be considered as exactly proportioned to the strictness of the functionary's dependence on *public opinion:* understand thereby the general tenor of the exercise given by the Public Opinion Tribunal to its power: exception made of any such aberrations from the path marked out by the greatest happiness principle, as, on the part of that body, happens, in the place and at the time in question, to have been produced and maintained, by deficiency in appropriate *intellectual* aptitude.

II. Singly seated, a functionary finds not any person on whom he can shift off the whole or any part, of the imputation, of a mischievous exercise given to any of his functions. Not so, when he has a colleague.

III. No person does he find to share with him in the *weight* of that odium.

IV. No person does he find in the same situation with himself, engaged by the conjunct ties of self-regarding interest and sympathy, to support him under the apprehension of it, by the encouragement given by their countenance.

V. He has it not in his power, without committing himself, to give to an indefensible exercise made of his functions, half the effect of a vote,——namely, by purposed absentation and non-participation.

VI. He finds not, in the same situation with himself, any person to share with him, and in proportion draw off from him, the whole, or any part, of any lot of approbation, whether on the part of his superiors in office, or the public at large, that may come to be attached to extra merit, in any shape, manifested on the occasion of any exercise given to his functions.

VII. His reputation stands altogether upon the ground of his actions. He finds not in the same situation, any person to help him, as numbers help one another, to raise a schism in the public,——and, by the mere force of prejudice,——without evidence, or in spite of evidence, in relation to specific actions,——to draw after them the suffrages of the unreflecting part of it.

*Ratiocinative*

ART. 4. II. APPROPRIATE INTELLECTUAL APTITUDE, cognitional and judicial.

VIII. By a single seated functionary, intellectual aptitude is likely, from the above-mentioned causes, to be acquired and maintained in a higher degree than by a conjunctly seated functionary, in so far as aptitude in this shape is the fruit of *exertion*.

*Ratiocinative*

ART. 5. III. APPROPRIATE ACTIVE APTITUDE.

IX. On the part of a singly-seated functionary, appropriate active aptitude is likely to be acquired and maintained, in a higher degree than by a conjunctly seated functionary, in so far as aptitude in this shape depends upon the joint power of intellectual aptitude and exertion.

*Ratiocinative. Expositive*

ART. 6. IV. COLLATERAL END OR ENDS OF ADMINISTRATION: exclusion of *delay*, *vexation*, and *expense*.

X. Only in the case of a singly-seated functionary can *promptitude*, or say *despatch*, be maximized.

XI. A singly-seated functionary has but one opinion, and one set of reasons, to give.

XII. No person's opinion has he to wait for.

XIII. No person has he to debate with, to gain over, or to quarrel with.

XIV. No person has he to put unnecessary questions to him,—to propose unnecessary steps,—or to necessitate useless adjournments.

XV. To *suitors*—that is to say, to persons having business at the office,—causes of *delay* are, in a large proportion of the number of individual cases, to a greater or lesser amount, causes of *expense*.

*Ratiocinative*

ART. 7. The addition made, as above, to the above-mentioned evils by plurality, bears a pretty exact proportion to the *number* of the seats.

*Ratiocinative*

ART. 8. So many seats, so many sets are there of persons, who, by community of sinister interest, stand engaged to secure the possessor of the situation against responsibility in every shape, for delinquency in every shape.

### Ratiocinative. Expositive

ART. 9. In each set of persons thus linked together by a community of sinister interest, distinguishable component members are the following—

I. All persons, connected by any tie of self-regarding interest or sympathy, with any of the several *actual* incumbents.

II. All persons having any prospect of *succeeding* to those same situations.

III. All persons, connected, as above, with any such successor in expectancy.

### Ratiocinative

ART. 10. The *higher* the situation in the scale of power, the stronger of course the support given to delinquency, by addition of sets of persons, united, as above, in support of it.

### Expositive

ART. 11. In English practice, where, in the Administration Department, in an official situation, Members, more than two, have place, the aggregate of them is commonly styled *a Board.*

### Ratiocinative

ART. 12. *A Board* keeps concealed deficiency, in any amount that can be desired, in appropriate intellectual aptitude in both its shapes, —with the addition of that of appropriate active aptitude.

### Ratiocinative. Instructional

ART. 13. A Board furnishes means and pretext, for bestowing, to the largest amounts in use, the matter of remuneration, on a number of persons equal to that of all its members except one—all of them in any degree destitute of appropriate aptitude in any or every one of its shapes.

### Ratiocinative

ART. 14. By vacancy or temporary incapacity, if effectual provision against it were not made, a considerable objection to single-seatedness would indeed be afforded. But by §6, *Self-suppletive function*, such provision *is* made; and in that way, without expense: instead of being made, as above, with increase of expense in exact proportion to the additional number of seats.

176

## Ratiocinative

ART. 15. Whatsoever beneficial effects can be expected from a multiplicity of functionaries in the same situation, may, and in a much greater degree, be insured, and in this Code are accordingly insured, by means of other agents: namely, by superordinates, (the Public Opinion Tribunal included) for controul; by Subordinates, for information.

## Exemplificational. Instructional

ART. 16. In the Central Government of the Anglo-American United States, the situations in the Executive Department are every one of them single seated. Of the thirteen here proposed Subdepartments, some have there no place; the rest are consolidated into four: each filled by a Minister, locable and dislocable by the President of the State, whose power, in so far, is that of the here proposed Prime Minister. Denominations of these Ministers, in the case of the Army Subdepartment, Foreign Relation Subdepartment, and Finance Subdepartment, *Secretary;* in the case of the Navy Subdepartment, *Commissioner*. Denomination of the Foreign Relation Minister, *Secretary of State*, to whose office some other functions of a miscellaneous nature may perhaps also be found attached. Subdepartments, conjointly in the hands of the functionary *here* named *Finance Minister, there* Secretary of the *Treasury* Department,—those *here* denominated the *Finance Subdepartment* and the *Trade Subdepartment.* Sub-departments, for which, as not belonging to the logical field of service of the Central Government, *there* is no place, these which follow:—I, The Election Subdepartment; II, The Preventive Service Subdepartment; III, The Interior Communication Subdepartment; IV, The Indigence Relief Subdepartment; V, The Education Subdepartment; VI, The Domain Subdepartment; VII, The Health Subdepartment.—Subdepartment, not in the contemplation of that Government, the here proposed *Legislation Subdepartment.*[1]

## Instructional. Exemplificational

ART. 17. In the case of the relation between the President, as above,

[1] Bentham's information here is not entirely correct in detail. When the American Navy Department was created in 1798 its head was, like those of the Departments of State, Treasury, and War, designated Secretary, not Commissioner. See p. 212, where Bentham is correct on this point. Again, in referring to these Cabinet officers as 'locable and dislocable by the President', Bentham overlooks the important proviso in Article II, Section 2 of the Constitution that in such appointments the President must act 'by and with the Advice and Consent of the Senate'.

and his immediate subordinates,——the power of the superordinate, in relation to subordinates, is not only as to location, but as to dislocation, absolute: and, at the accession of each President, the power of dislocation is commonly exercised as to those whom he finds in office, and that of location at the same time, as to new ones: in regard to each, effectual responsibility is secured, by the power expressly given to him to require of each of them an opinion in writing, in relation to all points belonging to their respective offices: and, by this arrangement are produced all the good effects, the production of which is professed to be expected from Boards. To this power, the exercise thus given is as a matter of course; and, accordingly, does not to the eye of the public at large convey any unfavourable imputation; nor in the breasts of the functionaries thus eliminated, produce any pain of disappointment.[1]

### Instructional

ART. 18. In this proposed Code, to both powers——that of location and that of dislocation——those limitations are attached which will be seen,——to the power of location, in §16, *Locable [who]*, and §17, *Located how;* to the power of dislocation, in §21, *Oppression obviated*. Thus, then, a sort of competition for the preference may be seen having place. In the case of this Code, in regard to *location*, the limitations to the power of effecting it in the instance of these situations, form part of an all-comprehensive system, and are necessary to the exclusion of inaptitude: as to *dislocation*, the one arrangement may be best in some countries, the other in others.

### Ratiocinative

ART. 19. Any beneficial effects, that can by accident have resulted from any addition to number *one*, will not be found attributable to any thing but the chance it affords of an appeal, formal or virtual, to superordinate authority, as just mentioned.

### Ratiocinative

ART. 20. That which, in the exercise of official functions, constitutes *arbitrary power*, is——not the unity of the functionary, but his exemption from controul, including the obligation, contemporary or eventual, of assigning *reasons* for his acts.

[1] Article II, Section 2 of the Constitution provides that 'The President . . . may require the Opinion, in writing, of the principal Officer in each of the executive Departments, upon any subject relating to the Duties of their respective Offices.' There is no constitutional provision as to the power of 'dislocation', but the position Bentham describes did become established practice at an early stage.

### Ratiocintative

ART. 21. The circumstances which render plurality indispensable in *legislation* apply not to the case of *administration*. For the purpose of legislation, it is not physically possible for the Supreme Authority ——the Constitutive——to act, in one body and in concert and coopera- tion, in the location and dislocation, periodical and eventual, of an immediate subordinate: nor, in this way, were it physically possible so to act, would it be possible so to act with advantage towards the proper ends of government: but, to its locators and representatives in the Legislature, this conjunctness of action is possible, and is accord- ingly here ordained.

### Exemplificational. Ratiocinative

ART. 22. In English practice, this Department swarms with Boards. And this practice——does it not (it may be asked) form a presumption in favour of many-seatedness? *Answer.* A presumption: yes. But, of this presumption the probative force is completely overborne: over- borne——by that of the above *reasons*, with the addition of the coun- ter presumption afforded by the counter practice of the United States, as per Art. 16, with or without the consideration of the *ends* to which the many-seatedness has been directed, and the *purposes* which have accordingly been, and continue to be, served by it.

### Exemplificational. Ratiocinative

ART. 23. End in view of the here proposed Code, the greatest happi- ness of the greatest number: *means*, or say *subend*, so far as regards the whole Official Establishment, maximization of official appropriate aptitude, coupled with minimization of expense: for the connexion between which two branches, see §15, *Remuneration;* §16, *Locable who;* §17, *Located how.* End in view in the case of the English form of government, greatest happiness of the *ruling one*, in conjunction with that of the *subruling few: means* and *subends*, on the part of the whole Official Establishment, in relation to appropriate aptitude, minimization of the quantity necessary to the possession of a situa- tion in it; in relation to expense, maximization,——for the sake of the profit, to the *one* and the *few*, extractible out of the expense. Of the truth of the position, that the here assigned main end and subends are the real ones,——the above mentioned ratiocinative matter, as far as it goes, operates in demonstration: for further proof, see whatso- ever, in the course of this Code, is said of that same form of govern- ment, and in particular in the several sections just referred to.

### Exemplificational. Ratiocinative

ART. 24. In practice, in some of the above instances, partition of the business would probably be found to have place: and, in the course of this partition, more or less of the business would be found lodged in single hands. But, by no such instances of single-seatedness, are the mischievous effects of many-seatedness, as above particularized, diminished: on the contrary, rather are they increased. General result, a mixture of responsibility and irresponsibility, both contributing to misrule: on the part of all subordinate Boards, responsibility—and that complete—as towards the Cabinet Ministers, who are in the same way responsible (dislocationally, to wit,) to the completely irresponsible and thence arbitrarily ruling Monarch; irresponsibility, as towards the Public Opinion Tribunal, exemption from its influence being in so great a degree the result of the many-seatedness, as above.

### Exemplificational. Ratiocinative. Instructional

ART. 25. For many-seatedness, in no one of all these several instances, can there be any necessity or use. So far as single-seatedness, as above, has place,—for producing its good effects, it has but to be rendered, as here, permanent, and at the same time notorious: so many exemplifications of it[,] so[1] many distinct official situations being established, each with its appropriate denomination. To the Public Opinion Tribunal, each functionary would then be responsible for *every* thing that he does: on the present footing, no one is responsible for *any* thing that he does.

### Instructional

ART. 26. Rule. Be the situation what it may,—if there be more business than a single functionary is sufficient for,—according to the nature of the business, keep for the principal member a certain portion of it, establishing additional single-seated situations, one or more, either in co-ordination or in subordination, with reference to the original one. The distribution, the declared existence of which forms the only alledged reason in support of the Board system, will thus be to a certainty effected: whereas, otherwise, it may be pretended to be effected, without being so in reality.

### Ratiocinative. Instructional

ART. 27. In the case of the English Boards, what there is of irresponsibility, as above, though in every instance it keeps the Members in

---

[1] 1830, 'it so': Bowring inserts the comma to clarify the passage.

a great degree exempt from the authority of the Public Opinion Tribunal, and in that same degree deprives the public of that security for appropriate aptitude and good conduct,—does not exempt them in any degree from the absolute and arbitrary power of the Monarch. In the Chief of each Board, under whatever name, he beholds the sole and all-sufficient instrument of his will; and, for the purpose of giving effect to it by the direction given to the proceedings of the Board, the object of his confidence. By him, every Member of every Board may at any time be dislocated at pleasure: all but the Chief, in case of non-compliance with the direction of the Chief: the Chief, in case of non-compliance with the direction of the Supreme Board, the Cabinet, the Members of which are, every one of them, at every instant dislocable by that same universal Master; and, for this purpose, though to the public nothing is on any occasion known of the part taken by *any* one of them,—yet by him, through the medium of the Chief, every thing is known of the part taken by *every* one of them. Under this form of government,—a Board, though in so great a degree unapt as a security for good rule, is, as may be seen, completely apt as a security for misrule. What then is it that prevents the despotism from being in that one hand consummate? The answer belongs not to this place. See as to this matter, Ch. xvi. QUASI JURY.[a]

[a] Of the Members of this Supreme Board, the number has within these forty-four years received an augmentation, to the amount of what may be stated as one half. At present, it is fourteen. In the year 1782, what is certain is—that it was not more than ten: what seems highly probable is—that it was not more than nine.* [For Bentham's note see p. 182.] Of this change, the causes, could they be ascertained, would be instructive: the consequences may be in no small degree influential, if so it be that by the same causes, a gradual further increase to an indefinite extent, is a probable result. But, any endeavour to reach them, would require a dissertation which belongs not to the present subject.

Note, in the several Boards following, number of Members as follows—

### I. HIGHEST BOARD.

1. Cabinet Ministers . . . . . . . . . . . . . . . . . . . . . . . . . . . . . . . . 14

### II. SUB-BOARDS.

1. Treasury Board. . . . . . . . . . . . . . . . . . . . . . . . . . . . . . . . . 7
††2. Exchequer Bill Loan Office. . . . . . . . . . . . . . . . . . . . . . . . . .29
†3. Board of Trade. . . . . . . . . . . . . . . . . . . . . . . . . . . . . . . . .21
4. Admiralty Board. . . . . . . . . . . . . . . . . . . . . . . . . . . . . . . . 5
†5. India Board . . . . . . . . . . . . . . . . . . . . . . . . . . . . . . . . . .12

### III. *Bis-sub-boards under the Treasury Board.*

1. Customs Board. . . . . . . . . . . . . . . . . . . . . . . . . . . . . . . . .13
2. Excise Board . . . . . . . . . . . . . . . . . . . . . . . . . . . . . . . . .13
3. Stamp Office . . . . . . . . . . . . . . . . . . . . . . . . . . . . . . . . . 7
4. Tax Office . . . . . . . . . . . . . . . . . . . . . . . . . . . . . . . . . . 5
5. Hackney Coach Office . . . . . . . . . . . . . . . . . . . . . . . . . . . . . 4
6. Woods and Forests Board . . . . . . . . . . . . . . . . . . . . . . . . . . . 3
††7. Consolidated Army Clothing Board . . . . . . . . . . . . . . . . . . . . . .52

*Instructional. Ratiocinative*

ART. 28. Correspondent and opposite to the case of the union of
divers persons in one official situation, is that of the union of divers

---

IV. *Bis-sub-boards under the Admiralty Board.*
1. Navy Board . . . . . . . . . . . . . . . . . . . . . . . . . . . . . . . . . . . . . 9
2. Victualling Board . . . . . . . . . . . . . . . . . . . . . . . . . . . . . . . . 7
Number of these boards . . . . . . . . . . . . . . . . . . . . . . . . . . . . . . . . .15
Total number of Members of these Boards . . . . . . . . . . . . . . . . . . . . .208
Average number of Members in a Board. . . . . . . . . . . . . . . . . . . . . . . .13

Note—that, to the purpose of *diminution of responsibility*, the whole number applies in every one of the above instances. Not altogether so to the purpose
of *increase of expense*. In the case of those marked with two crosses, no one of
the Members has any emolument in quality of Member of the Board: in the case
of those marked with *one* cross, only some small number, such as two or three.
But, in every one of these Boards, subordinates there are in single-seated situations, who, all of them, have salaries.[1]

* Ground of this persuasion. Anno 1782, the Earl of Shelburne became Prime
Minister. On that occasion, *eleven*, the Author of these pages perfectly remem-
bers spoken of with much warmth by a friend of his—a Member of the opposite
party—as being the result of an addition, by which the number of the Members
was swelled to an altogether astonishing, as well as unexampled magnitude.[2]

In that Supreme Administration Board, there were, at that time, three grades
of power, distinguished by appropriate denominations: the *Cabinet* simply; the
Cabinet with the *circulation*; and the Cabinet with the circulation and the *Post*

---

[1] On the basis of the *Royal Kalendar* for the mid-1820s, Bentham's figures
here are correct, except that there were five, not four, Commissioners at the
Hackney Coach Office. Bentham is also broadly correct in his references to 'subordinates in single-seated situations'. It was normal for a Board to have a Secretary, with the following exceptions: the Hackney Coach Office had a First and
a Second Clerk, but no Secretary; the Admiralty had a First and a Second Secretary; the Treasury and the Board of Trade each had two joint Secretaries. The
'Highest Board', however, the Cabinet, was not to have a Secretary until 1916.

[2] Bentham's information on these matters is substantially correct. North's
Cabinet in 1781 had nine members, according to E. R. Turner, *The Cabinet
Council of England in the Seventeenth and Eighteenth Centuries, 1622-1784*,
2 vols., London, 1932-4, ii. 18; but Shelburne formed a Cabinet of eleven members, as Bentham says, when he took office in July 1782, and this was increased
to twelve in the following February. On the other hand, Bentham's friend in
1782, whom it is not possible to identify, was mistaken in thinking that the size
of Shelburne's Cabinet was 'unexampled'. Its immediate predecessor, in which
Shelburne himself had served under the premiership of Rockingham, had also
had eleven members. See J. Steven Watson, *The Reign of George III*, Oxford,
1960, pp. 578-83. As for the period when Bentham was writing, see J. P. Mackin-
tosh, *The British Cabinet*, 2nd edn., London, 1968, p. 70: 'After the turn of the
[nineteenth] century, Cabinets varied between fifteen in 1818 and eleven in
1828, Earl Grey's total of thirteen in 1830 being a fair average for the period.'

official situations in one person. Cases in which a demand for this union may have place are the following—

CASE I. For the business of the several situations, the applicable time of one individual sufficient. Of causes of demand in this case, examples are—

1. On the part of all,—need of the service of one and the *same subordinate* or set of subordinates, at the same time.

2. Saving of the *time* necessary for *conveyance* of appropriate information from one to another, in so far as information, necessary to all, is, in the first instance, received by any number less than all.

3. Saving of *expense:* more particularly expense in remuneration.

For eventual instances of all these causes of demand, see §2, *Ministers and Subdepartments.*

## Instructional

ART. 29. Case II. By reason of the smallness of the local field of service and the logical field taken together,—unfrequency of the individual instances of demand, for the exercise of the functions belonging to the several situations.

For examples, see Ch. xxvi. *Local Headman;* Ch. xxvii. *Local Registrar.* In the situation of *Local Headman*, number of functions belonging to the Administrational Department, eleven; to the Judicial Department, five; total, sixteen: many of them widely dissimilar.

---

*Office.* By the *circulation*, was meant the privilege of a key to the *box*, in which the foreign despatches, with or without other documents of the day, went [their] rounds: by the *Post Office*, the power of ordering the letters of individuals to be opened at the Post Office. Such is the information given by that Minister to the Author of these pages, when present at the opening of one of these receptacles, and reading of the contents. How the matter stands at present, he cannot say.[1]

---

[1] The information Bentham recalled from his conversation with Shelburne is broadly confirmed by an account to be found in the papers of Francis Willes, Under Secretary to Lord Rochford, who was Secretary of State for the Southern Department in North's administration in the 1770s (BL Add. MS 32,254, fo. 17). This describes a tripartite division of Cabinet papers into the 'Hanoverian Box' (Hanoverian despatches and interceptions of diplomatic correspondence made in Hanover) available only to the Secretaries of State for the Northern and Southern Departments; 'Secrets' (the most secret despatches and interceptions made in Britain) seen only by the Prime Minister and the Secretary of State for the Northern Department; and the 'Common Correspondence', circulated to all Cabinet members. As for the power to order the opening of letters, this had been given to the Secretaries of State by an Act of 1711, 9 Anne c. 10, but was occasionally exercised by other leading ministers such as the First Lord of the Treasury and the First Lord of the Admiralty during the eighteenth century. See K. Ellis, *The Post Office in the Eighteenth Century*, London, 1958, pp. 62-3.

### Ratiocinative. Instructional

ART. 30. Thus it is—that, at the top and at the bottom of the official climax, the greatest scope for the union of functions of different natures has place: at the top, because there the functions are chiefly of the *directive* kind; and to the directive function, exercise may, in minute portions of time, be given to the operations of functionaries, in indefinite number: at the bottom, because, for the performance of the functions, though of the executive kind, the demand for performance will generally be so unfrequent.

### Instructional

ART. 31. At the first formation of the official establishment, on no other ground than that of conjecture can any determination be formed, as to the number of distinguishable sets of functions, to which the service of one and the same individual will be sufficient to give exercise. Thereafter, a more substantial and appropriate ground will be afforded, by experience, observation, and experiment. But, in the nature of the case, at one time the demand for augmentation, at another time the demand for diminution, will be presented by incidental occurrences.

Suppose the maximum of frugality attained in the first instance, yet thereafter increase of population, whether in the whole territory of the State, or only in this or that section of it, will naturally become productive of a demand for augmentation in the number of official situations,—and this, without any infringement of the *expense-minimization* rule.

### Exemplificational. Instructional

ART. 32. In English practice, in regard to the number of official situations, the same Official Establishment exhibits, in one department— the Administrational—a vast redundancy;—in another department —the Judiciary—a vast deficiency. Of two systems in appearance so inconsistent, a common efficient cause may be seen in the all-ruling sinister interest. In the Administrational Department, all functionaries being, in every situation, in effect, dislocable, as well as locable, at the command of the supreme authority,—and at the same time endowed with emolument, mostly in vast excess,—the greater the aggregate mass in number and value, in the greater degree is the sinister interest on the part of locating rulers, benefited: and note, that in this Department, the emolument is in general composed exclusively of salary without fees; and is thence not increasible by any act on the part of incumbents.—In the Judiciary Department, on the contrary, —the emolument being increasible and increased, by fees exacted by locators for themselves and their locatees,—the greater the number of judicatories of subordinate grades, the incumbents of which would not be locable by them, the greater would be the quantity of business intercepted, and prevented from finding its way to their shops. Hence a compound, composed of *sale* of what is called *justice*, and *denial* of it; denial, to wit, to all those who cannot afford to buy it: and by both sale and denial, the sinister interest benefited: shape of the benefit, in so far as the *sale* has place, *emolument:* in so far as *denial*, ease.

## Instructional

ART. 33. A memento for which, on this occasion, a demand might seem to have place,—is a caution not to unite, in the hands of one and the same person, two or more offices, termed, for shortness, *incompatible:* an appellation, by which have been designated offices, the possessor of one of which is in any way subordinate, or in any way immediately responsible, to the possessor of the other. *Reason,* the controul would, by any such arrangement, be annihilated. But, an arrangement thus palpably absurd—scarcely could it be realized but in a more or less disguised form: as where the two official situations are, one or both of them, many-seated: and in the present Code have been inserted, even without any design directed to this end, two arrangements, either of which would, so long as it lasted, suffice to exclude all demand for any such caution. One is—the non-existence of any many-seated official situation under that of the Legislature: the other—the dislocability, of the possessor of every official situation under the Legislature, by any one of several authorities.

## Instructional

ART. 34. More obviously to the Judiciary Department than to the Administrational belongs the caution here given: and but for English practice, scarcely could there have been any demand for it. Under this form of government, an all-ruling, although, (as may be imagined,) not a declared principle is—what may be termed the *self-judication principle:*—*Every man judge over himself.* Examples follow.

## Exemplificational

ART. [35]. I. In case of breach of official duty, from the lowest to the highest degree of enormity, in the highest situations—the *Cabinet,* for example,—no penal Judicatory but the House of Lords, no accuser but the House of Commons: and, of the Cabinet, every Member is so either of the House of Lords, or of the House of Commons.[1]

## Exemplificational

ART. [36]. II. Anno 1826. In the House of Commons, complaints after complaints, during a long course of years, (grounds of complaint having existed during a much longer), of inaptitude, intellectual and active, on the part of the head of the law: complaints of moral inaptitude,—(conniving at, and profiting by, extortion practised to vast amount, on false pretences), though so much more flagrant as well as notorious, being, as usual, studiously suppressed. To stop the enquiry in the House of Commons, a fellow Member of the Cabinet proposes a Board of Commissioners to be named for enquiry into the aptitude of the system of procedure, under which the Judge in question is acting: the proposal, acquiesced in of course. Locator of these Judges,—in name the King; in effect—and sole Locator—and by his countersignature, even in name,—the Judge so complained of.[2]

Connected with this principle, and constituting a ground for it, is an article in the political creed, not the less universally professed by not being subscribed to, in the political creed:—impeccability of all persons whose situations in the official establishment are of a certain altitude. Exemplifications and proofs might fill a volume: for, by these principles, is practice, throughout, and in particular judicial practice, as well as language, determined.

## SECTION 4

### FUNCTIONS IN ALL

## Instructional. Expositive

ART. 1. To the several sorts of *operations*, which in every one of these Subdepartments will need to be continually *performed*, correspond so many *functions* which will need to be *exercised*. By the name of the function, the name as well as nature of the operation will in general, with the help of a short definition or exposition, where necessary, be sufficiently indicated: where not, it will be added.[3]

---

[1] Bentham is referring to the process of impeachment, last used in 1805 in the case of Henry Dundas, 1st Viscount Melville (1742-1811), who was acquitted on charges of malversation of public funds. See Ch. IX, § 25, Art. 56n, p. 436n.

[2] See Ch. VI, § 27, Art. 55n, p. 110n.

[3] 1830 and Bowring, 'where not, it will be added'. This phrase seems to be redundant.

### Instructional. Expositive

ART. 2. Previously to the enumeration of these functions, note requires to be taken, of the distinctions, which have place, in regard to the sorts of *subject matters*, on or in relation to which these same functions, and in particular the *registrative*, as per §7, will have to be exercised.

### Expositive

ART. 3. Only by their *names* or more ample descriptions, can the subject matters of political functions be designated. All names are, in their grammatical appellation, *nouns substantive*.

### Expositive

ART. 4. [I.] Names of *real* entities—names of *fictitious* entities:— under one or other of these denominations will all names of the subject matters in question be found comprised.

### Expositive

ART. 5. Names of *persons*—names of *things:*—under one or other of these denominations will all names of real entities be found comprised.

### Expositive

ART. 6. Names of fictitious persons—names of fictitious things— under one or other of these denominations will all names of fictitious entities be found comprised.

### Expositive

ART. 7. [II.] On one class of *fictitious entities* is by lawyers bestowed the denomination of *things incorporeal.* These are *obligations* and *rights:* of which two correspondent fictitious entities, *rights* alone are commonly spoken of, though they are not explainable or intelligible otherwise than by reference to the respectively correspondent obligations; while obligations are capable of having place without any correspondent right.

### Expositive

ART. 8. By the *absence* of correspondent *obligation, right* is in some instance[s] constituted: by the *presence* of obligation, in other instances: by the absence of obligation in one quarter, coupled with the presence of it in another, in another set of instances.

187

*Expositive*

ART. 9. By the absence of obligation to forbear meddling with it, is constituted your *simple*, or say *natural* or *naked*[1] right to any thing that is yours: by the obligation imposed on your neighbour to forbear meddling with it, and to forbear obstructing you in the use of it, is constituted whatever factitious, or say *sanctional* and *exclusive* right you have to it.[a]

For further exemplifications, see the Penal[2] and Procedure[3] Codes.

*Expositive*

ART. 10. III. *Immoveables* and *moveables*——to one or other of these denominations will every thing that is not a fictitious entity be found referrible. Clear and eminently useful is this distinction: source of it, *Rome-bred* law: source of endless confusion, the denominations which come nearest to the above——the denominations——*realty* and *personalty*, in English-bred law.

*Expositive*

ART. 11. IV. *Moveables* at large, and *money:* to one or other of these denominations will be found referrible every *thing* that comes under the denomination of *moveables*. What, on the present occasion, renders the division and distinction necessary is——that, between *money* on the one part, and all *other things moveable* on the other, such will be found, in several respects, the diversity,——that, although, between the sets of functions respectively exercisible in relation to them, little, if any, difference will be found requisite to be made in *name*, yet, in the effects respectively produced upon the two sorts of subject-matters, by the exercise given to these same functions, great difference will be seen to have place: a difference, which has for its cause the comparative simplicity of the sort of thing denominated *money*, and the *necessary* diversifications which have place in the remaining part of the aggregate, denominated *things moveable*.

---

[a] *Moral rights* belong not to this place. A thick cloud envelopes the discourse, under it endless confusion reigns——wherever they are confounded with *legal* rights.

---

[1] 1830 and Bowring, 'natred'; but this is evidently a misreading. For Bentham's use of the phrase 'naked rights', see *Pannomial Fragments* (Bowring, iii. 211–30), Bowring, iii. 218.

[2] See Ch. V, § 6, Art. 2n, p. 39n, and Table 2.

[3] See Ch. V, § 5, Art. 6n, p. 38n.

*Expositive*

ART. 12. V. *Occurrences*——to this denomination will be found referrible all *fictitious entities*, considered as presenting themselves to human notice: that is to say, in each instance, the matter of fact consisting in their so presenting themselves.

*Expositive*

ART. 13. VI. *States* (understand *quiescent* States) of *persons* or *things*, and *motions* of the same——to one or other of these denominations will be found referrible every *occurrence* that requires to be taken for the subject of the hereinafter explained registrative function, the exercise of which is composed of that of the hereinafter mentioned *minutative*, and that of the *conservative* function, and, exceptions for special reasons excepted, is followed by that of the hereinafter explained *publicative* function.

*Expositive*

ART. 14. VII. *Interior* and *exterior*——to one or other of these denominations, or both together, will be found referrible every occurrence, which, to an eye placed in any office belonging to any department of the Official Establishment, can present itself. By *interior*, understand those alone which have taken place in relation to some *person* or *thing belonging* to the department, subdepartment, or office in question; by *exterior*, every *other* occurrence and sort of occurrence whatsoever.

*Expositive*

ART. 15. VIII. *Important* and *unimportant*——to one or other of these denominations will be found referrible every *occurrence* to which it can happen to be taken for the subject of registration, as above. By *important*, understand of a nature to exercise an influence, augmentative or diminutive, on the net sum of happiness.

*Expositive*

ART. 16. IX. *Relevant* and *irrelevant*——understand to the purpose of registration, as respectively applied to the service of the several abovementioned Subdepartments: and thence (as presumed) to the purpose of exercising an augmentative influence on the net sum of happiness, as above.

*Instructional*

ART. 17. Of such occurrences as are *relevant*, an object of endeavour will be, in the business of each Subdepartment, to maximize the *number* and *value*, minimizing, at the same time, the number of such as are deemed irrelevant. To the exercise given to the hereinafter mentioned *statistic* and *registrative* functions, this distinction is more particularly applicable.

### Expositive

ART. 18. X. Written (including quasi written) instruments. By written instruments, understand any *things*, immoveable or moveable, which are distinguished from things at large, by being applied to the purpose of giving expression to discourse. *Real*, considered in themselves, they are *personal* when considered in respect of the expression given by them to the thoughts of *persons:* the information conveyed by them having thus the effect of *personal information*, or say *evidence*.

### Expositive

ART. 19. XI. Like the *occurrences*, which they are capable of being employed in giving expression to, those same instruments may be distinguished into *interior* and *exterior*, *important* and *unimportant*, and the important again into *relevant* and *irrelevant:* distinguished in the same manner, and for the same practical purposes.

### Expositive

ART. 20. XII. In so far as applied to the purposes of law and government, they may be distinguished according to the Departments and Subdepartments, to the service of which they are or ought to be respectively applied: and, in each individual case, the person whose discourse they exhibit will be either a *functionary* or a *non-functionary*.

### Expositive

ART. 21. XIII. On the occasion of each such instrument, there will be a person or set of persons, *by* whom the discourse is addressed, and a person or set of persons, *to* whom the discourse is addressed.

### Expositive

ART. 22. The instruments, to which existence is given by an *act* of *registration*—by the exercise of the *registrative* function,—might, to a first glance, present themselves as constituting an exception: but, on further observation, being all of them destined for publication, at a time either certain and immediate, or eventual and more or less distant,—these also will be seen to be addressed *to a set of persons:* to wit, those of whom the *public* at large is composed.

*Expositive*

ART. 23. XIV. Considered as addressed, by or from a functionary, in any department of the State, to a functionary subordinate to himself, or to a non-functionary, subject, on the occasion in question, to his authority, an instrument may be termed a *mandate*.

*Expositive*

ART. 24. *Transitory* and *naturally permanent:*——considered in respect of possible *duration*, under one or other of these denominations will all *mandates* be found comprised.

*Expositive*

ART. 25. By *transitory*, understand those in the case of which, at the end of a certain length of time, by some circumstance or other belonging to the nature of the act, giving *ulterior* execution and effect to the mandate is rendered impossible: as where the mandate having for its sole object the exercise of a certain act, on a certain person or thing, such exercise has been performed, and the object of the mandate accomplished. In this case, the mandate may also be styled *ephemeral*.

*Expositive*

ART. 26. By *naturally permanent mandates*, understand those, the execution of which continues possible, and, bating revocation, will continue actual, for an indefinite length of time. Such are those which have for their respective subject-matters persons or things, or the one *and* the other, taken in *classes*.

Of this kind, for the most part, are those mandates, which, emaning from the Legislative authority, are called *Laws*.

*Expositive. Instructional*

ART. 27. Note however, that, in case of necessity, there is nothing to hinder the Legislature from issuing mandates, as above, of the ephemeral kind, as well as those of the naturally permanent kind. '*Bring hither forthwith this or that person, or this or that thing.*' Of this transitory and ephemeral complexion will, generally speaking, be those mandates, for example, by the issuing of which, exercise is given to the characteristic function of the *[Legislation] Enquiry Judicatory*, as per Ch. vi. §27. So again, 'Convey to this or that *prison*, and cause to be enclosed, and till further orders kept therein, this or that *person*.'

## Expositive. Instructional

ART. 28. But, in the ordinary course of things, the situation of the person, by whom utterance is given to a mandate of this ephemeral sort, will be that of some functionary subordinate to the Legislature; say the Prime Minister, say a Minister, especially the Army Minister, the Preventive Service Minister: say lastly a Judge.

## Expositive

ART. 29. *Spontaneous* and *elicited;* considered in respect of its *origin*, under one or other of these denominations will every mandate, in and from whatsoever department issued, be found comprised. By *spontaneous*, understand brought into existence without having been preceded and produced by application, in any shape, from any other quarter; *elicited*, when by such application *ab extra*, brought into existence.

## Expositive

ART. 30. When the mandate, being elicited, has been produced by an instrument, composed of a portion of written discourse, whether ready written, or minuted down as uttered, call the instrument an *application instrument*.

## Expositive

ART. 31. *Ordinance*. This appellative is sometimes employed to designate any *Government mandate* of the *permanent* kind; but is most commonly the result of the exercise of *Legislative* authority either in the supreme or in a subordinate grade. In this case, at any rate if in the supreme authority, it is commonly considered as having for its synonym the word *law*. In the present Pannomion, however, need has been found for making exclusive application of the term *law*, to a purpose in certain respects different: to wit, to the giving clearness to the idea designated by that word, by employing it to designate exclusively a species of *command;* and this, in such sort as on no occasion to designate either more or less than the entire matter of *one command:* whereas, by the term *ordinance* is continually designated matter belonging to distinguishable commands in any number, yet perhaps without embracing completely the whole matter of any *one*. The employment thus given to the appellative *law*, is (in a word) the designation of an abstract idea, having for its object the marking out the distinction between the matter of a *penal* and that of a *non-penal* Code. But, for that detail this is not the proper place.

*Expositive*

ART. 32. *Rules, Regulations, Orders*. Without any as yet settled distinction, these words are commonly employed, almost promiscuously, to denote mandates emaning from any constitutional authority subordinate to that of the Legislative,——as also to mandates delivered by bodies incorporated, and bodies or say associations unincorporated, or even by ruling members of private families:——for the designation of a set of mandates belonging to one and the same batch, the word *Rules* being employed sometimes in conjunction with the word *Regulations*, sometimes with the word *Orders*. Thus confused and disorderly is as yet the phraseology of current practice.

*Expositive*

ART. 33. By the word *Rule*, a mandate of the permanent kind is more generally presented to view, than a mandate of the ephemeral and transitory kind. But, in the confused language of English procedure, it is equally and indiscriminately applied to both. When employed to designate mandates of the permanent kind, the word *order* is spliced on to it.

*Expositive. Instructional*

ART. 34. The distinction is not a mere speculative one. In those established seats and sources of extortion and oppression, in which what is called *justice* is sold to the relatively opulent few, and denied to the relatively indigent many,——no rule, at the instance of an individual, is ever issued *gratis:* none but on payment of a price put upon it, which price is called a *fee*, and pocketed either by a Judge, or by some subordinate *locatee* of his, whose profit is at the same time the profit of the Judge: *elicited*, accordingly on the part of the Judge, not *spontaneously issued* is the *mandate* or other instrument in this case.

*Expositive*

ART. 35. *Rules and Orders* on the other hand are issued——not at the instance of any party to any suit, but *spontaneously* by the Judges themselves, in whom the power of imposing, without stint, for their own benefit, taxes on all suitors, has lately been conferred by the self-constituted representatives of the people:——trustees who, on that same occasion, thus officiated in such numbers in the two self conjoined characters of oppressors and depredators. Nevertheless, intimate in this case is the connexion between the *permanent* sort of mandate and the *ephemeral*. *Rules and Orders* are the remote and original instruments of the abuse, *Rules*, the immediate and derivative.

### Expositive

ART. 36. *Mandate*, (it may be observed,) being a word not belonging to the vocabulary of English procedure,——it has, on the present occasion, been taken from the body of the language, for the purpose of infusing, if possible, a ray or two of light into the den of Cacus. On a particular occasion——and *that* rather a narrow one——a *Rule* issuing from a Common Law Judicatory, is indeed called a *mandamus:* but, neither on that occasion nor any other is any employment given to the word *mandate*. When issued under the notion of giving termination to a suit,——a mandate receives in one sort of Judicatory, the name of a *judgment*, in another, that of a *decree:* in any other stage of the cause, a *writ*, an *order*, or else a *rule:* in Judicatories of other sorts, it may perhaps be found to go by this or that other name: nor yet without reason: the more various the denomination, the less intelligible.

### Instructional

ART. 37. Of the above explanations it will be seen that some part belongs more particularly to the Judiciary, than to this which is at present on the carpet——the Administration department. But, in this place, the subject being unavoidably begun upon,——in this same place (it was thought) it might with some advantage be concluded.

### Instructional

ART. 38. For giving expression to all these several mandates, together with the *responses*, expressive of the respectively appropriate *answers* or say *returns*,——appropriate *written forms* will, in the course of this *Pannomion*, as far as practicable, be prepared: to the whole of the *generally applicable* matter, expression being given in *printed* forms: while, for the reception of the *individually applying* matter, adequate *spaces* will, of necessity, be left in blank. Thus will *uniformity* and *certainty* be maximized; *expense* minimized.

### Instructional

ART. 39. In a more particular degree, to the business of the Judiciary Department, will the *All-comprehensive Formulary* thus composed be found applicable: and, to the portion composed chiefly of mandates with their responses, will therein be added that composed of *conveyances* and *contracts: instruments* which, while to the judge they serve in the character of eventual *evidences*, serve, in the mean time, to the parties respectively interested, in the character of so many particular *laws:* the parties contributing the *directive* matter, the Legislature the *sanctionative.*

### Expositive

ART. 40. By an *arrangement* understand the result, whatever it be, of any human *act*, and consequently of any *mandate* emaning from the Legislative, or any other department of the State. Fictitious is the sort of entity of which this word is the name. In so far as *execution* and effect have been given to any law—or to any mandate of the Prime Minister—of a Minister—or of a Judge,—an *arrangement* may be said to have been *made* by it. The effects will, as above, be of the *ephemeral* or of the *permanent* kind, according to the nature of the case.

### Expositive

ART. 41. *Institutions* and *Establishments*. Both these fictitious entities are comprised under the generic appellative *arrangement*. How far soever their respective imports may be from being determinate, —most usually conveyed by the word *institution* seems to be the idea of an arrangement, carried into effect *without* any concurrent operation on the part of *government*, in any of its departments; by the word *establishment*, an arrangement carried into effect *by* government. Witness the all-comprehensive aggregate styled the *Official Establishment*, with its several branches: the Official Establishment, —the vast fictitious receptacle, in which are considered as included all *functionaries.*

### Instructional

ART. 42. Such are the *subject-matters*, which, as will be seen, require to be kept constantly in view, on the occasion of the *ordinances and mandates*, by the issuing of which those *arrangements* will be made, by which the several *functions* will be created, and at the same time allotted to the correspondent classes of *persons*, thence denominated *functionaries*. In §7, *Statistic function*, exemplifications of the several different sorts of these subject-matters will be found.

### Instructional

ART. 43. *Uses* looked to, in and from this analysis, are the following—

1. Affording ground and invitation for judgments to be passed, as to what, if any, portions of matter, properly belonging to this part of the field of government, have been omitted.

2. By survey thus taken of the points of *agreement* and *diversity* between the several objects,——maximizing, on the part of the conceptions respectively formed and entertained in relation to them, the desirable properties of *clearness* and *correctness*, at the same time with *comprehensiveness*.

### Enactive. Expositive

ART. 44. First, as to functions regarding PERSONS. These are——

I. The *Locative:* exercised by placing individuals in the several official situations. It is as to persons what the presently mentioned *procurative* is as to things and money. As to this function, see §16, *Locable who;* and §17, *Located how.*

II. The *Self-suppletive:* exercised by giving location, actual or eventual, to Deputes, and thus providing for the insufficiency in number or aptitude on the part of Principals: another mode of the *procurative.*

III. The *Directive:* exercised by giving direction to the conduct of Deputes or Subordinates, in relation to the business of the Sub-department.

IV. The *Dislocative:* exercised by removing Deputes or Subordinates out of their several situations. This is as to *persons* what the presently mentioned *eliminative* is as to *things.*

Sub-modes of location are——

1. *Allective*, or say *remuneration[al]ly operating*, or say *engagement;* to wit, by free *consent* and *contract:* function, the *conductive.*

2. Compulsive, or say *punitionally operating*, or say *pressing;* to wit, without consent: function, the *compulsorily procurative.*

Bis-sub-modes of location, allective and compulsive together, are——
1. Promotion in the same line.
2. Simple dislocation.
3. Suspension.
4. Transference permanent to a superior grade in a different line.
5. Transference temporary to a superior grade in a different line.
6. Transference permanent to an inferior grade in a different line.
7. Transference temporary to an inferior grade in a different line.
8. Transference permanent to an equal grade in a different line.
9. Transference temporary to an equal grade in a different line.

### Enactive. Expositive

ART. 45. Next as to functions regarding THINGS: things immoveable, things moveable, and money, included.

V. The *Procurative:* exercised by procuring and attaching to the service the things in question. It is, as to *things* and *money*, what the *locative* is as to *persons*.

### Enactive. Expositive

ART. 46. Sub-modes of *procurement* are—
1. *Purchase:* function, the *emptive.*
2. *Hire:* function, the *conductive.*
3. *Fabrication:* function, the *fabricative.*
4. *Requisition:* to wit, from some other Department or Subdepartment: function, the *requisitive:* followed (in so far as the requisition effects its object) by
5. *Receipt:* to wit, *ab intra:* function, the *transreceptive:* wherein is supposed, and of necessity included, as exercised in the other Department or Subdepartment.
6. *Transmission:* to wit, to this Department: function, the *transmissive.*
7. If the article so received had been antecedently issued, receipt is *retroacception:* function, the *retroacceptive;* correspondent the *retrotransmissive.*

### Enactive

ART. 47. Requisite exceptions excepted, the exercise of the *procurative* function will be constantly preceded by a correspondent exercise given to a correspondent preliminary function, styled the *requisitive*, and a thereupon consequent mandate, styled a *procurement mandate:* as to which, see §8, *Requisitive function.*

### Enactive

ART. 48. VI. The *Custoditive:* exercised by keeping the things in a condition fit and ready for service. As to the person or persons to whom it should be committed, see §7, *Statistic function.* Bissection II, Original Outset Books.

### Enactive

ART. 49. VII. The *Applicative:* exercised by the actual application of the things to the purpose of the service, according to the nature of the service, and the things. It is as to *things* what the directive is as to *persons.* Applied to money, it coincides with the [*eliminative*]; which see. As to this function, see §7, *Statistic function.* [Bis]section III, *Journal Books.*

### Enactive

ART. 50. VIII. The *Reparative:* exercised by causing the things to be again fit for the service, after they have ceased to be so.

*Enactive*

ART. 51. IX. The *Transformative:* exercised by the giving to the *matter* of the thing in question another *form*. As to this function, see §7, *Statistic function.* [Bis]section III.

*Enactive*

ART. 52. X. The *Eliminative:* exercised by removal of the thing in question out of the custody of the functionary in question.

It is as to *things* and *money*, what the *dislocative* is as to *persons*.

*Enactive*

ART. 53. Submodes of elimination are——

1. As to things, in the case in which application to use consists in rapid and destructive *consumption,*——for example, in the case of things applied to the purpose of food, drink, heating, lighting, explosion,——application accordingly: function, the *consumption-authorizing.*

2. *Sale:* function, the *venditive.*

3. *Donation*, or say *gift:* function, the *donative.*

4. *Letting out to hire:* function, the *lease-letting*, or say the *mercede-locative.*

In this case, in so far as the contract has been fulfilled, follows *retroacception:* function, the *retroacceptive:* a submode, as above, of the *procurative.* If the lessee be——not an individual at large, but the appropriate functionary belonging to some other Subdepartment or Department,——correspondent and precedent to such *retroacception* will have been *retrotransmission* from the last-mentioned Subdepartment or Department, as above: function, the *retrotransmissive.*

5. *Commodation*, or say *lending out:* function, the *commodative.*

6. *Ejection*, without making use of it in any shape, or transmitting it to any other Subdepartment or Department: *ejection*, to wit, on the supposition of its being valueless: function, the *ejective.*

*Enactive. Expositive. Instructional*

ART. 54. XI. The *Inspective:* exercised by surveys made, preparatory to exercise eventually given to the *directive* function. To it must be added, or in it included, the *quasi-inspective.* As to this, see §11, *Information-elicitative function.* It has for its objects, in a more particular manner than any of the former, two distinguishable, howsoever intimately connected, operations or courses of action: to wit, 1, maximization of the aggregate of good, producible by *serviceable* dispositions made of the subject-matters in question: 2, minimization of the aggregate of evil, producible by the *dis*serviceable dispositions and accidents to which they stand respectively exposed.

### Instructional. Expositive

ART. 55. As often as, for the exercise of the Inspective function, change of place is necessary, a different denomination may be of use in speaking of it: to wit, the *visitative*. As to this, see §9, *Inspective function.*

### Enactive. Expositive. Instructional

ART. 56. Now, as to functions regarding PERSONS, THINGS, MONEY, and OCCURRENCES. These are—

XII. 1. The *Statistic:* exercised by statements made of the state of *persons, things,* and *money,* belonging to the Subdepartment at the time in question, and of such knowledge-worthy *occurrences* as have taken place in relation to those objects respectively: including not only such *occurrences* as, with reference to the Subdepartment in question, and the Official Establishment of which it makes a part, may be styled *interior,*—but also, among those which, with relation to it are *exterior,* all such by which a demand may be produced, for exercise to be given, in this or that particular manner, to any of the functions belonging to it: say accordingly—*exterior* relatively *important,* or relatively *influential* occurrences: with mention made of the *times* and *places* at which the occurrences respectively occurred: together with deductions, exhibiting such *contingencies,* or say *eventually succeeding occurrences* of the like nature as seem most reasonably to be expected, and the exercise most proper to be given to the *directive* function in contemplation of them.

### Enactive. Expositive

ART. 57. XIII.—2. The *Registrative,* or say *Recordative:* exercised, by the arrangements and operations, by which, in conformity to corresponding ordinances and mandates, the accounts, given at different periods by the exercise of the statistic function, are kept in contiguity, and in a regular series, for the purpose of reference and comparison. As to this, see Ch. viii. PRIME MINISTER; §10, *Registration System.*

### Enactive. Expositive

ART. 58. XIV.—3. The *Publicative:* exercised, by the publicity given to the produce of the correspondent part of the *Registration* system. See Ch. viii. §11, *Publication System.*

*Enactive. Expositive*

ART. 59. XV. [4.] The *officially informative*, or say *Report-making* function: exercised by a subordinate functionary, by communication, made to his superordinate, of a discourse called a *Report:* in which expression and arrangement are given to a body of evidence, having for its purpose the constituting, or contributing to constitute, an appropriate ground in point of *fact*, for exercise to be eventually given on some particular occasion, to some function or functions, by the superordinate. It may, in the whole or in any proportion, consist of evidence, elicited by the thus *information-giving functionary*, with or without *comments*, having for their object the affording assistance to judgment, and consequent action on the part of the *information-receiving* functionary. See further, §10, *Officially informative function;* and §11, *Information-elicitative function.*

*Enactive. Expositive. Instructional*

ART. 60. Lastly, as to functions regarding PERSONS, THINGS, MONEY, INSTRUMENTS OF STATISTICATION REGISTRATION and PUBLICATION, ORDINANCES, and consequent ARRANGEMENTS, having place in relation to the several above-mentioned *subject matters.*

*Enactive. Expositive*

ART. 61. XVI. The *Melioration-suggestive:* exercised in so far as,— any of those same subject matters presenting themselves as needing *reform*, or being susceptible of *improvement*,—indication is given of a *change*, supposed to be adapted to one or other of those two intimately connected, often undistinguishable, ever beneficial, and, so far as possible, desirable, purposes.

*Enactive. Expositive. Instructional*

ART. 62. Of the sorts of *things* here in question, some there are, the need of which has place, in every Department and Subdepartment, whatsoever be the nature of the business of it: others, the description of which will be different according to the nature of the several branches of service carried on in the several Subdepartments.

*Enactive. Expositive*

ART. 63. By the *instruments of statistication and registration*, understand—the several portions of written discourse and other permanent signs, if any, employed in the exercise of those same functions. They will be found distinguishable into—1, the *elementary*, to wit, the several individual *entries;* 2, the *aggregate*, to wit, the several *Register Books*, in which the several entries are inserted.

### Enactive. Expositive

ART. 64. Of the sorts of *things*, the need of which will have place in *every* Department and Subdepartment, examples are as follows:—
I. Things unmoveable.
I. The *edifice* or *apartment*, in which the business of the Department or Subdepartment is carried on. As to this, see §26, *Architectural arrangements.*
II. The *land*, if any, attached to it.
II. Things moveable.
III. 1. *Furniture*, and other such part[s], of the moveable stock as are put to use otherwise than by rapid consumption.
IV. 2. *Stationery* ware: that is to say, instruments and materials employed in writing.
V. 3. Instruments and materials employed in lighting, warming, and cooling. As to these several matters, see §7, *Statistic function*—Bissection IV. *Loss Books.*

### Expositive

ART. 65. Functions mutually *competitional*, or say *antagonistic*. Understand by this denomination those functions, as to which, on this or that occasion, option may require to be made, by the appropriate functionary, as to which of them, exercise shall, on that same occasion, be given [to].

### Expositive. Instructional

ART. 66. Of functions capable of thus coming into competition, examples are the following:—
I. Under the *procurative*, its several modes, to wit, the *emptive*, the *conductive*, the *fabricative*, and the *transreceptive*.

### Expositive. Instructional

ART. 67. Of subject matters in relation to which such competition is most apt to have place, examples are the following:—1, Edifices and ground works of various sorts; 2, Navigable vessels; 3, Ship-stores of various sorts; such as masts, yards, sails, and cordage; 4, Arms and ammunition of various sorts: in particular, gunpowder.

### Expositive. Instructional

ART. 68. [II.] So likewise, during the continuance of the *custoditive*, will be apt to antagonize the *applicative*, the *reparative*, the *transformative*, and the several modes of the *eliminative;* to wit, as above, the *venditive*, the *lease-letting*, the *transmissive*, and the *ejective*.

### Expositive. Instructional

ART. 69. [III.] So, in the Domain Subdepartment in particular, antagonizing functions will be the *applicative* and the *lease-letting*, or say the *mercede-locative*.

### Expositive

ART. 70. By the *applicative*, understand in this case the function, exercised by the keeping in hand the aggregate mass of the things which are the subject matters of the property in question,——on account of the Government and the public, applying them to their respective uses,——and, on account of Government, and thereby of the public, making, in respect of money, the appropriate *expenditure*, and reaping therefrom the *profits*.


### SECTION 5

#### SUBORDINATION-GRADES

### Instructional

ART. 1. In the several Administration Subdepartments established by this Code, divers *degrees*, or say *grades*, in the scale of subordination, will be found necessary: necessary thereupon will be found expository matter, under the subheads following:——

　1. Subordination——its *efficient causes*.

　2. *Superordinateness* and *superiority*——their difference.

　3. Super and subordination——their *grades*.

　4. Subordination——*accountability*——*responsibility*——their mutual relation.

　5. Ulterior grades——*efficient causes of demand* for them.

　6. Connection between demand for *grade* and demand for *pay*.

### Expositive

ART. 2. Subordination supposes *superordination*. Subordinateness is a mode of inferiority; superordinateness, of superiority: for the modes, see Art. 4.

### Expositive

ART. 3. Of subordination, the efficient cause is——*power:* viz., of the superordinate in relation to the subordinate.

*Instructional. Expositive*

ART. 4. *Modes* of power necessary, are the following—

1. Power of *direction:* corresponding *function*, the *directive*.
2. Power of *suspension:* corresponding function, the *suspensive*.
3. Power of *dislocation:* corresponding function, the *dislocative*.
4. Power of *punition:* corresponding *function*, either the *punitive*, or the *punifactive*.
5. Power of *suppletion*, that is to say, of fresh location, in case of suspension or dislocation: corresponding *function*, the *suppletive*.

Modes of power, not necessarily but incidentally capable of being usefully employed, are, in this case, powers *transferential*, permanent or temporary, to an equal or inferior grade, and *sistitive*, or say *promotion-stopping*. As to these, see §20, *Insubordination obviated*, and §21, *Oppression obviated*.

*Instructional*

ART. 5. In the hands in which the directive function is, must be the *suspensive* and *temporarily suppletive:* in the superordinate's must be the permanently suppletive: in the superordinate's, to a certain extent, must be either the *punitive*, or the *punifactive:* in a Judicial functionary must, for this same purpose, be the punitive to an ulterior extent.

*Instructional. Ratiocinative*

ART. 6. Either with the *directive*, the superordinate must have the *suspensive* function, or he cannot be made *responsible* for misconduct on the part of the subordinate. But, the degree of the necessity will depend upon the nature of the work, coupled with the distance between the grade of the directing functionary and that of his next superordinate.

*Instructional. Enactive*

ART. 7. In respect of *punitive* power, the Judiciary functionaries are superordinate to the Administrational in all Subdepartments: not so, in respect of directive, suspensive, dislocative, transferential, or suppletive.

*Expositive*

ART. 8. To the several grades in the scale of subordination, one beneath another, taking that of the Minister for the highest and the common object of reference, attach the several denominations following, taken from the numeration table.

1. Minister's immediate subordinate, call his *Prime Subordinate:* correspondent grade of subordination, grade the first.

2. Minister's immediate subordinate's immediate subordinate, call Minister's *Bis-subordinate:* grade, the second.

3. Minister's immediate subordinate's immediate subordinate's immediate subordinate, call Minister's *Tris-subordinate:* grade, the third: and so on through the *numeration* table.

### *Instructional. Ratiocinative*

ART. 9. In the present case, of necessity is the highest grade taken for the common object of reference in forming the scale of corresponding denominations. For, in every department, the name of the highest will at all times be the same. But the number of the grades,—and consequently in this mode of denomination, the name of the lowest, —will continually be liable to be on the change.

### *Expositive*

ART. 10. Without and instead of the word *superordinateness*, the word *superiority* would not, on this occasion, have answered the purpose. Superordinateness is not either identical or co-extensive with superiority; subordinateness, with inferiority: *superordinateness* is but *one mode* of superiority, subordinateness, of inferiority. Without superordinateness, superiority may have place even by means of legal power; as well as without being accompanied with legal power: I. by means of legal power: to wit, over a third person: the third person being or not being in a state of subordinateness as to either or both the superiors, having in relation to such third person, more power than the inferior has.

### *Expositive*

ART. 11. Example. If by directive and suspensive power, a superordinate in the Administrative Department can produce more suffering on the part of a subordinate, than, in execution of a law, bearing upon any part of his conduct, the Judge can,—the superordinate member of the Administrative will, in so far, be superior in power to the Judge.

### *Expositive*

ART. 12. [II.] So, to an indefinite extent is superiority universally considered and spoken of as having place, without being accompanied with legal power in any shape on the part of the superior over the inferior. In this case, the field and line of comparison may be the quantity possessed by the superior and inferior respectively of any desirable quality or possession. Examples of such qualities and possessions are as follows:—

1. Personal strength.
2. Personal beauty.
3. Moral accomplishments.
4. Intellectual accomplishments, (cognitional).
5. Intellectual accomplishments, (judicial).
6. Useful or graceful activity in any line.
7. Skill in pastimes of any sort.
8. Agreeableness in conversation, and private intercourse, say *urbanity*.
9. Opulence.
10. Factitious honour and dignity.
11. Influence of will on will.
12. Influence of understanding on understanding.

### Instructional

ART. 13. Note here the distinction and difference between *subordinateness* with the attendant *specific inferiority* in respect of *power* on the one part, and *inferiority* at large on the other part.

### Expositive

ART. 14. Example. Foreign Relation Department: *political missionary* line, Scale of Grades in rank, beginning with the highest;[a] in no one of them correspondent subordinateness on the part of the inferior.

### I. *Rank*

1. Ambassador extraordinary.
2. Ambassador ordinary.

### II. *Rank*

3. Envoy.
4. Minister Plenipotentiary.

### III. *Rank*

5. Minister.

[a] From [Martens's] Précis du Droit des Gens, &c., Gottingen, 1801, section 191: in some of the instances the distinction not altogether determinate.[1]

---

[1] Georg Friedrich von Martens, *Précis du Droit des Gens Moderne de l'Europe fondé sur les traités et l'usage*, 2nd edn., Göttingen, 1801, pp. 18-21, mentions only Ministre Plénipotentiaire, Ministre Résidant, and Ministre Chargé d'Affaires; pp. 21-4 list the subdivisions of the three ranks set out below by Bentham.

6. Resident.

7. Chargé d'Affair[e]s.

### Ratiocinative

ART. 15. Even in a Representative Democracy, observance of these distinctions is necessary: cause, the need which, under this as under every other form of Government, there is, of keeping up communication with the Governments of other states.

### Instructional. Expositive

ART. 16. In the Anglo-American Union, the highest grade for which provision is made in this line, is that of Envoy Extraordinary and Minister Plenipotentiary. It rests with those to whom it belongs, to show why even the lowest grade might not as well suffice as under Frederic styled the Great of Prussia, an Envoy or Resident of the lowest grade (the Chevalier Mitchel) sufficed: sufficed, even at the Court of London, on which the monarch was dependent for his existence.[1] In that case, the importance of the *sending* state, and of its business to the state *sent to*, was trusted to as a sufficient security for the requisite degree of attention. With those to whom it belongs, it rests to show why the case should be otherwise in the instance of the Anglo-American Democracy.[2]

### Expositive. Ratiocinative

ART. 17. Correspondent and concomitant to subordinateness is *accountableness*. By *accountableness* understand subjection to the obligation to exercise the *statistic* function, (as to which see §4), as to operations performed by the subordinate, in consequence of, and compliance with the corresponding exercises given to the *directive* power of [the] superordinate: for, without such accountableness, the *directive* power cannot be efficient.

---

[1] Sir Andrew Mitchell (1709-71), MP successively for Aberdeenshire and for Elgin Burghs, was sent as envoy to the court of Frederick the Great of Prussia in 1756, and represented Britain there during the critical period of the Seven Years' War. Bentham's point is however somewhat weakened by the fact that Mitchell's post at Berlin was raised to the rank of Minister Plenipotentiary in 1759.

[2] Although the Constitution of the United States authorised the President, 'by and with the Advice and Consent of the Senate', to appoint 'Ambassadors, other Public Ministers, and Consuls' (Article II, Section 2), no diplomatic representative with a title higher than that mentioned by Bentham at the beginning of this article was appointed until 1893, when the first American Ambassador was accredited in terms of an Act of Congress passed in that year.

### Expositive. Instructional

ART. 18. Such obligation, on the part of the accountable *subordinate*, supposes correspondent *powers* or *rights* on the part of the *superordinate; powers*,[1] in so far as exercisible without recourse to a Judge: viz. by means of suspensive power and punifactive power, as per Art[s]. 4, 5, 6, 7: *right[s]*, in so far as not exercisible but by means of recourse to a Judge, for the purpose of giving to the *punifactive* power the effect of *punitive*.

### Instructional

ART. 19. Of *accountableness* at large, accountableness in respect of *money* is the mode most frequently brought to view.

### Instructional

ART. 20. Eventual obligation of making *transfer* of the subject matter is a natural and frequent, but not necessary accompaniment of it.

### Expositive

ART. 21. Correspondent and concomitant to subordinateness, and accountableness is *responsibility:* efficient causes the same.

### Instructional. Ratiocinative

ART. 22. By superordinateness, no increase of pay is rendered necessary or requisite. Pay, as per §17, *Located how*, is, by the pecuniary competition, minimized. Power being, as well as money, part and parcel of the matter of reward,—of any *addition* to *power*, the effect in respect of demand for emolument, is—not addition, but subtraction.

### Instructional. Ratiocinative

ART. 23. Nor, by superiority in *factitious dignity:* under this Code, no factitious dignity being admitted.

### Ratiocinative. Instructional

ART. 24. Nor, by need of official intercourse: the manifold writing system, as per Ch. viii. PRIME MINISTER, §10, *Registration System*, minimizing the expense of transmission of statistic matter, wheresoever the information conveyed by it can be of use.

---

[1] 1830 omits the semi-colon between 'superordinate' and 'powers': it is supplied in Bowring as a necessary clarification.

*Expositive*

ART. 25. In every case where, between one functionary and another,
—intercourse, either for the purpose of direction, that is to say of
*directiveness* and *directedness*, is needful, a grade in the scale of
subordination has place.

*Instructional. Ratiocinative*

ART. 26. In any Subdepartment,—in the shape of constant *account-
giving*, need of subordinateness may have place, on the part of a functionary, in whose instance there is no need of his taking constant
*direction* from the superordinate to whom he is thus accountable.

Uses of account-giving in this case.

1. Securing constancy of supply,—in respect of appropriate stock
in all shapes, and money, necessary and sufficient for the branch of
service under his charge.

2. Prevention of needless delay.

3. Prevention of misconduct in every other shape; to wit, by fear
of eventual punishment.

*Expositive*

ART. 27. Examples.

1. Army Subdepartment: appropriate operation, construction of
fortifications.

2. Navy Subdepartment: appropriate operation, construction of
navigable vessels, ships, docks, &c.

3. Interior Communication Department:[1] appropriate operation,
construction of canals, bridges, tunnels, &c.

4. Domain Subdepartment: appropriate operation, working of
mines. In all these cases the operations of planning, and directing the
execution, will naturally be performed—not by the Minister, but by
an appropriate skilled functionary. Not only to such his immediate
superordinate, will account be accordingly given by such his subordinate, but also to the Minister; including a regular account of progress.

*Instructional*

ART. 28. By mere distance, without need of any such determinate
superiority as per Art. 26, in respect of appropriate skill, a demand
may be created for a grade in the scale of subordination for the purpose of *direction*.

[1] See Ch. VIII, § 11, Art. 6n, p. 164n.

### Expositive

ART. 29. Examples. Foreign Relation Department: station of *Commercial State Missionaries*, or say Consuls. For the service of two stations,—at the same distance, the one as the other, from the Foreign Relation Minister's official residence,—no demand can have place for a Consul at the one, and a Vice-consul at the other. But between station and station suppose a certain distance,—it may be necessary that, under one such agent, there may be one or more, —taking direction from him, and even eventually undergoing dislocation by him, followed by temporary location of a substitute, before those functions can respectively be exercised by the Minister.

### Instructional. Expositive

ART. 30. So perhaps it may happen in the case of the *Letter-post* branch of the business of the *Interior Communication Minister's* Subdepartment. Examples.

1. Residence of the Foreign Relation Minister, in *Europe*, Stations of Consul and Vice-consuls in *America*.

2. Residence of the Foreign Relation Minister on the borders of the Atlantic, as in the *Anglo-American United States*, Station of Consul and Vice-consuls, on the borders of the *Pacific*.

### Instructional. Ratiocinative

ART. 31. To the *Finance Minister*, in respect of his Subdepartment, in no other Subdepartment is any one of its functionaries in a state of *subordinateness*. But, in relation to that same *Minister*, in every Subdepartment, all functionaries are in a state of *accountableness:* of accountableness in regard to *money*, and thence in regard to the state of receipts, issues, losses, needs and expectancies as to money,—that by his care, in so far as depends upon him, supply may at all times be at their command, as to what is needed by them respectively in the shape of *money:* in regard to appropriate *stock* in all shapes, and thence in regard to the state of receipts, issues, losses, needs, and expectancies, as to such appropriate stock—that, by the same care, supply may at all times be at their command, as to what is needed by them respectively as to stock in those several appropriate shapes, by means of *money:* of money employed in the *procurement* of it.

### Instructional

ART. 32. At the outset, the Legislature will, in each Subdepartment, establish such grades of subordination as at that time appear needful:

adding to, or subtracting from, the number, at all times, in any such manner as experience, or change of circumstances, may indicate.

### Expositive

ART. 33. Of Subdepartments in which the number of grades needful will naturally be smallest, Examples are—

I. *Election Minister*—Subordinates to him needful.

1. Election Clerks, at the several *District Election Offices*, as per Ch. vi. [LEGISLATURE]; §7, *Election Offices*.

2. Vote-receiving Clerks at the several *Subdistrict Election Offices*.

### Instructional

ART. 34. II. *Legislation Minister*. What may happen is—that, under him no class of functionaries may be needful, other than that of *Writing Clerks*, in addition to his own Depute, as per §6, *Self-suppletive function*. But, neither will it be extraordinary, if other intermediate subordinates should be found needful.[1]

### Instructional. Expositive

ART. 35. Of Subdepartments, in which the number of grades will necessarily be the greatest, Examples are—

The *Army Subdepartment*. For the efficient causes of the demand, see Ch. x. DEFENSIVE FORCE, §1, *Branches*, §[4], *Stipend[i]aries who*, and [6], *Promotion*.

### Instructional

ART. 36. Where, as to this matter, the end of government is *maximization of official expense*, coupled with indifference as to official aptitude,—the *number* of the highest-paid grades will be maximized, for maximization of the expense.

### Expositive

ART. 37. Example from the *English Army Subdepartment*.

1. Superordinate of the highest grade,—Supreme Commander in chief,—the King.

2. Subordinate of the highest grade, the Secretary for Colonies and War.[2]

---

[1] For a slightly different version of this article see Art. 42 in this Section, p. 213. Bowring omits the last sentence of this article and inserts '(See Art. 42)'.

[2] The additional (third) Secretaryship of State created in 1768 for colonial affairs was abolished in 1782 in the movement for administrative economy and reform. A third Secretary of State, for war, was appointed in 1794, and responsibility for colonial affairs was transferred to this Secretary's department in 1801. After the Napoleonic wars the post became largely concerned with colonial

### Professional Functionaries

3. Bis-subordinate, the *Commander in chief* so styled Duke of York, Brother of the King and Successor Presumptive.[1]
   4. Tris-subordinates, the Field Marshals: as per Royal Calendar, anno 1825, number of this grade. . . . . . . . . . . . . . . . . . . .  6
   5. Quadries-subordinates, the Generals: number . . . . . . . . . . .  86
   6. Quinquies-subordinates, the Lieutenant-Generals: number . 215
                                                                  ———
   Together . . . . . . . . . . . . . . . . . . . . . . . . . . . . . . . . . . . . 307
   7. Sexties-subordinates, the Major Generals: number . . . . . . . 259

### Instructional

ART. 38. Where, as to this same matter, the end of government is maximization of official aptitude, coupled with minimization of expense, the number of the highest-paid grades will be *minimized*, for minimization of the expense.

### Expositive

ART. 39. Example in the Anglo-American United States' Army Subdepartment.
   1. Superordinate of the highest grade, officiating as the English King, only in case of *necessity*, the *President*.
   2. Subordinate of the highest grade,—a non-military functionary, —Secretary of the War Department.

### Professional Functionaries

3. Bis-subordinates, the Major-Generals: number, 1.
   Commander in chief, Field Marshals, Generals, and Lieutenant-Generals, none.[2]

affairs, though the Secretary of State was still, as Bentham says, the minister responsible for the army. There was also, however, the much older position of Secretary at War, which had existed since 1661 and which co-existed with the Secretaryship of State until the period of the Crimean War.

[1] Frederick, Duke of York (1763-1827), second son of George III, was appointed Commander-in-Chief of the Army in 1798 and retained the position until his death, except for the years 1809-11.

[2] Bentham is largely correct, although the President is also formally designated the 'Commander-in-Chief', and the post of 'Commanding General of the Army' had existed since 1821. It was not until 1864 that Congress established the rank of Lieutenant General, and 1866 that the rank of full General was created. See Russell F. Weigley, *History of the United States Army*, London, 1968, pp. 249, 285, 558-9.

*Instructional. Expositive*

ART. 40. Example from the English Navy Subdepartment.

1. Superordinates of the highest grade under the King, the Lords Commissioners of the Admiralty, acting in the form of a Board,— accordingly no otherwise than conjunctly: number, 5.

*Professional Functionaries*

[2]. Subordinate of the highest grade, Admiral of the Fleet and General of Marines, Duke of Clarence, Brother of the King.[1]

| | | |
|---|---|---|
| [3]. | Bis-subordinates, the Admirals of the Red: number...... | 16 |
| [4]. | Tris-subordinates, the Admirals of the White: number.... | 17 |
| [5]. | Quadries-subordinates, the Admirals of the Blue: number. | 18 |
| [6]. | Quinquies-subordinates, the Vice-Admirals of the Red: number ........................................ | 21 |
| [7]. | Sexties-subordinates, the Vice-Admirals of the White: number ........................................ | 22 |
| [8]. | Septies-subordinates, the Vice-Admirals of the Blue: number ........................................ | 21 |
| [9]. | Octies-subordinates, the Rear-Admirals of the Red: number........................................ | 22 |
| [10]. | Nonies-subordinates, the Rear-Admirals of the White: number ........................................ | 24 |
| [11]. | Decies-subordinates, the Rear-Admirals of the Blue: number........................................ | 25 |

Together ........................................ 186
[12]. Superannuated Admirals ......................... 29

Total ........................................ 215

In the case of the superannuated admirals, pay mentioned, twenty-five shillings per day: in the other cases, pay not mentioned.[2]

*Instructional. Expositive*

ART. 41. Parallel examples from the United States' Navy Subdepartment, anno 1824.

1. Superordinate under the President, the Secretary of the Navy.

---

[1] William, Duke of Clarence (1765-1837), third son of George III, afterwards King William IV (1830-7). He entered the navy in 1779, and rose to the rank of Admiral of the Fleet in 1811. He held the revived office of Lord High Admiral in 1827-8.

[2] Bentham's figures again come from the *Royal Kalendar* for 1825. *The British Imperial Calendar* for the same year gives a total of 214.

2. Subordinates of the highest grade, the Commissioners of the Navy, acting in the form of a Board: accordingly no otherwise than conjunctly: number, 3.

## Professional Functionaries

[3]. Subordinates of the highest grades, Captains: titles, when in the command of divers vessels composing a squadron,—as in the English service, *Commodores*. *Admirals*, of any grade, not one.[1]

## Instructional

ART. 42. The Subdepartment in which the number of the grades will naturally be the least, is the *Legislation Minister's*. Under him, decidedly necessary, it will perhaps be seen, are no other functionaries than a *Registrar*, and under him *Writing Clerks* in indefinite number.

But, for the assistance of this Minister, either in the capacity of Deputes, or immediate Subordinates, functionaries in any number may be found necessary: necessary, according to the magnitude of the State, and the nature and quantity of the business allotted to that same Subdepartment.[2]

## Instructional. Ratiocinative

ART. 43. To every considerable *directive* situation, an indispensable Subordinate will be a *Registrar*. But, in that office, the mode and degree of subordination requires a mode of limitation that has not place in any other. As to *omission*, it must not be in the power of a Registrar's immediate Superior whose acts he records, to compel, whether in a direct or indirect way, the *omission* of any apt entry: in an indirect way, for example, by so taking up his time with useless or needless entries, as not to leave time sufficient for needful ones.

As to *insertion*—compelling the *insertion* of false or otherwise improper entries—the mischief cannot be near so great as that of compelling the omission of true and appropriate ones: for, in this case, the misconduct presents to view its own evidence: all that the Registrar

---

[1] The Board of Commissioners of the United States Navy was established by Act of Congress in 1815, under the control of the Secretary of the Navy. See p. 177, n. 1. The highest rank in the service was, as Bentham states, that of Captain: 'Commodore' was merely a courtesy title given to a captain in command of two or more vessels. In 1824 Congress had rejected a presidential proposal for the establishment of the ranks of Vice Admiral, Rear Admiral, and (as a substantive grade) Commodore; and not until 1862 did Congress approve the creation of the ranks of Rear Admiral and Commodore. See Dudley W. Knox, *A History of the United States Navy*, New York, 1936, pp. 13n, 249n.

[2] See Art. 34 & n, p. 210.

213

will have to prove, is——the fact of the compulsion: and of this fact, the entry may accompany the other entries.

### Instructional

ART. 44. Wheresoever, for the despatch of the business belonging to an official situation, need has place for *writing*, in greater quantity than the occupant of that situation can himself perform within the time requisite,——need has place for a *Writing Functionary* styled a *Clerk*, by whom, for this purpose, direction cannot but be taken from the other and first-mentioned functionary. In every Subdepartment, the grade of *Writing Clerk* will in this way be the lowest, as will that of *Minister* be the highest, whatsoever be the number of intermediate grades.

### Instructional. Ratiocinative

ART. 45. But it follows not that the *pay* of the *directing* must be greater than that of the *writing* functionary. The reverse will generally be the case. For, without pay, the Writing Clerk, having no power, can scarcely ever have any adequate inducement for bestowing his labour: whereas the functionary, to whom his office gives power, may, in many cases, as per Art. 22, find, in that same power alone, an adequate inducement.

### Instructional

ART. 46. Note the distinction between the number of *grades* and the number of *official situations* necessary.

### Instructional. Expositive

ART. 47. Instance, the Finance Subdepartment. In that Subdepartment, for every office at which revenue is collected, a subordinate, with a correspondent *Registration System*, as per Ch. viii. §10, will naturally be indispensable: while, in all those instances, the grade of these several functionaries in the scale of subordination may be the same.

### Instructional. Ratiocinative

ART. 48. Rule, as to the proper number of grades in a Subdepartment. Unless for special and preponderant need,——between the grade occupied by the functionary by whom the course of operation is carried on, and the Minister of the Subdepartment, establish no intermediate grade.

Reason. Of every such intermediate grade, necessary concomitants are——complication, delay, vexation, and expense.

## SECTION 6

### SELF-SUPPLETIVE FUNCTION

#### *Enactive*

ART. 1. Lest the business of his office should at any time, though it were but for a day, be at a stand,——to every Minister, as to the Prime Minister, belongs the *power of self-supply*, with the *obligation* of keeping it in exercise. It is exercised by the location of an at-all-times-dislocable *Depute*, with powers and duties as per Ch. viii. PRIME MINISTER, §4, *Self-suppletive function*. Art[s]. 2, 3, 4, 5, 6, 10.

#### *Enactive*

ART. 2. In so far as of the several Ministerial Situations, as per §[2], *Ministers and Subdepartments, union* shall have place,——the Minister will, at his discretion, locate one Depute to serve in all, or distribute them, in such manner as he sees most convenient, amongst Deputes more than one.

#### *Enactive*

ART. 3. Within {           } days after his own location, a Minister is expected to make such location as per Art. 2: and thereafter, immediately upon the dislocation of any such Depute, to locate a succeeding one.

#### *Enactive*

ART. 4. The instrument of location, with the year, month, and day of the month, will be signed by the Principal, and, in token of acceptance, by the Depute.

#### *Enactive*

ART. 5. Of every such instrument, exemplars, as per Ch. viii. PRIME MINISTER, §10, *Universal Registration System*,[1] will be disposed of as follows:
1. Kept in the Registrar's Office of the Subdepartment, one.
2. Transmitted to the Prime Minister's Office, one.
3. Kept by the Locator, one.
4. Delivered to and kept by the Locatee, one.

#### *Enactive*

ART. 6. In case of emergency,——created, for example, by sudden calamity or hostility,——lest time for acceptance be wanting, a Minister

---

[1] See Ch. VI, §27, Art. 8n, p. 95n.

may, by appropriate instruments, constitute *Deputes occasional*, in any number, without any such acceptance: a second to serve in default of the first, a third in default of the first and second, and so on. But, only in case of emergency will he execute any such instrument: and, on his responsibility, he will cancel it, having, if issued, called it in, so soon as the emergency has ceased.

### Expositive

ART. 7. Examples of cases producing a demand for the service of a Depute, permanent or occasional, are the following:

1. A sudden influx of business, with particular need of despatch.

2. Infirmity, whether of body or mind, on the part of the Principal, rendering him unapt, either altogether or in part, for the performance of the business.

3. Need of his attendance, at a place where the business cannot accompany him without preponderant inconvenience: for instance, when absent from Office, on an *Inspection progress*, as per §[9]: or when on attendance in the *Legislation Chamber*, as per §[24].

### Enactive

ART. 8. Locable in the situation of Minister Depute permanent are all those, and those alone, who are so in that of Minister Principal, as per §16, *Locable who.*

### Enactive

ART. 9. Dislocable or suspendible at any time is the Minister Depute by the Principal, as likewise by any of the authorities by which the Principal is dislocable as per §18, *Dislocable how:* and this without the judicial forms such as those made requisite in and by §21, *Oppression obviated.*

### Enactive

ART. 10. Exceptions excepted, this same power of self-supply, together with the obligation of exercising it, and the dislocation and suspension powers, as above, attached to it,—will be possessed— not only by the *Minister* of every Subdepartment, but by the several functionaries, occupying the several situations, in the several grades, *subordinate* to that of Minister.

### Enactive. Instructional

ART. 11. Exceptions are—

1. In the *Army* Subdepartment, the offices belonging to the *Military*, or say *Professional* branch.

2. So, in the *Navy* Subdepartment.

3. Such offices, if any such there should be, in the case of which, by special reasons, it shall have been made appear to the Legislature that this institution is unsuitable.

### Instructional. Ratiocinative

ART. 12. Beneficial effects resulting from the allotment of this function to functionaries belonging to the Administrative Department, are the following—

1. Number of functionaries at all times sufficient, at no time redundant.

2. Frugality secured, by exclusion of pay for superfluous and needless number of principal and paid functionaries.

3. Frugality secured, by the gratuitous obtainment of all but one of whatsoever number of functionaries may happen to be respectively needed for the several offices.

### Instructional. Ratiocinative

ART. 13. No ground has place for any such apprehension as that of a deficiency in the number of apt persons ready and willing to serve as Deputes, in any office in which there are persons serving as Principals. Reasons are—

1. Of the office[s], to which either power or honour in any shape are attached,—in few, if in any, would be found (it is believed) any deficiency in the number of individuals, whose services remuneration in both these shapes, or even in no more than one of them, would be sufficient to engage, without remuneration in a pecuniary shape, either in possession or expectancy: and, proportioned in value to whatever remuneration there is in possession, will be remuneration in expectancy: always understood, that, because remuneration in these non-pecuniary shapes might suffice for official service, with the laxity of attendance, which, under other systems, is to a great extent tolerated, it would not follow, that remuneration in these shapes would suffice for procuring the closeness of attendance, which, under the present system, is uniformly exacted.

2. In point of experience, generally speaking, whatsoever profit-seeking occupation persons of adult ages are engaged in, in the situation of *masters*,—other persons in adequate number are, in a non-adult age, ready and willing to learn and carry on in the situation of *apprentices*.

In every office, the relation of a Depute to the Principal is analogous to that of an Apprentice to a Master in a non-official occupation.

## SECTION 7

### STATISTIC FUNCTION

#### BIS-SECTION THE FIRST. ALL BOOKS TOGETHER

##### *Instructional*

ART.1. This Section has for its object the bringing together in the aggregate, all the several *operations*, which, in the exercise given to the *statistic* and *recordative functions*, as applied to the business of the *Administrative* Department, can require to be performed: the *operations* themselves, and thence the *subject-matters* in relation to which, the *instruments* by the help of which, and the *official places* in which, those same operations are carried on.

For any such purpose as that of *original information*, many of the particulars which it will here be necessary to present to view, will be apt to appear, and indeed would be, needless and useless: none however are there, to which, incidentally, it may not happen to be found needful and useful, for the purpose of *reminiscence*. This distinction should never be out of view. Moreover, as to information, between the *needful* and the *needless*, the distinction will always be, in great measure, not *absolute* but *relative;* that which is needless to one person, being needful to another: and, to complete a whole, and render every part intelligible, particulars, which, taken each of them by itself, would be altogether trivial, may, to a considerable extent, be necessary.

##### *Instructional. Expositive*

ART. 2. In regard to this function, and the exercise to be given to it, topics for consideration are as follows—

1. *Objects*, or say *ends in view, uses*, and thence *purposes*, of the several *operations*, in this as in every other part of the business of this and the several other Departments[1] enumerated in §2, Art. 1. Expressed in the most general terms, these objects may be distinguished into—1, maximization of appropriate good;—2, minimization of relative evil.

2. *Subject-matters*, in relation to which the operation is performable. As to this, see §4, *Functions in all*.

3. *Relative times*, of the existence of those same subject-matters, in such their character. These are—1, entrance; 2, continuance; 3, exit.

---

[1] See Ch. VIII, § 11, Art. 6n, p. 164n.

4. *Entries*, that is to say, portions of written discourse, by the penning of which, the act of registration, as to those several subject-matters, is performed.

5. *Books:* Register Books, composed of so many aggregates of those same entries.

6. *Uses* in detail, derivable from the matter of these several Books: relation had to the respective businesses of the several Subdepartments.

7. *Offices:* Official Residences, in which this system of registration will be carried on.

8. *Securities* for *correctness* and *completeness* in the aggregate mass of the above-mentioned entries.

Under these several heads, follow in the order here expressed, the appropriate details.

### Ratiocinative

ART. 3. I. *Ends in view.* [1.] *Maximization of appropriate good.* Way in which registration contributes to this end:——presenting to view such information as to the *past*, as is necessary to the making, in regard to each several business, appropriate provision, of the several *subject-matters*, for the *future*.

### Instructional. Ratiocinative

ART. 4. Proportioned to the *clearness, correctness,* and *completeness*, given to the results, will be the *usefulness* of this operation, and those its results. Under the worst-constituted governments, more or less of information, in relation to these several subject-matters, is obtained and preserved: here, the endeavour is——1, to optimize the quality; 2, to maximize the quantity. Yet, on no occasion, except in so far as the benefit from the operation promises to be preponderant over the burthen of the expense.

Instruments employed in relation to this end——are the proposed *Outset Journal, Loss,* and Subsidiary *Books:* as to which, see [Bis]-sections II, III, IV, and V.

### [Instructional. Ratiocinative]

ART. 5. [2]. *Minimization of relative evil.* Way in which registration contributes to this end:——presenting to view past burthens in the shape of *losses*, with their causes:——on the part of directing functionaries, appropriate aptitude,——moral, intellectual, and active, being supposed the same in all cases,——the more clear, correct, and complete, the information possessed by them, under the several appropriate heads, the greater the probability of their preventing the like losses in future.

Instruments employed in relation to this end——are the proposed *Loss Books:* as to which, see [Bis]section IV.

### Expositive

ART. 6. II. *Subject-matters of registration.* As to these, see §4, *Functions in all.*

### Instructional. Expositive. Ratiocinative

ART. 7. III. *Relative time.* Periods of relative time, as above, are these: to wit, 1, *entrance;* 2, *continuance;* 3, *exit.*

Whatsoever be the Subdepartment,——only in so far as *employment,* or say *application to use,* is made of it, can any such article of stock be made contributory to the good of the service of that same or any other Subdepartment. In every case, entrance and continuance have therefore, or at least ought to have, and are supposed to have, for their design and end in view, employment, or say application to use.

### Instructional. Expositive

ART. 8. Of application to use, the description will, of course, be variable, according to the business of the Subdepartment, and the nature of the article.

Of some sorts of articles, application to use is made during their *continuance* in the service; examples are——instruments of all sorts, employed in works of all sorts: of others, no otherwise than by means of their *exit:* examples are——1, articles employed in nourishment; 2, articles employed in the production of heat and light; 3, missile articles employed in war; 4, money.

### Instructional

ART. 9. IV. *Entries.* As in all other portions of discourse designed for instruction, so in these,——*properties* desirable will be in each——1, *clearness;* 2, *correctness;* 3, *comprehensiveness;* 4, in the aggregate of all, taken consecutively and collectively, 1, *comprehensiveness;* 2, *symmetry.*

### Instructional

ART. 10. Applied to the present case, an operation, which appropriate *symmetry* presents itself as requiring, is the following——

In case of any change of method as between any succeeding year and the preceding years,——for convenience in respect of reference, to each aggregate of entries penned before the change, substitute for use a *fresh Book*, exhibiting the same matter in the form given to those penned *after* the change: for security against errors, *preserving*, at the same time, in the original form, those penned *before* the change.

### Enactive. Expositive

ART. 11. V. *Books. Register Books*. Taken in the aggregate, [those] which present themselves as adapted to the present purpose will be found distinguishable, in the first place, into 1, *Service* Books; 2, *Loss* Books. In the *Service Books* will be recorded the *operations*, by which the business of the respective Subdepartments is carried on: in the *Loss Books*, indications concerning the *loss*, which, in its various shapes, has been taking place in relation to the several subject-matters, as above, in the course of the service.

### Enactive. Expositive

ART. 12. Distinguishable will the *Service* Books be into 1, *Outset Books*, or say *Inventories:* 2, *Journal Books*, or say *Diaries.*

*Outset* Books again, into 1, *Original* Outset Books; 2, *Periodical* Outset Books: these Periodical Books commencing, each of them, at the commencement of some *period*, subsequent to the date of the *Original Outset* Book, which is also that of the earliest *Journal* Book.

Divisible into *Specific* Books will be each of the above-mentioned Books: *principle* of division, the subject-matter of registration.

The *Original Outset Book* into four Specific Books, to wit, the *Personal, Immoveable, Moveable*, and *Money* Books: so likewise the *Periodical Outset Book*, and the *Loss* Book.

The *Journal*, into the same four Books, with the addition of the *Occurrence* Book.

Relation had to these *Specific* Books, those within which they are respectively contained may be styled *Generic* Books. Of these same Specific Books, each will moreover be divisible, according to the three periods of relative time, into three *Subspecific* Books: to wit, *Entrance, Continuance*, and *Exit* Book.

### Enactive. Expositive

ART. 13. [1]. *Original Outset Book*. This will consist of an *Inventory* of the whole *stock* of the Subdepartment, or Subordinate Office in question: such stock being distinguishable into the four above-mentioned subject matters, as they exist on the day of the commencement of the System of Registration here delineated.

### Enactive

ART. 14. [2]. *Journal*. This will consist of entries recordative of the *occurrences* styled *interior*, which, on the several days of the year, take place in respect of those same subject-matters: added will be such other occurrences of which, under the name of *exterior* occurrences, mention is also made in §4, *Functions in all*, Art. 14.

### Enactive. Expositive

ART. 15. [3]. *Periodical Outset Books*. Of these the description could not be given, till after mention made of the *Journal Book*. At the end of a certain length of time, the same causes, which produced the demand for the *original Inventory*, will produce a demand for *another*, and so successively for *others*: if between each the lengths of time are the same, they will constitute so many *Periodical Outset Books*. Distinction between *Solar Year* and *Service Year*.——If the day, on which the Original Outset Book bears date, is the first day of that year,——the time, intervening between the date of the *Original Outset Book* and that of each succeeding Outset Book, will be a year, commencing on the same day with the *solar* year: if it be any other day, the year which commences with it will require a different denomination, and may be termed a *service year*. Simplicity will require that the need of these distinctions be excluded: this will be done, by placing on the first day of the next solar year, the date of the *second* Outset Book, and so of every *successive* Outset Book.

### Instructional. Expositive

ART. 16. *Super-books* and *Sub-books*. By *Super-books* understand the books kept in the Minister's office: by *Sub-books*, the books kept in the Offices subordinate to his. Correspondent to the denominations of the Offices considered with reference to their *Grades*, will be those of the Books; Offices,——Super-offices, Sub-offices, Bis-sub-offices, Tris-sub-offices; Books,——Super books, Sub-books, Bis-sub-books, Tris-sub-books.[1]

### Instructional. Ratiocinative

ART. 17. VI. *Uses:* to wit, of the above several Books; and, in the first place, of the *Service Book[s]*.

Aggregate, all-comprehensive and ultimate use, maximization of appropriate *good*, or say *benefit*, as above, to and by the service.

### Instructional. Ratiocinative

ART. 18. Particular, elementary, and instrumental uses, these——

---

[1] Bowring alters the 1830 punctuation in the last sentence of this article in order to clarify it: see the 1830 Collation, p. 469. The Bowring changes have been followed above.

1. On each day, showing the *stock in hand* for the next and succeeding days of that same year.

2. Contributing to form a ground for estimation of the *ordinary demand* and correspondent *supply* for the service of the succeeding years.

3. Contributing to present to view, within time, instances of *extraordinary* demand and extraordinary supply.

4. Thence, contributing to the making of timely provision for similar *succeeding* demands.

5. Indicating, in relation to the *real* stock, immoveable and moveable, belonging to the office, the most economical mode of *procurement*, as between *fabrication, purchase*, and *hire*, as to the several articles of which it is composed.

6. Furnishing data and standards of comparison, with a view to improvements in *fabrication*, in respect of *serviceableness* and *cheapness*: whether by substitution of more *economical employment* of the same materials, in the same modes,—or of different *modes of fashioning* or putting together those same materials,—or of *more apt* or *cheaper* materials.

7. In regard to *purchase* or *hire*, indicating past *prices* paid, with a view to economy by obtaining the article from the same or other dealers, in better *quality*, or at less *price* paid.

8. In regard to application of stock by *sale* or *lease-letting*,—indicating *past prices* obtained, with a view to *increase of profit* by disposing of the article to the same or other purchasers or hirers, at an increase of price received.

9. In respect of *stowage*, to wit, in *receptacles*, fixed and moveable, (as to which see Bissection II. Art. 8), for the several moveable articles of stock,—indicating the *demand*, present and future probable, with a view to the prevention of *deficiency* at the several *places* where needed, or the more *economical* stowage of the quantity, actual or future probable.

10. As between *place* and place of *stowage*,—indicating the distribution made of the aggregate amount of stock in hand, as well *personal* as *real*, for the purpose of securing the correspondency between need and supply at each, as against deficiency in one place and redundance in another: this being what may happen, notwithstanding that in the aggregate of the quantity in all places taken together, the correspondence between need and supply, is complete.

11. In case of *redundance*, affording indication of it, with a view to the *stoppage* of any works, the fabrication of which may be in progress,—the *prevention* of any, the fabrication of which, for want of due observation, might otherwise have been commenced,—or the

purchase or hire, of any which otherwise might have been purchased or hired; or with a view to the disposal by *sale* or *lease-letting*, of any part, at present needless, and not likely to be needed in future soon enough to warrant the keeping it in hand.

12. Affording evidence of *misconduct*——wilful, or through negligence or rashness——on the part of subordinate *functionaries*, with a view to transference, degradation, dislocation, and punition.

13. Affording evidence in case of misconduct, in the shape of *fraud* or *non-performance of contract* on the part of *non-functionaries*, with whom the office has had dealings: with a view to the obtainment of *remedy* by *satisfaction*, with or without punishment. See Art. 20, as to uses of the *Loss Book*.

14. In case of *extra merit* on the part of subordinate functionaries, indicating demand for *extra remuneration*, see Art. 20.

For more particular uses, so far as regards the *personal* stock, see [Bis]section the second, Art. [2].

### *Instructional. Ratiocinative*

ART. 19. [Secondly,][1] *Loss Books*. Their *Uses* are——

All comprehensive and ultimate use, minimization of relative *evil*, or say *burthen* to the service, in the shape of *loss*.

### *Instructional. Ratiocinative*

ART. 20. Particular, elementary, and instrumental uses, these——

1. As to each *individual* loss, preventing or minimizing the instances of its *renewal*, by pointing the attention of those whom it may concern, to its nature, efficient causes, and authors.

2. So, to the *aggregate* annual or other *periodical* amount.

3. Serving for comparison between each and each other year's loss: thereby, for increasing of preventive attention where loss is upon the increase.

4. For the purpose of prevention in future, pointing the attention of inspecting superordinates to loss by *negligence* or *wilfulness* on the part of their *subordinates*, and to loss by *wilful delinquency*, on the part of *non-functionaries*.

5. So, to loss, by the disadvantageous *bargains* with non-functionaries, on the occasion of *purchase* or *hire, sale* or *lease-letting*.

6. So, to *extra merit* on the part of subordinates, in respect of the prevention or diminution of loss, with a view to *extra remuneration*.

---

[1] 1830, 'II'; Bowring, 'Second.': see Art. 17 above——'in the first place, of the *Service Book*[*s*].

7. Exciting and keeping up *emulation* among subordinates as to the *minimization* of loss.

8. Pointing the attention of the *Public Opinion Tribunal* to the prevention of loss by the apprehension of its censure, and furnishing it with matter to operate upon.

## [*Instructional. Ratiocinative*]

ART. 21. *Efficient causes* of loss may be thus enumerated—

1. Unpreventible *accident* or casualty. Unpreventible accidents, though by the supposition they cannot be *prevented*, may yet be *foreseen* as more or less probable, and accordingly, in the way of *supply, provided against*.

2. On the part of a directing and custodient functionary, *want* of appropriate *information*.

3. Or, want of adequate and due *attention*.

4. On the part of a directing and custodient functionary, *embezzlement* or *peculation*.

5. On the part of a non-functionary, *stealing* or *fraudulent obtainment*.

## Instructional. Ratiocinative

ART. 22. In a proportion more or less considerable,—the *causes*, the *authors*, and even the *amount* will be out of the reach of ascertainment: for a time at least, even out of the reach of *conjecture*. But, from these uncertainties, no reason results for forbearing or omitting to put upon record, in any case, so much as *is ascertained*, and in some cases, the subject-matter and result of *conjecture*. For the omission of these indications, the only sufficient cause will be—what may have place in regard to supposed *authors* of loss, and is produced by the danger of injury to the reputation, of persons, on whose part no blame, in any shape, has had place. Note here, that evidence not sufficient to warrant legal punishment at the hands of the *Constituted Judicatories*, may yet be sufficient to produce and warrant *censure*, or at least *tutelary suspicion*, at the hands of the *Public Opinion Tribunal:* and, in this case, as well as the other, the *publicity* given to the *past* transgressions will contribute to the *prevention* of *succeeding* ones.

For the several *shapes* in which loss is liable to have place with relation to the several *subject-matters* of registration, to wit, the several species of *stock*, see [Bis]section IV.

*Instructional. Expositive. Ratiocinative*

ART. 23. VII. *Offices*, in which this system of registration will be carried on.

By the *Office*, understand here the building or apartment in which the business of the functionary in question is carried on. Allotted to every Subdepartment, or, as per §2, *Ministers and Subdepartments*, aggregate of united Subdepartments, there will be at least one *building* or *apartment*. In a Subdepartment, to which, under the Minister, belong functionaries in other *grades*, acting each in a separate Office at a distance from his,—his will be the Head Office; [theirs,] Sub-offices, of the several grades,—Bis-suboffices, Tris-suboffices, and so on. If, in any one such Office, need of this registration has place, so, with little or no difference, will it have in every other: in each will accordingly be kept a set of Books, with entries under the same or correspondent heads: call them, according to the grade of the Office, Sub-books, Bis-sub-books, or Tris-sub-books, as above, Art. 16.

BIS-SECTION THE SECOND. ORIGINAL OUTSET BOOKS

*Enactive*

ART. 1. *Original Outset Book*. I. *Specific Book the first. Personal Stock Book*. Heads of Entry. Examples—

1. Name of the official situation.

2. Name of the individual in all its parts.

3. Time of birth, as far as known: year, month, and day.

4. Place of birth, so far as known: District, Subdistrict, and Bis-subdistrict: if in a foreign country, indications analogous.

5. Condition in respect of marriage, whether Bachelor, Married-man, or Widower.

6. Time of location: year, month, day of the month, and week.

7. Other official situation, or situations, if any, in which he has successively been employed.

8. Remuneration to be received by him: shapes and yearly amount.

9. Office or offices, or other place or places, at which, on the day of entry he is, or at some future days, and what days, is destined to be, employed.

10. Locator, who: designated by his official and personal names.

11. Recommender, if any distinct from the Locator, who; designated in like manner,—for example, a functionary superordinate to the Locatee, but subordinate to the Locator.

12. If, and so soon as, the system of Official *Instruction*, or say *Education*, shall have been established, as per §16, *Locable who,*

226

mention of the *Examinations* undergone by him, together with the clusters of branches of art and science, and his rank in each, as per Office Calendar therein mentioned.[a]

As to the personal stock of the Military branch of the Army and Navy Subdepartments, see Ch. x. DEFENSIVE FORCE.

### Ratiocinative

ART. 2. *Uses* of Entries under the above heads, considered in the aggregate.

1. Maximizing and optimizing the service derivable from each such person.

2. Minimizing the loss from him.

3. Indicating his degree of appropriate aptitude in all its several elements.

4. Giving additional efficiency, to the responsibility, imposed in respect of him, on the functionaries by whom he was recommended and located.

5. Crediting him in case of his extra-aptitude.

6. Indicating the aggregate strength and value of the entire personal stock at the outset, with relation to its several purposes.

### Instructional

ART. 3. Subdepartments, in the service of which, the application of this registration system to the *personal* part of the aggregate stock possesses, to wit, in respect of the natural magnitude of their number, a more particular degree of importance. Examples—

---

[a] In the official Office Calendar of the American United States for the year 1817, the heads stand as follows—

| Names and Offices. | Compensation, Pay, and Emolument. | State or Country where born. | Where employed. |
|---|---|---|---|

Title, as follows:—'A REGISTER OF OFFICERS AND AGENTS, *Civil, Military, and Naval*, in the service of the *United States*, on the 30th day of September, 1817; together with the *Names, Force*, and *Condition of all the Ships and Vessels*, belonging to the United States, *and when and where built.* Prepared at the Department of State, in pursuance of a Resolution of Congress, of the 27th of April, 1816.'*[1]

* To precede this long title, might not a short one, such as *Office Calendar*, be a matter of convenience?

---

[1] Bentham's citation of the title is correct in all essentials. The *Register* was published in Washington biennially between 1818 and 1874, and subsequently continued as the *Official Register of the United States.*

1. Army Subdepartment.
2. Navy Subdepartment.
3. Preventive Service Subdepartment.
4. Interior Communication Subdepartment: to wit, in respect of the functionaries belonging to the *Letter-post.*

*Enactive*

[ART. 4. Original Outset Book continued.]
II. *Specific Book the second. Immoveable Stock Book.* Heads of Entry, in relation to each article. Examples—
I. The portion of land—its name.
  1. Situation.
  2. Dimensions.
  3. Elevation above the sea.
  4. Form of the surface.
  5. Nature of the soil.
  6. State in respect of culture.
  7. State below the surface, in so far as known or inferred.
II. Erections on the whole or a part.
  1. Aspect.
  2. Exterior form.
  3. Exterior materials.
  4. Exterior dimensions.
  5. Separate Apartments: their lights and dimensions.
  6. Condition, in respect of fitting up.
  7. Furniture.
III. Appurtenances, or say ground-works superficial: as yards, fences, bridges, &c.
IV. Appurtenances, or say ground-works subterraneous: as wells, drains, &c.
V. *Obligations intervicinal,* if any:—obligations of affording partial use of the land or ground-works to the occupiers of contiguous lands.
VI. *Rights intervicinal,* if any:—rights of making partial use of contiguous lands or ground-works.
VII. Uses made of the whole together: separate uses, if any, made of the several parts.
VIII. Persons employed in or about the land and building.
IX. Each person, how employed.
X. Things moveable from time to time brought on the land and stationed, at the day of date, in the buildings respectively.
XI. Keeper or keepers having in charge the whole, or the several parts. Function, the custoditive.

XII. Need, if any, and particulars, of reparation,—as per inspection and estimate.

XIII. Inspector or Inspectors, Estimator or Estimators, who, in this case.

XIV. Aggregate saleable value, as per estimate.

XV. Estimator or Estimators, who.

XVI. Aggregate leaseable value, as per estimate: Estimator or Estimators, who.

XVII. Capacity, and use, of increase, if any; with particulars of the nature, and estimated cost, of the means.

### Ratiocinative

ART. 5. Use, derivable from the confrontation of antecedent estimated cost with consequent actual cost—serving as a security against *waste*: to wit, by commencement of a work with insufficient funds: consequence, either *abandonment* of the work, with waste of the whole expense down to the time of stoppage, value of the materials alone deducted; or else continuance, under the pressure of a burthen unexpected and unprepared for.

On the footing of a mode of payment customarily exemplified in England, the interest of a professional person employed in building is in a state of natural opposition to that of his employer: the particulars of the work needed being settled, the interest of the employer calls upon him of course to minimize the cost; that of the employee to maximize it. Hence, peculation *pro ratâ*; in which case, to gain a comparatively small profit, the *employee* is under the necessity of imposing on the employer an expense many times as great. In this case, the less the apparent and avowed, the greater the unseen and unavowed amount of the remuneration.

For elucidation, take the case of the planning Architect. Intended cost, say £100,000: remuneration of the planning, if he be also the directing Architect, 5 per cent.: at this rate, if the actual cost is exactly equal to the estimated cost, his profit is £5,000. Suppose him then able and determined to extract for himself an additional profit of £1,000, to do this, he must impose upon his employer an additional expense of £20,000.

### Expositive

ART. 6. Original Outset Book continued. III. *Specific Book the third. Moveable Stock Book.* Heads of Entry. Examples.

1. Sorts, as indicated by the names.
2. Quantities.

3. Quality and conditions, whether perfect, or in any and what degree deteriorated.

4. Purchase, if any, in what instances.

5. If purchased, or hired, price.

6. If manufactured by the strength of the subdepartment in question, or any other,——cost of manufacture, as known or conjectured.

7. Year, month, and day of the month, when deposited in the custody of the official keeper.

8. In case of any such articles as are liable to be in a particular degree deteriorated by age, without the deteriorations being readily visible——for example, medicines,——year, when gathered, or brought into a state for use.

9. Place, where stowed: including, according to the nature of the article, as well the outermost place, for example, the *yard* or the *building*, as the inmost, for example the *shelf* or the *drawer*, say in both cases the *fixed receptacle:* as to which, see the Articles following.

### *Expositive*

ART. 7. Follows a subsidiary *mimographical* mode of registration, which, in aid of the ordinary *verbal* mode, will be employed in so far as the benefit in respect of appropriate information, is deemed to outweigh the burthen of the expense. Call it moreover the *receptacle-employing*, or for shortness the *receptacular*, or otherwise the *mimetic* mode: *receptacle-employing*, because, in making the entries, indication is given of the *fixed receptacle*, say *yard* or *building*: and, in the case of the *building*, the interior subreceptacles, one within another, ——say apartment, closet, platform, shelf, chest of drawers, and drawer, *into* which the article is *received*, and out of which it is *issued: mimetic*, because, for this purpose, *draughts*, or say *diagrams*, are employed, exhibiting to view so many *representations*, or say *images in outline*, of the outermost fixed receptacle, as above, with the several interior fixed receptacles and subreceptacles, down to the innermost, contained in it: *fixed*, in contradistinction to any such *packages* as it is enclosed in, while in its passage to or from, or while in, the official warehouse. Use, presenting at all times and to any number of persons at once, in any number of different places at once, a more adequate conception of the state of the moveable stock in all its parts, than could otherwise be obtained.

### *Ratiocinative*

ART. 8. *Usefulness* of this auxiliary mode of registration. Proportioned to the quantity, variety, and frequency of *entrance* and *exit*, on the part of the aggregate of the articles composing the species of stock here in question,—will, to each directing functionary, be the importance of his having at all times in his mind a conception, and to that end before his eyes a display,—of the quantity he has need of, and of the correspondent supply he has at hand or at command. The things themselves no such functionary can have always before his eyes: still less can the whole number of such other persons, by whom it would be of use that such information should be possessed. But, of the receptacles, in which, at each given point of time, the articles are respectively stowed,—every such functionary, whose business has need of it, may at all times have before his eyes an appropriate imitative substitute,—superficial or solid, draught or model: and, by reference therein made to the original, a conception of the quantity and situation of the thing therein contained: a conception, in some cases even more prompt, correct, and adequate, than the things themselves, if present to him, could furnish him with.

### *Expositive. Exemplificational*

ART. 9. Subdepartments, in which the benefit of this mode of manifestation presents itself as being most likely to outweigh the burthen. Examples.

I. *Army Subdepartment*. Species of stock.

1. Cannon. 2. Mortars. 3. Cannon-balls. 4. Bombs: these four in open areas: Balls and bombs, in piles, in each a determinate number.

5. Firelocks. 6. Pistols. 7. Lances. 8. Swords: these, in appropriate fixed receptacles, with or without the intervention of moveable ones, in which they are stowed: in each a determinate number as above.

9. Gunpowder. 10. Provisions. 11. Drinks: these by the barrel, or other moveable receptacle, number in each receptacle always determinate.

12. Clothing: in each moveable receptacle, sort of article one: number of that sort, determinate as above.

II. *Navy Subdepartment*. The like as to the several component parts, inflexible and flexible, of the vessel and rigging, that are in use to be kept, a number of each sort in the same fixed receptacle: for example, masts, yards, sails, cordage.

So, at each port, number, of each rate, each day in the port, with mention of arrivals and departures.

III. *Health Subdepartment*. At the Head Dispensary in the Metropolis,—stock in hand, of the several elementary matters, of which the medicines, in the state in which they are administered, are composed. Examples—

1. Mineral substances:—as, 1. Mercury. 2. Antimony. 3. Zinc.

2. Vegetable substances in natural state:—as, 1. Seeds, 2. Barks. 3. Roots. 4. Gums. 5. Resins, and gum-resins of various sorts.

3. Animal substances:—as, 1. Vaccine matter. 2. Living leeches.

4. Products of chemical analysis:—as, 1. Acids in a liquid state. 2. Alkalis. 3. Salts in a crystallized state. 4. Oils, expressed and essential.

In each fixed receptacle, moveable receptacle, and subreceptacle, if any,—quantity always determinate, to wit, in number or by weight, as the case may be.

### Instructional. Exemplificational

ART. 10. Present usage—progress made by it towards this mode of registration. Of the exterior receptacles in question, to wit, *Areas* and *Buildings*, in the business of some of the Subdepartments, draughts are in common use, models not altogether unexampled. Not so, of those inmost and other interior fixed receptacles, in which,—whether unpacked, or in their several appropriate packages, or say *moveable* receptacles, packed,—the several moveable articles of the stock are lodged.

In present practice, to the business of very few of the whole number of the here-proposed Subdepartments, does even the first-mentioned usage extend itself: in no instance, perhaps, does it go beyond the *area* or *exterior building:* in no instance does it extend to the Suboffices of the Subdepartment in question, or to any Offices belonging to any other Subdepartment: to no such Office, how intimate soever the connection between Subdepartment and Subdepartment, and how dependent soever for its success the business of one Subdepartment may be, on information, respecting the stock possessed by this or that other.

### Instructional. Ratiocinative

ART. 11. In the here-proposed mode,—by the extension of the *imitative* mode, in each instance, to the inmost fixed receptacle,—the places, in which, in their several sorts and quantities, the moveable articles of stock are lodged, are at all times presented to view in that same more vividly and promptly expressive mode; while, to the information thus afforded, any degree of extent which the business is deemed to require, may be given by the *manifold* system in this as in all other cases.

### Instructional. Ratiocinative

ART. 12. Thus far as to *original disposition:* now as to *changes*. In present practice,—of the *changes* continually taking place in the quantity of the articles stowed in each building or apartment, no otherwise than by verbal description is any conception ever conveyed in the here-proposed *receptacular* mode, all such changes may, at all times, receive immediate exhibition and communication, as per Art. 7.

### Instructional

ART. 13. Subdepartments, to the business of which this same auxiliary mode of registration and continual intercommunication is most obviously assistant. Examples—

1. Army Subdepartment.
2. Navy Subdepartment.
3. Ordnance Bis-subdepartment, respectively included in those Subdepartments.
4. Finance Subdepartment: to wit, on the occasion of the demands made on it by the above mentioned Subdepartments.
5. Health Subdepartment: to wit, in respect of the Medical Stock, Surgical Apparatus included.

### Instructional. Ratiocinative

ART. 14. Moreover, to every Subdepartment will belong a continually increasing stock of *written instruments*, styled in one word *papers*: and, in relation to these papers, in each Subdepartment, to the Minister, seated in his Head-office, there will be a convenience, in possessing, at all times, by means of the here-proposed mode of indication, the most perfect conception possible of the aggregate mass of these documents in the several Suboffices under his direction.

### Instructional

ART. 15. Mode of adapting this *receptacular* mode of registration to the two distinguishable cases, to which, as above, it presents itself as applicable.

Case 1. By its bulk, the article not exposed to ordinary theft, and by its nature little exposed to spontaneous deterioration by weather. Receptacle, in this case, no other than an open *area*, or say *Yard*. Articles thus stowed. Examples—

1. Navigable vessels.
2. Timber: in readiness to be employed in the construction, either of navigable vessels or edifices.
3. Stones and bricks, for edifices and groundworks.
4. Cannon, cannon balls; mortars and bombs.

### Instructional

ART. 16. Modes of adapting, to the purpose of appropriate delineation, the draught of a *yard* thus employed. The plan being delineated in the ordinary mode, divide the whole surface into squares of the same size. As often as any article or aggregate of articles is received into the yard,—when entry of such receipt is made in the Journal Book, show on the draught, the squares in which the article is deposited: so, on issuing, the squares left vacant.[a]

### Instructional

ART. 17. By any one of a variety of devices,—the changes made in the *stock* of the yard, might, as soon as made, be represented, in such manner as to be intelligible without the help of words; as in a map, the portions of territory are by lines and colours. The difference is—that whereas in a map the picture is always the same, in the appropriate draught it will be frequently varied and continually variable.

In the draught, the *squares* will be left in blank: the *boundary lines* alone expressed. For the purpose of the registrative operation, provide,—for the covering of each such square or aggregate of squares, a piece of card, of a size exactly to cover it: each card, with a pin in the centre, to lift it on and off by. On each card, the sort of article, it is destined to express, is expressed by its *image:* and, to the several different images may moreover be allotted so many different *colours.* In this way, for example, may be distinguished from each other—Cannon, Cannon Balls, Mortars, and Bombs: different calibres, expressed by figures, exhibiting in the usual mode the weight or diameter of the missiles.

In this way, a deficiency or redundancy would be manifested in a more impressive manner than by words; thus affording a correspondently greater probability of a timely remedy.

In the margin of the draught, the change will be registered by verbal description, as in the ordinary mode.

---

[a] Some 40 or 50 years ago, a map of Paris was on sale,—in which, to enable a person to find the street or other place he wanted,—the name of the places being inserted in alphabetical order, one under another, in the margin,—the whole area was in this way divided into parallelograms: an instant or two sufficed for applying it to use. Recently, no such map was found obtainable: in lieu of it was to be found one in which the compartments were so few and consequently so large, that to a pair of weak eyes it was found nearly useless.[1]

---

[1] It is not possible to identify the maps Bentham refers to here. The first was presumably one he used when visiting Paris either in 1764 or in 1770; or perhaps one used by his brother Samuel during his visit to Paris with his parents in 1775. Maps of this kind were by no means uncommon in the eighteenth century. Bentham's encounter with a less satisfactory street-map would have been on his visit to Paris in 1826 at a time when he was experiencing a good deal of trouble with his eyesight.

*Instructional*

ART. 18. Case 2. The sort of article requiring an enclosed exterior fixed receptacle, such as a warehouse, with or without interior sub-receptacles, one within another: for example, apartments, closets, piles of shelves, chests of drawers, fixed boxes, or platforms.

In this case, the plans and elevations in the ordinary mode serve for the exterior of the building with its several apartments, and for the closets, if any, within the several apartments. For exhibition of the above-mentioned innermost receptacles, ulterior and appropriate sections and elevations will in this case require to be added.

In the draught, in each such receptacle, if large enough, the *name* of the sort of article for the reception of which it is destined, may be expressed in the appropriate compartment, as above: if not large enough, instead of the name the figure or figures expressive of a number: in the margin will in this case be given the *name*, with that same number prefixed to it. Images and colours may be employed in this case as in the others, as above.

*Instructional. Enactive*

ART. 19. Note, that on every change made, in the number, dimensions, or mode of partition of the several *interior fixed receptacles*—platforms, shelves, drawers, &c.—a fresh draught will require to be made, to wit, in the *manifold* mode: exemplars transmitted, in this as in other cases.

*Instructional*

ART. 20. Things not capable of being stowed, but in *moveable* receptacles, in which they may be conveyed to, deposited in, and conveyed from, the *fixed* receptacles. To the reception of these same moveable receptacles will the several inmost fixed receptacles be to be adapted. Examples—

1. Drinks, and other matters in a liquid state.

2. Provisions and other matters, in a solid state, stowed with liquids, for preservation and conveyance.

3. Matter in the shape of grain, or powder.

4. Articles, natural or artificial, so circumstanced, as to be usually stowed and indicated in an aggregated way, by number, weight, or measure: as gun-flints, nails, belts, locks and keys, &c.

5. Piece goods of all sorts.

6. Medicines and most of the ingredients employed in the composition of medicines.

*Instructional*

ART. 21. Particular case, in which this receptacular mode of registration, as applied to articles kept in warehouses, may perhaps be employed to advantage. Example—

For all the offices belonging to all the several Subdepartments, materials of *writing* and *delineation*, as well in the ordinary mode as in the manifold mode, will at all times be needed: exceptions excepted, a stock for use, whether procured by *fabrication* or *purchase*, will need to be kept in a *central office*, naturally under the direction of the Finance Minister: exception may be—where, by reason of vicinity to the several places of manufacture, the expense of conveyance from them to the central office, and from the central office to the several offices in which supply is needed, may in part be saved: the article being conveyed from the place of manufacture to the office where the need is, without passing through the *central* office.

*Instructional*

ART. 22. Materials requiring Registration in the mode in question in this case. Examples—

I. For ordinary writing,—paper, pens, and ink.

II. For manifold writing,—1, appropriate paper; 2, appropriate silk; 3, appropriate oil; 4, lamp-black.[a]

*Instructional*

ART. 23. In the case of the Health Subdepartment may be seen a sort of stock, which at the same time exhibits the greatest variety and nicety, as to the manner of stowage, and requires the greatest care to obviate natural deterioration.

*Ratiocinative*

ART. 24. Uses of the receptacular mode of notification particularized.—

[a] In English practice, under the name of the *Paper Office* an appropriate office is, or at least has been, kept on foot, for the supply of that article to the several Government Offices: should the maintenance of such an office be found to be in England disadvantageous in point of economy, in comparison of *purchase* made at each office from the nearest manufactory, of the stock requisite for that same office,—it follows not but that it might be advantageous in the case of this or that other State.[1]

[1] The Stationery Office, originally called the Paper Office, was established in 1786 for the purpose of supplying books and paper for use in government departments. At a later stage its functions were extended to include the printing of official documents.

1. Facility given, to the application of the articles, on each occasion, with the maximum of *promptitude*, to their respective uses: *function* aided, the *applicative*.

2. Like facility to the minimization of *expense* and *loss* in respect of them: *function* aided, the *custoditive*.

3. In accordance with, and in proportion to, *consumption*, and other modes of *serviceable elimination*, with the assistance of the *Journal Books*,—facility given to the keeping up at all times the stock requisite, for present and future use, without deficiency or excess: function aided, the *procurative*.

### Instructional

ART. 25. Precautionary rule, as to *stowage* of articles sent to a distance: to wit, whether by land or sea, more especially if by sea.—
When articles of two or more sorts are so connected, that those of the one cannot be put to use without those of the other, send an assortment of each by the same conveyance: thus, if one conveyance miscarries, those which go by another will, in proportion to their quantity, not be the less serviceable. Send not the whole stock of one sort by one conveyance, of another by another: for thus, if one conveyance miscarries, the consequence is—the whole of the stock sent by both conveyances is found unserviceable.[a]

### Instructional

ART. 26. General heads, under one or other of which, for aid of conception, every article,—belonging to the aggregate of the moveable stock belonging to all the Subdepartments taken together, and to several of them taken singly,—may be found included—

I. *Articles in a state fit for use*. Examples—

1. *Furniture* of the several official residences. Articles of this description will of course have been bought, not home made.

2. Provisions of all sorts, liquors for drink, gunpowder, ready-prepared medicines; other articles, put to use by appropriate consumption in the *rapid*, or say *immediate* mode: Subdepartments, those of the Army, Navy, and Health Ministers.

3. Clothing, sails, cordage of navigable vessels, and the vessels themselves—put to use by consumption in the *gradual* mode. Subdepartments, those of the Army and Navy Ministers.

[a] In the course of the revolutionary war, under English Government management, instances occurred of this oversight. Instances stated to the author by an official authority, under whose cognizance they had just fallen: these, cannon in one vessel; balls in another; powder in a third: disasters, known at the time, had been the consequence.

II. *Materials*. Examples—

1. Corn, and other seeds employed when in a manufactured state, as food.

2. Materials of gunpowder.

3. Drugs, employed in the composition of medicines.

4. Paper, and other wares employed in writing.

III. *Instruments*, employed in work: in bringing the *materials* into a state fit for use. Examples—

1. Machines, of various sorts.

2. Carpenter's, joiner's, and turner's tools, of various sorts.

3. Blacksmith's and whitesmith's tools, of various sorts.

IV. *Vehicles*. Examples—Those employed in the conveyance of any part of the *personal* stock, or of the *moveable* real stock: in particular those belonging to the Letter Post establishment.

V. *Beasts* employed in conveyance as above.

VI. *Works in hand*: or say, articles of the above or any other sorts as yet unfinished, but in a state of preparation.

The particulars will be indefinitely variable, according to the modes of *procurement* respectively employed: to wit, sale, hire, or fabrication.

*Instructional. Enactive. Expositive*

ART. 27. Original Outset Book continued—

IV. *Specific Book the fourth. Money Stock Book*. Heads of Entry. Examples—

1. Stock *actually* in hand in the office, distinguishing between metallic and paper: and as to metallic, between gold and silver.

2. Stock supposed *virtually* in hand: to wit, in other and what offices.

3. Stock in *expectancy:* distinguishing *whence*: whether from the same or another Subdepartment or Department, or from a non-functionary.

In general, it will be from the Finance Minister, under direction from the Prime Minister and Legislature.

*Instructional. Enactive. Expositive*

ART. 28. Expectation, from a non-functionary. Heads. Examples—

1. From whom. His *description*. For heads, see above, Art. 1.

2. On whose account—*his* or what other's.

3. Ground of expectation; whether debt due to the office, or what other ground.

4. If debt, day when due.

5. If not on *that*, on what other day or days *expected*.

6. *Causes* of the uncertainty—if any determinate.

*Instructional. Enactive. Expositive*

ART. 29. Issues in *expectancy. Sub-heads* of entry.

1. Demand, *on whose account* expected—a functionary's or a non-functionary's.

2. Ground of demand,—debt, or what other.

3. Day, when *due*, or *expected* to be received.

4. Day or days, if different, when proposed to be transmitted from the office.

5. Causes of the uncertainty and retardation.

*Enactive. Expositive. Ratiocinative*

ART. 30. Where it is by a sub-office that the money is to be transmitted,—in that sub-office, correspondent entries will be made: thus, each will behold a check to it in the other.

### BIS-SECTION THE THIRD. JOURNAL BOOKS

*Expositive*

ART. 1. So much for the day of *Outset*. Now as to all *interior occurrences subsequent* to that day:—occurrences, which, in the office in question,—in relation to persons at large, or to persons belonging to any office in the Subdepartment, or any other Subdepartment or Department,—shall come to have taken place on the several succeeding days.

*Expositive*

ART. 2. In relation to these occurrences, relative *periods*, or say *portions of time*,—requiring distinct mention, as being occupied by so many different operations and correspondent sets of *occurrences*,—are the following—

1. Time of entrance: to wit, of the moveable article in question into the mass of stock contained in the fixed receptacle in question.

2. Time of continuance therein.

3. Time of exit.

*Expositive*

ART. 3. Correspondent to *entrance* is *receipt:* entrance, the operation, performed—as it were, by the *article: receipt*, the operation performed—*literally*, by some appropriate functionary; *figuratively*, by the receptacle and the aggregate mass of stock contained in it.

*Instructional*

ART. 4. Contemporaneous with *continuance*—to wit, on the part of the article of stock—*ought* to be as extensively as may be, and is accordingly of course *supposed* to be—on the part of the directing functionary, *application to use:* application to the most *appropriate* use.

*Expositive*

ART. 5. Correspondent to *exit* is an occurrence, which, relation had to the article of stock, demands different appellatives, according to the nature of the article.

Case 1. Stock, *personal:* appellative, *elimination:* to wit, from the office in question. Modes of elimination, as per §4, *Functions in all*, four: to wit, 1, promotion; 2, transference; 3, degradation; 4, dislocation.

Case 2. Stock, *immoveable:* appellative, *alienation*, or say *expropriation*. Modes of alienation, if perpetual and [indefeasible], *sale* or *donation:* if temporary, *lease-letting*.

Case 3. Stock, *moveable:* appellative, *issue*, or say here again *elimination*.

Case 4. Stock, *money:* appellative, *issue:* modes of issue in this case—

1. Payment; to wit, on purchase, or extinction of debt.
2. Transference to some other office.
3. Donation.
4. Loan.
5. Exchange: to wit, for *money* of some other *species.*

*Enactive. Expositive*

ART. 6. In the Journal, as in the Outset Book, *Specific Books* will be the *Personal, Immoveable, Moveable*, and *Money Stock* Books.

*Enactive. Expositive*

ART. 7. In the Journal, comprised in each Specific Book will be three Sub-specific Books: to wit.

1. The *Entrance Book*, or say *Receipt Book.*
2. The *Application Book.*
3. The *Exit Book*, or say *Issue Book.*

*Enactive*

ART. 8. Journal Books. Specific Book the first. I. *Personal Stock Book*, or say *Individual Service Book.*

I. Subspecific Book the first. *Entrance Book*, Heads of Entry, in relation to each functionary—

1. Day of location, as per year, month, and week.

2. For other heads, see [Bis]section [II.] Art. 1.

### Enactive

ART. 9. II. Subspecific Book the second. *Application Book*. Heads of Entry.

1. Day, on which attendance, being due, is paid.

2. Hour of entrance.

3. Hour of departure.

4. Place or places of service.

5. Subject matter, or subject matters of service.

6. Where the nature of it admits, particulars and estimated value of work done.

7. In case of non-attendance *absolute*, appropriate mention thereof.

8. So, in case of non-attendance at the proper place, or on the proper service.

9. Excuse, if any, what.

10. Evidence, if requisite, as to the truth of the excuse, what.

### Enactive

ART. 10. III. Subspecific Book the third. *Exit Book*, Heads of Entry.

1. Mode of exit: to wit, 1, promotion; 2, transference; 3, degradation; 4, resignation; 5, suspension; or 6, dislocation.

2. *Causes* of the exit: to wit, according to the mode in which, as above, it took place.

### Ratiocinative

ART. 11. Uses of these Books, in relation to this species of stock.

1. Securing attendance, thence service.

2. Securing the public against loss of the service and pay.

3. Securing the public against inaptitude, in respect of the service allotted.

4. —— against inaptitude in performance.

5. Securing responsibility on the part of the superordinate.

6. Securing the functionary in question against non-receipt of the pay due.

7. Securing the public against embezzlement of the pay, by the functionary, by whom it should have been paid to the functionary in question.

8. Affording indication as to the general value of the functionary's

service,——with a view to promotion, transference, degradation, or dislocation.

9. By reference to the Money Journal, as below, indicating the comparative value of his service compared with ditto of pay.

10. Indicating the different value, if any, on different days.

11. As to alledged places of attendance, indicating truth or falsity, by evidence of others, alledged to have attended at the same time and place.

12. Affording indication, as to whether he could be better employed in any other *service*, or at any other *place*.

### Ratiocinative

ART. 12. Not accompanied with any preponderant hardship is the obligation of furnishing and seeing furnished the evidence elicited under the above heads, and furnished by the entries.

1. If one party is charged and thereby burthened, another is discharged and thereby benefited.

2. Only in case of delinquency does the burthen attach.

3. The burthen imposed by the exaction of service in the shape in question——to wit, giving of evidence——is no other than in *judicial* practice, is, as often as occasion calls, imposed on all persons without distinction: in that case, without consent or equivalent: in the present case, with consent and equivalent——to wit, official remuneration.

### Instructional

ART. 13. Degrees of facility as to estimation of value of service of different functionaries; thence, of loss, by want of ditto. Examples——

I. *Maximum* of facility.

1. Copying-clerk's service.

2. Next, Directive or Inspective functionary's service.

3. Next, purely mental labour, unaccompanied with corporal, and employed in formation of some utensil. Examples.

1. Ship.

2. Engine.

3. Surgical instruments.

4. Article of furniture.

II. *Minimum* of facility.

1. Purely mental labour in various cases, in which no result in a physical shape can, in an immediate way, be produced by it.

### Instructional

ART. 14. [Journal continued.] Specific Book the second. *Immoveable Stock Book.*

I. Subspecific Book the *first. Entrance Book*. This book will not have place except in the case where, for the use of the Subdepartment, in addition to the *immoveable* stock as entered in the original Outset Book, acquisition of an article or articles of stock in this shape has happened to have been made: as to which case, see below, Art. 17.

*Enactive*

ART. 15. II. Subspecific Book the *second. Application Book*—Heads of Entry. Examples—

I. *Application to service, or say profit.*

1. Uses made of the whole, and, if different, of the several parts.

2. Day of each use.

3. Persons employed on each day, in or about the land and buildings respectively.

4. Keeper or keepers, having in charge the whole or the several parts, at the several times. *Function* the *custoditive*.

II. *Application belonging to the head of Loss.*

1. Repairs, if any—days of commencement, continuance, completion.

2. Causes by which the need of the repairs was produced.

3. Costs, as per pre-estimate—Estimator or Estimators, who.

4. Costs, as per experience.

N.B. These four entries belong also to the Loss Book, which see.

5. Inspection made, if any, from time to time, with a view to repair and estimate. Inspector or Inspectors who, and on what days:—their Report or Reports, on what day or days delivered.

*Enactive*

ART. 16. III. Subspecific Book the *third. Exit Book*. In case of Exit, Heads of Entry. Examples—

1. Mode of exit—to whom alienated or lease-let.

2. Cause of exit: to wit, according to the mode in which, as above, the exit took place.

*Enactive*

ART. 17. On the occasion of any *addition* to the Immoveable Stock, Heads of Entry. Examples—

I. For those relative to the state at the time of acquisition, see the Original Outset Book. [*Bissection* II].

II. Additional Heads of Entry, in case of acquisition by *Fabrication*. Examples—

1. Cost of building—of the *whole*, if built for the service, in all its particulars: so, of the several *parts*, if built at several times.

2. Functionary, by whose *direction* the building was *undertaken:* functions, the *directive* and *fabricative*.

3. Day or days, on which the building or buildings were respectively *commenced*.

4. Day or days, on which the building or buildings were, as per Report, respectively *complete*. Reporter or Reporters, who.

5. Day or days, on which the building or buildings, were, as per Report, respectively *fit for use*. Reporter or Reporters, who.

6. Antecedently expected cost in each case, as per pre-estimate. Estimator or Estimators, who.

III. Additional Heads of Entry, in case of acquisition by *Purchase*. Examples—

[1]. Cost and terms of purchase, in all particulars.

[2]. Purchase money, day or days of payment.

[3]. Of whom purchased.

[4]. Original estimate, on the ground of which, on behalf of the service, the purchase was made. Estimator or Estimators, who.

[5]. Directing functionary, at whose recommendation the purchase was made, who.

IV. Additional Heads of Entry in case of acquisition by *Hire*. Examples—

1. Terms of hire, in their several particulars, as per *contract*.

2. Of whom hired.

3. Original estimate, on which, on behalf of the service, the contract was made. Estimator or Estimators, who.

4. Functionary, by whose direction the contract was entered into, who.

5. State in respect of *repair*, as per *Report*, on behalf of the service. Reporter or Reporters, who.

6. As to *repairs*, if any, *during the lease*, for heads of entry, see above, in the case of an immoveable, belonging to the outset stock, as per Original Outset Book, Bissection [II., Art. 4,] page 228.

7. On the expiration of the time for which the hire was made, mention of the surrender or renewal, and on what terms. Person or persons who, on whose report the surrender or renewal was grounded.

*Expositive. Enactive*

ART. 18. Journal continued. Specific Book the third. *Moveable Stock Book*.

[I. Subspecific Book the first. *Receipt Specific Book*: for ] Heads of Entry, see in the Outset Book, Subspecific Book the third. *Moveable*

*Stock Book*, page 229. Follow those peculiar to the *Journal*. Examples—

1. Day of receipt, viz. day of year, month, and week.
2. Name, of the subject matter received.
3. Quantity.
4. Quality, if variable and ascertainable.
5. Moveable receptacles, or say *package[s]*, if any, in what received. Wood, glass, paper, &c.
6. Delivered, by whom.
7. Received, by whom.
8. Source, whence.
9.  1. If fabrication, from whose custody.
10. 2. If purchase, from whom.
11. 3. If hire, from whom.
12. 4. If transreception, from what office.
13. [5.] So, if retroacception.
14. [6.] If *ex-dono-acception*, from whom.
15. In what area, edifice, apartment, and fixed interior receptacle deposited.
16. In case of subsequent inspection by an appropriate functionary, —his names, official and proper, with his signature.
17. So, of every other person present.

*Expositive*

ART. 19. [II. Subspecific Book the second. *Application Book.*]

The *period* being that of the *continuance* of the moveable article in question in the employ of the office in question, the *function* exercised by the functionaries in question, in relation to the article during that period, is the *applicative*.

For an all-comprehensive conception, of the *modes* in which application is capable of being made of any article of this class, note the distinction between two modes, to wit, the *principal* and the *subsidiary* or say *instrumental: principal*, the *mode* employed, where the article is *not* considered as being of a nature to be employed in[1] the composition of other articles, or in the putting them to use: *subsidiary*, or say *instrumental*, where it *is* considered as being of a nature so to be employed: for example, materials, machines, tools, and other instruments; vehicles, employed in conveyance of these same materials and instruments; beasts employed in like conveyance, or in giving motion to machinery; receptacles, fixed and moveable, employed in giving stowage to the several above-mentioned, or any other,

[1] 1830, 'employed otherwise than in'. Bowring omits 'otherwise than', as the sense of the passage seems to require.

component parts of the aggregate of the moveable stock belonging to the office. See Bissection the fourth, Art[s]. [18, 19]¹ in which these same articles are considered as subject matters or sources of *loss*.

With the exception of *materials*, as above,—these same subsidiary articles, being applied or applicable, employed or employable, on any and *every* day, the application made of them will not, generally speaking, need to be registered on any day in particular.

*Expositive*

ART. 20. Where the mode of application is the *principal* mode, the subject-matter may be brought into use, either 1, singly, or 2, conjunctively with others: forming therewith a composite subject-matter, of which they are the component elements.

1. Where, by the operations employed in the fabrication, the article is rendered capable of being applied to use,—without being, in conjunction with articles of a different sort, formed into a compound body,—call the mode of application and fabrication *transformative:* as in the case of iron or brass formed into cannon, mortars, balls, or bombs: [2.] where it is brought into use in conjunction with others, —forming therewith, as above, a compound, or say a complex body, —call the mode of application and fabrication *conjunctive:* when conjunctive, the mode will be either 1, by simple *apposition*, as in the case of the elementary parts of the carriage of a cannon or mortar: or 2, by *mixture*, as in the case of the elementary ingredients of the gunpowder. In some cases, in the formation of the thing for use, —materials, which enter not into the composition of it, are employed by being consumed. Example, *fuel:* in particular, when employed in *fusion* or *refusion.*

*Enactive. Expositive*

ART. 21. Of the stages of the PROGRESS, to wit, of the progress made in the course of *formation*, the description will, of course, depend upon the nature of the *article formed*. But, be it what it will, among the HEADS OF ENTRY applicable to it will be the following—

1. Elementary subject-matters, what.

2. Days, on which they are respectively delivered into the custody of the person or persons employed in the work: as to whom, see above, the Original Outset Book, Specific Book the first, Personal Stock Book.

3. Their names, quantities, and qualities.

¹ 1830 and Bowring, 'Art. 16', but a reference to Arts. 18 and 19 seems more appropriate.

4. By whom respectively delivered.

5. Persons who, employed in the work.

6. Each day, progress made in the work.

7. Persons, if any, ceasing, and when, to be employed in the work, and in what capacities.

8. In case of unexpected retardation and delay,——mention of the *causes*, and of the persons concerned in the producing of it.

### Instructional

ART. 22. By these entries, with the addition of the mention made of the *apartments* in which the work is carrying on,——the superordinate functionaries will at all times be enabled to follow in mind each article, formed, as above, throughout the whole course of its progress.

### Enactive. Expositive

ART. 23. III. Subspecific Book the third. *Issue Book*. Heads of Entry.

1. Day of issue; to wit, day of year, month, and week.

2. Name of the subject-matter issued.

3. Quantity.

4. Quality, if variable and ascertainable.

5. Moveable receptacles, or say *packages*, if any, in which packed when issued.

6. Delivered out, by whom.

7. Delivered, on what account.

### Instructional

ART. 24. Note, that of transmission from fixed receptacle to fixed receptacle, though in the same apartment and in the same person's custody, mention may require to be made, lest the Superordinate's conception, as deduced from the *imitative sketches*, or say *diagrams*, should be erroneous.[1]

### Enactive

ART. 25. Journal continued. Specific Book' the fourth. *Money* [*Book*.] Subspecific Book the *first. Receipt Book*. Heads of Entry.

[I]. Day; to wit, day of year, month, and week.

[II]. Money in hand.

[III]. Receipts, as per *expectation*. Heads of Entry in relation thereto.

1. On what account received.

2. From whom received.

---

[1] This article should logically follow Art. 22.

3. By whom delivered.
4. By whom received.

[IV]. Appendage to the *Receipts*.

I. *Non-receipts:* that is to say, sums which, though the receipt of them was expected for that day, were not received accordingly. (See below [Bissection] 4. [Loss Books]. Art. [20].) Heads of Entry here—

1. Day, when the money should have been received.
2. On what account, it should have been received.
3. From whom.
4. Causes of non-receipt, to wit, blameless misfortune or misconduct: as ascertained, presumed, or conjectured.
5. If misfortune, how: if misconduct, by whom, and in what shapes.

II. *Unexpected Receipts:* Sums, if any, unexpectedly received, with like entries, as above in the case where *expectedly* received.

### Enactive

ART. 26. Subspecific Book the *second. Application Book*, none: other than the *Issue Book*, which see.

### Enactive. Expositive

ART. 27. Subspecific Book the *third. Issue Book*. Heads of Entry—
1. Days of issue.
2. Sums issued, as per expectation.
3. On whose account delivered.
4. To whom delivered.
5. By whom delivered.
6. Sums issued in compliance with *unexpected* demand.

### Enactive. Expositive

ART. 28. Appendage to the *Issues*. I. *Non-issues*, or say *Expected demands not fulfilled.* Heads of Entry.

1. Day, when the demand should have been fulfilled and issue made.
2. On what account the money should have been issued.
3. To whom it should have been issued.
4. Causes of non-issue, blameless accident or misconduct, as ascertained, presumed, or conjectured.
5. If misfortune, how: if misconduct, by whom, and in what shape.

II. *Unexpected demands fulfilled.* Heads of Entry.
1. On what account or ground made.
2. By whom made.

3. Causes of non-expectation.

III. *Unexpected demands not fulfilled.* Heads of Entry, the same.

## Instructional

ART. 29. Note, that these same heads of entry relative to non-receipts, demands unexpected, and issues unexpected, might, on occasion, be applied to *moveables* as well as *money.*

## Instructional. Expositive. Exemplificational

ART. 30. JOURNAL continued. Specific Book *the fifth. Exterior Occurrence Book.* Subdepartments, to the business of which, receipt and registration of evidence of exterior occurrences will be more particularly apt to be needful. Examples—

1. *Army* Subdepartment. Time, war-time. Examples—1. Occurrence, war-engagement: result, favourable or unfavourable. 2. Occurrence, arrival or miscarriage of a convoy.

2. *Navy* Subdepartment. Time and occurrences, as above.

3. *Preventive Service* Subdepartment. Occurrence, arrival of a calamity or commotion. For examples of calamities, see Ch. xi. MINISTERS SEVERALLY, §[5], *Preventive Service Minister.*

4. *Health* Subdepartment. Occurrence, breaking out or importation of a disease regarded as contagious.

5. *Foreign Relation* Subdepartment. Occurrence, symptoms observed of hostility on the part of a Foreign State.

6. *Trade* Subdepartment: to wit, in respect of states of things and events regarded as presenting a demand for fresh regulations relative to the manner of carrying on trade, or as obstructing or facilitating the giving execution and effect to existing regulations.

## Instructional. Expositive. Exemplificational

ART. 31. Heads of Entry. Examples as to occurrences.

1. Place of the occurrence: description as particular as may be.

2. Time of the occurrence: description as particular as may be.

3. Time,—to wit, *day*, and in some cases *hour*,—of the receipt of the information of the occurrence, at the Office by which it is recorded.

4. Name and description of the person or persons, by whom the information is delivered at the Office: distinguishing whether by personal appearance and oral discourse, or by epistolary discourse.

5. Nature of the evidence by which the fact of the occurrence is more or less probabilized.

*Instructional. Enactive*

ART. 32. With a solicitude proportioned to the importance of the occurrence,—on the receipt of the information at the Office, it will be the endeavour of the directing functionary to trace it up to its *sources*,—i.e. to trace each alledged fact up to the person or persons, who, in relation thereto, are stated as having, by means of any one or more of the five senses, been *percipient* witnesses. For the mode of making this investigation, see Ch. vi. [LEGISLATURE], §27, *Legislation Enquiry Judicatory:* and *Procedure Code*,—title, EVIDENCE.[1]

BIS-SECTION THE FOURTH. LOSS BOOKS

*Instructional. Expositive*

ART. 1. Loss, considered as liable to befall the service of a Subdepartment, may be considered as receiving division from two sources: to wit, the *subject-matter* and the *efficient cause.*

*Instructional. Expositive*

ART. 2. Subject-matters, as above, may be—
    1. Personal service, or say services of persons.
    2. Things [immoveable].
    3. Things moveable.
    4. Money.

*Instructional. Expositive*

ART. 3. Efficient causes of the loss may be—
    1. Purely *human* agency: to wit, on the part of functionaries or non-functionaries: on the part of functionaries belonging to the Office in question, or on the part of functionaries belonging to other Offices.
    2. Purely *natural* agency, as in the case of calamity or casualty: as to the different sorts of calamities, see Ch. xi. MINISTERS SEVERALLY, §[5], *Preventive Service Minister.*
    3. *Mixed* agency, or say partly natural, partly human agency: to wit, where the loss has for its efficient cause calamity or casualty, produced or aggravated by misconduct, culpable or criminal, positive or negative, on the part of some person or persons, functionaries or non-functionaries.

---

[1] Although Ch. XI, 'Evidence', of the *Principles of Judicial Procedure* (Bowring, ii. 3–188), does not discuss modes of investigation, it does contain a discussion of different forms of evidence. On modes of investigation, see also generally the *Equity Dispatch Court Bill* (Bowring, iii. 319–431) and the *Rationale of Judicial Evidence* (Bowring, vi. 189–585, vii. 1–600). On the Procedure Code, see Ch. V, § 5, Art. 6n, p. 38n.

*Instructional. Expositive. Enactive*

ART. 4. Subject-matter or source of loss, I, *Personal service*. Modes of loss. Examples—

1. Non-attendance, or say *absentation, absolute:* the functionary not being attendant or occupied in any place, on business belonging to his Office.

2. Non-attendance *relative:* attendance and occupation in a place in which his service was not so profitable as it would have been in some other place.

3. Application *uneconomical*: the work, to which his service was applied not so profitable as some other to which it might have been applied.

4. Non-operation, during attendance.

5. Operation *careless* or *rash* during attendance: thence, service not so profitable as it might have been.

*Instructional. Expositive. Enactive*

ART. 5. Incontestably proveable are—

1. Non-attendance absolute.

2. Non-attendance relative.

3. Non-operation during attendance.

Not incontestably proveable are—

1. Application uneconomical.

2. Operation careless or rash.

*Instructional. Expositive. Enactive*

ART. 6. Subject-matter or source of loss, II, a thing *immoveable*. Examples—

I. Land adapted to Husbandry. Modes of loss. Examples—

1. Non-culture.

2. Culture uneconomical.

II. Land covered with Buildings, or employed in Ground-works. Modes of loss. Examples—

1. Non-occupation.

2. Application uneconomical.

3. Deterioration spontaneous, for want of appropriate reparation.

4. Deterioration by positive human agency.

5. By natural causes,—inundation, fire.

6. Mode of reparation uneconomical.

III. Land, the value of which is constituted by application made of portions of its substance, after converting them from their [immoveable] to a moveable state: as in the case of mines, quarries, chalk-pits, gravel-pits. Modes of loss. Examples—

251

1. Non-application.
2. Application uneconomical.

IV. Land in any one of the above conditions.

Appropriate source of profit, self-dispossession temporary, by *lease-letting*. Modes of loss. Examples—

1. Non-lease-letting.
2. Lease-letting gratuitous.
3. Lease-letting at under price.
4. Lease-letting to a Lessee, by whom it is deteriorated.
5. Lease-letting to a non-solvent Lessee.
6. Lease-letting to a Lessee, by whom, at the end of the term, it is not surrendered.

### *Instructional. Expositive. Enactive*

ART. 7. Subject-matter or source of loss, III, a thing *moveable*. Modes of loss. Examples—

1. Non-receipt, in a case in which the article should have been received: with the cause of such non-receipt, whether pure accident or human agency, positive or negative, as in case of deterioration, as per No[s]. 4, 5, 6.
2. Non-application.
3. Application uneconomical.
4. Deterioration or destruction spontaneous for want of appropriate custody.
5. Deterioration by positive human agency.
6. Deterioration for want of reparation.
7. Miscollocation: stowage, in a place not conveniently accessible: whence, loss of labour.
8. In case of an article not applicable to use but by consumption, as food, fuel, etc., consumption useless.
9. Consumption excessive.
10. Consumption uneconomical.
11. Loan gratuitous.
12. Loan at under price.
13. Loan to a borrower, by whom it is deteriorated.
14. Loan to a non-solvent borrower.
15. Loan to a borrower, by whom it is not returned.
16. Elimination by accident, without blame to the custodient functionary.
17. Sale at under price.
18. Elimination through negligence or rashness on the part of the custodient functionary.
19. Embezzlement by the custodient functionary.

20. Theft by another person, functionary or non-functionary.

21. Fraudulent obtainment by ditto.

22. Peculation: that is to say, from loss in any one of the above or other shapes, profit derived by a directive or custodient funcationary.

### Instructional

ART. 8. Note that, in regard to sale, even where *auction* is the mode, the nature of the case keeps open a door to fraud, in two distinguishable shapes.

1. By accident or contrivance, the article, though in comparatively good condition, has been made to wear a deteriorated appearance: to the party meant to be favoured, information as to its true value is given, and at the same time concealed from others: by this means, it is sold to and bought by him at under value.

2. By confederacy with each other, with or without the participation of the functionary in question, divers persons, who otherwise would have been bidding one against another—say for six several articles, these being the only persons who could have bid for them—agree; and thus leave, to each of them, one of the articles, at the under price at which it has been put up.

### Instructional

ART. 9. Subdepartments, the business of which lies exposed to fraud in these shapes. Examples—

1. Navy Department:[1] in respect of sale of *old stores*.

2. Finance Subdepartment: in respect of sale of articles confiscated as contraband.

### Instructional

ART. 10. Against fraud in these shapes, the Members of the Public Opinion Tribunal will be on the alert, watching the offices belonging to the Subdepartment, in their several grades.

### Instructional. Expositive

ART. 11. Efficient causes and modes of spontaneous deterioration. Examples—

1. Evaporation.
2. Exsiccation.
3. Humectation.
4. Induration.
5. Emollition.

[1] See Ch. VIII, § 11, Art. 6n, p. 164n.

6. Fermentation,——saccharine, acetous, or putrifactive.

7. Discoloration.

### Instructional

ART. 12. Efficient causes or modes of spontaneous destruction. Examples—

1. [Subject-matter] vegetable, in a natural state, in large masses. Efficient cause, combustion in consequence of fermentation.

2. Subject-matter vegetable, in a manufactured state, sails or cordage heaped together in a humid state, with or without contiguity to oleaginous matter. Efficient cause, combustion, as above.

3. Subject-matter, mineral with vegetable in a manufactured state, gunpowder. Efficient cause of destruction by explosion, in window glass, a bubble, having the effect of a lens.

### Instructional

ART. 13. Subject-matters, considered in respect of their degrees of natural durability, independently of their application to use. Examples—

I. Articles of *greatest* durability.

1. Precious stones crystallized.

2. Stones (accretions of earths) in general.

3. Metals in general.

4. Shells of shell fish, by naturalists ranked under the head *vermes*.

5. Bones and horns of animals.

6. Alcohol, saline bodies, and other products of chemical analysis, if kept from evaporation and communication with the atmosphere.

II. Articles of *least* natural durability: though, for a greater or lesser length of time, preservable by art. Examples—

1. Flesh of animals.

2. Herbaceous parts of vegetables.

III. Articles of *intermediate* degrees of natural durability. Examples—

1. Wood of ligneous plants.

2. Seeds of plants, as wheat and other grain.

3. Roots, tuberose and bulbose.

### Instructional

ART. 14. Effect of *age* on the value of an article of stock; of age, and thence of the *time* during which it has continued in the service. In most cases, it will thus be *deteriorated*, but in some, it is, or may be *improved.*

*Instructional*

ART. 15. As to *persons*, up to a certain age, their value will naturally be increased by experience: beyond a certain age, it may be diminished by weakness.

*Instructional*

ART. 16. As to *things*. Of most things, the value regularly decreases by age: but of some, before it decreases, it commonly increases: witness, many fermented liquors. Of quadrupeds below the age of full growth, the value generally increases, up to that age.

*Instructional*

ART. 17. Hence, a memento, where the effect of the age is important enough to be worth the trouble:——establish a column, headed *'when introduced'*: with or without another, headed *'when produced'*: to wit, where the time of *production* is known, and the difference between that and the time of *introduction* into the service is considerable.[a]

*Instructional*

ART. 18. Subject-matters, considered as to the length of time, during which the use, made of them respectively, continues. Examples—
I. Articles of quickest consumption.
1. Gunpowder and shot.
2. Combustible matters used for heating and lighting.
3. Matter of food and drink.
II. Articles of slowest consumption.
1. Articles composed of gold, silver, and platina.
2. Articles composed of other metals.
3. Materials employed in building.

[a] For an indefinite length of time, in a perfectly closed vessel, by determinate and unvarying degrees of heat, the flesh of animals has been found preservable from the putrefactive, vegetable matter in the soft and moist state from the acetous as well as the putrefactive fermentation. What other changes they would undergo, and whether any for the better, in greater heat, and for greater length of time, remains for the most part to be tried. Of late, wine has been improved by heat: so, by cold. For heat, the instrument would be steam: for cold, ice.[1]

[1] For Bentham's much earlier interest in ways of preserving perishable foodstuffs, see UC cvi. 17–75, MSS written at various dates between 1794 and 1809 and largely connected with his plans for the economical management of institutions for the poor.

4. Materials employed in receptacles for liquids, and for solids, in a state of powder:——glass and earthenware.

5. Materials employed in the composition of the *steadiments*, or say unmoving parts of fixed machinery.

6. Utensils——articles of household furniture, employed as *receptacles* for smaller articles: chests of drawers, bookcases, etc.

7. Articles of household furniture used for repose: the ligneous parts——chairs, tables, bedsteads.

8. Artillery.

III. Articles of intermediate quickness of consumption.

1. Articles of household furniture: those composed of the oxydable metals, pure and mixed, as iron, copper, brass, etc.

2. Articles composed of matter in a filamentous state, employed as furniture of ships or houses.

3. Tools, and the *moving* parts of machinery.

4. Beasts employed in conveyance, or in giving motion to machinery.

### Instructional

ART. 19. In the business of each subdepartment, immediate subaggregates——of the aggregate stock of moveables, kept in custody, and applied or waiting to be applied, and as such considered as liable to be subject-matters or sources of loss,——are

1. Articles of work finished for use.

2. Materials for the formation of work, finished for use.

3. Machines, tools, and other instruments, employed in the formation of work finished for use, or in the formation of other instruments so employed.

4. Receptacles, fixed and moveable, of all sorts.

5. Vehicles of all sorts.

6. Beasts, employed in conveyance, or in giving motion to machinery. See Art[s]. 16, 17, and Bissection the [second], Art. 26, page 237.

### Instructional. Expositive. Enactive

ART. 20. Subject-matter or source of loss, IV, *Money*. Modes of loss. Examples——

I. Loss by disserviceable *procurement*. Modes. Examples——

1. Taxation misseated.

2. Borrowing on terms less advantageous than might have been obtained.

3. Payment or repayment postponed, on terms less advantageous than might have been obtained.

256

II. Loss by disserviceable *non-receipts*. Modes. Examples—

1. Non-receipt *definitive*, or say *absolute*, through negligence.

2. Non-receipt *temporary* through negligence: the money not received till after the day on which it might have been, and ought to have been received.

3. Non-receipt, *definitive* or *temporary*, through favour to, but without concert with, a party, from whom it might have been and ought to have been received.

4. Non-receipt for reward, in concert and by complicity with, a party from whom it might and ought to have been received.

III. Loss by disserviceable *application* or *non-application*. [Modes. Examples—]

1. Purchase of personal services, things immoveable, or things moveable, at an over price.

2. Non-purchase of ditto, till after the commencement of the time when needed: thereby, loss of the value of the use, minus the interest of the money.

3. Purchase on credit instead of for ready money: thence loss by the overprice.

4. Omission to employ it in loan, when received in quantity exceeding the demand for purchase.

5. Note, that if exacted in greater quantity than needed, or before needed, the loss falls on the contributors.

6. Non-application definitive, or say *hoarding*.

IV. Loss by *transformation*. Modes. Examples—

1. Transformation uneconomical, by simple refusion: subject-matter of loss, the expense of coinage, and pay for labour employed in calling in the current stock.

2. Transformation uneconomical, and *fraudulent:* to wit, by diminution of quantity, or deterioration of quality by alloy, without correspondent change of denomination.

3. Augmentation uneconomical of the aggregate quantity: to wit, by addition of *paper money*, consisting of promises, to the stock of *actual money*, thereby lowering its value.

V. Loss by disserviceable elimination of money, including expenditure in purchase or supposed purchase of *Personal services*. Modes. Examples—

1. Pay attached to *needless Offices:* offices, in their nature useful, but, by and in proportion to over number, superfluous, and so far useless.

2. Pay attached to *useless* offices: useless in their nature: the labour, if any performed in them, being useless.

3. Pay attached to *sinecure* offices: to an official situation, instituted

or continued, on pretence of services rendered, when in fact no labour is performed in respect of them in any shape.

4. *Over-pay*, attached to *needful* offices.

VI. Loss by purchase or hire, of *things*, immoveable or moveable. [Modes. Examples——]

1. Purchase or hire of things needless, as above.

2. Purchase or hire of things useless, as above.

3. Expenditure on the pretended purchase or hire of a thing not procured, as above.

4. Expenditure, during an unnecessarily protracted series of years, in the fabrication of a thing not completed for use till the end of the series: at which time it may or may not be needed.

In this case, the loss consists in the loss of the interest of the money expended in making the several instalments.[a]

### Enactive. Ratiocinative

ART. 21. For prevention of loss,——on receipt of an article, into what custody shall it be delivered? that of some *one* person, or that of persons in any and what number *greater* than one?

*Answer.* Into the custody of one person and no more.

*Reasons.* 1. As the number of co-responsibles increases, the effective force and efficiency of the responsibility decreases. As to this, see § 3, *Number in an Office*.

[a] In former days, in the English Navy Subdepartment, a practice had place, of expending money in this way, in a work which, at the intended rate of progress, could not have been completed, or so much as been expected to be completed, earlier than at the end of perhaps half a century. But if, without the work in question, the service could be sufficiently provided for during any such term, so might it thereafter for ever more. Some hundred thousands of pounds was that which, according to a calculation made at the time, would, at the end of the term, have been the amount of the loss: not to speak of the case, in which, by that time, the work might, by any one of a number of contingencies, be rendered useless, the demand being superseded, or being better provided for by other means. Representation to this effect was made, and the calculation exhibited by a functionary, to whose office it belonged: to this representation no regard was paid at the time: whether since, cannot here be stated.[1]

[1] The functionary mentioned here is almost certainly Bentham's brother Samuel Bentham (1757–1831), who was appointed in 1796 to the office of Inspector General of Naval Works and later served on the Navy Board, retiring in 1812. In 1813 he published *Services rendered in the Civil Department of the Navy in investigating and bringing to Official Notice Abuses and Imperfections* . . . , London, 1813, where (pp. 18–21) he noted the defects of the prevailing method of financing protracted building schemes. He added (pp. 21–4) that he had given evidence on the point to a Commons committee in 1798, but implies that he failed to bring about reform.

2. Blame is by each laid to the account of the other.

3. As their number increases,——so, in case of delinquency, the strength of the sinister support, afforded to all by their several connections.

### Instructional. Enactive. Ratiocinative

ART. 22. But, so as the person responsible is but one, no matter how many others concur *with* him in the operation belonging to custody, so they be assistants chosen by or for him, or by a Depute chosen by him, or a Depute chosen for him.

### Instructional. Enactive. Ratiocinative

ART. 23. So, the greater the number of *subsequently* attesting Inspectors, one after another, the better: since, by their attestation, they are responsible for the existence and condition of the article: responsible, that is to say at the *time* of such their *inspection:* not at any *subsequent time:* for, thereafter, in respect of the existence and condition of the things in question, the responsibility will rest exclusively on the custodient and subsequently inspecting functionaries; on the custodient at all times; on the inspecting, at the time of inspection.

### Instructional. Ratiocinative

ART. 24. Principle of these observations, the *individual responsibility principle*. Corresponding rule.——Of responsibility, in whatever shape, imposed upon a trustee, the efficiency is *diminished* by every *co-trustee* added to him.

### Enactive

ART. 25. In the Loss Book, in every page,——in which entry is made of an article of loss, as above,——at the end of the lines will be provided five columns; the first, headed with the words *'Present value in money;'* the second with the word *'Ascertained;'* the third with the word *'Supposed;'* the fourth with the word *'Conjectured;'* and the fifth with the word *'Unconjecturable:'* the day indicated by the word *present*, being the day on which the entry under that head is made.

### Enactive. Instructional

ART. 26. In each of these columns, it will in each office be for the care of the directing functionary to cause to be made, on the occasion of each article of loss, in addition to the sum expressive of the *amount*, or say *money value* of the loss, an entry under that one of the four last heads which, in his judgment, is the proper one: except that,—where it is under the word *unconjecturable* that the entry is made,—the line, in the column headed '*present value in money*,' will of course be blank.

### Enactive

ART. 27. In each Subdepartment, to the directing functionary of each office it will belong—to secure the regular making of the above entries,—by the'directing functionary—of the office, if one,—or if more than one, by the several directing functionaries of the several offices, one under another, subordinate to his own.

### Enactive

ART. 28. To the Prime Minister it will belong—to secure the regular making of these same entries, by the care of the Minister in each Subdepartment, as above.

### Instructional

ART. 29. To the several Members of the Public Opinion Tribunal it will belong—upon occasion, to judge of the propriety and verity, of the indications afforded by the several entries, as above.

### Ratiocinative

ART. 30. The allowance given by the word *unconjecturable* considered,—no obligation of insincerity will in any case be imposed, by the obligation of making entry under some one of the four heads, at the option of the person in question, as above: nor yet, will an entry under that head be without its use: for, when, under that same head, an entry is made,—the propriety and sincerity of it will lie open to the judgment of the several above-mentioned constituted authorities.

### Instructional

ART. 31. Causes or occasions of loss, by *human agency* on the part of supreme functionaries. Examples—

### I. *Incidental Expenditures*

1. Expenditure, of persons, things moveable, and money,—in commencement, continuance of, or preparation for, needless *wars*.

2. Expenditure, of ditto, in the purchase, foundation, or maintenance, of *distant dependencies*.

3. Expenditure, of money, on articles, for the accommodation or amusement of the comparatively *opulent few*, at the expense of all,

including, in prodigiously greater number, the *unopulent many*, who are incapable of participating in the benefit: production[s] of the *fine arts*, for instance, and books, the uselessness of which is demonstrated by their rarity. The expense, however, is in this third case but as a drop of water to the ocean, compared with what it is in the two former: and the mischief consists——not so much in the absolute expense as in the preference given to it over *needful* expenses, leaving thereby the *correspondent evils* in a state of continuance and increase, ——and in its operation in the character of an instrument of *corruption*, by means of the official situations carved out of it,——and in that of an instrument of *delusion*, contributing, by the awe-striking quality of the object, to beget and maintain a habit of blind and unscrutinizing submission on the part of the subject-many.

## II. *Permanent Expenditure*

4. Expenditure, in the pay attached to needless and sinecure offices, and the overpay attached to useful and needful ones: and note well, on each occasion, the *corruptive* and *delusive* influence, inseparably attached, by the nature of the case, to every particle of such waste.

For the course taken for the minimization of such waste——and, by that in aid of other means, for the maximization of appropriate aptitude,——with reference to the functionaries belonging to each office, see the several ensuing Sections, headed *Remuneration, Locable who, Located how, and Dislocable [how]*.

### *Instructional*

ART. 32. *Stock-in-hand Books*. Whatsoever be the *subject-matter*, and the *place*,——the manner of ascertaining, on each day, the quantity of the stock in hand, of each of the above four species of stock, on that day, will be the same.

On the day, next to that on which the original Outset Stock Book and the first Journal Book bore date,——the stock in hand will, in regard to each species of stock, be composed of the stock as per *Original* Outset Book, *adding* the amount of receipts, if any, on the first day, and deducting the amount of issues and losses, if any, on that same day.

If, for the purpose of presenting to view the *balance* of the stock in hand applicable to the service of each day, a set of books were instituted, they might bear the name of *Stock-in-hand Books*. The matter in question being, as above, entered,——the whole of it——in the Journal, the only question will be, as to the copying it, in this form and method, into a separate set of books.

## Instructional

ART. 33. To the *immoveable stock*, unless it be in respect of the moveable stock attached to it, this operation will not have application. Applied to the *personal* stock, and the *money* stock, it is simple, and accordingly attended with little difficulty. Not so in the case of *moveable* stock: unless it be of a sort, the importance of which, with a view to the purposes in question, is sufficient to warrant the time and expense of keeping a separate account of it. In so far as this degree of importance has place,—above may be seen the mode.

### BIS-SECTION THE FIFTH. SUBSIDIARY BOOKS

## Instructional

ART. 1. Of books which there may be found a convenience in employing as subsidiary to the above examples, are the following—[1]

V. I. RETROACCEPTION BOOK. Heads of Entry for this Book, names of the Offices from which the several articles have been *received back* after transmission thereto. For Subheads see [Bissection] 3, Art. [18, *Receipt Book*].[2]

VI. II. RETROTRANSMISSION BOOK. For Heads and Subheads see above *Retroacception Book*, and page 247, *Bissection* 3, Art. 23, *Issue Book*.

## Instructional

ART. 2. Other Subsidiary Books a demand may perhaps be found for, created by local or temporary circumstances. To keep on the look-out for such demand will be among the objects of the Legislature's care.

---

[1] The numerals V and VI before the two books listed in this article do not fit readily into any previous sequence. One possibility is that they refer back to the fourfold classification of 'Generic Books' in Art. 12 of the first Bissection (p. 221): Original Outset Books, Periodical Outset Books, Journals, and Loss Books. ('Periodical Outset Books' were not in fact examined in detail, perhaps because the particulars were supposed to have been subsumed under those for Original Outset Books.) This explanation remains highly tentative, however; and it is clear that Bentham failed to work out fully and systematically the various enumerations in this section.

[2] This cross-reference follows the Bowring emendation of the 1830 text, which reads, '§ 3 [probably a misprint for "§ 2§ 3", the abbreviation occasionally used in 1830 for "Bissection 3"], Art. 8, *Entrance Book*'. This 1830 reference fails because in fact the article cited does not list subheadings but gives a reference to another article for such a list (p. 240). The Bowring alternative is an improvement inasmuch as the article now cited (p. 244) does list some of the subheadings, giving a reference to yet another article for the remainder.

BIS-SECTION THE SIXTH. ABBREVIATIONS

## Instructional

ART. [1].[1] *Abbreviations*. Antecedently to the organization of the several Subdepartments, or subsequently, on report from the several directing and registering functionaries,—it will be for the consideration of the Legislature, whether, in every Subdepartment, or in any one or more, and which of the Subdepartments,—in the making of the entries, *abbreviations*, in any and what cases, and if in any, in what form and tenor, shall be ordained or allowed.

## Ratiocinative. Exemplificational

ART. [2]. Antagonizing consideration for and against the practice. Examples—

[I]. *For the practice*. [1.] Saving of time and labour of writers: thence of expense to Governments.

2. Saving of time and labour of readers: to wit,

1. Functionaries belonging to the office.

2. So, among suitors, all to whom the abridging characters have become as familiar as the unabridged.

3. In the abbreviations commonly employed in manuscripts before printing had come into use,—saving, in respect of time, labour, and thence expense employed in writing, was manifestly the advantage, by the contemplation of which the practice was produced: had not such advantage been actually obtained, the practice, it may be thought, would not have continued.[a]

II. *Against the practice*. Disadvantage to such suitors, in whose instance, in the capacity of readers, more time and labour is consumed by the abridged form than by the unabridged.

[a] As in *writing* and *reading*, more particularly in writing, so in pronunciation. In the corresponding advantage of despatch may be seen the cause of the continually increasing deviations of the pronunciation at each point of time of a great part of the aggregate stock of words, as compared with the pronunciation still indicated by the written characters: for example, in French, at the end of the third person plural of verbs, the omission of the entire syllable *ent*, the sound of which is in other positions so strong and marked.

[1] 1830 numbers the six articles in this section from 27 to 32. The reason may be that Bentham originally envisaged this material as part of the first Bissection, though that in its final form had only 23 articles. This is suggested by the reference in Art. 6 (p. 266) to 'Art. 4' with no indication as to which section or bissection is intended. The reference is in fact clearly to Art. 4 of the first Bissection, and the form of reference would be normal within the same section or equivalent division of the text.

Antagonizing advantages—on the part of the *abridged* form, *conciseness;* on the part of the *unabridged* form, *clearness.*

### Instructional

ART. [3]. Means of compromise. Rule 1. As to words singly taken. For the abbreviated form, take not forms altogether unanalagous, such as are the *algebraic*, but fragments of the respective words: to wit, *initial letters*, with or without final or other succeeding ones.

### Instructional

ART. [4]. Rule 2. Employ no abbreviated word, without inserting it in an alphabetical list of abbreviated expressions, followed and explained by the corresponding unabbreviated ones: that list being entered, on a page opposite to the page on which the title of the book is entered.

### Instructional. Ratiocinative

ART. [5]. Rule 3. So, in regard to *propositions*, and *locutions* composed of *fragments*, or *aggregates*, or aggregates with fragments, of propositions.

Rule 4. In written instruments, addressed to, or designed for the perusal of, individuals at large, who are not in the habit of attendance at the office,—employ not any abbreviations, which are not perfectly familiar to individuals at large.

Rule 5. In the case of the books kept at the offices, employ not any abbreviations, by which, on the part of individuals at large, in their capacity of Members of the Public Opinion Tribunal, facility and clearness of conception will be diminished.

Rule 6. Leave not, to functionaries in each or any office, the faculty of employing, at pleasure, abbreviations of their own devising.

*Reasons.* If *yes,*—1. There might, in this particular, be as many different languages as there are offices.

2. Abbreviations would be liable to be employed for the express purpose, of eluding the scrutiny, and diminishing the tutelary power of the Public Opinion Tribunal.[a]

[a] In a Subdepartment of the Finance Subdepartment of England—to wit, in an office called that of *Clerk of the Pells*, (*Pells* means *parchments*), belonging to what is called the *Receipt of the Exchequer*, the money accounts used to be kept, and, it is believed, still continue to be kept, in characters composed of abridgments of Latin words: characters such as were in use before the introduction of the Arabic numerals. In this form, the difficulty attached to the operation of *summing up*, how moderate soever were the number of the items it was applied to, was such as may be left to be imagined. On various occasions, propositions having been made for the discontinuance of it,—to what a degree the

## Instructional. Ratiocinative

ART. [6]. Securities for correctness and completeness in *entries*. Properties, desirable on the part of each such entry, as per [Bissection

functionary, who was the chief if not the sole adept in this mysterious language, clung to it and resisted the discontinuance of it,——may also be left to be imagined.[1]

In some of the Oxford Colleges, at any rate in Queen's College, accounts of the articles of diet, as bespoken and delivered, are, or at least used to be, entered in the like and no other mode: entered by the cooks, the under-cook, and the keeper of the bread and beer. On a certain occasion, complaint, well or ill-grounded, was made of the cooks, as having charged the under graduate Members for articles never delivered. The defence was true and simple. The books were constantly open to all members. True, but the characters being more repulsive than even algebraical ones, the books might almost as well, to the purpose of the security in question, have been kept closed.[2]

Note, that *arithmetical* expression is throughout but an abridgement of ordinary ditto: *algebraical*, of arithmetical and ordinary mixed.

Note also, that of whatever matter is expressed by arithmetical and algebraical signs, there is not a particle that could not be expressed by the signs employed in ordinary discourse; and note that in this case it would be intelligible, and without effort, to non-mathematical readers at large.

And yet, of that stock of information which has been obtained by the use of

---

[1] Already in the 1780s the Commissioners of Inquiry into the Public Accounts had criticised the use of Latin, Roman numerals, and unintelligible hieroglyphics in the Exchequer, of which the Pells Office was part; and the complaint was repeated by several subsequent parliamentary committees. An Act passed in 1821, 1 & 2 Geo. IV c. 121, sought to enforce the use of the English language and of Arabic numerals; but Exchequer officials continued to use Latin wherever they were not expressly required by the statute to do otherwise, as was discovered by a Select Committee on Public Accounts in 1831. The Pells Office itself was abolished in 1834 as part of the sweeping Exchequer reforms introduced in that year. See E. W. Cohen, *The Growth of the British Civil Service 1780-1939*, London, 1941, pp. 31, 37, 49-51; H. Roseveare, *The Treasury*, London, 1969, pp. 133-4.

[2] What Bentham says here is partly true, but not the whole truth. The Buttery Books in the archives of Queen's College show that in Bentham's time there the butler, the cook, and others similarly concerned, used Arabic numerals to record sums of more than a penny, and had done so for at least a century before. They did however use the standard Latin abbreviations for halfpennies (*ob.* = *obolus*) and farthings (*qa.* = *quadrata*). Since most of the daily entries seem to have been for items costing a halfpenny or a farthing each, the books are studded with these abbreviations; and this may have misled Bentham into thinking that all the entries were composed of Latin abbreviations. In the termly accounts, summarising all the daily items extracted from the Buttery Books, Arabic numerals were used. Thus Bentham's own account for the Hilary term of 1765 is:

| | in promptu[ario] | in lardario | summa totalis |
|---|---|---|---|
| D[S] Bentham | 0:10:6½ | 6:0:11½ | 6:11:6 |

(Queen's College Archives, Kitchen and Buttery Accounts, 1756-85).

265

the first], Art. 4,[1] *correctness, clearness,* and *comprehensiveness:* on the part of the aggregate of all, comprehensiveness and symmetry. Correspondent errors—opposite to correctness, *false entry:* to wit, either by simple addition of false statements, or substitution of false

those signs,—more especially that most formidable sort, composed of letters of the alphabet,—it seems clear enough, that not more than a comparatively small part could have been obtained without them.

The reason is—that, but for these modes of compression, to such a bulk would the matter have swollen, that, before the result had been obtained, the minds of writers and readers would have been bewildered and put to a stand: the conceptive faculty not being able to grasp, at once, the whole quantity necessary to the obtainment of the result.

Newton could never have been Newton, had he lived in Grecian or Roman days.

By development given to this conception, considerable facility might, it is believed, be given to instruction in this branch. For this purpose a few problems would be to be chosen; and, of the deduction employed in the solution, translations made into the language employed in ordinary discourse; with indication given of the use by which each stage or step in the process was suggested.

### Italian Book-keeping Nomenclature.[2]

1. In no book kept in the here-proposed mode, are the words *Debtor* and *Creditor* employed, as in that, as heads.

2. To the mode of expression, in which, by the heads here employed, the information is thus given, belong the properties following—

1. It is *intelligible* to all alike.

2. It conveys not any idea *contrary to truth:*—inconsistent with the idea meant to be expressed.

3. Not so the language in which *Debtor* and *Creditor* are employed.

4. In the mode of expression ordinar[ily] and universally employed, and accordingly here employed, *Debtor* and *Creditor* mean *persons* only: nor do they express other subject-matters, either received or issued, or expected to be received or issued.

In the technical language which has obtained currency among mercantile men, namely, that employed in the *Italian Method of Book-keeping, things* are absurdly styled *Debtors* and *Creditors*. Wine, for example, is stated $D^r$. to Cloth, or Cloth to Wine; and both to *sundries*.

5. These forms of expression are misrepresentative and perfectly useless: they can no otherwise be made intelligible, than by translation into correspondent portions of the universally employed language. To what end then employ, on

---

[1] See p. 263, n. 1. Bowring emends 1830, 'Art. 4' to read 'Art. 5'—that is, presumably, of the present Bissection. But this is unlikely to represent Bentham's intention.

[2] See also *Official Aptitude Maximized; Expense Minimized* (Bowring, v. 263-386), Bowring v. 383-6. The basic double-entry technique of the Italian system of book-keeping can be found in 1340 in the accounts of the Massari of Genoa, though it is believed to date back for a further century before that. The first explicit exposition of the system seems to be in Luca Paccioli, *Summa de Arithmetica Geometria Proportione et Proportionalita*, Venice, 1494.

to true: opposite to completeness, *non-entry:* omission of matter that ought to have been inserted.

In the one shape as well as in the other, the error may have had for its cause either matter foreign to the conduct of the functionary in question, or misconduct on his part: if misconduct, it may have had for its cause a deficiency, either in moral, intellectual or active aptitude: if in moral, either, 1, evil intention, with correspondent evil-consciousness——the result of misdirected attention: or 2, *negligence,* or say *carelessness*——the result of want of due attention.

Against misconduct in both these shapes, the direct and appropriate security will be *punishment,* as to which, see the Penal Code.[1]

For securities as well against misconduct through *moral* inaptitude, as above, as against deficiency in respect of appropriate *intellectual* and appropriate *active* aptitude, see in §25, *Securities, etc.* those which apply to the due exercise of this function, together with all others belonging to functionaries in this Department.

any of these occasions, the generally unintelligible, to the exclusion of the universally intelligible locutions?

6. To non-professional eyes, they keep the subjects involved in darkness: to professional they afford no additional light.

7. Practical mischievous effects are——

1. Concealing the nature of the transactions, from many to whom the information would be of use.

2. Waste of time: to wit, of time employed by men in rendering intelligible to them this useless, and, to all but the initiated, unintelligible, or, at the best, perplexing phraseology.

On this occasion, as on so many others, sinister interest in a pecuniary shape is not by any means the sole cause of the adherence to ill-adapted practice. Self-esteem, from the possession of a supposed valuable acquirement, in which a comparatively few are sharers,——unwillingness to regard as wasted, so considerable a portion of a man's time——are sentiments, which concur with authority-begotten prejudice in strengthening the attachment to the practice, even in the most highly cultivated minds.

At any rate, so long as, on his part, the need of reference to documents expressed in this language continues, by no degree of original inaptitude can a man be warranted in leaving it unlearnt. But, to enable him to *read* it in the books of other commercialists, no necessity is there for his *writing* it in his own.

To a question concerning the particular *shape* in which the supposed *usefulness* of this distorted language may be seen to manifest itself, *brevity* was the answer returned. For a trial of its title to this useful property a short enough process might suffice. In a parallel column, opposite to each of the several technical phrases, write its import in ordinary language: adding in each case an exemplification or two of the use of it as applied to the details of so many individual transactions. It would thus be seen——in the first place, whether by the employment given to the technical language, any saving at all were made in respect of quantity of matter: in the next place, if yes, what may be the amount of it.

---

[1] See Ch. V, §6, Art. 2n, p. 39n, and Table 2.

## SECTION 8

### REQUISITIVE FUNCTION

#### Expositive

ART. 1. Necessary to conception of the *function* styled *requisitive*, is that of the *administration* MANDATE, styled a *procuration-mandate*. By a *Procuration* Mandate, understand a written instrument, by which, for the service of the public, certain supplies therein mentioned are ordered to be *procured.*

#### Enactive

ART. 2. Exceptions excepted,—for the service belonging to any Administration Subdepartment, to the *Legislature* alone it belongs, on each occasion, to issue, for the procurement of a supply in any shape, a Procuration Mandate.

#### Enactive

ART. 3. Exceptions are the several occasions, on which, by some precedent act of the Legislature, authority for issuing Procuration Mandates, for the purposes, and to the effect therein mentioned, has been given to the Prime Minister or a Minister within his Subdeparment.

#### Ratiocinative

ART. 4. Exercising this function without authority from the Legislature, any functionary would, to the extent of the supply ordered by him, be acting as *Legislator:* to the amount of the expense thereof, he would be *imposing a tax.*

#### Instructional. Ratiocinative

ART. 5. The person, by whom such indication is afforded, will naturally be a functionary, and *he* the functionary for the service of whose office the article in question is needed.[1] In addition to whatsoever may be the function, to the exercise of which the supply in question is needful,—now comes the additional function, distinct from and in its exercise preparatory to, that of the *procurative* function, necessarily called into exercise—call it the *requisitive.*

---

[1] The clause 'by whom such indication is afforded' does not seem to refer very directly to anything Bentham has said so far in this section: he presumably had in mind an indication of whatever need for supply had arisen.

### Enactive

ART. 6. Accordingly, in so far as, for any supply that comes to be needed, no sufficient procuration mandate remaining in force has been issued by the Legislature,—exercise will be given to this same *Requisitive function.*

### Expositive

ART. 7. By the *Requisitive function* understand *that* to which exercise is given by a functionary, when, conceiving, that for the due exercise of some other function belonging to him, the faculty of giving direction to the labour of some *person*, or that of making application of some *thing* to the public service is necessary,—he makes application to the Legislature, or to some other functionary, in whose power it is to place the article of supply at his disposal for that purpose.

### Expositive

ART. 8. Name of the written instrument, by which such application is made, a *requisitional instrument;* or for shortness, a *requisition: requisitor*, the functionary *by* whom,—*requisitee*, the functionary *to* whom, it is addressed.

### Expositive

ART. 9. The procuration mandate in this case not being valid or attainable, otherwise than by means of a correspondent requisition-instrument,—the faculty of issuing the *requisition-instrument* is, to that of issuing the correspondent *procuration-mandate*, what, in the case of a law at large, the *initiative* is to the *consummative*, or say the *effective.*

### Instructional. Ratiocinative

ART. 10. Whatsoever be the respective situations and ranks of *requisitor* and *requisitee*, the name of the instrument will be a requisitional, or say *requisition instrument*, or say *a requisition*, and no other. By any such distinction as that between *requisition* and *petition*, jealousies and contests might probably, useless complication would certainly, be introduced.

### Enactive

ART. 11. The *places*, from which requisition instruments will be issued, are the several *offices, in* which, for their several businesses, the need of the subject-matters required, is deemed to have place. Of all such need, indication will at all times be given, by means of the

269

mimographical documents, as per §7, *Statistic function*, [Bissection] 2, Art. 7, with or without the aid of the *Inspection-visits.*

### Instructional. Enactive

ART. 12. Of the *heads*, under which the matter of a requisition instrument will, in all cases, be contained, examples are as follows—

1. Supplies needed what, according as they are *persons, things*, or *money*.

2. If *persons*,—*names* and *descriptions*, with the *expense*, as known or estimated, on the occasion of each.

3. If *things*,—*names, qualities*, and *quantities*, with their respective *prices* as known or estimated.

4. Proposed best *mode* of procurement, as per §4, *Functions in all;* and §7, *Statistic function*, [Bissection 1, Art. 18.]¹

5. *Times*, within which respectively needed.

6. *Times*, within which supposed capable of being made *forthcoming* at the place where needed, in a state fit for use.

7. Statement of the *stock in hand*, if any, of the article *required*, with reference to the *mimographical* documents, if any, as per §7, *Statistic function*, on the face of which the state of the stock appears.

### Enactive

ART. 13. When the Requisitor is the Minister, and the Requisitee the Prime Minister, the Requisitee will either reject the requisition, or confirm it: if he confirms it, he does so either simply, or with amendment: and, in either case, issues a correspondent *procuration mandate:* and so in the case of any other requisitor or requisitee.

### Instructional. Enactive

ART. 14. Checks on the requisition will be—the exemplars of the mimographical documents and other statistical matter, in the hands of the functionaries, to whom, in each case, it will belong—to reject, simply confirm, or substitute, as above.

### Enactive

ART. 15. Such procuration mandate will be transmitted to the Requisitor, either immediately, or through the medium of the Finance Minister, as the case may require.

¹ 1830 ends the reference to §7 with the symbol '§2§' (= Bissection). Bowring supplies the rest of the reference but mistakenly refers to Bissection 2 instead of Bissection 1, which Bentham seems to have intended. See Art. 27, p. 274, where the same reference is correct and complete in both editions.

*Enactive*

ART. 16. To the Minister of each Subdepartment it belongs, at all times, on his responsibility, to transmit, to the Prime Minister, appropriate and timely requisition instruments, for the procurement of such supplies, the need of which, for the business of his Subdepartment, has, from time to time, come to have place.

*Instructional. Expositive*

ART. 17. Service *permanent* and *occasional;* or say *ordinary* and *extraordinary*. In each several instance, in which the need of an article or aggregate of articles of *supply*, is regarded as having place,—it will belong either to the *permanent*, or to the *occasional* branch of the service: either to the *ordinary* or to the *extraordinary* branch.

*Instructional*

ART. 18. At the commencement of this Code, the Legislature will have to make provision of the *first* supply provided: call it the *outset supply*. On that occasion, it will be considered—whether any, and if any, what part, of that which is provided, shall be distinguished from the rest by any such denomination as the *occasional*, or say *extraordinary* supply.

*Instructional. Expositive*

ART. 19. The particulars of the *outset supply* being settled, the Legislature will determine and declare—at what point of time the provision thus made shall, for the first time, be *renewed:* say at the expiration of the then current solar year, and thenceforward at the expiration of each ensuing solar year. If the point of time be any other than the last moment of the solar year, and the recurrence of the renewal *annual*,—here then will be constantly employed and necessarily referred to, a sort of year different from the solar: call it the *service year*. If, in this case, to outweigh the burthen of the complication, there be any preponderant convenience,—any Subdepartment, or any office, may accordingly have its own *service year*, different from that of every other office, as well as from the *solar year*.

Name of the day on which, for the service of the then next ensuing year, whether solar year or service year, the consideration of the supply to be provided for that same ensuing year commences, say *The General Supply Day*.

*Instructional*

ART. 20. On this occasion, the Legislature will determine and declare

—whether, in the interval between the time of this first supply and that of the next, provision may, to any and what amount, by any and what functionary or functionaries be made: and in each case, if yes, [whether] by *spontaneous* mandate,[1] or not otherwise than in consequence of a *requisition instrument;* declaring, in this case, from what office or offices, for the obtainment of the corresponding procurement mandate, it may be addressed.

### Instructional. Expositive

ART. 21. Diversifications, which, on this occasion, the nature of the case admits of, are the following.

1. *Procurement spontaneous*—that is to say effected without *antecedent* requisition; namely, by an occasional *mandate*, issued *by the Legislature*, and directed either to the *Prime Minister*, or to this or that *Minister*, or *subordinate* of any grade belonging to the Administration department: and, in this last case, either *directly*, or through the *medium* of the Prime Minister's office.

2. In virtue of appropriate general and *permanent* powers conferred by the Legislature, procurement mandate *spontaneous*, emanating from, and issued by, the *Prime Minister*, and addressed to such subordinate functionary or functionaries, as the nature of the case is thought by him to indicate.

3. The like from the *Minister* of any subdepartment.

4. The like from a *subordinate* of the Minister in any subdepartment.

### Enactive. Ratiocinative

ART. 22. If, in this way, from any office, [a] procurement mandate, whether spontaneously issued or in consequence of requisition, be sent down to an office of any other than the next immediate grade, exemplars will, at the same time, be transmitted to the intermediate office or offices. Reasons—

1. That, in case of neglect or delay, compliance with the mandate may be enforced by the intermediate superordinate.

2. That no functionary may, without his knowledge, be divested of any part of the stock, personal or real, of which he may have need, and for which he is responsible.

### Instructional

ART. 23. On the occasion of the first *general supply day* that ensues

---

[1] 1830, 'if yes, by *spontaneous* mandate . . .'; Bowring adds 'whether' to bring out the sense of the two alternatives, that is, the use of the spontaneous mandate or the requisition instrument.

after provision made of the *outset supply*,—the Legislature will have before its eyes, or at its command, the result, in all its parts and elements, of the *Statistic* and *Registration* system, carried on during that interval, as per §7, *Statistic Function*. It will thereby, on appropriate and substantial ground, be in a condition to draw a more determinate line, between the *ordinary* and all *extraordinary* service,—and to determine—by what offices, if by any, and for what purpose, procurement mandates may be issued, without antecedent and correspondent requisition; and from and to what offices, *requisition instruments* may be transmitted, in such sort, that, from those to which they are transmitted, correspondent procurement mandates may be issued, and followed by the transmission of the correspondent supplies, when accordingly procured.[1]

## Instructional

ART. 24. Of the considerations, by which, on these occasions, the determination, of the Legislature will naturally be guided, examples are as follows—

1. The importance of the branch of service in question.

2. The quantity of the stock, in whatsoever shape, of which, in the interval, need is capable of having place, and likely to have place.

3. The degree of suddenness, of which the demand is susceptible.

4. The expense necessary for procurement.

Note, that by the uninterruptedness of the labours of the Legislator, as per Ch. vi. LEGISLATURE, §18, *Attendance,*—the *latitude* of the powers necessary to be given for procurement, as above, with or without antecedent requisition, will of course be *minimized.*

## Instructional

ART. 25. To a subordinate, scarcely will the importance of the service afford any sufficient reason for giving the power of procurement, in any other case than that in which, by his waiting for authority from his superordinate, the performance of the service to which the article was necessary, would have been prevented or materially delayed.

## Instructional

ART. 26. Examples of cases, in which, in a subordinate situation, power of *self-supply*, as above, may be necessary, are the following—

1. *Military necessity*, in the *land* defensive service.

2. So, in the *sea* defensive service; see Ch. x. DEFENSIVE FORCE.

---

[1] This article seems out of place and should properly follow Arts. 17 and 18.

*Instructional. Expositive*

ART. 27. Modes of procurement, as per §4, *Functions in all*, and §7, *Statistic function*, [Bissection] 1, Art. 18.

*Exemplificational*

ART. 28. Cases in which, between mode and mode, as to certain articles, *competition*, or say *antagonization*, may have place: Examples are as follows—

1. Army and navy subdepartments: requisites, arms and ammunition; antagonizing modes, *fabrication*, and *purchase*.

2. Navy subdepartment: requisites, navigable vessels: antagonizing modes, *fabrication, purchase*, and *hire*.

3. Health subdepartment: requisites, various medicines; antagonizing modes, *fabrication*, or say *preparation*, and *purchase*.

4. All subdepartments: requisites, appropriate edifices: antagonizing modes, *fabrication, purchase*, and *hire:* and as to *fabrication*, antagonizing modes, *Government account* and *contract*.[1]

*Instructional*

ART. 29. To the Legislature, in regard to each subject-matter or class of subject-matters, it will be a matter of consideration—whether of itself to determine between the several antagonizing modes, after receiving appropriate information by *reports*, from the subdepartment to which it belongs,—or to commit the determination to the Prime Minister, or the Minister[2] of the subdepartment, to the service of which the subject-matter in question belongs; always observing, that as the act of procurement by a functionary without authority from the Legislature, involves in it, as per Art. [4,] a power of *taxation*, so in an indirect way, does the determination as between two different modes: to wit, by determination in favour of the more expensive in preference to the less expensive.

*Instructional*

ART. 30. For giving expression to the several sorts of *instruments* employed in the exercise of the function, as per §4, *Functions in all*, Art. 18, by direction from, and under the care of, the Legislature— appropriate and apt *formulas* will be framed: useful qualities therein to be specially aimed at—*clearness, conciseness, uniformity, legibility*, and *cheapness*.

[1] 1830 and Bowring, '*Government account and contract*'; but by printing 'and' in italics the sense of the two 'antagonizing modes' is lost.

[2] 1830 and Bowring, 'Prime Minister of the subdepartment'; but Bentham clearly intends to refer to the Minister of the subdepartment.

*Expositive*

ART. 31. 1. By clearness, understand exclusion of *obscurity* and *ambiguity*.

*Expositive*

ART. 32. 2. By conciseness, understand exclusion of all needless words; for example, complimentary phrases.

*Instructional*

ART. 33. Under this head will be considered the employment to be given to *abbreviations*, as per §7, *Statistic*, [Bissection 6], instead of words at length: care being taken that they be sufficiently and promptly intelligible to all who have need to read them.

*Instructional*

ART. 34. [3.] Rules for *uniformity* as to *expression*.

Rule 1. For giving expression to the same ideas, employ on each occasion, the same words.

Rule 2. For giving expression to different ideas, employ on each occasion, different words.

*Instructional. Ratiocinative*

ART. 35. Uniformity as to *paper*, or other physical ground of the signs employed,——exceptions, for special reasons, excepted,——to every exemplar, written manifold-wise, as per Ch. viii. PRIME MINISTER, §10, *Registration system*,——give the same dimensions; that in every office, exemplars may be put together in form of a book. In this particular, as between office and office, and book and book, no variation but for special cause.

*Instructional*

ART. 36. 4. *Legibility*. 5. *Cheapness*. For these conjunct purposes, *printing* will of course be employed, in so far as, by reason of the number of exemplars needed, they are more effectually accomplished, than by writing *manifold-wise*.

*Instructional*

ART. 37. *Stamping*. For saving labour and time, it will be for consideration——whether in any, and if in any, in what cases, to employ it instead of *writing:* for instance, where, in a *formula*, of which the greater part has been expressed by *printing*, expression is to be given to signatures, such as *names* and *dates*, the expression of which may require separate application to each several sheet. Regard will, on this

275

occasion, be had to elaborateness of the figure, as a means of render-ing forgery more difficult and rare. A subject for consideration and inquiry may be, whether the human countenance, as exemplified in the person of some extensively known individual, be not the sort of figure, in which imitation made by an ordinary hand, will by ordi-nary eyes, be most generally detected.

### Instructional

ART. 38. *Sublegislatures*. With respect to exercise given to the several Administrative functions, as per §4, and in particular the *statistic, recordative, publicative,* and *requisitive,* to the Legislature it will belong so to order matter[s] that, *mutatis mutandis,* within their respective fields of service, the like course shall be pursued by the several sublegislatures.


## SECTION 9
### INSPECTIVE FUNCTION
### Expositive

ART. 1. *Inspective function*. In so far as, in the exercise given to it, *migration* from the official residence of the functionary in question has place, this function may be styled the *visitative* function. Con-sidered in respect of a number of *visits* successively made, each in a different place, the *visits*, or say *visitations* thus performed, may be styled *progresses:* considered, in respect of the form of the line of march described by the making of such progresses, they may be styled *circuits*.

### Enactive

ART. 2. In the exercise of his Inspective function, once at least in every year, and as much oftener as need may require and home busi-ness permit,—so far as may be in person, as to the rest, each time by a *Depute*, permanent or occasional, *spontaneously*, or by direc-tion as to *time* and *place* from the *Prime Minister*, the Minister of each Subdepartment will visit the several offices, and any such other *places* as lie within his charge.

### Instructional. Ratiocinative

ART. 3. *Uses*, thence objects and *purposes* of this visitation system. Examples—

1. Securing execution and effect to the system of statistication, registration, and publication, ordained by Ch. viii. PRIME MINI-STER, §10 and §11, and by this Chapter, §7, *Statistic function:* to

wit, in relation to each individual subject-matter of registration,—
that is to say, persons, immoveables, moveables, money, or occurrences, and whatsoever class it belongs [to], ascertaining whether it
ought to be registered, and if yes, whether it has been registered, and
if yes, how far the mode of registration is conformable to the existing ordinances.

2. In relation to each office inspected,—doing what the nature of
the case admits of, towards providing a supply, as adequate as may
be, for any such deficiency as shall have been observed in respect of
the execution and effect which should be given, as above, to that end;
taking personal cognizance of any such appointed subject-matters of
registration and publication, as shall either have been left altogether
unregistered or unpublished, as the case may be,—or not registered or
published, as the case may be, in conformity to the appointed mode.

3. Taking, by *immediate perception*, cognizance of the state of
those several subject-matters, in so far as the conception derived no
otherwise than from the report of other persons, cannot be, or shall
not have been, rendered adequate.

4. Taking cognizance of the degree of appropriate aptitude, absolute and comparative, in its several branches, on the part of the
several functionaries belonging to each office: to wit, with a view to
ulterior direction and instruction; as also to continuance in office,
transference to another office of the same grade, promotion, transference temporary or definitive, or suspension, or dislocation, as the
case may appear to require.

5. Taking cognizance of any such *complaints* as any person may be
desirous of making, as per §21, *Oppression obviated*, and of any
such other indication, of *misconduct* on the part of functionaries, as
any person may be willing to afford: to wit, for the purpose of eventual admonishment, transference, suspension, or dislocation, as the
case may appear to require: as per §20, *Insubordination obviated*;
and §21, *Oppression obviated*.

6. With a view to *extra remuneration*, by promotion, or otherwise,
—taking cognizance of any such *extraordinarily meritorious* service,
as may happen to have been rendered, in relation to the business of
the Subdepartment in question, or any other Subdepartment or Department, by any person, functionary, or non-functionary. As to
this, see §15, *Remuneration*, [Arts. 18 to 29,] and §25, *Securities,
etc.*, Art. [5].

7. By appropriate instruction and direction,—solving any *doubts*,
that may be found to have place on the part of functionaries, in respect of the exercise to be given to their respective functions; and,
with a view to eventual transference in default of reconciliation,

settling any *disagreements* that may be found to have place between functionary and functionary.

*Instructional*

ART. 4. Places, and Offices therein, which, in the exercise of this function, may require to be visited by the Ministers of the respective Subdepartments. Examples—

1. *Election* Subdepartment. Places, the stations of the several District Election Clerks, and Subdistrict Vote-receiving Clerks.

2. *Legislation* Subdepartment. Places, the residences of the several Sublegislatures.

3. *Army* Subdepartment. Places, the several fortified places, barracks, hospitals, and magazines.

4. *Navy* Subdepartment. Places, the several ports.

5. *Preventive service* Subdepartment. Places, the several places, in which functionaries, in bodies subject to the direction of the *Preventive Service Minister*, are stationed.

6. *Interior communication* Subdepartment. Places—

1. The several Post offices, in so far as *time* sufficies: where *not*, the aggregate of the several stations may be divided into *Circuits*, and the circuit progresses performed in the course of the year, together with the *times*, at which they shall respectively be performed, may, from time to time, be determined, as per Art. [8],[1] by *lot*, publicly drawn, as per §16, *Locable who*. Supplement.

2. Edifices, and groundworks, belonging to the Subdepartment: in particular, such as, having been commenced, remain at the time unfinished.

7. *Indigence relief* Subdepartment. Places—

1. The seats of any Eleemosynary establishments maintained by Government at public expense.

2. The seats of Eleemosynary establishments, maintained at the expense of bodies corporate, or of individuals. If *time*—expense of conveyance being moreover considered—should not suffice for all, determination by *lot*, as above.

8. *Education* Subdepartment. Places—

1. The seats of any education establishments maintained by Government at public expense: as to which, see §16, *Locable who*, and §17, *Located how*.

2. Those, if any, maintained by the several Sublegislatures, at the expense of their respective districts.

---

[1] 1830, 'as per Art. 3'; Bowring omits this reference because Art. 3 is not concerned with the use of a lottery. But Bentham may have intended to refer to Art. 8 which deals with the use of chance in inspection visits. See Art. 8, p. 281.

3. Those maintained by bodies corporate, or by individuals. See §16, *Locable who*.

9. *Domain* Subdepartment. Places——

1. The several portions of land, edifices, and groundworks, kept in hand, or leased out, by Government, at the expense and for the profit of, the public.

10. *Health* Subdepartment. Places——

I. Dispensaries.

1. Central, in the metropolis.

2. Those in the metropolises of the several Election Districts.

3. Incidentally, in case of appeal, apothecary's or chemist's shops, in relation to which any censure shall have been passed, or direction delivered, by the *Health Subminister* within his district; as to which, see Ch. xi. MINISTERS SEVERALLY, §10, *Health Minister*.

II. Hospitals.

1. Those maintained by Government at the expense of the whole state.

2. Those maintained by the several Sublegislatures, at the expense of their respective districts.

3. Those maintained by bodies corporate, or by individuals.

11. *Foreign Relation* Subdepartment. Places. Examples——

1. Of the habitations of the several Agents, Political and Commercial, of the several foreign powers, resident within the territory of this state, the residences maintained at the expense of the respective governments. This, with a view to eventual repair merely, and not without permission given by the respective residents.

2. Those, if any, which are supplied to them gratuitously by *this* state.

12. *Trade* Subdepartment. Places——

1. The several Docks, other Groundworks, if any, employed as receptacles for shipping, and the several other instruments of water communication from place to place, at which goods are exported to, or imported from, the dominions of *foreign* states.

2. The several inland barriers, if any, at which goods are exported into, or imported from, other ports, or barrier places, belonging to *this* state.

13. *Finance* Subdepartment. Places——the several Offices, at which, on account of Government as trustee for the public, money is received or paid.

For other examples and particulars, see Art. 7.

*Instructional. Ratiocinative*

ART. 5. For different purposes, and on different occasions,——

Inspection *visits*, and even *Progresses* and *Circuits*, may, by different Ministers, in various numbers be made, to one and the same establishment, public or private.

REASONS. Uses, thence objects and purposes, of this arrangement.

1. For different purposes, the same establishment, it will be seen, may require to be inspected, by so many different Ministers, in order to [its] being inquired into for those several purposes, and contemplated in so many different points of view: in each case, with reference to different branches, or even the same branch, of the public service.

2. By the cognizance thus taken in relation to the same subject matter by divers functionaries, independent of each other,—the information furnished by each, will serve as a check upon the conduct pursued, and information furnished, by every other.

3. By this conjunction, no *collision* of authority will be produced: the *directive* function being, in each Subdepartment, in the hands of *one* person alone,—no obstruction need be afforded to it by any exercise given to the *inspective* and *statistic* function, by whatsoever number of different functionaries exercised, in relation to one and the same object.

### Instructional. Ratiocinative

ART. 6. Exceptions excepted,—for the second of the above reasons, it will be for the care of the Prime Minister so to arrange the visits of the several Ministers, in such sort that no two shall perform any *Inspection visit* at the same time one with the other.

Exception is—where, for some special, preponderant, and *declared* reason,—it appears to him that, for mutual explanation, information, and discussion, the purpose requires, that by two or more [Ministers],[1] by whom, by his direction, a visit is made at the same time, the inspective function should be exercised by them in each other's company, and thereby at the same time.

### Instructional

ART. 7. Cases, in which the good of the service may require that, by the Minister[s] of two or more different Subdepartments, one and the same establishment should be visited. Examples—

1. Army Minister and Navy Minister. Subject matters requiring

---

[1] 1830 and Bowring, 'Members', but 'Ministers' is required by the context.

inspection by each, with a view whether to conjunct or separate service. Examples—artillery, ammunition, and small arms.

Note, that as to the adequacy of the aggregate of the supply, the two interests are here *united:* in case of deficiency, *antagonizing.*

2. Army Minister, Navy Minister, and Preventive Service Minister. Subject-matters demanding inspection by each—troops, small vessels and their crews, arms and ammunition.

3. 1, Army Minister; 2, Navy Minister; 3, Preventive Service Minister; 4, Trade Minister; and 5, Finance Minister. Subject-matters requiring inspection by each, as above: on the part of the Preventive Service Minister, Trade Minister, and Finance Minister, where the casual cause of demand is forcible resistance, experienced or apprehended, in relation to execution and effect required to be given to ordinances and arrangements respecting imports, exports, or collection of revenue.

4. The same five Ministers, with the Interior Communication Minister. Subject-matters requiring inspection by each—the several instruments of communication, immoveable and moveable, by their several diversifications, for the purpose of giving effectual and adequately prompt *communication* to the several above-mentioned instruments of *defence*, together with the instruments of *subsistence* for men and beasts of *conveyance*, occupied in the correspondent branch of the public service.

5. 1, Indigence Relief Minister; 2, Education Minister; 3, Health Minister. Subject-matters requiring inspection by each—all such establishments as have for their ends in view the administering the benefit of education, in conjunction with relief to indigence; especial care of health being alike needful in the two first-mentioned sorts of establishments.

6. Domain Minister, and every other Minister: to wit, in so far as the Land, Edifices, and Ground-works employed in these several branches of the public service, belong to the Public Domain.

7. All the several other Ministers, and the Finance Minister: in consideration that it is from or through his hands that every expenditure of money, and thence of money's worth, must come. Upon the expenditure of every other Subdepartment, without exception, his care is a needful and indispensable check.

### Instructional

ART. 8. The Legislature, the Prime Minister, and the Minister will have in consideration the advantage, derivable in some cases from the use of *chance*, for the purpose of securing unexpectedness to inspection visits, and thence constancy of good order in the places visited.

For the mode of taking the decision of chance, see §16, *Locable who. Supplement.*

### Instructional. Ratiocinative

ART. 9. To the constant application of this security to establishments under government management,—the addition liable to be made to the quantity of time spent on the road, by fortuitous migrations made without regard to distance, would, by expenditure of time and money, oppose such a body of disadvantage, as would leave no adequate prospect of compensation: such being the security, afforded in all shapes, by the universal *registration and publication system*, coupled with the correspondent facility, afforded to individuals, for the indication of imperfection and abuse in all shapes.

But, on this or that occasion, this instrument of security presents itself as being, even in this case, capable of being employed with advantage by the above-mentioned constituted authorities.

### Instructional. Ratiocinative

ART. 10. Establishments under private management, as per Art. 4, are those, in regard to which the service capable of being rendered by it is most conspicuous: the light of publicity not being otherwise capable of being thrown, with adequate intensity, upon those minor objects.

### Instructional. Ratiocinative

ART. 11. Yet, not even in this case[1] is the advantage clear of opposite disadvantage. On the one side, stands the advantage derivable from *unpreparedness* on the part of *Inspectees*: but this case supposes disorder already to have place: the remedy *suppressive* only, not *preventive*. On the other side stands the advantage derivable from *preparedness* on the part of eventual *accusers*. True it is that, in the form of written discourse, accusation is open to all at all times. But it is by indication of individual facts that accusation will in this case be performed. For this operation, to some persons written discourse, to others *oral*, is the most convenient instrument. But those to whom *oral* is so will always be the most numerous. Mutes excepted, all are able to speak: but to a purpose such as that in question, few in comparison will, in any state of things, be able to write.

---

[1] The phrase 'in this case' takes up the argument from the end of Art. 9.

## SECTION 10

### OFFICIALLY INFORMATIVE FUNCTION

#### *Instructional*

ART. 1. As in all private so in all public business, necessary on every occasion to apt *operation* is appropriate and correspondently extensive *information*, or say *evidence*. 'What can we *reason*' (asks the poet) 'but from what we know?'[1] With correspondent and equal propriety,—to *reason*, he might have added *act*.

#### *Expositive*

ART. 2. To the import of the word *evidence* the word *information* adds a reference made to some mind, as being one into which the evidence has been *received*.

In English practice, with a view to the business of the Administration Department, *information* is, throughout, the word most commonly employed. In the business of the Judiciary Department, the word *evidence*, and not the word *information*, is in most cases employed; the word *information*, and not the word *evidence*, being employed in some cases, in those, to wit, in which for insuring veracity in what is uttered, no security is applied. But, in the Judiciary Department, wheresoever it has not been the desire of the constituted authorities that falsehood should be elicited, as in the cases where a disguised licence for encouragement of mendacity has been purposely granted, some known security for veracity has of course been applied.

As to the *mendacity licence*, see the *Procedure Code* and *Scotch Reform*, Letter i, p. 19.[2]

#### *Instructional. Expositive*

ART. 3. Of whatsoever a man knows, whatsoever portion he has not derived from his own experience or observation, he must have *received* from some other person. If received from another person, it must by that other person have been *furnished*, or say *communicated*.

---

[1] Alexander Pope, *Essay on Man*, 4 pts., London [1732-4], i. 18.

[2] For the first of these references see *Principles of Judicial Procedure* (Bowring, ii. 3-188), Ch. VIII, 'Judicial Application', and Ch. XI, 'Evidence', Bowring, ii. 48-9, 58. On the Procedure Code generally, see Ch. V, § 5, Art. 6n, p. 38n. Bentham's second reference is to Letter I of his *Scotch Reform; considered with reference to the Plan proposed in the late Parliament*, London, 1808 (Bowring, v. 1-53): see Bowring, v. 6, 11. The 'mendacity licence' is also discussed in *The Rationale of Judicial Evidence* (Bowring, vi. 189-585, vii. 1-600), Bowring, vii, as index.

*Expositive*

ART. 4. If *communicated*, it must have been so either in compliance *with* application for that purpose by some other person, or *without* any such application; in this last case the operation by which it is *furnished*, is termed *spontaneous*.

*Expositive*

ART. 5. When, on the part of the possessor of the information,—the possession of it has *not* been preceded by any operation, other than that of concurrence, for that purpose, in so far as correspondent action is necessary, with a person by whom it has been communicated, and with whom the communication of it has in so far *originated*,— it is said to be *received.*

*Expositive*

ART. 6. When, on the part of such possessor,—it *has* been preceded and produced by application made *by him* to the person by whom it has been communicated to him, and from him as above received,— in this case it has been *extracted*, to wit, from the person by whom it has been communicated; and in both cases, as per Ch. vi. § 27, Art[s]. 3, 7, it has been *elicited.*

*Instructional*

ART. 7. So obvious, upon the bare mention of it, does the necessity of all this appear, that the mention will be apt to appear useless and frivolous. But upon a closer view, it will be found, that of this necessity, the perception has, to a great extent, been generally wanting; and that, not only has it been an object of sinister policy with legislators to obtain for themselves the information necessary for their own particular and sinister purposes, while the information, necessary to be communicated to, and for the benefit of the community at large, has been studiously kept concealed,—but, for want of due attention to the necessity, they have every where, to a greater or less extent, left themselves destitute of that portion of information, by the possession of which, service would have been rendered to their own particular and sinister interest.

*Instructional. Expositive*

ART. 8. In Ch. vi. § 27, *[Legislation] Enquiry Judicatory*,—on allotting to the *Legislature* its several functions, it became necessary to allot to it the *information-elicitative* function, in which is included the *extractive;* and, for that purpose, to organize the institution on

284

that occasion denominated *a [Legislation] Enquiry Judicatory*. In Ch. xii. JUDICIARY COLLECTIVELY, and the succeeding chapters relating to the *Judiciary department*, and thereafter in the *Procedure Code*,[1] directions will be seen given for the elicitation of appropriate *information*, under the name of *evidence*, for the origination and guidance of the exercise given to the *judicial* function.

### Instructional. Expositive

ART. 9. What the *present* occasion calls for, is——to provide the *information* necessary for the apt exercise of the powers allotted to the *Administrative* Department: and, for that purpose, to determine how far such information shall, by the functionaries of the several grades, be spontaneously furnished to the other functionaries belonging to that same department respectively, as well as to the Legislature, in addition to that which is conveyed, constantly and of course, by the exercise given to the *registration* and *publication* system. As to this, see § 11, *Information-elicitative function*,[a] and Ch. viii. PRIME MINISTER, §[§]10, 11.

### Instructional. Expositive

ART. 10. So likewise how far and by what *means*, in addition to the supply thus afforded, it shall on that occasion be *elicited*. As to this, see § 11, *Information-elicitative function*, Art[s]. 4 to 14.

### Enactive. Instructional

ART. 11. Exceptions excepted,——*by* the several Ministers, information of all *occurrences*,——relevant, and with relation to the business of their several offices adequately material,——will (it is hereby ordained) be furnished as well *to* the Legislature as *to* the Prime Minister.

### Enactive. Instructional

ART. 12. The exceptions will be made by the Legislature, consideration had of the incumbrance and expense, of registration and custody: and determination will be made accordingly——what part, if

[a] This all-comprehensive view of the *information* necessary to the apt exercise of the functions of government, and of the means of its being obtained, should have been given in speaking of the functions of the Legislative Department; that being the first of the Departments, in which, on the part of the functionaries, appropriate action was necessary for the obtainment of it: but the views of the author had not at that time received the correspondent extension.

[1] See Ch. VI, § 27, Art. 11n, p. 96n. On the Procedure Code generally, see Ch. V, § 5, Art. 6n, p. 38n.

any, of such information shall not, unless called for, be transmitted to the Legislature and the Prime Minister respectively. In so doing, it will take care, that to each of the two authorities, all such information as is necessary as a ground for its *habitual action*, shall be *habitually transmitted.*

### Enactive

ART. 13. *To* the several Ministers, such information will be furnished by the several functionaries respectively belonging to the several official situations subordinate to theirs.

### Instructional

ART. 14. In what cases, from this or that office, information shall be furnished,—to this or that other office of a grade *superior* to that of its immediate superordinate,—at the same time with, or in lieu of the furnishing it to such *immediate* superordinate,—the Legislature will determine, regard being had to the businesses of the several Subdepartments.

### Instructional

ART. 15. By whatsoever need of the exercise of the officially informative function has place, as above—is produced the correspondent need of the exercise of the correspondent information-elicitative function. As to which, see the next section, §11.

### Expositive

ART. 16. Correspondent and correlative to the *officially informative*, as per Art. 8,[1] is the *information-receptive function:* the two functions being not only in their general nature thus correspondent and correlative, but on each individual occasion, accidents excepted, the exercise of the former being accompanied or followed by the exercise of the other.

### Instructional

ART. 17. By an exercise given to the *officially-informative function*, suppose adequate ground made for the exercise of any other function,

[1] 1830, '*officially informative*, as per § 10, Art. 8,'. Bowring omits the reference to § 10 as being redundant. Nevertheless, both 1830 and Bowring may be mistaken, as the discussion not only here, but also in Art. 8, is concerned with the information-elicitative function and not the officially-informative function. Bentham may have included the redundant reference to § 10 to remind the reader that he is thinking not of § 11 where the information-elicitative function is mainly discussed, but of Art. 8 in the present section. In the process, however, he seems to have inserted the name of the wrong function.

to which it is, or is designed to be, subservient,—correspondent exercise given to the correspondent *receptive function*, is a matter of fact, which must have been established: but, for this purpose, presumptive evidence, arising out of the nature of the case, will, without additional express evidence, be in general found sufficient to produce adequate credence.

### Expositive

ART. 18. Example. A letter, sent by the Letter-post, cannot, by him to whom it is addressed, be acted upon, unless and until it has been received by him: but, for the purpose of judging whether what he has done since the time at which it ought to have been received by him has been right or no,—the *presumption*, except in case of special reason for belief of the contrary, must on each occasion be—that it *has* been received.

### Instructional. Ratiocinative

ART. 19. But, forasmuch as, comparatively speaking, small indeed is the number of cases, in which it cannot happen, that by accident, expectation, how well-grounded soever, has been frustrated,—hence, in every case, in which official action has for its sole ground such presumptive evidence, care will universally be taken that, in case of wrong, produced to the public or to an individual, by want of due attention, and correspondent action on the part of the Administration functionary,—means of compensation, as adequate as may be, shall be provided, and eventually applied.

### Instructional. Ratiocinative

ART. 20. In the case of this department (the Administrative as in the others,)—for the appropriate supply of the information, on each occasion necessary or serviceable, provision is made, as far as may be, by the application made of these same systems to the business of this department. The function, by the exercise of which such information is afforded, may however require to be considered and spoken of, as a distinguishable and accordingly distinct function: to wit, for the reasons which follow.

1. On this or that occasion,—over and above all *information* or say *evidence* furnished by the exercise given to the *registrative* function,—it may happen, that *ulterior* evidence may, for the particular purpose of the particular occasion, require to be *elicited;* and, in conjunction with it, *arranged* and *commented* on.

2. In the event of the *non-employment*, or only partial employment, of the *registration* system, on this or that particular occasion,

—the exercise given to this same officially-informative function will be—in proportion the more necessary.

### Instructional. Exemplificational

ART. 21. Accordingly, the nature of the case will not admit of a doubt—but that, under every form of government, exercise is, with more or less frequency, comprehensiveness, and symmetry, actually and habitually given to it.

### Instructional. Exemplificational

ART. 22. In English practice, no such all-comprehensive or generally-comprehensive system of appropriate information-furnishing, from the Administrative authorities to the Legislature, has place. Generally speaking, no information is furnished to either of the two Houses, without its having been ordered: nor, for any information to be furnished in a ready-written form, is any order commonly issued, but in obedience to a special order by the House, with or without an intermediate order from the Monarch, to whom a petition from the House in question is addressed for the purpose, and with whom it rests to give or not to give such orders at pleasure: nor is such petition addressed, but in consequence of a resolution made, and expressed in writing for that purpose: which motion,—though scarce ever negatived, when made by a member of the Administration,—is frequently negatived, when made by a member, who is not specially connected with the party in office.[1]

### Instructional. Exemplificational

ART. [23]. From this state of things cannot but result the consequences following:

1. Forasmuch as, rare and extraordinary accidents excepted, the will and agency of both houses of the Legislature is determined by

---

[1] Bentham's opening statement in this article is correct. Both the House of Commons and the House of Lords are entitled to call for the production of documents and papers. Where the royal prerogative is not involved, either House can call for the production of papers by a direct order, which must be obeyed. Where the exercise of the prerogative is involved, an Humble Address to the Crown is required, and the Crown through its ministers may refuse the request. As a rule of thumb for distinguishing the two sorts of case, it can be said that information from or through any Revenue department, any department under the Treasury, or any department constituted or regulated by statute, is obtained by order; whereas information from or through departments headed by a Secretary of State, or from the Privy Council, must be prayed for by Humble Address. See Josef Redlich, *The Procedure of the House of Commons*, 3 vols., London, 1908, ii. 39–42.

that of the administrative authority, and no condemnation can be passed on the conduct of any person, but on the ground of appropriate and adequate information,—nor can any such information be furnished, but by consent of the party in office,—hence it is, that, on the conduct of no member of that party, can any censure be passed, nor so much as inquiry be made without the consent of that same party: and, by this state of things, without need of anything more, the *self-judication principle* is constituted an all-determining principle; and all show of effective responsibility, except to the Public Opinion Tribunal, is mere pretence and mockery.

2. Even where the party in Administration has no aversion to the exhibition of the information in question, it is matter of accident whether the House ever receives possession of it.

3. In consequence,—to an indefinitely great extent, evil in various shapes cannot but have been habitually taking place for want of some information, by the receipt of which, by both or either of the two Houses, it would have been prevented.

4. Of the information, by which are determined the proceedings, of the House, in which, with few exceptions, all laws originate, to wit, the House of Commons,—it is only in a small part of the whole number of instances individually taken, that the whole stock is possessed by the other House. Thus it is that, in relation to one and the same matter, the two Houses are, on almost every occasion, acting on different grounds: the one House, on grounds frequently partial and inadequate, the other House rarely on grounds other than partial and inadequate: the whole Legislature acting under a system of delusion, and in an habitual course of more or less mischievous operation, even when not thereto purposely determined by any sinister interest.

5. By this system of partial information,—whatsoever be the system of maleficence carried on,—not only is all due punishment at the hands of the legal tribunal impossibilized, but so is all cognizance, and consequently all censure, on the part of the Public Opinion Tribunal, likewise.

### Instructional

ART. [24]. To the case of provinces situated at great distances from the seat of legislation, applies the mischief liable to result from deficiency of timely information. Proportioned to that distance, in respect of place, and thence in respect of time, of communication,—is the degree in which these dependencies are, by the nature of the case, rendered scenes of habitual misfortune and abuse: and it is for the sake of the sinister profit derived and derivable from the abuse, that, at the expense of the *subject many*, such dependencies situate at a certain distance, are kept in subjection by the *ruling few*. Hence one cause of demand for *Sublegislatures*.

### Instructional. Exemplificational

ART. [25]. In English practice, deficient in appropriate aptitude in every shape, this or that lord or other member or adherent of the ruling few, is sent to exercise tyranny over the distant provinces; and, when at length complaints have reached and annoyed the ear of the Legislature, *percipient* witnesses have, on this or that pretence, been sent out of the way, of being rendered, for the information of the Judicial and Legislative authorities, *narrating* witnesses.

## SECTION 11

### INFORMATION-ELICITATIVE FUNCTION

### Enactive

ART. 1. Exceptions excepted,——to every functionary belongs the information-elicitative function, exerciseable at the hands of every other person, functionary or non-functionary, in so far as the receipt of the information in question is necessary or useful.

### Enactive. Instructional

ART. 2. For exceptions, see cases for secrecy, as referred to in Ch. xii. § 14, *Publicity*, &c.[1]

### Expositive. Ratiocinative

ART. 3. As between the *simply receptive* mode of elicitation, and the *extractive*,——in so far as the communicator and the receiver are both of them functionaries belonging to the official establishment,——any distinction that may be observable between them, will, comparatively speaking, be of little moment.

Reasons. 1. By the general *registration and publication* system, as per Ch. viii. § [ § ]10, 11, every functionary, as such, stands pre-engaged to furnish whatsoever appropriate information may, on whatsoever occasion, be needful, or, as such, appropriately required of him.

2. To a considerable extent, reception and communication are works of the same hand, and thus in a manner consolidated into one. Thus, for example, in every office to which a Registrar is attached,

---

[1] Secrecy is not in fact discussed in § 14 of Ch. XII as published in Bowring, ix. 493–4. Bentham might have referred here to the discussion in Ch. VIII, § 11, pp. 162–8.

the several functions, *minutative* and *transmissive*, are, on each occasion, by the Registrar exercised, as of course, and thus, in that same hand, united with the *receptive*, and the *custoditive*.

### Instructional

ART. 4. Far different is the case, where, the *proposed receiver* of the information being a *functionary*, the *proposed communicator* is a *non-functionary*. In this case, between elicitation by simple *reception*, and elicitation by *extraction*, in effect as well as in mode, wide indeed may be the difference. On the part of a *spontaneous* communicator, *willingness* is indeed at least *apparent*, naturally *presumable*, and in most cases *actual:* but, on the part of him, who communicates not but in compliance with requisition, and from whom the communication, if obtained, is accordingly extracted, *unwillingness* in every conceivable degree,—for any length of time, even *non-compliance*, —may have had place. The surmounting, in all cases, this unwillingness, and substituting to it the correspondent *compliance*, belongs, in a more particular manner, to the *Judiciary* Establishment; and forms the most difficult of the tasks imposed upon it.

### Instructional

ART. 5. In the business of *that* department, this difficulty is all pervading and continual; and so it will be, whatsoever is, in this proposed Code, done,—or *can*, in any Code, be done,—for the lessening it. Happily, in the business of the *Administration* Department, it need be but incidental and casual. In the quantity, which, for forming a ground for action, is strictly necessary and proportionably sufficient, appropriate information [is] provided for, as above.

### Instructional

ART. 6. In the hands of the *Minister* in each Subdepartment, this power presents itself, as indispensable. On a view taken of the several official situations, in their several grades, established in each Subdepartment, in *subordination* to that of Minister,—to the Legislature it will belong to determine, to which of them this power shall be attached: in each case, subject to all such restrictions and conditions as may be deemed necessary for security against abuse.

### Instructional

ART. 7. For securities against *disturbance* given to the exercise of this function, see §20, *Insubordination obviated*; for securities against oppression by abuse of power in the exercise of it, see §21, *Oppression obviated;* against extortion, §22, *Extortion obviated.*

*Instructional*

ART. 8. As to the number of *possible sharers* in the exercise of these functions,—the *extractive* function is, in the nature of the case, susceptible of the being exercised by *any* number of persons, on the same proposed communicator, or say *examinee*, on the same *occasion*, or any number of different occasions. Witness, in judicature, under every system, the examination of supposed *Evidence-holders*, by the Judge, and the parties or their Advocates on both sides: not to mention the other classes of persons, to whom the power is imparted by the present proposed Code. So also, at *exactly* the same time, while the *extraction process* is going on, by any number of *note-takers*.

*Instructional*

ART. 9. To the Legislature it will belong,—to determine in what cases, if any,—or by what classes of functionaries, if by any, belonging to the Army and Navy Subdepartments respectively,—power shall be possessed—of extracting, from persons at large, information requisite for the defence of the country against hostility, commenced, or regarded as impending.

*Instructional*

ART. 10. On the occasion of the several obligations, of spontaneous information furnishing, and information furnishing in compliance with interrogation,—special care will be taken by the Legislature, to avoid the producing of preponderant evil, by the divulgation of facts, by the disclosure of which more evil will be produced than prevented: regard being at the same time had to the evils producible by the practice termed in French *espionage*, and to those produced by abuse of the power termed *inquisitorial*.

*Enactive. Ratiocinative*

ART. 11. In particular, care will be taken not to comprise under the obligation the disclosure of any opinions, entertained by any individual on the subject of religion.

Reason. In this case, if the profession of such opinion is regarded and treated as a crime, the authors of the crime, such as it is, are the Legislature itself, or the functionaries acting in pretended obedience to its ordinances.

*Instructional*

ART. 12. To the Legislature it will belong,—to determine in what cases, if in any, it shall be matter of obligation to persons at large, to furnish, to the several Administration offices, information relevant and material to the business of those same offices. In so doing, regard will be had, as well to all expense and vexation necessarily attached to the furnishing of such information,—as also to the difficulty of making sure, that the knowledge of the existence of such obligation has been presented to the mind of the individual, at whose hands it is required: and for this purpose, care will be taken, that no such obligation shall extend to any species of information, in regard to which, mention of such obligation has not been inserted in the Code, appertaining to the situation in life in which the party is placed.

### Instructional. Expositive

ART. 13. Of cases in which the obligation of spontaneously furnishing information may,—in so far as duly notified, as above, be reasonably imposed, examples are the following:

1. Information of calamity, recent or impending, to the *Preventive-service Minister*.

2. Information of hostility, recently committed or impending, to the *Army* Minister or *Navy* Minister, as the case may be; and, in both cases, to the *Prime* Minister.

### Instructional. Exemplificational

ART. 14. In English practice, such obligation is imposed, upon all persons without exception, in the case of all offences, to which the denomination of *High Treason* is applied. *Misprision* is the denomination in that case given, to the offence consisting in the non-fulfilment of that same obligation.

# SECTION 12

## MELIORATION-SUGGESTIVE FUNCTION

### Enactive

ART. 1. *Melioration-suggestive function*. In the exercise of it, as often as, in respect of any part of the business of his office, the practice thereof presents itself to the view of the Minister, as needing correction, or as being susceptible of improvement,—it belongs to him— to draw up, and transmit to the Prime Minister, an appropriate *Melioration-suggesting Report*.

### Enactive

ART. 2. Included in the melioration-suggestive function are the elementary functions following:

293

I. *Indicative* function: exercised by a statement made, in general terms, of the supposed amendments proposed.

## *Enactive*

ART. 3. II. *Ratiocinative*, or say *Reason-giving* function: exercised by adding, in the form of *reasons*, a statement of the *beneficial* effects, looked for from the several proposed changes; prefacing them with an indication of the *maleficial* effects, if any, resulting from the actual state of things.

## *Enactive. Ratiocinative*

ART. 4. III. *Eventually emendative function*: exercised, by a written instrument, by the authorization whereof in the *very terms* therein employed, it appears to the writer that the change, if approved of, may most aptly be accomplished: together with an indication of the *authority*, whose sanction will, it is supposed, be necessary, and sufficient, for the accomplishment of it: whether, for example, the authority of the Legislature be requisite, or any and what authority subordinate thereto may be sufficient. For the *reasons* why, for the designation of a proposed change, the *very terms* of the appropriate regulations require in this case to be employed, see Ch. xii. JUDICIARY COLLECTIVELY, § 20, *Judges' eventually emendative function;* and Ch. vi. § 29.

## *Enactive*

ART. 5. Exemplars will be disposed of as follows:
   1. Kept in the Office, one.
   2. Kept by the Minister for his own use, one.
   3. Transmitted to the office of the Prime Minister, one.
   4. At the same time to the office of the Legislation Minister, one.
   5. So, to that of the Finance Minister, one.

## *Instructional*

ART. 6. Whatsoever benefit,—may from time to time have been derived from the exercise given to this function,—will be as it were the fruit, and *that* the ripest fruit, of whatsoever labour has been employed, in the exercise of the several before-mentioned functions.

## SECTION 13

### TERM OF SERVICE

*Enactive. Ratiocinative*

ART. 1. Dislocation excepted, as per §18, *Dislocable how*,——a Minister's term of service is the term of his life.

### *Ratiocinative*

ART. 2. *Question*. Why, in the situation of Minister, render the length of a man's term of Service eventually and probably the same as that of his life; instead of rendering it no more than annual, followed by temporary non-relocability, as in the case of a member of the Legislature?

*Answer. Reasons.*

I. Because, in every one of the thirteen subdepartments,——in the situation of Minister, the field of service being, in comparison with what it is in the situation of Legislator, narrow,——and the subject-matter of consideration and operation, matter of detail,——appropriate knowledge, judgement and active talent will necessarily be kept in a state of *constant* exercise, and thence, receiving *increase*, in proportion to the length of the course of practice and experience: whereas, in the situation of Member of the Legislature, to no one of the above faculties is any exercise given of necessity: nor, in the case of the great majority, under the *discontinued relocability* system, is it likely to be given in such sort as to be productive of public benefit, unless it be under some special stimulus; such as that which has place, in the case of those Members who possess, or look to possess, the faculty of exercising influence on the proceedings, in the character of speakers,——and such, to whom it may have happened to be continued for a number of years together in the situation of Continuation Committee men.

### *Ratiocinative*

ART. 3. II. Because, in case of deficiency in appropriate aptitude in any of its shapes,——for the dislocation of a Minister, as per §18, *Dislocable how, facilities* have place, much greater than those which apply to the case of a Member of the Legislature; and, for the existence of that same aptitude in the meantime, *securities*, as per §25, more numerous and still more efficient: the dislocatedness, a loss to which a Member of the Legislature will in comparatively but a very slight degree stand exposed. Yes: slight in comparison it would still be, should he even be, all the while, carrying on, in conjunction with

295

the Prime Minister, a plan of depredation, by exercise all along given to the quantity of the matter of corruption placed at his disposal, and the facility of making application of it to evil purposes.


## SECTION 14

### ATTENDANCE

*Enactive. Expositive*

ART. 1. *In-door* service and *out-door* service. Between these two modes, or say branches of service, will the attendance time of the several Ministers, taken in the aggregate, be divided.

By *In-door* service, understand whatsoever service is performed by the Minister in his official residence; by *Out-door* service, whatsoever service is performed by him any where else: for example, by inspection progresses, as per §9, *Inspective function.*

*Instructional*

ART. 2. By the principles and reasons brought to view in the case of the Members of the Legislature in Ch. vi., §20, *Attendance and remuneration, how connected*, will the aggregate quantity of time, employed by them in both branches taken together, be determined; in what proportion it shall be divided between the two, the Legislature, regard had to the different nature of the several services, will determine.

*Ratiocinative*

ART. 3. For the uninterruptedness of attendance on the part of the Legislature taken in the aggregate, and the punctuality of attendance on the part of its several Members, individually considered—special grounds, over and above those brought to view, as above, in the chapter having for its subject-matter the Legislative Department, are furnished by the need of receiving the several communications made from the offices of the several Ministers in the exercise of the officially informative functions, as per §11.[1] To the end that, in every instance, at the earliest moment requisite, all such arrangements may

---

[1] 1830 and Bowring, 'officially informative functions, as per §11'. The reference may be to the exercise of the officially informative function, as per §10, Art. 11, where Ministers are required to furnish information to the Legislature and Prime Minister. Alternatively, Bentham may be referring more generally to the several functions connected with the extraction, receipt, and publication of information discussed in §§10 and 11.

be taken for which, at the hands of the Legislature, the nature of the communication may have produced a demand.

So likewise by the need of receiving, and eventually operating in consequence of, Reports from the Judiciary Department, as per Ch. xii. JUDICIARY COLLECTIVELY; §19, *Contested interpretation reporting function;* §20, *Eventually emendative function;* §21, *Sisitive, or say Execution-staying function;* and §22, *Preinterpretative function:* also of taking the requisite cognizance of the proceedings of the several Sublegislatures.[a]

## SECTION 15[1]

### REMUNERATION

*Ratiocinative. Instructional*

ART. 1. *Aptitude maximized; expense minimized.* Indicated in these few words are the leading principles of this Constitution on the subject of remuneration.

*Ratiocinative. Instructional*

ART. 2. As to maximization of official aptitude in this department, for the course taken in this view, see also the next section, §16, *Locable who.*

---

[a] Of the matter of this Article, entry should have been made, and would have been, had it occurred, in the Chapter having for its subject-matter the Legislative Department.[2] For the importance of the uninterruptedness of its attendance, with a view to the business of the Sublegislatures, see Ch. [xxx]. SUBLEGISLATURES—§[1], *Fields of Service.*

---

[1] §§15–17 and Supplements appeared in two additional versions besides the 1830 and the Bowring editions of the *Code.* The first was the *Extract from the Proposed Constitutional Code, Entitled Official Aptitude Maximized, Expense Minimized,* London, 1826, which will be referred to subsequently as the 1826 *Extract.* This pamphlet (wrongly dated 1816) included the texts of §§15–17, the Concluding Instruction to the Public Opinion Tribunal, and a few articles from a proposed §18. The second version appeared in 1830 as a part of *Official Aptitude Maximized; Expense Minimized.* The 1830 *Off. Apt. Max.* (as it will be called) largely reprints the 1826 *Extract* but adds at the end the two lengthy supplements to §§16 and 17, and omits the few articles from §18. Bowring does not reprint this material in his edition (Bowring, v. 263–386) of *Official Aptitude Maximized; Expense Minimized* because it also appears in the *Code.* For full collations of these two versions, see pp. 520–8. Important variants are noted in the textual notes. For a fuller discussion of the order of publication of these versions, see pp. xxxix–xl.

[2] See Ch. VI, §18, pp. 38–9.

*Ratiocinative*

ART. 3. Subservient even to the maximization of aptitude is minimization of expense. For,

1. Whatever be the occupation belonging to the office, the greater a man's relish for it is, the greater his aptitude for it is likely to be.

2. The less the remuneration, in consideration of which he is willing to exercise these same occupations, the greater is his relish for them.

3. Greater still, if, instead of receiving, he is willing to pay for the faculty of exercising them.

*Ratiocinative*

ART. 4. So, on the other hand, the greater the expense employed in remuneration, the greater will be the opulence of the functionary so remunerated. But the greater his opulence, the less his appropriate aptitude will naturally be. For,

1. The less will be his activity.

2. The greater his facility for engaging in merely pleasurable and other rival occupations.

3. The greater his facility for obtaining accomplices in transgression, and supporters to shield him against dislocation, punishment, and disrepute.

4. The more apt to form an exaggerated estimate of the quantity of the expense for which, at the charge of the public, there may be, on each several occasion, a demand.

5. Altogether fallacious is the notion, by which, to the purpose of repression of wrong, responsibility is regarded as increased by opulence. By man's nature, every the poorest individual is rendered susceptible of more suffering, than, in any case, is ever thought fit to be inflicted for the purpose of repression by means of punishment: altogether fallacious this notion, and, under a corrupt form of government, invented for no other purpose than that of affording a pretence for needless, wasteful, and corruptive remuneration; remuneration, and to a vast extent, in cases where the absence of all service is notorious and undeniable.

*Ratiocinative*

ART. 5. Minimization of expense is therefore an object here pursued, not only as being itself an end, but as being a means of attainment, with relation to that other end. One and the same, accordingly, as per §16, is the road that leads to the attainment of both these ends.

### *Ratiocinative*

ART. 6. So far as regards remuneration, minimization of expense, in relation to all, can no otherwise be effected, than by minimization in relation to each. In relation to each, in each official situation, note this rule: Having by appropriate courses, as per §16, *Locable who*, maximized the number of persons possessed of the maximum of appropriate aptitude, ascertain from each the minimum of remuneration for which he will be content to charge himself with the official obligations. Modes of ascertainment are every where in use. Competition is no less applicable to the price of labour than to the price of goods; to one sort of labour than to another; to labour in the service of the public than to labour in the service of an individual. So much for minimization of expense, separately considered. As to the arrangements of detail, for the union of minimization of expense with maximization of aptitude, see the next sections, §16, *Locable who*; §17, *Located how.*

### *Ratiocinative*

ART. 7. Exercised, by a public functionary, at the expense of the public, *liberality* is but another name for waste. Combined in its essence are breach of trust, peculation, depredation, oppression, and corruption. Exercised, to a good end, and at a man's own expense, liberality is a virtue: exercised, at the expense of others, and without their consent, it is a vice: laudation bestowed upon it, hypocrisy and imposture: its fruits, the above evils: the good, if any, on the smallest scale; the evil, upon the largest.

### *Ratiocinative. Instructional*

ART. 8. Repugnant accordingly to these principles is remuneration, in any shape, on any occasion, *arbitrarily* conferred: repugnant, even if for service really rendered, or about to be rendered; much more if on false pretence of service.

### *Ratiocinative. Instructional*

ART. 9. Arbitrarily conferred, consistently with these principles, can neither good nor evil be by the hand of Government: neither reward nor (as per Penal Code)[1] punishment: nor (as per Ch. xxv. JUSTICE MINISTER, §[5], *Dispunitive Function*) exemption from punishment.

---

[1] See Ch. V, §6, Art. 2n, p. 39n, and Table 2.

*Expositive*

ART. 10. *Arbitrarily* conferred is the matter of reward, so far as by the hand of Government it is otherwise than *judicially* conferred. Judicially conferred will accordingly be seen to be all official situations, in relation to which location is performed, as per §17, *Located how.*

*Ratiocinative. Instructional*

ART. 11. On no other account than that of service to the public, can the matter of reward be conferred by the hand of Government, except in so far as it is bestowed in waste.

*Expositive*

ART. 12. *Ordinary* and *extraordinary*: under one or other of these denominations comes all service rendered, or supposed to be rendered, to the public.

*Expositive*

ART. 13. In the case of a public functionary, by ordinary service understand all such service as, by acceptance of his office, he stands bound to render.

*Expositive*

ART. 14. By extraordinary service, all such service as, by such acceptance, he does not stand bound to render.

*Expositive*

ART. 15. *Pecuniary* and *honorary:* by one or other of these denominations may the matter of reward be designated, in every shape in which it is usually bestowed by the hand of Government.

*Ratiocinative. Instructional*

ART. 16. For extraordinary service rendered to the public, reward in a *pecuniary* shape may, with as much facility and propriety, be demanded at the hands of a Judicatory at the charge of the public, as in the like shape it is so demanded at the charge of an individual.

*Ratiocinative. Instructional*

ART. 17. With not less facility and propriety, so may it in an *honorary* shape.

### Enactive. Instructional

ART. 18. Honorary reward in no shape does this constitution allow to be conferred, but in the shape of *natural honour augmented*: augmented by the hand of Government; and in this case the hand of Government is, as per Art. 20, the hand of justice.

### Expositive

ART. 19. By *natural honour*, understand that which, in consideration of service, in this or that extraordinary shape, rendered to the community, or to this or that section of the community, the members of it, in their quality of members of the *Public Opinion Tribunal*, spontaneously render to the *benemeritant:* render, that is to say, by means of appropriate sentiments of love and respect, entertained in relation to him, with the occasional addition, of the special good will, good offices, and services, in whatever shape, tangible or untangible, naturally flowing from these sentiments.

### Enactive. Expositive

ART. 20. *Judicially augmented* will *natural honour* be by two conjunct and correspondent appropriate judicial decrees; the first *opinative*, the other *imperative*, in this as in other cases: as to which, see Art. [23], and Ch. xii. JUDICIARY COLLECTIVELY, §9, *Judges' Elementary Functions*.

### Enactive

ART. 21. Efficient causes of the augmentation in this case, are, authoritative *recordation* and authoritative *publication*.

### Enactive

ART. 22. Authoritative recordation is by entry made in an appropriate Register Book: say, in the *Extraordinary Service Register*, or say, *Public Merit Register*.

### Enactive

ART. 23. Of such entry, the matter is composed of an abstract of the record of the proceedings in a suit, in conclusion of which the judicial decrees, as per Art. 20, have been pronounced: 1. the *opinative*, stating the act deemed meritorious, the *shape* in which the service has been rendered to the public, and the fact that the individual, by or for whom the demand of the reward is made, is *he* by whom the service has been rendered, with the *evidence* on which the decree has been grounded;——time, place, and manner mentioned: 2. the *imperative*, ordering entry to be made of this same abstract in the above-mentioned Merit Register.

### Enactive

ART. 24. The commencement of the suit is by application, made to the Judicatory, demanding for the alleged *benemeritant* a place in the *Public Merit Register*, on the ground of the extraordinary service thereupon stated; as in the case of an ordinary application for money, alleged to be due from defendant to applicant on the ground of work performed.

### Enactive

ART. 25. The *applicant*, that is to say *demandant*, may be either the alleged *benemeritant*, or any person for him, with or without his consent, and with or without his knowledge.

### Enactive

ART.26. The *defendant* will be the functionary, who would be defendant, were the subject of the demand——money alleged to be due from Government for goods furnished, or work done, otherwise than in the way of official service; namely, the *Government Advocate* of the immediate Judicatory, as per Ch. xviii. IMMEDIATE GOVERN-MENT ADVOCATE[S]; or the Government Advocate-General, as per Ch. xix. GOVERNMENT ADVOCATE-GENERAL, if so he thinks fit.

### Enactive

ART. 27. The *Judicatory* will be the immediate Judicatory of the sub-district in which the metropolis of the state is situated; unless, for special reasons, assigned by the Legislature, or the Prime Minister, the immediate Judicatory of some other subdistrict shall have been appointed.

### Enactive. Instructional

ART. 28. *Authoritative publication* is by publication, given, in such way as the Legislature shall have appointed, to the matter of the recordation-entry, made as per Art. [22], in the *Public Merit Register.*

### Enactive. Instructional

ART. 29. Repugnant, accordingly, to the principles of this Constitution, is all *purely factitious honour* or *dignity*, in whatever shape, conferred, as hitherto it has every where been, *arbitrarily*; that is to say, otherwise than *judicially*, as above.

302

*Expositive*

ART. 30. *Titles of honour*, or *ensigns of dignity*. To one or other of these denominations may be referred the instruments, by which factitious honour or dignity has usually been conferred. Combined, to a considerable extent, they have been with one another, and in many instances with masses of power, or wealth, in various shapes, or both.

*Expositive*

ART. 31. Examples of *titles of honour* are——
1. Prince.
2. Arch-Duke.
3. Grand Duke.
4. Duke.
5. Marquis.
6. Count or Earl.
7. Viscount.
8. Baron.
9. Baronet.
10. Knight——to wit, of any one of a variety of *orders*.
11. Knight——of no order.

*Expositive*

ART. 32. Examples of ensigns of dignity, worn about the body of the individual, are——
1. Stars.
2. Crosses.
3. Ribbons.
4. Garters.
5. Gold and silver sticks.

*Expositive*

ART. 33. Examples of *ensigns of dignity*, exhibited on utensils of various sorts, employed by the individuals, are as follow:——
1. Coronets, of various shapes, corresponding to the several titles of honour.
2. Armorial bearings.
In this latter case, the assertion conveyed, though in most instances contrary to truth, is——that some ancestor of the individual had employed himself in an enterprise of unprovoked slaughter and devastation. For a symbol, if requisite, a *gibbet*, substituted or added, would have been more suitable.

*Ratiocinative. Instructional*

ART. 34. To the purpose of remuneration, whether for ordinary or extraordinary service,—unsuitable, in comparison of *natural honour augmented*, as above, would merely *factitious honour* be, as above, even if *judicially conferred*. For, with the utmost conceivable accuracy, in each individual instance, does the quantum of natural honour adjust itself to the quantum [of]¹ merit, in every shape, of the service: the lots of reward, attached to the aggregate number of services rendered within a given time, thus rising, one above another, in gradations which may be as numerous as the individual services themselves. Thus it is, that, in this mode of remuneration, not a particle of injustice can ever have place, except that which, as in all other cases, is liable to be produced by deceptiousness on the part of the evidence, or want of aptitude on the part of the Judge; and, by the supposition, this danger is the same in both cases.

On the other hand, where it is of *factitious honour* that the reward is composed, no such accuracy of adjustment can have place. Between grade and grade, how numerous soever the grades, there must always be a space more or less considerable; each such space is consequently a field of possible injustice, the magnitude of which is as the amplitude of such space. But, proportioned to the magnitude of each such space, is the discouragement, applied to the most meritorious of two or more services, to which the same lot of *factitious reward* is applicable. For if, for the rendering of each of them, sacrifice in any shape is necessary, in such sort that greater sacrifice is necessary in the case of the most than in the case of the least valuable of the two, the identity of the reward in both cases operates as a premium on the least valuable—as a prohibition on the most valuable. Moreover, in the case of the *factitious* honour, the justice of the decree is exposed to a degree of disbelief, and the Judge to a degree of disrepute, for which, in the case of the *natural honour*, there is no place. In the case of the *factitious honour*, it is by *the Judge* that the exact place in the scale of honour is determined, since it is by him that it is conferred, in the shape of some *title of honour*, or some *ensign of dignity*, which has a specific name. In the case of *natural honour*, it is not by the Judge, but by the *Public Opinion Tribunal*, that, in each individual instance, the *benemeritant's* place in the scale of honour is determined. The Judge may be corrupt, or (what, so far as regards the individual case, amounts to the same thing) may be suspected of being so; the *Public Opinion Tribunal* cannot.

¹ 1830, 1826 *Extract*, 1830 *Off. Apt. Max.*, 'quantum and merit'; Bowring, 'quantum of merit' as more appropriate after 'quantum of natural honour'.

### Enactive. Ratiocinative. Instructional

ART. 35. Sufficient of itself for the destruction of this Constitution might an instrument of corruption of this sort be, if arbitrarily conferrible. To the Prime Minister alone could the power of conferring it be allotted; for to no other functionary could any one propose to allot it. In the hands of a man of ordinary ambition and superior ability, sufficient then might this one instrument be, for the conversion of the here-proposed commonwealth into an arbitrary monarchy: at the least, into a monarchy operating by an all-pervading and all-vitiating system of corruption, waste, and unpunishable depredation, as in England. Into his lap, in return for these *objects* of *general desire*,—for themselves, or, what would amount to the same thing, for their connexions,—would continually be poured power in various shapes, impunity for various transgressions, and money from various sources, by the Legislature, that is, by the acting majority of the members. Immoveable he would remain, how flagrant soever were his inaptitude.

### Enactive. Expositive

ART. 36. Exceptions excepted, repugnant to these same principles is all *ultra-concomitant* remuneration. By *ultra-concomitant* remuneration, understand all habitual remuneration for habitual service, after the cessation of the habit of service.

For exceptions, apparent rather than real, see Ch. xi. MINISTERS SEVERALLY, §3, *Army Minister*; Ch. xi. MINISTERS SEVERALLY, §4, *Navy Minister*.[1]

### Ratiocinative

ART. 37. Completely needless, and thence unjustifiable, is all such ultra-remuneration. A baker is not paid for supplying food when he has ceased to do so; a medical practitioner for attending patients; a law practitioner for assisting litigants. Yet never is there any want of bakers, of medical, or of law practitioners: as little, in any official situation, would there be any want of occupants,—if, in the case of service rendered to the whole community, as in the case of service rendered to individuals, the habit of receiving the remuneration were to expire with that of rendering the service. But, bakers have it not in their power thus to load customers; medical practitioners, patients; law practitioners, litigants: while, in a Government which has for its end in view the good of the few, and, for the subject-matter of its

---

[1] Remuneration is not in fact discussed in the sections to which Bentham refers, but is dealt with in § 10 of Ch. X.

sacrifice, the good of the many, placemen have it in their power thus to load subjects. In the Anglo-American United States, waste in this shape has no place.

### Expositive. Ratiocinative

ART. 38. Of *modes* of *ultra-concomitant remuneration*, examples are as follow:——

1. Superannuation pensions, granted on presumption of relative inaptitude, through infirmity caused by age.

2. Pensions of retreat, granted on the score of casual inaptitude, through infirmity.

3. Pensions of retreat, granted without so much as the pretence of infirmity, on the score of a certain length of past service, balanced all along and requited already by concomitant remuneration.

Remuneration thus located is a premium on inaptitude. Men flock into the situation in contemplation of inaptitude: the infirmity, if it occurs, is exaggerated: if worth while, fostered or even produced: for the plea of it, naturally ready assistants may be looked for in all third persons, who are, or regard themselves as exposed to be, sufferers by it; most strenuous of all, the patron to whom the right of location accrues.

### Enactive. Instructional

ART. 39. Repugnant to these same principles is all *artificially mislocated* remuneration, so located, at the expense of the community, by the hand of Government. It is universally needless; it is essentially unfrugal.

### Expositive

ART. 40. By *artificially mislocated*, understand conferred on an individual, other than him by whom the service was rendered.

### Expositive

ART. 41. *Mislocated:* it is either *mislocated in toto* or *extravasated.*[a]

### Expositive

ART. 42. It is *mislocated in toto*, where, to a person by whom the service in question was not, in any part, rendered, reward is given; to him by whom it was rendered, none.

[a] By anatomists, blood which has flowed out of its proper vessels is said to be *extravasated:* if into other vessels, the *error loci* is spoken of as having place; as in the case of a blood-shot eye.

## Expositive

ART. 43. It is *extravasated*, in so far as, to reward given to the person by whom the service was rendered, is added, on that same account, reward given to some person, by whom, on the occasion in question, no service was rendered.

## Ratiocinative. Expositive

ART. 44. On the contrary, purely beneficial, and by the whole amount of it, is all remuneration in so far as *naturally extravasated*. *Naturally extravasated* it is, in so far as, without expense to Government, in virtue of pre-established connexions, the benefit of it diffuses itself among any, who, by any tie of interest, self-regarding or sympathetic, are in any way connected with the remuneratee. In this case, having place without expense to the community, it is so much pure good, and the more there is of it the better.

## Ratiocinative. Instructional

ART. 45. Of reward *mislocated in toto*, an example has place as often as, for service rendered by a Subordinate, the Superordinate not having contributed any thing to the performance of it, the Superordinate reaps the reward, the Subordinate no part of it.

In monarchies, injustice in this shape naturally and habitually pervades the whole of the official establishment: the more abundantly, the more absolute the monarchy is, and thence the more perfectly the light of the public eye is excluded from all official operations.

From this code, by the exclusion of all *arbitrarily conferred* reward, as per Arts. 8, 9, injustice in this shape will be seen effectually excluded. Every man will be judged of according to his works.[1]

## Expositive. Ratiocinative

ART. 46. Of reward *artificially extravasated*, at the expense of the community, by the hand of Government, examples are the following:——

1. Pensions, receivable by the widow of the functionary, on his decease.

2. Pensions, receivable by a child or children of the functionary, on his decease.

3. Pensions, payable to any more distant relative of the functionary, on his decease.

These may be styled *post-obituary*, or *post-obit* pensions.

[1] There is a multiple biblical echo here: see Proverbs 24: 12; Matthew 16: 27; 2 Timothy 4: 14.

4. An income in perpetuity, derived from land or otherwise, with power given to the supposed benemeritant and his representatives to hold in hereditary succession, as if so purchased by him. In this case, for the benefit of one individual, generations, indefinite in number, are subjected to depredation.

### Enactive. Ratiocinative. Instructional

ART. 47. Pre-eminently repugnant would be any such compound, as that which is composed of *factitious* dignity, with fractional masses of supreme power, legislative and judicial together; the whole rendered extravasate, running in the blood of the first remuneratee, from generation to generation, through a boundless line of descendants, from no one of whom could any part have been borne in the supposed public service so remunerated: those same generations being, moreover, loaded with the obligation of keeping repaired all breaches, made by dissipation, in the originally excessive mass of wealth, originally combined with that same inordinately rich compound[a] the whole for the perpetual saturation of appetites essentially unsaturable.

### Expositive. Ratiocinative. Instructional

ART. 48. For examples, see Art. [31]: those appellations, which elsewhere designate little more than the *gaseous* dignity, designating, in one nation——many of them——the above-mentioned substantial compound: for, in the race of waste and corruption, it was ordained of old, that the foremost of all other Governments should be distanced by that, of which it is the distinguishing character to be (in the words of its own so indefatigably trumpeted proclamations), 'the envy and admiration of all surrounding nations.'

### Enactive

ART. 49. In respect of any extraordinary public service, analogous to the ordinary service attached to any official situation in this department,——any person whatever, by whom any such extraordinary service has been rendered, may be considered as belonging, on that

[a] For two successive demonstrations of this truth, see the Author's Defence of Economy against Burke, in Pamphleteer, No. XVII. anno 1817; and Defence of Economy against Rose, in Pamphleteer, No. XX. anno 1817.[1]

---

[1] Bentham's 'Defence of Economy against the late Mr Burke' was published in *The Pamphleteer*, ix (1817), 3–47; and his 'Defence of Economy against the Right Hon. George Rose' in x (1817), 281–332. Both were reprinted in *Official Aptitude Maximized; Expense Minimized* (Bowring, v. 263–386) as papers V and VI: see Bowring, v. 278–328.

occasion, to that same office, and, in proportion to the value of the service, be remunerated.

### Enactive. Expositive

ART. 50. Service, which, to a functionary in the situation in question, would be *ordinary*, and sufficiently requited by the remuneration attached to it, may, if rendered by a person not in that situation, be *extraordinary*, and as such be remunerated.

### Expositive

ART. 51. Examples are as follow:——

1. Service, by defence of any portion of the territory, or of a Government or private vessel, or any individual inhabitant of the territory, against aggression by any pirate or foreign enemy. Subdepartment, the Army or Navy.

2. Service, rendered, at the peril of life, by the apprehension of a depredator or other common malefactor, while engaged in the commission of a crime. Subdepartment, the Preventive Service.

3. Service, rendered, at the peril of life, by the extinction of an accidental conflagration. Subdepartment again, the correspondent section of the Preventive Service Subdepartment.

### Enactive

ART. 52.[1] But, in a case of this sort, the Judge will be upon his guard against a fraud, to which, by its nature, it stands exposed: that is to say, service left unperformed by an appropriate functionary, that a confederate non-functionary may perform it, and thus, by the fraudulent display of pretendedly meritorious service, receive appropriate remuneration.

### Enactive

ART. 53. *Judicially*, in a pecuniary shape, may reward to any amount, be thus conferred.

### Enactive

ART. 54. A minister's pay is {—— ——} a year, paid quarterly {in advance}. From unwilling hands, receipt of ulterior emolument is *extortion*: from willing ones, corruption. This pay is the standard of reference in the case of the pecuniary competition, as per §17, *Located how*, Art. 1.

---

[1] This article should logically follow Art. 53, not precede it.

*Enactive*

ART. 55. In every Subdepartment, the pay of the minister is the same.

*Enactive*

ART. 56. Whatsoever is the number of subdepartments allotted to one and the same minister, pay is not given for more than one.

*Enactive*

ART. 57. To his stated pay is added indemnification money, for the expense of inspection visits, at the rate of {— —} per mile, actually travelled; with {— —} for each day or part of a day so employed, for diet and lodging while out. By the care of the Finance Minister, after each visit, immediately on his return, the money is paid to every other minister, on his signing a receipt.

## SECTION 16

### LOCABLE WHO

*Enactive*

ART. 1. This section has for its object the providing, as soon as may be, and in so far as is necessary,—but no further, at the public expense, in relation to the business of all the several Subdepartments comprised in the Administration Department, a system of arrangements, whereby in the several official situations, appropriate aptitude in all its branches shall be maximized, and at the same time expense minimized; say, a SYSTEM OF OFFICIAL LOCATION, or, for shortness, THE LOCATION SYSTEM.

*Instructional*

ART. 2. As to what regards instruction, in so far as this system is well adapted to the instruction of persons destined to become public functionaries, so will it be, according to the nature of the business belonging to the several subdepartments, to the instruction of persons at large, foreigners as well as natives. Any benefit thus derivable from the system, call it the COLLATERAL BENEFIT.

*Enactive. Ratiocinative. Instructional*

ART. 3. Of this system of location the leading features are as follow:—

A choice will, at any rate, be to be made, out of a number of candidates or persons proposed. According to this Constitution, for

310

reasons elsewhere given, by a single person, and not by a number, the location must on every occasion be made. That person can be no other than the person, on whom, in case of a bad choice, as demonstrated by relative inaptitude, the responsibility, legal or moral, or both, will fall; in a word, the *Prime Minister*. By no legal restriction is he, therefore, prevented from choosing any person at pleasure: but, by a moral restriction, by the circumscribing eye of the Public Opinion Tribunal, his choice (as per §[17], *Located how*) will naturally be confined within limits comparatively narrow. The person whose degree of appropriate aptitude, in all its several branches, as certified by the votes of a set of appropriately determined Judges, stands highest, will have been made known——made known to him and every body. Thus it is that provision is made for *maximization of aptitude*.

Remains now the *minimization of expense*. Of those persons who, in the scale of aptitude, stand on or near the same level, it is made known by public competition who those are who, in the situation in question, are willing to serve the public on the lowest terms. Provision for moral aptitude is at the same time made, by a scrutiny, performed at the same time, in the course of the same examination, and with equal publicity.

If, to a person who, in the eyes of the universal public, is seen to stand foremost in the line of appropriate aptitude, and in that of cheapness of service, taken together,——he prefers a person not distinguished in either way, it is at his peril——at the peril of his reputation——that he does so. Nor can an improper choice afford any promise of producing to him any permanent advantage; for, in the case of every office, the power of *dislocation* is confided to a number of hands, each acting separately, with full power, and who, not adding to it (any one of them) the power of *location*, stand (every one of them) altogether divested of all inducement to abuse a power so thankless and unprofitable to the possessors.

For calling into exercise this dislocative power, there will be the motive afforded by the affection of envy in the breasts of disappointed rivals:——a check not capable of being brought into operation in the ordinary case of a purely arbitrary power of patronage.

The choice being thus narrowed, not only expense, but with it, power of corruption, is minimized: the benefit thus bestowed is the produce——not of favour, but of right; though not of legally binding, yet of morally binding right.

### Enactive. Ratiocinative

ART. 4. Under this system, two periods there are, in relation to which, separate provision requires to be made; the *preparation* period, and the *consummation* period. The consummation period, though last in the order of time, requires to be first described; the other not being otherwise capable of being made intelligible.

### Expositive

ART. 5. By the *consummation period*, understand *that*, during which the courses of proceeding regarded as necessary to the production of appropriate aptitude in the several official situations, in the degree of perfection regarded as desirable and attainable, will be carrying on, each of them during the whole length of time regarded as desirable. Of this period, the *commencement* will coincide with the termination of the preparation period: determinate *end* it will have none.

### Expositive

ART. 6. By the *preparation period*, understand *that* during which those same courses will have been going on, but will not have continued long enough, it is supposed, to have produced, with sufficient certainty, the whole of the desired benefit.[1]

### Instructional. Ratiocinative

ART. 7. If in any degree beneficial, these same courses will, however, almost from the first, have been productive of some degree of appropriate aptitude, which benefit will have continued on the increase up to the point of time at which the preparation period terminates, and the consummation period commences. This increase, at every distinguishable stage of it, the Legislature will turn to profit, as per Arts. [55], and those which follow it.

### Instructional

ART. 8. For these several courses, the several times of commencement will be appointed by the Legislature.

### Instructional. Ratiocinative

ART. 9. On these principles, throughout the official establishment, proceed the several arrangements, in virtue of which, so soon, and so long, as any person is to be found by whom appropriate proof has been given of his having reaped any distinguishable portion of the benefit in question, no person by whom like proof has not been given will be locable: and, by the whole amount of the thus acquired aptitude, how small soever, this system of location will be preferable to any in which no security at all is given for appropriate official

[1] The distinction between the preparation and consummation periods is further clarified at Arts. 57-9, pp. 327-8.

aptitude. Thus it is, that not by doubt, nor even by despair, as to the practicability of carrying the system to the height of perfection here exhibited to view, can any tenable reason be given, for omitting to carry it so far as it shall be found capable of being carried into effect.

### Instructional

ART. 10. For this, as well as other purposes, the Legislature will have caused to be made, and published, an all-comprehensive list of the several situations, belonging to this, as well as the several other departments: name of it, *The Office Calendar:* as to which, see also §[25], *Securities for Appropriate Aptitude.*

### Instructional. Expositive

ART. 11. General heads, under which, for the present purpose, these may be ranged, are—
  I. Situations of talent.
  II. Situations of simple trust.
  III. Situations of trust and talent.

### Expositive. Instructional

ART. 12. By situations of talent, understand those so circumstanced, that, for the apt fulfilment of the duties attached to them, appropriate *knowledge, judgment,* and *active talent,* in some special shape or shapes, as per Art. 15, over and above appropriate *moral* aptitude, are regarded as necessary.

These situations will be formed into groups, corresponding to the several groups of branches of art and science, proficiency in which shall have been regarded as necessary to the apt exercise of the several functions respectively belonging to the several situations.

### Expositive

ART. 13. By situations of simple trust, understand such, for the apt performance of the duties whereof no such proficiency is necessary.
  Examples are—
  1. Situations, the duties of which are discharged by the receipt, custody, and transmission, of money.
  2. Or of [messages][1] from a central part of the territory of the state to every other: as in the case of Post-office situations.
  3. Or of stores of any kind: except in so far as, according to the

---

[1] 1830, 1826 *Extract,* 1830 *Off. Apt. Max.,* 'messengers'; Bowring, 'messages'. The context clearly requires the emended reading.

nature of the article, chemical knowledge respecting the causes and preventives of deperdition[1] may be necessary.

4. So, situations, in virtue of which the *custoditive* function is exercised with relation to an immoveable subject-matter: excepting as above.

*Expositive*

ART. 14. By situations of talent and trust, understand such situations of talent, for the apt performance of the duties whereof the disposal of the services of men in considerable numbers, or of things, for public use, to considerable value, is necessary.

*Instructional. Expositive*

ART. 15. Of groups of talents, proficiency in which may be regarded as necessary to the apt exercise of the functions belonging to correspondent groups of situations, examples are as follow:—

| I. *Talent-requiring Situations* | II. *Talents therein more especially requisite.* |
| --- | --- |
| 1. Army Minister, and his various subordinates, in the several situations of Commander of Engineers, of Artillerymen, and Cavalry; Commissary, for the purchase, preservation, and conveyance of military stores and provisions; Medical Curator; Military Judge. | 1. Mechanic and Chemical Art and Science, various branches. Mathematics, in so far as subservient thereto. Fortification. Military Tactics. Medical Art and Science, in most of its branches. Judicature, as applied to Army Service. |
| 2. Navy Minister, and his various subordinates. | 2. Mechanic, Chemical, and Medical Art and Science, various branches, as in the case of Army Service. Astronomy, in so far as applied to the determining the place of a navigable vessel, whether at anchor or in her course. Mathematics, in so far as subservient thereto. Naval Architecture. Naval Tactics, Judicature, as applied to Navy Service. |
| 3. Interior Communication Minister, and his subordinates in | 3. Mechanical and Chemical Art and Science, various branches; |

---

[1] 1830 and Bowring, 'deperdition'; 1826 *Extract* and 1830 *Off. Apt. Max.*, 'deperition'. Both words are recorded in *OED*.

various situations belonging to this subdepartment.

4. Indigence Relief Minister.
5. Domain Minister.

6. Health Minister, and his various subordinates.

7. Foreign Relation Minister, and his subordinates, in the several situations of Envoy for General Purposes, and Consuls for the special purpose of protection of trade.

8. Finance Minister, and his various subordinates.

more particularly Hydrostatics and Hydrodynamics. Mathematics, in so far as subservient thereto.

4. Political Economy.

5. According to the nature of the several Domains, Agriculture, Geology, Mineralogy, and the several branches of Mechanical and Chemical Art and Science subservient thereto.

6. Medical Art and Science, all its branches. Chemical Art and Science, all its branches. Mechanical Art and Science, various branches. Natural History, most of its branches. Geography, in so far as regards climate and temperature, in countries which the members of the community may have occasion to visit, either for war or trade.

7. Branches of Art and Science, corresponding to the faculties of reading, speaking, and writing, in various languages. Political Economy, in respect of the affairs of trade. History and Geography. National Statistics. International Law.

8.—1. Political Economy, as above.

2. Branches of Art and Science to which belong the several processes of the several manufactures and other branches of profit-seeking industry, the operations of which are liable to become subject-matters of taxation, restriction, prohibition, or compulsory obligation. History, Geography, National Statistics, and International Law, as above.

*Enactive*

ART. 16. Except as per §[17], *Located how*, Arts. 16, 17,[1] antecedently to his admission into any office belonging to this department, the name of the individual must have been entered upon a
certain list, called *the Locable List.*

*Enactive*

ART. 17. For determining, in regard to each individual whether he
be qualified to be admitted; and accordingly, whether he shall be
admitted, into this list,—and if yes, in what rank, a Special Judicatory will be formed, under the name of the *Qualification Judicatory*,
or say, *Examination Judicatory.*

*Enactive*

ART. 18. Of this Judicatory the composition will be as follows:—
    1. *Presiding Judge*, the Justice Minister or his depute.
    2. *Other Judges*, the *Prime Minister* and the several *Ministers*, or
their respective deputes.
    3. *Quasi-jurymen*, the several *instructors*, as per Arts. 42 to [54],
under whose instruction the several *locables* have acquired their
proficiency in the several groups of branches of art and science.
    As to Quasi-jurymen and their functions, see, in the part belonging
to the Judicial Department, Ch. [xvi.] QUASI-JURY.

*Enactive*

ART. 19. Included in the supposition of the sitting of a Judicatory
of this sort, are the suppositions following:—
    1. Returns made to the *advertisement*, as per Art. 42.
    2. To the several places in question, pecuniary supply, afforded by
Government; or ascertainment of the needlessness of such supply.
    3. Time elapsed, sufficient for the obtainment of instruction, more
or less extensive, in the several branches of art and science in question, or some of them; observation being at the same time made,
that, how small soever, the instruction obtained in consequence of
this plan will, by the whole amount of it, have been so much more
than would have had place otherwise. More will always be better
than less, but the least will always be better than none.

*Enactive. Instructional*

ART. 20. Mode of procedure in these examinations:—in the main
this will be the same as in an ordinary *Immediate Judicatory.*

---

[1] The references Bentham provides do not in fact take up the exceptions to
the general rule stated here.

Examples of points of *agreement* and coincidence are as follow:——

1. On the *pursuer's side, applicants* and demandants (the several scholars) demanding admission into the *locable list*, and to [that] end presenting themselves for examination.

2. Subject-matter of demand, the *judicial service*, which the Judicatory will have rendered to the applicant, if, being placed on the list, he is at the same time placed at the head of it, or in any such inferior place as shall have been thought fit.

3. *Defendants*, in like manner, these same several scholars, each contesting the demand made by every other of the highest station, and the several next stations, one below another, as above.

4. *Evidence* in favour of his own aptitude, spontaneously adduced by each scholar in the character of *demandant*,——any such marks of proficiency, as, according to the nature of the case, the regulation shall have allowed to be exhibited.

5. *Other evidence* in his favour, elicited by *interrogation*, addressed to him by any Judges, or Quasi-jurymen, or fellow-candidates, so disposed.

6. Other evidence, elicited by *counter-interrogation*, addressed to him in pursuance of the opposite disposition.

7. Also, whatever *evidence* operates, in a *direct* way, in favour of any one of his several *competitors*, as above.

8. *Publicity*, throughout maximized.

### *Expositive*

ART. 21. Examples of points of *diversity* on the part of this as compared with an ordinary Judicatory, are as follow:

1. Substitute or assistant, none, gratuitous or professional, to any such candidate, either as demandant or defendant.

2. Co-demandants or co-defendants, none *compelled* or *compellable* to be.

3. Extraneous witnesses, none compelled or admitted, except in case of necessity, on an examination into moral aptitude, as per Art. [34].

4. Costs, that is to say, compensation to a party on the opposite side for expenses of demand or defence, none exigible.

### *Enactive*

ART. 22. Of the Qualification Judicatory the *opinative* decree will be thus formed:——*Modes of votation*, two: the *secret mode;* then, before the result of the secret mode has been disclosed or ascertained, the *open mode*.

*Enactive*

ART. 23. Of the way in which votation in the *secret* mode may be conducted, an example is as follows:—

1. A roll of paper or parchment is provided: length such as to contain the names of all the several candidates, one under another.

2. In this roll are so many *columns*, placed abreast of one another, headed each by the names of such *groups of branches of art and science* as, for this purpose, have been assorted into groups, as per Art. 15.

3. Under each of these heads, in each column, follow the *names* of the several *candidates*, in the alphabetical order of their surnames.

4. To each voter have been delivered *tickets*, in card or paper, equal in number to that of the *candidates*, multiplied by the number of the above *groups* of branches of art and science.

5. Underneath, or at the back of the name of each candidate, according to the space provided, the *voter pins a ticket*, exhibiting the number, expressive of the relative rank which it is his desire the candidate should occupy.

6. Say, for instance, voters (Judges and Quasi-jurymen together), 25; candidates, 200; groups of branches of art and science, 4: thence, total number of tickets requisite for each voter, 800.

7. Breadth of each ticket, say about one-fourth of an inch; hence, length of each roll, exclusive of the heading, 50 inches—4 feet 2 inches. Divide the roll into two equal parts, placing them abreast; length of each will be 2 feet 1 inch.

8. The words and figures employed being, all of them, in print, and printed in the same press, the person of the voter cannot thus be made known, as by hand-writing it might be.

9. The two half-sheets of each sheet being folded one over the other, in the manner of a sheet of paper in folio, the *numbers* attached to the names, will *not* in any instance, be *visible*.

*Enactive*

ART. 24. Mode of *giving in the votes*. On a day pre-announced, *the Judges* in presence of each other, *deliver in* to the Registrar, each of them, his *voting roll*, at the same time: as delivered in, these rolls are *shuffled*, in the manner of a pack of cards, that it may not be known by what person they have respectively been delivered in. They are then *deposited*, one upon another, in a box. The box is *sealed*, by an impression from each Judge's seal.[a]

[a] Note by an East India Proprietor. At the India House the forms of secrecy are established; but it is regarded as a signal of hostility to the Directors if, on

*Enactive. Expositive. Instructional*

ART. 25. Mode of scrutiny. For performing the arithmetical operation, the course taken is as follows:——

1. For the assistance of the Registrar, *scrutineers*, two or more, are
*elected by the Judges*.

2. In case of equality, the *President* has a casting vote.

3. At the commencement of the scrutiny, and not before, the seals
are broken. Thus, by the shortness of the time, all *unduly partial disclosure*, indicating by means of secret marks, which roll was delivered
in by which Judge, is rendered *impracticable*.

4. In relation to each such group of subject-matters, the figures expressive of the ranks, assigned to the several candidates by the several
voters, being summed up,——he, in regard to whom the sum is least, is
thus seen to stand highest in the judgment of the whole Judicatory
taken together.[a]

the delivery, the vote is not made visible to him who presides. Secrecy is thus an
imposture. Allowance of liberty of suffrage professed; tyranny and corruption
practised.[1]

[a] Note by a highly distinguished Officer of Artillery, bred up in the Government Academy at Woolwich, near London.

Such is the practice at the Woolwich Academy. Of the proceedings of the
examinations, a register is there kept, and monthly returns of the contents made.
By these returns, the earliest commissions in the service are determined, and pro-
motions are determined by seniority in service.[2]

For the quieting of the anxieties liable to be produced on such occasions,
respecting the correctness of the vote, the nature of the case does not shut the
door against ulterior expedients. Suppose a voter hesitating as to the comparative aptitude of two or more candidates; in this case, to give the preference to
any one above the other may seem to him an act of injustice.

Modes in which he may exempt himself from self-condemnation on this
score:——

1. One is the determining by *lot* which shall be placed.

2. Another, which will naturally be correctly expressive of the desired equality,
is, the adding together the numbers, that would be expressive of the ranks, given

[1] For this note and those on Woolwich Academy and Glasgow University
which follow below, see UC xxxix. 95-6, headed 'Notes by Col. Young'. James
Young (1782-1848), second son of John Young, Professor of Greek at Glasgow,
matriculated there in 1793, was a cadet at Woolwich 1798-1800, and served
in India from 1801 until he resigned his commission in 1818, being by then
Lieutenant-Colonel and Secretary to the Military Department. After leaving
the service he held various other positions in India, notably in banking and as
editor of the *Bengal Hurkaru*, the leading liberal newspaper in Calcutta. For
further details see Major V. C. P. Hodson, *List of the Officers of the Bengal
Army 1758-1834*, 4 vols., London, 1927-47, iv. 547-8.

[2] See n. 1, above: James Young saw active service in the Mahratta wars with
the Horse Artillery.

5. Example. Candidates, as above, say 200: voters, 12: if, by all 12, Candidate A is meant to be ranked highest, 12 will be the number expressive of such his rank: if lowest, 2,400. To facilitate conception, in an appropriate column, in a line with number 12, may be inserted number 1: so also in regard to the several other candidates.

*Enactive*

ART. 26. In the *open* mode, the votation will be performed in nearly the same manner; sole difference, the name of the voter will be in his *own* hand, written at the top of his voting-paper.

*Enactive*

ART. 27.—It will be performed, after performance in the secret mode: and before the time, when, by the breaking of the seals, the result thereof is begun to be disclosed.

*Enactive*

ART. 28. In the same manner, as per Art. 23, will be expressed, in the *secret* mode, the aggregate of the opinions of the *Quasi-jurymen.*

*Ratiocinative. Instructional*

ART. 29. In their instance, the *secret* mode alone will have place. On their votes, favour or disfavour of candidates and their friends will operate, it is presumed, with more force than on those of the Judges. In the case of the *Quasi-jurymen*, they being the several Instructors, the interest which they respectively have in the aptitude of the persons located in the several official situations, is not so immediate and clear as in the case of the *Judges*. Each Quasi-juryman being an *Instructor*, it is for the interest of his reputation that his pupils, qualified or not qualified, be in the greatest number possible, placed in the highest ranks possible.[a]

to the several supposed equally apt candidates, if they were placed one above another, and then dividing the sum by the number of those same candidates: the quotient resulting from this division is the number which, on this plan, he attaches to the name of each. Thus much as to these particular candidates. By this mode his opinion will be correctly expressed in relation to these several candidates; nor, in this way, would the rank of those above or those below them be affected.

[a] Note by a person of distinction, bred in the University of Glasgow. When prizes were given, votes, expressive of the degrees of proficiency, were delivered by the candidates themselves; each thus acting as Judge in relation to every other: justice was universally acknowledged to be the general, not to say the constant, result.[1]

Addition by the Author. At Hazelwood School, near Birmingham, at which

--------

[1] See p. 319 n. 1.

## Enactive

ART. 30. Of the votation, in both modes, in a Table styled the *Ranking-table*, the results will be published at the same time.

## Enactive

ART. [ 31 ].[1] The effect of priority being, as per §17, not peremptory, in such sort as to exclude the faculty of choice on the part of the locating superordinate, the result of both modes will lie, and will be seen to lie, before him, for his guidance.

## Enactive. Instructional

ART. [ 32 ]. When time has brought into existence a sufficient body of experience, the Legislature will choose between the three modes: to wit, the secret mode alone; the open mode alone; and the two compounded, as above. In regard to the whole number of official situations, or this or that portion thereof, it will, if it see reason, ordain that they shall all three be employed: to wit, one during the first; another during the second; and the third during the third, of three successive years.

## Enactive

ART. [ 33 ]. Of the comparative aptitude of the several instructors, presumptive evidence, more or less probative, will thus be exhibited. The rank of each several candidate being thus ascertained,—on a line with each, in an appropriate column, will be inserted the name

two Greek youths are educating by the Author of this Code, punishment is never administered, unless the accused has been found guilty by his fellow-scholars. Note, that in no shape is corporal punishment there practised.[2]

In the present case, the multitude of the persons in question would with difficulty, if at all, admit of so extended a Judicatory.

---

[1] 1830, 1826 *Extract*, and 1830 *Off. Apt. Max.*, repeat the numeral '30' for this article, and the resulting mistake persists to the end of the Supplement to §16.

[2] For Bentham's concern in the education of the two Greek boys, Eustratios Rallis and Stamos Nakos, see Bowring, iv. 588 and x. 544-7; and see UC xii. 321, which indicates that in 1824 Rallis was fourteen, born at Constantinople, the son of a merchant, while Nakos was twelve, born in Livadia, the son of an exarch and member of the provincial assembly. (Bowring, iv. 588 reads 'eparch' for 'exarch'.) The two boys' arrival at Hazelwood School in January 1825, as to which see UC x. 146-7 and xviii. 178, 183-7, is recorded in the *Hazelwood Magazine*, iii (1825), quoted in *Plans for the Government and Liberal Instruction of Boys, in large numbers, as practised at Hazelwood School*, 2nd edn., London, 1825, pp. 77-8.

or names of the *instructor* or *instructors*, under whose instruction he had studied, together with the *time* or times at which, and the length or *lengths of time during which*, such his study had been continued.

## Enactive. Instructional

ART. [34]. For appropriate *moral* aptitude, the Legislature will, if it sees reason, appoint a limited list of topics, in relation to which, to the exclusion of all other topics, the several *Judges* and *Quasi-jurymen* shall or may interrogate the several competitors: and the several competitors, with the leave of the judges, one another.

Into any alleged irregularities of the sexual appetite, all scrutiny, as being irrelevant, and pregnant with useless and mischievous annoyance to third persons, will be interdicted.

## Enactive

ART. [35]. Till such list has been framed and published, the liberty of interrogation will be unlimited. Power in this case to the majority of the judges, spontaneously, or at the instance of the candidate who is the subject of the interrogation, to inhibit answer, or declare the interrogatee at liberty to answer or not, as he thinks best. As to this, see Ch. xii. JUDICIARY COLLECTIVELY, §[28], *Locable who.*

For falsity committed in this Judicatory, the interrogatee is responsible, as if it were in any other. So the interrogator, for any falsity asserted on the occasion of, or implied in, his interrogation.

## Enactive

ART. [36]. Of the result of this scrutiny into moral aptitude, entry will be made in an appropriate register book, styled the *Candidate's Character Book.*

## Enactive. Ratiocinative

ART. [37]. Appropriate moral aptitude being, in this case, mostly negative,—and where no imputation attaches, as will mostly be the case, not susceptible of degrees,—appropriate aptitude in this shape will not be subject to votation. Of this scrutiny, as of the other, the result will lie in the view of each locator, and will assist him in the formation of his choice.

## Enactive

ART. [38]. From the result of the votation process, as above, will be framed, printed, and published by the *Registrar*, under the direction of the President, the aggregate *opinative decree*, by which the ranks

of the several *candidates*, say the several *probationary locables*, will
be determined.

### Enactive

ART. [39]. Consequent upon, and determined by, the opinative decree, will be the *imperative decree*, by which order will be given for
their insertion in the *locable list*, and for the printing and publication
of it.

### Enactive

ART. [40]. To the name of no *probationary locable* will insertion be
refused, on the ground of *intellectual* inaptitude, unless by an express
decree of the majority of the officiating Judges. In case of imputed
inaptitude, the degree thereof will be exhibited by the rank occupied
by the individual's name in the list of *probationers*, as per Art. 25.

### Enactive

ART. [41]. So neither, on the ground of *moral* inaptitude. But in
the printed list, to the name of each probationer, to whose conduct,
on the score of moral inaptitude, an objection has been made, a mark
will be attached; and of what has passed, on the occasion of every
such scrutiny, a *record*, under the care of the Registrar, will be made
and *published*.

### Enactive. Ratiocinative

ART. [42]. For obtainment of *instructors* in the several branches as
above,—for maximizing the aptitude of those employed, by maximizing the number of those competing for the employment,—and,
moreover, for preascertainment of the expense to Government, *advertisement* will, by direction of the Prime Minister, be made of the
several places at which it is proposed that the instruction shall be
administered; together with questions, to which every person desirous of administering it may give answers. Name of this instrument
—*The Prime Minister's Advertisement for Instructors;* or, for shortness, *The Advertisement for Instructors.*

### Enactive

ART. [43]. Examples of these questions are the following:

1. At the time of answering, have you under your instruction, any
and what pupils, and of what ages respectively, in any and what
branch or branches of instruction contained in this advertisement; and
during what length of time have you so had them respectively, mentioning in each instance the year, month, and day of commencement?

2. To any and which of them do you supply lodging and diet, or either, and which, and on what terms?

3. As to what other branches, if any, of art and science, in the groups stated in the advertisement, as per Art. 15, or in any and what other groups, or separately, do you regard yourself able, being also willing, to administer instruction?

4. What remuneration do you require for each pupil, with variations, if any, according to age, or any and what other circumstance?

5. Shall you be able and willing, and when, for any and what number, to supply lodging and diet, or either, and which, and on what terms?

### Enactive

ART. [44]. Of an advertisement to this effect, the object will be, to ascertain, in the first place, in what branches of instruction, and in regard to each, for what number of pupils apt instruction, may be expected, at the charge of the *individuals* more immediately benefited, and thence, what part of the expense will be required to be borne or advanced by *Government*.

### Enactive. Ratiocinative

ART. [45]. As to the Government's share of the expense, the primary distinction will be between that part which must be advanced in the shape of *capital*, and that part for which an annual or other periodically received allowance, in the manner of *interest on capital*, may suffice: periodical allowance being preferable as far as it will go: preferable, inasmuch as, if ineffective or become needless, the expense may at any time be made to cease.

### Enactive

ART. [46]. Of the *purposes* for which *capital* may be requisite, the principal, are *house-room, ground-room*, and appropriate *apparatus*: relation being, in this case, had to the several branches of art and science.

For house-room and ground-room, it will be the care of Government that no advance shall be made in the shape of *capital*, any further than room, suitable and adequate to the purpose, cannot be obtained for hire.

### Enactive. Ratiocinative. Instructional

ART. [47]. For the maximization, not only of *frugality* and *extent of provision* as above, but, moreover, of appropriate *aptitude* on the part of the *Instructors*,—it will be the care of the Legislature, to minimize, in the instance of each Instructor, all such supply in a pecuniary and quasi-pecuniary shape as will be independent of the number of his pupils, and thereby of the strenuousness and constancy of his exertions.

### Instructional. Ratiocinative

ART. [48]. In this view, it will be the care of the Legislature, that whatsoever remuneration is needed for engaging apt Instructors shall, in as large a proportion as may be, be defrayed, not by Government, but by the pupils, and their relatives: considering that, in so far as salary is provided at a fixed rate, independent of the number of the pupils, motives for adequate exertion on the part of the alleged Instructors are altogether wanting; while the love of ease is an inducement, by the force of which, the absence of exertion will be secured: considering, moreover, that even if remuneration were made to rise in proportion to the number of the pupils, adequate motives for adequate exertion might still be wanting; the number being kept up for appearance sake, and the exertion no greater than what would be regarded as necessary to save the Instructor from disgrace; and that thus, in both cases, every allowance, thus made, operates as a premium on negligence, and as a prohibition on appropriate attention and exertion.

### Instructional. Ratiocinative

ART. [49]. On the other hand, cases may have place, in which, on pain of leaving the service unprovided with the necessary instruction on matters of indispensable necessity, it may be necessary to provide extra remuneration, in a quantity such as to free the Instructor from any such dependance, as above, on the number of his pupils. But against this case provision, in a great degree effectual, will have been made:——made, by the inevitable constancy of attendance, and performance of the appropriate functions, at the seat of duty, on principles and by means, as per Ch. vi. [LEGISLATURE], §20, *Attendance and Remuneration, how connected*; and §23, *Self-suppletive function*: so far as consists in the reading of lectures, performance being thus secured, although the motives for exertion may not be in quite so high a degree efficient as they might be rendered by emolument, rising in proportion to the number of the pupils, still may they be sufficiently effective, to make ample return for the expense; delivery of the instruction, in some state or other, being by the supposition inevitable, regard for his own character will prevent a man from exhibiting the instruction in any such state as should expose his character to disgrace; and, in situations such as those in question, this will, on the part of most men, suffice to call into action nearly all such appropriate aptitude as they are conscious of being in possession of.

### Instructional. Ratiocinative

ART. [50]. Of cases in which, in addition to bare subsistence, remuneration, rising in regular proportion with, and thence dependent on, the number of the pupils, may, as above, fail of being sufficient, examples are as follows:——

1. On the one hand, the branch of instruction, on the other hand, the state of the country such——that an extra mass of emolument, to a certain degree ample, may be necessary to attract instructors from *foreign countries*.

2. Or, in the country in question, from *rival pursuits*.

3. The branch of instruction such that, in the country in question, at the time in question, notwithstanding the multitude of those by whom it is, on account of the public, desirable that it should be possessed,——proficiency in it may not afford to pupils,——in number sufficient to make up such remuneration, as above, to the instructor, ——inducement sufficient in their eyes to pay for the time, labour, and expense, necessary to acquirement.

### Instructional

ART. [51]. In a case in which, under the persuasion of necessity, as above, any such extra rate of remuneration has at the outset been allotted,——it will be for the care of the Legislature so to order matters, that along with the necessity the overplus shall cease. Preserving, therefore, for the sake of good faith, to the first professor his agreed-for remuneration——such reduction will, accordingly, upon his decease, resignation, or dislocation, be made, as the consideration of the probable desirableness of the situation in the eyes of apt instructors,—— consideration being moreover had of the habitual probable number of pupils,——appears to admit of.

### Instructional. Ratiocinative

ART. [52]. If, in this or that *place*, it should be found necessary to employ *public money*, in providing *pay* for the engaging of apt Instructors, care will at the same time be taken, *not* to make it *larger* than the pay customarily regarded as necessary for the subsistence of the lowest-paid class of labourers: for, if at the *place* in question, at the expense of parents and relatives, pupils cannot be obtained, in number sufficient to afford an adequate inducement to an apt instructor, it will follow, that that same place is not so fit as some other that might be found. For the mode, in which, on the part of instructors, comparative aptitude will be exhibited by the examinations, see Art. [33].

### Instructional. Ratiocinative

ART. [53]. In this same view, the propriety will be seen of abstaining altogether from making any allowance for *lodging* or *diet* of pupils, considering, that in no part of the territory, in which any population has place, can there be any want of parents or other relatives, by whom persons, apt in respect of age to become pupils, are already maintained at their own expense: and that, in so far as allowance were made for any such purposes, such allowance would operate as a premium, or bounty, on the production of population in excess.

### Instructional. Ratiocinative

ART. [54]. As to *clothing*, if any Government allowance is made, it will be in the view of preventing the comparatively opulent from being excluded from the benefit of the instruction, by disgust produced from the spectacle of deficiency or uncleanliness, on the part of the comparatively indigent.

### Enactive. Instructional. Expositive

ART. [55]. When, in consequence of the advertisement, as per Art. 42, answers, at the end of a sufficient interval of time, have been received,—the Legislature will, by a succeeding advertisement, fix a day, distant not less than {one year} from the day on which such last-mentioned advertisement is issued; on which succeeding day, at the appointed place or places, the *first examination* or examinations will be to be made. These days may respectively be denominated, the *examination-appointing* day or days, and the *examination* day or days; the advertisement, the *examination-appointing* advertisement.

### Enactive. Instructional

ART. [56]. On the occasion of such examination-appointing advertisement, if not before, the Legislature will have determined, and will then declare its determination, as to whether the several branches of art and science, comprised in the several groups, shall be included all in one examination, or shall, in any and what manner, be distributed among divers examinations: those examinations to be performed by the same or divers *Qualification Judicatories*, at the same or divers times.

### Enactive

ART. [57]. Length of the *consummation period*, say {seven} years.

Day of commencement, either the day of the first examination, or some anterior day—say the examination-appointing day, as above. In each place if there be places more than one, the number of examinations in the course of that period will be, if annual, 7; if semi-annual, 14; if quarterly, 28. By the last examination will have been produced a complete set of functionaries, by whom the full benefit of the system will (it is presumed) have been reaped.

### Instructional. Ratiocinative

ART. [58]. Coincident with the *earliest consummation period* that has place, will be the *preparation period*. So many years, half-years, or quarters, so many *stages*, into which it may be considered as divided. By whatever considerations the Legislature will have been determined to cause the course of instruction to be administered in its entire length, by the same will it have been determined to cause to be administered whatsoever smaller portion the interval of time will, at each stage, have admitted. For,

1. In relation to appropriate aptitude in official situations, any quantity of time, employed in appropriate instruction for the obtainment of it, will be better than none.

2. Of any given degree of such aptitude, any such *direct* evidence will be better than none.

3. On grounds unknown to all men, *no man's* bare opinion, in affirmance of another man's aptitude, can be so well grounded as that of *all men* will be, after *a* public examination, though there were no more than *one*, followed as it will be by collective judicial opinion, having such examination for its ground, and expressed by secret, and thence by free votation, as above.

### Enactive

ART. [59]. Accordingly, when one year's instruction has been received, no person, those excepted who are already in office, will be placed on the *locable list*, unless he has been receiving the benefit of that same instruction throughout that one year: when two years, no person by whom it has not been received during those two years, those persons excepted who are then already in office, and those by whom the instruction had been received during the second year: and so on during the whole of the period—the quantum of appropriate instruction receiving every year an increase, until what is regarded as a sufficiency has been secured to all functionaries, in all lines, and the door perpetually shut against all those whose inaptitude stands self-confessed, and thus conclusively proved, by their shrinking from the test.

## Instructional

ART. [60]. In relation to appropriate *moral* aptitude, the Legislature will consider—whether the course of examination relative thereto shall commence at the same *time* with the examination relative to the other branches of appropriate aptitude, as above,—or not till at some and what later point of time; as also whether the acts of the examinee, which, on the examination, may be permitted to be brought to light, may commence at *any* point of time, or whether a time shall be assigned, to the end that no such act, anterior to that time, shall be endeavoured to be brought to light.

### Supplement to §16. Locable who.[1]

USE OF LOT AS AN INSTRUMENT OF SELECTION

## Instructional

ART. [61] or 1. Purposes, to which, on the occasion of a probationary examination, *chance*, substituted to *choice*, is capable of being employed, with advantage, as an instrument of selection, for the selection of a *part* of the whole number of desirable subject matters of examination, in a case where want of time renders the employment of the *whole* impracticable.

1. Maximization of the *inducement* afforded to *exertion* on the part of learners, by impossibilizing the knowledge as to what part of the field of exercise the trial will be applied to, and thence making *aptitude* of equal necessity in relation to every part: thus, on the part of each, in so far as depends on exertion, maximizing the probable degree of *absolute* appropriate aptitude.

2. In respect of the degrees of *comparative* aptitude ascribed to the several competing probationers by the aggregate judgment of the examination judicatory,—minimizing the probability of injustice, by impossibilizing the faculty of giving exercise to undue *disfavour*, by the selection of subject matters of examination;—or *favour*, by the

[1] In 1830 and 1830 *Off. Apt. Max.*, this Supplement is printed at the end of § 17, and is followed by the Supplement to that section. As §§ 15-17 were already in print in the form of the 1826 *Extract*, Bentham found it more convenient to add the Supplements to the end of the material already in print rather than to re-edit the sections already printed. He justifies this briefly in a footnote at Ch. IX, § 25, Art. 1n, p. 419n. In the Bowring edition, the two Supplements were separated, each being placed after the section to which it refers; and this arrangement has been followed here. For discussion of this arrangement and of the various versions of this part of the *Code*, see Ch. IX, § 15n, p. 297, and the Introduction, pp. xxxix-xl.

like selection,—foreknowledge of it being given or not given to the favoured candidate.

### Instructional

ART. [62] or 2. *Responses* and *exhibitions:*—to one or other of these denominations, will, it is believed, be found referable every token of appropriate aptitude, of which, on the part of a probationer, as such, in any branch of art and science, the nature of things admits the manifestation. Correspondent *function*, the exercise of which, on the part of examiners, is necessary,—in the case of responses the *extractive;* in the case of exhibitions, the *simply receptive:* as to which, see §11, *Information-elicitative function.*

### Instructional

ART. [63] or 3. Points, determined antecedently to the manifestation either of responses or exhibitions, will require to be the following:—

1. *Length of time*, intended and expected to be occupied in the whole process of the examination.

2. *Probationers*, entitled and expected to be examined—their whole number.

3. *Functionaries*, entitled and expected to take part in the examination, their several classes, and the number of individuals in each. As to this, see Art[s]. 17, 18.

4. *Classes of Examiners:* as per Art. 18, three.

5. *Number*, of individual *examinees* in each class.

6. *Aggregate number*, of the individuals in the aggregate of the classes.

7. *Time*, intended to be occupied in the elicitation of the appropriate information in the extractive mode, to wit, by *interrogations* followed by correspondent *responses.*

8. *Time*, proposed to be occupied in elicitation in the *simply receptive* mode: to wit, by *inspection* applied to *exhibition.*

For the several modes of elicitation, as applied to appropriate information, or say evidence in general, see above, §11, *Information-elicitative function.*

### Instructional. Enactive

ART. [64] or 4. Mode of procedure for the elicitation of *responses.*

For each branch of art and science, provide a *book*, in which the whole matter of it, or such portion as shall have been deemed necessary and sufficient, has been cast into the form of *questions, with correspondent answers:* say, for distinction, *responses*. Name, common to each such book, the *Question Book;* name of each such question book——that same generic name, with the addition of the name of the branch of art and science in question prefixed to it. Examples, *Chemistry Question Book: Mechanics' Question Book.*

### Instructional

ART. [65] or 5. For the purpose of obtaining the instruction[1] afforded by it, the assumption is, that, by each probationer, the whole matter of it may have been stowed in his memory: but that, for the purpose of their making proof of such portion of instruction as they have respectively obtained from it, only a part of the instruction so obtained can be brought to view; brought to view, to wit, by responses, delivered in compliance with the corresponding questions propounded; only a part by the aggregate of them; consequently, not more than a much smaller part by any one. Such, accordingly, is the course here supposed to be determined on,[2] and universally known to be so.

### Instructional

ART. [66] or 6. This being assumed,——one consequence is——what person soever it be, by whom, for the purpose of his undergoing the scrutiny in question, it is deemed necessary that he should enable himself to make apt response to any one of these same questions, by that same person will it be deemed necessary for him to enable himself to make response to all alike; whereas, supposing him to regard any one part of the whole number as being more likely to be propounded to him than others, in any number,——he would be tempted to content himself with qualifying himself for making answer to this most probably propounded part, leaving the remainder in a state of absolute or comparative neglect.

### Instructional. Ratiocinative

ART. [67] or 7. In the following mode, *lot* may be seen to be made effectually instrumental to the exclusion of partiality, as well unfavourable as favourable, on the part of *examiners.*

1. So far as it depended upon the choice of the examiner to determine the questions, or other tests of aptitude, that shall be propounded to a probationer,——the consequence would be a power of favouring or disfavouring, without any regard to appropriate aptitude, the pretensions of probationers, in any number, at his pleasure. To favour

---

[1] 1830, 1830 *Off. Apt. Max.*, and Bowring, 'instructions'; but the singular form seems better suited to the context: see just below, the phrase 'such portion of instruction'.

[2] 1830 *Off. Apt. Max.*, 'course here determined on'. By omitting 'supposed to be' which appears in 1830 and Bowring the passage is improved.

any probationer, he might propound such questions alone, how little probative soever of aggregate aptitude, as the probationer was best prepared to answer; or, to disfavour another probationer, he might propound such questions alone as,——to his (the examiner's) knowledge,——the probationer[1] would be unqualified, or, at any rate, least qualified to respond to.

2. If, of the whole number of the questions that ought to have had place in the lottery, any part were omitted,——the lottery would, in proportion to the magnitude of the omitted part, fail to be as probative a test of aptitude as it would be otherwise; and such would be the case, although it had been by *chance*, not *choice*, that the omission had been produced.

If, on the other hand, there were any person, by whose choice any such omission could take place,——it would, in this indirect way, be in the power of that person to give effect to undue partiality, favourable or disfavourable, as above.

*Instructional. Enactive*

ART. [68] or 8. Mode of proceeding, by which choice is excluded, and to all eyes shewn to be so. Example:——

Manner of arranging the questions, for the purpose of its being, in each instance, determined by *lot* which of them shall be propounded.

In the *Question Book*, the questions being designated, each of them, by a number prefixed to it, and the numbers following one another in numerical order,——a set of square tickets, (of card, suppose) all of equal size, marked with the correspondent numbers, are provided. These tickets, in the appointed manner, and in numerical order, are ranged together in juxta-position——in the manner of squares in a *chess* or *draught* board, and, like them, enclosed in a square frame. Total number of questions (suppose) 1000: number of the above square tickets in each frame, as in a Polish draught board, 100: on this supposition, number of *boards* requisite, 10: size of the tickets such as shall suffice to render it manifest, to the requisite number of eyes, at one view, that for every question there is a ticket: and that for no questions there are tickets more than one.[2]

Name of a ticket of this sort, a *question-indicating ticket;* or, for shortness, a *question-ticket.*

---

[1] 1830 and Bowring, 'alone as,——to his (the examiner's) knowledge,——the probationer'; 1830 *Off. Apt. Max.*, 'alone, as, according to what he had learnt, the probationer'. The latter version seems to simplify the passage.

[2] The Polish version of the game of draughts uses a larger number of pieces and, as Bentham indicates, a board with 100 squares instead of the standard 64.

## Instructional. Enactive

ART. [69] or 9. Manner of drawing out the *question-tickets*.

A box is provided, figure square or cylindrical; size, such as to admit of the tickets being thoroughly shaken in it, in such manner that
no traces of the order in which they are originally deposited shall be
perceptible: for a cover, it has a cloth, in which is a slit, long enough
to admit a hand:—fittest hand, that of a child, not old enough to be
exposed to the suspicion of having received instructions enabling it
to act with discrimination. When the tickets have been dropt into the
box, and a stiff cover substituted to the flexible one,—the box is
handed over to a number of persons successively, to be shaken for a
sufficient time by each: the inflexible cover being replaced by the
flexible one, the hand is introduced into the aperture, and the question-tickets, in the predetermined number, drawn out, and, as they
are drawn out, exhibited to all present,—and, in the eyes of the
same person, lodged, as expeditiously as may be,—and now likewise,
in so far as the necessary gaps admit, in numerical order—in an
appropriate frame. The frame is thereupon covered up and sealed;
and, either by the numerical order, or by fresh lot, may now be
determined—which of the several questions shall be presented to the
several probationers.[a]

[a] *Reform in the English Style.*[1]—In the Act, anno 1825, 6 G. 4, ch. 50,
relative to *Jury Trial*, and commonly called Mr. *Secretary Peel's Act*, §26, the
following are the words, in which the mode of selection there appointed is
described:—'Such pieces of parchment or card, being all as nearly as may be of
equal size, shall be delivered unto the Associate or Prothonotary of such court,
(viz. King's Bench, Common Pleas, or Exchequer), by the under Sheriff of the
county, or the Secondary of the city of London, and shall, by direction and care
of such Associate or Prothonotary, be put together in a box to be provided for
that purpose, and when any such issue shall be brought on to be tried, such
Associate or Prothonotary shall in open court draw out twelve of the said parchments or cards, one after another.'[2]
On this occasion, what, on the part of the prime author of this act, and the
draughtsmen respectively, was the design—whether to continue the present
practice of *selection by choice*, called *packing*, or to substitute *chance* to it—is
more than the author of the present work, by whom a volume on the subject
had been published,[3] can take upon him to say: what he *does* say is—that if,

[1] In 1830 *Off. Apt. Max.* this note does not appear at the end of Art. 69 or 9,
but is placed at the end of n. a, p. 335.
[2] This act is entitled 'An Act for consolidating and amending the laws relative
to Jurors and Juries'. Bentham's quotation, apart from minor typographical
variations, is correct save for the mistaken insertion of 'such' before 'issue'.
[3] *Elements of the Art of Packing, as applied to Special Juries, particularly in
cases of Libel Law*, London, 1821 (Bowring, v. 61-186), was written and printed

## Instructional

ART. [70] or 10. In the same manner may be determined whatsoever *exhibitions* the several probationers shall have to perform.

having the act to draw, it had been his design to continue the reality of choice, with the appearances of chance to serve as a veil to it,—unless the fear of being detected by the choice made of means so palpably adverse to the professed end had stayed his hand,[1]—similar to the above wording, probably identical with it, is that which he should have employed.

In the new House of Commons,[2] should any such *chance* happen to it as the containing so much as a single member, to whom the difference between *packing* and *non-packing* were any thing different from a matter of entire indifference, —a motion will be made for an amendment, having for its object the substituting *chance* to *choice*. In this case, *mutatis mutandis*, unless aptitude for the professed purpose be religiously avoided, the wording in the text, or something not dissimilar to it, may, by another chance, be found to answer the purpose.

Thus much as to theory: now as to practice. In the natural course of administration and judicature, supposing, on this or that occasion, *choice* regarded as more conducive to *expediency* than *chance*,—gratification will not probably be given to the desire, but on some few, and those adequate occasions: for, in some nine cases out of ten, either the course taken by the verdict will be a matter of indifference, or the verdict suggested by *expediency* will be deemed sufficiently secured by other causes. By the multitude of the occasions, on which no point would be to be gained by unfairness, the habit of fairness being thus rendered a matter of notoriety,—a high ground will thus have been formed, from which to thunder down the charge of insincerity, on whosoever shall have had the audacity to speak of any such intention as that of ever putting, to their obvious use, the instruments provided as above. Thereupon, should peradventure any *packing-worthy* occasion happen to take place, there are they at hand—the effectual means of choice, and the obvious manner of giving effect to them, much too simple to present any demand for instruction in the nimble-fingered art. Nothing is there to hinder a mark from being put on one side of a ticket, on the other side of which a name is written: not that any such trouble is necessary; for nothing is there to hinder the names—one and all—from being uppermost.

In the formation of the immediately acting list, a sort of gauze veil, with a colouring of *chance* upon it, is thrown over the packing machinery, as above. But, the *original* list, out of which this immediately acting list is thus to be packed —by whom, and how is it to be formed? Answer. By the *Sheriff*—a member of the aristocracy, named every year by the King. This, per § §13, 14, without disguise. And, lest this original garbling should not suffice, by whom is this garbled list to be regarbled? Answer. By the very judicatories, whose power of garbling was the grievance, to which this statute is the professed and supposed remedy:

---

in 1809 (see UC xxvi. 68-136). See also Bowring, x. 450-1, and A. Bain, *James Mill: a Biography*, London, 1882, pp. 98-103.

[1] 1830, 1830 *Off. Apt. Max.*, and Bowring, 'had not stayed his hand', but the negative seems to reverse Bentham's meaning.

[2] Parliament was dissolved on 2 June 1826 and writs for a General Election, returnable on 25 July, were issued at once. The new Parliament met for the first time on 14 November 1826.

*Institution*, in the practice of which this same *fortuitous* mode of selection, for the probation of appropriate aptitude, is exemplified —the *Health subdepartment* at Berlin.[a]

### Instructional

ART. [71] or 11. A mode—the surest and most commodious of all that presented themselves—being thus proposed, for obtaining a decision at the judicatory of *Fortune*,—this, as well as any other, may be the place, for taking and exhibiting a supposed all-comprehensive view of the *occasions* on which, and the *purposes* to which, beneficial application may be made of it.

### Instructional

ART. [72] or 12. Cases, in which this same mode of selection is

for, by §20, all the great criminal courts, commencing with 'the King's Bench,' are expressly confirmed in the power of doing whatever they please in regard to the selection of jurors—'in manner heretofore used and accustomed,'—by 'order, orally or otherwise . . . amending or enlarging the pannel of jurors returned for the trial of any such issue.'[1] And this *heretofore known and accustomed manner*—supposing the existence of any possibility of knowing it—by whom is this possibility possessed? By the judges, and by them alone: by the judges, who, on each individual occasion, cause this supposed check upon their conduct to be whatsoever best suits their purpose.

Thus, by this statute is the acknowledged grievance—instead of being, as professed, remedied—aggravated to the very uttermost; and the jury system—the supposed check to despotism—and, so far as it is a check, the only check by law established,—converted, from a feeble and very imperfect *check*, into a most powerful *instrument*.

[a] Work, from which the indication of it was taken—'A Corrected Report of the Speeches delivered by Mr. Lawrence,' in 8vo. London, 1826, p. 102. Sole indication of *lot* there furnished—'*taking out of an urn*;' no ulterior indication being, on that occasion, regarded as necessary. This little work of the illustrious Therapeutist would form a highly instructive supplement to the present section: *Uses* of it,—1. Obstacles to official aptitude in general, indicated: 2. Established modes of trial, exemplified.[2]

---

[1] Bentham's quotations from the 1825 Act (see p. 333 n. 2) are again substantially correct apart from such details as the spelling 'pannel' for 'panel'.

[2] The full title of the work cited is *A Corrected Report of the Speeches delivered by Mr Lawrence, as Chairman, at two meetings of Members of the Royal College of Surgeons*: the passage to which Bentham refers occurs in Appendix V, 'Course of Study etc. at Berlin', § 1, dealing with the procedure in Berlin for obtaining the rights and privileges of a medical and surgical practitioner. William Lawrence (1783–1867), who was to be created a baronet in the last year of his life, had been appointed in 1815 Professor of Anatomy and Surgery at the College of Surgeons. In 1826 he was the leader of a campaign of protest at the management of the College, of which his speeches and their publication formed part.

susceptible of being employed with advantage in the attribution and distribution of benefits in other shapes besides the above:——the benefit too small in value to be administered in the shape of the smallest denomination of coin; or at any rate to pay for the unavoidable expense of *requisition* or *transmission*, with the intermediate and subservient operations included in that of *communication*. Examples——

Division of a fund constituted by, and composed of——

1. The effects of a *proprietor deceased.*
2. The effects of an *insolvent*, extraneously declared such, or self-declared.
3. The subject-matter of a *bequest* or *donation*, ordaining money, from a certain source, to be divided among persons of a certain description.
4. *Prize-money:* money produced by the division of a mass of specie, or sale of a mass of property in other shapes, taken in *war.*

### Instructional

ART. [73] or 13. Cases, in which it is susceptible of being applied to the *location* of a *burthen:* the burthen, (suppose) *that* which is imposed by the obligation of rendering service, burthensome to the individual rendering it, but regarded as serviceable to the community at large, or this or that section of it.

Case I. Delinquency not imputed. Examples:
1. Militia service. As to this, see Ch. x, DEFENSIVE FORCE.
2. Quasi-jury service. As to this, see Ch. xvi. QUASI-JURY.

### Instructional

ART. [74] or 14. In these cases, the supposition is——that the burthen is not divisible. In itself it certainly is not; but, in respect of time of duration, personal service, in any shape, is susceptible of division. Moreover, where the burthen itself is *not* divisible, the hardship attendant on it *is* divisible: to wit, by grant of pecuniary compensation, coupled with the division of the burthen of paying the money, among the several persons among whom the correspondent benefit is shared.

### Instructional

ART. [75] or 15. Case II. Delinquency imputed, and regarded as proved.

Of delinquents, convicted or convictible, the number so great, that, if punishment were applied to every one, the benefit of the remedy, applied by the aggregate mass of it, would be outweighed by the sum

336

of the burthens imposed by it on the delinquent individuals and their several connexions.

### Instructional

ART. [76] or 16. Physically speaking, in the nature of things, *chance* is capable of being employed either *in lieu* of *choice*, or *in association* with it: in association with it, either, 1, by being made to *precede it*, or 2, by being made to *follow* it.

The being employed with it *at the same time* in a decision on the same point, was scarce worth noticing; on *exactly* the same point at the same time, it cannot be: if, of any proposed subject-matter, one part be placed under the dominion of *choice*, the other under that of *chance*,—by this arrangement, nothing more is done than the taking of the two thus distinct cases and confounding them into one.

### Instructional

ART. [77] or 17. What is called a *lottery*, may be constituted—1, by the act of the parties interested:—*i.e.* by a *contract*, to which, as to other contracts, the sanction of law is applied: or else 2, by the law itself, without waiting for any consent of parties.

### Instructional

ART. [78] or 18. The case, in which the consent of *parties* is *not* waited for—the institution of the lottery being the act of the *law*— is the only case that belongs to the present subject. The other case belongs to the *expositive* matter of the *Penal Code*,[1] and has no place here. Note always, that, in the case of a Government lottery, in the same manner only as an individual contracting party, does the Government act,—not in its coercive character. In a Government lottery, no man is compelled to purchase tickets, any more than in a private one.

### SECTION 17

#### LOCATED HOW

#### *Enactive. Expositive*

ART. 1. *Pecuniary Competition.* So soon as, by the records of the Qualification Judicatory, candidates, apt for official situations, and thence placed on the *locable list*, have been made known,—the Prime Minister will, by advertisement, give notice, of the day on or

---

[1] See Ch. V, § 6, Art. 2n, p. 39n, and Table 2.

before which, but not after which, the offers of persons desirous of filling the several situations are to be delivered in at his office. These offers will be so many biddings in the *office competition process.* Name of this advertisement, *the pecuniary—competition—inviting,* or *official pecuniary—competition, advertisement.* The *pay* annexed to each office having been predetermined by an ordinance of the Legislature, each *bidding* will be either *reductional,* or *emptional* or *compound.*

### Expositive

ART. 2. By a *reductional bidding* understand—an offer, to accept, along with the situation, a quantum of pay, less than the appointed quantum, by a sum therein named.

### Expositive

ART. 3. By an *emptional bidding* understand—an offer to give, for the situation, with the appointed quantum of pay, a sum therein named.

### Expositive

ART. 4. By a *compound bidding* understand—a bidding, in which the reductional and the emptional offers are combined.

### Enactive

ART. 5. On the occasion of this same pecuniary competition,—from no person other than those on whose claims a judgment has been passed in the Qualification Judicatory will any bidding be available. No person, by whom a trial in the Qualification Judicatory has not been undergone, is in any one of these situations locable.

### Enactive. Instructional

ART. 6. *Pecuniary Security.* In relation to the several *simple trust* and *talent and trust* situations, as per §16, Arts. 10, 11, 12, 13, [14], the Legislature will have determined—in what instances, and in what shapes, *pecuniary security* shall be required at the hands of Locatees: and, at the biddings, made on the occasion of the pecuniary competition, each bidder, making reference to such determination, will add in detail the pecuniary security he is able and willing to give.

### Expositive

ART. 7. Of every Minister, the situation is one of *talent* as well as *trust.*

*Enactive*

ART. 8. No person will be admitted, either as Principal or as Deputy, to the exercise of the functions belonging to any situation standing upon the list of official situations in this department,——or to any pay as Principal, until an appropriate *instrument of location*, signed by Locator and Locatee, has been lodged in the records of the office.

*Enactive*

ART. 9. In this instrument, matter will be to be entered under the several heads following: to wit,

1. *Name*, at full length, of the person located.

2. *His age* (mentioning the year, month, and day of the month, when born, so far as known) on the day of the signature of the instrument.

3. *Time*, that is to say year, month, and day of the month, on which he was *admitted* into the *Locable List*.

4. *Rank*, assigned to him on that occasion, as evidenced by the *Ranking-table*, as per §16, *Locable who*, Art. 30.

5. *Bidding*, if any, made by him for the situation, with the particulars, as above, per Arts. 1, 2, 3, 4, annexed.

6. *Biddings*, if any, respectively made by whatsoever other persons were, for that same situation, candidates. Of these biddings, designation will be made, either by transcript, or abridgment, or simple reference to a separate instrument according as they are more or less numerous.

7. If preferred to any whose *ranks* were respectively superior to his, mention of them, with brief indication of the *grounds of preference*.

8. So, if there were any whose *biddings* were superior.

9. Service, in quality of Depute in that same situation, may be a sufficient ground:——the actual length of such service being specified, together with the year, month, and day of the month, on which it commenced.

*Enactive*

ART. 10. Of each such *location instrument, exemplars* will be disposed of as follows:——

1. Delivered into, and kept in the office into which the Locatee is located, one.

2. Delivered into, and kept in the office of the Locator, one.

3. Delivered to the Locator for his own use, one.

4. Of the several functionaries, if any, who, in their several grades, are *superordinate* to the Locator, to each, one.

## Instructional

ART. 11. The Legislature will consider——whether, to the checks thus applied, any other and what checks on mislocation shall be added: as for example, a statement of the several connexions of the several candidates in the way of relationship, whether by consanguinity or alliance, fixing in that case the degrees. As to this matter, see Ch. xii. JUDICIARY COLLECTIVELY, §16, *Partiality obviated.*

## Enactive

ART. 12. When a situation subordinate to that of Minister is to be filled, the Minister will advertise for candidates, and receive biddings as per Arts. 1, 2, 3, 4, 5, 6; the faculty of bidding with effect being confined to *tried* persons, as per Art. 5.

## Enactive. Instructional

ART. 13. In the Location Instrument, the matter will be entered under heads, as per Art. 9, together with any such others as the Legislature shall from time to time have added.

## Enactive. Expositive

ART. 14. Exceptions excepted, as per §16, *Locable who*, Art. [59], no person who has not undergone trial in the Qualification Judicatory (as per §16) will (as above Arts. 5, 12) be locable. But, in the case of a situation of *simple trust*, notwithstanding any inferiority in the scale of *talent*, the preference may, without reproach, be given to a candidate,——in consideration of the comparative advantageousness of his *bidding*, and the sufficiency of the pecuniary security, *self-seated* and *extra-seated*, proffered by him.

By *self-seated*, understand property possessed by himself; by *extra-seated*, property possessed by any such other persons, as have consented to stand bound for the eventual supply of any loss to the public, judicially proved to have had misconduct on his part for its cause.

## Instructional

ART. 15. As to pecuniary and quasi-pecuniary *security*, the Legislature will determine——in regard to what, if any, situations, the property, required for this purpose shall be required to be in such sort bound, as to be rendered inalienable in the hands of the possessor.

## Enactive

ART. 16. Exceptions excepted, in no situation of trust, or talent and trust, will any person be locable, until his age (whatsoever have been the number of his examination years) is that, at which a man is entrusted by law with the entire management of his own concerns: say {21} years.

### Enactive. Ratiocinative

ART. 17. Exceptions for consideration are—

1. Army service; the military branch: in this branch, an officer is locable in the lowest grade at the age of {——} years.

For, in this grade, the functionary, though he has the command of some, is himself constantly under the command of others.

### Enactive. Ratiocinative

ART. 18.—2. Navy service; the military branch: in this branch, an officer is locable in the lowest grade at the age of {——} years. Reason, as per Art. 17.

### Instructional

ART. 19. On a comparative survey of the several subdepartments, and the several situations in each subdepartment, the Legislature will consider, in what instances demand for difference in grades has place, and, in so far as it is established, how far succession to a vacancy shall be influenced by it: that is to say, in what instances, in regard to any grade above the lowest, biddings under the pecuniary competition system shall have place.

### Instructional. Ratiocinative

ART. 20. On this occasion, the considerations following will be borne in mind:—

1. Of two persons, the one, suppose, has been habitually subject to the direction of the other. In this case, if, by a fresh arrangement, it happens to the superordinate to find himself subjected to the direction of his quondam subordinate,—a natural consequence is—on the part of the thus relatively depressed superordinate, a pain of *humiliation*—say, in this case, *a pain of degradation*—a pain produced by the comparison made of his antecedently elevated, with his subsequently depressed state.

2. Where no such subjection has had place, no such pain is produced in a man's mind by the mere view of the rise of a person, who, not having been subject to his direction, comes to be located in a situation more eligible than his: in this case, therefore, that same reason, in favour of *settled succession*, has no place.

### Enactive. Expositive. Instructional

ART. 21. As to every situation subordinate to that of Minister, there will be two locators—the *initiative* and the *confirmative*. Exceptions excepted, as to every office in his subdepartment, the initiative locator is the Minister; confirmative, the Prime Minister. Exceptions, if any, remain to be excepted by the Legislature.

### Enactive. Expositive. Ratiocinative

ART. 22. If, in any subdepartment, any *initiative* locator, subordinate to the Minister, is established,—it will be in consideration of distance, lest, during the interval between the day on which the vacancy at the place in question takes place, and the day on which information of the *confirmative* location reaches that same place, the service belonging to the situation, so vacated, be left unperformed. In this case there may be *two initiative locators; temporarily initiative locator*, the next superordinate of the functionary by whose dislocation the vacancy is created; definitively initiative locator, the Minister.

### Expositive. Instructional

ART. 23. Examples of subdepartments, in which, in respect of *distance*, a demand for *initiative location*, in hands other than those of the Minister, and thence for *temporarily initiative location*, is more particularly apt to have place, are the following: to wit—
  1. The Army Minister.
  2. The Navy Minister.
  3. The Foreign Relation Minister.

### Enactive. Ratiocinative

ART. 24. In the Army subdepartment, in so far as regards command over functionaries in the military branch, vacancies, in respect of *function*, are, in effect, for the occasion, without special appointment, filled of course; to wit, by the universally and necessarily established relation between rank and rank; as to which, see Ch. x. DEFENSIVE FORCE.

### Instructional

ART. 25. Not so, in so far as regards situations in the non-military, styled the *commissariat branch;* those, to wit, by whom, with relation to the matter of warfare, and the matter of subsistence, are exercised the several functions, *procurative, custoditive, applicative, reparative,* and *eliminative*: as to which functions, see Ch. ix. MINISTERS COLLECTIVELY, §[4].

## Instructional

ART. 26. Nor in so far as regards the command of fortified places.

## Instructional

ART. 27. Nor in the Navy department,[1] in which, in the establishments of the great maritime powers, in so far as regards the matter of subsistence, the above functions, as per Art. [25], are, in each ship, commonly exercised by a single functionary, styled the *Purser*.

## Enactive

ART. 28. In the Foreign Relation subdepartment, at each missionary station, as on the incapacity or absence, so on the death, of the principal functionary,—his functions will be exercised by a depute of his, as per Ch. viii. PRIME MINISTER, §4, *Self-suppletive function*. Failing such depute, if an established subordinate of the principal is on the spot, under a denomination, for example, such as that of *Secretary of Legation*, such subordinate will, for the time, except in case of special provision to the contrary, succeed as if located by a temporarily initiative locator, as above, Art. 22.

## Enactive

ART. 29. On a vacancy in the situation of *Vice-Consul*, by the *Consul* will the function of *temporarily initiative locator* be exercised.

## Instructional

ART. 30. In what stations, and on what footings, the power of deputation shall be exercised by a Vice-Consul, the Legislature, having regard to distance, and to the state of society in the foreign nation, in each case, will determine.

## Enactive

ART. 31. Of the locative function, the mode of exercise is as follows:——By the Minister, he being the initiative locator, an appropriate *location instrument* is prepared and conveyed to the office of the Prime Minister. After the lapse of {— —} days exclusive, reckoned from the day of its being received in that office, the location will have become confirmed:[a] unless, under the signature of the Prime

---

[a] On this occasion, the *rationale* will have to speak of this sort of expeditive arrangement, as generally applicable, for remedy, to the practice of indeterminate and indefinite *suspension*, through negligence or indecision:——a practice

[1] See Ch. VIII, §11, Art. 6n, p. 164n.

343

Minister, an instrument, in correspondent form, locating some other locable, or an order, suspending the effect of such initiative location, has, in the mean time, in the office of that same Minister, been received.

### Enactive. Ratiocinative

ART. 32. In case of any such substitution, reasons for the rejection, and the consequent location, will be expected: if none are given, the conclusion of the Public Opinion Tribunal, and of the Legislature, will be——that none can be found.

### Enactive

ART. 33. *Deputes permanent.*——Without special reason, no person, who has not been upon the *general locable list*, as per Art. [8], is capable of being located as *depute permanent*, in any office belonging to this department.

### Enactive

ART. 34. Special reason is——where, in the *location instrument* by which the depute is constituted such, the names of all persons on that list being by recital or reference designated,——the locator states, on the part of each, either *refusal* or *inaptitude* actual or virtual, absolute or comparative: adding, in what particular shape or shapes such inaptitude has place.

### Enactive

ART. 35. In the *location instrument*, matter will in this case be inserted under the four first of the heads enumerated as per Art. 9, in the case of a person located in the situation of *principal* in the office.

pregnant with distress to all individuals interested, as well as indefinite public mischief. Apply it also to appeals. See Ch. xxii, APPELLATE JUDICATORIES. Refer to Morning Chronicle, 27th May, 1824, mentioning Secretary Canning's indefinite suspension of an ordinance of the East India Direction, in the debate of the 26th.[1]

---

[1] The *Morning Chronicle* report actually appeared on 26 May 1824, and the debate in which Canning spoke had taken place on the 25th. The subject under discussion was the freedom of the press in India, arising from a petition on behalf of the traveller and journalist James Silk Buckingham (1786-1855), presented by John George Lambton (1792-1840), later 1st Earl of Durham. George Canning (1770-1827) was at this time Foreign Secretary, but had been President of the Board of Control (see p. 000 n. 0) and thus responsible for Indian affairs from 1816 until 1822. The relationship between Canning's speech (*Hansard's Parliamentary Debates*, n.s., xi (1825), 879-80) and Bentham's comment here is not entirely clear. See also § 19, Arts. 18, 19 & n, p. 372.

### Enactive

ART. 36. Of the *deputation* instrument, *exemplars* will in this case be disposed of, in number and destination the same as in the case of the *principal*, as per Art. 10.

### Enactive

ART.37.[1] In any subdepartment, in the situation of Minister, or any situation thereto subordinate, should any person be located who has no right so to be,—such mislocatee, as also the functionary by whom he was mislocated, will, for such act of mislocation, be responsible: compensationally, if, through temerity, the act was culpable; compensationally and punitionally, if, through evil consciousness, it was criminal: so also their respective accomplices, if any, as per Penal Code.[2]

### Enactive

ART. 38. But, on no such account, will any act done by such mislocatee, in the exercise of any function belonging to the office, be *null and void*, or say *invalid.*

### Ratiocinative

ART. 39. Reason. In so far as the exercise given to the function, though by an usurper, is apt, the end for which it was allotted to the office is attained, and no evil is produced; whereas, by nullification of the act, an infringement of the *disappointment-preventing* principle,—on which, as per Penal Code,[3] the law of property rests,—would be committed, and, on the part of non-offending persons, suffering to an indefinite amount, produced.

### Expositive

ART. 40. Examples are as follows:
1. Acts of *sale*, performed in the exercise of the *venditive* function.

[1] In the 1826 *Extract,* § 17 ended with Art. 36, and this pattern was followed in the 1830 *Off. Apt. Max.* Arts. 37–41 were added for the 1830 edition of the *Code.* When Bentham added the Supplement to § 17, he omitted to renumber the articles and the Supplement wrongly began with Art. 37 or 1.

[2] Pt. I, Ch. X of the Table of Contents of the proposed Penal Code is headed 'Co-Offenders and Co-Delinquency'. 'Evil consciousness' is placed in Pt. I, Ch. VII. See Table 2. On the Penal Code generally, see Ch. V, § 6, Art. 2n, p. 39n.

[3] In the Table of Contents of the proposed Penal Code, the disappointment-preventing principle would most likely be discussed in Pt. I, Ch. III, 'Ends in view'. See Table 2. For a discussion of the significance of the principle, see Bowring, iii. 388 & n.

2. Acts of *lease-letting*, performed in the exercise of the *mercede-locative* function.

3. Act[s] of purchase, done in the exercise of the *emptive* function.

4. Any act of *hire*, done in the exercise of the *mercede-conductive* function.

### *Enactive*

ART. 41. But, in such case, all persons, who have derived or would derive profit from the wrong,—whether privy thereto, and accomplices with the wrong-doing functionary or not,—will, as per Penal Code,[1] be divested of all profit therefrom, provided they be exempted from all positive loss.

### *Supplement to §17. Located how*

### *Ratiocinative*

ART. [42] or 1. *Pecuniary competition* principle. Reasons, in support of it as hereinabove employed: employed, to wit, not as decisive, but as contributing, in subordination as above, to the *aptitude manifestation system*, to the guidance of the decisive choice given to the responsible locating superordinate.[2]

### *Ratiocinative*

ART. [43] or 2. I. Reasons, direct and intrinsic, deduced from the greatest happiness principle applied to the nature of the case.

Case I. The situation, a *situation of simple trust*, as per §16, Art. 13: for appropriate *moral* aptitude, adequate provision being supposed to have been made: to wit, by §16, *Locable who* (Art[s]. 34, 35, 36, [37, 41]), and no special appropriate intellectual or active aptitude being regarded as necessary.

---

[1] Remedies would be treated in Pt. I, Chs. XV and XVI of the Penal Code. See Table 2. See also Ch. V, § 6, Art. 2n, p. 39n.

[2] In the Bowring text (see Collation, p. 508) this article is not numbered as such but treated as an introductory paragraph to the Supplement as a whole. The words 'Pecuniary Competition Principle' are used as a title for the Supplement, which (see § 15n, p. 297) in 1830 and 1830 *Off. Apt. Max.* immediately follows the Supplement to § 16. In those editions, both Supplements follow the 'Concluding Instruction to the Public Opinion Tribunal' (pp. 362–4) at the end of § 17. Here, as above, the Bowring order has been followed as more appropriate, but the 1830 treatment of this article has been restored. Neither 1830 nor Bowring numbers the articles in this Supplement correctly in sequence with those of § 17. The Bowring numeration is thrown out by the omission of a numeral for the first article. The 1830 series begins wrongly with '37 or 1' instead of '42 or 1', the reason for which is noted above at § 17, Art. 37n, p. 345.

The presumption here is, that, but for some special reason, assignable and assigned, to the contrary,—the choice of the locating superordinate will fall upon that candidate, in whose instance the result of the pecuniary competition is most favourable to the public purse. On this supposition, all parties will have cause to be pleased: to wit,

1. The *community* at large; because that choice has been made, which is most beneficial to its aggregate pecuniary interest.

2. The *locating* functionary: the candidate's aptitude, and thereby the locator's responsibility, [being] alleviated by the result of the probationary trials, [as] above;[1] say then the *locating functionary*: unless it be his desire, at the expense of the community, in breach of his duty and engagement, and at the risk of his own fortune and reputation, to gain to himself an undue benefit, in the shape of *patronage*.

3. The candidate, by whose own offer the situation is procured for him.

### Ratiocinative

ART. [44] or 3. Case II. The situation, a *situation of trust and talent:* to wit, after the manifestation made, of the grade acquired by the candidate, in the scale of manifested appropriate aptitude in all its branches, as certified by the certificate given by the *Examination [Judicatory]*,[2] as per §16, Art. 17; that document contributing, in conjunction with the result of the pecuniary competition, to the guidance of the decision entrusted to the responsibly-locating superordinate.

Reason, grounded, as in the former case, on *intrinsic utility*. Only where, to the purpose of the practical conclusion, the claims of the two candidates, on the ground of the manifestation made as to *appropriate aptitude*, as above, are, in the opinion of the *Examination*, or say *Qualification Judicatory*, virtually equal,—does it seem likely, that the determination will be made, in favour of him, whose offer, on the ground of its favourableness to the *pecuniary interest* of the community, is accepted. The locating superordinate being, by §6, *Self-suppletive function*, responsible for the conduct of his subordinate,—he is thus, by a personal interest of no inconsiderable strength, urged to have due and adequate regard to the thus manifestly demonstrated *appropriate aptitude*. By a deficiency in the

---

[1] 1830 and 1830 *Off. Apt. Max.*, '. . . responsibility, alleviated . . . trials, above'. The Bowring insertion of 'being' and 'as' has been followed here in order to justify the passage.

[2] 1830 and 1830 *Off. Apt. Max.*, 'Jury'; Bowring, 'Judicatory'. The Bowring version has been followed as clearly required by the context.

aptitude, he would stand exposed to be more or less a sufferer: in the small saving to the public purse, he would have no perceptible share.

The arrangement affords therefore a prospect of good, and this without a prospect of evil in any shape.

### Ratiocinative

ART. [45] or 4. II. Reasons extrinsic, deduced from authority and practice.

In England, among the highest of the ruling few, the tide of events has of late years borne up some, in whose declared opinion, not only the price of labour,—in whatsoever shape—unskilled or skilled,—but also the price of commodities in general, and in particular of those means of sustenance which are worth all other commodities put together,—should be minimized; and that, as the only instrument of minimization, the competition principle should be uniformly and steadily employed.

### Instructional

ART. [46] or 5. These same distinguished statesmen—would they—durst they if they would—accede to the application of this same instrument to the reduction of the price of the labour performed by themselves and their present colleagues? or—not to insist upon that which could not reasonably be proposed—of the like labour when performed by their successors, and the colleagues of those same successors? O yes: when the energy of the people is to such a degree troublesome, that, in the high places in question, regard for consistency, and the comfort of the subject-many, cannot, consistently with the comfort of these same ruling few, be refused.

### Instructional

ART. [47] or 6. At present, engaged, by so efficient an interest, to *maximize*, instead of minimizing, the expense of *official* labour,—they stand engaged by a no less efficient interest, to *minimize*, instead of maximizing, all need, and thence all proof, of *appropriate aptitude* with relation to such labour. If by competition—that competition being at the same time free and unrestrained—the degree of aptitude on the part of all competitors were made known,—the chance, in favour of the objects of their care, would, instead of being equal to certainty, be but as one to ten, or twenty, or whatsoever greater multiple of their own number might be that of their fellow competitors. Moreover,—as natural talents, and other means being supposed equal,—*proficiency* will be in the direct ratio of *exertion*, and exertion in the ratio of degree of *need*—those who, without exertion, are sure of having, in this shape, what they have need of, will not bestow any exertion at all on the acquisition of *appropriate aptitude*: and their natural *place*, instead of being certainly at the *top*, will be probably at the *bottom*, of the scale. Thus it is, that, to the ends which the greatest happiness principle requires to be pursued, will be substituted the direct opposites of those exclusively justifiable ends: and while, for the benefit of the hands in question, the *expense* of official service, or of the appearance, or the false pretence of it, without so much as the pretence of it, is *maximized*,—appropriate *aptitude* for the performance of it will be *minimized*.

### Instructional. Exemplificational

ART. [48] or 7. The more immediately education for office is under the direction of the ruling few, in whose hands the fixation of the quantum of remuneration, and the location of those by whom it is to be received are conjoined,—the more striking and instructive will here be the exemplification of the relation between cause and effect.[a]

### Instructional. Expositive

ART. [49] or 8. Note that, in the case of pecuniary competition is comprised in a certain way the case of *gratuitous service;* gratuitous service constituting *one point* or say *degree*, in a scale of indefinite length, established by pecuniary competition; at the same time there is a necessity in marking the distinction between them; the difference in point of efficiency and extent of application being so great; the application of gratuitous service, (including that which is so in appearance, and is always called so,) being widely extensive, while the application of pecuniary competition to personal service in this branch of the public business is, nearly if not altogether, as yet without example.

Applied to the expense of the Official Establishment taken in its totality,—(expense of remuneration for personal service included,) it is not in the power of pecuniary competition, by reduction of expense, to carry on good economy any thing near to the point of gratuitousness—the point at which expense is equal 0.

At the same time, if applied to the purpose of engaging personal service in particular official situations, it is capable of carrying that same benefit not only up to the gratuitous point, but to a degree to an [indefinite] amount higher; the matter of wealth being but one of

[a] For exemplifications, see the work intituled 'Official Aptitude maximized, Expense minimized.'[1]

---

[1] Bentham is referring to *Off. Apt. Max.* published in 1830. See Ch. IX, § 15n, p. 297.

divers instruments, by the application of which personal service is engaged; others being *power, reputation*, and *dignity;* the dignity, that which results from the *nature* of the *occupation*, with or without *factitious* honor and dignity, superadded: in such sort that, instead of receiving money in compensation for the service rendered by him, in taking upon himself the obligation of exercising the functions of the office considered as *a burthen*——a man will be content to give money, for the faculty of exercising those same functions, that same faculty being regarded by him as a *benefit.*

But, in the instances of gratuitous service here alluded to, in so far as remuneration in a pecuniary shape has place, neither is it paid avowedly by the hands of Government for service performed in the situations in question; nor is service in any shape rendered to the whole community, nor otherwise than to a small particular and sinister interest of a small part, at the expense of the interest of the whole, which is thereby accordingly *disserved*, instead of *served:* in so much that, in so far as this same [alleged]¹ service is performed, the remuneration derived from it belongs not to the present case; and, being so completely unfit or adverse to the purpose of the pecuniary competition,——required to be, with proportionable care, distinguished from it.

In English practice, to this head belongs the situation of *Member of the House of Commons*, and Member of the *Unpaid Magistracy*, styled *Justices of the Peace*. In these instances, nominally the service is uniformly gratuitous; really so, according as abuse does not or does take place.

### Instructional. Ratiocinative

ART. [50] or 9. To the proposed aptitude-securing and expense-minimizing system, as composed of the public examination system and the pecuniary competition system taken together, but followed by the choice left to the locating functionary,——various considerations, in the character of objections, present themselves, as having been, or being more or less likely to be, urged. With all employable diligence they have been searched for, and found reducible under the heads following——

I. Objection[s] to the public examination part of the system.
1. Timid merit excluded.
2. The unopulent excluded: thence, equality violated.
II. Objections to the pecuniary competition part of the system.
3. Venality established.

¹ 1830 and 1830 *Off. Apt. Max.*, 'illegal'; this seems clearly mistaken and the Bowring emendation to 'alleged' has therefore been followed.

4. Munificence or say *liberality* excluded.

5. Depredation, sharpened by indigence, invited.

6. Aptitude diminished: aptitude being *as* opulence.

Of these in their order; with their answers.

### Ratiocinative

ART. [51] or 10. Objection 1. *Timid merit excluded*:

Answer. In the case of a more or less considerable proportion, of those who otherwise would be candidates for office, this effect may ensue. But, it presents not, to any precise amount, so much as a deduction from the aggregate of the good effects expectable from the system; nor any thing more than the shadow of a reason for the rejection of it; yet entire rejection, if any thing, is what it calls for. Proportional number of the individuals excluded by this their misfortune, say at random, and only for argument's sake, *one-tenth*. Suppose then the system to be in other respects a beneficial one,—such it will be—in the first place to the whole body of the unexcluded candidates, on their several individual accounts; in the next place, to the whole community, on the aggregate account. Give effect, then, to the objection, and for the sake of the unliquidated benefit to the one-tenth, the [remaining nine-tenths] will be deprived of that same benefit in one shape, and the [whole] of the community in the other.[1] On the other hand, suppose the system rejected, this same one-tenth for whose sake it is rejected, in what determinable way will they respectively be benefited by the rejection? To this question, all answer is impossible.

Then, as to the *existence* of the alleged justificative cause of the proposed rejection—the supposed *merit*. In the instance of this tenth part, where is or can be the proof of it? True it is, that in whatever line of study or instruction the merit is supposed to have place,—timidity, to the degree and to the effect in question, is not incompatible with it; but, on the other hand, of the existence of the merit, neither conclusive, nor any how weakly soever presumptive evidence, does the timidity afford. Of merit, in a word, timidity *may be* an *accompaniment*, but *is not a cause*.

This, and all other objections notwithstanding,—suppose now the *public examination* system established,—observe what, with regard to *merit* and *timidity*, will be the consequence. The trial to be submitted to being alike visible to all eyes, each individual, who might

---

[1] 1830 and 1830 *Off. Apt. Max.*, 'the rest of the community will be deprived of that same benefit in one shape, and the rest of the community in the other'. Bowring emends the passage to read as above, which is clearly correct in view of the context.

otherwise feel disposed to enter upon this career, will consider and ask himself whether he has *nerve* enough to undergo it. Let the answer be in the negative, he will then bid adieu to a pursuit, for which his own judgment pronounces him unfit, and betake himself to one, for which it pronounces him fit. So doing, where will be his loss? Answer—No where: for proof, see answer to Objection 1.[1] Before him lie, for his choice, all professions and other profit-seeking occupations, the profit from which is—not, as here, confined within the narrowest limits possible, but altogether unlimited. So much for proofs in a *pecuniary* shape. As to *reputation*, and esteem for services rendered to the public by intellectual labour,—the press is open to him,—and timidity,—at any rate, the sort of timidity here in question,—is no bar to any use he may feel disposed to make of it.

### Ratiocinative

ART. [52] or 11. But the proposed system—does it not hold up to view *unopulence* as an efficient cause of aptitude?

Answer. True: but only when in a certain degree, and, in that degree, only as a partially contributing cause, and that a remotely operating one, operating through the medium of *appropriate examination*. True it is, that in the character of a learner, looking to be one day a probationer and competitor for offices,—a man, whose pecuniary supplies are scanty, is *likely* to use more exertion than a man whose pecuniary circumstances are abundant:—to use more *exertion*, and thence, in so far as depends upon exertion, to acquire a greater degree of appropriate intellectual and active aptitude. But the immediately applying probative test of this same appropriate aptitude, is—not the situation in the scale of opulence, but the result of the *examination* undergone; and, by this immediately applying *direct* evidence, what little probative force belonged to the faint and remotely applying *presumptive* evidence, is superseded and reduced to nothing.

### Ratiocinative

ART. [53] or 12. Objection 2. *The unopulent excluded: thus, equality violated.* Answers—

1. The provision for equality must always be subordinate to that for security, or society cannot subsist. See *Leading Principles*, &c.[2]

---

[1] Bentham's reference here is somewhat confusing, since this *is* the answer to Objection 1.

[2] *Leading Principles of a Constitutional Code, for any State* (Bowring, ii. 267-74) was originally published in 1823 in *The Pamphleteer*, xxii (1823), 475-86. This was the first public appearance of any part of the *Code*, although the

2. Supposed relation of equality not real. The supposed loss to the classes in question will not have place. *Into* this source their industry could not be turned in quest of profit, without being turned aside *from* other sources much more lucrative: to the quantity obtainable by them from this source, there would be limits, and those rendered as narrow as, by application made of the frugality-maximizing principle, appropriate aptitude on the part of rulers could render them: to what is obtainable by every man from other sources, there are no such limits.

3. The bar, opposed to the unopulent by the proposed instrument of frugality, is not—like the bar opposed under some Governments, by want of nobility—an impassable one. By raising himself to a degree of opulence adequate to the purchase of the office,—the most unopulent man, supposing him demonstrated to be, by intellectual attainments, qualified for it, will be able to acquire it.

4. By the access, which, by the objection, is proposed to be left to the unopulent,—entrance into office would neither be secured to them, nor rendered so probable to them, as to the more opulent: the greater the opulence, the greater the means of access to patrons, who, of course, belong to the opulent class.

5. From the rejection of this necessary security, great would be the quantity of incontestable *evil* pressing upon this very class:— evil, pressing upon them in a much more tangible and sensible shape than any *good*, of the chance of which it is charged with depriving them, can be shown to wear: *burthen of taxation*, to the amount of the money which the competition would save is in proportionable quantities added to that of the matter of patronage, with its corruptive influence. Mass of pecuniary remuneration saleable, say £1,000,000 a year: saving effected by the competition, £200,000. To reject this instrument of economy, would thus be to impose *a tax* of £200,000 a year on opulent and unopulent together: and this for no better purpose, than the turning aside the profit-seeking industry, of the unopulent, from other channels into this.

6. By the rejection of this proposed instrument of frugality, an exclusion would be put—not only upon the frugality, but upon the bringing into play a main security for, and thence instrument of, appropriate aptitude; namely, *relish* for the business. The less the emolument,—in other words, the more a man gives for the office,— the greater is thus proved to be his relish for the business of it: while to him who gives nothing for it, it may be an object of disgust: of disgust, not surmountable but by the extreme of indigence.

material did not in the end form part of the published *Code* as such. See the Introduction, p. xviii.

No, says another *objection:* what is proved is—not the alleged relish, but a plan for getting possession of the office, for the purpose of converting into an instrument of depredation the powers belonging to it. *Reply.* Of no such plan is the formation in any degree probable. This objection is Objection 5, *Depredation*, &c. which, with the answers, will be found in its place.

### Ratiocinative

ART. [54] or 13. Objection 3. *Venality established.* The plan makes offices *venal*: it introduces venality into office.

Answer. 1. Source of the objection, confusion of ideas: confusion produced by the misapplication of the word. What is proposed to be sold is—not to individual suitors at the office the *acquiror* of it, but to the acquiror himself, the *emolument*, in a particular shape, attached to it.

2. To find such a form of words, as should give to the objection, as above, a sort of superficial colour of reasonableness, required some industry. That which the objection applies to is—not the arrangement itself, but a particular word or two, which are capable of being employed in speaking of it. For example, the modes in which the amount of the pecuniary part of the remuneration is capable of being reduced and minimized, are, as above shewn, two: to wit—1, The *reductional* mode; according to which, mention is made of the greatest *reduction* the bidder will consent to see made from a determinate salary proposed: 2, the *emptional* mode; according to which, mention is made of the greatest sum he will give for it, if *unreduced.* Employ the reductional form of expression, the objection vanishes: but, the emptional being in effect precisely the same thing as the reductional, so likewise does [the objection to] the emptional.[1]

3. The party, to whom *service* in any shape is rendered by the arrangement, is the *public* alone: not any individual whatsoever: of no individual is any service *bought by*, of none any *sold to*, any other.

4. Associated with the idea of *venality* is that of *corruption*; and by the objection is meant, if any thing, that, by the arrangement, as often as it is exemplified, *corruption*, in some shape or other, has place, or at the least is *probabilized;* and that thence, in some shape or other, so is relative *inaptitude.*

5. But, the real effect of the arrangement is precisely the reverse: for, 1, Minimizing the pecuniary value of the situation, it minimizes the quantity of the matter of corruption which the patronage places in the hands of the locating functionary.

---

[1] 1830 and 1830 *Off. Apt. Max.*, 'so likewise does the emptional'; the Bowring insertion of 'the objection to' is evidently required by the sense.

6. 2, Minimizing the value of the pecuniary remuneration, it maximizes, as above, the degree of *relish* which the candidate is likely to have for the functions which he is desirous of having the exercise of: for, the less the inducement he requires in the shape of *money*, the greater is the inducement he possesses in the shape of *relish*, or he would not make the offer, which, by the supposition, he does make.

7. [3,] Minimizing the value of the situation, and thence of the patronage, it minimizes the probability of its being given by the patron to a *protégé*, whose sole *relish* is for the *money*, and who, in regard to the *functions*, has neither *relish*, nor *aptitude*, in any shape.

8. As to corruption, so far then from acting as a *ferment* to it, the competition system is, in the emptional as well as in the reductional mode, a *specific* against that disorder: it is for want of such a specific, that corruption takes place, when it *does* take place.

9. In vain would it be said—a man, who sees sinister profit, in this or that shape, as being capable of being made, from an abuse of the powers attached to the situation,—will offer and give more for it than one who sees no such prospect. In vain; for, by the reduction thus made, in the quantity of money the man will have at command, no addition is made to whatever facility he will have for such abuse: on the contrary, as above, that facility is diminished by the diminution of whatever facility he may have as to the finding associates and supporters for the abuse: the greater the *reduction* he will thus submit to,—and still further, if so it be that he offers to give more for the salary than it is worth, the more he offers to *give* for it,—the more strongly he draws upon himself the attention of all concerned, and puts them upon the watch to find out—by what course, he expects, and proposes to himself to endeavour, to reap the sinister profit supposed to be in contemplation. Suppose even, that, as applied to the state of things under this or that existing Government, the objection would be a fatal one,—it would not follow that it would amount to any thing, when applied to the one here proposed: for, in no existing Government can any system of securities for appropriate aptitude be found, comparable in point of efficiency to what may be seen proposed here.

### Ratiocinative

ART. [55] or 14. Objection [4.] *Munificence*, or say *liberality, excluded:*——Exclusion put upon that virtue in one quarter, by which *merit* in other quarters, and in all manner of shapes, is brought into existence.

Answer. Let but misapplication of words be argument—argument, affording in the present case justification for useless and pernicious expense,—true it will be, that, as good argument may be made out of the word *munificence*, or the word *liberality*, as out of the word *venality*. *Liberality* may perhaps serve still better than *munificence*. Being more extensively in use, especially on the popular side, it is more strongly as well as extensively associated with the sentiment of approbation; and, by the laxity of its import, better adapted to the purpose of delusion. But, such being the nature of the arguments, see now on what ground stands the title of either of them to the property of giving birth to merit.

When, on the *one* part, what is called *liberality* is exercised, the existence of *merit* on the *other* part—on the part of him or those in favour of whom the self-styled virtue is exercised, is constantly alleged.[1] Constantly alleged,—so far from being constantly proved, it is seldom so much as attempted to be proved. The place of proof is occupied by assertion: of the assertion, when orally delivered, the probative force is as the loudness and reiteratedness of it, joined to the force and number of eulogistic epithets and phrases bestowed on the alleged possessor of the asserted merit; and scorn, with the imputation of envy and insincerity, on all who presume to question it.

In the Official Establishment of the City of London, conquests have, it has been said, been of late years made of official situations more than one by the virtue of *liberality* from the vice of *venality;* these conquests made, and the source of them—a correspondent quantity of patronage—put into official pockets. The substance has now been seen of the eloquence by which these conquests were achieved.[2]

### Ratiocinative

ART. [56] or 15. Objection 5. *Depredation sharpened by indigence, [invited].*[3] When a man has paid the purchase-money (says the objection) he will be left in a state of indigence, such as will render it, as it were, a matter of necessity to him to commit depredation at any hazard. Answers—

1. The objection supposes, that, by a certain, or an ascertainable, quantity of emolument attached to the office, the endeavour to commit depredation may be prevented, or at least in an adequate degree improbabilized. Altogether groundless is this supposition. Draw the

---

[1] 1830, 1830 *Off. Apt. Max.* and Bowring, 'the alleged existence of *merit . . .* is constantly alleged', where the first 'alleged' is evidently redundant.

[2] It is not possible to provide any specific elucidation of what Bentham says here; such strictures on City politics were commonplace at the time.

[3] 1830, 1830 *Off. Apt. Max.* and Bowring omit 'invited'; but see Art. [50] or 9, p. 351.

line where you will, true it is, the comparatively unopulent functionary will, it is probable, endeavour to commit depredation: and
commit it he will, if in his eyes the benefit of the depredation is
greater than the burthen from detection: probability in regard to
detection being taken into account. This will the comparatively unopulent do; but so will the comparatively opulent. The most opulent
of functionaries have always been the most voracious of depredators.
Witness monarchs almost without exception, and more particularly
the most absolute. Witness even *the best of kings,* as he was so commonly called: witness he, whose debts, it was asserted in Parliament,
had been nine times paid by Parliament, notwithstanding his million
a year,[1]—the exemption he gave himself from the income tax,—and
his seventeen millions, obtained for his own particular use,—without
previous declaration of war,—by the instrumentality of a richly-
remunerated Judge,—in point blank contradiction to an act of the
Legislature, passed in the year 1744: the decrees issued without
other warrant than the words *Droits of Admiralty*, the assertion that
the king is *Lord High Admiral*, with reference made to an order of
the *King alone*, dated in the year 1665–6, and that King, *Charles the
Second.*[a]

[a] Brown's Civil Law, ii. 57.[2]

---

[1] George III's debts were paid by Parliament in 1769, 1777, 1784, 1786,
1802, 1804, 1805, 1814, and 1816. Bentham returns repeatedly to this theme:
see Bowring, ix. 141–2 (part of Doane's introductory 'Book I' to the *Constitutional Code*); and *Jeremy Bentham to his Fellow Citizens of France on Houses
of Peers and Senates*, London, 1830 (Bowring, iv. 419–50), Bowring, iv. 431. Of
the title 'the best of kings', Bentham says (Bowring, ix. 141), 'George the Third,
because he behaved well to his wife, was proclaimed *the best of kings*.'
[2] Bentham is here referring in a somewhat confused way to a distinctly complicated subject. On 6 March 1665/6 an Order in Council clearly distinguished
between the Droits of Admiralty and the Droits of the Crown. In regard to the
former, all captures made during periods of hostilities, either in port or by non-
commissioned vessels (privateers without letters of marque), belonged as of right
to the Lord High Admiral; and the proceeds of such prizes became Droits of
Admiralty. The Droits of the Crown, on the other hand, consisted of captures
made *before* hostilities, whether by commissioned or by non-commissioned
ships, and of captures made *during* hostilities by commissioned ships. It was,
however, usual at the start of a war either for a Crown proclamation to be issued
or for a Prize Act to be passed, granting the Droits of the Crown, that is, the proceeds of prizes taken by commissioned vessels, to the vessels taking prizes. The
1744 act to which Bentham refers, 17 Geo. II c. 34, was precisely a Prize Act of
this kind, lapsing like all such acts on the cessation of hostilities. Prize Acts did
not apply either to the Droits of Admiralty as defined above nor to that part of
the Droits of the Crown comprising captures made *before* the outbreak of hostilities. However, in these cases, it was customary for the Crown, on receipt of
a memorial from the captors, to grant a varying proportion (between 1799 and

2. In the situation of the comparatively opulent, the probability of depredation is greater than in the case of the comparatively unopulent, on two accounts.

1. In consideration of, and in proportion to his opulence, and the erroneously but commonly and naturally entertained supposition, of the security afforded for his probity by that same opulence, he will be less suspected——less closely watched.

2. In proportion to his opulence, will be (as per §15, *Remuneration*, Art. 4) his facility for obtaining accomplices in transgression, and effectual supporters to screen him against punishment, dislocation, and even disrepute. Instances, see every where.

3. Of the absence of any such degree of indigence, as can probabilize a sharpness of appetite sufficient to produce depredation,——a highly probative evidence is afforded by the very nature of the transaction here proposed: what a man gives for the office with the emolument attached, he would not give, if in his eyes the emolument, with his remaining income, if he has any, will not be sufficient for his exigencies.

*Instructional. Ratiocinative. Exemplificational*

ART. [57] or [16]. This was the argument against economy, brought out and made the most of, on the occasion of his sham Economy Bill, by *Edmund Burke*, foaming with rage at *Necker's* disinterestedness, then staring him in the face:——Edmund Burke, on whose principle

1804 usually two-thirds) of the prize money to those who had taken the prize. The particular case Bentham has in mind arose from the capture of Spanish bullion ships in the closing months of 1804, before the formal declaration of war on Spain on 11 January 1805, and not therefore covered by the Prize Act (45 Geo. III c. 72) of 1805. These captures, which did indeed yield very large sums to the Crown, were Droits of the Crown, not of Admiralty; and a proportion was in fact granted to the captors, though it was, in view of the amounts involved, a smaller share than had been customary. Both here and in a fuller MS discussion (UC xxxiv. 316-17) Bentham seems either to have misunderstood or to have misrepresented the matter. For the above account see H. C. Rothery, *Prize Droits being a Report to H.M. Treasury on Droits of the Crown and of Admiralty in time of war*, London, 1915, 53-8. Bentham's own footnote reference is to a two-volume work by Arthur Browne (1756?-1805), who became Regius Professor of Civil and Canon Law at Trinity College, Dublin, in 1785. The book has a complex bibliographical history, and it has not been possible to identify Bentham's specific reference, which is evidently not to the first edition. This was published in 1798-9: vol. i, *A Compendious View of the Civil Law*, London, 1798; vol. ii, *A Compendious View of the Ecclesiastical Law*, Dublin, 1799. The latter, despite its title, opened with Book III of Browne's *Civil Law*: this is followed by the separately paginated *Ecclesiastical Law*, where Ch. V, pp. 149-200, is entitled 'Of the Practice of the Admiralty Law'. Droits of Admiralty are discussed mainly in nn. 30-1 on pp. 177-8.

thus displayed, the accidentally divulgated depredation committed
by two of his *protégés*,[a] formed, not long afterwards, so instructive
a comment. A document, in no small degree instructive to the great
body of the people would be a list of at length notified depredators,
with the particulars of their respective crimes, under a system of sinecure and overpay, with an assurance of support and protection. With
the commencement of the reign of George the Third, it might commence, and be continued onwards, as occasion called, till the time,
should it ever arrive, when, the eyes of the people having been sufficiently opened, the scene had closed.

### Instructional. Ratiocinative

ART. [58] or [17]. In this objection, what there is of truth, or at
least of the semblance of it, rests altogether upon a state of things, in
respect of official management and remuneration, in its whole tenor
the direct opposite of the one here proposed. A man, whose life has
been a life of luxury without any thing of his own to support it—
the dependent of some patron, whose habits have been correspondently luxurious—is put into an office, with the emolument which
has been attached to it for the purpose of enabling him to continue
in the same habits. If then this same emolument is *not*, by more than
to a certain amount, beneath his habitual expenditure,—he confines
himself within the bounds of it, and neither peculation nor extortion
have place. But, if it *is* to a certain amount lower, he finds himself to
such a degree uncomfortable, that rather than continue so, he risks
the engaging in some one or more of the forbidden practices, and exposing himself to the consequences.

  'But,' it may be asked, 'knowing his own propensities, how came
he to take upon himself the office, and thus subject himself to this
risk?' Answer. Nothing better offered; the situation of absolute dependence was uncomfortable; the mass of emolument in question,

  [a] Powel and Bainbridge.[1]

------

  [1] John Powell (d. 1783), a cashier in the Pay Office, and Charles Bembridge
(d. 1794), an accountant in the same office, were charged in 1783 with frauds
by which the estate of Henry Fox (1705-74), 1st Baron Holland, had been considerably enriched. Powell committed suicide while awaiting trial, but Bembridge, despite Burke's efforts in his defence, was eventually found guilty of
having fraudulently concealed certain items in the Paymaster General's accounts
for 1783. See *A Complete Collection of State Trials*, ed. T. J. Howell, 34 vols.,
London, 1816-28, xxii. 1-160; also *The Correspondence of Edmund Burke*, ed.
T. W. Copeland *et al.*, 10 vols., Cambridge, 1958-78, v. 87-9. What Bentham
calls Burke's 'sham Economy Bill' was the measure introduced in parliament in
1780 aimed at the abolition of fifty 'offices of profit under the Crown' held by
members of one House or the other.

how inadequate soever, constituted, by the whole amount of it, a *portion* at any rate of the means of independence—and the general character of the whole establishment of which this office forms a part, was that of maximizing the facilities for *ease* on the one hand, combined with accustomed, though unlegalized profit in every shape, on the other. As to the punishment, he saw it altogether without example. Dislocation, and that self-effected, and in the quietest and most unobserved mode, the worst that could ensue: dislocation, and from what? from an office which, after experience, was found not to give what was expected from it.

Such is the state of things—such the frame of Government, in which the objection originated, and on each occasion will be reproduced. But, of the whole multitude of securities *here* proposed against abuse, scarcely will *that* system be found to exhibit so much as a single *one*.


*Ratiocinative*

ART. [59] or [18]. Objection [6]. *Aptitude diminished. Aptitude being as opulence, lessening opulence you lessen aptitude.*

Thus, for shortness: for precision, a few more words are necessary. By *opulence*, understand—not opulence already possessed by the functionary, but opulence *given* to him: given to him *at public expense*. This being understood, say once more aptitude is *as* opulence. This is the whole theory, on which all practice is grounded. This, being an *axiom*, may without difficulty be taken for a *postulate*. If therefore in any situation you have not aptitude enough, it is because you have not given out money enough: give money enough, the aptitude comes of course: all other care is superfluous. Whatsoever be the situation, if you want twice the aptitude in it that you have at present,—give the man who is in it twice the money you had given him, you have twice the aptitude.

Note also, that, on divers occasions, the more he has, the more of it must be given to him. Instance, the metamorphosis of an indiscriminate defender of right and wrong into a Judge. The stronger the repugnance between the two characters, the greater the force necessary to effect the transition from the one to the other.

Giving out money is, in English Treasury language, *making exertions*. If any where you want more aptitude, you must make proportionable *exertions*. Giving out money being the cause,—establish this cause, the effect follows of course. Of a barrel full of spirits, turn the cock, out [flow] the spirits. Into the pocket of the functionary, in with the money,—in with it flows the aptitude. As to *how* this happens, this is, in both cases, matter of *theory;* no need have you to trouble yourself with it.[1]

This objection comes in aid of the one last preceding, by which economy is presented in the character of a sure cause of depredation. Instead of *giving, receive* money, as the price,—of the power or other object of desire attached to the office,—you will (says the objection) have the reverse of aptitude; and the more money you receive from him, the more flagrantly unapt in every respect he will be. On the other hand (says the basis of the present objection) aptitude being *as* opulence,—give twice the emolument you give at present, you will have twice the aptitude: and so on, *ad infinitum.* Put the two objections together, you have a triumphant *dilemma.* Offer (it says) with the office any less emolument than that which you will find attached to it,—either no person whatever will accept of it, or, if any one will, his acceptance of it will be a certain proof of his inaptitude for it; with no other purpose than that of employing it as an instrument of depredation, will the acceptance have been given to it. —The offer will not be accepted:—so says *horn* the first of this same irresistible dilemma. Good. But why will it not be accepted? Answer. Because, to be accepted, it must have been made: and it will not have been made. But *why* will it not have been made? Answer. Because by nobody but the maker of the dilemma can it have been made: and what *he* has made is—not the *offer*, but *the determination not to make it.* And why this determination? Answer. Because he has always been so perfectly convinced, that the offer, if made, would be accepted, and when accepted, followed by consequences, the opposite to those which his dilemma assigned to it: to his own assertion his own conduct gives the lie.

Tell him of any other country in which the rate is less, then come two other objections.

1. *That* country *differs* from this.

2. Of the smallness of the remuneration, the result is actually, in that country, a proportionable degree of inaptitude:—then, for proof, comes the assumption just disposed of.

As to the *difference*,—propose any enquiry into it; whether, for example, it is so great as to warrant, in the whole or in any part, the practical conclusion deduced from it,—Oh no: this would be too much trouble. So will say the objector: and in this instance what he says may be admitted for true: a Committee would not be very

---

[1] 1830 and 1830 *Off. Apt. Max.* places Bentham's footnote a, p. 362, at this point; but it seems clearly related to Art. 1 of the 'Concluding Instruction to the Public Opinion Tribunal', where, following Bowring, it has accordingly been placed. See also p. 362 n. 1 on the placing of the 'Concluding Instruction' itself.

instructively employed, in the enquiry whether it be true——that, when a man breaks a contract, for the performance of which no such securities as might be are provided, it is because it does not give him all he would have been glad to get from it, and not for want of those same necessary securities.

CONCLUDING INSTRUCTION TO THE PUBLIC OPINION
TRIBUNAL [1]

### Instructional

ART. 1. To the Public Opinion Tribunal it will belong, with all its energies, to urge the commencement, and urge on the progress, of the system of appropriate instruction here delineated.[a] By the most powerful particular and sinister interests,——the several Ministers, with their several dependents and other connexions, whoever they are, will at all times be urged to do their utmost for the retardation, and, if possible, the frustration of it. Of this repugnance the cause is no less manifest than the existence is unpreventable. Till the tests of aptitude thus furnished are in operation, the locating functionaries will, of necessity, remain in possession of a power of choice, altogether

---

[a] Designed directly and principally for *official*, this system will, as far as it goes, operate as a system of *national* instruction, and *that*, without additional cost: not to speak of education in other respects. Assistant to *that* its least extensive, will be this its most extensive though indirect influence. The better they are themselves instructed, the better will individuals, in quality of auditors at the several examinations, be qualified for the judging of the degrees of appropriate aptitude on the part of probationary *locables*.

Even in England,——among the suggestions in question, if considered merely in their application to national *instruction at large*, to the exclusion of *official instruction*, with a view to *location*,——some there may be which, even to the ruling few, will not be altogether an object of abhorrence. For, in the conduct of the majority of that class, the wish to shut out all intellectual light without exception, whatever possession it may have taken in some minds, does not appear to have manifested itself, by any conclusive evidence. Delusion, by means of false lights,——and the encouragement given for the reception of them by the application of the matter of reward in the character of matter of corruption,—— are the principal means employed for preventing the *subject many* from endeavouring to substitute a form of Government favourable, to one, hostile, to their interests.

---

[1] In the 1826 *Extract*, this 'Concluding Instruction' was placed at the end of the extract, following the main text of § 17. When Bentham added the two Supplements to §§ 16 and 17, in 1830 and 1830 *Off. Apt. Max.*, the 'Concluding Instruction' was left in an anomalous position between the end of § 17 and the beginning of the Supplement to § 16: see § 15n, p. 297. It has seemed best to follow Bowring in placing the 'Concluding Instruction' after the Supplements as well as the main texts of §§ 15-17.

arbitrary: apt, or in ever so high a degree unapt, their several dependents and connexions will remain located and locable, in all situations under them respectively, from the least to the most highly desirable. On the other hand, no sooner are these tests of aptitude in operation, than, by the influx of tried minds, whose aptitude has been made manifest to all eyes, the sceptre of arbitrary power will be swept out of their hands, and the feelings of a dethroned despot will be theirs.

### Instructional

ART. 2. The whole artillery of *fallacies* will be drawn out and employed; in particular, the better the plan is in *theory*, the more incapable it will be pronounced of being carried into effect *in practice:* and to the thus predicted impracticability, all imaginable exertions will be employed to give fulfilment.

### Instructional

ART. 3. If, and in proportion as, in the dominion of the State, apt instructors, whose native language is the national language, are wanting,—either the functionaries must remain uninstructed and unapt, or, under the disadvantage of having to learn, at a more or less advanced period of life, a foreign tongue, foreigners must be called in and employed. But, unless in case of temporary calamity, men will not for nothing quit their old accustomed habits and connexions, for those of a strange land: and thus, under the double mask of patriotism and frugality, sinister interest will seek, and with but too much probability of success, a cover for mischievous and anti-patriotic exclusions.[1]

### Instructional

ART. 4. Unhappily, no sooner has the system come into operation, than a dilemma, in no small degree unwelcome to every feeling eye, will have taken place: either, to an incalculable amount, sacrifice of the public good—of the good of every branch of the service—must have place; or, notwithstanding any, the most perfect, degree of moral aptitude, a more or less considerable number of functionaries will have to quit their several situations.

### Instructional

ART. 5. For minimizing the evil from these two opposite sources,— one means, however, there is, the application of which will be completely in the power of those functionaries whose situation exposes

---

[1] 1830 and Bowring, 'exclusions'; 1826 *Extract* and 1830 *Off. Apt. Max.*, 'exertions'. The former is retained as being more apt in the context.

them to it. According to their several situations, let those in possession participate in the instruction administered to their successors in
expectancy: at this price they will add those titles, whatever they be,
in which others are sharers with them, to that experience which is
peculiar to themselves.

Should pride be troublesome, let this fact quiet it. Anno 1824, in
London, John MacCulloch, having acquired the reputation of proficiency in the art and science of political economy, instituted a course
of lectures. Among his audience were Frederick John Robinson and
William Huskisson, both Members of Parliament, both Cabinet Ministers: Robinson, under the name of Chancellor of the Exchequer,
Finance Minister in the House of Commons; Huskisson, under the
title of President of the Board of Trade,[1] Trade Minister, in the language of this Code, as per Ch. xi. MINISTERS SEVERALLY, [§12].


## SECTION 18[2]

### DISLOCABLE HOW

*Expositive*

ART. 1. Dislocation is either *unmodified* or modified. By *unmodified*, or say *simple* dislocation, understand definitive removal from
an official situation, without consent of the dislocatee, and without
his being located in any other.

*Expositive*

ART. 2. Modes of modified dislocation, as per §4, *Functions in all*,
are these—

[1] John Ramsay MacCulloch (1789-1864), afterwards Professor of Political
Economy at University College London, delivered the Ricardo Memorial Lectures in the spring of 1824, David Ricardo having died in the previous year. See
MacCulloch's *A Discourse on the Rise, Progress, Peculiar Objects and Importance of Political Economy; containing an outline of a course of lectures on the
principles and doctrines of that Science*, Edinburgh, 1824. F. J. Robinson (1782-
1859), later Viscount Goderich and 1st Earl of Ripon, was Chancellor of the
Exchequer from 1823 to 1827 and Prime Minister in 1828. William Huskisson
(1770-1830), was President of the Board of Trade from 1823 to 1827. For
another reference to their attendance at MacCulloch's lectures, see MacCulloch
to Macvey Napier, 2 May 1824, *Selections from the Correspondence of the late
Macvey Napier, Esq., edited by his son*, London, 1879, pp. 39-40.
[2] Bentham included three brief articles from §18 in the 1826 *Extract*, but
these were superseded by the more extensive discussion in the 1830 edition of
the *Code* which appears here. See the Collation of the 1826 *Extract*, p. 523
below, for the text of these earlier articles. They were omitted entirely from
1830 *Off. Apt. Max.*

1. Promotion, to wit, in the same subdepartment.

2. Suspension.

3. Transference, *permanent*, to the same grade in another subdepartment.

4. Transference, *temporary*, to the same grade in another subdepartment.

5. Transference, *permanent*, to a *superior* grade in another subdepartment.

6. Transference, *temporary*, to an *inferior* grade in another subdepartment.

## Expositive

ART. 3. Wheresoever the word *dislocation* is employed, dislocation *unmodified* is what is intended: wheresoever dislocation *modified* is intended, the denomination of the modification so intended is employed.

## Enactive

ART. 4. In both ways, every Minister is at any time dislocable by the Prime Minister.

## Enactive

ART. 5. So, by the Legislature.

## Enactive

ART. 6. Other efficient causes of dislocatedness are the same as in the case of a member of the Legislature, as per Ch. V. CONSTITU-TIVE, §2, *Powers*, Art. [5]. For security against undue dislocation, —unmodified, and without consent of the [dislocatee][1] modified, see §21, *Oppression obviated.*

## Enactive

ART. 7. A Minister is not dislocable by the sentence or decree of a Judge.

## Ratiocinative

ART. 8. Reasons are the following:

Reason 1. It may happen that a Minister,—notwithstanding some offence, for which a Judge Immediate, and the Judge Appellate, his superordinate, might be disposed to dislocate him,—might be fitter for his situation than any other person that could be found. By a

[1] 1830 and Bowring, 'dislocative'; but 'dislocatee' seems correct, as in Art. 1 above.

Judge, for the forming and entertaining a right estimate of an Administration functionary's aptitude for such his situation,—no more than a small part can be possessed, of the means, which will, at all times, be in the hands of his superordinates in his own line.

### *Ratiocinative*

ART. 9. Reason 2. By confederacy,—between a Judge Immediate and his superordinate the Judge Appellate,—with any other person, acting,—spontaneously, or at the instigation of either of them, the part of an accuser—any Administration functionary, how apt soever for his own line of service, might to a certainty be dislocated. In the case of any functionary, in a situation subordinate to that of Minister (Army and Navy subdepartments excepted), small, it is true, might be the probability of any such confederacy. Not equally so however, by a great deal, in the case of a Minister: for instance, a Minister of the Army, Navy, Foreign Relation, or Finance Subdepartment. Well might it be worth the while of a foreign enemy, to employ,—in engaging by bribery the two Judges to concur in a judgment to that effect,—a sum too vast to be resisted by any ordinary degree of moral aptitude.

### *Ratiocinative*

ART. 10. Reason 3. Such would be the danger,—supposing the exemption, limited as it is, not established. On the other hand, [suppose] it established,—small, if any, is the danger of continuance in office, on the part of an unapt Administrative functionary. In the course of a prosecution of the functionary in question, suppose facts such as demonstrate his inaptitude for that same situation made known to the whole community,—his dislocation by a [superordinate][1] in his own line, is a consequence, which may be relied on with comparative confidence: especially considering the responsibility of superordinates for their subordinates, as per §25, *Securities*, &c.

## SECTION 19

### SUBORDINATES

### *Instructional*

ART. 1. *Fields of service.* In §2, *Ministers and subdepartments*, are allotted to those functionaries their several fields of service. In §4, *Functions in all*, may be seen matter, *enactive* and *instructional*,

---

[1] 1830 and Bowring, 'subordinate', but Bentham is clearly referring to a superordinate.

relative to such functions, as require, all of them, to be exercised for the carrying on the business of every subdepartment. In §5, may be seen instructional matter in relation to the several *grades*, which,— in quality and number differing or agreeing, as it may happen, in the several subdepartments, compared one with another,—may require to be instituted. To the Legislature, regard being had to circumstances local and temporary, it will belong,—in each such subdepartment, to give existence to the several *grades* requisite: allotting to each its distinctive field of service, and its functions.

### Enactive

ART. 2. Exceptions excepted,—on each occasion, in the exercise of his several functions, subject is each subordinate functionary, to the exercise given to the *directive* function of his immediate superordinate: subject however to any counter direction, given by any superior superordinate, and so on upwards in the *scale of subordination*.

### Instructional

ART. 3. Exceptions, if any, to this enactment, it will belong to the Legislature to apply, regard being had to circumstances, local and temporary, as well as to the general nature of the service of the subdepartment and the office.

### Instructional

ART. 4. *Statistic function*. Regard had to the matter, ratiocinative and instructional, of §7, *Statistic function*,—and to the nature of the business of each official situation, of each grade, in each subdepartment,—to the Legislature it will belong to determine—what the Register Books, kept in each such situation, shall be, and in what manner they shall respectively be kept.

### Instructional

ART. 5. *Self-suppletive function*. Regard being had to the ratiocinative matter of §[6], *Self-suppletive function*,—to the Legislature it will belong to determine—in what official situations, in the several grades, if in any, the power corresponding to this function needs not, and therefore shall not, be possessed and exercised.

### Instructional

ART. 6. So, in regard to the *requisitive function*.

### Instructional

ART. 7. So, in regard to the *melioration suggestive:* and, in this case,

the Legislature will not, it is presumed, see any material difference
—either in respect of the relative utility, or in respect of the mode
of exercise, as between office and office; any more than as between
subdepartment and subdepartment.

### Enactive

ART. 8. *Term of service.* Exceptions excepted, and subject to dislocation, simple and modified, as per §18, *Dislocable how;* §20, *Insubordination obviated;* and §21, *Oppression obviated,*—a subordinate
of every grade continues in his official situation during his life.

### Enactive

ART. 9. Persons excepted, are—

1. Persons belonging to the *Military*, or say *professional* branch of
the service of the Army subdepartment. As to these, see Ch. x.
DEFENSIVE FORCE, §5, *Term of Service.*

2. Persons belonging to the *Military*, or say *professional* branch of
the service of the Navy Subdepartment: as to these, see Ch. x. §5,
*Term of Service,* and §16, *Sea [Defensive] Force.*

3. Persons engaged in any branch of the service of the subdepartment in question, for a length of time, in any other way determined,
and by special designation expressed.

4. Persons therein engaged for the performance of a particular and
temporary service: for example, artists, handicrafts, and labourers.

### Ratiocinative

ART. 10. Question. Why, subject to eventual dislocation, give to the
term of service in grades subordinate to that of Minister, a duration
equal to that of their respective lives?

Answer. Reason. End in view—the affording, in the case of every
functionary, the only efficient security which can be afforded against
his being,—notwithstanding any the highest degree of appropriate
aptitude in relation to the business of his situation,—removed out of
it, at any time, by the operation of self-regarding interest, or ill-will,
or good-will towards any other person, or erroneous judgment,—
in the breast of any individual, in whose hands the *dislocative* power,
in the case in question, is reposed. This security consists in the rendering the act of dislocation *judicial*, in contradistinction to *arbitrary.*
As to the mode of rendering it judicial, see §20, *Insubordination
obviated*, §21, *Oppression obviated*, and §25, *Securities*, &c.

### Instructional

ART. 11. *Attendance.* Regard being had to circumstances local and temporary, as well as to the general nature of the service of the sub-department and the office,—to the Legislature it will belong, in relation to each office, to examine and determine in what manner application of the general principles and rules laid down in regard to *official attendance* in §14, and in Ch. vi. LEGISLATURE, §18, *Attendance*, and §20, *Attendance and Remuneration, how connected*, shall be made to the several subordinate situations.

### Instructional. Ratiocinative

ART. 12. *Remuneration*. In the case of a functionary—in any, and if in any, in what, grade or grades—should any, and, if any, what, increase be given, to remuneration, at the expense of the public, on the account of length of *continuance* in the several *situations* separately taken, or any of them?

Answer. No such increase, on this account, in any instance. Reasons for the negative in every case are—

1. Of any mass of emolument that could be appointed for this purpose, the receipt would be prevented by the *pecuniary competition*, in so far as it operated.

2. In so far as such prevention failed to have place, the increase in question would give correspondent increase to public expense.

3. Of no increase in the amount of the reduction made in the expense by increase given to the reductional biddings, does such an arrangement afford any prospect. By a prospect of future contingent emolument at a distance, men in general are not so numerously or so strongly influenced, as by a prospect of emolument of the same value, immediate or near at hand.

By it, no increase would be given to appropriate aptitude: either in a direct way, or in an indirect way, by increase given to competition.

4. The reasons against it present themselves as not differing materially from those which have place, in the case where, instead of continuance in the office, dislocation out of it by resignation has place: that is to say, in compliance with request made by the person himself, as per §15, *Remuneration*, Art[s]. 37, 38.

5. On the occasion of his *biddings* under the *pecuniary competition principle*, he will be at liberty, of course, to stipulate for an eventual provision of this nature, if in his judgment his interest will, by such an arrangement, be preponderantly served.

### Instructional. Ratiocinative

ART. 13. Should any, and if any, what, increase be in this case given to remuneration, at the expense of the public, on the account of *length of service*, in the official establishment, taken in the aggregate?

Answer. Reasons for the negative.

The same as those which apply to the case, where, as per Art. [12], the situation continued in is a *single* situation, separately considered.

### *Ratiocinative*

ART. 14. Should any, and if any, what, increase be in this case, given to remuneration, at the expense of the public, on account of length of continuance *in life*, or say longevity?

Answer. Reasons for the negative.

1. With no material difference, the reasons are those which have place in the case of continuance in the *service*, as per Art[s. 12, 13].

2. To those, to whose interior dispositions and exterior circumstances any such distant increase is adapted,——means of producing the effect are open, other than that of a provision, appointed, as in the case here in question, for all persons without exception, as well for those to whose case it is *not*, as to those to whose case it *is*, adapted.

3. If settled by any general rule,——it would, in the case of every individual, be liable to be either too great or too small: too great, the difference being thereby, to the detriment of the whole community, bestowed in waste; or too little, not sufficient for the exigencies of the individual, whatever they were, that were thought fit to be provided for.

4. In no case will the exigencies of the individual be altogether dependent upon the number of years during which his life has continued. But, supposing that it is, the smaller the remuneration he receives at the expense of the public service, the greater is the regard he thus manifests for the good of that same service.

5. The *quantum*, if not determined by any such just and inflexible standard, would be required to be determined by the individual will of some other functionary. In this case, the determination would be much more arbitrary, than when, as in the case of dislocation, the question is——whether a man shall or shall not be deprived of the *whole*. The eye of the Public Opinion Tribunal would not be so jealous and watchful in this case as in that.

6. In this case, misdirected sympathy, real or pretended——regard for the happiness of the few, at the expense of that of the many—— would, in the situation of *locating patrons*, be for swelling the demand, and working, to this end, upon the sympathy of others. For the purpose of engaging sympathy in support of excess, a commonly-employed notion is——that a sort of *moral merit* is manifested by the employing time and labour in the service of the public, in contradistinction to the service of the individual. Erroneous and fallacious

is this notion. Naturally small and altogether incalculable exceptions excepted,—no more is the good of the public service taken into the calculation of him who gives his *time* and *labour* for what he gets from it, than by him who gives his *goods* for what he gets from it. But, supposing that it is, the smaller the remuneration he receives at the expense of the public, the greater is the regard he thus manifests for the good of that same service.

7. The annexing to official situations remuneration to any greater amount, than, in the estimation of the individual functionary himself, is needful, is, in the breasts of patrons more *likely* to have had self-regard than *benevolence* for its *cause*, and is sure to have a net balance—not of *beneficence*, but of *maleficence*, for its *effect*.

8. It would tend to people the establishment with individuals, who, at entrance, were more advanced in life,—to the exclusion of those less advanced: and, in that way, to give not only useless, but worse than useless, increase to the expense.

9. The less the pecuniary provision exacted by the proposed functionary, at the expense of the public, as necessary for his exigencies, —the greater will be the quantum of that which he has already of his own: and the greater thereby his pecuniary responsibility, to the purpose of eventual satisfaction, for loss occasioned by him to the service.

10. The greater the provision for eventual addition on the account of length of *age*, the more efficient would be the tendency of the system to people the establishment, with individuals, absolutely or comparatively, destitute of responsibility in the *pecuniary* sense.


## Instructional

ART. 15. *[Locable who]*. To the Legislature it will belong to consider—in what, if in any subdepartments, and in each subdepartment, in what official situations subordinate to that of Minister, the principles, applied as per §[16, *Locable who*], to the situation of Minister, will be applicable with beneficial effect; and, in each instance, with what, if any, modifications: regard being had, in particular, to the exemplification given, in Art. 15 of that section, of the groups of talents necessary to the apt performance of the businesses belonging to the several subdepartments.


## Enactive

ART. 16. *Located how*. Exceptions excepted, as per §17, *Located how*, Art. 31,—as to every situation subordinate to that of Minister,

371

the initiative function will be exercised by the Minister, the consummative, as per §17, Art. 21, by the Prime Minister.[1]

### Enactive

ART. 17. To this case likewise applies the provision, made by §17, Art[s]. 22 to 29, of the temporary initiative function exercisible in consideration of *distance*.

### Enactive

ART. 18. To this case likewise extends the provision made by §17, Art[s]. 31, 32, for securing the filling up vacancies. For this purpose, —in the present case (so also in that of the day, on which the *location instrument* is delivered in at the Prime Minister's office,) recordation will thereon be made, under the conjunct signatures, of the person by whom *delivered*, and the person by whom *received*.

### Enactive

ART. 19. After the day, on which location, consummated by lapse of time, has place, as per Art. 8,[2]—the locatee will not be liable to be dislocated by the Prime Minister, otherwise than subject to the limitations attached to the dislocative power, by §21, *Oppression obviated*.[a]

### Ratiocinative. Instructional

ART. 20. Question. To what end this security for despatch?
Answer. Reasons—
To prevent the superordinate functionary from suffering vacancies to continue unfilled for indefinite lengths of time, and thereby suffering the functions to remain unexercised, and the business to be either put to a stand, or exercised by functionaries, whose responsibility to the Public Opinion Tribunal is diminished, for want of its seeing in what manner exercise is given by them to the powers, which in fact

[a] Note, that the particular security, given by these two Articles, [18 and 19], should, in Section 17, *Located how*, have been applied to the location of *Ministers* themselves.

---

[1] In §17, Art. 21 Bentham calls the consummative function the confirmative function.

[2] Bowring substitutes for this reference 'Sect. 17, Art. 31'—where Bentham does indeed deal with the consummation (or confirmation) of appointments 'by lapse of time'. But the reference to Art. 8 in the present section may be what was intended, being concerned with the point made in the present article after, rather than before, the cross-reference—tenure, 'exceptions excepted', for life.

are exercised by them. As to this matter, see [ §17 ], Art. 31, as applied to the situation of Minister.

### Instructional

ART. 21. On the occasion of the filling up of situations, become, from whatever cause, vacant,—questions which will naturally present themselves for consideration, are the following—

1. The situation—shall it devolve, as of course, upon the Depute permanent of the last occupant? or, upon one, and which,—if there be Deputes permanent more than one?

2. The *qualification examination*, the result of which, as per §[16], Art. 17, every admission into the list of locables, and thence every admission into the Official Establishment for the first time, has had for its efficient cause—shall it be undergone anew,—by whatsoever candidates, for location in the recently vacated office, there may be?

3. The *pecuniary competition*, if any, which in the instance of each official situation, has, on the occasion of the first location therein made, had place, between the successful candidate and his competitors—shall it, antecedently to the filling up of the vacancy, have place anew?

4. *Promotion*—in what shape, if in any, can it, and shall it, in this case, have place?

### Ratiocinative

ART. 22. Question 1. In this department, in any instance, on a vacancy, shall the situation devolve, of course, upon a Depute permanent, without power to the Minister to make any other choice?

Answer. *Reasons* for the negative.

1. The obligation, which would thus be imposed upon the Minister, would not be compatible with the need there is, for the arrangement, by which, as per §25, he is rendered in a greater or less degree responsible for the conduct of his subordinates.

2. Unless some particular reason to the contrary presented itself, whether in disfavour of a Depute, or in favour of some locable person other than a Depute,—a Depute would be the person towards whom, in the first instance, the eyes of the Minister in his character of locator would naturally direct themselves. The greater the advantage thus possessed by the Depute under a system of free choice, the less the advantage that would be secured to him by securing to him the succession to it, to the exclusion of free choice.

3. Under a system of free choice,—the whole number, of the

persons, whose names have place on the locable list, will, at all times, remain, as under all eyes in general, so in particular under those of the locating Minister. Should any other person, whose name is on that list, present himself to the conception of the Minister as possessing appropriate aptitude in a degree superior to what has been deemed to have place on the part of the Depute——the Minister's responsibility, as above, will operate on him as an inducement to the giving to such more apt candidate the preference.

## Instructional. Ratiocinative

ART. 23. Question 2. The *Qualification examination*——shall it as above, be in any case repeated? If yes, shall the repetition of it be, by the Legislature, ordained to have place in all cases,——or should power *without obligation* be given to [the minister]¹ for the repetition of it?

*Answer.* To the Minister's having it in every instance in his power to receive the information which would be furnished by the examination in question, there seems no possible objection: by him, in his situation, no sinister advantage could be derived from it. The interest of the public requires that, for the guidance of his judgment, he should be in possession of the completest stock of appropriate information obtainable: and, for his possessing it, this is the most effectual, if not the only adequate means. The only danger to be apprehended, is——his not giving to this instrument of instruction exercise so frequent as the interest of the public would require.

## Instructional

ART. 24. Note, that, for enabling the locating functionary to give to himself this information,——no additional judicatory, and thence no considerable addition to delay and expense, would be necessary. Under §16, *Locable who*, the Qualification Judicatory will be in existence, and periodically at work, for the purpose of giving admission into the *Locable list*. In this state of things, candidates for admission into the vacant situation will, if not prohibited, be at liberty to aggregate themselves to the body of examinees, for the purpose of making manifestation of their respective degrees of appropriate aptitude. Having it thus still in their power, some there will naturally be, who, if they see a probability of thereby eclipsing the Depute or Deputes belonging to the several situations, will, of their own accord, subject their own aptitude to this fresh test; and, to this number, an express

¹ 1830, 'to him': Bowring changes to 'to the minister' to make clear that Bentham is referring to the minister.

invitation, given by the Minister, might have the effect of making addition.

### Instructional. Ratiocinative

ART. 25. In this way alone can appropriate provision have place, for the case where the vacancy leaves, in the situation of Deputes, persons more than one; for, in this way alone,—to wit, by the course taken by them respectively as to the affording or forbearing to afford to him this information,—can the locating Minister obtain, for the guidance of his judgment, such lights as (they being the most instructive which the nature of the case affords) it may happen to him really to desire. In this way alone, can the tutelary influence of the Public Opinion Tribunal, as applied to the securing of appropriate aptitude on the part of functionaries belonging to the classes in question, be maximized.

### Instructional

ART. 26. Note, that the situations to which the question bears reference, cannot be any others than those which, as per §16, *Locable who*, Art. 15, are situations of *talent*: applied to situations of mere *trust*, the result of the operation would be time and labour expended without use: of any imposition, of labour in the shapes in question, on candidates,—the effect might be—a reduction more or less considerable in the number of those who would otherwise take part in the pecuniary competition; and thence an increase in the expense.

### Instructional. Ratiocinative

ART. 27. Question 3. The *pecuniary competition*, shall it, in these same cases, or any and which of them, be repeated?

*Answer*. 1. The result of *pecuniary competition* being, with relation to the locating functionary,—in the same manner as the information afforded by *qualification examination*,—instructional merely, not obligatory,—it is accordingly as completely free from objection as that has been seen to be.

2. The minimization of the expense,—or at the worst the proof that in that line of improvement the utmost that can be done has been done,—is a beneficial effect, which, so long as no preponderant evil has been shown to have place, will suffice to decide in favour of this case.

3. Were any objection to be found that could apply to the admission of the pecuniary competition,—it would be removed, by the consideration of the inadmissibility of any comprehensive arrangement, by which, on the occasion of a vacancy, the location in it

would be secured to the occupant of the situation next below. To establish as a general rule that, in all branches of the civil, as well as in the two branches of the military service, superiority of grade shall be accompanied with a correspondent superiority of emolument,—would be to establish a system of boundless waste.

4. In this or that station in this subdepartment may be seen a situation of talent, to which,—by reason of the smallness of the number of persons possessed of adequate appropriate talent necessary, and the magnitude of the remuneration obtainable in the same line of art and science from service to individuals,—it may be necessary to attach emolument to an indefinitely large amount: next above may be a situation, to which no such superiority of talent being necessary, but which, being a situation of high trust, with or without incidental patronage, might find persons willing to fill it, for the sake of the power and honour, with emoluments in small quantity, or even without any.

### Instructional. Ratiocinative

ART. 28. Question 4. *Promotion*. Consistently with the above-mentioned proposed arrangements,—so far as regards service other than military, can any such system or practice as that indicated by the word *promotion* be with propriety said to have place?

*Answer*. It should seem not. Reasons.

1. The objections which, as per Art. [22], inhibit the necessitating the location of a Depute into a vacancy created by the dislocation of the Principal, apply also to this case.

2. They do so with increased force. For, be the situation what it will,—evidence, more probative, as to appropriate aptitude of the functionary, will have been afforded by the manner in which he has performed the business of the situation in question,—than any that can in general have been afforded by the manner in which he has conducted the business of another and subordinate situation, the business of which may happen to be in any degree different.

3. To any degree of extent it might happen—that, in the scale of directive power and correspondent superordination and subordination,—in this or that instance, the higher grade would, to persons in general, all circumstances considered, be not so acceptable as the grade next below it in that same subdepartment, or even a grade inferior to the next below it.

4. It would be a negative upon spontaneous migration, and upon the transference of a functionary from a situation in one subdepartment, to a situation, which, though it belonged to another subdepartment, might, on good grounds, be deemed more congenial to his

faculties as well as his inclinations; and, if the inhibition were *not* thus all comprehensive,——to reduce it within the most apposite bounds, would necessitate a system of complicated arrangements, such, that the evil, produced by the complication and the addition thereby made to the bulk of the rule of action, would outweigh the utmost possible good producible by it.

## *Instructional*

ART. 29. On the nature of the distribution proper to be made, of power, grade and emolument, in non-military situations,——the distribution necessary to be made in military situations may, in the way of contrast, throw some light. In the Army service, it is of necessity, that power, and thence grade, should rise in proportion to extent of command, as determined and measured by the number of individual functionaries subjected to it. Confusion and anarchy would be the result, if a functionary having under his command a comparatively larger number——say a thousand men——were subjected, constantly or incidentally, to the directive function of another, having under his command no more than a comparatively smaller number,——a hundred men for example. Superiority of grade and power thus keeping pace of necessity with extent of command,——and in a stipendiary army, emolument to an amount more or less considerable being an essential and inseparable feature,——addition to emolument——an addition keeping pace with addition to grade and power,——was an obvious and *natural* accompaniment, and hitherto has perhaps universally been an *actual* one.

It follows not, however, that, even in that line of service, it is a *necessary* one in the *general* nature of the case, howsoever in the instance of this or that particular political community it may have been rendered so by local and temporary circumstances. Even when not combined with pecuniary emolument, or with the matter of good applied as matter of reward, in any other shape,——*power* has its value; and, as has been shown in §17, *Located how,*——is capable of operating, not only as *an* inducement, but of itself, as an *adequate* and effectual one, to the application of time and labour, to courses of operation, to which, but for the inducement, they would not be applied. But, of the adequacy of the mass of inducement in one shape, the consequence is——not *needfulness*, but *needlessness* of inducement in any other shape.

If, in any *one* instance, military subordination has place without being accompanied with emolument in any shape,——this one instance suffices to prove, that, in that line of public service, no such *correspondent* superiority in the scale of emolument, is matter of necessity; and, of such gratuitous service, the examples are numerous and extensive. The result, therefore, appears to be—that, of the degree of correspondency which has hitherto had place, the cause is to be looked for—rather in habit, and the propensity to imitation, than in the necessity of the case.

### Instructional

ART. 30. If to necessity, it is to necessity in another shape—it is to necessity of a local and temporal character—that, in the case of a stipendiary Army and Navy,—more particularly a stipendiary Army, —the customary all-comprehensive correspondence between altitude in the scale of power, and altitude in the scale of emolument, is to be attributed. In this or that country—whatever, at the time in question, were the proportions,—if an arrangement were expected to be made, for reducing, to a certain amount, the scale of emolument,— the proposed conjunct scales of grade and power remaining unreduced, —*resignation*, to an extent having the effect of *dissolution*—*resignation*, or even *revolt*—might be the consequence.

To the case of non-military functionaries, however, no such danger applies. The consequence is—that, to the complete disregard of *symmetry*—as exemplified in a mutual correspondency in the three scales of grade, power and emolument,—no objection on the ground of *necessity*, has place.

### Instructional. Exemplificational

ART. 31. For elucidation, a glance at an arrangement, made in Russia by *Catherine the Second*, may perhaps, on this occasion, have its use. From the military situatons, *analogy* conducted her, or her advisers, to the non-military: and, a scale of superiority and inferiority in rank, with or without correspondent subordination and superordination in respect of exercise given to the *directive* function, was the result. It was borrowed (it has been said) from the practice of some other state or states in her native country—Germany; but, by the conspicuousness of her situation, her name has been stampt upon it.[1]

---

[1] Catherine II (1729-96), Empress of Russia from 1762, was the daughter of the German prince of Anhalt-Zerbst. The administrative reform initiated in 1775 established, among other things, an 'exact gradation' of ranks in the government of the empire. See *The Life of Catherine II, Empress of Russia, An Enlarged Translation from the French*, ed. W. Tooke, 3 vols., London, 1798, iii. 28-9. Writing to his brother from St. Petersburg on 28 May 1780, Samuel Bentham asks whether he should send the French translation of the *Règlements* for these reforms, published there in 1778: *Correspondence* (*CW*), ii. 468. But Bentham subsequently cited an earlier edition published at Liège in 1777: *Of Laws in General* (*CW*), p. 151.

Be this as it may,——in two respects it was a system of no small importance: beneficial, to a considerable extent, it was and is; maleficial to a much greater extent. Beneficial, inasmuch as it is, in its nature, a vast *source* or *mine* of *hope*. So many situations in the whole Official Establishment,——so many objects of desire, endeavour, competition and hope, open, as at first sight might appear, to the entire of one of the sexes, and thence it might seem, to one half of the whole population. Here, then, was a good, placed, within possibility of acquirement, before the individuals in question, considered in their individual capacity. But, by it was maximization given to the quantity of the matter of *good*, applicable in the shape of matter of *reward*, which, by misapplication, operates, and continues to operate, as matter of *corruption*, placing within the hope of every individual of the male sex, the capacity of serving his own particular interest, by contributing, to the sacrifice made of the universal interest, to the particular interest, real or supposed, of the Monarch, by the maximization and perpetuation of arbitrary power in his hands.[a]

### Instructional

ART. 32. Like as between the *fabricational* and the *emptional* modes of procurement, antagonization, as per §4, *Functions in all*, Art[s]. 65, 66, has place,——so may it as between fabrication on *government* account, by fabricating functionaries, occupying a permanently, and (repeal excepted) *perpetually*, established situation in the official establishment, and functionaries occupying situations not continuing any longer than till completion has been given to this or that individual work. Regard being had to circumstances local and temporary, to the different natures of the services in the several subdepartments, and to the situation in each several subdepartment,——to the Legislature it will belong,——in relation to any such works as may come to be proposed,——to determine, to which of the two modes of procurement to give exercise.

---

[a] This system of arrangement may perhaps serve, in some sort, for the exemplification and elucidation of the distinction and alleged opposition, so often alluded to, between *theory* and *practice:* that is to say, in so far as the notion and the language is any thing better and other than a fallacy, employed for the purpose of opposing the shadow of an objection, in the case where none, of any substantial nature, can be found. *Analogy* being one of the great instruments in the hand of inventive genius,——and, this being an application of analogy upon a widely-extended scale,——the system of arrangements deduced from it was so far *good in theory*. But, an adequately close and separate examination of particulars ——of the particular arrangements comprised under this general head——was wanting; and therefore it is, that it would be found (it is believed) *bad in practice*. For the grounds of this opinion, see Art[s]. 28, 29, 30.

### Instructional. Exemplificational

ART. 33. Of such antagonization, examples are the following—

1. Fabrication, or say construction, of a bridge over a wide and rapid river.

2. — of an under-ground tunnel, especially if under water.

3. — of navigable vessels on the old accustomed plans, for war purposes.

4. — of steam-boats for non-military, as well as military purposes.

By survey taken, of the branches of art and science brought to view in §16, *Locable who*, other examples might be found.

### Instructional

ART. 34. In this or that instance, what may happen, is—that, where, for the exercise of the *fabricative* function, unpermanent situations may be most eligible,—for the exercise of the *custoditive* and *reparative*, the exercise of permanent functions, in relation to the same subject-matter,—and thus the institution of permanent, and even perpetual situations,—may be necessary, or at any rate, preferable.

### Instructional. Ratiocinative

ART. 35. Under a form of government, of which corruption is the main instrument, and under which, on the part of superordinates, appropriate aptitude is, in a proportion correspondent to the degree of it, rare,—both the inclination and the ability to make apt choice being accordingly rare,—succession, determined, in ordinary cases, by seniority in *official age* as contradistinguished from *natural age*, —may afford a less bad chance for appropriate aptitude on the part of locatees, than would be afforded by an habitual exercise of the power of unrestrained choice by superordinate locators, in whose instance, to such their power, an unrestrained and irresponsible power of dislocation is conjoined.

### Instructional. Ratiocinative

ART. 36. In such a state of things, succession by seniority, as above, —with correspondent augmentation of emolument, on such terms as above,—is, on several accounts, obviously beneficial to the particular, personal, and sinister interest of the locating Superordinate.

1. It gives proportionable increase to the value of his patronage.

2. It gives proportionable increase to the power and efficiency of *allective*[a] corruptive influence.

[a] (*Allective*) operating by inducement composed of hope of reward expected, or gratitude for reward received. See §4, *Functions in all*, Art. [44].

3. It gives proportionable increase to the power and efficiency of *intimidative* corruptive influence.

If suspected of want of devotedness to the will, declared or presumable, of the superordinate,—the superordinate, if not dislocated, may, at any rate, without scandal and censure by the Public Opinion Tribunal, remain unpromoted.

Under a form of government, of which corruption is the essence, —power, through whatever channels it runs, having been converted into poison,—there and thence it is, that [for] appropriate aptitude, as between choice and *lot, lot* would afford the least bad chance.[1]

### Instructional

ART. 37. For obtainment of ordinarily meritorious service,—no need nor use is there for augmentation of emolument, on account of, and in proportion to, seniority in *age*, natural or official: no more than, for the obtainment of commodities good in quality or cheap in price, there is for paying for the same commodities to a shopkeeper who is sixty years old, more money than to a shopkeeper who is but thirty years old, or to a shopkeeper who has been keeping shop for thirty years, more money than to one who has been keeping shop for no more than ten years.

### Instructional

ART. 38. For ordinarily meritorious service,—an individual master may, in this or that instance, have good reason for giving, to a servant of his own, extra remuneration, on the score of length of continuance in life or service. But, it follows not—that, at the expense of the public, a superordinate functionary should have the same power as to the augmentation of the emolument received by a subordinate. Any such power will be sure to be employed for the benefit of the superordinate; and, in case of antagonization, will be little less than sure to be employed, for that purpose, at the expense, and by the sacrifice, of the interest of the public service.

### Instructional

ART. 39. No need is there for any such augmentation, but for [obtainment] of extra-merit; and when it is for that purpose that it is given, it is for that purpose and on that account declaredly that it should be given; not on the account of length of continuance either in life or of Government service. *Bounty*, on length in either track, is *prohibition* of extra-merit. The reward that should have been

---

[1] 1830, '—for there and thence it is, that appropriate aptitude,'; the Bowring emendation which is followed here seems required by the sense.

appropriated to extra-merit, a man gets without it: and, in proportion as this has place, labour and self-sacrifice in the endeavour to make proof of extra-merit would be thrown away. See §15, *Remuneration*, Art. 37: and §25, *Securities*, &c. Art. [13], *Extra despatch.*

### Enactive

ART. 40. Exceptions excepted,—in every subdepartment, dislocable are all subordinates by the Minister,—subject to restrictions, as per §21, *Oppression obviated;* also, by the several authorities by which the Minister is dislocable, as per §18, *Dislocable* [*how*], Art[s]. 4, 5, 6; but, for reasons, as per Art[s]. 7, 8, 9, 10, not by a Judge.

### Enactive

ART. 41. Exceptions are as follows:

1. The several grades in the Military branch of the Army Minister's subdepartment: as to which, see Ch. xi. MINISTERS SEVERALLY, §3, *Army Minister.*

2. The several grades in the Military branch of the Navy Minister's subdepartment, as to which, see Ch. xi. §4, *Navy Minister.* In relation to these branches of the Administrative service, separate arrangements are made, as per Ch. x. DEFENSIVE FORCE.

### Instructional

ART. 42. Regard being had to circumstances local and temporary,—to the Legislature it will belong to consider and determine, in what cases to give, to a superordinate of a grade inferior to that of Minister, the power of *suspending* a subordinate, on account of *distance* in *place*, until circumstances shall have rendered it practicable to take the decision of the Minister, respecting the exercise of the powers of dislocation, simple or otherwise modified: and this, not only for this or that *individual* instance of misconduct in a determinate shape, but, in case of need, for general deficiency of appropriate aptitude in any one of its shapes. See §21, *Oppression obviated*, Art. [47].[1]

### Instructional. Exemplificational

ART. 43. Examples are—

1. In the territory of a foreign state, suspension of a vice consul by a consul.

2. In a remote part of the territory of this state, suspension of a deputy commissary by a commissary, employed in the *procurement,*

---

[1] In §21, Art. 47 the power of suspension is given directly to the superordinate and the role of the legislature is not mentioned. See p. 403.

*custody*, *distribution*, and, incidentally, *sale*, of provisions or war stores, for the use of an army belonging to the state.

3. Or, in war time, in the territory of a foreign enemy.

## SECTION 20

### INSUBORDINATION OBVIATED

### *Instructional*

ART. 1. The Legislator will, on this occasion, consider, whether, to the *professional* or say *military* branch of the Army and Navy services respectively, any, and if any, which, of the arrangements brought to view in this section and the two next, to wit, §21, *Oppression obviated*, and §22, *Extortion obviated*, are applicable with advantage.

### *Instructional*

ART. 2. This section and the three next have for their object the giving,——to functionaries of all grades, as per §5, in the exercise of their several functions, as per §4, and to the [members]¹ of the community at large——in a word to *non-functionaries*, in their several capacities of *suitors*, [*inspectees*],² and *evidence-holders*,——security against such wrongs as they stand exposed to at the hands of each other; as well as to this branch of the Government service, against such wrongs as it is exposed to at the hands of persons acting in these several capacities.

### *Expositive*

ART. 3. By a *suitor*, understand——any person, who, in virtue of any business which he has, with a functionary belonging to any sub-department and acting as such,——has need of any act or forebearance on his part: whether it happen or not to such suitor to attend, or to have need to attend, at the official residence of such functionary.

### *Expositive*

ART. 4. By an *Inspectee*, understand——any person, whose conduct, in respect of some concern he has in the management of some establishment, or institution, private or public, placed under the inspection of the Minister of some subdepartment in this same Administration department,——is thereby in that respect placed under the inspection

¹ 1830, 'numbers'; the Bowring emendation to 'members' seems to be required by the sense.

² 1830 and Bowring, '*inspectors*'; but '*inspectees*', as in Art. 4, seems correct.

of that same Minister: and this, whether the establishment or institution in question is or is not, in the whole or in part, carried on at the expense of the state or any district thereto belonging: and thence, whether such establishment or institution is or is not in any respect subject to the exercise of the *directive* function of such Minister.

*Expositive*

ART. 5. By an *Evidence-holder*, understand——any person, considered as having at his command *evidence*, or say *information*, the possession of which is necessary, or in a preponderant degree useful, to any functionary for his guidance in the exercise of any one of his functions: and this, whether the *source* of the evidence be *personal, real,* or *written*:——furnished by the oral discourse of a person, by the appearance of a thing at large, or by the appearance of that particular sort of thing, by the appearance of which, *discourse* in a written form is expressed.

As to *Evidence-holders* and their evidence, see Procedure Code under the head of *Evidence.*[1] Information, in so far as obtained by *inspection*, is obtained by inspection of some source of *real* or written evidence.

*Expositive*

ART. 6. By *insubordination*, understand hereinafter——any act whereby wrong is by a *subordinate functionary* done to the public service, by means of wrong done to some superordinate or co-ordinate functionary, in such sort that disturbance, in some shape or other, is given to the exercise of his functions.

*Expositive*

ART. 7. By *quasi-insubordination*, understand hereinafter——any act whereby wrong is done, by a suitor, an inspectee, an evidence-holder, or an individual at large, to the public service, by means of disturbances given to the exercise of some functions of some functionary as above.

*Expositive*

ART. 8. From *insubordination, quasi-insubordination* differs in this particular. The suitor, inspectee, or evidence-holder, not occupying

---

[1] While different kinds of evidence are discussed in Ch. XI, 'Evidence', of *Principles of Judicial Procedure* (Bowring, ii. 3–188), Bowring, ii. 57–62, 'evidence-holders' are not specifically mentioned. They are however mentioned in Ch. XV, 'Suits, Continuance Of', Bowring, ii. 69. On the Procedure Code generally, see Ch. V, § 5, Art. 6n, p. 38n.

any official situation under Government,—any wrong done or endeavoured to be done by him in the business of the subdepartment, cannot be obviated by dislocation, as in the case of a functionary, occupying, as such, an official situation under Government.

### Expositive

ART. 9. To the exercise of any function of any functionary, *disturbance* is capable of being produced in any one of the modes following—

1. By *personal annoyance*, or say by *vexation*, corporal or mental, in such sort that, for a length of time more or less considerable, it is rendered either utterly impracticable, or to a degree more or less considerable, less easy, for him to act with due effect in the exercise of such his function. As to the several modes of vexation, corporal and mental, see the Penal Code.[1]

2. By operation, performed on some *other* person or on some *thing*, in such sort that the exercise of the function in question is rendered impracticable, or less easy, as above.

3. By non-compliance with some mandate or requisition which, in virtue of his official situation, the functionary is empowered to address, and does accordingly address, to the *disturber*, as above.

### Ratiocinative

ART. 10. Under this Constitution, whatsoever be the establishment, institution, or foundation,—and howsoever *private*,—in no way can any interest which is not sinister be served, by screening it from public inspection, performed through the medium of the authorities hereby for that purpose constituted: always understood that, in relation to such establishment, institution, or foundation, the *inspective* function is not, in the hands of those same authorities, accompanied by the *directive* function, or by the [dislocative] function, simple or modified.

### Ratiocinative

ART. 11. If altogether exempt from inspection, as above,—any establishment, and, by means thereof, the founder or founders and their successors, might give an effective force to regulations repugnant in any degree to the greatest happiness principle, and to the ordinances of the state. For, no otherwise than by appropriate application of the matter of punishment and reward, can effective force be given to any

---

[1] In the Table of Contents to the Penal Code, modes of vexation are distinguished in Pt. II, Chs. I and VIII. See Table 2. On the Penal Code generally, see Ch. V, § 6, Art. 2n, p. 39n.

imaginable regulation. But, whosoever, for the creation, preservation, or extension of any institution or establishment, attaches a fund to the support of it, makes to that purpose a correspondent application, of the matter of reward, to the purpose of securing, on the part of all who share, or look to share, in the reward, conformity to the regulations, whatsoever they may be, by which the act of foundation is accompanied or followed: of the matter of reward, application is thus made avowedly and under that name: of the matter of punishment, not less effectually, though not under that name: for, of the various modes of punishment, subtraction of the matter of reward is *one;* and, whoso, subject to any such subtraction, gives his acceptance to the reward, renders himself thereby subject to the correspondent punishment. And in this way it is,——that, under the wing of any dominion, a dominion still more powerful than itself, is, but for appropriate precaution, liable, at any time, and any where, to be established.

### *Ratiocinative*

ART. 12. If, under a representative democracy, any secret establishment or institution is thus, in a greater or less degree, pernicious and dangerous, and at the best needless and useless,——in a still greater proportion is it salutary, supposing it capable of subsisting under an absolute monarchy, or aristocracy, or a mixture of both: for as, under such a form of Government, no open security can the people have against the most excruciating tyranny,——thence it follows that, if they have any, it must be a secret one: and by the mere suspicion, even supposing it groundless, of the existence of any such institution, some check, how inadequate soever, may be applied, to a tyranny to which there would otherwise be none.

Tyranny would be banished from the earth, could it but once be sufficiently known, that rest is every where banished from the pillow of the tyrant.

### *Expositive*

ART. 13. Of establishments or institutions, perpetual or temporary, which,——being, in whole or in part, maintained at the expense of individuals, singly or in numbers, or of bodies corporate or unincorporated other than the Government,——may, as above, present an adequate demand for their inspection by the Minister to whose subdepartment they respectively belong, instances are as follows:

1. *Indigence Relief* and *Health* subdepartments. Establishments or Institutions, having for their object or say end in view, real or professed, the relief of indigence, absolute or relative, with or without labour: for example, 1. Almshouses: 2. Workhouses: 3. Hospitals.

2. *Education and Health* subdepartments. Establishments or Institutions, as above, having for their object or end in view, real or professed, the *instruction* of individuals, of whatever age, in respect of any *beneficial acquirement*, on any part of the field of art and science.

3. *Health* subdepartment. 1. Hospitals. 2. Dispensaries. 3. Medical Museums. 4. Lectureships.

### Expositive

ART. 14. By a subordinate, in relation to a superordinate of his of any grade, an act of insubordination is capable of being committed in any of the three modes or shapes, in which, as above, an act of *quasi-insubordination* is commissible, as above, by a non-functionary, in relation to a functionary.

It is moreover commissible by non-compliance with any direction, delivered to him by the superordinate in the appropriate exercise of his *directive function*.

### Enactive

ART. 15. Remedies in the case of *quasi-insubordination*.

In a case in which the functionary, to the exercise of whose function disturbance is offered, is a Minister,—the *physical* remedies applicable on the spot will be the same as those applicable on the spot by a Judge Immediate, in the case of the like disturbance to the exercise of his functions: as per Ch. xii. JUDICIARY COLLECTIVELY, §11, *Sedative function.*

### Instructional

ART. 16. For prevention of disturbance producible in any other less effective mode, will be provided an appropriate set of *rules*. Title of these rules—'Rules *for the deportment of suitors, and other non-functionaries present on the occasion of exercise given to the functions belonging to any of the several official situations:*' or, for shortness, *Rules for the deportment of non-functionaries* in their intercourse with functionaries, in the several Administration subdepartments. If, by the circumstance of any particular subdepartment, any special alteration from the tenor of the above general rules shall appear to be called for,—such alteration will accordingly be made, to wit, by omission, addition, or substitution, as the case shall have been deemed to require.

### Expositive

ART. 17. These Rules of deportment on the part of suitors towards functionaries, will consist of such of the Rules styled *Rules of good behaviour, good manners, good-breeding*, or *decorum*, as apply to the species of superiority which, in this case, has place, and is necessitated by the nature of the case.

### Instructional

ART. 18. To these rules execution and effect will be given, in the *first* place, by the power of the *popular* or say *moral sanction*, as exercised by such persons, to whom, in the capacity of *Inspecting* members of the *Public Opinion Tribunal*, it shall have happened, by presence or otherwise, to have had cognizance of the facts.

### Instructional

ART. 19. On the occasion of the drawing up of those rules, the Legislature will consider and determine—whether, in the case of any, and if any, of which of them, for the better securing of execution and effect thereto, the force of the *legal* sanction shall in any shape be applied; as, for example, by moderate penal fine or imprisonment, or rather, for a first offence, exclusion or suspension from the right of being present in the character of Inspecting Visitors, as per §21, *Oppression obviated*, and §25, *Securities for appropriate aptitude*.

### Instructional

ART. 20. In this as in other cases, on the character of the system of *Judicial procedure* will depend, in considerable degree, whether,— in the case where the *legal* sanction, with the judiciary authority for giving execution and effect to it, shall be employed,—good or evil shall be preponderant: if in its several shapes of *delay, vexation*, and *expense*, the mass of evil opposite to the *collateral* ends of justice be minimized,—the advantage, of making application of this power to the purpose and the occasion, will be much more unquestionable, than where the magnitude of it is left to stand, even at the very lowest pitch at which it has hitherto been customarily placed under the best constituted Governments.

### Enactive

ART. 21. For remedy, in case of non-compliance on the part of an *Inspectee*,—a Minister, acting within his subdepartment,—subject to the operation of the securities against depredation and oppression, as per §21,—has power, in case of necessity, to employ physical force: in the first place upon *things*, and, if by resistance rendered necessary, against *persons*.

*Enactive*

ART. 22. For remedy, in case of non-compliance on the part of an *Evidence-holder*,—a Minister, acting as above, and subject as above, has the same powers, as, by Ch. vi. LEGISLATURE, §27, *Legislation Enquiry Judicatory*, are given to the Legislature; and by Ch. xii. to Immediate Judges: for details, see the Procedure Code.[1]

*Enactive*

ART. 23. Against *insubordination*, committed in any one of the shapes, in which, as above, *quasi-insubordination* is commissible,—remedies employable are the same as in that case.

*Instructional*

ART. 24. To the Legislature it will belong to consider and determine, —to what *grades*, if any, subordinate to that of Minister, shall, in the several subdepartments, be imparted the benefit of the *securities* hereinafter afforded against *disturbance* and *non-compliance*, on the part of *Suitors, Inspectees*, and *Evidence-holders*.

*Enactive*

ART. 25. In case of non-compliance, on the part of a subordinate, in relation to a *direction* delivered in the exercise of the *directive* function belonging to his office,—to every superordinate, subject as above, as per §21, *Oppression obviated*, [belongs] the power of *suspension*: also, to the appropriate superordinate, the additional powers of unmodified dislocation, transference to an equal or inferior grade, or stoppage of promotion: and in each case exercisible either definitively or for a time. For remedy to mis-exercise of these several powers, see §21, *Oppression obviated*.[2]


SECTION 21

OPPRESSION OBVIATED

*Instructional. Expositive*

ART. 1. Relation had to the business of the several departments of the *Official Establishment*, and to that of the *Administrative* Department

---

[1] Remedies for non-compliance by evidence-holders do not seem to be discussed specifically in the *Principles of Judicial Procedure* (Bowring, ii. 3–188), although there are materials relevant to the problem presented in various chapters. On the Procedure Code generally, see Ch. V, §5, Art. 6n, p. 38n.

[2] For additional material relevant to this section, see §21, Art. 77, p. 409.

in particular,——persons at large require, on various occasions, and for various purposes, to be distinguished from each other, into *non-functionaries* and *functionaries*: so also *functionaries* into those who, in relation to one another, are *superordinates, subordinates,* and *co-ordinates.* By the constitution of human nature, persons of all these several classes stand exposed to suffer wrong in all shapes, from human agency: at the hands of every other, each one: and, through the medium of such private wrong, or in a direct way, so does the public at the hands of every one.

### Instructional. Expositive

ART. 2. Correspondent to wrong done *to* a functionary, and thence to the public service,——if *by* a functionary inferior to himself, is, as above, §20, *insubordination*: if by a non-functionary, *quasi-insubordination*: correspondent to wrong done *to* a functionary *by* a functionary superior to himself, or *to* a non-functionary *by* a functionary of any grade, by means of the power belonging to him as such,——is *oppression.* In the case where, and in so far as, *oppression* has *profit* for its fruit, it is *extortion*: profit, pecuniary or quasi-pecuniary——money or money's worth.

### Instructional

ART. 3. Against *insubordination*, provision is made in the section last preceding: against *oppression* at large, in this present section: against oppression in the particular shape of *extortion*, in the next.

### Instructional. Expositive

ART. 4. Take any human act whatsoever,——in so far as oppression is the result of it, the agent is an *oppressor*, the patient an *oppressee.*

Persons, who, on the present occasion, are considered in their capacity of becoming *oppressors*, are——functionaries belonging to the Administration Department: all persons so situated, and no others.

Persons liable to be rendered *oppressees* are——1, non-functionaries; 2, functionaries: non-functionaries in their several capacities of, I, suitors, II, inspectees, III, evidence-holders, as per §20, *Insubordination obviated*, Art[s]. [3, 4, 5], by all functionaries; functionaries, by their respective [superordinates].[1]

Oppressed by a superordinate, any subordinate functionary is liable to be in any one of three ways: to wit, 1, in his capacity of suitor, having need of intercourse with the superordinate, in the same manner as a non-functionary; 2, by abuse of the superordinate's *directive*

[1] 1830, 'subordinates': the Bowring emendation to 'superordinates' is required by the context.

power; 3, by abuse of the superordinate's *dislocative* power, simple or modified, as per §18, *Dislocable how*, Art[s]. 1, 2.

Abuse of power may be either *positive* or *negative*: *positive* is committed by mis-exercise; *negative*, by non-exercise, where exercise is due: *non-user* is among the terms employed in English-bred law, and is applied to *power*; and, still more extensively, to *right* at large.[1]

### Expositive. Exemplificational

ART. 5. Follows exemplification in the above-mentioned four several cases.

CASE I. Alleged oppressee, a suitor. Examples—

1. On the part of the alleged *oppressor*, refusal, or omission to render an official service, on the occasion in question, due to him.

2. Needless suffering, inflicted on him on any such occasion, in the shape of *delay, vexation*, or *expense*.

3. Needless and ungrounded contempt or disrespect, expressed in relation to him; to wit, whether by discourse or deportment.

4. Any other wrong or wrongs, which the suitor may prefer submitting to at his hands, rather than be subjected to sufferings such as the above.

5. Wrongs, exercisible by contravention of the *Rules of Official Deportment*, as per §20, *Insubordination obviated.*

### Expositive. Exemplificational

ART. 6. CASE II. Oppressee, an *inspectee*. Examples—

1. Useless or needless suffering, in any shape, inflicted on him, on occasion of the process of inspection: of whatsoever nature the subject-matter of it, if a *thing*, may happen to be: the subject-matter, if *one*, damaged: subject-matters, if *divers*, damaged or thrown into confusion.

2. *Profit-extinguishing disclosure*: disclosure made—of a beneficial process in manufacture, or plan of management in commerce, not obtained without expenditure of time and capital, but productive of, or pregnant with, net profit, the amount of which would be lessened, or the source of it altogether dried up, were the same process employed by other persons, by whom the expenditure had not

---

[1] The term non-user may be less than wholly appropriate to Bentham's point about abuse of power, since it denotes essentially the neglect to exercise a *right*, by which that right may become void. See *Halsbury's Laws of England*, 4th edn., London, 1973– , vi. 240: 'If a person who has acquired a right of common fails for a long period of time to exercise it, he may lose the right if circumstances permit of the presumption that he has abandoned it; but mere non-user, though evidence of abandonment, is not conclusive evidence.'

been shared: the disclosure being accordingly followed by extinction of profit, as above, in consequence of such competition.

For other examples, see above, Art. 5.

### Expositive. Exemplificational

ART. 7. CASE III. Oppressee, an *evidence-holder*. Examples—

1. The evidence, *personal* evidence, *orally* to be elicited: for the extraction of it, the *evidence-holder* subjected to forced attendance from distant parts, with uncompensated expense, of journeys to and fro and demurrage.

2. The evidence, *epistolarily*, to be elicited: for the extraction of it, the *evidence-holder* subjected to the obligation of furnishing more or less lengthy written answers, to correspondently long strings of questions.

3. The evidence, *real* evidence: for the obtainment of it, the *evidence-holder* subjected to the burthen of a more or less protracted course of search, inspection, and examination, followed by the burthen of reporting the result: also travelling, the source of the evidence being immoveable, for instance, an edifice or tract of land; or if moveable, bringing it or sending it to the official residence.

4. The evidence *ready written*: necessary to the exhibition of it, a more or less protracted course of search, examination and methodization. In each case, the evidence either useless or needless: or the burthen to the individual not adequately compensated by payment to him, or benefit to the public.

### Expositive. Exemplificational

ART. 8. CASE IV. Oppressee, a *functionary*. For examples of oppression, which functionaries at large are exposed to at the hands of functionaries at large,—see those which non-functionaries are exposed to, as per Art[s]. 5, 6, 7. For examples of oppressed*ness* by abuse of dislocative power, see the several modes thereof, as per §18, *Dislocable how*, and the articles which here follow.

Note, that by oppression at large, if not sufficiently obviated, the effect of dislocation, dishonour excepted, is not incapable of being produced: rather than endure any longer the vexation he is subjected to, the resignation of the oppressee is tendered and accepted. On the occasion of the oppression, this result may have been in contemplation, and have operated as the final cause of it.

### Expositive

ART. 9. So much for the *disorder*—its *shapes*, *authors*, and *patients*: now as to *remedies*.

Case I.[1] Oppressee, a [*non-functionary*].[2] Remedies applicable in this case are either—1, generally applying, or 2, specially applying. By the *generally applying*, understand those which apply to oppression, *by* whomsoever, *on* whomsoever, exercised, and are furnished by the Penal Code,[3] and applied by the judiciary authority. By the *specially applying*, understand those which apply to oppression, in no other case than where *functionaries* are the *oppressors*, and the authority by which the remedy is applied is—*not* the Judiciary authority, otherwise than as called in and employed in aid of the Administrational.

### Expositive

ART. 10. The *specially applying* remedies, are either—1, *directly applying*, or 2, *indirectly applying*. By the *directly applying*, understand those which are constituted in the ordinary mode, to wit, by prohibition, and are specially applying no otherwise than because, instead of those alone who belong to the Judiciary Department, the functionaries by whom they are applied, are those who belong to the Administration Department, with or without aid from those belonging to the Judiciary. By the *indirectly applying*, understand such as are applied otherwise than by prohibition and judicature, applied, as above, to the abusive act. They will be seen to consist chiefly in the applying to this purpose the power of the *Public Opinion Tribunal*, —and for the use of that as well as to the legal tribunals, providing appropriate *evidence* and means of *publicity*.

### Enactive

ART. 11. Follow, in the several cases, the directly-applying remedies.

CASE I. Alleged oppressor, a functionary of a grade *inferior* to that of Minister.

[1.] Power, in this case, to the alleged oppress*ee*, to prefer his

---

[1] In the remainder of this section, 1830 conflates and confuses several series of numerals: Bowring substantially resolves this, and the Bowring adjustments are in the main followed here. For details see the 1830 Collation, p. 476. A further source of confusion is the fact that Bentham uses the term 'Case' in two different ways. In this article and in Art. 34, p. 400, it is used to distinguish two broad categories, according to whether the 'oppressee' is a non-functionary or a functionary. In Arts. 11, 18, and 19, however, it is used to refer to 'sub-cases' within the first of these two main groups.

[2] 1830, '*suitor*', as though the sequence of 'cases' in Arts. 5–8 were to be followed; but the context shows that the Bowring emendation to '*non-functionary*' is correct: see the latter part of n. 1 above.

[3] Remedies are listed in Pt. 1, Ch. XVI in the Table of Contents of the Penal Code: see Table 2. On the Penal Code generally, see also Ch. V, § 6, Art. 2n, p. 39n.

demand for redress, either to the ordinary Judicatory,——or to the Minister, to whose situation that of the alleged oppress*or* is subordinate.

### Enactive

ART. 12. [2]. In so far as is necessary for giving execution and effect, to redress, at the charge of the alleged oppressor,——invested, in this case, is the *Minister*, with the powers and obligations attached to the situation of a Judge immediate, with right of appeal, on both sides, to the Judge appellate.

### Enactive

ART. 13. [3]. As in the case of the ordinary permanent Judicatory, ——power and obligation to the Judge of this occasional and transient Judicatory, to administer *satisfaction*, in whatever shape it is provided by law, in case of oppression at large, for damage, in whatever shapes resulting, from the oppression; and this, whether to the oppressee, or, through him, to any other person.

### Enactive

ART. [14]. [4]. So likewise to subject the oppressor to dislocation, *simple* or *modified*, as per §18, *Dislocable how*.

### Enactive

ART. 15. [5]. Of his own motion,——or at the instance of the complainant, or the party complained against,——power, in this case, to this same special Judge, to *call in*, or say *invoke*, the assistance of the *Judge immediate*, of the *sub-district*, within which the official residence of the functionary complained against, is situated.

### Ratiocinative

ART. 16. Reasons, purposes, and uses of such *invocation*. Examples——
 1. Obtainment of evidence, at the hands of *evidence-holders*, in relation to whom the special Judge has no *evidence-elicitation power*.
 2. Avoidance of the appearance, or suspicion, of undue *favour* or *disfavour*.
 3. Increase given to the *publicity* of the proceedings: thence, to the security against any deficiency of appropriate aptitude, in any particular, on the part of the special Judge.

### Enactive. Ratiocinative

ART. 17. By the Judge *invoked*, as above,——as well as by the Judge invoking,——will in this case be exercised the several *elementary*

394

*Judicial functions*, as per Ch. xii. §9, *Elementary Judicial Functions:* the ultimate *imperative* function excepted. This will be exercised by the special Judge alone: REASON, *responsibility undivided.*

*Enactive*

ART. 18. CASE [II]. Alleged oppressor, a *Minister*. Special Judge in this case, the *Prime Minister*. Power of invocation in this case, as per Art. [15].

*Enactive*

ART. 19. CASE [III]. Alleged oppressor, the *Prime Minister*. Special Judicatory in this case, the *Legislation Penal Judicatory*, as per Ch. vi. §28.

*Enactive*

ART. 20. Indirectly-applying remedies, in these cases, are as follows:

1. *Rules of deportment for functionaries*: analogous to those applied, as per §20, *Insubordination obviated*, Art[s]. 16 to 20, to the situation of non-functionaries having need of official intercourse with a functionary.

In the case of the *Army* and *Navy* subdepartments, respectively, whether any, and what variation should have place, the Legislature will consider and determine.

2. Enumerated cases for *secrecy* excepted, *publicity* of all official intercourse between functionaries and non-functionaries. For architecture adapted to these two opposite purposes, see §26, *Architectural arrangements*.

3. In the *audience chamber* of each Minister, and that of each functionary his subordinate of every grade,—in situation and characters conspicuous,—suspended by the side of the table of *Rules of deportment for suitors*, etc., a table exhibiting the *Rules of deportment*, as above, for *functionaries*. In many points, the two sets of rules will coincide: in some points, they will diverge.

4. As in the proceedings of the Judicial Department, as per Ch. xii. §14, and Ch. xxi. JUDICIARY REGISTRARS, §[5], *Minutation how*,—as in the public, so in the secret audiences, minutation and registration applied to every thing that passes. See Ch. vi. §21.

5. As in the Judiciary Department, so in this,—securities the same for *clearness, correctness*, relative *completeness*, and thence *undeceptiousness*, in the *evidence* so elicited.

6. As in every *justice chamber*, so in every *administration functionary's audience chamber*,—the sort of *register*, styled an *Incidental Complaint-Book*, as per Ch. xii. §18, will be ready for the reception

of any complaint, which, at the charge of the functionary,——the suitor, inspectee, or evidence-holder, as the case may be——may think fit to make: or, at the charge of the non-functionary, the functionary.

7. Thus, as in judicial business, as per Ch. xii. and Ch. xvii. JUDI-CIAL INSPECTORS, and the correspondent Procedure Code,[1]——so in administration business,——to the hitherto customary, ungrounded, and *arbitrary* mode, a determinately and *judicially-grounded* mode of procedure, is throughout, substituted.

### Instructional. Expositive

ART. 21. First, as to the above *Rules of deportment*. For the more effectual comprehension of them, take the analysis following:

Rules.——1, of purely self-regarding prudence;——2, of extra-regard-ing prudence;——3, of negative effective benevolence;——4, of positive effective benevolence:[a]——under one or other of these four heads, may be ranked every rule, by the observance of which increase can be given to the sum of human happiness: call them *Rules of Ethics*,[b] or say, *Morality*, rightly understood.

### Instructional. Expositive

ART. 22. Of these four sets of rules, the aggregate may again be dis-tinguished into two groups: the first, composed of those, in regard to which, for securing observance to them, the sanctions belonging to the *Penal Code*[2] may be employed with advantage: the others, of those in regard to which those same sanctions cannot be, or at any rate, at the time in question have not been, so employed.

### Instructional. Ratiocinative

ART. 23. Rules, not thus advantageously enforceable as between in-dividual and individual taken at large, may be thus enforceable, when

---

[a] Note that, to express what is here expressed by effective benevolence, the single word *benevolence* would not have sufficed: for, by benevolence alone, no contribution can be made to happiness: nor would *beneficence* alone, because beneficence may, to any extent, be exercised, without a particle of *benevolence:* by pecuniary expenditure it accordingly is thus exercised, and to an amount cor-responding to the quantum of such expenditure.

[b] More significant than *Ethics*, were it equally familiar would be another appellation of Greek origin, *Deontology*.[3]

---

[1] On the Procedure Code generally, see Ch. V, § 5, Art. 6n, p. 38n.

[2] See Ch. V, § 6, Art. 2n, p. 39n, and Table 2.

[3] 'Deontology' was of course the term Bentham eventually adopted as the title of his unfinished work on ethics, posthumously published in a version edited by Bowring in two volumes in 1834. The 'rules of deportment' referred to here form a major theme of that work. See also p. 400 and n. a.

applied to the conduct of persons, brought into a state of constant and inevitable contact with each other, by their particular correlative situations. The reason is—that, in this latter case, a *wrong*, which, as between persons capable of keeping themselves separate from each other, would be of little or no importance, may, by means of such constant and inevitable contact, be rendered an instrument of constant and intolerable annoyance.

### Instructional

ART. 24. Between the respective fields of these two sets of rules, the proper place of the line of demarcation depends, in no small degree, upon the state of the system of *judicial procedure*. The less the quantity of factitious delay, vexation, and expense, engendered by it, the less will, in this case, be the evil of the remedy which they are respectively calculated to administer, and the slighter the disease to which application may be made of it to advantage.

### Instructional

ART. 25. In the Procedure Code[1] belonging to this present Constitutional Code, evil in this shape is endeavoured to be minimized. In the codes of several nations, and in that of England in particular, the endeavour has been rather to maximize it, and has been but too extensively successful: expense has been maximized for the sake of the profit, official and professional, extractible out of it: delay and vexation increased for the maximization of the expense.

### Instructional

ART. 26. As for the rules of purely *self-regarding prudence*, *extra-regarding prudence*, and *positive effective benevolence*,—they belong not to the present occasion. As to the rules of *negative effective benevolence*,—many, which, under a system directed to the ends of justice, might be enforced with advantage,—and, in domestic procedure, with a success proportioned to the degree of appropriate aptitude, on the part of the domestic legislator and judge, actually are enforced with advantage,—must, under a procedure-system directed to ends opposite to those of justice, be left unenforced, and *wrong* in the several corresponding shapes left unopposed, and, by any force other than that of the *popular* or *moral* sanction, unrepressed.

### Instructional. Exemplificational

ART. 27. The distinction thus brought to view has not altogether

---

[1] See Ch. V, § 5, Art. 6n, p. 38n.

escaped the observation of the authors of the existing codes. The service of the two military subdepartments,——those, to wit, of the Army and Navy Ministers,——being that in which the contact between functionary and functionary is, in the highest degree, close and constant,——and moreover, the quantity of mischief liable to be produced to the *public service* by mutual and unredressed wrongs, greatest,—— endeavours, more or less successful, have, in the correspondent parts of the aggregate code, been directed to the repression of such comparatively petty wrongs, the repression of which was not, as it seemed, called for by any such necessity, in the case of any other subdepartment.

## Instructional

ART. 28. Take, for example, in English practice, an ordinance, to which, for the purpose in question, a place is given in a *Monarchically-established Code*, styled the *Articles of War*, which,——with the addition of the annually enactive *Parliamentarily-established Code*, styled the *Mutiny Act*,——constitutes the whole body of the *regulations*, by which the stipendiary functionaries belonging to the Army are governed.[1]

It is comprised——the whole of it——this same *Code of good manners*, in one article——Article 30th——of those same Articles: and is in these words——

'Whatsoever commissioned officer shall be convicted before a General Court-Martial, of behaving in a *scandalous infamous* manner, such as is *unbecoming* the character of *an officer* and a *gentleman*, shall be discharged from our service: Provided, however, that in every charge preferred against an officer for such scandalous or unbecoming behaviour, the *fact* or *facts* whereon the same is grounded shall be clearly specified.'[2]

## Instructional. Ratiocinative

ART. 29. In and by this exposition, such as it is, is plainly enough meant to be expressed, the substance of the above-mentioned *rules*

---

[1] Articles of War for the regulation of the armed forces were first issued as an act of royal prerogative. After the Revolution of 1688–9, however, the issuing of such articles was authorised by the annual Mutiny Act, which was the constitutional basis for the maintenance of a standing army in peacetime. But it was not until 1715 that the Mutiny Act mentioned the issuing of Articles of War in time of peace.

[2] According to E. Samuel, *An Historical Account of the British Army, and of the Law Military*, London, 1816, pp. 645-52, the passage Bentham quotes is Article 28 of Section XVI of the Articles of War.

*of deportment*, as applied to the class of functionaries therein mentioned. To the ordinary judicatories,—in their stationary situations,
and with their endlessly-protracted courses of procedure,—of no
such indeterminate and unparticularised rules could the enforcement
have been committed, with any sufficiently-grounded prospect of
preponderant advantage. To the extraordinary judicatory, to which,
as above, the enforcement of them is actually given, yes: for, as in
other countries, so even in England, whatsoever, if any, may have
been the imperfections in the organization of that extraordinary judicatory, to no ends other than those of justice can the procedure system attached to it ever have been directed. Never, like the system,
organized for and by the ordinary judicatories,—never has it been
directed to ends diametrically *opposite* to the ends of justice: maximization, to wit, of the wealth, power, and reputation of lawyers,
official and professional, at the expense, and by the sacrifice of the
comfort and security, of the rest of the community.

### Instructional

ART. 30. If, in the practice of these military Judges, instances of a
contravention of the rules of justice are ever produced, it is by favour
or disfavour, by hope or fear derived from distant sources: it is not
by masses of fees, the enormity of which, as in English non-military
judicature, rises in regular proportion to the enormity and constancy
of the habit of contravention, as applied to the very rules, the contravention of which the judges in question pretend to be endeavouring
to prevent.

### Instructional

ART. 31. Inadequate as is the above-exhibited skeleton, in the
character of a substitute to a *Code of good manners*, such as legislation, in its present less immature state, might be capable of providing,
—there seems little doubt of its having answered its purpose in practice with a considerable degree of efficiency. Of such a result the
smallness of the number of prosecutions that have ever occurred
under these same *Articles of War*, compared with the length of time,
and the number of the persons subject to them, affords no inconsiderable presumption. True it is—that, by the unwieldiness of the
judicatory in this case,—and, in particular, the difficulty of getting
together the required number of judges—the force of the presumption is somewhat lessened: but, in addition, comes the general propriety of the deportment, on the part of the functionaries of this

class, as compared with that of individuals of correspondent rank, taken at large.[1]

### Instructional. Ratiocinative

ART. 32. As to the two corresponding *Codes of good manners* here spoken of, neither of them can be inserted here. Reasons are as follows—

1. For any such minute details, the Constitutional Code is not, it should seem, the proper place.

2. Scarcely is the art-and-science sufficiently in advance for the exhibition of them.

3. To a more or less considerable extent, variations would be indicated, by the diversity of sentiments, manners, and customs, in different regions and communities.

4. As the public mind [matures] itself, the matter of *private*, will be removed into the field of political, *deontology*.[a][2]

### Instructional

ART. 33. Of the comparatively broad features, by which, to the purposes of *satisfaction* and *punishment*, at the hands of the *ordinary* judicature, delinquency, in its coarser and most prominent shapes, is characterised,—no adequate portrait—no adequate set of definitions—is as yet to be seen in the code of any nation: till these have been settled and delineated, as in the Penal[3] connected with the present Constitutional Code, they are endeavoured to be,—scarcely, in the minds of public men, will appropriate aptitude be sufficiently ripe, for the adequate performance of the still more delicate and difficult task, brought to view as above.

### Enactive. Instructional

ART. 34. CASE [II. Oppress*ee* a *functionary*. He can be none other than] a subordinate functionary; to wit, a subordinate, belonging to

---

[a] (*Deontology*) From the Greek—the branch of art-and-science, having for its subject-matter that which, on each occasion, is *proper* to be done.[4]

[1] W. Hough, *Precedents in Military Law: including the practice of Courts-Martial*, London, 1855, pp. 222–40, selects between the years 1803 and 1823 eighteen cases of general courts martial under the Article cited by Bentham.

[2] Bentham discusses political deontology at some length in MSS written in 1816. See UC xv. 3–80.

[3] See Ch. V, § 6, Art. 2n, p. 39n, and Table 2.

[4] See Art. 21 & n, p. 396.

the same subdepartment, and subject to the power exercised by the exercise of his [superordinate's] directive function.[1]

In this case, in respect of the need there will be for the subordinate to hold intercourse with the superordinate,—the relation of the situation of the subordinate to that of the superordinate, is, as per Art. 4, the same as that of a suitor to any functionary with whom he has business. Remedies, direct and indirect, will accordingly be the same.

### Enactive

ART. 35. So likewise, when the power, the abuse of which is alleged, is the power exercised by the exercise of the *directive* function.

### Enactive. Instructional

ART. 36. Remain, the remedies to the abuse of the power exercised by the exercise of the *dislocative* function.

1. *Directly* applying remedy in this case, right of complaint exercisible as per Articles [11] to [19]; but, as to satisfaction by *relocation*, the power, if exercised by a Judge ordinary, recommendatory only (as will be seen)—not *imperative*.

2. *Indirectly* applying, the same in this case as in *that;* but, in this case, with the addition of the preliminary fixation, of the authorities, by which alone the several modes of dislocation shall respectively be exercised.

### Enactive. Ratiocinative

ART. 37. For [the] purpose [of hearing the complaint],[2] exceptions excepted, the Judicatory employed will be that of the metropolis.

*Reason.* In that situation will naturally be found the best instructed section of the *Public Opinion Tribunal*, and thereby the most efficacious security against abuse.

### Instructional. Ratiocinative

ART. 38. But, for saving expense, vexation, and delay, or even [for] avoidance of partiality,[3] and thus misdecision or non-decision,—it may happen that a Judicatory, preponderantly preferable upon the whole, may be found in some other subdistrict. Consideration had of all circumstances, permanent and temporary,—to the Legislature it

---

[1] Case II follows the Case I of Article 9. For the amendments to Bentham's text which Bowring introduces here, see the 1830 Collation, p. 477.

[2] 1830, 'For this purpose': the Bowring emendation, followed here, clarifies the passage.

[3] 1830, 'or even avoidance of partiality': the Bowring insertion of 'for' seems required by the context.

will accordingly belong to determine, what if any exceptions to establish: and whether *actual*, by exercise of its own immediately applying authority, or *eventual* by the giving powers to that effect to the *Prime Minister* or the *Justice Minister*, or recommending the exercise of such powers to succeeding *Legislatures*.

### Enactive

ART. 39. For the formation of the decrees of such dislocation Judicatory, optional courses are the following—

1. Confirmation of the act of dislocation, simplified or modified.

2. Declared forbearance to exercise the *opinative* function.

For the distinction between the *opinative* and the *imperative* function in a judicial sense, see Ch. xii. JUDICIARY COLLECTIVELY, §9, *Judges' Elementary functions*.

3. Recommendation given to the disclocating functionary,—to substitute, to the mode of dislocation exercised, dislocation in some other mode, mentioning *what*.

### Ratiocinative

ART. 40. Uses of such recommendation are the following:

1. By the prospect of it, and the publicity attached to the procedure,—affording a security against ungrounded, and insufficiently grounded, and thence oppressive, dislocation.

2. Affording to the dislocatee the means of clearing his reputation from ungrounded imputations.

### Ratiocinative

ART. 41. The due exercise of the functions of a functionary would be liable to be much impeded, if so it happened that he were unable to give exercise to them without the instrumentality of a subordinate regarded by him as relatively unapt: and, by the apprehension of seeing himself laid under this difficulty by this or that subordinate of his, his operations might, to an indefinite degree, be obstructed.

### Enactive. Ratiocinative

ART. 42. But to no such recommendation is any obligatory effect attached.

*Reasons.* The inconvenient effects of which such attachment might be productive:—too obvious to need description, too various and numerous to admit of description here.

### Enactive. Ratiocinative

ART. 43. In every such case, to the Minister it will belong, either to give effect to such recommendations, as per Art. [39], or to adjust the matter by exercise given to the *transferential* function; that is to say, applied——either to the subordinate functionary, or to the superordinate, as the case may appear to require.

### Enactive

ART. 44. Simply *dislocated*, a functionary, of a grade *subordinate* to that of a Minister's, cannot be, by any person other than the Minister of his subdepartment, the Prime Minister, or the Legislature.

### Enactive

ART. 45. Nor *stopped* in the course of promotion.

### Enactive

ART. 46. Nor, without his consent, *transferred*, either *definitively* or *temporarily*, to an office, either of an inferior, or of the same, grade, or even of a superior grade.

### Enactive. Ratiocinative

ART. 47. *Suspended* a functionary may be, either by his *immediate* superordinate, or by his superordinate of any *superior* grade.

*Reasons*. 1. Responsibility of superordinates for subordinates, as per §25, *Securities*, &c.

2. Distance of the spot, on which, at the moment of supposed misconduct, the subordinate happens to be, in such sort that, unless the act of suspension could be exercised before there was time for its being exercised by the Minister, irreparable damage might ensue. See §19, *Subordinates*, Art[s]. 42, [43].[1]

### Enactive

ART. 48. Follows here [an][2] *indirectly* operative remedy. Exceptions excepted,——in no subdepartment is any act of dislocation, simple as above or modified, valid,——unless expressed in and by an appropriate written instrument. Name of the instrument——in case of *simple* dislocation, a *Dislocative*, or say *Dislocation instrument:* in each case of *modified* dislocation, the corresponding name.

### Enactive. Instructional

ART. 49. Exceptions excepted are——

[1] Bentham here seems to qualify his earlier statement in §19, Art. 42, by giving the power of suspension directly to superordinates. See p. 382.

[2] 1830, 'the'; the Bowring emendation to 'an' seems justified as there are other indirectly applying remedies and the one given here does not seem to refer exclusively to the preceding article.

1. The Army subdepartment, so far as concerns the situations belonging to the military branch of the service.

2. The Navy subdepartment, so far as concerns the situation[s] belonging to the military branch of the service.

In relation to these situations, separate arrangements are made, as per Ch. x. DEFENSIVE FORCE, §13, *Military Judicatories.*

*Enactive*

ART. 50. [I. Shape, *simple dislocation.*][1] *Dislocation instrument.* Among the heads, under which the matter of this instrument is entered, will be the following—

1. Time of the operation: designation made of it, by mention of the year, month, day of the month, day of the week.

2. Dislocatee, who: his names—personal and official.

3. Dislocator, who: his names—personal and official.

4. Supposed *justificative cause* of the dislocation: supposed justificative portion of the *law:* supposed justificative *facts*, with their application to the law.

5. *Evidence*, by which the existence of the supposed justificative matters of fact is supposed to have been ascertained: in general terms, brief indications of the *source* or *sources* from which the evidence was obtained:—*sources;* that is to say, *Evidence-holder or holders*, who: evidence *what*—*personal, real,* or *written*, furnished by each.

6. Time, as above, and down to the *minute,* from and after which it is intended that the dislocation shall be considered as having taken place.

7. *Shape*, in which the inaptitude, the existence of which has been regarded as a sufficient justificative cause for the dislocation, is regarded as having place:—a deficiency to wit, in respect of appropriate aptitude in one of its four shapes: that is to say *moral, cognitional, judicial, active:*—probity, knowledge, judgment, active talent.

*Enactive*

ART. 51. In case of deficiency in respect of appropriate cognitional, judicial, or active aptitude, instead of an act of simple *dislocation*, emanating from the *dislocating* functionary, may be employed an act of *resignation*, exercised by the dislocatee, with an act of *acceptance* thereto annexed by the *dislocator*, as attested by his signature; in this case, such *resignation* may be assigned as the sole cause of the

---

[1] The 1830 presentation of the series of topics which begins here is evidently confused, and the Bowring alterations, which serve to clarify matters, have been followed: see the 1830 Collation, p. 477, for details.

dislocation:——in case of deficiency in respect of appropriate *moral* aptitude, resignation will not be accepted; in this case the dislocation will be stated as having had the deficiency for its justifying cause.

### Ratiocinative

A R T. 52. *Reason.* By causes in great variety other than inaptitude in any shape,——resignation is alike capable of being produced. Examples are——

1. Ill health.
2. Better provision in some other shape.
3. Avoidance of separation from domestic or other social connections.
4. Disagreement with other persons, functionaries or non-functionaries, with whom the nature of the resigner's business unavoidably brings him into habitual or frequent contact.

### Enactive

A R T. 53. Added to the *Dislocation instrument*, but on a separate paper, will be the *Minutes of the record*, including the *Evidence*, constituting the ground of the decree, in execution of which the *Dislocation instrument* has been signed.

### Enactive

A R T. 54. [II]. Shape, *suspension:* heads for entries, as above. Examples——

1. Time of the operation, designated as per Art. 50.
2. Suspendee, who: as per Art. 50.
3. Suspender, who: as per Art. 50.
4. Justificative cause, as per Art. 50.
5. Evidence, as per Art. 50.
6. Time from which the suspension is to reckon, as per Art. 50.
7. Time, at which it is to cease, as per Art. 55, [when], in case of *renewal*,[1] the *instrument* of renewal will be delivered for the information of the *Suspendee*. This, upon the principle of the *Future-communication-securing arrangement:* as to which, see the Procedure Code.[2]

---

[1] 1830, 'Art. 55. in which, in case of such *renewal*,'; the Bowring emendation clarifies the passage.

[2] See Ch. X, 'Judicial Communication', especially § 6, in *Principles of Judicial Procedure* (Bowring, ii. 3-188), Bowring, ii. 52-7, especially p. 57. On the Procedure Code generally, see Ch. V, § 5, Art. 6n, p. 38n.

*Enactive. Ratiocinative*

ART. 55. Rules for the *Suspender*.

Rule 1. Take, for the duration of the suspension, the least time which affords any promise of being sufficient; reserving, and declaring yourself to have reserved, power of unlimitedly repeated renewal, yet so that no *subsequent* suspension shall be for a term longer than the *first*.

*Reason*. Preventing the *suspension* from having the effect of *dislocation*, or being continued for an inordinate length of time, by forgetfulness, indolence, or ill-will.

*Enactive*

ART. 56. Rule 2. On each such renewal, add the justificative cause: and whether it be the *original* justificative cause as per Art. 54, or some *fresh* cause. Particularize, in this last case, such fresh cause.

*Enactive*

ART. 57. By any of the causes following, the suspension will be terminated.

1. Failure of the renewal.
2. Failure of the mention of the justificative cause thereof.
3. Failure of sufficient *notification*, as per Art. 54.

*Enactive*

ART. 58. In the case of *suspension*, as in that of dislocation, added to the instrument will be an exemplar of the *record*.

*Instructional*

ART. 59. To warrant *dislocation*, the evidence will need to be *conclusive:* for *suspension, presumptive* or say *suspicion-inducing*, may suffice.

*Enactive*

ART. 60. [III]. Shape, *transference permanent*, to a grade *not* inferior. Heads for entry, *mutatis mutandis*, the same as in case of simple dislocation, as per Art. 50.

*Enactive*

ART. 61. [IV]. Shape, *transference temporary*, to a grade *not* inferior. Heads for entry, *mutatis mutandis*, the same as in case of *suspension*, as per Art. 54.

### Instructional

ART. 62. With or without *blame* on the part of the transferee,—transference, whether permanent or temporary, so it be to a not inferior grade, may have place. For examples, see the case of *resignation*, as per Art[s]. 51, 52. Note, that inaptitude with reference to this or that office, in this or that *situation*, may not have place with reference to a similar office in this or that *other* situation.

### Instructional

ART. 63. The case of a recent vacancy excepted,—transference of one functionary supposes simultaneous transference of another: nonexistence of detriment to the public service being supposed, such transference, may in this case, have for its justificative cause, *mutual convenience.*

### Enactive

ART. [64].[1] [V]. Shape, *transference permanent* to an *inferior* grade. Heads for entry, *mutatis mutandis*, the same as in case of dislocation, as per Art. [50].

### Enactive

ART. [65].[VI]. Shape, *transference temporary* to an *inferior* grade. Heads for entry, *mutatis mutandis*, the same as in the case of *suspension*, as per Art. [54]: so, arrangements, as per Art[s. 55, 56, 57].

### Instructional. Ratiocinative

ART. [66]. Note, that by a familiar and single-worded appellative—to wit, *degradation,*—*transference* to an *inferior* grade might have been designated. *Reason* for not employing it—Danger of a degree of *opprobrium*, more than sufficient for the occasion and the purpose. Of such opprobrium, one consequence might be—in name, *transference;* in effect, dislocation. By the necessity of passing his time in contact with persons, to whose knowledge his punishment had been characterized by this word,—uncomfortable, in such sort and degree might the situation of the intended transferee be thus rendered, that dislocation produced by resignation might, as a less evil, be embraced by him in preference. In this case, to the loss of the official situation in question would naturally be added the loss of all hope of being placed in any *other.*

[1] The sequence of article numbers in 1830 omits Art. 64 so that the remainder of the articles in the section are misnumbered.

*Instructional. Expositive*

ART. [67]. Cases in which, transference, if temporary,[1] though it be to an inferior grade, might be a not inapposite punishment: Examples—

1. Offence insubordination, by disrespectful deportment towards an immediate superordinate in the subordinate's subdepartment: object of the transference, satisfaction and punition for a course of contempt or disrespect persevered in.

2.——Or towards a functionary of a grade superior to his, in any *other* subdepartment or department.

*Enactive*

ART. [68]. [VII]. Shape, *stoppage of promotion*: stoppage *definitive*. Heads for entry, *mutatis mutandis*, the same as in case of dislocation, as per Art. [50]: so, arrangements, as per Art[s. 48, 49].

*Enactive*

ART. [69]. [VIII]. Shape, *stoppage of promotion:* stoppage *temporary*. Heads for entry, *mutatis mutandis*, the same as in case of suspension, as per Art. [54]: so, arrangements, as per Art[s. 55, 56, 57].

*Enactive*

ART. [70]. Special cases for *secrecy* excepted, the *publicity* given to the whole proceeding will be *maximized*, as in the case of ordinary Judicial procedure, as per Ch. xii. JUDICIARY COLLECTIVELY, §14, *Publicity*, &c.

*Enactive*

ART. [71]. Cases for secrecy. Example—

War, existing or supposed impending. To avoid furnishing information serviceable to hostile purposes, on the part of an enemy, or apprehended enemy,——the Special Judge or any superordinate of his may, in this case, locate a *Special Registrar*. Of the proceedings, entry will, in this case, be made in a *special* and *secret* Register, as per Ch. xii. §14, *Publicity*, &c.

*Enactive. Instructional*

ART. [72]. Power to the Special Judge Appellate to *invoke* the assistance of the ordinary Judge, or *transfer* to him the cognizance of the

---

[1] 1830, 'if not temporary': the Bowring emendation is necessary, as Bentham is referring to temporary transference.

cause, as per Art. [15]. Whether this power shall be given, the Legislature will consider and determine.

## Enactive

ART. [73]. Exceptions excepted, as per Art[s]. [74, 75, 76], in the several cases following, exemplars of the Record will be disposed of in manner following:

These cases are

1. Judicature, on complaint of oppression at large.

2. Judicature, for the purpose of warranting the exercise of dislocative power in any one of its shapes.

Judicature, on *appeal*, against an exercise of *transferential* or say *locomutative* power.

Modes of disposal will be the following—

1. Kept in the office of the Special Judge, one.

2. Delivered to each of the parties, one.

3. Transmitted to the office of every functionary, if any, superordinate to the Special Judge, one.

## Enactive

ART. [74]. In the case of *suspension*, unless it be at the instance of *suspender* or *suspendee*, *exemplars* of the *suspension instrument*, or of the record, will not be transmitted to any other office.

## Enactive

ART. [75]. So, in the case of simple *transference* to an office, not inferior:—transference whether definitive or temporary.

## Enactive

ART. [76]. So, in the case of *stoppage* of promotion.

## Instructional

ART. [77]. In the application made of the matter of this and the last preceding Section, the Legislature will have due regard to the circumstances following—

1. Extent of the whole territory of the state.

2. Distance of the seats of the several offices from the metropolis.

3. Facility or difficulty of communication.

4. Smallness or magnitude of the number of grades of subordination in the several subdepartments respectively considered.

## SECTION 22

### EXTORTION OBVIATED

*Expositive*

ART. 1. By *extortion* understand, on the present occasion, extortion, committed at the charge of any person whatsoever, non-functionary or functionary, by a functionary belonging to the *Administration* department, by means of the power attached to the official situation occupied by him, whatsoever it may be.

*Expositive*

ART. 2. If, by oppression or fear thereof, in any one of the four cases, as per §21, above exemplified, profit to himself or any other person is obtained by a functionary at the charge of any other person whatsoever,—*predatory oppression*, or in one word *extortion*, is thereby committed.

*Expositive*

ART. 3. By *oppression* at the charge of one person, *extortion* at the charge of another is capable of being committed: as where, to save any person from ulterior oppression, another gives money or renders service in any other shape, to the supposed eventual oppressor, or to any other person on his account.

*Instructional. Enactive*

ART. 4. For the remedies, applicable, in the *direct* and *general* way to the prevention of *extortion*, see the title thus denominated in the *Penal Code*:[1] for those applicable in a *less direct*, and to a certain degree *peculiar* way, see §21 of this present chapter.

*Instructional*

ART. 5. Of extortion and fraudulent obtainment combined, an example, as striking perhaps as any that history ever did, or human nature ever could afford, may be seen in English Judicature.

*Exemplificational*

ART. 6. By a species of subordinate Judges, styled *Masters in Chancery*, acting under the Lord Chancellor, sole Judge of the highest single-seated judicatory, suitors are constantly compelled to pay

---

[1] Extortion appears in the Table of Contents of the Penal Code in Pt. II, Ch. III, §11. See Table 2. On the Penal Code generally, see Ch. V, §6, Art. 2n, p. 39n.

money, and to a prodigious amount in the whole, to the said Master[s],
for attendance alleged by them to have been bestowed by them, and
known not to have been so bestowed: at the same time, to a still
greater amount, to the *Solicitors* (a class so called of professional
assistants) of the parties on both sides, for *attendances* alleged to
have been, at those same times, bestowed by these same Solicitors:
and, in this case likewise, known not to have been bestowed by any
one of them, by or for whom payment is compelled for their so men-
daciously pretended services. In this way it is, that, in the constant
and full view of the English public, *fraudulent obtainment* is combined with, and aggravated by, *extortion:* justice being to a certainty
denied to all who should refuse, or be unable, to comply with the
demand: the victim not having, in any case, any possible means of
escape. Of criminality in this double shape, the profit goes into the
pockets—in the first place of these subordinate *Judges*, and of their
thus protected and even compelled accomplices, the *Solicitors:* in
the next place, into that of the Lord Chancellor, by whom, for the
extraction of profit from this and other sources in such disastrous
abundance, a relative, or any other dependent or connection of his,
is, on each occasion, located at pleasure: all this, without so much
as the pretence of application made of any test of appropriate aptitude, other than the pretended judgment of the patron, to whom,
were it only by want of time, the actual exercise [of]¹ it would be
rendered physically impossible.

This enormity is matter of perfect notoriety, and out of all dispute. It has not only been denounced over and over again in various
publications, but, though without any the least token of disapprobation, has, of necessity, been exposed to view in the pages of a Report,
communicated to the House of Commons, by a commission, composed of men appointed by the present Lord Chancellor to sit in
judgment on the system of Procedure of which this practice forms
a part, and on his conduct in the direction of it.

Were it possible that prosecution should ensue,—the defence,
(for no other imaginable defence could there be,) would consist
in the extent, long continuance, and constancy of the practice. The
practice of poaching, and that of smuggling, though neither of
them so deeply stained with immorality, are both of them still
more extensive, inveterate, and constant: but, among their accomplices, neither have the Poachers, nor the Smugglers, men sitting in
Parliament, to secure to them the continuance of the profit,—to
secure them for ever against punishment, and as long as possible from

¹ 1830 and Bowring, 'by'; but 'of' seems to be required, since it is to the
exercise of judgment that Bentham is referring.

411

reproach and ignominy; of ignominy at the hands of all men to whom justice is not an object of either hatred or indifference.[1]

## SECTION 23

### PECULATION OBVIATED

#### *Expositive*

ART. 1. Peculation is where, in an indirect way—a *Trustee* obtains, for himself or another, undue profit, in a pecuniary or quasi-pecuniary shape, at the charge of an *intended Benefitee:* producing thereby *loss*, pecuniary or quasi-pecuniary, or *sufferance* in some other shape, in manner or quantity not intended by the law, by, or in virtue of which, the *trust* was created.

#### *Expositive*

ART. 2. The *trust* thus *violated* may be either *private* or *political: political*, it may be either *public* or *semi-public*. On the present occasion, trust in both these its *branches* is the object in question: *public*, in so far as the loss, being pecuniary or quasi-pecuniary, falls upon the public at large: *semi-public*, in so far as it falls upon the population of this or that particular class or district.

#### *Expositive*

ART. 3. Of the *mode[s]*, in which, by a *person at large*, undue profit may, in a direct and criminal way, be made at the charge of another, examples are as follows:
 1. Theft.
 2. Fraudulent obtainment.
 3. Extortion.
 4. Robbery.

#### *Expositive*

ART. 4. That which would be called *theft* if committed at the charge of a person at large, is called *embezzlement*, when committed by a *trustee*, at the charge of an *intended benefitee*.

#### *Expositive*

ART. 5. For the *direct* remedies against peculation, see the Penal Code, title *Peculation*:[2] for *indirect*, the measures of security brought

---

[1] See p. 110 n. 1.
[2] Peculation appears in the Table of Contents of the Penal Code in Pt. II, Ch. III, § 12. See Table 2. On the Penal Code generally, see Ch. V, § 6, Art. 2n, p. 39n.

to view in §7, *Statistic function*, [Bis-section 4], *Loss-Books*. See also what follows.

### Enactive

ART. 6. Whatsoever articles come to be *procured* for the public service, by exercise given by a Minister, or by any subordinate of his, to the *procurative function*,—if the person of whom they are procured be, by consanguinity, affinity, patronship on the one part, and aspirancy on the other, immediately or interventionally connected with such Minister,—the Minister will, in the instrument of contract, cause declaration of such connection to be attached to the other contracting party's name.

### Enactive

ART. 7. Moreover, with respect to any supposed but not generally-known tie of connection,—any person may, in any public print,—leaving with the printer, his name and abode, in such manner as that communication may be sure to reach him, as per Procedure Code,[1] —address to the Minister any question tending to impute partiality on that account: and, to all such questions, the Minister will either make such answers as to him shall seem meet, or else abide all such inferences as may come to be drawn from silence.

### Ratiocinative

ART. 8. So it be but avowed,—from no such connection can any adequate reason be deduced for inhibiting any such contract, or imputing improbity as of course, in respect thereof, to the functionary, or such his relative, as per Art. 6. The person, of whom it can be obtained best and cheapest, is the person, of whom, in every case, the article ought to be procured: and, if between one dealer and another, there is not, in these respects, any difference,—[of] which of them the article is procured, is to the public, and ought to be to the government, a matter of indifference.

### Ratiocinative

ART. 9. So it be but avowed and publicly known,—so far from being conducive to peculation, a connection of this sort would rather be a security against it: for, by this means, the public eye which, in the case of a person not supposed to be thus connected, might remain closed upon the transaction, would naturally be wide opened to it.

[1] See the *Principles of Judicial Procedure* (Bowring, ii. 3-188), Ch. VIII, § 13, 'Applicant's accessibility secured, how', Bowring, ii. 43-4. On the Procedure Code generally, see Ch. V, § 5, Art. 6n, p. 38n.

*Ratiocinative*

ART. 10. Under these circumstances,—if a participation, in any such contract as that in question, ought to be interdicted, even to the Minister himself,—the proper ground for the interdiction would be —not the danger of *peculation*, but the draught, which a private business of this sort would naturally, if not necessarily, be making upon him, for that *time* and *attention*, of which, by acceptance of the office, he has engaged to transfer to the public service the whole benefit.

*Ratiocinative*

ART. 11. By any endeavour, pretended or real, to apply a remedy in any other shape, to this always impending disorder,—the disorder would not be lessened but increased. That which a Minister would naturally fear to do with his own hand, no cause can he have for fearing thus to do by another hand. For all such purposes, relative situations are sufficient: no concert being necessary; by no evidence need he expose himself to be reached. In that situation, as in every other, —without the most flagrant and mischievous injustice, for no misdeed in which he had not been proved to have participated, could any man be punished: for, by punishment in any such case, the sense of security would, in the breast of every person who knew of it, be weakened, if not destroyed: in the fate of any man so punished, any other man would be apt to read his own.

*Ratiocinative*

ART. 12. On the other hand, against no such disclosure as is here required, can any person feel reluctance, unless it be his wish and desire, upon favourable occasion, to do or see done the very thing— to be guilty or see others guilty of the very crime—which it is the purpose of the disclosure to prevent: and the more ardent the desire, the more intense will, of course, be the reluctance. Functionary! this desire—is it not yours? Then what is it you can suffer by any difficulty opposed to the gratification of it? 'But the imputation.' . . . Yes, if it were to you alone, but it is to the whole species, without exception, that it applies itself. Say you—'I am *not* as other men are?'[1] Well then—if not, it is—not because you are better than they, but because you are so much worse. If, in your case, suspicion is not necessary—necessary in exactly the *same* degree as in that of the generality of men—it is because it is so in a *greater* degree. This

---

[1] Luke 18: 11.

is what, by this very claim of yours—this claim of exemption and
privilege—you have proved. It is the very claim, which every malefactor, if he saw any chance of its being granted, would be sure to
make: and, the more incontestably as well as the more atrociously he
were guilty, the more anxious would he be to obtain it. Your wealth
—your factitious dignity—your political power—your power in all
shapes—is it on these that this claim of yours grounds itself? Rightly
understood, all these are but so many *bars* to it. All these are so
many instruments of possible delinquency in all these shapes:—of
delinquency, in the case of every man, possible; in the case of every
man, more or less, probable. Thus, from beginning to end, saith the
Penal Code.[1] Yes: so says it every where: for if any where there be
a *person* exempt from suspicion as being incapable of delinquency,
—it is because he is—not man, but God upon earth: which being
granted, that which in a man would be *wrong*, is in this God *exercise
of right*. To abuse power is, upon occasion, the wish of every man:
the greater the power, the greater the facility he has for giving effect
to that wish, and therefore, the *more*, not the *less*, needful, is this
and every other bar and check that can be opposed to it. The greater
the power, the stronger indeed is the ground . . . the ground? but for
what? for suspicion and precaution surely: for any thing rather than
confidence. Are you sincere and honest? You will now give up this
exclusive claim of yours: you will submit, with resignation, to the
common lot. Are you insincere and crafty? Your mask is now off,
and will no longer serve your purpose.

### Instructional

ART. 13. As to *situations of mere trust*, in which the business consists in the receipt and disbursement of money,—by the following
rules, unless for special and preponderant reason to the contrary, will
the conduct of the Legislature be guided—

1. In the case of each such situation, *minimize* the quantity of
*money*, placed at the disposal of the occupant.

2. Minimize the *time* during which it is left at his disposal.

3. As a condition precedent to his location,—require *security* for
the eventual forthcomingness of a sum, as near as may be to equality,
with the maximum of the money so placed at his disposal.

4. Such security may be composed—partly of property of his
own, remaining at his own disposal, partly of property belonging to
persons, consenting to become *bondsmen:* bound, in case of deficiency, to provide, to an extent, in each case limited, for the filling

---

[1] See Ch. V, § 6, Art. 2n, p. 39n, and Table 2.

it up: or it may be given—partly in the one shape, partly in the other.

5. To the fact of his receipt of the money in each instance, give *recordation*,—together with whatever degree of *publicity* the regard due to frugality admits of.

6. So, to the *time* and *place* of its being transferred into his hands: with a sufficient description of the *person*, by whom it was so placed, and of the *cause* and *purpose* of such transfer.

7. So, on its passing out of his hands,—to the time, cause, and purpose, of such its subsequent transfer.

### Instructional

ART. 14. For the exclusion of sinister profit by public loss,—a consideration that will be kept in mind, is—that *money's worth*—in all its several shapes, immoveable and moveable—is more exposed to be made an instrument of such loss, than *money* itself is: that, accordingly, generally speaking, in the exercise of the *procurative, reparative, eliminative,* and *venditive* functions,—in relation to land, edifices, vessels, or goods,—more facility is afforded for such malpractice, than in the exercise of the *receptive, custoditive,* and *transmissive* functions, in relation to *money:* in a word, that *peculation* is attended with less difficulty and danger than *embezzlement:* on this, as on other occasions, proportioned to the demand, will be the Legislator's vigilance.

### Instructional

ART. 15. Of the ways in which such sinister profit may be made by a *peculator,*—examples are as follows:

1. Purchasing from a confederate or favourite, he gives over value.

2. Selling to a confederate or favourite, he accepts under value.

3. In case of competition between vender and vender, he over-rates the quality of the goods tendered by a confederate; he under-rates the quality of those tendered by a rival dealer.

4. In case of competition between purchaser and purchaser, he assorts the articles, in a manner suitable to the demand of the confederate or favourite, unsuitable to the demand of the competitor.

### Instructional

ART. 16. By the united powers, of recordation, publication, and unrestricted interrogability, as per Art[s]. 6, 7,—an effectual bar may, in every instance, be opposed, to breach of trust in both those forms:[1]

[1] It is not clear what Bentham means by 'both these forms': he may be referring to peculation and embezzlement. See the end of Art. 14.

improbability of accomplishment, and probability of detection, will concur in excluding the attempt.

## SECTION 24

### LEGISLATION-REGARDING FUNCTIONS

#### *Enactive. Expositive*

ART. 1. Exercisible, in an appropriate seat, in the assembly of the Legislature, by himself or a Depute permanent,——to every Minister, subject to the orders of the Legislature, belong the functions following——

1. *Argumentative* function: exercised by taking part in a debate on the same footing as a member.

2. *Initiative* function: exercised by making a *proposition*, or say *motion*, in relation to any subject, in any shape.

3. *Responsive* function: exercised by answers given to all questions put to him by members, or fellow-ministers, as above, with the permission of the assembly.

#### *Enactive. Expositive*

ART. 2. But, by no Minister, even though it be with the consent of the Assembly, can the *votative* function be exercised: the function exercised by the delivery of a vote.

#### *Enactive*

ART. 3. By himself or Depute permanent, every Minister is bound to attend throughout the sitting of the Assembly: to wit, in readiness to answer questions, as per Art. 1.

#### *Enactive*

ART. 4. To the several Ministers as well as to Members, apply the several provisions in Ch. vi. [LEGISLATURE], §29, *Members' motions:* as also the provision made in Ch. xi. MINISTERS SEVERALLY, §2, *Legislation Minister*, for giving to the *Pannomion*,——through whatsoever channel the several portions of it may, from time to time, come to be introduced,——the benefit of the official experience, and consequent appropriate aptitude, in the department in question endeavoured to be secured: whether it be the Legislative immediately, or the Legislative with the intervention of the Judiciary authorities, as per next Article.

417

*Enactive*

ART. 5. In Ch. xii. JUDICIARY COLLECTIVELY, §19, *Judge's contested-interpretation-reporting function*, §20, *Judge's eventually emendative function*, and §21, *Judge's sistitive*, or say *execution-staying function*, will be seen the provision made, for preserving the rule of action against deterioration; and, in the *melioration-suggestive function* allotted to all functionaries, may be seen the provision made for securing the *Pannomion* against deterioration from that source, and the continual melioration thereof from that same source. *Mutatis mutandis*, to the situations of the several Ministers in their several subdepartments, apply the several provisions therein contained: except that the several reports will be transmitted through the office—not of the Justice Minister, but of the Prime Minister.

*Enactive*

ART. 6. To every administrative situation *subordinate* to that of Minister,—belongs the *contested interpretation-reporting* function, as well as the *melioration-suggestive*.

*Enactive*

ART. 7. To the Legislature it will belong to consider and determine, —to what situations, if any, shall be allotted, and through what channels, as above, shall be exercisible,—the *preinterpretative* function, as per Ch. xii. §22, with reference to that portion of the matter of the *Pannomion* which applies to their several offices.

*Enactive. Instructional*

ART. 8. So likewise, to what situations, if any, the *sistitive* or *execution-staying function*, shall belong.

*Instructional*

ART. 9. In so doing, regard will, in each case, be had—on the one. hand, to the quality and quantity of the irreparable evil liable to have place, for want of the exercise of this function; on the other hand, from the exercise of it: and, in both cases, to the degree of probability of the result: to the end that thus, on every occasion, evil may, in every shape, be minimized.

## SECTION 25

### SECURITIES FOR APPROPRIATE APTITUDE

*Instructional*

ART. 1. *Securities for appropriate aptitude*. Under this head, subject-matters for consideration are the following:[a]

1. *Elements* or *branches* of appropriate aptitude, the existence of which, on the part of the functionaries in question, as on other occasions so on this, is endeavoured to be secured: Here, as elsewhere, *moral, intellectual*, and *active:* intellectual, including *cognitional* and *judicial*——knowledge and judgment.

2. *Motives*, the operation of which, as on other occasions so on this, trusted to, for the giving effect to the securities here provided: Desire of pleasure in all shapes, desire of exemption from pain in all shapes. For the several pleasures and pains, considered as objects of desire or aversion,——and thence as *motives*, creative of correspondent *interests*,——and as constitutive of the only sort of matter of which motives can be composed,——see *Springs of Action Table*.[1]

3. *Sanctions*, or say *sources*, from which the motives here employed take their rise: the popular or *moral*, and the *legal:* to the popular, or say *moral* sanction, execution and effect being given by the *Public Opinion Tribunal:* to the *legal* sanction, by the *legal* tribunals: to wit, the several judicatories, whose operation applies to functionaries as

---

[a] This analytic sketch should, by right, have been exhibited at an earlier point of time: that is to say, in Ch. vi. LEGISLATURE, §31, *Securities*, &c. But the conception of the draughtsman had not, at that point of time, received the correspondent degree of extent and maturation.

In a work of this kind, to no person assuredly can it be matter of surprise——if new, and it is hoped, more correct views, and consequent demands for amendment, should, from time to time, be seen presenting themselves. In the composition of the present work it has happened in some instances that the time, at which the demand has presented itself, has been when the part in question of the work has been still unprinted, and, by that means, in a condition susceptible of correction; to wit, in the mode, designated in Ch. vi. [LEGISLATURE], §29, *Members' motions*, Art[s]. 5, 6, by the appellation of the *reeditive*. But, in the present instance, besides the expense of time that might be necessitated by the operation of working up the matter anew,——the references antecedently made to articles destined for the section thus amended, would have been misnumbered. Thence it is, that in and for this section, as well as §16 and §17, the *corrective*, or say *directive* mode,——the mode employed by the insertion of added matter, is here employed in preference to the *reeditive*.[2]

---

[1] See p. 122 n. a.

[2] For the application of these principles to §§16 and 17 and the Supplements, see the note to §16, Supplement, p. 329.

well as non-functionaries, and the several administrational and *virtually* judicial tribunals,[1] whose operations, performed through the medium of the several powers locative and dislocative, is mostly confined to functionaries and locables looking to become functionaries.

4. *Persons*, to whose conduct, as on other occasions so on this, for the purpose of securing, on their parts, the existence of the elements of aptitude, or say the *qualifications*, here in question:——on *former* occasions, the members of the legislative body, and the Prime Minister: on the present occasion, the several Ministers, and their several subordinates.

5. *Persons*, by whose agency, as on other occasions so on this, the power of the above-named several *sanctions*, is applied to the production of the *effect* looked to from these several *securities:*——persons at large, members of the political community, together with those of all other communities, considered as members of the Public Opinion Tribunal; and the several superordinate functionaries, belonging to the several *legal tribunals*, judical and administrational, just mentioned.

6. *Purposes*, to which, as designated by their most extensive and comprehensive denominations——that is to say, *maleficent* modes of conduct, in the *prevention* of which, as on other occasions so on this, the operation of the securities here provided, and the aptitude here endeavoured to be ensured, are endeavoured to be employed:—— 1, *misuse* of the official powers in question—2, *nonuse* of those same powers, in cases where the declared end in view of the institution requires that *use*, and thereby *right and proper use* of them should be made.

7. Relative point of *time*, at or during which, as on other occasions so on this, the operation of the several efficient causes of security has place:——1, *antecedential*, 2, *concomitant*, 3, *consequential;* relation had to the exercise given by the several functionaries to their several functions, in their several official situations. As to this, see in particular Ch. xii. JUDICIARY COLLECTIVELY, §32, *Securities*, &c.

### Instructional

ART. 2. To the Legislature it will belong, on survey made of the several securities provided in the case of the situation of Member of the Legislature, as per Ch. vi. §31, and that of Prime Minister, as per Ch. viii. §12, *Securities*, &c., Art. 1,——to consider——whether any

---

[1] 1830 and Bowring, 'and by the several administrational . . .'; but the word 'by' implies that there is another category in addition to the legal tribunals. Bentham, however, in paragraph 5 of this article, considers judicial and administrational tribunals as two parts of the larger category of legal tribunals. See also Art. 32, p. 428.

of them, and which, are, with promise of benefit, applicable to the situation of Minister.

## Instructional

ART. 3. Apply, of course, the securities following—

1. Registration system.
2. Publication system.
3. Dislocability, by the Legislature.
4. Dislocability, by the constitutive authority.
5. Responsibility, for insufficiency in the exercise of the several functions—*informative, indicative,* and *initiative:* as per Ch. viii. §3, *Relation to the Legislature,* Art[s]. 3, 4, 5, 6.
6. Dislocability, for acceptance of any other office.
7. Dislocability, for acceptance of any office, gift, or factitious honour or dignity, at the hands of any foreign government.
8. Obligation to keep in exercise a Depute or Deputes, coupled with responsibility for their aptitude.
9. Responsibility for the aptitude of their immediate subordinates respectively, as per Art[s. 26 to 29], of this section.
10. Securities afforded by §16, *Locable who:* in particular, that afforded by the examinations undergone in the Qualification Judicatory, Art[s]. 17 to [41].
11. Securities afforded by §17, *Located how:* in particular, the provision for minimization of expense, by means of the pecuniary competition, as per Art[s]. 1 to 13.
12. Subjection to the authority of the Public Opinion Tribunal, as exercised by the exercise given to its functions statistic, censorial, and melioration-suggestive.

## Instructional

ART. 4. *Instruments* of Security already brought to view, and on that account needing but to be referred to, are the following:

I. *Character Index:*—a species of document, affording, in relation to a functionary belonging to the department in question,—information serving to convey a conception of his habitual condition in respect of appropriate aptitude in its several branches; and his conduct on particular and individual occasions.

To both purposes taken together will serve—the entries made in the several books denominated PERSONAL STOCK BOOK, as per §7, *Statistic function,* Bissection 2, Art. 1, p. 226; INDIVIDUAL SERVICE BOOK, Bissection 3, Art[s]. 8 to 13, pp. 240, 242; and LOSS BOOK, Bissection 4, Art[s]. 4, 5, p. 251.

*Instructional*

A R T. 5. II. *Official Merit Register*, or say *Extraordinary Service Register* or *Public Merit Register*: a document—serving to convey, in relation to this or that functionary, a conception of his conduct, on this or that individual occasion, on which, in effect or tendency, it has been, in this or that extraordinary mode or degree, beneficial to the service of the public, and in that respect laudable. As to this, see § 15, *Remuneration*, Art[s]. 18 to 29, pages 301-2.

*Enactive*

A R T. 6. Additional securities, on this present occasion instituted, are the following—

III. *Demerit Register*. At the end of each edition after the first, will be inserted an Appendix, intituled the *Delinquent List, Convicted List, Transgression List, Official Delinquency Calendar*, or *Official Demerit Register*.

*Enactive*

A R T. 7. Heads, under which the appropriate matter will be inserted are the following—

1. Offence or say *delinquency*, or *transgression*—its denomination —generic and specific: with the characteristic individualizing circumstances extracted from the Record.

2. Judicatory in which convicted and sentenced.

3. Offender—or say, delinquent, or transgressor, styled on this occasion the *malemeritant*—his name at length.

4. Year, month and day of the month of the conviction and sentence.

5. Judicial Register, in which the record of the proceeding may be seen.

6. Added to these heads will be those published in connection with his name in the last preceding Office Calendar, as to which, see § 16, *Locable who*.

*Enactive*

A R T. 8. In the Office Calendar of each succeeding year, will be inserted the Convicted Lists of the several preceding years.

*Instructional*

A R T. 9. Should the accumulated matter of this list ever swell to an inconvenient bulk, the Legislature will ordain the closing of the series, and the commencement of a new series: of the several preceding series thus eliminated, to the entire matter will thenceforward be substituted an *abstract*.

### Enactive

ART. 10. IV. *Deportment Rules*. In the *Audience Chamber* or say *Business Chamber*, of every functionary, of whatever grade,—kept constantly hung up, in a conspicuous place and characters, will be two correspondent *Tables*: the matter being on one side only of the page; the whole presenting itself thus to the eye at the same time.

### Enactive

ART. 11. Table I. *Functionary's Deportment Rules*. At the head of it will be inserted, in relation to the functionary for the time being, the several heads mentioned in Article 4, as above.

Thereupon will follow the existing regulations for the direction of the conduct of functionaries in that situation: as to which, see §21, *Oppression obviated*, Art. 20. Among them will be rules, recommending attention and kind deportment towards all visitors; those especially, whose particular business brings them to the Official Chamber.

### Enactive

ART. 12. Table II. *Visitor's Deportment Rules*. Herein will be inserted all regulations for the direction of the conduct of persons at large, attendant at the office; whether in quality of *suitors* having business of their own to transact with the functionary, or as Inspectors, in their quality of members of the *Public Opinion Tribunal*, to keep watch over his conduct, exercising the *inspective function* with relation to it; and on their part correspondent kindness will herein also be recommended. As to these rules, see §20, *Insubordination obviated:* Art[s]. 16 to 19.

### Enactive. Expositive

ART. 13. *Extra Despatch*. Exceptions excepted,—for *extra despatch*, gift and acceptance of remuneration, in any shape, is *corruption:* gift, corruption active—*corruptingness*: acceptance, corruption passive—*corruptedness:* for, though on that *one* occasion it is a premium for despatch, it operates as a premium on delay on all others. Thus is business made to stagnate,—that, first for extraordinary, then for no more than ordinary despatch, habitual remuneration may be necessitated. By *extra-despatch* understand employment of a quantity of the functionary's time over and above that during which, by his agreement, he stands bound to occupy himself in the service for which he is engaged.

*Enactive*

ART. 14. Ulterior Securities now for the first time proposed for institution, are the following—

I. Security, against extortion and factitious delay, by inhibition of remuneration for extra despatch.

*Enactive*

ART. 15. Exception is—where, in a case of urgency, the minister, at the head of the subdepartment, by a written instrument, styled a *remuneration draught*, as per Art[s]. [18 to 24], makes application in favour of the *benemeritant* to the Finance Minister, recommending the grant of the remuneration desired to be bestowed.

*Enactive*

ART. 16. But, in every such case, the fact of the extra despatch must have been established by *quasi-judicial* assertion, and appropriate recordation and publicity, as per Ch. xii. JUDICIARY COLLECTIVELY, §14, *Publicity*, &c.

*Expositive*

ART. 17. II. By *Quasi-judicial* assertion, understand assertion, the verity of which is sanctioned by the same responsibility as that which has place in the case of testimony delivered before a Judge. See *Procedure Code*, title *Evidence:*[1] mean time, see above, Ch. vi. LEGISLATURE, §27, *Legislation Enquiry Judicatory*, Art[s]. 50, 51, 52.[2]

*Enactive. Expositive*

ART. 18. III. By appropriate recordation, understand, in this case, entry in a book styled the *Extra Despatch Book*. Follow the heads under which the matter will be entered.

1. Nature of the business on the occasion of which the extra service was rendered.

2. Person by whom rendered.

3. Whether of his own motion, or at whose instance rendered.

4. Year, month, and day or days on which it was rendered.

5. Number of extra hours of service in which it consisted.

[1] On evidence generally, see Ch. XI of the *Principles of Judicial Procedure* (Bowring, ii. 3–188), Bowring, ii. 57–62. On the Procedure Code, see Ch. V, § 5, Art. 6n, p. 38n.

[2] Bentham's cross-reference to § 27, Arts. 50, 51, 52 deals solely with the elicitation of evidence in the House of Commons and House of Lords. A more general reference to the discussion of evidence and evidence elicitation in § 27 would have been more appropriate.

*Enactive*

ART. 19. At the bottom of every such *Remuneration Draught*, as per Art. [15], will be, a transcript of the above-mentioned correspondent entry in the *Extra Despatch Book*.

*Enactive*

ART. 20. Of every such *Remuneration Draught*, exemplars will be disposed of as follows:

1. Transmitted, to the Finance Minister's office, one.

2. Transmitted, to every office superordinate to that from which the Draught was issued, ending with the Prime Minister's inclusive, one.

3. Delivered, to the *benemeritant* to be, by him or any Agent or Representative of his, exhibited to the Finance Minister, one.

4. Kept, by the functionary by whom the draught was drawn, one.

*Enactive*

ART. 21. On the face of the Draught, immediately on its being presented, the Finance Minister will, by his signature, acknowledge the receipt of it.

*Enactive*

ART. 22. The drawer of the draught will, in the tenor of it, have mentioned some day, on or before which it may, in his judgment, be paid without detriment to the service. If, on or before such day, it be not paid,——the Finance Minister will, on that day, transmit to the office from whence it issued, a *non-payment excuse:* if no such excuse has thus been transmitted, or if of an excuse so transmitted the sufficiency is denied, the *benemeritant* may transmit to the Prime Minister an instrument styled a *non-payment complaint*, giving thereto such publicity as he deems expedient.

*Enactive. Instructional*

ART. 23. To the whole of this, as of every other transaction belonging to the business of the Administrative department, constant *publicity* will be given: that is to say, by all such means, whereby it can be given, without preponderant evil in the shape of hindrance to the business, or burthen in the shape of expense: and, in particular, by means of general facility of *access* to the *Register Book*, for the purpose of the lective, inspective, commentative and melioration-suggestive functions; as to which, see §4, *Functions in all*, and Ch. xii. §9, *Judges' Elementary Functions*.

## Instructional

ART. 24. To the cases, if any, in which,—for example with a view
to war, actual or apprehended,—publicity, given to the fact of the
extra dispatch, might occasionally be in a preponderant degree detrimental to the public service,—the Legislature will have regard, and
provide accordingly: namely, as per Ch. xii. JUDICIARY COLLEC-
TIVELY, §14, *Publicity*, &c.,—by *secrecy*, so it be not *closer* nor
*longer* than the necessity of the case requires.

## Instructional

ART. 25. To extra *service*, rendered by any other means than that of
*extra despatch*, as per Art. 13, the provisions of this section do not
apply.

## Enactive. Ratiocinative

ART. 26. IV. *Responsibility for subordinates.* By acceptance,—with
power *self-suppletive*, and power *suppletive, locative, dislocative* and
*suspensive*, in relation to his subordinates,—a Minister undertakes
for the apt and complete performance of the business belonging to
his office: and this, not only on his own part, but also on the part of
such his several subordinates. Were he not responsible for their mis-
doings,—he might, to his own sinister profit, by their hands, screening them by his own power, do evil in any shape, and to any amount.

## Enactive

ART. 27. Responsible accordingly he is, for all such detriment as, in
any assignable form, shall have accrued to the public service, through
deficiency, in any assignable shape, in respect of appropriate aptitude in any assignable shape, on the part of any subordinate in his
subdepartment, to wit, in so far as, by any vigilance on his part, any
such deficiency might have been prevented from having place.

## Enactive. Expositive

ART. 28. Of cases, in which a presumption of culpable deficiency in
respect of such vigilance, may justly have place, examples are as follows—

1. If, on the part of this or that culpable subordinate, any such deficiency in appropriate aptitude has been judicially proved, or is
become generally known or suspected.

2. If, after apt information received of such deficiency, the superordinate has omitted to take timely arrangements for preventing
the recurrence of the like in future: viz. by dislocation, suspension

performed, or judicial examination instituted, and with as much despatch as is consistent with justice, carried on; or by simple admonition, in a case in which there is reason to expect that such admonition will prove sufficient.

3. If, antecedently to, or without such information,—timely arrangements, such as ordinary prudence would suggest, had not been taken by him.

### Instructional

ART. 29. By any such want of vigilance on the part of the superordinate,—apt ground may be afforded to the *Public Opinion Tribunal*, for inquiry into the cause thereof, through the medium of the *periodical press* or otherwise:—whether, for example, in consideration of the location or the continuance of the subordinate in his office, service in some shape, pecuniary or miscellaneous, at the hands of the subordinate or some *connection* of his, to the *superordinate* or some *connection* of his, may not have been received or looked for: *service*, which, how truly soever sinister, and how extensively soever mischievous, will, in the nature of the case, for want of sufficient proof coming home to the superordinate, commonly be unsusceptible of legal punishment judicially applied.

### Enactive

ART. 30. V. *Completeness of the subjection to the power of the Public Opinion Tribunal.* As for all other good purposes, so for this, —as in the other departments, so in this,—under the authority of the *Public Opinion Tribunal*, for the information of the Supreme [Constitutive], through the medium of the press,—by any person, on the conduct and character of any public functionary, comments may be made,—in so far as clear of falsity in respect of facts, and made without disturbance of the business:—and, for bringing to light, grounds for just censure,—*interrogatories* may, in like manner, be uttered and made public: answer or silence will remain to the *interrogatee:* the Tribunal will draw its conclusions.

From expressions of *vague vituperation*, the appropriate and sufficient punishment will, in the shape of the appropriate disrepute, recoil on the *vituperator:* in so far as *ungrounded*, the vituperation will be regarded as *groundless*. But, for the purpose of judicial satisfaction or punishment, or both, in so far as a demand has place, it will rest with the functionary to provide evidence; to wit, by minutation, as per Ch. xxi. IMMEDIATE REGISTRARS, §[§]5, 6, *Minutation [how, Attestation how]*.

*Enactive*

ART. 31. As, for *past* misconduct, *censure* may thus be administered, and the individual placed under the *surveillance* of the public, for the prevention of the like in future,——so, with still better effect and prospect, may be held up to view——cause of *suspicion*, on the score of apprehended inaptitude *antecedently* to location. So far as regards moral inaptitude,——the security thus sought to be established has been seen in §16, *Locable who*, on the occasion of the Probationary Examinations. In relation to the *Judiciary* department, see the like provision in Ch. xii. §[28], *Locable who:* and the like, in the chapters relative to the several particular offices in that department.

*Enactive. Ratiocinative*

ART. 32. VI. *Completeness of the subjection to the power of the legal tribunals.* As to the Prime Minister it belongs (as per Ch. viii. PRIME MINISTER, §12, *Securities, &c.* Art[s]. 2, 3, 4,) to receive information of inaptitude on the part of any Minister, and to act accordingly,——so, to every Minister does it belong——to receive information of inaptitude, on the part of every functionary in his subdepartment, who, as such, is subjected either to his *dislocative*, or to his *directive* power; and to proceed accordingly: together with the provision as to secrecy in Art. 3 of that section, and the extension established, as per Art. 4, with relation to the Minister's official predecessors.

*Instructional*

ART. 33. VII. *Provision for securing the completeness of the necessary mass of responsible power*, together with the exclusion of all irresponsible exercise of power, by functionaries belonging to this department. To the Legislature it will belong, throughout the whole field of the Administrative department, to look out for,——and, subject to the requisite conditions, to establish,——all such powers, the existence of which shall be necessary and sufficient: and thereby to minimize all demand on the score of necessity, for the exercise of powers not thus legalized.

*Expositive. Exemplificational*

ART. 34. Examples of need of the exercise of such powers are as follows——

Temporary inhibition, restriction, or permission——of commercial intercourse with foreign nations,——with a view to security against calamity, in the shape of famine, dearth, contagion, &c.: as to which, see Ch. xi. MINISTERS SEVERALLY, §5, *Preventive Service Minister.*

### Instructional

ART. 35. Note, that [on] no Minister under the *undiscontinued session* system, established by Ch. vi. [LEGISLATURE], §18, *Attendance*, and §20, *Attendance and Remuneration,*—can there be any use in conferring any such power: the Legislature being, at all times, in the exercise of its functions,—and every Minister, by self or depute, present in the Assembly: [on] subordinates alone, that is to say, [on] such subordinates of the several Ministers, as, at the time in question, happen to be—in places, in such sort distant from the seat of the Legislature, that the evil, the exclusion of which is the object of the exercise given to the extraordinary power, would take effect, before the exclusion of it, by exercise given to the power of the Legislature could be accomplished,—[is it necessary to confer it.]¹

### Instructional

ART. 36. For his guidance in the exercise of such extraordinary powers,—and for his indemnity in respect of the exercise given to [them],—the functionary will frame to himself an estimate of the two antagonizing evils:—the several elements of *value*,—to wit, *magnitude, propinquity,* and *probability*, being taken into account: that is to say, the mass of evil liable to take place, if the power in question be *not* exercised, and the mass of evil liable to take place if the power *be* exercised.

### Enactive

ART. 37. Conditions, the fulfilment of which is necessary to the obtainment of exemption from punishment, and from the burthen of satisfaction, with or without extra remuneration on account of exercise given to such extraordinary power,—are the following—

1. With as much promptitude as may be,—information, as far as may be, clear, correct and complete,—given to the Legislature, respecting the evil, and the supposed remedy so applied.

2. In case of any need of ulterior powers, to be given by the Legislature for the exclusion of the like evil in future,—indication given, of the terms proposed to be employed in the making of such appropriate amendment as shall appear requisite to be applied to the text

¹ Throughout this article, 1830 uses 'to' with the verb 'confer'; the Bowring emendation to 'on', in accordance with normal construction, has been followed, and also the insertion at the end of the article of the words 'is it necessary to confer it', which serve to complete the sentence.

of the law. As to this matter, see Ch. vi. [LEGISLATURE], §29, *Members' motions;* Ch. xi. MINISTERS SEVERALLY, §2, *Legislation Minister;* and Ch. xii. JUDICIARY COLLECTIVELY, §20, *Eventually emendative function.*

## Instructional

ART. 38. For elucidation by means of contrast,—an artifice, congenial to an aristocracy-ridden and corrupt mixt Monarchy, is an object, a glance at which may have its use. It consists in the leaving the provision made of administrative power, purposely, in a state of scantiness and insufficiency: to the end that,—on the plea of necessity, power, on any occasion at pleasure,—to any effect at pleasure,— may be exercised without previous exposure to the scrutiny of the public eye, through those ordinary forms of debate, which are conformed to, in so far as legislation is not only practised but professed: power, exercised without any special and appropriate warrant from law: power which, under any aptly and adequately-penned constitutional code, could not be exercised without violation of some assignable and specially-applying enactment.

## Instructional

ART. 39. A power of this sort may be exercised, *so it may seem,* in either of two ways, according to the state which the *Pannomion* is in with relation to the subject: to wit, either simply without *authority,* or say *warrant* from the law as it stands, or in direct and declared contrariety to some express enactment of the same law. In this last case, the power thus exercised is commonly designated by the appellation of a *dispensing power.* So it may seem: and in practice, as yet, so perhaps everywhere it *is.* In the nature of the case, however, the diversity depends upon that which, in the political community in question, at the time in question, is the state, and the tenor, of the written rule of action: for, suppose it to contain an enactment, to a certain degree comprehensive,—the case will be—that no power not expressly given by law can be exercised, without being exercised by an infringement of some assignable article in the body of the law; nor, therefore, without the exercise of a dispensing power setting itself above the law.

By every individual instance in which this device is practised,— practised on the one part and submitted to on the other,—exercise and strength are given to secret and silent despotism, at the expense of open, and preparatorily, and freely, and publicly discussed legislation.

### Instructional

ART. 40. In pursuance of this same artifice,—for prevention of opposition and discontent, a natural and common practice is—in the first instance,—on each several occasion, so long as the particular noxious purpose can, without greater inconvenience, be effected in some other way,—to forbear giving exercise to this power, otherwise than for a purpose, which, in itself, or at any rate according to received opinions, is of a beneficial nature; whereupon (when, by a little experience, accustomed to see the usurpation applied to good purposes) the people are insensibly led into the habit of regarding it as intrinsically not only innoxious, but beneficial: and in that character, paying, in opinion and action, the same deference to the executive as to the legislative authority, to the subordinate as to the superordinate, to anticonstitutional insubordination as to constitutional legislation, to acts by which law is violated as to acts by which law is made: thereby aiding those, who should be the under servants of their servants, in their endeavours to put themselves over the upper servants, and thereby over those, in whom both upper and under servants ought to behold their masters.

### Instructional. Exemplificational

ART. 41. In especial manner and frequency, this artifice may be seen employed in English practice; employed, and with such success, that public men—those even, who, on other grounds, are all the while acting in declared opposition to those usurpers—may be seen and heard speaking of the exercise of a *dispensing power* as one of the ordinary operations of Government, in so much that, on this or that occasion, it is even matter of charge against them, their not having had recourse to it.

### Instructional. Exemplificational

ART. 42. Continually-increasing extent given to this abuse, is a relative use of, and motive for, two other congenial abuses: 1. One is— minimization of that portion of time, during which, in each year, legislation business is carried on;—as to this, see Ch. vi. [LEGISLATURE], §20, *Attendance and Remuneration;* 2. the other is—maximization of that portion of the field of law, in which the rule of action is left in the state of *fictitious*, alias *judge-made* law; and, at the same time, minimization of the clearness and correctness, and thence the cognoscibility, as well as the extent and comprehensiveness, of that part which has been brought into the state of really-existent and *legislature-made* law.

*Instructional*

ART. 43. A circumstance which, under a tyranny of the few over the many, giving peculiar facility and commodiousness to the practice of carrying on the business of government in this pernicious mode, is—that, in this way, the power of legislation—supreme and all-comprehensive legislation—is exercised without expense of time or thought, and without controul from opposition on the ground of the greatest-happiness principle. '*Whatever is, is right*'—(whatever is—that is to say, whatever, by men in the situation in question, has been done)—being tacitly assumed as a postulate,—the *rectitude* of doing the same thing, on any and every subsequent occasion deemed a similar one, is stated and acted upon, as a necessary consequence. This is called *following precedents:* and this course it is that is constantly held up to view, not only as a safe course, but even as the only safe course: acting, in consequence of all-comprehensive views taken of the same subject, under the guidance of the greatest-happiness principle, being at the same time marked out for a mixture of abhorrence and contempt, under the name of *theory*, and spoken of as an *unsafe* course: that course which, in truth, is the most *opposite* to the only safe one, being thus represented and acted upon as if it were *itself* the only safe one.

*Instructional*

ART. 44. Thus it is—that, by the comparative blindness of man in each preceding period, the like blindness in each succeeding period is secured: without the trouble or need of reflection,—men, by opulence rendered indolent, and by indolence and self-indulgence doomed to ignorance, follow their leaders,—as sheep follow sheep, and geese geese.

*Instructional*

ART. 45. To the purpose to which this mode of governing is applied, nothing can be more commodious; the labour of thought is saved to all who, by indolence or incapacity, or both, stand excluded from the exercise of it: the operation of judging of the mere similitude of one mode of action to another, without confronting either the one or the other with whatever, on the occasion in question, is the proper end in view and standard, being that sort of mental operation, for which the lowest degree of intellect—the lowest degree in the conjunct scales of cognitional and judicial aptitude—is sufficient.

*Instructional*

ART. 46. And what is the class of persons, for the giving effect to whose will this mode of legislation is, in so eminent a degree, well adapted? It is the class of those, of whom, under such a form of government as that in question, the great majority of the legislature is so sure to be composed: men who being, by opulence, rendered destitute of all motives for mental exertion, are, by the very nature of man, from the beginning to the end of life, kept, as above, in a state of relative ignorance and mental impotence.

*Instructional*

ART. 47. Thus it is, that of the thousand persons or thereabouts, on whose will the prosperity of the millions depends, the action of the whole number (an accidentally-introduced few excepted, or not excepted) is determined by a particular and sinister interest, on almost all points, standing, and working, in direct opposition to that of the millions. This class may be divided into two subclasses: those with *misemployed*, and those with *unemployed* faculties: to the *misemployed* (meaning with relation to the universal interest) belong the *lawyer* subclass, the *mercantile* subclass, and the *official* subclass: to the unemployed, headed and led on by men in *possession* and men in *expectancy* of situations in the peerage, belong those who, though distinguished as above, by pre-eminence in mental imbecility, are, by this device, enabled to do the work of depredation and oppression, with the mask of wisdom on their visages, and the praise of virtue in their ears, sung on each occasion by the whole company in chorus.

*Instructional*

ART. 48. One point however there is——on which a representative democracy and an aristocracy-ridden monarchy do (it must be confessed) agree: under both forms of government, the possession of power is secured to one class, to the perpetual exclusion of another class. In the *character* of the *power-holding* class in the two cases, lies the sole difference. In the democracy,——the individuals of whom it is composed, are the most *apt* of all whom the whole population of the country furnishes: in the monarchy, as above, the most *unapt*: and thus lodged must the powers of government continue,——and, thus disposed of the lot of the governed millions,——until these same millions, roused at length by the smart of the sufferings thus continually increased, rise up in a mass, and take the care of their own welfare into their own hands.

*Instructional*

ART. 49. *Precedent* and *practice*——no head too empty or too weak, to make the tongue say *aye*, at the sight, or the sound, of both or either of these two so nearly synonymous and so aptly-associated words:——precedent, *set* by the distinguished few whose characteristic is political and moral wickedness: precedent, *followed*, practice persisted in, by those comparative many, whose characteristic is a compound, composed of political wickedness, combined, as chemists phrase it, *in excess*, with mental weakness.

This mode of acting——acting by *precedent* (understand always, instead of, and in preference to, *enactment*)——what is it? It is acting without reason, to the declared exclusion of reason, and thereby in declared opposition to reason: acting in a more particularly anticonstitutional manner, when it is by the *Executive* or the *Judiciary*, in opposition to the acts of the Legislature.[1]

The more flagrant is the anti-[r]ationality and absurdity, the more *antique* the *precedent*: the more antique the precedent——that is to say, the more barbarous, inexperienced, uninformed, and prejudiceled the race of men, by and among whom the precedent was set:—— the more unlike that same *past* state of things, to that which, at the time in question, is the *present* state of things.

To act thus——to argue in defence of action in this way——is it not as much as to say, *I will have it so*, because this or that other man, still more profoundly ignorant than myself, and still less restrained from evil by the tutelary controul of public opinion than myself,—— said in *his* day——said some scores or some hundreds of years ago—— *I will have it so*? These declarations, are they not such as every man who acts and argues in this way should be regarded, and dealt with, as having made?

By these arguments is endeavoured to be set up an everlasting bar against *reform*, be the abuse ever so mischievous——against *improvement*, be it ever so beneficial and unobjectionable.

*Instructional*

ART. 50. Observations on the system of judicial controul, employed in this section and in [ § § ]20, 21, in preference to that of arbitrary will.

Of the substitution here made of judiciary to purely arbitrary procedure in the Administration Department, examples are not wanting in the practice of any civilized nations of Europe.

---

[1] Bentham presumably means, in his own terminology, the Administrative and Judiciary Departments, since he defines the term Executive as including both the Administrative and the Judiciary. See Ch. IV, Arts. 1-6, pp. 26-7.

Witness, in every nation the *Courts Martial*.

Witness, in English practice the *Courts Martial* and *Military Enquiry Courts*.

In none of these cases, without reasons regularly assigned, accusation on specific grounds, elicitation of evidence, and conjunct deliberation, by a body of judges,—is dislocation commonly pronounced, or suspension, or so much as forced transference. How averse soever, —not altogether deaf are these judicatories to complaints preferred by subordinates against superordinates. How comes it then—that, in the case of the non-military subdepartments of the Administration Department, the security, afforded by the essentially-necessary judicial forms as above, is almost without exception denied?

### Instructional

ART. 51. Instead of it may be seen—in absolute monarchies, in relation to all non-military administrational situations, dislocation altogether arbitrary; in the English, an incongruous and pernicious mixture, of arbitrary dislocability with virtual undislocability, how flagrant soever the wrongs done to individuals, to the public, or to both. General rule, dislocability altogether arbitrary: exceptions made, here and there, with great parade, by the Latin phrase, *quamdiu se bene gesserit*; in English, *during good behaviour*: alias, *at the pleasure of the Judge*.[1] Note too, that in this case the mode of procedure is not, as above, the natural, summary, and naturally-effectual mode; but the technical and never-effectual mode pursued in the ordinary high judicatories.

### Instructional

ART. 52. Referring his complaint to the one great penal justice shop, the King's Bench, a man by whom a wrong is sustained, places his complaint in the hands of a Judicatory, to which every one of the requisites necessary for the administration of relief is completely wanting.

### Instructional

ART. 53. Law, by which the wrong in question is defined, and prohibition attached to it, none: disposition, none on the part either of Judge or even of Jury (not to speak of the secretly acting instrument of impunity the *Grand Jury*), to give relief against the wrong, had it been so marked out and combated by the law: both situations filled by members of the aristocracy, bound by the chains of corrupt

[1] The Latin phrase (with the verb in the plural: *gesserint*) is from the Act of Settlement of 1701, 12 & 13 Wm. & Mar. c. 2, § 7.

dependence on the Monarchy, and predetermined to give, on every occasion, the most effectual support, to power howsoever exercised. In relation to evidence, arrangements, such as in effect to put in great measure an exclusion upon all testimony but that of *willing* witnesses: and the situation of all actually percipient witnesses such, as to render it, on every occasion, in a high degree improbable, that among them should be found any willing witnesses.

### Instructional

ART. 54. In this state of things, if the whole system of intercourse between functionaries and non-functionaries on the one hand, and superordinate and subordinate functionaries on the other hand, is not one unvaried scene of oppression, it is owing—not assuredly to the state of the law, but to the species and degree of good morals and good manners, which,—under the fostering care of the popular or moral sanction, as applied by the Public Opinion Tribunal,—has been nurtured and kept on foot, in spite of the law, and of whatever has the force of law.

### Instructional

ART. 55. In the depths of the great pitfall, in which the tickets in the lottery called *Justice* are openly sold—sold at never preascertainable, and continually increasing prices,—anxious indeed must that evil-doing functionary be to experience a stroke from the rod of punishment, if he can so much as prevail upon the hands that hold it, to gratify him with a touch of it: addressing himself to them, he will be addressing himself to men, to whom he will find *his* impunity scarce less dear than their own.

### Instructional

ART. 56. Hence, when, in the highest judicatory of all, accused of having pocketed £10,000 of public money, an Ex-Cabinet Minister, knowing the men he had to deal with, stood up and said 'Yes—I have pocketed the £10,000,' '*No*' (was the answer of every one of the majority)—'*No, upon my honour you have not.*'[1]

[1] Henry Dundas, 1st Viscount Melville (1742–1811), was impeached in 1805, the last case of impeachment in British history, for alleged malversation of public funds as Treasurer of the Navy in Pitt's first administration. One charge, allegedly based on Melville's own admission, was that some £10,000 had been diverted to his personal use with the help of the then Paymaster of the Navy. Melville was acquitted on all charges; and Bentham's final phrase refers to the form of words in which individual peers give their verdict when the House of Lords sits as a court to try criminal charges, 'Not guilty, upon my honour'.

*Instructional*

ART. 57. Against oppression in no one shape, do the oppressed, (so it will be seen in detail,) find any tolerably efficient security, in English legislation coupled with English Judicature. Ask for *relief*,—what you receive is *aggravation*: oppression by partially assessed, and, to the vast majority of the people altogether unsupportable, expense. Complain of oppression,—the yoke is additionally loaded by irresistible depredation: sole relief against both, a sort of anarchy, creeping on by degrees, and raising up its head under the feet of tyranny.

*Instructional*

ART. 58. Highly advantageous in comparison is, in this respect, the situation of military men. To them justice could not quite so safely be denied as to their unarmed countrymen. Accordingly, from military procedure no profit finds its way into the pockets of the Judge: while, from non-military procedure flow into the correspondently situated pockets such immense and ever increasible profits. Hence, the purity of the one system, the corruption of the other. Hence, in the one case, the system is so *well-suited* to what in both cases is the sole proper and professed purpose—giving execution and effect to the substantive branch of the law: hence, in the other case, so utterly *hostile*. Remains, indeed, as a source of corruption in the military case, the despotism of the Commander in Chief: but, that despotism would have nothing to gain, on the contrary, much to lose, by poisoning the system with factitious expense and factitious delay for increase of the expense, and absurd arrangements in relation to evidence: these too for increase of the expense, and moreover of that uncertainty, from which the source of the expense, and the profit extracted from it, receive their increase. In that part of the present Code which applies to the *Judicial* department, and thereafter in the Procedure Code,[1] this state of things will come to be laid open in some detail; but even on the present occasion, reference to it could not be altogether omitted: those which belong to evidence, see in complete detail in the *Rationale of Judicial Evidence*.[2]

---

[1] On the Procedure Code, see Ch. V, § 5, Art. 6n, p. 38n.
[2] *Rationale of Judicial Evidence, specially applied to English Practice*, ed. John Stuart Mill, 5 vols., London, 1827 (Bowring, vi. 189–585, vii. 1–600).

## SECTION 26

ARCHITECTURAL ARRANGEMENTS

*Instructional*

ART. 1. Among the *ends in view,*—or say the *elements* or the *features* of appropriate aptitude,—in the mode of carrying on the business of the Administrative department and its several subdepartments, are some, which cannot be given to it in so high a degree, without, as with, that assistance, which is not derivable to it from any other source than the art-and-science of *architecture.*

*Instructional*

ART. 2. Here, as elsewhere—Main ends to be aimed at—those already brought to view, as per §7, *Statistic function*: namely—maximization of relative good, and minimization of relative evil:—of relative good; that is to say, of the value of the benefit, accruing to the public from the exercise given, by the several functionaries belonging to the several subdepartments, to their several functions:—of relative evil, that is to say, of its main branch—to wit, diminution of the benefit just mentioned; of its collateral branches, to wit, the several evils of *delay, vexation,* and *expense.*

Classes of persons, in different ways affected by these evils respectively, are—1, Suitors, at and to the several offices; 2, Functionaries, thereto belonging.

*Instructional*

ART. 3. By appropriate architectural arrangements, contribution, (it will be seen,) may be made at the same time to that same main end, and to those same collateral ends: for, by those same architectural arrangements, by which delay, vexation and expense are reduced in favour of suitors,—may delay, as well as vexation and expense, be seen reduced in favour of the directing functionaries; and through them, in favour of the public service.

*Instructional*

ART. 4. Intermediate purposes, to which, for maximization of good and minimization of evil, Architectural arrangements are applicable to official edifices, are—publicity and secrecy of intercourse: *publicity*, in the cases where publicity, *secrecy*, in the cases where secrecy, is in the highest degree conducive to those same desirable purposes: *secrecy*, or say *privacy.*

Narrow will have been seen to be the extent, to which secrecy,

438

compared with that [to]¹ which publicity, is productive of those
same pre-eminently and universally desirable effects.

### Instructional

ART. 5. With a view to the *choice* as between publicity and secrecy
—subject matters susceptible of diversification and requiring consideration, are—1, Occasions; 2, Persons; 3, Places; 4, Times; 5,
Points of time; 6, Lengths of time.

### Instructional

ART. 6. On one and the same *occasion*, what may happen is—that,
at or in the same place or places, at one and the same point of *time*,
for these desirable purposes, it may be requisite—that, during one
and the same length of time, as to persons two or more, the existence
and the matter of the intercourse should be known, and in so far
public, so to another or others unknown, and in so far secret or say
private.

### Instructional

ART. 7. According to the nature of the business, the demand, as
between publicity and secrecy, will be seen to vary, as between *department* and department; and, in the same department, as between
*subdepartment* and subdepartment: so also, in the same subdepartment, as between *office* and office.

### Instructional

ART. 8. As to secrecy—the department, in which the *usefulness* of
that state of things is at its maximum, the Constitutive. So also the
*extent*, to which this usefulness has place. This usefulness consists in
the need there is of secrecy of suffrage for the preservation of liberty
of suffrage: preservation of it, that is to say, against corruptedness,
by the influence of the matter of reward and punishment, applied to
the producing an opposition—between the choice in reality desired
to be made, and the choice which, in appearance alone, is that which
the person in question is desirous to make: as where, at an Election,
it being the desire of an Elector that A should be the candidate
chosen,—the case is—that, by contemplation of the matter of good
or the matter of evil, as eventually about to be received by him at the
hands of this or that other person, an Elector gives his vote in favour
of B: B being a candidate other than the one whom, on that same
occasion, it is his wish to see successful.

¹ 1830, 'with': the Bowring emendation as above is needed to clarify the
passage.

### Instructional

ART. 9. Upon the agreement or disagreement, or say upon the identity or the diversity,—as between the wish really entertained, and the wish expressed by the outward sign employed in giving expression to it,—depends the character or say the quality, of a *vote* or say *suffrage*, in respect of the difference between *genuineness* and *spuriousness*: if the two wishes point to the same object, the quality exemplified is *genuineness*: if, to two different objects, *spuriousness*.

### Instructional

ART. 10. The Department which, taken in its totality, presents itself as being that, in which the need of publicity, as compared with the need of secrecy, is most extensive,—is the Judiciary.

### Instructional

ART. 11. The Department which, taken in its totality, presents itself as being that, in which the need of [ publicity ] exists in an intermediate extent—less, to wit, than in the *Constitutive*, greater than in the Judiciary,—is the *Administrative*.

To the cases in which the demand for secrecy has place,—they being cases of exception,—occasion for making reference has, in the chapters and sections of this volume, been already frequent. Others will be seen in the several chapters, which have for their subject the Judiciary Department.

### Instructional

ART. 12. For the *uses* of *publicity*, by *whatsoever means* effected, see above, §25, *Securities, &c.* For the uses of *secrecy* by whatsoever means effected, see Ch. vi. [LEGISLATURE], §21, *Sittings public and secret*; Ch. xii. JUDICIARY COLLECTIVELY, §14, *Publicity, &c.* and other intermediate places therein referred to. Now, as to the mode, in which, to publicity and secrecy,—in the several cases in which they are respectively productive of *good*,—*architectural arrangements* in particular may, in quality of *means*, be made subservient.

### Expositive

ART. 13. By *delay*,[1] is meant, on this occasion, delay in respect of *communication*: of communication on the part of persons employed in the service of the subdepartment or subdepartments in question,

---

[1] Bentham here takes up the argument begun in Art. 3, but postponed for the discussion of publicity and secrecy.

with any of the several objects, whether *persons* with whom, or *things* with which, in and for the exercise of their several functions, it is necessary that communication should have place.

### Instructional. Expositive

ART. 14. As for other purposes, so for these,—instruments necessary to communication are—the psychological and the purely physical: psychological, the two are so intimately connected senses, *sight* and *hearing:* correspondent physical instruments, *light* and *air:* air, in that state of motion of which *sound* is the *result*. When and where, by means of both these senses, perception is rendered instantaneous, —delay is not only minimized, but excluded altogether; when and where, in regard to either of them, perception fails in any degree of being instantaneous,—delay, in a degree proportioned to that of the failure, fails of being excluded.

### Instructional. Ratiocinative

ART. 15. So simple, so obvious, so familiar, the appropriate arrangements;—so sure of being effectual, so easy to be employed, so cheap in comparison of all others;—shame might have prevented the mention of them, had not a justification but too sufficient been afforded, —not only by the utter neglect of them in *practice*, but even by the absence of all mention of them in discourse. *Principle* say the all-comprehensive *juxtaposition* principle.[a] Corresponding *Rule*. Place in *contiguity* the several *offices*—meaning here the several *apartments* allotted for the official abodes of the several proposed intercommunicants, during the time of such parts of their respective businesses as can in those several places be most conveniently carried on.

### Expositive

ART. 16. *Offices*—say then, as above, *thirteen*: understanding at the same time—that, under this name either so many entire and separate edifices, or so many apartments only,—and those in the same, or in any lesser number of edifices, are as yet alike capable of being designated.

---

[a] Not less simple, than in mathematics the *superposition* principle:—a principle employed in geometrical demonstration, and as such noticed by *D'Alembert* in his *Mélanges*.[1]

---

[1] Jean le Rond d'Alembert (1717–83), *Mélanges de Littérature, d'Histoire, et de Philosophie*, new edn., 5 vols., Amsterdam, 1773, iv. 262–3 (*Essai sur les élémens de philosophie, ou sur les principes des connoissances humaines*).

*Instructional*

ART. 17. *Relative situation of the offices.*

Of the thirteen Ministers, two, to wit, the Election Minister and the Legislation Minister, not being necessarily subject to the direction of the Prime Minister,——remains *eleven* as and for the *number*, of those, in the instance of each of whom, need may have place for an office within the reach of the common superordinate, for the purpose of instantaneous intercommunication with him.

Ministers' offices——say eleven, twelve, or thirteen, as above, disposed in a *crescent:* a *crescent,* or else——what, to the purpose here in question, would serve equally well,——instead of any such *fragment* of a circle, one entire circle, or rectilinear *quasi-circle*——a polygon of that same number of sides, circumscribing, or inscribed on, a circle: or an *oval* form correspondently diversifiable. So far as *ventilation* alone is regarded,——if protection against violent winds from particular quarters be not regarded as necessary,——an *unenclosed* space, such as that covered by a crescent, presents itself as obviously preferable to the above proposed or any other plan, by which a thorough draught of air, sweeping the whole, is excluded. In any case, though not necessarily, yet naturally, in the central situation with reference to the rest, would be placed the Prime Minister's office, from whence directions will have to be continually issued.

*Instructional. Ratiocinative*

ART. 18. With the exception of the saving in expense, by diminution of the quantity of matter and workmanship employed in the erection of boundaries,——as to the *Election Minister's* office, whether it does or does not form a part of the assemblage, presents itself as being nearly if not altogether a matter of indifference. As to the *Legislation Minister,*——the most convenient, if not the only convenient, situation for *his* office is obviously that of contiguity with the edifice appropriated to the use of the Legislature.

*Instructional*

ART. 19. In the apartment of the Prime Minister,——from an apt position within reach of the seat occupied by him, issue thirteen *conversation tubes,*[a] terminating in corresponding positions contiguous in like

---

[a] Note as to the *distance,* to which, for the purpose of *conversation,* sound is capable of being conveyed by means of these same *conversation-tubes.* Between thirty-four and thirty-five years ago,——on the occasion of an experiment, made, by the procurement and under the eye of the author of these pages,—— conversation, of course with a velocity which was that of sound, in the tone of

manner to the seats of the several Ministers in their several apartments.

From the apartment of each Minister to the apartment of every other Minister runs in like manner a conversation tube.

As between one and every other of these fourteen Administration functionaries,—thus is promptitude of oral intercourse maximized.

### *Ratiocinative*

ART. 20. *Collateral advantage*. By these same means, effectual security is afforded, against an imaginable mishap, the realization of which is not without examples. From office to office, official papers are of

ordinary discourse, was carried through a tube of about 350 feet in length, composed, of course, of a number of tubes, fitted one into another, air-tight: *diameter*, according to recollection, between one and two inches. The dimensions of the building were not such as to admit of the drawing out that length into a right line: but, between interlocutor and interlocutor such was the distance, as to render otherwise impossible any such communication, without the greatest exertion, if it could be held at all, at any such distance as that at which it actually had place.

Much about that time,—information was received from several quarters, of an interchange of sounds as having been produced at more than a mile's distance between the two ends of an antique watercourse, somewhere in the North of England.

About twenty years before that time,—observation had by the persons in question been made of conversation habitually carried on in a low tone, between the top and the bottom of a high house in *Cornhill*, London. The year, in which, in a work intituled *Panopticon*, or the *Inspection House*, the universal inspection principle, with this feature belonging to it, was published and circulated in government circles, was 1791. Since that time, this instrument has, in London, found its way into several public offices, among which is the *Custom House*.[1]

---

[1] The experiment mentioned in the first paragraph of this footnote evidently took place in September 1793 at 5 New Bridge Street, Blackfriars, the premises of Charles and John Wyatt, tinned copper manufacturers: see Wyatt to Bentham, 23 September 1793, Letter 929 in *Correspondence* (*CW*), iv. 480. Bentham sent an elaborate account of the experiment in his letter of 10 November 1793 to Evan Nepean, then Under Secretary at the Home Office (Letter 934, ibid., pp. 485–90), where he suggests the employment of conversation-tubes between the two Houses of Parliament and the Horse Guards, between the War Office and the Tower, and so forth. The account of the experiment shows that Bentham's memory here, though slightly at fault in one detail (the diameter of the tubes ranged from ¾ to 1¼ inches), was remarkably accurate: the length of the tubes (366 feet) was very much as he remembered it over thirty years later. The papers sent with the letter to Nepean also mention the 'antique watercourse' referred to in the second paragraph here. Bentham had heard on good authority, though not at first hand, that a voice had been audible at the distance of a mile through a leaden water-pipe. For Bentham's references to conversation tubes in *Panopticon; or, the Inspection-House: containing the idea of a new principle of construction*, London, 1791 (Bowring, iv. 37–172), see Bowring, iv. 41, 84–5.

course sent in locked boxes. The offices being, many of them, out of sight of one another, and situated at indefinite distances,—the bearers of these boxes have been way-laid, and for some sinister political purpose robbed of them.[a]

On the above construction,—the messengers, by whom papers are carried to and fro, need never be out of sight of the intercommunicators: by means of wheels within-doors,—boxes, if it were worth while, might even be borne to and fro, by ropes instead of messengers; at the immediately preceding moment, notice being given by accompanying *bells.*[b]

[a] In the London Offices, particular instances of this mishap have reached the ears of the author of these pages.

[b] So in the case of prisons. If, in any shape, abuse has existence in any place at any time,—it is because, to the extent which, with the utmost facility, in any place at any and every moment of time, [it] might be made to have place, *inspection*—say rather inspectedness—has not place: inspection, by individuals at large; inspectedness, on the part of *prisoners*, by the eyes of *prison-keepers*: inspectedness, on the part of prisoners and prison-keepers, by the eyes of individuals at large, in the character of members of the *Public Opinion Tribunal.* In this case, in England, in a manner of which history will have to speak, a plan, by which, on the part of all instruments, personal as well as real, appropriate aptitude would, as had been demonstrated, have been maximized, expense at the same time minimized,—was, even after having been sanctioned by the legislature, frustrated by personal antipathy, in the breast of an individual higher than the Legislature: instead of it was carried into effect, an establishment, in which, on the part of instruments of both sorts, inaptitude soon became so flagrant, as to break through the integument of Bastille secrecy in which it had been enveloped: expense, in capital more than decupled, expense annual several times multiplied. In general terms, as above, indication of this phenomenon was too analogous and apposite to be suppressed: particulars belong not to this place. In the above-mentioned individual instance, the extinction of the plan had for its cause an accidental and individual state of things. But the degree of neglect experienced by it thenceforward—not in England alone, but throughout the civilized world, and more particularly in France—and this, not a particle of objection to it being uttered any where, can scarcely be accounted for, otherwise than by that mixture of cold jealousy and apathy, the influence of which on human conduct is but too frequently visible. Before its receiving the above sanction in England, in France, Lewis the XVI saw it, and expressed his personal approbation of it: before the reign of that gentlest and least noxious of Monarchs had, along with his life, come to a close,—the inventor of the political part of this plan (the architectural being the invention of his brother,) was invited by authority to establish it in that country. In Ireland, at the hands of the local authority, adoption had been given to it and endeavour used towards its being carried into execution and effect,—even before it had received adoption in England, as above. In Spain, in the year 1823, it was recommended for adoption upon a national scale, by a Committee of the then existing Legislature. In England, and perhaps the Anglo-American United States,—the practical adoption of it awaits the death of the two inventors: no expense in the shape of misery and money being (one should think) in the minds of those on whom it depends, too

*Instructional. Expositive*

ART. 21. Thus much for promptitude of oral communication between functionary and *functionary*.

Now as to the promptitude as between functionaries and *suitors*, —together with exclusion of needless delay, vexation and expense: vexation, by haughty or negligent demeanour on the part of the functionary, and by unjust favour in respect of priority of audience. Follows now the remedy, in so far as applicable by architectural arrangements.

*Waiting-boxes*. By a *Waiting-box* in a Minister's office, understand —a compartment, into which a suitor or set of suitors are admitted, there to remain while waiting for audience: seats, in each, from two to eight: in *tiers*, one above another—one, two or three—as in the boxes of a theatre.

Form of each office—suppose, on the outside, a polygon of *thirteen* sides: *eleven* of them constituting the exterior boundaries of so many of these *Waiting-boxes*: the two others contiguous to each other, use—giving to suitors—the one entrance, the other, exit. As to these, see Art. 30.

Of the eleven, nine contiguous to each other, termed *Public boxes*: these, for the reception of suitors in whose instance no secrecy is required.

*Private* boxes, (as to which see Art. 26) two: one at each extremity of the line of Public boxes. Should the number be found or predetermined insufficient,—it might be increased by two or more, at the expense of that of the *Public boxes*.

In each Public box,—the interior boundary a correspondent parallel to the exterior.

About the centre of the polygon,—a counter, or rectangular table, with seats for the Minister, and one or two Registrars or Clerks for registration.

Between that part of the table which is nearest to the interior boundary of the annular or say quasi-annular line of Waiting-boxes, —an *open area*, of greater or less extent according to convenience, into which opens a door waist-high, by the opening of which any

great to pay for exemption from the mortification of seeing the inventors reap so much as the satisfaction of witnessing the adoption of it, unaccompanied by remuneration in any other shape.[1]

---

[1] For further particulars of the matters dealt with in this footnote, see the 'Selections from Bentham's Narrative regarding the Panopticon Penitentiary Project, and from the Correspondence on the subject', printed in Bowring, xi. 96–170.

person in the box may, in case of need, on permission, pass to the table.

Between the Minister's table and the exterior boundary of the line of Waiting-boxes, the distance not so great as to afford any obstruction to oral intercourse.

By this consideration, the necessary limit will be set to the diameter of the ground-floor of the whole building.

Exterior to the exterior boundary of this annular line of *Waiting-boxes*, a correspondent line of *passage*: along it the suitors make their way all round to the several Waiting-boxes: he who comes first, moving on to the box which is furthest from the entrance.

Height, not exceeding what is requisite for ventilation.

Light, received into it from the top.

The boxes distinguished from one another by *numbers*: each number expressed in figures over the exterior door of the box, to wit, that which opens into the passage, as also over the interior door, which opens into the above-mentioned area.

Without and within these Waiting-boxes,—in type and numbers such as to be visible to all eyes, are exemplars of the two Tables, as per §25, *Securities, &c.* Art[s]. 10, 11, and [12.] Table I. *Functionary's Deportment Rules*: Table II. *[Visitor's] Deportment Rules.*

### Ratiocinative

ART. 22. *Uses* of these same public Waiting-boxes. 1. Service rendered by the population of them, in securing and augmenting the *publicity* of every thing that passes: this, in like manner as by the [*Judicial Inspectors*] in a Justice chamber, as per Ch. xvii.

2. Like service, by securing observance to the above-mentioned rules of deportment.

### Instructional

ART. 23. Into the central part occupied by the Minister, light is let in, by windows running all round the roof, at an elevation higher than that of the *passage*.

### Instructional

ART. 24. All this, on the same level; that is to say, the *ground-floor:* over it, in stories of any number, are apartments or assemblages of apartments, called collectively the *Treasury*, appropriated to the purpose of giving stowage to the official books and papers. As to this, see below, Art[s]. 38, 43.

*Instructional*

ART. 25. To a set of these apartments may, if the situation be approved, be added another for the habitation of the Minister and his family: but see Art. 38.

*Instructional. Expositive*

ART. 26. *Private waiting boxes.* By a private waiting box, understand a box having for its destination the affording audience to suitors in such manner, that, in the instance of such suitor, not only the purport, but even the existence, of his intercourse with the Minister, while sitting in his central part of the room, as per Art. 21,—shall remain, for the requisite time, unknown to all persons, but such, if any, to whom the suitor or the Minister shall have communicated information of it.

*Instructional*

ART. 27. Number of these private waiting boxes, two: one at each extremity of the ring of public waiting boxes. But, from that part of the passage which gives admission into the public waiting boxes, the part which gives admission to the private ones is separated by a thick wall.

For the efficient cause or causes of demand for such privacy, see below, Art. 32.

*Instructional*

ART. 28. Across the Minister's office, in the direction of the *diameter* of a circle (the diameter being drawn at right angles to the middle part of the ring of the above-mentioned public waiting boxes) or of a *chord* parallel to the diameter, runs a partition, closed by a door or curtain, by the opening of which the Minister makes his entrance to the table, to give audience to any part of the population of the public waiting boxes. On his return at any time through the aperture,— he gives audience to the individual or individuals in either of the private boxes as above.

Between the construction of the *public* and that of the *private* waiting boxes, the only considerable difference is,—that in the *private* boxes, the side partitions, instead of being of any degree of thinness, must be of such a thickness, as to prevent the communication of *sound:* and, to the same purpose, like regard must be had in the construction of the floor and ceiling.

### Instructional. Ratiocinative

ART. 29. Moreover, in the case of the private boxes, the area between them and the Minister's table cannot be so spacious as in the case of the public boxes: nor would there be any use in its being so. A correspondent portion of space will thus be free, capable of being allotted to other purposes.

### Instructional

ART. 30. In that part of the circle which is opposite to the part occupied by the *public* waiting boxes,——and thence, with reference to *them, behind* the above-mentioned *partition,*——is a sort of *hall* or *vestibule*, equal in *extent* to at least two of those same public waiting boxes.

In the middle part of its exterior boundary,——which is that of the whole building,——is an outward door, which opens into the street, and thus gives admission to all persons indiscriminately.

After continuing undivided for some part of the space, this hall gives admittance to whatever staircase or passage may be deemed necessary for communication with the several parts of the building: for example, with the apartments of the several superior stories, and the annular exterior passage, which, as above, leads to the waiting boxes.

On his entrance at the above-mentioned outward door,——a visitant sees, on each side of the hall or vestibule, a *passage* with two *doors* in it, in a right line with one another, divided by a wall into two equal halves: the *outward* half gives admission to the public waiting boxes on that side; the *inward* half to the one private waiting box on that same side: the two doors which give admission, the one of them to the exterior, the other to the interior half passage, are both in the same right line: the half passage which leads to the private waiting box has, besides the just-mentioned door, another opening sideways into the half passage which leads to the public waiting boxes; by this means, at his exit into the vestibule, the secret suitor has his option ——whether to pass into it *directly*, or through the *medium* of the half passage that communicates with the public waiting boxes.

A suitor, whose audience in a private box has been finished,——to make his exit unperceived, watches the time when either there is no person at all in the vestibule, or no person in relation to whom he has any apprehension.

For enabling the *secret suitor*, at his exit, to see into the vestibule without being seen from it,——a small hole closed by a glass would suffice: the situation of it being at an elevation to a certain degree above that of the human figure, and a step or steps being provided for enabling him to ascend to it. Of the purpose here in view, a general conception being thus conveyed,—an intelligent architect will, it is supposed, find little difficulty in giving effect to it in any one of a variety of particular ways, adapted to local circumstances.

### Instructional

ART. 31. For further security, if deemed necessary, a passage *under ground* may be provided, opening into an exterior *open* passage, with a *sentinel* at the end of it, by whom all persons are precluded from the faculty of making observation of the persons coming into it, or going out of it.[a]

### Instructional

ART. 32. Cases in which justificative causes for privacy of the intercourse between minister and suitor may have place. *Examples*:—

*Loss*, already fallen—or, unless prevented, about to fall—on the public service. For a list of the several forms of which such loss is susceptible—a list endeavoured to be rendered all-comprehensive, see §7, *Statistic function*, Bissect. iv, *Loss Books*.

### Instructional

ART. 33. *Motives*, capable of giving birth to such information on the part of a suitor. *Examples*:—

1. Benefit *naturally* resulting to him: to wit, from the termination or prevention of the efficient cause of loss: as where, by a fair trader, information is given of contrabandism.

2. Benefit, sought in the shape of remuneration from *government* by the hands of the minister. *Example*:—Case the same:—except that the informant is not, in this case,—as in the other case it may happen to him to be,—in a situation to reap any such naturally resulting benefit, and *that* an adequate one. For illustration, this one example may suffice: the subdepartment, from the business of which

---

[a] Had the usual imitative means of representation been employed, the diversifications which the diversities of place and time may be found to require, might thus have been kept out of mind: and a peremptory objection to this or that particular diversification might have been regarded as constituting an equally peremptory objection to every other diversification that could have been employed.

In the shops of London pawnbrokers, a frequently exemplified mode of situation and construction has been—one door opening into an obscure court, for giving unobserved entrance to bashful *pledgers*: another, into a frequented street, for giving information and entrance to all classes indiscriminately, including purchasers and unapprehensive pledgers.

it is taken, is that of the *Finance Minister*: but the like example might alike have been furnished from most of the other subdepartments.

### Ratiocinative

ART.34. Question. Why, in a case of this sort, admit the information to be *secret?*

Answer. *Reasons.* I. Liableness of publicity to convey to a delinquent or to delinquents information, enabling them to elude the operation of the appointed *remedies*: to wit—

1. In *all* cases, the *punifactive* and thereby *subsequentially-preventive*.

2. In many cases, the *satisfactive*, including the *compensative*.

3. Where the offence is continuous, the *suppressive*.

4. In so far as the mischief is as yet in contemplation only, the *preventive*.

II. Need of temporary secrecy, to secure the information from being suppressed by fear of the disrepute liable to be attached to the exercise of the function of *informer*.

III. Ill will and ill offices on the part of the delinquent, and persons especially connected with him—by the tie of interest, self-regarding or sympathetic.

Be the act what it may,—where motives, adequate to the production of the requisite information, have place,—it may be presumed that a correspondent probability of such prevention or suppression will thus have place: where no such adequate motive has place, the evil practice will go on unpunished. Note, that the disrepute so generally attached to the character of informer can scarcely have any other cause than a correspondent depravity in the character of the laws. Of that depravity it is accordingly every where strongly presumptive at least, if not of itself conclusive, evidence.

### Instructional

ART. 35. *Objection answered.* No reward! (cries an objector:) no reward in this case. If true, the information will have been given by the pure motive of regard for the public good: given for the sake of *lucre*, it will have been false.

Answer. 1. But, this same *lucre*—what is it that the word designates? Nothing more than the matter of *reward*, that is to say, the matter of *good*, applied to the purpose in question, with intimation given—that, to him who is speaking of it, the application made of it is an object of disapprobation; but without any intimation, of the *ground* on which that sentiment is entertained.

2. Admit the objection to be a valid one, a consequence is—that

no offence—no mischief producible by an offence—should ever be prevented;—except in a case, which, for this purpose, presents persons in sufficient number, who are content to sacrifice, each of them, his own interest to a comparatively small interest on the part of the public,—and act accordingly.

### Ratiocinative

ART. 36. As in any other way, so in this—to oppose discouragement to the proceedings necessary to the prevention of an offence, is to act as an accomplice.—*Question*. You yourself,—have you ever made any such sacrifice?—out of a hundred such sentimentalists, not more perhaps than one is there whose answer would not be in the affirmative: yet not so much as one, perhaps, is there in whose instance it would be true: that which in the language of sentimentalism is a sacrifice of private to public interest, being but a sacrifice of a self-supposed private interest in one shape to a self-supposed private interest in another shape: for example, of an interest corresponding to the love of power, to an interest corresponding to love of reputation:—of that reputation, of which power is the expected fruit.

### Instructional

ART. 37. The determination to exclude *all false* evidence—is it an absolute one? included in it then is the determination to exclude *all* evidence. For where has ever been the piece of evidence, in relation to which, antecedently to examination, it could have been known not to be, false?

### Instructional. Ratiocinative

ART. 38. Attached to the official apartment of a Minister, (including the *treasury* thereto belonging,) and under the same roof—shall there be or not be, a mass of building, with the appurtenances, provided for the *habitation* of the Minister and his family?

Reasons for the affirmative.

1. Saving in respect of the roof.

2. Protection against *furtive abstraction*—or say *robbery*—particularly by night.

3. Assurance that, by this means, the Minister will be, generally speaking, on the spot.

Reasons for the negative.

1. If an *habitable part* be to be added,—there must be, for the subdepartments of the eleven or twelve Ministers taking directions from the Prime Minister, that same number of ministerial habitations. But, as per §2, (*Ministers and Subdepartments*), what may happen is—

451

that, for several subdepartments, one and the same Minister may suffice: in this case, so many unions or reunions, so many masses of superfluous expense.

2. The number of the persons, of whom the [family][1] of a Minister is composed, admits of an indefinite number of diversifications. But, of the habitations thus provided, the aggregate mass will require to be sufficient for the most numerous family; and, in this sufficiency will be included, a proportionate superfluity and excess, with the correspondent wasteful expense,—in every instance, in which the actual number falls short of the number thus arbitrarily assumed; and this excess may be to be repeated upon any number of habitations, not exceeding the eleven or twelve.

3. As to the Minister's being always on the spot,—by his having a *habitation* on the spot, no complete security will be afforded for his being himself *constantly* in that same habitation, nor of his being accessible when he *is* there. Other and more appropriate arrangements the nature of the case affords, as per §25, *Securities*, by which this accessibility is capable of being secured. Understand always—at the *times*, at which the business requires his presence at office hours in the official apartment. But, every year, a portion more or less considerable of his official time will be to be employed in *Inspection visits*, as per §9, *Inspective function*.

4. Suppose no such appendage attached,—the habitation, occupied by each Minister, will be that, which, in the judgment of the most appropriate judge, is best adapted to his wants and means in all respects. As to the expense,—it will, in both cases, be taken into the account, on the occasion of the offers made by candidates, on the occasion of the *pecuniary competition*, as per §17, *Located how*.

### Instructional

ART. 39. This same instrument might, and naturally would,—every part of it—serve, at the same time, for both the *matériel* and the *person[n]el* of both departments—the Legislative and the Administrative:—for the *personal* as well as *real* stock—for the functionaries belonging to the two departments, as well as for the dead portion of the public property.

### Instructional

ART. 40. Compare, with a view to comparative importance, the prime subject-matter of preservation in the case of a representative democracy as here, with the corresponding subject-matter of the like care

---

[1] 1830, 'faculty'; the Bowring emendation, 'family', is clearly correct.

so universally bestowed in the case of the Monarch: the absence of all expense in the one case, the enormity of the expense in the other: the needfulness in the one case, with the [uselessness]¹ in the other: more particularly in the case of those whose attendance is paid on his migration from place to place. Behold, in the case of the Monarchy, a virtual certificate——that, under that form of government, the state of perpetual insecurity,——into which, for the increase of the inordinate prosperity of that one individual, the subject millions are kept plunged,——is shared with them, at the same time by that same unit, to whose interest in this shape, a sacrifice, so enormous, of the universal comfort of those same millions, is not grudged.

### Instructional. Ratiocinative

ART. 41. Note well——that, in the organization of this compound instrument of security, an indispensable condition is——that the individual elements of the fictitious body be frequently changed. A Prime Minister for life——with an unchanging body of men——though in number, for example, not more than *fifty* under his command,—— encompassing at the same time his residence, and that of the most confidential and highly empowered servants of the people,——might sooner or later become a *Pisistratus* with his fifty yeomanry, or a *Roman Imperator* with his Prætorian guards.²

### Instructional. Exemplificational

ART. 42. Subsidiary arrangements, requiring to be connected with, and adapted to, those which belong strictly to Architecture alone, are——arrangements for the security of the buildings, their appurtenances, and contents, against *loss* by whatever causes——physical or psychological——produced.
  Of such loss examples are——
  1. Destruction by conflagration.
  2. Destruction [or] deterioration by other physical causes at large.
  3. Furtive abstraction.

¹ 1830, 'usefulness': the Bowring emendation, as above, is clearly required by the context.
² Peisistratus (*c.*600–528 BC), seized power in Athens about 560 BC and held it, with some interruptions, until his death. He is said to have acquired his bodyguard of Greek and Barbarian mercenaries by feigning an attempt on his life. The Praetorian Guard was the force established by the Emperor Augustus for the protection of Italy, where none of the legions was stationed. The force came to have considerable political power, especially during the 3rd century. It was abolished by Constantine in AD 312.

*Instructional*

ART. 43. Subject-matters, the preservation of which is of prime importance are—the literary contents of the *treasury;* more particularly those in manuscript. But, so far as regards the manuscripts, the evil from loss is already minimized: to wit, by the universal *registration* and *publication* system, as per Ch. viii. §[ § ]10, 11.[1]

*Instructional*

ART. 44. Of psychological causes of indiscriminate *destruction* and *deterioration*, examples are—

1. Ill will on the part of a *foreign* adversary.

2. Ill will on the part of *internal* adversaries, as in the case of popular commotions.

*Instructional. Exemplificational*

ART. 45. Of psychological causes of *furtive abstraction*, examples are—

1. Desire of the matter of wealth in the ordinary case: to wit, that in which the subject-matter possesses intrinsic marketable value.

2. Indirect advantage, from the loss of the subject-matter to a party on one side, or the acquisition of it to a party on the other side, over and above any marketable value which it may happen to it to possess.

Of furtive destruction or abstraction thus produced, individual examples have every now and then transpired.

*Instructional*

ART. 46. Follow *correspondent safeguards*. Even in a Republic, established with the best possible constitution, a purposed destruction of public property by popular commotion, should not be regarded as too improbable to need guarding against. The love and veneration of ten millions at a distance might be an altogether inefficient protection, against ten dozen of individuals, impregnated with effective malevolence in this shape, whether by inbred error, or by fraud and mendacity from without: in which case,—by resentment, produced by the conduct, real or supposed, justly or unjustly regarded as culpable on the part of this or that Minister,—the public treasure in this shape—the whole or any part of it—might be made a sacrifice.

[1] See Ch. VI, § 27, Art. 8n, p. 95.

### Instructional. Ratiocinative

ART. 47. Sole adequate as well as appropriate security in this case —a *military guard*. Minister, in this case, specially charged with the *directive* functions, and responsible for the exercise of it—the *Preventive Service Minister*.—Subordinates, draughted from the professional subordinates of the Army Minister. By the employment of *non-military* functionaries for the purpose,—for example, under the name of *Watchmen* or *Porters*,—appropriate aptitude would be lessened,—remuneration, the whole of it, expended in waste.

### Instructional. Exemplificational

ART. 48. Thus much, as to that which might have place—might, should, and every where, if the good of the whole community were the end aimed at, would have had, and have place. What can be more obvious? What more simple? What more effectual? What more easily effectible?

Look round now every where,—and every where behold what actually has place.

Turn first to Monarchy. Here, the all-determining principle is— that, as beasts in general are made for the use of men in general,—so, in each community are men—all of them but one—made for the use of that one: of this universal slave-holder, the *duty* (for he too has his duty) is—as in all other matters and on all other occasions, so in this matter and on this occasion—at every moment of time whatsoever, to do that which, at that same moment, is most agreeable to himself.

Of these two-legged beasts of draught and burthen, corresponding and proper state—that of *slavery* under that *one*: *domestic* slavery, did the nature of things admit of it: but, the nature of things not being thus tractable, then that which comes nearest to it,—to wit, *political* slavery.

### Instructional

ART. 49. Thus, as to all operations and all arrangements in general: this same all-comprehensive principle—apply it now to those arrangements in particular which apply to Architecture, and thence to the habitual *official residence* of the chief functionary, and his chief subordinates.

That which the greatest happiness of the greatest number requires, is—that at each moment of time, the residence of each functionary, and in particular of that one whose functions are of most importance, should be on that spot, on which his service, reference had to the greatest happiness of that same number, would be of the greatest use. Correspondent, howsoever opposite, is the arrangement as to place, in the case of this all-ruling *one*. That which *his* greatest happiness requires, is——that, without communication received of his will and pleasure, no operation which is regarded as being of adequate moment with reference to such his happiness, is ever to be performed. When, with the utmost possible despatch, the welfare of the community requires this or that thing to be done, which cannot be done but by this or that next highest functionary, nor by him without verbal communication with this highest,——how great between the two functionaries the distance is——distance in place and thence in time,—— with the consequent delay, vexation and expense,——is not worth a thought. His official abode being in the metropolis, is it at any time his pleasure to be at twenty miles distance, the *delay* correspondent to those twenty miles is to have place: if sixty miles, the delay correspondent to these sixty miles; and so in the case of 400 miles, whether by land only, or by land and sea, with all the uncertainties resulting from that mixture.

### Instructional

ART. 50. On this or that occasion, what is the evil that may not have had its origin in this cause? But why mention it? Who ever heard any thing about it? What Minister, except for the fatigue to self and friends, ever cared about it the value of a straw.

### Instructional

ART. 51. What then is the remedy? To have a Monarch, and keep him in a state of confinement? No surely. What then? Not to have any functionary, but one by whom, for the power and so forth attached to the office, the confinement would be submitted to with pleasure.

### Instructional

ART. 52. While the Monarch is upon his rambles in pursuit of pleasure,——wretches by dozens or by scores are kept suspended between life and death, waiting their doom. True it is——that, in this case, combined with the all but most unapt form of *government*, (for pure aristocracy is still worse), is the most unapt form of *punishment*. But this, though the most conspicuous, is but one drop, in the current of inscrutable evil, flowing from the same source.

### Instructional. Exemplificational

ART. 53. In the United States, the offices belonging to the subdepartments, together with the residence of the Prime Minister, styled

*President*, are under the same roof: the whole edifice being styled *the Capitol*. But, neither has the circular nor the polygono-circular plan of construction been employed: nor, for aught appears, the *Conversation-tubes*. For the designation of the several departments, four denominations and no more are there employed, namely, 1, State; 2, Treasury; 3, War; 4, Navy.——See the Plans in 'The New National Calendar' for 1821.[1]

### *Instructional. Ratiocinative*

ART. 54. As to the office of the Justice Minister,——this should rather be *remote* from, than contiguous to, the above-mentioned cluster of offices. Between the Administrative Department and the Judiciary, ——the less the unseen and unheard communication, the better.

---

[1] Bentham is mistaken in suggesting that the President and the administrative departments are housed in the Capitol, which has been from the beginning the seat of the Congress. The plans to which he refers are of four buildings, housing the departments of State, Treasury, War, and Navy, which were intended to surround the White House. See P. Force, *The National Calendar, for MDCCCXXI*, Washington City, 1821, pp. 218–23, especially p. 219. Bentham also seems to suggest that there were only four executive departments and omits to mention the offices of the Attorney-General and Postmaster-General.

# Sections.

# COLLATIONS

# A. 1830 COLLATION

Collation: Jeremy Bentham, *Constitutional Code; for the use of All Nations and All Governments professing Liberal Opinions* (London, 1830).

*Note.* The collation prints all variants (including variations in punctuation, spelling, italics, and capitalization) between the present edition and the 1830 text. Elaborate textual devices have been avoided. Where the present edition departs from 1830, the collation lists the original items by chapter, section (and bissection) and article. Major changes are also discussed in footnotes in the text, though at times the reader is referred to the collations for the full texts of the originals. A number of minor variations, most of which are based on printing conventions, are not recorded in the collation, but are listed here: (a) changes from lower to upper and upper to lower case roman numerals are not recorded, although changes from roman to arabic and arabic to roman numerals are noted; (b) variations in the form of footnote markers in the text are not recorded; (c) the use of full stops after chapter, section and article headings is not recorded; (d) the use of commas after chapter references (e.g. Ch. vii,) and full stops after section references (e.g. §17.) in cross-references is not recorded; (e) the use of double inverted commas in quotations has not been recorded; and (f) as the use of square brackets is confined to textual emendations in the present edition, Bentham's use of square brackets to indicate a point to be supplied by the country adopting the Code is replaced by braces.

## 1830 Collation

| | |
|---|---|
| N to title | [Constitutional Code.] |

**CHAPTER I**

| | |
|---|---|
| Art. 3 | District: as . . . LEGISLATURE: sending Ch. xxviii, |
| Art. 4 | Code, Ch. vi, . . . §4, a IMMEDIATE JUDGES. |
| Art. 6 | division; the |

**Instructional Dissertation**

| | |
|---|---|
| 1st para | Bis-subdistricts, |
| 8th para | Παροικὶα |
| 9th para | division, |
| 13th para | *departements*; *Justices de paix*, |
| 14th para | 1. Departements 2. Arrondissemens |
| 17th para | LOCAL HEADMAN'S REGISTRAR. |

CHAPTER II
   Art. 2                              Correspondent Rules.
   Art. 16  n                         [*Responsibility*.]
          9th para                maximixing
         13th para               facilities
   Art. 17                             examination, principle.
                                    location Principle—
                                    §13, ... §14, ... §15, *Locable how.*
                                    ... §26,
   Art. 20                           Public-Opinion Tribunal,
                                    *Public-Opinion*
   Art. 22                         dislocational,
   Art. 24                         Public-Opinion


CHAPTER IV
   Art. 2                              Constitutive
                                    §2, 3,
                                    CONSTITUTIVE. §2, 3.
                                    LEGISLATURE.
   Art. 11                         Ch. xxviii,
                                      severally:
   Art. 13                         Sub-legislature,


CHAPTER V

Section 1,
   Art. 2                              LEGISLATURE. §4 to 13.
   Art. 3                              §6,

Section 2,
   Art. 3                            I. Their
          n                       [*Deputy*.]
   Art. 4                          II. The

Section 3,
   Art. 1                          §4 to 13.
   Art. 4                          Constitutive, I. On
                                      *Powers*, Art. 4,
                                    SubDistricts
                                    §5,
   Art. 6                          Art. 4, 5,
   Art. 9                          *Legislative Penal Judicatory*.

Section 4,
   Art. 2                          §1. Art. 3.
   Art. 3                          Sub-committees.
                                    Sub-legislatures.
                                    COLLECTIVELY. §2. *Actors in*

| | | |
|---|---|---|
| Section 5, | Heading *omits* | *Public Opinion Tribunal:*— |
| Art. 1 | | I. *Statistic* |
| Art. 6 | | case they will |
| Art. 7 | | *Motions:* Of |

| | |
|---|---|
| Section 6, | |
| Art. 1 | *melioration suggestive* |
| Art. 5 | Public-Opinion |

## CHAPTER VI

| | |
|---|---|
| Section 2, | |
| Art. 2 | incidental, dislocative |

| | |
|---|---|
| Section 6, | §22, *Locable who.* |

| | |
|---|---|
| Section 17, | §4. |

| | | |
|---|---|---|
| Section 20, | | |
| Art. 5 | *omits* | is placed |
| Art. 17 | | —on no session |
| Art. 22 | | even |

| | |
|---|---|
| Section 22, | |
| Art. 1 | precipitation and duty, |
| Art. 3 | sitten on |
| | Legislature, as shall be sufficient to secure |

| | | |
|---|---|---|
| Section 23, | | |
| Art. 12 | | and almost |
| Art. 24 | *omits* | 2. |
| | | Depute, |
| Art. 32 | | *Legislative* |

| | | |
|---|---|---|
| Section 25, | | |
| Art. 1 | | [or twice?] |
| Art. 3 | | Art. 2, |
| Art. 6 | | course: the |
| Art. 8 | | fai |
| Art. 24 | | *Arch-corruptor* |
| Art. 37 | | *Question* 3. |
| | | *tried*, to |
| Art. 39 | | pursuits. 2, |
| Art. 40 | | circumstances |
| Art. 49 | | §24, *Securities,* |
| | *omits* | part of |
| Art. 52 | (Objections) | 1. . . . non re-locability |
| | (Answers) | 1. . . . non re-locability |
| | | 3. . . . Continuation-Committee |
| | | 3. . . . Continuation-Committee |

463

Art. 53                              Continuation-Committee
                                     Continuation-Committee
Art. 54                              *Question* 4.


Section 26,
  Art. 5                             CONSTITUTIVE. §2.


Section 27,
  Art. 1                             Art. 16, 18, 19, 29, 30.
  Art. 6                             §4,
  Art. 8                             MINISTER. §10,
  Art. 9                             REGISTRARS. §4, *Marriage-recording.* §5,
                                     *Birth-recording.* §6, *Full-age-recording.* §7,
                                     *Death-recording.* §8, *Post-obit-administra-*
                                     *tion-granting.* §9, *Conveyance-recording.*
                                     §10, *Contract-recording.* §11, *Prospective-*
                                     *evidence-recording.* §12, *Subjudiciary topo-*
                                     *graphical function.*
  Art. 11                            *eliciter,*
                                     *interrogater,*
  Art. 13                            Art. 23 to 26.
  Art. 14  *omits*                   5,
  Art. 15                            Government. *Agents*
  Art. 17                            definitive
  Art. 19                            wheresoeverd elivered,
  Art. 20                            REGISTRARS. §5,
  Art. 26                            JUDGES IMMEDIATE DEPUTE PERMA-
                                     NENT:
                                     Ch. xvi, JUDGES IMMEDIATE DEPUTE
                                     OCCASIONAL.
  Art. 27                            Elector
                                     §18, 20, and 25,
  Art. 28                            time,
  Art. 39                            *Methodization condensation,*
                                     *completenes,*
  Art. 41                            *Regularity*
  Art. 48                            *exclutionary*
                                     serve
                                     systems exemplified
  Art. 50                            1. Neither
                                     subjected to is—
  Art. 55  *omits*                   III.


Section 29,
  Art. 2   Heading                   *Instructianal.*
           n                         [Pannomion]
  Art. 5                             (Year, . . . as above.)
                                     "*Repealed* "on
                                     Instead, of
  Art. 9                             Art. 3, 4, 5, 6.

464

Section 30,
    Art. 1                              Judiciary,
                                      CONSTITUTIVE. §2,

Section 31,
    Art. 9                              *Adam* has on regard
    Art. 14                          it applied
    Art. 17                          exercised: in regard to no
    Art. 20   n                  andmother
    Art. 22                          Of that supposed
    Art. 24                          Art. 23
    Art. 25                          Art. 24
    Art. 26                          Art. 25
    Art. 27                          Art. 26
    Art. 28                          Art. 27
    Art. 29                          Art. 28
    Art. 30                          Art. 29
    Art. 31                          Art. 30
                                    abuse of its power
    Art. 32                          Art. 31
                                    in preventing . . . from opposing
    Art. 33                          Art. 32
    Art. 34                          Art. 33
    Art. 35                          Art. 34
    Art. 36                          Art. 35
    Art. 37                          Art. 36
    Art. 38                          Art. 37
    Art. 39                          Art. 38
    Art. 40                          Art. 39
    Art. 41                          Art. 40
    Art. 42                          Art. 41
                                    §4 to 13
              (3)                Elector:
                                    *service, accidental appendage.*
              (5)                *Legislature,*
              (8)                Ch. vii,
    Art. 43                          §15, *Remuneration;*
    Art. 44                          *Publicity-recordation publication;*
                                    SEPARATELY,
                                    COLLECTIVELY. §19,
                                    §2,
    Art. 45                          §2,

## CHAPTER VII

N TO CHAPTER                    dissention
                                    perhaps of war.

Section 1,
    Art. 4                           repealed

| | | |
|---|---|---|
| Section 5, | Heading | *all, promised.* |
| Section 6, | Heading | *Justice, accessible to all, promised.* |
| Section 9, | Heading | *Impartiality, in . . . power, promised.* |

## CHAPTER VIII

Section 1,
| | | |
|---|---|---|
| Art. 1 | Heading *omits* | *Enactive.* |
| Art. 2 | | Art. 4 and 5, |
| | | §2, 3, 4. |
| Art. 4 | | COLLECTIVELY. §1, |
| Art. 8 | | *in-correctness,* |

Section 2,
| | | |
|---|---|---|
| Art. 2 | *omits* | II. |
| Art. 3 | *omits* | III. |
| Art. 5 | *omits* | IV. |
| Art. 8 | *omits* | V. |
| | | Art. 8, 9, |
| Art. 9 | | *Stipendiary* |
| Art. 11 | | Art. 14, |
| | n | Article 11, Section 11, Clause 1, |
| | | Art. 13. |
| Art. 15 | | §9, |
| | | [*Exemplars.*] |
| Art. 16 | | COLLECTIVELY. §16, |

Section 3,
| | | |
|---|---|---|
| Art. 1 | | Art. 7. |
| | | COLLECTIVELY. §24, |

Section 4,
| | | |
|---|---|---|
| Art. 2 | | understand iu |
| Art. 7 | Heading *omits* | *Enactive.* |
| Art. 8 | | §1. Art. 14. No. 1, 2, 3. |
| Art. 10 | | §3, |

Section 5,
| | | |
|---|---|---|
| Art. 4 | | substitute a Representative Democray, |

Section 8,
| | | |
|---|---|---|
| Art. 5 | | COLLECTIVEY. §16, *Located how.* |

Section 9,
| | | |
|---|---|---|
| Art. 3 | | LEGISLATIVE. §30, No. 1, 2, 3, 4, 5, 7. |

Section 10,
  Art. 7                          §9, 11, 12;
                                  Cʜ. xi, . . . §1,
                                  §19, 20, 21, 22.

Section 11,
  Art. 6    4.                    4. The *Health*
            7.                    ᴄᴏʟʟᴇᴄᴛɪᴠᴇʟʏ. §14,
  Art. 10                         Lᴇɢɪsʟᴀᴛɪᴠᴇ;
                                  Jᴜᴅɪᴄɪᴀʀʏ ᴄᴏʟʟᴇᴄᴛɪᴠᴇʟʏ.
  Art. 14   Rule 3               their hands

Section 12,
  Art. 1    Heading *omits*       *Enactive.*
            6                     §31, *Securities*, Art. 13.
            7                     §31, Art. 14, 15,
            9                     Art. 2, 3, 4,
            10                    ᴄᴏʟʟᴇᴄᴛɪᴠᴇʟʏ. §25.
            12                    Cᴏɴsᴛɪᴛᴜᴛɪᴠᴇ. §5, *Function*
            13                    *Legislational*
  Art. 3                          at at his desire
  Art. 5                          ᴄᴏʟʟᴇᴄᴛɪᴠᴇʟʏ. §23, . . . Art. 13, 14, 15,
                                  16.


CHAPTER IX

Section 2,
  Art. 1    *Nos. 5 and 6 and* § §*5 and 6 reversed.*
            11                   §10.

Section 3,
  Art. 3    *omits para at*      ɪ.
  Art. 4    *omits para at*      ᴠɪɪɪ.
  Art. 5    *omits para at*      ɪx.
  Art. 16                        Foreign Relation, Subdepartment,
  Art. 18                        *Locable how,*
  Art. 25                        it so
  Art. 27   n*                   its rounds:
  Art. 35                        Art. 34.
  Art. 36                        Art. 35.

Section 4,
  Art. 4    *omits*              I.
                                 subject-matters
  Art. 7    *omits*              II.
  Art. 8                         instance
  Art. 9                         *natred*
  Art. 17                        herein-after
  Art. 27                        *Legislative*
  Art. 44                        *remunerationly*

| | | |
|---|---|---|
| Art. 47 | | 1. Requisite |
| Art. 49 | | elimination; |
| | | Subsection |
| Art. 51 | | Subsection |
| Art. 59 | *omits* | 4. |
| Art. 60 | | STATISTICATION, REGISTRATION |
| | | PUBLICATION ORDINANCES, |
| Art. 64 | | part, |
| Art. 65 | | be given. |
| Art. 68 | *omits* | II. |
| Art. 69 | *omits* | III. |

Section 5,

| | | |
|---|---|---|
| Art. 12 | *omits* | II. |
| Art. 14 | | line Scale |
| | | d'Affairs. |
| | n | Mertens's |
| | | Precis |
| | | &c. Gottingen, |
| Art. 17 | | function, as |
| | | of superordinate: |
| Art. 18 | | *superordinate powers*, |
| | | Art. 4, 5, 6, 7: |
| | | *right*, |
| Art. 27 | 1 | appropriate operations, |
| Art. 33 | | LEGISLATIVE; |
| Art. 35 | | III. The *Army* |
| | | §3, *Stipendaries* ... §5, |
| Art. 40 | | 1 ... 1 ... 2 ... 3 ... 4 ... 5 ... 6 ... 7 ... |
| | | 8 ... 9 ... 10 ... 11. |
| Art. 41 | | 1. Subordinates |

Section 6,

| | | |
|---|---|---|
| Art. 1 | | MINISTER. §4, |
| | | Art. 2, 3, 4, 5, 6, 10. |
| Art. 2 | | §1, |
| Art. 7 | | §29: ... §28. |
| Art. 13 | | office, |

Section 7, Bissection 1,

| | | |
|---|---|---|
| Art. 2 | | §2. Art. 1. |
| Art. 3 | *omits* | 1. |
| Art. 4 | | Subsections |
| Art. 5 | Heading | *Enactive.* |
| | | II. *Minimization* |
| | | Subsection |
| Art. 11 | | these |
| Art. 13 | | I. *Original* |
| Art. 14 | | II. *Journal.* |
| Art. 15 | | III. *Periodical* |

| | | |
|---|---|---|
| Art. 16 | | Books, Offices, Super-offices . . . ; |
| | | Books, Super-books, |
| Art. 17 | | *Book*. |
| Art. 18 | | *lease*-letting, |
| | | Subsection |
| | | Art. 23. |
| Art. 19 | | II. *Loss* |
| | | 1. All |
| Art. 21 | Heading *omits* | *Instructional. Ratiocinative*. |
| Art. 22 | | Subsection |
| Art. 23 | | their Suboffices, |

Bissection 2,

| | | |
|---|---|---|
| Art. 4 | *omits* | Art. 4. Original Outset Book continued. |
| | | *second, Immoveable* |
| | | *Rights intervicinal*; if |
| Art. 5 | | *pro* ratâ ; |
| Art. 6 | | Specific Book the third. |
| | | deterioration's |
| Art. 9 | | I. Mineral |
| | | II. Vegetable |
| | | III. Animal substances.— |
| | | IV. Products . . . 1, Acids |
| Art. 19 | | &c——a |
| Art. 20 | | keys. &c. |
| Art. 26 | I.2 | ready-preparedm edicines; |
| | | VI. Works in hand: |
| Art. 27 | | IV. Specific Book the fourth, |
| | | *Money* Stock Book. |
| | | I, distinguishing *whence*: |

Bissection 3, Heading

| | | |
|---|---|---|
| | | . . . III. JOURNAL BOOKS. |
| Art. 5 | | *immoveble*: |
| | | indefensible, |
| | | *moveable*; appellative, |
| Art. 7 | | Entrance Book, |
| | | *Application* Book. |
| Art. 8 | | I. *Personal*. |
| | *new para at* | *Stock Book*, |
| | | Subsection IV, |
| Art. 14 | *omits* | Journal continued. |
| | *omits para at* | I. *Subspecific* Book the *first*. |
| Art. 17 | | original Outset Book. |
| | | *Subsection* 2. |
| | | PURCHASE. |
| | | III. . . . I. . . . II. . . . III. . . . IV. . . . V. |
| | | HIRE. |
| | | out-set stock, |
| | | 2, Art. 3, page 289. |

| | | |
|---|---|---|
| Art. 18 | | *third*. Moveable Stock Book. |
| | *omits* | I. Subspecific Book the first. |
| | | For a *Receipt Specific Book*, Heads |
| | | page 291. |
| | | *package*, |
| | | 13. So, |
| | | 14. If . . . whom |
| Art. 19 | *omits* | II. Subspecific Book the second. |
| | *omits* | *Application Book.* |
| | | Art. 16, |
| Art. 20 | *omits* | 2. |
| Art. 23 | | third, *Issue* |
| Art. 25 | | IV. *Money* Subspecific Book the *first*. |
| | | 1. . . . 2. . . . I. . . . II. |
| | | (See below, Bis-sub-book 4, Art. 4. Loss |
| | | Book.) |
| Art. 28 | | III. Unexpected demands not fulfilled. |
| Art. 30 | *new para at* | 2. Occurrence, |
| | | SEVERALLY. §6, |
| Art. 32 | | LEGISLATIVE. |

| | | |
|---|---|---|
| Bissection 4, Heading | | III. LOSS BOOKS. |
| Art. 2 | | unmoveable. |
| Art. 3 | | SEVERALLY. §6, |
| Art. 4 | | I. Subject-matter . . . I, |
| Art. 6 | | II. Subject-matter . . . II, |
| | | unmoveable |
| | | Loss. |
| Art. 7 | | III. Subject-matter . . . III, |
| | | No. 4, 5, 6. |
| | | &c. consumption |
| Art. 11 | | Fermentation, saccharine, |
| Art. 12 | | Subject-matters |
| Art. 13 | | Subject matters, |
| Art. 17 | | "*when introduced*: |
| | | "*when produced*: |
| Art. 19 | | subject matters |
| | | Art. 16, 17, |
| | | third, |
| | | page 303. |
| Art. 20 | | IV. Subject matter . . . IV. *Money.* |
| | III. *omits* | Modes. Examples— |
| | VI. *omits* | Modes. Examples— |
| Art. 31 | | production |
| | | *Dislocable who.* |

| | |
|---|---|
| Bissection 5, | |
| Art. 1 | §3, Art. 8, *Entrance Book.* |
| | *Retro-acception* |
| | page 315, |

470

Bissection 6,

| | | |
|---|---|---|
| Art. 1 | | Art. 27. |
| Art. 2 | | Art. 28. |
| | | 1. *For the practice*. Saving |
| Art. 3 | | Art. 29. |
| | | 1. As to . . . Rule 1. For |
| | *new para at* | Rule 1. |
| Art. 4 | | Art. 30. |
| Art. 5 | | Art. 31. |
| | n a | ordinary |
| Art. 6 | | Art. 32. |
| | *omits* | Bissection the first, |
| | | Art. 4. |

Section 8,

| | | |
|---|---|---|
| Art. 9 | | correspondeut *procuration-mandate*, |
| Art. 11 | | §2§2, |
| Art. 12 | | §2§. |
| Art. 20 | | if yes, by |
| Art. 22 | | as procurement |
| Art. 23 | | §.7, |
| Art. 24 | | place |
| Art. 27 | | §2§ |
| Art. 28 | | *account and contract*. |
| Art. 29 | | Prime Minister of the subdepartment, |
| | | Art. iv. |
| Art. 33 | | §2§5, |
| Art. 34 | *omits* | 3. |
| Art. 38 | | matter |

Section 9,

| | | |
|---|---|---|
| Art. 3 | | belongs, ascertaining |
| | 4 | transference, temporary |
| | 6 | *Remuneration*, and . . . *Securities*, &c. |
| | | Art. 6, and 18 to 29. |
| Art. 4 | 6.1. | determined, as per Art. 3, by *lot*, |
| | | §16, *Locable who*. Supplement, Art. 65 or 6, |
| | | 66 or 7, 70 or 11. |
| | 12. | *Subdepartment*. |
| | 13. *omits para at* | For other |
| Art. 5 | | their |
| Art. 6 | | Members, |
| Art. 7 | | Minister of |
| Art. 8 | | *Supplement*. Art. 60. |

Section 10,

| | | |
|---|---|---|
| Art. 6 | | Art. 3, 7, |
| Art. 8 | | *Legislative* . . . *Legislative* |
| Art. 9 | | §11. *Information-elicitative* |
| | | §10, 11. |
| Art. 10 | | Art. 4 to 14. |

| | | |
|---|---|---|
| Art. 16 | | §10, Art. 8, |
| Art. 23 | | Art. 24. |
| | 5 | likewise, |
| Art. 24 | | Art. 25. |
| | | *subjectmany*, |
| Art. 25 | | Art. 26. |
| Section 11, | | |
| Art. 3 | | §10, 11, |
| Art. 5 | | action is |
| | | being provided |
| Art. 13 | | imposed examples |
| Section 14, | | |
| Art. 3 | n | Ch. xxviii, |
| | | §2, |
| Section 15, | | |
| Art. 2 | | *who* |
| Art. 4 | 3 | disrepute |
| Art. 9 | | §4, |
| Art. 20 | | Art. 22, |
| Art. 26 | | The defendant |
| | | demand-money |
| | | ADVOCATE; |
| | | Chap. xix. |
| Art. 28 | | recondation-entry, |
| | | Art. 23, |
| Art. 33 | | follows:— |
| Art. 34 | | quantum and merit, |
| Art. 48 | | Art. 30: |
| Art. 51 | | follows:— |
| | 2 | Sub-department, |
| Section 16, | | |
| Art. 3 | | follows:— |
| | | §15, |
| Art. 7 | | Arts. 54, |
| Art. 10 | | §31, |
| Art. 13 | | messengers |
| Art. 15 | I.3 | sub-department. |
| Art. 16 | | §18, |
| Art. 18 | | Arts. 42 to 53, |
| | | Ch. xiv, |
| Art. 20 | | what |
| | | fellow-canditates, |
| Art. 21 | | Art. 33. |
| Art. 31 | | Art. 30. |
| Art. 32 | | Art. 31. |
| Art. 33 | | Art. 32. |
| Art. 34 | | Art. 33. |
| Art. 35 | | Art. 34. |
| | | §26, |

| | |
|---|---|
| Art. 36 | Art. 35. |
| Art. 37 | Art. 36. |
| Art. 38 | Art. 37. |
| Art. 39 | Art. 38. |
| Art. 40 | Art. 39. |
| Art. 41 | Art. 40. |
| Art. 42 | Art. 41. |
| Art. 43 | Art. 42. |
| | either and |
| Art. 44 | Art. 43. |
| Art. 45 | Art. 44. |
| Art. 46 | Art. 45. |
| Art. 47 | Art. 46. |
| Art. 48 | Art. 47. |
| Art. 49 | Art. 48. |
| | LEGISLATIVE, |
| Art. 50 | Art. 49. |
| Art. 51 | Art. 50. |
| | eys |
| Art. 52 | Art. 51. |
| | examinations. See Art. 32. |
| Art. 53 | Art. 52. |
| Art. 54 | Art. 53. |
| Art. 55 | Art. 54 |
| Art. 56 | Art. 55 |
| Art. 57 | Art. 56. |
| | 7, if |
| Art. 58 | Art. 57. |
| Art. 59 | Art. 58. |
| Art. 60 | Art. 59. |
| Art. 61 or 1 | Art. 60 or 1. |
| Art. 62 or 2 | Art. 61 or 2. |
| Art. 63 or 3 | Art. 62 or 3. |
| | Art. 17, 18. |
| Art. 64 or 4 | Art. 63 or 4. |
| Art. 65 or 5 | Art. 64 or 5. |
| | instructions afforded |
| Art. 66 or 6 | Art. 65 or 6. |
| Art. 67 or 7 | Art. 66 or 7 |
| Art. 68 or 8 | Art. 67 or 8 |
| | 1. Manner |
| | question ticket. |
| Art. 69 or 9 | Art. 68 or 9. |
| | 1. A box |
| n | appearanccs |
| | had not stayed his hand,— |
| Art. 70 or 10 | Art. 69 or 10. |
| Art. 71 or 11 | Art. 70 or 11. |
| Art. 72 or 12 | Art. 71 or 12. |
| Art. 73 or 13 | Art. 72 or 13. |
| | QUASI JURY. |

| | |
|---|---|
| Art. 74 or 14 | Art. 73 or 14. |
| Art. 75 or 15 | Art. 74 or 15. |
| | 1. Of |
| Art. 76 or 16 | Art. 75 or 16. |
| Art. 77 or 17 | Art. 76 or 17. |
| Art. 78 or 18 | Art. 77 or 18. |

| | |
|---|---|
| Section 17, | |
| Art. 6 | Arts. 10, 11, 12, 13, |
| Art. 9 | say; year, |
| Art. 14 | Art. 55, |
| Art. 15 | quasi pecuniary |
| Art. 17 | considerations |
| Art. 18 | service, the |
| Art. 19 | sub-departments, |
| | sub-department, |
| Art. 21 | sub-department, |
| Art. 22 | sub-department, |
| Art. 23 | sub-departments, |
| Art. 24 | sub-department, |
| Art. 25 | §3. |
| Art. 27 | Art. 23, |
| Art. 28 | sub-department, |
| Art. 29 | *Vice-Consul* by |
| Art. 33 | Art. 18, |
| Art. 37 | sub-department, |
| Art. 38 | *null-and-void*, |
| Art. 39 | perPenal |
| Art. 40 | 3. Act |

| | |
|---|---|
| Section 17, Supplement, | |
| Art. 42 or 1 | Art. 37 or 1. |
| Art. 43 or 2 | Art. 38 or 2. |
| | Art. 12, 13: |
| | (Art. 33, 34, 35, 36, 40), |
| | responsibility, alleviated |
| | trials, above; |
| Art. 44 or 3 | Art. 39 or 3. II. Case II. |
| | *Examination Jury*, |
| | I. Reason, |
| Art. 45 or 4 | Art. 40 or 4. |
| | 1. In |
| Art. 46 or 5 | Art. 41 or 5. |
| Art. 47 or 6 | Art. 42 or 6. |
| Art. 48 or 7 | Art. 43 or 7. |
| n | intituled Official |
| Art. 49 or 8 | Art. 44 or 8. |
| | *or say* |
| | indefinitely amount |
| | illegal service |

| | |
|---|---|
| Art. 50 or 9 | Art. 45 or 9. |
| | I. Objection, to |
| Art. 51 or 10 | Art. 46 or 10. |
| | rest of the community . . . rest of the community |
| Art. 52 or 11 | Art. 47 or 11. |
| | *Answer.* |
| Art. 53 or 12 | Art. 48 or 12. |
| | £1,000000 |
| Art. 54 or 13 | Art. 49 or 13. |
| | 3, *Venality* |
| | does the emptional. |
| *omits* | 3, |
| | *protagé*, |
| Art. 55 or 14 | Art. 50 or 14. |
| | *Objection 14,* |
| | alleged existence |
| Art. 56 or 15 | Art. 51 or 15. |
| *omits* | *invited.* |
| Art. 57 or 16 | Art. 51 or 15. |
| | *protegés* |
| Art. 58 or 17 | Art. 52 or 16. |
| Art. 59 or 18 | Art. 33 or 17. |
| *omits* | 6 |
| | flew |

*Footnote to Concluding Instruction inserted after*      with it.

CONCLUDING INSTRUCTION TO THE PUBLIC
OPINION TRIBUNAL

| | |
|---|---|
| Art. 5 | it Anno |
| *omits* | §12. |

Section 18,

| | | |
|---|---|---|
| Art. 2 | 6 | Transference, temporary, |
| Art. 6 | | Art. 4. |
| | | dislocative modified, |
| Art. 10 | | supposed it |
| | | subordinate |

Section 19,

| | |
|---|---|
| Art. 1 | I. *Fields* |
| Art. 5 | §7, |
| Art. 9 | *Sea Stipendiary Force.* |
| Art. 11 | *Remuneration how* |
| Art. 12 | Art. 37, 38. |

| | | |
|---|---|---|
| Art. 13 | | Art. 10, |
| Art. 14 | | Question 2. Should |
| | 1 | Art. 11, 12. |
| | 7 | effect. |
| Art. 15 | | *Located how.* |
| | | §17, *Located how,* |
| Art. 17 | | Art. 22 to 29, |
| Art. 18 | | Art. 31, 32, |
| Art. 19 | n | 17 and 18, |
| Art. 20 | | 1. To |
| | *omits* | §17, |
| Art. 21 | | §17, |
| Art. 23 | | to him |
| Art. 28 | | Art. 21, |
| Art. 31 | n | elucidatiou |
| | | Art. 28, 29, 30. |
| Art. 32 | | Art. 65, 66, |
| Art. 36 | | ——for there . . . that appropriate |
| | n | Art. 41. |
| Art. 39 | | obtainments |
| | | Art. 16, |
| Art. 40 | | *Dislocable who,* |
| | | Art. 4, 5, 6; |
| | | Art. 7, 8, 9, 10, |
| Art. 42 | | Art. 48. |

| | | |
|---|---|---|
| Section 20, | | |
| Art. 2 | | numbers |
| | | *inspectors,* |
| Art. 10 | | dislocation |
| Art. 13 | | 3. *Health* subdepartments. |
| Art. 25 | | above, belongs, as per §21, . . . the power |

| | | |
|---|---|---|
| Section 21, | | |
| Art. 1 | | other; each |
| Art. 4 | | Art. 2, 3, 4, |
| | | subordinates. |
| | | *dislocative power,* |
| | | Art. 1, 2. |
| Art. 6 | | *Inspectee.* |
| Art. 7 | 4 | examinations |
| Art. 8 | | Art. 5, 6, 7. |
| Art. 9 | | a *suitor.* |
| Art. 11 | *omits* | 1. |
| Art. 12 | | II. |
| Art. 13 | | III. |
| Art. 14 | | ART. 15. IV. |
| Art. 15 | | V. |
| Art. 18 | | CASE V. |
| | | Art. 16 |
| Art. 19 | | CASE VI. |

| | | |
|---|---|---|
| Art. 20 | | Art. 16 to 20, |
| | 4 | §4, |
| | 7 | Chap. xvii, |
| Art. 21 | | *positive* |
| Art. 32 | | matured |
| | n | [*Deontology*] |
| Art. 34 | | CASE VII. The alleged oppres*s*or a *functionary*. Oppres*s*ee, in this case, none can there be but ... |
| | | his directive function. |
| Art. 36 | | Articles 12 to 20; |
| Art. 37 | | For this purpose, exceptions |
| Art. 38 | | expense vexation |
| | | even avoidance |
| Art. 43 | | Art. 40, |
| Art. 47 | | Art. 41, 42. |
| Art. 48 | | here the |
| Art. 49 | | situation |
| Art. 50 | *omits* | I. Shape, *simple dislocation*. |
| Art. 54 | | CASE VIII. |
| | | Art. 55. in which, |
| | | of such *renewal*, |
| Art. 60 | | CASE IX. |
| Art. 61 | | CASE X. |
| Art. 62 | | Art. 51, 52. |
| Art. 64 | | ART, 65. CASE XI. |
| | | Art. 51. |
| Art. 65 | | ART. 66. CASE XII. |
| | | transference temporary to an inferior |
| | | Art. 55, 56: |
| | | Art. 57, 58, 59. |
| Art. 66 | | Art. 67. |
| Art. 67 | | Art. 68. |
| | | if not temporary, |
| Art. 68 | | ART. 69. CASE XIII. |
| | | Art. 51: |
| | | Art. 49, 50. |
| Art. 69 | | ART. 70. CASE XIV. |
| | | stoppage of promotion: stoppage temporary. |
| | | Art. 55, 56: |
| | | Art. 57, 58, 59. |
| Art. 70 | | Art. 71. |
| Art. 71 | | Art. 72. |
| | | 1. War, |
| Art. 72 | | Art. 73. |
| | | Art. 39. |
| Art. 73 | | Art. 74. |
| | | Art. 65, 66, 67, |
| | 3 | special |
| Art. 74 | | Art. 75. |
| Art. 75 | | Art. 76. |

| | |
|---|---|
| Art. 76 | Art. 77 |
| Art. 77 | Art. 78. |

Section 22,
| | |
|---|---|
| Art. 6 | said Master, |
| | exercise by it |

Section 23,
| | |
|---|---|
| Art. 3 | *mode*, |
| Art. 5 | *subsection* intituled |
| Art. 8 | by which |
| Art. 16 | Art. 6, 7, — |

Section 24,
| | |
|---|---|
| Art. 4 | LEGISLATIVE, |
| | *Member's* |

Section 25,
| | | |
|---|---|---|
| Art. 1 | 3 | popular or moral, |
| | | and by the |
| | 6 | sames power, |
| | n | LEGISLATIVE, |
| | | Art. 5, 6, |
| Art. 3 | | Art. 3, 4, 5, 6. |
| | 9 | Art. 11, 12, 13, 14, 15, |
| | 10 | Art. 17 to 40. |
| | 11 | Art. 1 to 13. |
| Art. 4 | | *function*; §2§ II. Art. 1. p. 286, |
| | | *Book*; §2§ III. Art. 8 to 13. pp. 306 to 309, |
| | | §2§ IV. *Loss Book*, Art. 4, 5. p. 320. |
| Art. 5 | | Art. 18 to 29, pages 386, 387, 388. |
| Art. 12 | | Art. 16 to 19. |
| Art. 15 | | Art. 23, 24, |
| Art. 17 | | Art. 50, 51, 52. |
| Art. 19 | | Art. 19, |
| Art. 24 | | dispatch; might |
| Art. 27 | | subdepartment to |
| Art. 30 | | Supreme Constitution, |
| | | §5, 6, *Minutation*. |
| Art. 31 | | Ch. xii, §16, |
| Art. 32 | | Art. 2, 3, 4,) |
| Art. 34 | | 1. Temporary |
| Art. 35 | | to no |
| | | LEGISLATIVE, |
| | | to subordinates |
| | | to such |
| | *omits* | —is it necessary to confer it. |
| Art. 36 | | to it,— |
| Art. 37 | | clear correct |
| | | LEGISLATIVE, |

| | | |
|---|---|---|
| Art. 42 | | Legislative,<br>2, the |
| Art. 47 | | *mercantile* sub-class, |
| Art. 49 | | anti-nationality |
| Art. 50 | | sections 20, 21, |
| | | |
| Section 26, | | |
| Art. 4 | | with which |
| Art. 11 | | publication |
| Art. 12 | | Legislative, |
| Art. 20 | | messengers, at |
| | | moment: notice |
| | n b | time, might |
| Art. 21 | | Art. 10 and 11, |
| | | *Suitors'* |
| Art. 22 | | *Judiciary Visitors* |
| | | abovementioned |
| Art. 24 | | Art. 38. 43. |
| Art. 36 | | power; to |
| Art. 38 | *inserts* | *Ratiocinative.* |
| | | faculty |
| Art. 39 | | *materiel* |
| | | *personel* |
| Art. 40 | | usefulness |
| Art. 42 | | on |
| Art. 43 | | §10, 11. |
| Art. 45 | | subject matter possesses |

# B. BOWRING COLLATION

Collation: Jeremy Bentham, *The Works of Jeremy Bentham*, ed. J. Bowring (Edinburgh, 1838–43), Vol. IX, 146–333.

*Note*. See the note to the 1830 Collation, p. 461 above. In addition to the variations discussed in the note above, there are several further variants omitted from the Bowring Collation: (a) the use of the symbol '§' for the word 'section' has not been recorded; (b) the separation into two words of the following terms which Bowring combines is not recorded: 'anything', 'everywhere', 'anywhere', 'everybody', 'everything', 'thereby'; and (c) the omission of the hyphen in the following words is not recorded: 'all-comprehensive', 'Advocate-General', 'above-mentioned', 'a-year', 'bene-meritant', 'bis-sub-department', 'bis-sub-district', child-birth', 'committee-man', 'continuation-committee', 'co-operation', 'greatest-happiness', 'here-proposed', 'judgment-seat', 'many-seated(ness)', 'non-re-election', 'non-re-locability', 'pre-eminent', 'public-opinion', 're-election', 're-locability', 'single-seated', 'singly-seated', 'sub-department(s)', 'sub-district(s)', 'subject-many', 'subject-matter(s)', 'sub-legislative', 'sub-legislature(s)', 'sub-minister(s)', 'sub-office(s)', 'sub-receptacle(s)', 'sub-specific', 'waiting-box(es)', 'witness-box', 'writing-clerk'. Although Bowring usually inserts hyphens in the listed words, at times the text drops the hyphens and the 1830 version in turn adopts their use. This occurs most frequently with 'subdepartment(s)', 'subject-matter(s)' and 'continuation-committee'.

At the end of this Collation, the item from the Appendix to Bowring (ix, 648) which relates to Volume I of the *Constitutional Code* is reprinted.

## Bowring Collation

PREFACE

| | |
|---|---|
| Heading | TO THE ORIGINAL EDITION OF BOOK II |
| 1st para | volumes |
| | constitutional code |
| n | This first volume corresponds with Book II. chapter i. to ix. inclusive, of the present edition.—*Ed.* |
| | author |
| 2nd para | author |
| | first volume |
| | introductory dissertation, |
| | elgiibility |
| | monarchy, aristocracy, and democracy; |
| 3rd para n | The first book of the present edition has been arranged from the matter which the author had so prepared.—*Ed.* |

| | |
|---|---|
| 4th para | measures as |
| | government |
| | itself |
| | volume |
| 5th para | away, or |
| | empire. |
| 7th para | what |
| | table |
| 8th para | volume |
| | code:—— |
| n | See the Procedure Code at length, in vol. ii. |
| | —*Ed.* |
| 9th para | along what |
| | composition of |
| | system, destined |

10th para ff. to end *omits remainder of the preface*


CHAPTER I.

| | |
|---|---|
| Heading n | [Constitutional Code.] |
| | code: |
| | codes. |
| Art. 3 | Ch. xxix. |
| Art. 4 | say, *Voting* |
| Art. 5 | Ch. xxv |
| Art. 6 | |

INSTRUCTIONAL
DISSERTATION

| | |
|---|---|
| 1st para | be,——distant |
| | Bis-subdistricts, |
| 3rd para | not, however, increase |
| 5th para | Ch. xxv. |
| | functionary in |
| | functionary, who |
| | Ch. xxv., |
| | functionary, of |
| | functions some |
| | rough, and |
| | America, and |
| 6th para | made assumption, is——that in |
| | Judicatory, (so |
| | Judicatory,) there |
| | because on |
| | occasion impossible |
| 7th para | judicatory |
| 8th para | *parish*; in |
| | Παροικὶα |
| 9th para | division, |
| | twenty, |
| | territory,——whatsoever |
| | questions, divisions |

| | |
|---|---|
| 11th para | numeration-table |
| 12th para | here proposed |
| 13th para | *departements*; |
| | *Cantons* each |
| | *Canton*, |
| 14th para | 1. Departments |
| | 3. Cantons |
| 16th para | foreign with |
| 17th para | Ch. xxvi. |
| n a | far the |

CHAPTER II

| | |
|---|---|
| Art. 2 | maximized: expense |
| | maximization principle |
| | minimization principle. |
| Art. 10 | as a matter |
| Art. 12 | means, of |
| | otherways |
| Art. 15 | moral intellectual, |
| | judicial: knowledge |
| Art. 16   n | [*Responsibility*.] |
| | apt——(for |
| | legislator |
| | legislator, |
| | employed |
| | or, the |
| | money for |
| | imagined, |
| | that as |
| | facilities |
| | duty, and |
| Art. 17 | examination principle. |
| | competition principle. |
| | location principle |
| Art. 18   Heading | *Enactive. Instructional.* |
| Art. 19 | entituled |
| Art. 20 | public-opinion tribunal, |
| | *Tribunal——its Composition.* |
| Art. 22 | dislocational, |
| Art. 23 | is, in |
| | effect, constantly |
| Art. 24 | than such as it is agreeable |
| | alone that |
| | despotism, with |
| | parliament, he |
| | him, while |
| | Because, by |
| | be and |

CHAPTER III
    Heading n                          See above, p. 96.
    Art. 1                             exercised by


CHAPTER IV
    Art. 1                             Authorities which
                                       these:—
                                       follows:—
    Art. 2                             Constitutive Authority, it
                                       Section 2, 3,
                                       them, except
                                       them by
                                       CONSTITUTIVE.
                                       Section 2, 3,
                                       LEGISLATURE.
    Art. 3                             them: eventually
    Art. 4                             Legislative in
    Art. 6                             contradistinguished
    Art. 9                             District a
    Art. 11                            Ch. xxix.
                                       &c.,
                                       severally:
    Art. 12                            power, accordingly, *fractionized:*
                                       districts:
    Art. 14                            only,) frugality


CHAPTER V
    Heading n                          See p. 95, *et seq.*

Section 1,
    Art. 2                             classes. Mode
                                       Code: as
                                       Legislature. Section 4 to 13.

Section 2,
    Art. 3                             I. Their
              n                        [*Deputy.*]
                                       located,—some by
                                       theirs, the
                                       *Sheriff-Depute.*
    Art. 4                             II. The
    Art. 5                             following:

Section 3,
    Art. 1     *omits*                 hereunto-annexed
                                       Section 4 to 13.
    Art. 4     new para                On the
                                       (one fourth?)

| | |
|---|---|
| Art. 6 | Art. 4, 5, |
| | alleged |
| | appellatives dyslogistic |
| Art. 7 | *him*, and |
| Art. 8 | Art. 4., |
| Art. 10 | But should |
| | happen that |
| | functionary in |
| | partiality, and |
| | partiality, on |
| | Legislature, the |
| | |
| Section 4 n | See p. 41, *et seq.* |
| Art. 1 | *Tribunal* as |
| | Constitutive what |
| Art. 2 | individuals of |
| | classes which, |
| | Section 1. Art. 3., |
| Art. 3 | *Actors in* |
| | persons taking for |
| | functionaries, belonging |
| Art. 4 | authority, otherwise |
| | government, it |
| | civilisation |
| | |
| Section 5, Heading | *Tribunal. Functions.* |
| Art. 1 | 1. *Statistic*, or |
| | operate as |
| | proceeding, or |
| | conduct on |
| Art. 2 | *function.*——Exercise |
| | it in |
| Art. 3 | *function.*——Exercise |
| | it in |
| | addition——whether |
| | otherwise——is |
| Art. 4 | *function.*——Exercise |
| | it in |
| | amiss or |
| | better having |
| | has, as such, been |
| | end, that if |
| Art. 6 | *completeness* |
| | *completeness* |
| | *completeness* |
| | particular,——or |
| | *Code*; on |
| | misdecision: to |
| Art. 7 | *Motions*: Of |
| Art. 8 | be—— |
| Art. 9 | *apropriate* |

Section 6,
   Art. 2                                          civilian, who
   Art. 3     Heading            *Enactive. Expositive.*


CHAPTER VI

Section 1,
   Art. 1                                          Art. I.
   Art. 3                                          But, in
                                      confirmation of the acts, of
   Art. 5                                          Constitutive the
                                      also, on
                                      Legislature the
   Art. 6     Heading            *Enactive. Ratiocinative.*
                                      executive,
                                      incompetent.——Unfaithfulness,
                                      encroachment be
   Art. 8                                          exemplifications of
   Art. 9                                          judge until
   Art. 10                                         that in
                                        so. If, in
   Art. 12                                         and on
   Art. 13                                         be who,
                                        be who,
                                      assured that,
                                      afforded by
                                      Constitution by


Section 2,

   Art. 1     Heading            *Enactive. Ratiocinative.*
                                      is, that
   Art. 2                                          of as
                                        be to
                                      arrangement: and in
   Art. 3                                          Authority and, *that*
                                      observance of
                                      word to
                                      misdeeds, in
                                      purposes,——efficient
   Art. 4                                          persons, an
                                        do than
                                      engagement——say
                                      community——for
   Art. 5                                          judiciary
   Art. 9                                          alleged
                                        government
                                      judicatory

| | |
|---|---|
| Art. 10 | issued by |
| | judge |
| Art. 11 | But here, |
| | place for |
| | |
| Section 3, | |
| Art. 5 | states. |
| | |
| Section 4 n | The work called *Radical Reform Bill*, was first intended by the author to be termed *Election Code*. It appears near the end of vol. iii. in this collection, and a list of titles of sections virtually corresponding with the above will be found in p. 563.——*Ed.* |
| | |
| Section 10 | *pre-established.* |
| | |
| Section 20, | |
| Art. 5 | *Non-Attendance,* |
| | days on |
| Art. 8 | corporeal |
| | applied?——and |
| Art. 10 | artisan, |
| Art. 11 | many times |
| | But for |
| | place without |
| | or, at any rate, without |
| | traced to |
| Art. 12 | say, in |
| Art. 13 | are——1. The |
| | dependants; 2. His |
| | and, in particular, those |
| Art. 14 | dependants |
| | made which |
| | cause the |
| Art. 15 | month, or more, taken |
| Art. 16 | object of |
| | endeavour was |
| | purpose, and |
| | of, the |
| | business as |
| | whatsoever, coming |
| | and, in particular, all |
| | finished. As |
| | *Catechism*, vol. iii. p. 435.——*Introduction.* |
| Art. 17 | business-times |
| | *speaker*) the |
| | on no session, by |
| | attendance on |
| | day perhaps |

|  | those who |
|  | *slavery* the |
|  | those who |
|  | masters are |
|  | howsoever, by |
| Art. 18 | is, that |
| Art. 19 | so in |
| Art. 24 | course have |
|  | Judges,) know |
|  | comparison with |

Section 21,
| Art. 3 | belongs to |
|  | *sitting-book* |
|  | Alleged |
| Art. 6 | secrecy, as |

Section 22,
| Art. 1 | Assembly can be rendered, consistently |
|  | and performance of duty, the |
| Art. 2 | situated in |
| Art. 3 | districts, |
|  | sitten on |
|  | day,——as including the time occupied in the |
|  | journey from the District to the seat of the |
|  | Legislature, shall be sufficient to secure the |
|  | timely arrival of the elected Deputy at the |
|  | seat of the Legislature. |
| Art. 4 | accidents as |
| Art. 5 | say, the |
| Art. 6 | States is |
|  | Congress it |

Section 23,
| Art. 1 | power of |
|  | acting for |
| Art. 3 | deputy. |
|  | vote over |
|  | own might |
| Art. 4 | *Instruments*. |
| Art. 5 | person appointed |
|  | substitute, |
|  | *Substitute* may, |
| Art. 6 | that on |
|  | member |
| Art. 7 | substitute |
|  | deputy? |
|  | Deputy to |
| Art. 8 | *non-attendance*, involuntary through |
|  | voluntary through |
|  | section, |

487

| | |
|---|---|
| Art. 9 | himself, and |
| | Happily, though |
| | yet what |
| Art. 10 | uncommon where |
| | hence confusion |
| | uncertainty in |
| Art. 12 | expressed, and almost |
| Art. 13 | accident, over |
| Art. 15 | principle |
| Art. 17 | But it |
| Art. 24 | XI. So, |
| | Depute, |
| Art. 27 Heading | *Instructional. Ratiocinative.* |
| | above, considered,—it |
| Art. 28 | distinction's sake, |
| Art. 32 | case, have |
| | |
| Section 24, | |
| Art. 1 | legislature, |
| Art. 8 | completion would |
| Art. 9 | assigned may, |
| Art. 14 | *Legislation—regarding* |
| | |
| Section 25, | |
| Art. 1 | be in |
| | [or twice?] |
| Art. 3 | Art. 2, |
| Art. 6 | suppose an |
| | twenty-four: |
| | eighteen |
| | six |
| | six |
| | *Answer:* Every |
| | twenty-four, thirty: |
| | twenty-four |
| | six |
| | —thirty— |
| Art. 8 | body, the |
| | number—are |
| | yet, in |
| | number, rarely |
| | *Answer:*—What |
| Art. 9 | occur which |
| | and where |
| | mentioned but |
| Art. 10 | one-fifth |
| Art. 13 | cards, with |
| | "*Young* |
| Art. 15 | addition, and |
| Art. 18 | year has, |
| | who not |

| | | |
|---|---|---|
| Art. 19 | | *Minister*, and |
| | | deputy's electors. |
| Art. 20 | | Contents |
| | | included,) and |
| | | *distinction*, stands |
| Art. 21 | *no para at* | Here |
| | | for by |
| Art. 22 | | 1. Increase of power; 2. Diminution |
| | | *refrenative*, responsibility. |
| Art. 23 | | situation: 1. Such |
| | | connexions: 2. Gratification, |
| | | 3. Benefit |
| | | interest, or |
| Art. 24 | | 1. at |
| | | connexions, |
| | | Arch-corrupters: 2. Expectation |
| | | flattery at |
| | | *Arch-corrupter* |
| Art. 25 | | amount to |
| | | limit other |
| | | connexions |
| | | *speaking* and |
| Art. 26 | | cohesion of |
| Art. 28 | | dispositions as |
| Art. 31 | | which, more |
| Art. 32 | Heading | *Instructional. Ratiocinative.* |
| | | 1. To |
| | | Deputies; 2. To |
| | | expression, *appropriate aptitude*, substituted. |
| | | is, then, |
| Art. 33 | | Members, as |
| | | given, and that |
| | | provided at |
| Art. 34 | | *attention* bestowed |
| | | mind, will |
| | | say, to |
| | | seen, with |
| Art. 35 | | example, look |
| Art. 37 | | *Question* 3. |
| | | future, as |
| Art. 38 | | answer, are |
| Art. 39 | | 1. That |
| | | 2. Moreover |
| | | will for |
| | | long have |
| | | debarred from |
| | | electors |
| Art. 40 | | circumstances, by |
| | | situations which, |
| Art. 41 | | supreme legislature, |
| | | constitution, |

|  |  | Section 28. *Locable* |
| Art. 43 |  | child-birth |
|  |  | (the case of England and its emancipated Colonies excepted,) |
|  |  | can have had |
| Art. 46 |  | Monarchicho-Aristocratical |
|  |  | Despotic |
| Art. 47 |  | course in |
| Art. 48 |  | legislature |
| Art. 49 |  | COLLECTIVELY, (Ch. ix.); |
|  |  | is the |
| Art. 52 | [Objections] | time taken |
|  | [Answers] [1.] | degree conducive |
|  |  | non-re-locability |
|  | [3.] | 1. In the |
|  |  | Committee; 2. In |
|  |  | Sub-legislature; 3. At |
|  |  | expiration |
| Art. 53 |  | follows:— |
|  | [I.2] | expired, it |
|  | [I.3] | without doors, |
|  | [II.5]n | Cortes Ann. |
|  |  | not at |
|  |  | legislative department. |
| Art. 54 |  | provided in |
|  |  | *fixed* |
|  |  |  |
| Section 27, Heading |  | *Inquiry* |
| Art. 1 |  | *Inquiry* |
| Art. 2 |  | own, or |
| Art. 5 |  | were (as |
|  |  | Art. 17) desirable, |
|  |  | be, without |
| Art. 6 |  | inquiry, |
|  |  | time, which, |
| Art. 7 |  | *elicited*, comes |
|  |  | stock of |
|  | n | *Evidence*, in vols. vi. and vii.—*Ed.* |
| Art. 8 |  | MINISTER. Section 10, *Registration System.* |
| Art. 9 |  | Ch. xxvi. LOCAL REGISTRARS. |
| Art. 11 |  | *Code*, (vol. ii. p. 57.) |
| Art. 13 |  | Art. 23 to 26. |
| Art. 14 |  | and under |
|  |  | Inquiry |
| Art. 15 |  | Government. *Agents* |
| Art. 16 |  | non-penal, so |
| Art. 17 |  | limits, (and |
|  |  | limits are |
|  |  | ones,) to |
| Art. 19 |  | responsively—against |
| Art. 20 |  | REGISTRARS. |

| | |
|---|---|
| Art. 22 | Inquiry, |
| Art. 23 | Inquiry |
| Art. 25 | large——or, |
| | *doors*——or |
| Art. 26 | DEPUTE PERMANENT: |
| | DEPUTE OCCASIONAL. |
| Art. 27 | Elector |
| | sections 18, 20, and 26, |
| Art. 28 | inquiry |
| Art. 33 | its |
| Art. 35 | *secret*; as |
| | Inquiry, |
| Art. 36 | cases and |
| Art. 37 | member of |
| | Tribunal of |
| | design on |
| | Legislature——may |
| Art. 39 | *Inquiry* |
| | or, for shortness, say |
| | *application*,——by |
| | collecting and expressing, by |
| | inquiry. |
| | functions is |
| | Report thus |
| | *Inquiry* |
| Art. 40 | inquiry |
| | connexion |
| Art. 41 | light derivable, |
| | nation from |
| | *Regularity* |
| | say, *incidentally* |
| | elicited,——to |
| Art. 42 | monarch. |
| Art. 43 | next, as |
| | *compages* of government |
| | But seldom |
| | inquiry |
| Art. 44 | inquiry. |
| | thence *instructiveness* |
| | them: these |
| | rules which |
| Art. 45 | work |
| Art. 48 | systems |
| | serve |
| Art. 50 | appropirate |
| | 1. Neither |
| | connexion |
| | it——withholden, |
| | it——best |
| | improvement, in |
| Art. 51 | purpose but |

words, "*So*
Art. 52                          inquiry
dignity, it
Art. 53                          *exclusion,*—of
Art. 54                          persons at
Art. 55                          ART. 55. As
resource, when,—on
inquiry,
inquiries,
inquiry
Art. 56                          feature familiar
power on


Section 28,
  Art. 3                         persons who,—
  Art. 6                         function, the legislature
judge whether
  Art. 7                         members
part of
Inquiry,
  Art. 8                         still the
guilty—much
  Art. 10                        Legislature, have
  Art. 11                        For knowingly
those who,
it, be
  Art. 12                        guard, lest,
well in
vacancy which
  Art. 13                        case in
opinative,
alleged
  Art. 14                        occasion, if,
grounded, or
suit, proceed,—
  Art. 15                        Ch. xxiv.
redress of
  Art. 16                        or say, *execution-staying*
moreover, by


Section 29 n                     On the subject of this section see farther
Essay on Political Tactics, vol. ii. p. 301,
*et seq.*—*Ed.*
  Art. 1                         member
thereby, in
  Art. 2                         for thus
clear of
confusedness, and
         n                       [*Pannomion.*]
  Art. 3                         Section, and
  Art. 4                         Day.]"In"

Art. 5                               Month, and
                                     Thereupon comes
Art. 9                               Art. 3, 4, 5, 6.


Section 30,
    Art. 1    *omits*                Art. 1.
              [7.]                   Judiciary,
              [8.]                   Constitutive.


Section 31,
    Art. 2                           *control-maximization*
    Art. 3                           following:——I.
    Art. 7                           others, or say, *extra-regard*,
    Art. 8                           tenor
    Art. 11                          interest, (or
                                     such,) at
                                     otherwise, he be prevented
    Art. 16                          needless: for,
    Art. 19   *combines Arts. 19 and 20.*
    Art. 20   *omits heading*        *Instructional.*
              *begins at*            Are they the *ruling few?*
                                     theory) *are*
                                     affront, and
              n                      *Legislation,* (in vol. i. of this collection.)
    Art. 21                          Art. 20.
    Art. 22                          Art. 21.
                                     Ye who,
    Art. 23                          Art. 22.
                                     inverse, but
                                     possessed, is
    Art. 24                          Art. 23.
    Art. 25                          Art. 24.
                                     unfavourable in
    Art. 26                          Art. 25.
    Art. 27                          Art. 26.
                                     it which
    Art. 28                          Art. 27.
    Art. 29                          Art. 28.
                                     Monarch, by
    Art. 30                          Art. 29.
    Art. 31                          Art. 30.
    Art. 32                          Art. 31.
                                     be, in
    Art. 33                          Art. 32.
                                     particulars: Security
    Art. 34                          Art. 33.
                                     controlling
                                     Control——
                                     control,
    Art. 35                          Art. 34.

| | |
|---|---|
| Art. 36 | Art. 35. |
| | benefit without |
| | appetites without |
| | elements without |
| Art. 37 | Art. 36. |
| | cannot, easily |
| | on without |
| | another for |
| | say, to |
| Art. 38 | Art. 37. |
| | Establishment in |
| | Judicial; and, in particular, for |
| | Aristocracy all |
| | for there |
| Art. 39. | Art. 38. |
| | for without |
| | Judges, the |
| | power in |
| | *Justice*——half a minute——in |
| | man's, time,—— |
| | do in |
| | *words*, issued |
| | redress; take |
| | fathers; engage |
| | printers,——extinguish |
| | and not |
| | for wherever |
| Art. 40 | Art. 39 |
| | oppression too |
| Art. 41 | Art. 40. |
|     n a | Judicatory. |
| | prosecution the |
| | daylight: |
| | and though |
|     n * | *Eldon*, (vol. v. p. 348.) |
|     n * | G. II. Ch. 24, sect. 1. |
| Art. 42 | Art. 41. |
| | provided for |
| Art. 41 *ends at* | these—— |
|     Heading | *Instructional.* |
| | Art. 42. I. |
|     [1.] | section 4 to 13 |
|     [3.] | Elector: |
| | *service, continuance.* |
|     [4.] | persons who |
|     [7.] | Motions. Art. 6. |
|     [8.] | &c., in |
| | Ch. vii |
| | Ch. xxv. Local |
| | Ch. xxvi. Local Registrars. |
| Art. 43 [1.] | *Remuneration*; and, |

Art. 44  [3.]                    *Publicity-recordation publication*;
                                 IMMEDIATE AND APELLATE JUDICIARY
                                 Ch. xxvi. LOCAL REGISTRARS;
                                 *Inquiry*
        [4.]                     MINISTERS SEPARATELY,
        [5.]                     COLLECTIVELY.
                                 *eventually-emendative*
                                 *preinterpretive*


CHAPTER VII
            n                    Tribunal,
                                 perhaps of war.
                                 pleasure: for

Section 1,
    Art. 4                       commencemeut

Section 2                        following:
                                 recognise as
                                 number on
                                 impossible, by
                                 necessity to
                                 shape,——against
                                 internal, adversaries;
                                 aptitude, in

Section 3                        honour
                                 called *dignities*,

Section 4                        conclusive,——the
                                 particular, in
                                 subsistence are
                                 individuals; remembering
                                 customers,——nor
                                 Department the

Section 5    Heading             *all, promised.*
                                 interest being,

Section 6    Heading             *Justice, accessible to all, promised.*
                                 instruments, to
                                 vexation, introduced
                                 proceedings, produces

Section 7    Heading             *Elections, promised.*
                                 inquiry

Section 8    Heading             *Beneficence, promised.*
                                 wants of

495

| Section 9  Heading | *Impartiality, in . . . power, promised.* |
|---|---|
| | talent——natural |
| | countrymen, I |
| | |
| Section 10  Heading | *Assiduity, promised.* |
| | |
| Section 11  Heading | *Authority, promised.* |
| | |
| Section 12  Heading | *Authorities, abjured.* |
| | |
| Section 13  Heading | *Insincerity, abjured.* |
| | |
| Section 14  Heading | *Arrogance, abjured.* |
| | haughtiness |

## CHAPTER VIII

Section 1,

| Art. 1 | Heading *omits* | *Enactive.* |
|---|---|---|
| Art. 2 | | Art. 4 and 5, |
| Art. 3 | | exercised by |
| Art. 4 | | So, also, in |
| | | MINISTERS COLLECTIVELY. |
| Art. 5 | | denomination of |
| | | produced |
| Art. 6 | | immediative |
| Art. 7 | | Chief,) employed |
| Art. 8 | | say, of |
| Art. 9 | | is on |
| | | account inapposite. |

Section 2,

| Art. 3 | *omits* | III. |
|---|---|---|
| Art. 5 | *omits* | IV. |
| | | is by |
| Art. 8 | *omits* | V. |
| | | Art. 8, 9, |
| Art. 11 | | *Ingrafted,* |
| | | Art. 16. |
| n | | construction put |
| | | Article 11, Section 11, Clause 1,) |
| | | words, *"Commander* |
| | | because in that case there |
| | | Art. 13. |
| Art. 15 | | made, one. |
| | | made, one. |
| n | | [*Exemplars.*] |

Section 3,

| Art. 1 | MINISTERS COLLECTIVELY. |
|---|---|

Art. 3                                   exercisable
Art. 5        *inserts n marker*
Art. 6                                   Sanction
Art. 7                                   Minister, in

Section 4,
Art. 2                                   occasions on
Art. 7        Heading *omits*           *Enactive.*
Art. 8                                   Section 1.
Art. 10                                  Section 3,

Section 5,
Art. 2                                   [two ro three]
Art. 4                                   substitute a

Section 6,
Art. 2                                   wit, the
                                         forth, and

Section 8,
Art. 2     n                             see vol. iii. p. 577.
Art. 5                                   MINISTERS COLLECTIVELY. Section 17,
                                         *Located how.*
Art. 6                                   affections sympathetic
                                         experience——the

Section 9,
Art. 3                                   LEGISLATURE.
                                         No.

Section 10,
Art. 1     n                             In the original edition there is here a descrip-
                                         tion of the mode of executing manifold
                                         writing, which will be found already printed
                                         in vol. v. p. 406.——*Ed.*
Art. 7                                   MINISTERS COLLECTIVELY, Sections 9,
                                         11, 12;

Section 11,
Art. 6                                   Explanations (vol. iii. p. 558.)
Art. 9                                   limits,——other
Art. 10                                  COLLECTIVELY. Ch. xxv. LOCAL HEAD-
                                         MEN;
                                         Ch. xxvi. LOCAL REGISTRARS.
                                         Section 7. *Statistic*
Art. 11                                  question, and
Art. 14    Rule 2                        *persons* by
           Rule 4                        addition made
Art. 15                                  instances in

Section 12,
| Art. 1 | Heading *omits* | *Enactive.* |
| | 1. | acts, including |
| | 2. | whereby, with |
| | 6. | Section 31, *Securities*, Art. 13. |
| | 7. | Section 31, Art. 14, 15, |
| | 8. | Obligation to |
| | 9. | Art. 2, 3, 4, |
| | 10. | MINISTERS COLLECTIVELY. |
| | 11. | necessitated as |
| | 12. | exerciseable |
| | | *Function* |
| | 13. | Dislocability and |
| Art. 2 | | him, of indication |
| | | inquiry |
| Art. 3 | Heading | *Enactive Ratiocinative.* |
| | | falsehood accompanied |
| Art. 5 | | MINISTERS COLLECTIVELY. |
| | | Art. 13, 14, 15, 16. |

CHAPTER IX

Section 1,
| Art. | Heading | *Ends in View.* |
| Art. 2 n | | *parts,* (it |
| | | observed,) in |
| Art. 3 | | farther |
| Art. 4 | | 25, *Securities,* |

Section 2,
| Art. 1 | 11. | Section 10. |
| Art. 4 | | But though |
| Art. 6 | | *Sub-minister* |
| Art. 7 | | name of |
| Art. 10 n | | view to |

Section 3,
| Art. 9 | | expectancy |
| Art. 12 | | A Board |
| Art. 15 | | control; |
| Art. 16 | | I. ... II. ... III. ... IV. ... V. ... VI. |
| | | ... VII |
| Art. 20 | | control, |
| Art. 21 | | act would |
| Art. 24 | | single-seatedness are |
| | | Public-opinion |
| Art. 25 | | it, so |
| | | Public-opinion |
| | | *everything* |
| | | *anything* |
| Art. 26 | | alleged |

| | |
|---|---|
| Art. 27 | above,——though |
| | Master; * |
| n a | them have |
| n * | were at |
| | box, |
| | its rounds: |
| Art. 29 | Ch. xxv. . . . Ch. xxvi. |
| Art. 33 | appellation by |
| | control |
| Art. 36 | longer,) of |
| | pretences,) though |
| | inquiry |
| | inquiry |
| | Judges——in |
| | *effect*— |
| | *in name,*— |
| | practice——throughout——and |

| | |
|---|---|
| Section 4, | |
| Art. 3 | *nouns-substantive.* |
| Art. 4 n | For an exposition of the division of names of entities into real and fictitious, see Fragments on Ontology, vol. viii. p. 195, *et seq.* —*Ed.* |
| Art. 6 | denominations, will |
| Art. 8 | instance constituted: |
| Art. 9 | *natred* |
| n | [See vol. ii. p. 497, *et seq.*] |
| Art. 11 | every*thing* |
| | that although, |
| Art. 18 | any*things*, |
| Art. 27 | Note, however |
| | *Legislative Inquiry* |
| Art. 34 | *issued*, is |
| Art. 38 | *answers*, or say, *returns,*— |
| Art. 39 | meantime, |
| Art. 40 | law or |
| Art. 42 | persons, |
| Art. 44. IV. 1. | *remunerationly* |
| Art. 46  5. | Sub-department:—— |
| 7. | correspondent, the |
| Art. 47 | 1. Requisite |
| Art. 48 | Bissection II., |
| Art. 49 | *eliminative*, which |
| | Bissection III., |
| Art. 54 | XI.——The |
| Art. 56 | XII.——1. |
| Art. 59 | XV.——The |
| | *Information elicitative* |
| Art. 61 | XVI.——The |
| Art. 64 | part, of |

| | | |
|---|---|---|
| Art. 65 | | shall on |
| Art. 68 | | II.——So |
| Art. 69 | | III.——So in |
| | | |
| Section 5, | | |
| Art. 1 | | ART. I. |
| | | *degrees* or |
| | 3. | sub-ordination |
| | | Connexion |
| Art. 8 | 1. | him *Prime* |
| Art. 10 | | I. By |
| Art. 12 | *omits* | II. |
| | 4. | (cognitional.) |
| | 5. | (judicial.) |
| Art. 14 | | d'Affairs. |
| Art. 17 | | 4,) as |
| Art. 18 | | exercisable |
| | | Arts. 4, 5, 6, 7 : *right,* |
| | | exercisable |
| Art. 33 | Heading | *Instructional. Expositive.* |
| | | Election Clerks at |
| | | LEGISLATIVE; |
| Art. 34 | Heading | *Instructional. Expositive.* |
| | | (See Art. 42.) |
| | *omits* | But . . . needful, |
| Art. 35 | | III. The *Army* |
| | | Section 5, *Stipendaries* |
| | | Section 7, *Promotion.* |
| Art. 36 | | *maximized* |
| | | *maximization* |
| Art. 37 | 1. | grade, Supreme Commander-in-Chief,—— |
| | | PROFESSIONAL FUNCTIONARIES. |
| | 3. | *Commander-in-Chief* |
| | | styled, Duke |
| | | King, and |
| Art. 39 | | PROFESSIONAL FUNCTIONARIES. |
| | | Commander-in-Chief, |
| Art. 40 | *omits* | *Instructional.* |
| | | I. Superordinates |
| | | PROFESSIONAL FUNCTIONARIES. |
| | | I. . . . 1. . . . 2. . . . 3. . . . 4. . . . 5. . . . 6. |
| | | . . . 7. . . . 8. . . . 9. . . . 10. . . . 11. |
| Art. 41 | | PROFESSIONAL FUNCTIONARIES. |
| | | 1. Subordinates |
| Art. 42 | Heading | *Instructional. Expositive.* |
| | | minister, |
| | | |
| Section 6, | | |
| Art. 2 | | Section 1, |
| | | minister |
| Art. 5 | *omits* | *Universal* |

| | | |
|---|---|---|
| Art. 7 | | Section 8. |
| Art. 12 | | principal unpaid |
| Art. 13 | | is attached, |
| | | deficiency, in |
| | | master |

| | | |
|---|---|---|
| Section 7, | Heading n | For farther exposition of the function considered in this section, see the Rationale of Evidence in vols. vi. and vii. Index, *Statistics: Registration.*——*Ed.* |
| Art. 4 | | end are——the |
| | | Bissections II. III. IV. and V. |
| Art. 5 | Heading | *Ratiocinative. Enactive.* |
| | | end are——the |
| Art. 9 | | so, in |
| | | each,——1, |
| Art. 10 | | *preserving* at |
| Art. 13 | | (1.) *Original* |
| Art. 14 | | (2.) *Journal.* |
| Art. 15 | | (3.) *Periodical* |
| | | causes which |
| | | time intervening |
| Art. 18 | (9.) | Art. 8,) for |
| | (11.) | *lease*-letting, |
| | | Art. 23 |
| Art. 19 | | Second. |
| | | 1. All |

| | | |
|---|---|---|
| Bis-Section the Second, | | |
| Art. 1 | | Original Outset Book. |
| Art. 4 | | Specific Book the second. |
| Art. 6 | | Specific Book the third. |
| | (9) | *yard*, or |
| Art. 7 | | Use,——presenting |
| | | times, and |
| Art. 9. | III. | (1.) |
| | | (2.) |
| | | 1, Seeds. |
| | | (3.) |
| | | 1, Vaccine |
| | | (4.) |
| | | 1, Acids |
| Art. 10 | | offices |
| | | connexion |
| Art. 16 | n | forty or fifty |
| Art. 22 | | (1.) |
| | | (2.) |
| | n | *Office*, an |
| | | comparison with |
| Art. 24 | | requisite for |
| Art. 25 | n | fallen, these,——cannon |

|  |  | vessel, balls |
| --- | --- | --- |
|  |  | another, powder |
| Art. 26. | I. 1. | home-made. |
|  | II. 1. | enployed, when |
|  | VI. | Works in hand: |
| Art. 27 |  | Specific Book the fourth, |
|  | 3. | Distinguishing |

| | | |
|---|---|---|
| Bis-Section the third, | | |
| Art. 5 | Case 1 | 1. ... 2. ... 3. ... 4. |
|  | Case 3 | *issue*: or |
| Art. 6 |  | be,—the |
| Art. 8 |  | Bis-section IV. |
| Art. 9 |  | Entrance. |
|  |  | Departure. |
| Art. 10 |  | 1. ... 2. ... 3. ... 4. ... 5. ... 6. |
| Art. 11 |  | alleged |
|  |  | alleged |
| Art. 12 |  | is as |
| Art. 13 |  | Examples— |
| Art. 14 |  | Sub-specific Book the first. |
| Art. 15 |  | second. |
|  |  | *Book*. Heads of Entry—Examples— |
| Art. 16 |  | third. |
| Art. 17 | I. | original |
|  | II. 5. | buildings were, |
|  | III. | PURCHASE. |
|  | IV. | HIRE. |
|  | 6. | page 236. |
| Art. 18 | I. | Sub-specific |
|  |  | *Book*; for heads |
|  |  | page 237. |
|  | 5. | which received. |
| Art. 19 | *begins* | II. Sub-specific Book the second. |
|  |  | *Application Book*. |
|  |  | Art. 16, |
| Art. 20 | *omits* | 2. |
|  |  | 1. by ... 2. by |
| Art. 21. | 4. | delivered, |
| Art. 25 |  | I. Sub-specific |
|  |  | first. |
|  |  | Entry— |
|  |  | 1. ... 2. ... I. ... II. ... (1.) *Non-* |
|  |  | *receipts*: |
|  |  | Bissection 4. Loss Book. Art. 4. |
|  | 5. | shape. |
|  |  | (2.) *Unexpected* |
| Art. 26 |  | II. Subspecific |
|  |  | second. |
| Art. 27 |  | III. Sub-specific |
|  |  | third. |

| | | |
|---|---|---|
| Art. 28 | | (1.) *Non-issues,* |
| | | Entry— |
| | | (2.) *Unexpected* |
| | | Entry— |
| | | (3.) Unexpected demands not fulfilled. |
| Art. 29 | | *moveables,* as |
| Art. 30 | *new para at* | 2. Occurrence, |
| | | MINISTERS SEVERALLY. |
| Art. 32 | | alleged |
| | | LEGISLATIVE. |
| | | *Inquiry* |

Bis-Section the Fourth,

| | | |
|---|---|---|
| Art. 3 | | MINISTERS SEVERALLY. |
| Art. 4 | | I. Subject-matter |
| | | I. *Personal Service.* |
| Art. 6 | | II. Subject-matter |
| | | II. a |
| | | Loss. |
| Art. 7 | | III. Subject-matter |
| | | III. a |
| | 20. | Theft, by |
| | 21. | do. |
| Art. 11 | Heading *omits* | *Expositive.* |
| | | cause |
| Art. 17 | | headed, "*when introduced:* |
| | | another headed *when produced:* |
| | n | putrefactive, fermentation. |
| Art. 19 | 6. | page 241. |
| Art. 20 | | IV. Subject-matter |
| | | IV. *Money.* |
| | II. | Disserviceable |
| | 3. | been, and |
| | *omits* | Modes. Examples— |
| | V. 2 | labour if any, performed |
| | VI. *omits* | Modes. Examples— |
| Art. 21 | 3. | connexions. |
| Art. 25 | | page, in |
| Art. 27 | | belong, to |
| Art. 31 | | it, and |
| | | object,—to |
| | | *Dislocable who.* |
| Art. 33 | | place—above |

Bis-Section the Fifth,

| | |
|---|---|
| Art. 1 | above, examples are |
| | Subheads, see above, *Retroacception* |
| | page 245, |

Bis-Section the Sixth,

| | |
|---|---|
| Art. 2 | 1. *For the practice.* Saving |

503

|  |  |  |
|---|---|---|
|  |  | to wit—— |
|  |  | expense, employed |
| Art. 3 |  | 1. As to |
|  | *new para at* | Rule. 1. For |
| Art. 5 | Rule 5. | conceptionl wil |
|  | n a | *parchments,*) belonging |
|  |  | under-graduate |
|  | n | See Appendix viii. to Chrestomathia, vol. viii. p. 155.——*Ed.* |
| Art. 6 | *omits* | Bissection the first |
|  |  | Art. 5, |
|  |  | intellectual, or |
|  |  | or, 2, |
|  |  | &c., those |
| Section 8, |  |  |
| Art. 12 |  | Bissection 2, Art. 18. |
| Art. 16 |  | subdepartment, |
| Art. 21 |  | following—— |
| Art. 23 |  | requisition, and |
| Art. 28 | 4. | *account and contract.* |
| Art. 29 |  | Prime Minister of the Subdepartment, Legislature involves |
| Art. 31 | *omits* | 1. |
| Art. 32 | *omits* | 2. |
| Art. 34 | *omits* | 3. |
|  |  | occasion the |
|  |  | occasion different |
| Art. 36 | *omits* | 4 . . . 5 |
| Art. 37 |  | will, by |
| Art. 38 |  | matter |
| Section 9, |  |  |
| Art. 2 |  | permit (so |
|  |  | occasional) *spontaneously,* |
| Art. 3 | Heading | *Instructional. Expositive.* |
|  | 1. | belongs, ascertaining |
|  | 3. | been rendered |
|  | 6. | *Remuneration,* and Section 25, *Securities,* &c. Arts. 6, and 18 to 29. |
| Art. 4 |  | Places and |
|  | 6. 1. | Post-offices, determined, by |
|  | 10. 3 | district: as |
|  | 12. | *Subdepartment.* |
|  | 13. | which on |
|  | *omits new para at* | For |
| Art. 5 | 1. | their |
|  | 3. | produced; the |
| Art. 6 |  | Members, |
| Art. 7 |  | Minister |

504

Section 10,
   Art. 1    Heading         *Instructional. Ratiocinative.*
   Art. 2                         *Code*, (vol. ii.,) and
                                      Letter (vol. v.)
   Art. 8                         *Legislative Inquiry*
                                      *Legislative Inquiry*
   Art. 9                         Section
   Art. 10                      Art.
   Art. 12                      encumbrance
   Art. 20                      follow:
          2.                    be, in proportion, the
   Art. 23                      Art. 24.
          2.                    administration
          3.                    houses,
          4.                    House in
   Art. 24                      Art. 25
                                      that at
   Art. 25                      Art. 26.
                                      way of

Section 11,
   Art. 1                         exercisible
   Art. 3                         *simply-receptive*
          2.                    *receptive* and
   Art. 4                         proposed
                                      him who
   Art. 5                         action is
                                      being
   Art. 8                         case susceptible
   Art. 9                         any,——belonging

Section 12,
   Art. 1                         him to
   Art. 3                         II.——*Ratiocinative*,
   Art. 4                         III.——*Eventually*
   Art. 5                         4 At
   Art. 6                         benefit, may

Section 13,
   Art. 2                         service
                                    I.——Because,
                                    judgment, and
                                    talent, will
                                    nor in
                                    stimulus,——such
   Art. 3                         Because in
                                    and for

Section 14,
   Art. 2                         *connected*,——will
   Art. 3                         *interpretation-reporting*

505

|  |  |  |
|---|---|---|
|  |  | *Eventually-emendative* |
|  |  | *Pre-interpretative* |
|  | n | xxix. |
| **Section 15,** |  |  |
| Art. 2 |  | section; Section |
| Art. 6 |  | two sections; Section |
| Art. 7 |  | 7, Exercised, |
|  |  | exercised at |
| Art. 9 |  | xxiv. |
| Art. 14 |  | understand all |
| Art. 19 |  | render that |
| Art. 24 |  | *bene-meritant*, a |
| Art. 25 |  | *bene-meritant* or |
| Art. 26 |  | defendant |
|  |  | demand, money |
| Art. 28 |  | *publication*, is |
|  |  | given in |
|  |  | made as |
| Art. 33 |  | follows:—— |
|  |  | Coronets of |
| Art. 34 |  | with *natural* |
| Art. 35 |  | sources by |
| Art. 36 |  | *Army Minister* and Section 4, *Navy* |
| Art. 37 |  | of |
| Art. 39 |  | remuneration,——so |
| Art. 46 | 3. | *post-obituary* or |
| Art. 47 | n | XX., anno |
|  |  | [See these in "Official Aptitude Maximized, |
|  |  | Expense Minimized," in vol. v. p. 263, et seq. |
|  |  | ——*Ed.*] |
| Art. 51 |  | follows:—— |
| Art. 54 |  | [——] |
|  |  | advance.] |
| Art. 55 |  | way |
| Art. 57 |  | [————] |
|  |  | [————] |
|  |  | Minister,——after |
| **Section 16,** |  |  |
| Art. 3 |  | follows:—— |
|  |  | Public-opinion |
|  |  | who in |
|  |  | right: though |
| Art. 7 |  | Art. 42, |
| Art. 15 | II. 5 | Domains——Agriculture, |
| Art. 17 |  | say *Examination* |
| Art. 18 |  | 53, |
| Art. 19 | Heading | *Enactive. Instructional.* |
| Art. 20 | 1. | *applicants*, and |
|  | 2. | if being |

|  |  |  |
|---|---|---|
|  | 3. | other, of |
| Art. 21 |  | follow:— |
|  | 3. | aptitude as |
| Art. 23 | 6. | together) 25; |
|  | 8. | employed, being, |
| Art. 24 | n | *Note by an East India Proprietor.* |
| Art. 25 | n | *Note by a highly distinguished officer of Artillery, bred up in the Government Academy at Woolwich, near London.* |
|  |  | condidates; |
|  |  | is the |
| Art. 27 |  | Art. 27. It |
| Art. 29 | n | *Note by a person of distinction bred in the University of Glasgow.* |
| Art. 42 |  | pre-ascertainment |
| Art. 46 |  | principal are, *house-room,* |
| Art. 49 |  | dependence |
|  |  | LEGISLATIVE, |
|  |  | expense. Delivery |
| Art. 51 |  | pupils, appears |
| Art. 52 |  | examinations. See Art. 32. |
| Art. 53 |  | relatives by |
| Art. 55 |  | (one year) |
| Art. 57 |  | (seven) |
| Art. 60 |  | aptitude as |

|  |  |
|---|---|
| Supplement to Section 16. *omits* | *Locable who.* |

|  |  |  |
|---|---|---|
| Art. 65 |  | instructions |
| Art. 68 |  | shown |
|  |  | 1. Manner |
|  |  | *question ticket.* |
| Art. 69 |  | 1. A |
|  | n | IV., ch. |
|  |  | Mr *Secretary* |
|  |  | Exchequer,) |
|  |  | (see the Art of Packing Juries in vol. v.) |
|  |  | say is |
|  |  | had not stayed |
| Art. 70 | n | Mr Lawrence," |
|  |  | Section: |
| Art. 73 |  | (suppose,) |
| Art. 75 |  | 1. Of |
| Art. 76 |  | *in lieu of choice,* |
|  |  | arrangement nothing |
|  |  | cases, and |

|  |  |  |
|---|---|---|
| Section 17, |  |  |
| Art. 6 |  | Arts. 10, 11, 12, 13, |
| Art. 9 | 3. | say; year, |
| Art. 14 |  | above, Arts. |

507

| | |
|---|---|
| Art. 17 | considerations, |
| Art. 18 | service, the |
| Art. 27 | Art. 23, |
| Art. 31 | [———] |
| n | [See for farther securities here omitted Sec- 9, Arts. 18, 19, and Note.——*Ed.*] |
| Art. 31 | meantime, |
| Art. 33 | Art. I8, |
| Art. 40   3 | Act |
| Supplement Heading *omits* | *Located how.* |
| Art. 42   Heading *omits* | *Ratiocinative.* Art. [42] or. 1. |
| | PECUNIARY COMPETITION PRINCIPLE. |
| | above to |
| Art. 43 or 2 | Art. 42 or 1. I.——Reasons, |
| | Arts. 12, 13: |
| | (Arts. 33, 34, 35, 36, 40,) |
| Art. 44 or 3 | Art. 43 or 2.——Case |
| | intrusted |
| | I. Reason, |
| Art. 45 or 4 | Art. 44 or 3. II.——Reasons |
| | 1. In |
| Art. 46 or 5 | Art. 45 or 4 |
| Art. 47 or 6 | Art. 46 or 5. |
| | interest to |
| | *need,*——those |
| Art. 48 or 7 | Art. 47 or 6. |
| n | entituled |
| | minimized, "in vol. v. |
| Art. 49 or 8 | Art. 48 or 7. |
| | *or say* |
| | totality, (expense |
| | honour |
| Art. 50 or 9 | Art. 49 or 8. |
| | Objection, to |
| Art. 51 or 10 | Art. 50 or 9. |
| | system: nor |
| | Nowhere: |
| Art. 52 or 11 | Art. 51 or 10. |
| | belong, to |
| Art. 53 or 12 | Art. 52 or 11. |
| | 2, *The* |
| | sccurity, |
| | impassible |
| | save, is |
| Art. 54 or 13. | Art. 53 or 12. |
| | 3, *Venality* |
| | shown, |
| *omits* | 3, |
| Art. 55 or 14 | Art. 54 or 13. *Objection* 4, *Munificence,* the alleged existence corresponding |

508

| | |
|---|---|
| Art. 56 or 15 | Art. 55 or 14. |
| | *indigence.* When |
| | *Kings,* |
| | richly remunerated |
| | point-blank |
| Art. 57 or 16 | Art. 56 or 15. |
| | *protegés,* |
| Art. 58 or 17 | Art. 57 or 16. |
| | it, for |
| Art. 59 or 18 | Art. 58 or 17. |
| | If, therefore, in |
| | flows |
| | receive from the functionary, |
| | inquiry |
| | inquiry |

| | |
|---|---|
| Concluding Instruction  Heading | PUBLIC-OPINION |
| Art. 1 | dependants |
| | dependants |
| n | influencee, |
| | *larye,* |
| | taken of |
| | one hostile, |
| Art. 3 | land; and |
| Art. 5 | minister, |
| | Section 11. |

| | |
|---|---|
| Section 18, | |
| Art. 2      6. | temporary, |
| Art. 6 | dislocative, modified,——see |
| Art. 9 | them,——the |
| | accuser, any |
| | excepted,) small, |
| Art. 10 | subordinate |

| | |
|---|---|
| Section 19, | |
| Art. 1 | I. *Fields* |
| Art. 11 | *Remuneration how* |
| Art. 12 | and if |
| | account in |
| Art. 14 | what increase |
| | dependant |
| | shall, or |
| | not, be |
| Art. 15 | Section 17, |
| Art. 17 | provision made |
| | Art. 22 to 29, |
| Art. 19 | Sect. 17, Art. 31,—— |
| n | securities, |
| Art. 20 | 1. To |
| | which, in fact, are |

| Art. 21 | | situation has, |
| Art. 22 | | Minister, to |
| | | obligation which |
| | | is for |
| | | Minister, in |
| Art. 25 | | affording, or |
| Art. 26 | | labour, in |
| Art. 27 | | which, by |
| Art. 29 | Heading | *Instructional. Ratiocinative.* |
| | | power grade |
| Art. 30 | Heading | *Instructional. Ratiocinative.* |
| Art. 31 | | placed within |
| | n | nature can |
| | | close aud separate |
| Art. 32 | | Arts. 45, 46, |
| Art. 36 | n | Art. 41. |
| Art. 38 | | an antagonization, |
| Art. 42 | *omits* | otherwise |
| | | *obviated.* Art. 48. |

| Section 20, | | |
| Art. 2 | | *inspectors,* |
| Art. 4 | | Minister; and |
| Art. 9 | 2. | or some *thing,* |
| | | easy as |
| Art. 13 | | which, being, |
| | | Institutions as |
| | 3. | *Health* subdepartments. |
| Art. 18 | | Rules |
| Art. 19 | | legislature |
| | | Visiters, |
| Art. 21 | | oppression and depredation |
| Art. 22 | | *Inquiry* |
| Art. 23 | | commissable,— |
| Art. 25 | | superordinate belongs, |
| | | to the provisions of Section 21, |
| | | *obviated,* the |
| | | exercisable |

| Section 21, | | |
| Art. 4 | | I. non-functionaries; |
| | | II. functionaries: *non-functionaries,* |
| | | I. suitors; |
| | | II. inspectees; |
| | | III.   evidence-holders——(as   functionaries;) |
| | | functionaries, |
| | | be, in |
| | | 1. in |
| | | 2. by |
| | | 3. by |

| | | |
|---|---|---|
| Art. 5 | | *suitor.* |
| | | refusal or |
| | | omission, to |
| Art. 7 | 1. | expense of |
| | 4. | examinations |
| Art. 8 | | effects |
| | | are not incapable |
| Art. 9 | | Case I. |
| | | 1. generally applying; or 2. specially |
| Art. 10 | | 1. *directly applying;* or 2. *indirectly* |
| Art. 11 | | *directly-applying* |
| | *omits* | 1. |
| Art. 12 | *omits* | 2. |
| Art. 13 | *omits* | 3. |
| | | oppress*ee,* |
| Art. 14 | *omits* | 4. |
| Art. 15 | *omits* | 5. |
| Art. 17 | | *Judges' Elementary Functions:* |
| Art. 20 | | *Indirectly-applying* |
| | 1. | Art. 16 to 20, |
| | 3. | subordinate, of |
| | | conspicuous, suspended |
| | 6. | *register* styled |
| | 7. | Ch. xii. JUDICIARY COLLECTIVELY, |
| Art. 21 | *omits* | First, |
| | | *deportment,* for |
| | | *positive* |
| Art. 25 | | official, and |
| Art. 26 | | *prudence* and |
| | | and by |
| Art. 28 | | *fact,* or |
| Art. 29 | | particularized |
| Art. 32 | n | [*Deontology*] |
| Art. 33 | | characterized,— |
| Art. 36 | | Articles 12 to 19; |
| | | only—(as |
| Art. 37 | | *Opinion-Tribunal,* |
| Art. 38 | | nondecision,— |
| | | *Minister,* or |
| Art. 47 | | Arts. 41, 42, 43. |
| Art. 50 | 5. | say *Evidence-holder* |
| Art. 52 | *omits* | *Reason.* |
| | | connexions. |
| Art. 54 | 2. | Art. 50. |
| | 4. | Art. 50. |
| | 7. | Code, Ch. x. |
| Art. 59 | | *presumptive,* or |
| Art. 64 | | *transference, permanent* |
| Art. 67 | | 2. Or |
| Art. 71 | | 1. War, |
| | | proceedings entry |

| | | |
|---|---|---|
| Art. 73 | | excepted, in are— 2 Judicature, |
| Art. 76 | | So in |
| Section 22, | | |
| Art. 6 | | Judicatory, dependant connexion exercise by it but—though Commons by defence (for be) would |
| Section 23, | | |
| Art. 1 | | way, a |
| Art. 2 | | branches |
| Art. 6 | | connexion |
| Art. 7 | | connexion |
| | n | Ch. viii. Section 13; see vol. ii. p. 43. |
| Art. 8 | | connexion |
| Art. 9 | | connexion |
| Art. 11 | | endeavour pretended minister necessary, by |
| Art. 12 | | upon a and the more incontestibly |
| Art. 13 | | purpose of |
| Art. 15 | | underrates |
| Section 24, | | |
| Art. 2 | | assembly, |
| Art. 3 | | assembly: |
| Art. 5 | | *function*, allotted |
| Art. 9 | | thus on |
| Section 25, | | |
| Art. 1 | n | LEGISLATIVE, [In the original edition the supplemental matter of Section 16 from p. 279 to p. 283, as well as that of Section 17 from p. 286 to p. 293, was printed so as to follow Section 17.] |
| Art. 1 | 2. | *Table*—(in vol. i.) |
| | 3. | moral, non-functionaries,—and by |
| | 5. | agency as |
| Art. 2 | | Art. 1.— |
| Art. 3 | 10. | Art. 17 to 41. |
| | 11. | Art. 1 to 13. |

512

| | |
|---|---|
| Art. 4 | *function*; Bissection |
| | Art. 1, p. 236; |
| | B o o k; Bissection |
| | Art. 8 to 13, pp. 242, 243, |
| | B o o k; Bissection |
| | Arts. 4, 5, pp. 246, 247. |
| Art. 5 | Art. 18 to 29, pages 267, 268. |
| Art. 7 | following: |
| | month, and |
| | connexion |
| Art. 11 | visiters; |
| Art. 12 | *Visiter's* |
| | Art. 16 to 19. |
| Art. 14 | following: |
| Art. 15 | Art. 18 to 24, |
| Art. 17 | *Evidence* (Ch. xi.:) meantime, |
| | *Inquiry* |
| Art. 18 | extra-service |
| Art. 20 | *benemeritant*, to be by |
| Art. 23 | other transaction |
| | given without |
| Art. 24 | despatch, |
| Art. 27 | wit. in |
| Art. 28 | follows: |
| Art. 29 | *connexion* |
| | *connexion* |
| Art. 30 | *Minutation Attestation.* |
| Art. 32 | belong, to |
| | accordingly, observing the provision |
| | Art. 3. of |
| | Art. 4., with |
| Art. 35 | Minister, under |
| | L e g i s l a t i v e, |
| | functions, and |
| | alone,——that |
| | be in |
| | it by |
| Art. 36 | given to it, |
| Art. 37 | following: |
| | matter see |
| | L e g i s l a t i v e, |
| Art. 38 | purposely in |
| Art. 39 | be, that |
| Art. 40 | is, in |
| | innoxious but |
| | authority,——to |
| | superordinate,——to |
| | legislation,——to |
| Art. 42 | ᴸegislative, |
| | 2, the other |
| Art. 43 | control |

|              |                              |
|--------------|------------------------------|
|              | contempt under               |
| Art. 46      | kept as                      |
| Art. 48      | democracy, the               |
| Art. 49      | *enactment*) what            |
|              | anti-nationality             |
|              | control                      |
| Art. 50      | this Section                 |
|              | *Inquiry*                    |
| Art. 53      | *Jury*) to                   |
| Art. 55      | pre-ascertainable,           |
|              | punishment, who can          |
| Art. 57      | oppression, the              |
| Art. 58      | *well-suited*, to            |
|              | evidence,——these             |
|              |                              |
| Section 26,  |                              |
| Art. 2       | main                         |
| Art. 3       | vexation, and expense, are   |
| Art. 4       | *secrecy*, or say *privacy*, in |
|              | secrecy is                   |
|              | purposes.                    |
| Art. 6       | secret, or                   |
| Art. 8       | maximum, is the Constitutive. |
|              | corruptedness by             |
| Art. 12      | LEGISLATIVE,                 |
|              | &c., and                     |
| Art. 15      | comparison with              |
| Art. 16      | name, either                 |
|              | edifices,——are               |
| Art. 20  n b | *prisoners* by               |
|              | XVI. saw                     |
|              | brother) was                 |
|              | [The correspondence, illustrative of the author's attempt to put in practice his Panopticon, and its failure, with a narrative of the circumstances, will be found in the memoirs and correspondence, as printed in this collection. The Panopticon plan will be found at length in vol. iv.——ED.] |
| Art. 21      | audience.——Follows the remedy, |
|              | two, or                      |
|              | other,——use, giving          |
|              | these see                    |
|              | 26,) two:                    |
|              | insufficient, it             |
|              | *Public-boxes*.              |
|              | clerks                       |
|              | &c., Arts.                   |
|              | *Visiter's*                  |
| Art. 24      | Arts. 38. 43.                |
| Art. 26      | *Waiting-boxes*.             |

Art. 28                          aperture, he
Art. 30                          stair-case
Art. 31  n                       indiscriminately including
Art. 32                          all comprehensive,
                                 iv. *Loss*
Art. 33                          trader information
Art. 34                          I.——Liableness
                                 Ill-will
Art. 35  Heading                 *Ratiocinative.*
Art. 37                          be false?
Art. 38                          *Subdepartments*,) what
                                 arrangements, the
                                 *times* at
Art. 39                          *personel*
Art. 41                          *fifty*, under
Art. 42                          Destruction on
Art. 50                          minister,
Art. 52                          worse,) is
Art. 53                          aught that appears,
                                 1. . . . 2. . . . 3. . . . 4.

## No. I.

Collectanea relating to Book ii. Ch. vi. LEGISLATURE, Section 20, *Attendance and Remunderation*, Art. 18. (Supra, p. 165.)

Extract from an anonymous work, intituled the History of the United States. London, 1826. Published by John Miller, New Bridge Street, Blackfriars.

Speaking of New Orleans in the year 1814, some time in the month of December,——'Disaffection' (says the author, p. 434) 'growing bolder, martial law was proclaimed: the authority of the Civil Magistrate was suspended: and arbitrary power was assumed and exercised by the Commander-in-Chief. May no emergency hereafter occur, in which a military officer shall consider himself authorized to cite as a precedent this violation of the Constitution.'

To all appearance, it was by this proclamation of martial law that New Orleans was saved: saved from capture, perhaps from destruction: but for this substitute to regular legislation, one or other catastrophe would have taken place.

This is but one of divers accidents to which every Government stands exposed, and by which on pain of suffering, boundless in amount, a demand for immediate action on the part of the all-embracing Legislature may be produced. Foreign war, civil insurrection, pestilence, famine: here are already four, every one of them but too frequently brought to view by experience.

The following information, relating to this subject, the author received from John Neal, Esq., an advocate in the Supreme Judicatory of the Union, January, 1826.

'The members of Congress, of the United States, are elected for two years. They meet in the first Monday in December, and rise at the end of about four months, upon the average. They sit, therefore, only one-third of the time. They may be called together on forty days' notice, however, at any intermediate period. But, although it requires time to make a good law, and the President has power to provide for such events, whatever they may be, as are likely to require

515

extraordinary power—as if the country be invaded, or if a rebellion should break out,—still, cases have occurred where much distress might have been saved to the people, if the chief Legislature had been in session, with power to pass a law quickly.

'By the Constitution of the United States, it is provided that no State of the Confederacy shall pass a law "to impair the obligation of contracts." By the same Constitution, power is given to the United States to pass a *general Bankrupt Law*.

'The several States, or the majority of them, have been in the habit of passing *insolvent laws*, which had the effect sometimes of discharging both the person and property of a debtor. This habit continued for thirty years. At last, however, a question was made for the Supreme Court of the United States. That Court decided, that all discharges granted under *State* authority, under such and such circumstances, were void; the law, under the authority of which they were granted, being void, as *impairing the obligation of contracts*. The effect was terrible. The country was agitated in every direction. Houses were entered and stripped—the houses of wealthy men, who had been discharged years and years before. Nothing was heard but complaint. Hundreds and hundreds of old judgments were revived, a multitude of executions issued, and thousands of new suits brought.

'A national bankrupt law was required. But the Legislature were not in session, or, if in session, they had not time enough left before they were to break up, for passing a uniform system of bankrupt law.

'The distress continued, therefore, till it found a remedy, or died away, as the outcry did. So that when the Congress did meet, they were not much pressed about the matter. A law was half prepared, but they broke up, and went home before it was finished—and so was it the next year—and the year after, and so it is now. Up to this hour they have no *bankrupt law in the United States of America*, though thousands and thousands of people are praying for it as their only hope.'

### ADDITIONS TO BOWRING COLLATION:

| | |
|---|---|
| VI.25.A28 | antisceptic |
| IX.4.A46 | 5 receipt |
| 8.A21 | addressd |
| A28 | Art. 28, |
| A29 | Art. 4. |
| 15.A37 | practioners, |
| 19.A12(3) | competition, |
| A28 | Art, 28. |
| A36 | I. |
| 25.A3 | 10, |
| A50 | control, |

# C. BENTHAM ON
# HUMPHREYS' CODE COLLATIONS

Collations of Ch. VIII. §10, Arts. 1–7 and note with: 'Bentham on Humphreys' Property Code', *Westminster Review*, VI, No. XII (October, 1826), p. 487; Jeremy Bentham, *Article Eight of the Westminster Review No. XII. for October 1826, on Mr. Humphreys' Observations on the English Law of Real Property, with the Outline of a Code,* &c. (London, 1827), pp. 42–4; Bowring, v. pp. 406–7.

*Note.* See the introductory notes to the 1830 and Bowring Collations, pp. 461 and 480 above.

'Bentham on Humphreys' Property Code', the *Westminster Review*, VI, No. XII (October 1826), p. 487. The reprint of this passage, Jeremy Bentham, *Article Eight of the Westminster Review No. XII. for October, 1826, on Mr. Humphreys' Observations on the English Law of Real Property, with the Outline of a Code,* &c. (London, 1827), pp. 42–4, contains the same variants.

[Note: Inverted commas appear at the beginning of each article and paragraph. All headings, 'Enactive' &c. omitted.]

| | |
|---|---|
| Art. 1 | performance, of |
| | sub-departments—as |
| | office—he |
| | established, and |
| | practice, in |
| | Sub-departments, the Sub-legislative |
| Art. 1 n Heading | "MANIFOLD WRITING.—1. *Mode of Execution.* |

[Note: Inverted commas appear at the beginning and end of the note and at the beginning of each paragraph.]

| | |
|---|---|
| | over some |
| | taken, at |
| | time by |
| | exemplar by |
| | London this |
| | applied to |
| | employed under |
| | practice in |
| | means; for |
| | *sarsenet.* |
| New para. at | "As to the |
| | thinness, it |
| | England; nor |
| | thence in |

517

Art. 2
                             
legibility are
half of the
be, or
paper; to
one; the
paper; to

Art. 2
                             
follows:
expense which,

Art. 3
                             
other, the
skilled labour

Art. 4
                             
office,

Art. 5
                             
effected in
writings emanating
judicatory,—
protection afforded
judication
form,—to
evidence,—will

Art. 6
                             
unexampled against
*delinquency*—may
exemplars in
Justice-Minister
*inspective*
*melioration-suggestive*

*omits*                              
So also in the other Departments.

Art. 7
                             
taken, for
*statistic*
*melioration-suggestive*
ch. ix. §11, MINISTERS COLLECTIVELY:
*Legislative Minister*: and ch.
§19, *Judge's contested-interpretation-reporting function:* §20, *Judge's eventually-
emendative function:* §21, *Judge's sistitive
or execution-staying function:* §22, *Judge's
pre-interpretative function:* §23, *Judge's
non-contestational-evidence-elicitative function.*

'Bentham on Humphreys' Real Property Code.', printed in *Bowring*, v. pp. 406–7.

[Note: In addition to the variants recorded above in the *Westminster Review* article, the following are further variants.]

Art. 1
                             
registration
sub-departments, the sub-legislative

|         |                        |
| ------- | ---------------------- |
|         | *manifold*             |
| n       | style of               |
| Art. 2  | mode it                |
| Art. 6  | immediate judicatories |
|         | appellate judicatory,  |
|         | justice-minister,      |
| Art. 7  | legislature            |

# D. OFFICIAL APTITUDE MAXIMIZED, EXPENSE MINIMIZED COLLATIONS

Collations of Ch. IX. §§ 15–17 and Supplements with: Jeremy Bentham, *Extract from the Proposed Constitutional Code, Entitled Official Aptitude Maximized, Expense Minimized* (London, 1816?, 1826); Jeremy Bentham, *Official Aptitude Maximized; Expense Minimized: As shewn in the Several Papers Comprised in This Volume* (London, 1830) which contains the above 'Extract' plus Supplements.

*Note.* See the notes to the 1830 and Bowring Collations, pp. 461 and 480 above. Another variant not recorded in this collation is the use of 'and' in the headings to articles (e.g. *Instructional and Ratiocinative*).

Jeremy Bentham, *Extract from the Proposed Constitutional Code, Entitled Official Aptitude Maximized, Expense Minimized.* (London, 1826).

CHAPTER IX

| | |
|---|---|
| Section 15 Heading | §15. *REMUNERATION.* |
| Art. 2 | section, §16. *Locable* |
| Art. 6 | §16. *Locable* |
| | 16. *Locable who,* §17. *Located, how.* |
| Art. 9 | punishment; nor |
| | §4. *Dispunitive* |
| Art. 10 | §17. *Located, how.* |
| Art. 20 | Art. 22, |
| | §9. *Judges'* |
| Art. 26 | demand-money |
| | ADVOCATE; |
| Art. 27 | other sub-district |
| Art. 28 | recondation-entry, |
| | Art. 23, |
| Art. 34 | quantum and merit, |
| Art. 35 | Immovable |
| Art. 36 | MINISTERS COLLECTIVELY, §3. |
| | Ch. xi. MINISTERS COLLECTIVELY, §4. |
| Art. 45 | subordinate . . . superordinate |
| | subordinate . . . superordinate |
| Art. 47 | compound; the |
| Art. 48 | Art. 30: |
| Art. 51 | Sub-department, |
| | Sub-department, |
| | Sub-department |
| | Sub-department. |

| | |
|---|---|
| Art. 53 | reward, to |
| Art. 54 | [———] |
| | §17. *Located* |
| Art. 55 | Sub-department |
| Art. 56 | sub-departments |
| Art. 57 | [———] |
| | [———] |

| | |
|---|---|
| Section 16  Heading | §16. *LOCABLE WHO*. |
| Art. 1 | Sub-departments |
| | whereby, in |
| Art. 2 | sub-departments, |
| Art. 3 | *Enactive, Ratiocinative, Instructional.* |
| | follows:—— |
| | §15. *Located* |
| Art. 7 | increase, up |
| | Arts. 54, |
| Art. 10 | *Calendar*; as |
| | §31. *Securities* |
| Art. 12 | groupes, |
| | groupes |
| Art. 13 | messengers |
| | deperition |
| | immovable |
| Art. 15 | groupes |
| | groupes |
| I. 3 | sub-department. |
| Art. 16 | §18. *Located* |
| Art. 17 | admitted, and |
| Art. 18 | Arts. 42 to 53, |
| | groupes |
| | Ch. xiv. |
| Art. 21 | follow:—— |
| | Art. 33. |
| Art. 23 | length, such |
| | *groupes* |
| | groupes, |
| | *groupes* |
| | groupes |
| Art. 24 | *Judges*, in |
| Art. 25 | indicating, by |
| | groupe |
| Art. 31 | Art. 30 |
| Art. 32 | *Enactive or Instructional.* |
| | Art. 31 |
| Art. 33 | Art. 32 |
| | studied; together |
| Art. 34 | Art. 33 |
| Art. 35 | Art. 34 |
| | §26. *Locable* |
| Art. 36 | Art. 35 |

521

| | |
|---|---|
| Art. 37 | Art. 36 |
| Art. 38 | Art. 37 |
| Art. 39 | Art. 38 |
| Art. 40 | Art. 39 |
| Art. 41 | Art. 40 |
| Art. 42 | Art. 41 |
| Art. 43 | Art. 42 |
| | either and |
| | either and |
| Art. 44 | Art. 43 |
| Art. 45 | Art. 44 |
| Art. 46 | Art. 45 |
| Art. 47 | Art..46 |
| Art. 48 | Art. 47 |
| Art. 49 | Art. 48 |
| | instructor |
| | LEGISLATIVE, §20. *Attendance* |
| | §23. *Self-suppletive Function:* |
| | expense: delivery |
| Art. 50 | Art. 49 |
| | instruction; on |
| Art. 51 | Art. 50 |
| Art. 52 | Art. 51 |
| | can not |
| | Art. 32. |
| Art. 53 | Art. 52 |
| | seen, of |
| Art. 54 | Art. 53 |
| Art. 55 | *Enactive, Instructional, or Expositive.* |
| | Art. 54 |
| Art. 56 | *Enactive or Instructional.* |
| | Art. 55 |
| Art. 57 | Art. 56 |
| Art. 58 | Art. 57 |
| Art. 59 | Art. 58 |
| Art. 60 | Art. 59 |
| *omits* | Supplement to §16. |
| | |
| Section 17  Heading | §17. *LOCATED HOW.* |
| Art. 1 | *emptional*, or |
| Art. 6 | *Enactive or Instructional.* |
| | §16. Arts. 10, 11, 12, 13, |
| Art. 9 | §16. *Locable* |
| | instrument, according |
| Art. 10 | who, in in |
| Art. 11 | §16. *Partiality* |
| Art. 14 | §16. *Locable who*, Art. 55, |
| | Arts. 5. 12.) |
| | reproach be |
| Art. 19 | Sub-departments, |
| | sub-department, |

| | | |
|---|---|---|
| Art. 21 | | sub-department, |
| Art. 22 | | sub-department, |
| Art. 23 | | sub-departments, |
| Art. 24 | | sub-department, |
| Art. 25 | | §3. |
| Art. 27 | | Art. 23, |
| Art. 28 | | sub-department, |
| | | §4. *Self-suppletive Function.* |
| Art. 29 | | *Vice-Consul* by |
| Art. 31 | n | applicable for remedy to |
| | | Ch. xxiii. APPELLATE JUDICATORS. |
| Art. 33 | | Art. 18, |
| Art. 34 | | byrecital |
| | *omits* | Arts. 37–41 inclusive, as well as the Supplement. |

CONCLUDING INSTRUCTION TO THE PUBLIC OPINION TRIBUNAL

| | | |
|---|---|---|
| Art. 1 | | of, the |
| | *omits* n a | |
| Art. 3 | | exertions |
| Art. 5 | | sources, one |
| | *omits* | Finance Minister in the House of Commons; |
| | *substitutes* | principal Official Minister of Finance; |
| | *omits* | Trade Minister, in the language of this Code, as per Ch. xi. MINISTERS SEVERALLY, Section 11. |
| | *substitutes* | executing other functions in the Sub-department of Finance. |
| | *adds* | §18. *DISLOCABLE HOW.* |
| | | *Enactive.* |
| | | ART. 1. Every Minister is at any time dislocable by the Prime Minister. |
| | | *Enactive.* |
| | | ART. 2. So by the Legislature. |
| | | *Enactive.* |
| | | ART. 3. Other efficient causes of dislocatedness are the same as in the case of a member of the Legislature, as per Ch. vi. §1. Art. 1. For other checks, see §31. *Securities for appropriate Aptitude.* |

Jeremy Bentham, *Official Aptitude Maximized; Expense Minimized: As shewn in the Several Papers Comprised in This Volume* (London, 1830): *Extract from the Proposed Constitutional Code, Entitled Official Aptitude Maximized, Expense Minimized* (London, 1826).

The 1830 text is like that of the 1826 text, with the following minor variations:

| | | |
|---|---|---|
| Section 15, | | |
| Art. 18 | | Constitution |
| | | Government, is |

| | |
|---|---|
| Art. 19 | community or |
| Art. 31 | Baronet |
| Art. 32 | individual are—— |
| | |
| Section 16, | |
| Art. 49 | Instructor |
| Art. 50 | emolument to |
| | |
| Section 17, | |
| Art. 16 | intrusted |
| Art. 34 | by recital |
| | |
| Concluding Instruction, | |
| Art. 1 | progress of the |
| Art. 5 | title of Chancellor |
| | principal Minister of Finance, acting as such |
| | in the House of Commons; |
| | Minister of the Sub-department of Trade |
| *omits* | §18. Arts. 1–3 |

In addition, the 1830 text, unlike that of 1826, contains the Supplements to Sections 16 and 17. Variants from the text of the *present edition* are as follows:

| | |
|---|---|
| Supplement to | |
| Section 16, Heading | Supplement to §16. *LOCABLE WHO.* |
| | USE of LOT as an INSTRUMENT of SELECTION. |
| Art. 61 or 1 | Art. 60 or 1. |
| | Purposes to |
| | employed with advantage as |
| | knowledge, as |
| | aptitude, ascribed |
| | selection, foreknowledge |
| | it given, or not given, to |
| Art. 62 or 2 | Art. 61 or 2. |
| | science the |
| | *function,* (as per §10. *Information elicitative function,*) the |
| | *receptive* |
| *omits* | as to which, see Section 11, *Information-elicitative function.* |
| Art. 63 or 3 | Art. 62 or 3. |
| | *Functionaries* entitled |
| | Art. 17, 18. |
| | Art. 18. three. |
| | *Number* of |
| | *number* of |
| | *information,* |
| | *evidence* |
| | §10. *Information elicitative* |

| | |
|---|---|
| Art. 64 or 4 | Art. 63 or 4. |
| | science provide |
| | *answers*; say, |
| | Name common |
| | *Book*; the names |
| | book, that |
| Art. 65 or 5 | Art. 64 or 5. |
| | instructions |
| | it,——the assumption is—— |
| | that for |
| | view:——brought |
| | propounded: only |
| | course determined on, |
| Art. 66 or 6 | *Instructional and Ratiocinative.* |
| | Art. 65 or 6. |
| | assumed, one |
| | is,——what |
| Art. 67 or 7 | Art. 66 or 7. |
| | *partiality*, |
| | be——a |
| | alone, as, according to what he had learnt, |
| *omits* | ——to his (the examiner's) knowledge,—— |
| | otherwise: and |
| | person by |
| | place, it |
| Art. 68 or 8 | Art. 67 or 8. |
| | 1. Manner |
| | of the squares |
| | manifest to |
| Art. 69 or 9 | Art. 68 or 9. |
| | 1. A |
| | hand;—— |
| | one, the |
| | present, and in |
| | persons lodged, |
| | be——and |
| | sealed, and, |
| | may be |
| *omits* | *note following the end of Art. 69 or 9, which* |
| | *appears after note to Art. 70 or 10.* |
| Art. 70 or 10 | Art. 69 or 10. |
| | exemplified, the |
| n a | Work from |
| | Lawrence." 8vo. |
| | *urn:"* |
| | Supplement |
| | it—— |
| n | *style.——* |
| | words in |
| | Exchequer,) |
| | Under |

|                            |                                    |
|----------------------------|------------------------------------|
|                            | say, is, that                      |
|                            | had not stayed his hand,—          |
|                            | taken place,                       |
|                            | packed, by                         |
|                            | accustomed," .. by                 |
|                            | and them                           |
|                            | Thus by                            |
|                            | established, converted,            |
| Art. 71 or 11              | Art. 70 or 11.                     |
|                            | *Fortune*, this                    |
|                            | place for                          |
|                            | purposes                           |
| Art. 72 or 12              | Art. 71 or 12.                     |
|                            | *benefits*                         |
|                            | Examples:                          |
|                            | money from                         |
|                            | source to                          |
|                            | *Prize money:*                     |
| Art. 73 or 13              | Art. 72 or 13.                     |
|                            | Cases in                           |
|                            | QUASI JURY.                        |
| Art. 74 or 14              | Art. 73 or 14.                     |
|                            | cases the                          |
|                            | *itself*                           |
|                            | not: but                           |
|                            | *time*                             |
|                            | duration,—personal                 |
|                            | *hardship*                         |
|                            | money among                        |
| Art. 75 or 15              | Art. 74 or 15.                     |
|                            | 1. Of                              |
|                            | burthens, imposed                  |
| Art. 76 or 16              | Art. 75 or 16.                     |
|                            | 1. ... 2.                          |
|                            | noticing: on                       |
|                            | exactly                            |
|                            | point, at                          |
| Art. 77 or 17              | Art. 76 or 17.                     |
|                            | 1. ... 2.                          |
|                            | interested—                        |
|                            | *contract*; to                     |
| Art. 78 or 18              | Art. 77 or 18.                     |
|                            | case in                            |
|                            |                                    |
| *Supplement to Section 17* | *Located, how*                     |
| Art. 42 or 1               | Art. 37 or 1.                      |
|                            | *Pecuniary-competition*            |
|                            | contributing in                    |
|                            | *aptitude-manifestation*           |
| Art. 43 or 2               | Art. 38 or 2.—I. Reasons           |
|                            | Art. 12, 13:                       |

|  |  |
|---|---|
|  | *Locable, who* |
|  | Art. 33, 34, 35, 36, 40), |
|  | responsibility, alleviated |
|  | trials, above; |
| Art. 44 or 3 | Art. 39 or 3.——II. Case II. |
|  | *Examination Jury*, |
|  | I. Reason, |
|  | say, *Qualification* |
|  | likely that |
|  | made in |
|  | affords, therefore, a |
| Art. 45 or 4 | Art. 40 or 4.——II. Reasons |
|  | 1. In |
| Art. 46 or 5 | Art. 41 or 5.——These |
| Art. 47 or 6 | Art. 42 or 6.——At |
|  | that to |
| Art. 48 or 7 | Art. 43 or 7.——The |
|  | received, are |
| *omits n* |  |
| Art. 49 or 8 | Art. 44 or 8.——Note |
|  | *point, or say* |
|  | indefinitely |
|  | dignity superadded: |
|  | illegal service |
| Art. 50 or 9 | Art. 45 or 9.——To |
|  | I. Objection, to |
|  | excluded thence, |
| Art. 51 or 10 | Art. 46 or 10.——Objection |
|  | other-would |
|  | rest of the community . . . rest of the community |
|  | him, and timidity, |
| Art. 52 or 11 | Art. 47 or 11. But |
|  | *Answer.* |
|  | abundant;——to |
| Art. 53 or 12 | Art. 48 or 12.——Objection 2. |
|  | governments, |
|  | class: evil, |
|  | 1,000,000 *l.*, |
|  | 200,000 *l.* |
|  | 200,000 *l.* |
|  | put, not |
|  | *Reply*: Of |
| Art. 54 or 13 | Art. 49 or 13.——Objection |
|  | does the emptional. |
| *omits* | 3 |
|  | *protegé* |
|  | made in |
|  | abuse:——the |
|  | course he expects and |
|  | endeavour to |

|  |  |
|---|---|
|  | government, |
|  | government |
|  | found comparable |
| Art. 55 or 14 | Art. 50 or 14.——Objection 14, |
|  | alleged existence |
| Art. 56 or 15 | Art. 51 or 15.——Objection |
| *omits* | *invited.* |
|  | of the functionaries |
| Art. 57 or 16 | Art. 51 or 15.——This |
|  | *protegés* formed, |
|  | ths particulars |
| Art. 58 or 17 | Art. 52 or 16.——In |
|  | it, for |
| Art. 59 or 18 | Art. 33 or 17.——Objection. *Aptitude* |
|  | *expence.* |
|  | course; all |
|  | flew |

|  |  |
|---|---|
| *Footnote to Concluding Instruc-* | |
| *tion, Art. 1, is inserted after* | with it |
|  | Because to |
|  | made; and |
|  | accepted followed by consequences the |
|  | it; to |
|  | inaptitude; then, |
|  | objector; and |
|  | true; a |
| Art. 59 or 18 n | cost; not |
|  | examinations be |
|  | favourable to one hostile to |

# INDEX OF SUBJECTS

*Note.* The subject index covers Bentham's text of the *Constitutional Code*, and the various entries refer to the chapters, sections (at times, bis-sections), and articles and not to the page numbers. For example, a reference to Chapter VIII, Section 3, Article 1 will appear as VIII.3.A1. Where a series of articles appear in the index, the chapter and section are not repeated. There are two kinds of cross-references. Where a reference appears in the middle of an entry in square brackets, e.g. [19, See SUBORDINATE AND SUPERORDINATE], this means that to save space and avoid undue repetition, the relevant material will be found under the referred subject at the same point, i.e. at SUBORDINATE AND SUPERORDINATE at Section 19. The cross-references at the end of the entry refer more generally to related material.

The symbol 'v.' is used below to indicate 'as distinct from' or 'as opposed to'. Other abbreviations for frequently occurring words and phrases are:

| | |
|---|---|
| legislature | leg. |
| sublegislature(s) | subleg(s). · |
| exercise(s)/ed | ex. |
| function(s) | f(s). |
| appropriate aptitude | app. apt. |
| public opinion tribunal | p.o. trib. |
| prime minister | p.m. |
| department(s) | dept(s). |
| subdepartment(s) | subdept(s). |
| maximize(d)/maximization | max. |
| minimize(d)/minimization | min. |

ABBREVIATION(S): IX.7.6th.A1, use of abbreviations in ex. of statistic f. determined by leg.; A2, arguments for and against practice; A3–5, rules for abbreviations enumerated; A5n, Italian bookkeeping nomenclature criticized; A5n, use of Latin abbreviations in English practice criticized; A6, securities for correct and complete entries enumerated; IX.8.A33, abbreviations and requisitive f.

ABILITY: *See* APTITUDE AND INAPTITUDE

ABSTRACT(S): IX.25.A9, use of abstracts in preparing registers

ABUNDANCE: VII.2, max. of abundance as positive end of government

ADMINISTRATIVE AUTHORITY: IV.A1, administrative authority one of four in state; A3, leg. to locate and dislocate chiefs of administrative depts. and upon occasion to give individual and general direction; A4, administrative dept. to give execution and effect to ordinances of leg.; A6, administrative and legislative depts. compose government; A6, administrative and judiciary depts. compose executive; A6, executive and legislative depts. compose the operative; A7, use of word 'supreme' discussed; A8, for each authority, a dept.; A10, within administrative dept., there are 13 subdepts.; A11, administrative dept. and local and logical fields of service; A13, single-seated arrangements in administrative dept.; VI.1.A5, administrative authority dependent on legislative authority; A6, where non-performance or inaptitude, leg. can

529

take over fs. of administrative authority; VII.12, encroachment by leg. on administrative authority; VIII.2.A2, administrative authority and p.m.'s ex. of directive f.; IX.26.A11, publicity and secrecy in administrative dept.; A54, offices separate from judiciary. *See* MINISTER(S)

ADVOCATE(S): VI.27.A33-4, use of professional advocates before legislative enquiries. *See* LAWYER(S)

AMENDMENT(S): V.5.A6, headings relevant to formulation of amendments; A7, amendments and the preservation of symmetry; A8, reasons and effects to be given for proposing amendments; VI.29.A1-6, emendative ordinances; VII.1.A3-5, provision for amendment to legislator's inaugural declaration; IX.25.A37, amendments and securities against ex. of extraordinary power by functionaries. *See* MOTION(S)

ANALOGY: IX.19.A31n, 'one of the great instruments in the hand of inventive genius'

ANARCHY: II.A24, 'spice of anarchy' in English government; VII.6, anarchy and tax on judicial services; IX.19.A29, and distribution of grades in army; 25.A57, and relief against oppression

ANTI-CONSTITUTIONAL OFFENCE(S): V.6.A3, prohibition or taxation of political tracts is anti-constitutional offence; VI.2.A2, ordinances of leg. which are contrary to constitution; VIII.5.A4, failure to hold election for p.m. *See* ARBITRARINESS; CONSTITUTION; LEGISLATION PENAL JUDICATORY

APPLICATION FUNCTION: VI.27.A39, ex. in preparation of legislation enquiry report. *See* MANDATE(S); WRITTEN INSTRUMENT(S)

APPLICATIVE FUNCTION: IX.4.A49, ex. by ministers collectively in regard to things; A49, A70, defined; A49, applicative v. directive f.; A49, and eliminative f.; IX.7.2nd.A24, and use of mimographical or receptacular mode of registration; 3rd.A19, and application book

APPOSITENESS: VI.27.A44, as desirable property of evidence. *See* EVIDENCE

APTITUDE AND INAPTITUDE: II.A2, apt. max., as means to greatest happiness; A14, app. apt. for rulers v. rulees; A15, branches of appt. apt.: moral, intellectual (cognitional and judicial), active; A16, rules for max. of app. apt.; A17, app. apt. and the min. of expense, principles employed; A19, securities and max. of app. apt.; A22, punishment for moral inaptitude, dislocation for active and intellectual inaptitude; VI.1.A6-7, app. apt. and fs. of leg. in relation to subordinate authorities; A9, app. apt. and differences of opinion between constituents and deputy; 23.A23-6, app. apt. and deputy's substitute; 24.A1, app. apt. and continuation committee; A18, leg. best judges of app. apt. of continuation committee; 25.A8, temporary non-relocability system and apt.; A17-19, undiscontinued relocability and inaptitude; A32-7, temporary non-relocability, experience, and app. apt.; A42-5, app. apt. and period of founding new states discussed; A50, moral apt., p.o. trib., and liberty of press; A52, temporary non-relocability, freedom of choice and app. apt.; A53, app. apt. and temporary non-relocability v. undiscontinued relocability; 28.A8, moral and intellectual apt. and appointment of judges to legislation penal judicatory; A16, app. apt. and appellate judicatory; 31.A1, abuse of power, securities and app. apt.; A24, reception of securities as test of app. apt. of person; A41n, apt. and English judicial practice; VII.2, app. apt. and the ends of government; 4, legislator's duties in ensuring app. apt. of functionaries; 7, app. apt. and elections by leg. of p.m., justice minister, and legislation minister; 12, leg. and inaptitude of subordinate authorities; VIII.7.A1, app. apt. and location of p.m.; 12.A1, p.m. and securities for app. apt.; A2-4, p.m. to act on information of misconduct or inaptitude of ministers; IX.3.A3, moral apt. and number in office; A4, intellectual apt. and number in office; A5, active apt. and number in office; A12-13, inaptitude in boards in English practice; 9.A3, app. apt. of functionaries noted in ex. of inspective f.; 10.A26, inaptitude in English practice with distant dependencies; 15.A1-3, apt. max. in remuneration and location; A3, apt. dependent on man's relish for occupation; A3-4, apt. in inverse proportion to remuneration; A38, ultra-concomitant remuneration, a premium on inaptitude; 16.A3, app. apt. and location system; A3, 'scale of aptitude' in location system; A7, courses of instruction increasing app. apt.; A9, those reaping benefit from courses preferred in location over those without acquired apt., as security for app. apt.; A12, apt. and situations of talent; A33, comparative apt. of instructors exhibited in ranking table; A34, leg. will limit topics for interrogation by qualification judicatory regarding moral apt.; A34, judges, quasi-jurymen and competitors (with permission) may interrogate; A34, for app. moral apt., irregularities of sexual appetite, prohibited subject of enquiry; A35, until leg. limits topics, unlimited liberty of interrogation; A35, interrogation regarding moral apt. may be limited by majority of judges or by candidate; A35, responsibility for false statements indicated; A36, results of enquiry into moral apt. entered in candidates' character book; A37, app. moral apt. not subject of voting; A37, but results available to each locator; A40-1, no candidate refused entry on locable list on grounds of intellectual and moral inaptitude unless by express decree of majority of judges; A41, record of moral inaptitude printed and published by registrar; A47-9, max. of app. apt. of instructors; A58, app. apt. and preparation period; A59, after one year, to exclude inaptitude, no one placed on locable list without instruction, when available; A60, leg. to make arrangements for examination of app. moral apt.; A61, use of chance to max. apt. in examination system; A62, responses and exhibitions, as tokens of app. apt.; 17.A43, pecuniary competition and app. moral apt. in situation of simple trust; A47, in English practice, as expense of official labour max., app. apt. min.; A52, unopulence as a cause of apt. discussed; A53-6, pecuniary competition system an instrument for app. apt.; A59, apt. does not increase with increase of pay and opulence; 17.Con.Inst.A1n, application of instruction system to nation and app. apt.; 19.A12, app. apt. and increase in remuneration while in office; A24-5, repetition of qualification examination in filling vacancies and app. apt.; A35, securing app. apt. in corrupt government; A36, lot preferred to choice in corrupt government; 21.A33, app. apt. and adequate penal code; A50, and dislocation instrument; A51, and resignation; 24.A4, app. apt. of ministers as well as legislators used to secure pannomion from deterioration; 25.A1, elements of app. apt. distinguished: moral, active, intellectual (cognitional, judicial); A45, lowest degree of cognitional and judicial apt. necessary for following precedents; 26.A1, importance of art-and-science of architecture to app. apt. of administrative dept.; A20n, app. apt. and Panopticon; A47, app. apt. and military guards v. watchmen and porters. See LOCATION AND DISLOCATION; MAXIMIZATION AND MINIMIZATION; MORAL; PUBLIC OPINION TRIBUNAL; SECURITIES

ARBITRARINESS: VIII.12.A1, checks to arbitrary appointments by p.m.; IX.15.A8, arbitrary remuneration repugnant to constitution; A9, arbitrary remuneration neither good nor evil; A10, arbitrary remuneration defined as that not judicially conferred; A35, arbitrary conferring of factitious dignity sufficient to destroy constitution; 16.A3, dislocative power a check to arbitrary patronage by p.m.; 17.Con.Inst.A1, location system, apt. and arbitrary power; 19.A10, arbitrary v. judicial dislocation; A14, arbitrariness and remuneration for longevity; 21.A20, arbitrary v. judicially-grounded modes of procedure. *See* MONARCHY

ARBITRATIVE FUNCTION: VI.3.A1, A4, ex. by leg. in relation to sublegs.

ARCHITECTURE: VI.20.A24, good government depends on architecture; IX.21.A20, architectural arrangements, publicity, and indirectly-applying remedies against oppression; 26.A1, importance of art and science of architecture to app. apt. of administrative dept.; A2, ends in view; A3, app. arrangements to reduce delay, vexation, and expense for both functionaries and suitors; A4, importance of publicity and secrecy to max. good and min. evil; A5-6, subjects for consideration in choosing publicity and secrecy; A7, varying demands for publicity and secrecy as between depts., subdepts., and offices; A8-9, greatest secrecy required in constitutive dept. in secret ballot; A10, greatest publicity required in judiciary dept.; A11, intermediate publicity in administrative dept.; A12, uses of publicity and architectural arrangements as means thereto; A13-14, delay in communication discussed; A14, delay min. where there is direct communication; A15, importance of contiguous offices; A16, offices defined; A17, ministers' offices arranged in a crescent with p.m.'s office in centre for instant communication; A17-18, except for election and legislation ministers' offices; A19&n, use of conversation tubes for instant communication; A20, contiguous offices have additional advantage of security for transfer of papers; A20n, importance of inspection noted; A21, arrangements for oral communication between suitors and functionaries with use of waiting boxes, public and private; A22, uses of waiting boxes to augment publicity and secure observance of deportment rules; A23, arrangements for light; A24, arrangements for treasury to store official books and papers; A25, arrangements for apartments where ministers and families live; A26-7, private waiting boxes; A28-9, arrangements for minister to attend to public and private waiting-boxes; A30, admission to and exit from public and private waiting-boxes; A31&n, extra security for secret suitors; A32-4, justification of secret meetings between ministers and suitors discussed; A35-7, reward for informers discussed; A38-9, arrangements for living accommodation for ministers discussed; A40, expense in representative democracy v. monarchy; A41, importance of frequent change of ministers; A42, arrangements for security of buildings and contents against loss, examples given; A43, loss of manuscripts in treasury min. by registration and publication system; A44, causes of indiscriminate destruction and deterioration stated; A45, causes of furtive abstraction stated; A46, need in republic to protect public property from popular commotion; A47, military guard v. watchmen and porters for security; A48, in monarchy, all but one become slaves; A49-52, greatest happiness requires residence of functionaries located where of most use; A53, offices of functionaries, U.S. practice; A54, offices of judiciary should be separated from administrative dept.

ARGUMENTATIVE FUNCTION: IX.24.A1, ex. by ministers in debates in leg.

ARISTOCRACY: II.A24, and English government; VI.31.A34-5, and reception to securities; VIII.5.A4, representative democracy changed to monarchy and aristocracy where leg. fails to elect p.m.; 11.A6, democracy altered to aristocracy by publicity given to secret voting; IX.20.A12, aristocracy and secret institutions; 25.A47-8, as sub-class opposed to universal interest; A53, and

corruption; 26.A52, pure aristocracy worst form of government. *See* ENG-
LISH PRACTICE; MIXED MONARCHY; MONARCHY

ARMY MINISTER: IX.2.A1, serves under p.m.; 9.A7, joint visits with navy
minister in ex. of inspective f.; 16.A15, requisite talents for post; 19.A40-1,
and power of dislocation; 26.A47, provides subordinates for maintaining
security of public property. *See* ARMY SUBDEPARTMENT; MILITARY
SERVICE; MINISTER(S)

ARMY SUBDEPARTMENT: VI.27.A15, functionaries in field and powers of
legislation enquiry judicatory; VIII.2.A8, A10-12, A14-16, ex. of imperative
f. by p.m. as commander-in-chief; 11.A6-7, where publicity may be harmful;
A15-17, and time-limits on secrecy; IX.2.A10, potentially joined with navy
and preventive service subdepts.; A10n, army courts martial and judiciary;
5.A35, largest number of grades in subdept.; A37, English practice of large
numbers in higher grades max. expense; A39, English v. U.S. practice; IX.9.A4,
offices to be visited in ex. of inspective f.; 11.A9, extraction of information
for defence purposes; 16.A15, talent-requiring situations and requisite talents,
examples given; 17.A17, minimum age for service as lowest grade of officer;
A23-6, need for temporarily initiative location; 20.A1, legislator to consider
applicability of arrangements for obviation of insubordination, oppression,
and extortion to military branch of army services; 21.A20, leg. to consider
whether variation in rules of deportment is necessary for army subdept. as
indirectly-applying remedy against oppression; A27, military codes and
repression of wrongs between functionaries; A49, use of dislocation instruments. *See* ARMY MINISTER; MILITARY SERVICE

ARRANGEMENT(S): IX.4.A40, fictitious entity——the result of any law or
mandate, permanent or transitory; A41, institutions and establishments, as
arrangements; A41, defined and distinguished; A61, f. regarding arrangements:
melioration-suggestive. *See* ENTITIES

ARTS AND SCIENCES: VII.4, encouragement to arts and sciences at expense of
the indigent not the object of legislator; IX.7.4th.A31, expenditure on fine
arts and books as form of loss

ASYLUM: VII.8, asylum to all granted

ATTENDANCE AND NON-ATTENDANCE: VI.18.A1-2, leg. sits every day
except vacation days (every 7th day); 20.A1-3, arrangements for entry and
departure from assembly chamber; A4, remuneration for days attended only;
A5, absentation book and publication of record of absences of legislators;
A6, arrangements for sickness; A7, suspicion of using sickness as a pretence
obviated; A8, withholding remuneration for non-attendance; A11, non-
interrupted attendance v. interrupted attendance of legislators discussed;
A12-14, effect in mixed monarchies of non-attendance; A15-17, and in English practice; A18, A20-1, and U.S. practice; A19, importance of uninterrupted sittings; 23.A30, notice of non-attendance by deputy and substitute
to be posted by election clerk of district; 25.A54-5, effect of pecuniary
punishment for non-attendance in leg. discussed in light of other securities;
26.A1, exclusion from leg. by force, fraud, or accident; A2, legislative authority belongs to majority present at meeting; A3, effect on majority where
members excluded; A4, responsibility of those involved in exclusion; A5, if
wrongful exclusion by member, dislocation by constitutive authority; 27.A27,
elicitation process not to conflict with attendance at leg. by deputies and
continuation committee; A50, attendance by witnesses at elicitation of evidence by House of Commons not secured; A54, nor by monarch's commissions;

31.A43, attendance and securities for app. moral apt. of leg.; A45, and securities for app. active apt. of leg.; VII.1.A2, arrangements for unavoidable absence of legislator from reading legislator's inaugural declaration; 10, attendance by legislator promised in legislator's inaugural declaration; IX.14.A1, ministers' attendance time: in-door and out-door service; A1, in-door and out-door service defined; A2, leg. to determine time devoted to each; A3, attendance of legislators to receive communications from ministers; 19.A11, leg. to apply rules of attendance to each subordinate situation. *See* REMUNERATION; SELF-SUPPLETIVE FUNCTION
AUDIENCE(S): V.4.A3, audiences of official bodies serve as committees of p.o. trib. *See* ARCHITECTURE; CHAMBER(S); PUBLIC OPINION TRIBUNAL
AUDIENCE CHAMBER(S): *See* CHAMBER(S); LEGISLATURE
AUSTRIA: II.A24, England v. Austria, moral responsibility, and p.o. trib.
AUTHORITY(IES): IV.A1, four authorities in the state: constitutive, legislative, administrative, and judiciary. *See* ADMINISTRATIVE AUTHORITY; CONSTITUTIVE AUTHORITY; JUDICIARY AUTHORITY; LEGISLATURE

BENEFICENCE: *See* BENEVOLENCE
BENEFIT(S) AND BURDEN(S): IX.1.A2n, defined. *See* GOOD AND EVIL
BENEVOLENCE: VII.8, beneficence and effective benevolence promised by legislators; IX.19.A14, and remuneration for longevity; 21.A21, A26, negative effective benevolence v. positive effective benevolence and rules of deportment; A21n, benevolence v. beneficence
BIS-SUBDISTRICT(S): *See* LOCAL HEADMAN; SUBDISTRICT(S)
BOOK(S): *See* STATISTIC FUNCTION

CALAMITY: VII.2, security against physical calamity as a positive end of government; VIII.10.A6, security against destruction of judicial documents by calamity; IX.25.A34, security against calamity and ex. of power by leg.
CAPITAL: IX.16.A45-6, capital v. interest on capital and government funding of instruction; 21.A6, capital and extinction of profit by disclosure, as oppression of inspectees
CENSORIAL FUNCTION: V.5.A2, ex. by p.o. trib.; 6.A2, all members of human species have right to ex. censorial f.; VIII.12.A1, ex. by p.o. trib. as security for app. apt. of p.m.; IX.25.A3, ex. by p.o. trib. as security for app. apt. of ministers; A30-1, and power of p.o. trib. *See* PUBLIC OPINION TRIBUNAL
CHAMBER(S): IX.21.A20, administrative functionaries' audience chamber, presence of rules for deportment and incidental complaint book; 25.A10, rules of deportment displayed in functionaries' audience chamber, as security for app. apt. *See* ARCHITECTURE; AUDIENCE(S); LEGISLATURE
CHANCE: IX.9.A8, use of chance for unexpected visits in ex. of inspective f.; A9, as a security, how best used; 16.A61, use of chance v. choice in examination system; A69n, in English practice; A76, chance and choice used in association. *See* CHOICE; LOCATION AND DISLOCATION; LOT
CHARACTER INDEX: IX.25.A4, composed of personal stock book, individual service book and loss book, and used as instrument of security for app. apt.; A11, character index and functionary's deportment rules. *See* APTITUDE
CHECK(S): V.4.A4, public opinion a check to pernicious ex. of power of government; VI.1.A1, power of supreme leg. is unlimited but checked by securities;

25.A49, securities as checks to p.m.'s power; 27.A14, checks on legislation enquiry judicatory considered; A38, securities as checks applicable to legislation enquiry judicatory; VIII.11.A16, check on p.m.'s report by legislative committee; 12.A1, checks to arbitrary appointments by p.m.; IX.7.2nd.A30, checks on transmission of money; 8.A14, checks on requisitions; 9.A5, inspection visits as checks; A7, finance minister and checks on expenditure; 16.A69n, jury system as check to despotism; 17.A11, checks on mislocation; 20.A12, secret institutions as checks to tyranny; 23.A12, need for suspicion and precaution as checks to delinquency. *See* SECURITIES

CHOICE: VI.25.A12–13, two candidates for leg. required for effective choice; A39, period of non-relocability and choice between 'tried men'; A49, responsibility and freedom of choice of electors; A52–3, temporary non-relocability and freedom of choice; IX.16.A3, choice and location by p.m. in location system; A3, improper choice at peril of p.m.'s reputation; A31, choice and ranking table in location system; A61, use of chance v. choice in examination system; A69n, in English practice; A76, chance and choice used in association; 17.Con.Inst.A1, apt. system and arbitrary power of choice; 19.A22, ministers and choice in filling vacancies; A35, in corrupt government succession by 'official age' better than unrestrained choice; A36, choice v. lot for succession in corrupt government. *See* CHANCE; LOCATION AND DISLOCATION; LOT; RELOCATION

CLASS(ES): VI.31.A27–30, lawyer class in representative democracy; A41n, English practice and professional lawyers of all classes; VII.9, legislator promises impartiality toward individuals and all classes; IX.16.A52, payment to instructors and to lowest-paid class of labourers; 17.A53, unopulent classes excluded by pecuniary competition; 25.A46, class of persons to whom system of following precedents is well adapted; A47, class divided into two subclasses, mis-employed lawyers, mercantile, and official subclass; unemployed peerage subclass; A48, power-holding class in representative democracy v. mixed monarchy

CLEARNESS: VI.27.A18, A44, clearness as desirable property of evidence; A39, in legislation enquiry report; 31.A44, and securities for app. intellectual apt. of legislators; VII.5, as desirable characteristic of laws; IX.7.6th.A6, of entries in ex. of statistic f. *See* EVIDENCE; LAW OR MANDATE; MOTION(S); STATISTIC FUNCTION; WRITTEN INSTRUMENT(S)

COERCION: *See* INDUCEMENT AND COERCION; REWARD AND PUNISHMENT

COLONIES: *See* DEPENDENCIES

COMMENTATIVE FUNCTION: IX.25.A23, importance of access to register book for ex. of

COMMODATIVE FUNCTION: *See* ELIMINATIVE FUNCTION

COMMON LAW: *See* ENGLISH PRACTICE

COMMONWEALTH: IX.15.A35, constitution called a 'commonwealth'; A35, subversion of by arbitrary conferring of factitious dignity

COMMOTION(S): IX.26.A44, popular commotions as cause of loss of public buildings and contents; A46, need in republic to protect public property from popular commotions

COMMUNICATION: *See* ARCHITECTURE; EXEMPLARS; LEGISLATURE; PUBLICITY AND SECRECY

COMPENSATION: *See* REMUNERATION; RESPONSIBILITY; REWARD AND PUNISHMENT

COMPETITION: VI.25.A4–5, non-relocation and competition for legislative office; A6–11, examples discussed; A52–3, temporary non-relocability and competition for leg.; VII.8, competition between states and between individuals discussed; IX.15.A6, competition and remuneration of labour; 16.A3, 17.A1–59, pecuniary competition system; 17.A45, competition principle applied to min. price of commodities; A46–7, application to official labour resisted in English practice; 19.A12, and increase of remuneration during office; A31, competition and arrangements in Russia; 23.A15, peculation in competitive situations. *See* LOCATION AND DISLOCATION

COMPLETENESS: *See* COMPREHENSIVENESS

COMPREHENSIVENESS: II.A1, greatest happiness of greatest number as all-comprehensive end of constitution; VI.27.A18, A44, comprehensiveness as desirable property of evidence; A39, comprehensiveness in legislation enquiry report; A54, comprehensiveness of evidence elicited by monarch's commission; 31.A44, comprehensiveness in securities for app. intellectual apt. of legislators; VII.2, greatest happiness of greatest number as all-comprehensive end of government; 5, completeness as desirable characteristic of law; VIII. 10.A1, comprehensiveness in registration; IX.7.6th.A6, of entries in ex. of statistic f. *See* EVIDENCE; LAW OR MANDATE; MOTION(S); STATISTIC FUNCTION; WRITTEN INSTRUMENT(S)

COMPULSORILY PROCURATIVE FUNCTION: *See* LOCATION AND DISLOCATION

CONCISENESS: VI.31.A44, in securities for app. intellectual apt. of legislators; VII.5, as desirable characteristic of law. *See* EVIDENCE; LAW OR MANDATE; MOTION(S); WRITTEN INSTRUMENT(S)

CONDENSATION FUNCTION: VI.27.A39, ex. in preparation of legislation enquiry report. *See* MANDATE(S); WRITTEN INSTRUMENT(S)

CONDUCTIVE FUNCTION: *See* LOCATION AND DISLOCATION; PROCURATIVE FUNCTION

CONFIRMATION FUNCTION: *See* CONSUMMATIVE FUNCTION

CONSENT: VI.25.A52, consent to temporary non-relocability and suffering; 27.A27, consent and participation in evidence elicitation process v. attendance at leg.; VII.1.A2, consent and unavoidable absence at legislator's inaugural declaration; 8, grounds for legislator's consent to war; IX.15.A7, consent and liberal expenditure; A25, consent of persons not required for application for entry in public merit register; 16.A77–8, consent and use of lotteries; 21.A46, consent and transfer of functionaries; 24.A2, consent of leg. and vote of ministers

CONSERVATIVE FUNCTION: *See* REGISTRATIVE FUNCTION

CONSTITUENT(S): *See* CONSTITUTIVE AUTHORITY

CONSTITUTIONAL CODE OR CONSTITUTION: I.A1n, first in importance in the Pannomion; VI.1.A13, variable by legislative and constitutive authorities; 2.A2, ordinances of leg. repugnant to constitution, what effect; 25.A16, obstruction to the introduction of code by existing legislators; A20, exclusion of corruption from code; A39, and preparation period; A42, problem of app. apt. when states first founded; VIIn, provision for dissent to code in legislator's inaugural declaration; VII.11, basis of power in people; IX.8.A18, at commencement of code, leg. makes provision for outset supply; 15.A1, leading principles of code enumerated; A35, arbitrary conferring of factitious dignity sufficient to destroy constitution; A36, ultra-concomitant remuneration repugnant to constitution; A39, artificially mislocated remuneration also repugnant; A45, all arbitrarily conferred reward excluded from code; 16.A3, location by one person as principle of code; 20.A10, code and importance of inspection of public and private institutions; 21.A25, and system of judicial procedure; A32, no insertion of codes of deportment into constitutional code, reasons given; A33, constitutional code and penal code; 25.A1n, use of re-editive v. corrective or directive modes in code; A38, constitutional code and limits to abuse of power in ex. of extraordinary power; A49, acting on precedent is anti-constitutional when by executive and judiciary in opposition to leg. *See* ANTI-CONSTITUTIONAL OFFENCES; CONSTITUTIVE AUTHORITY; LEGISLATURE; STATE

CONSTITUTIVE AUTHORITY: III.A1, sovereignty in people, ex. by constitutive authority; IV.A1, constitutive authority is one of four authorities in the state; A2, constitutive authority to depute, locate, dislocate, and relocate members of the leg.; A2, not to give individual or specific direction to leg.'s measures; A7, use of word 'supreme' discussed; A7-8, constitutive authority supreme over others; A8, for each authority, a department; V.1.A1, constitutive authority defined; A2, vested in electors of state; A3, females, non-adult males, illiterates, and non-residents excluded; 2.A1, all other authorities subordinate to constitutive authority; A1, immediate v. interventional dislocation by constitutive authority; A2, constitutive authority ex. by locative, dislocative, punifactive fs.; A3-4, location of deputies to leg. and subleg.; A5, dislocative f., in relation to which functionaries exercised; A6, functionaries in relation to whom dislocative f. is ex. within each district; 3.A1, locative f., how ex. in relation to leg.; A2-3, and sublegs.; A4, dislocative f., how ex. in relation to leg.; A5, in relation to subleg.; A6, grounds for dislocation to be clearly stated, fallacies avoided; A7-9, punifactive f. how ex.; VI.1.A5, dependence of leg. on constitutive authority; A9, communication between constituents and deputy; A9, duty of deputy to constituents; A10, duty of deputy where interests of constituents conflict with national interest; A11-12, deputy's duty to public v. duty to constituents; A13, constitution variable by legislative and constitutive authorities; 2.A1, leg. to give execution and effect to the will of constitutive authority to max. happiness of greatest number; A2, constitutive authority and anti-constitutional ordinances of leg.; A3, constitutive authority and enforcement of contracts of leg.; A8, A11, constitutive authority to ex. dislocative and punifactive fs., where breach of public faith in contracts; 21.A1, sittings of leg. are public, p.o. trib. reports to constitutive authority; 23.A14-26, reasons given for suppletive f. belonging to deputy rather than to constitutive authority; 26.A5, constitutive authority and dislocation of members of leg. for wrongful exclusion of other members; VI.27.A27, service to constitutive authority and attendance of deputy v. participation in elicitation process; 28.A7, deprivation of constitutive authority of deputies by service on legislation penal judicatory; 30.A1, constitutive authority and dislocation of members of leg.; 31.A42, and securities for app. apt. of legislators; VII.11, the people are 'the only legitimate source of power'; 14, legislator but an agent of constituents; VIII.2.A1, constitutive authority and p.m.'s ex. of executive f.; 9.A2, constitutive authority and dislocation of p.m.; 11.A6, constitutive authority and evils of publicity in voting; 12.A1, registration system and constitutive authority and security for app. apt. of p.m.; A1, dislocation by constitutive authority as security for app. apt. of p.m.; IX.18.A6, constitutive authority and dislocation of ministers; 25.A3, as security for app. apt.; A30-1, constitutive authority and power of p.o. trib.; 26.A8-9, in constitutive authority, greatest need for secrecy in suffrage. *See* CONSTITUTION; ELECTION CODE; LEGISLATURE; PUBLIC OPINION TRIBUNAL

CONSUMMATIVE FUNCTION: IX.17.A21, 19.A16, ex. in location. *See* INITIATIVE FUNCTION

CONSUMPTION AUTHORIZING FUNCTION: *See* ELIMINATIVE FUNCTION

CONTAGION: *See* CALAMITY

CONTESTED INTERPRETATION REPORTING FUNCTION: IX.24.A5, judges' contested interpretation reporting f. and application to ministers; A6, in every situation subordinate to minister belongs the contested interpretation reporting f. as well as melioration-suggestive f.

CONTINUATION COMMITTEE: VI.20.A25, as remedy for deprivation of benefit of work of preceding legs.; 23.A29, distinctive dress for members of continuation committee discussed; 24.A1, located by leg. at end of session; A2, eligibility for continuation committee; A3, member has right of argumentation and initiation, but not the vote; A4, same remuneration as for deputy; reasons for provision of continuation given: (i) A5, time otherwise lost; (ii) A6, good measures otherwise lost; (iii) A7, time of functionaries otherwise wasted; (iv) A8, information already obtained, otherwise wasted; (v) A9, improvements requiring considerable preparation otherwise prevented; (vi) A10, the shorter the life of the leg., the greater evils of wasted time and information; (vii) A11, experience of legislators enhanced by successive relocation of continuation committee men; (viii) A12, absence of instance of continuation committee in governments, no bar to adoption; (ix) A13, practice in earlier societies; reasons for denying vote to continuation committee: (i) A14, more like ministers than legislators; (ii) A15, not chosen by electors; (iii) A16, number not fixed, effect on voting; (iv) A17, no grounds for objection to mode of location; reasons for leg. locating continuation committee: (i) A18, best judges of app. apt.; (ii) A19, best judges of the number of committee men needed; (iii) A20, committees in general are chosen by the body from which they come; (iv) A21, emblem of Sisyphus explained; 25.A3, continuation committee and relocation; A15, and discontinued relocability; A33, and maintaining app. apt. in leg.; A52-3, and temporary non-relocability; A53n, and evolution of Bentham's idea; 27.A25, members eligible for position as legislation elicitor; A27, elicitation process not to conflict with legislative duties. *See* LEGISLATION REGARDING FUNCTIONS

CONTRACT(S): VI.2.A3, enforcement of contracts of leg. by constitutive authority; A4, observance of contracts discussed; A5, judicial enforcement of contracts between government and individual of state; A6, between government and foreign state; A7, between government and subject of a foreign state; A8, constitutive authority to ex. dislocative and punifactive fs., where breach of public faith; A9, remedy for wrong done to foreign government; A10, and action of leg.; A11, and constitutive authority; IX.16.A77-8, lotteries and contracts; 23.A6-12, provisions in contracts for prevention of peculation

CONVERSATION TUBES: *See* ARCHITECTURE

CONVICTED LIST: IX.25.A6, as security for app. apt.; A7, headings employed; A8, inserted in office calendar; A9, arrangements for new series when list becomes of inconvenient size

CORRECTIVE FUNCTION: VI.3.A1, A3, ex. by leg. in relation to sublegs.

CORRECTNESS: VI.27.A18, A44, as desirable property of evidence; A39, in legislation enquiry report; 31.A44, and securities for app. intellectual apt. of legislators; VII.5, as desirable characteristic of law; VIII.10.A1, in registration; IX.7.6th.A6, of entries in ex. of statistic f.; 25.A1n, corrective and reeditive modes. *See* EVIDENCE; LAW OR MANDATE; MOTION(S); REEDITIVE MODE; STATISTIC FUNCTION; WRITTEN INSTRUMENT(S)

CORRUPTION: II.A16n, corruption as evil in government; VI.19.A1, ulterior remuneration and extortion v. corruption of legislators; 20.A17, corruption and English practice; 23.A9, absentation, corruption, and self-suppletion; A26, patronage without corruption; 24.A1, corruption of leg. by executive; 25.A8, relocability, stagnation in office, and corruption; A19-27, A46, corruption and undiscontinued relocability; A48, temporary non-relocability system as security against corruption; 27.A49, corruption in House of Commons; A54-5, monarch's commissions in English practice and corruptive influence; VII.4, sources of corruption discussed in legislator's inaugural declaration; VIII.6.A1, ulterior remuneration of p.m. and corruption v. extortion; IX.7.4th.A31, corruption and needless expense; 13.A3, corruption and dislocation of functionaries; 15.A4, remuneration, opulence, and corruption; A7, liberality and corruption; A34, corruption and conferring factitious honour by judges; A34, p.o. trib. not corruptible; A35, arbitrary conferring of factitious dignity, an instrument of corruption; A48, and hereditary titles of honour; A54, remuneration of ministers and extortion v. corruption; 16.A3, power of corruption min. through location system; A24n, corruption at India House; 17.A54, corruption and venality in pecuniary competition; A54, corruption min. in competition system; 17.Con.Inst.A1n, delusion and corruption rather than ignorance keep the subject many in England from changing governments; 19.A31, corruption and Russian practice; A35, to secure app. apt. in corrupt government, succession by official age; A36, ways this form of succession benefits sinister interests of superordinate; A36, allective v. intimidative corruptive influence; A36, use of lot, better to secure app. apt. in succession in corrupt government; 25.A13, gift or remuneration for extra despatch is corruption; A13, corruptingness v. corruptedness; A53, corrupt dependence of aristocracy on monarchy; A58, corruption and military v. civilian procedure in English practice; 26.A8-9, secret suffrage and avoidance of corruption. *See* APTITUDE; DEPREDATION; ENGLISH PRACTICE; EXPENSE; EXTORTION; GOOD AND EVIL; REMUNERATION; SECURITIES; WASTE

CUSTODITIVE FUNCTION: IX.4.A48, ex. by ministers collectively in regard to things; A48, defined; 7.2nd.A24, and use of mimographical or receptacular mode of registration; 3rd.A15, ex. by keepers; 19.A34, and use of permanent v. temporary functionaries; 23.A14, peculation v. embezzlement and ex. of custoditive f.

DEBATE: *See* FALLACIES; LEGISLATURE; MOTION(S)

DECEPTION: VI.27.A17-18, deception in elicitation of evidence; A18, A44, non-deceptiveness as desirable property of evidence; A19-21, securities against deception; VII.13, no deception in formulating ordinances and in debate promised in legislator's inaugural declaration

DECREE(S): *See* JUDICIAL DECREES

DEFAMATION: V.6.A2, and ex. of censorial f. by p.o. trib.; A3-4, and free circulation of political tracts

DEFENSIVE FORCE: *See* ARMY MINISTER; ARMY SUBDEPARTMENT;

IMPERATIVE FUNCTION; MILITARY SERVICE; NAVY MINISTER; NAVY SUBDEPARTMENT; PRIME MINISTER

DELAY: VI.23.A11, A19, deputy's substitute and prevention of delay; 24.A5, delay prevented by continuation committee; 27.A17-18, delay, vexation and expense and limits to extraction of evidence by leg.; A28, delay, vexation and expense and arrangements for extraction of evidence; A34, avoiding delay in legislation enquiry; 31.A29, factitious delay, vexation and expense and common law; VII.6, delay in judicial proceedings is equal to a tax; IX. 19.A24, prevention of delay in filling vacancies; 25.A13, remuneration for extra despatch acts as premium for delay in ordinary despatch; A14, prohibition of remuneration for extra despatch acts as security against factitious delay; A58, military procedure and factitious delay; 26.A13-14, delay in communication and architectural arrangements. See EXPENSE; GOOD AND EVIL; VEXATION

DELUSION: VI.24.A8, delusive information without continuation committee; VII.8, 'honour', 'glory', 'dignity'—words of delusion; 13, no delusion in formulating ordinances or in debate; IX.7.4th.A31, expenditure on fine arts and books as instrument of delusion; 17.A55, 'liberality' more suited than 'munificence' for the purpose of delusion; 17.Con.Inst.A1n, delusion and corruption rather than ignorance keep the subject many in England from changing governments. See DIGNITY; HONOUR

DEMERIT REGISTER: IX.25.A6, as instrument of security for app. apt.; A7, headings of entry

DEMOCRACY: See REPRESENTATIVE DEMOCRACY

DEONTOLOGY: IX.21.A21n, word of Greek origin, used for 'ethics'; A32, private v. political deontology; A32n, deontology defined. See DEPORTMENT

DEPARTMENT(S): IV.A8, for each authority, there is a dept. See AUTHORITY(IES)

DEPENDENCIES: VII.8, dependencies discussed; IX.7.4th.A31, needless expenditure on distant dependencies

DEPORTMENT: IX.20.A16-20, rules of deportment of non-functionaries before functionaries; 21.A5-6, rules of deportment and oppression of suitors and inspectees; A20, rules of deportment for functionaries as indirectly-applying remedies against oppression; A20, rules of deportment for functionaries and suitors displayed in functionaries' audience chambers; A20, rules for functionaries and suitors may diverge on some points; A21, rules of deportment analysed as rules of ethics; A22, and sanctions of penal code; A23, enforceability of rules; A24, and importance of system of judicial procedure; A25, English system of procedure contrasted; A26, enforcement of rules of negative-effective benevolence; A27, military codes as codes of deportment; A28-31, military codes in English practice; A32, reasons for not inserting codes of deportment into constitutional code; 25.A10, rules of deportment as instruments of security for app. apt., displayed in every functionary's audience chamber; A11, insertion of information from character index into functionary's deportment rules; A12, visitor's deportment rules for suitors and inspectors; 26.A21-2, rules of deportment displayed in waiting boxes

DEPREDATION: II.A16n, depredation as form of evil; VI.2.A4, depredation and use of oath by monarch; 27.A37, and secrecy in legislation enquiry judicatory; 31.A28, and lawyer class in representative democracy; A31, A33, and pure monarchy; A34-5, depredation and pure aristocracy; VII.4, depredation, economy and corruption discussed; 6, depredation and tax on judicial services; 8, 'honour' and 'glory' used for depredation; IX.15.A7, liberality as depredation; A35, unpunishable depredation in English monarchy and destruction of constitution; A46, depredation and hereditary succession; 17.A56, depredation not increased by indigence; A56, most opulent also most voracious; A56-8, reasons given; 25.A47, depredation and peerage; A57, depredation and English justice. *See* CORRUPTION; ENGLISH PRACTICE; OPPRESSION

DEPUTE: IV.A2, constitutive authority to depute members of leg.; A14, auxiliaries and self-suppletive f.; V.2.A3n, 'deputy' v. 'depute'; A3n, depute defined, examples given; A5, deputes and ex. of dislocative f. by constitutive authority; VI.23.A1-32, and ex. of self-suppletive f. by leg.; VIII.2.A5, deputes and ex. of dislocative f. by p.m.; 4.A1, location of depute by p.m. in ex. of self-suppletive f.; A2, depute defined and fs. stated; A3, occasions for assuming power listed; A4, power of principal and depute; A5-6, responsibility of principal for depute; A7, arrangements for location of depute; A8, instrument of location; A9, arrangements for power passing between principal and depute; A10, arrangements for death of principal; A11, dislocability of depute; IX.6.A1-13, self-suppletive f. ex. by location of depute by ministers; 17.A9, service as depute may be grounds for preference in location system; A33-4, deputes permanent must be chosen from locable list; A35-6, location instrument for deputes; 19.A21-2, deputes permanent not automatic choices for vacancies in office; 24.A1, depute permanent may ex. legislation-regarding fs. for minister in leg.; A3, minister or depute bound to attend sessions of leg. to answer questions; 25.A3, obligation by ministers to use deputes and be responsible for their apt., as security for app. apt. *See* SELF-SUPPLETIVE FUNCTION

DEPUTY(IES): I.A3, each district sends one deputy to leg.; A4, each subdistrict, as voting district, sends deputy to subleg.; V.2.A3n, 'deputy' preferred to 'representative', reasons given; A3n, 'deputy' v. 'depute'; VI.1.A9, communication between constituents and deputy; A9, duty of deputy to constituents; A10, duty of deputy where interests of constituents conflict with national interest; A11-12, deputy's duty to public v. duty to constituents; 23.A1, ex. of self-suppletive f.; A2, deputy responsible for substitute; A3, eligibility for location as substitute, other members excluded; A4-6, arrangements for appointment and admission of substitute to assembly chamber; A7-13, reasons given for appointment of depute by each deputy; A14-26, reasons given for suppletive f. given to deputy instead of constitutive authority; A27, option left to deputy whether deputy or substitute will attend; A30, notice of non-attendance by deputy and substitute to be posted by election clerk of district; A31, in absence of excuse paper, new election arranged; A32, leg. to determine validity of excuse paper; 25.A19-29, deputies and corruption by undiscontinued relocability; A49, deputies and responsibility; 27.A25, deputies eligible as legislation elicitors; A27, elicitation process not to conflict with legislative duties; VIII.3.A7, deputies and ex. of initiative f. by p.m. in relation to leg. *See* LEGISLATOR'S INAUGURAL DECLARATION; LEGISLATURE; SUBLEGISLATURE(S)

DEPUTY'S SUBSTITUTE: *See* DEPUTE; DEPUTY; LEGISLATURE; SELF-SUPPLETIVE FUNCTION

DESIRE AND AVERSION: IX.25.A1, as motives for securities for app. apt.;

A1, pleasure and pain, as objects of desire and aversion. *See* PLEASURE AND PAIN

DESPATCH (DISPATCH): IX.19.A20, in filling vacancies among functionaries as security; 25.A13, for extra despatch, gift, or remuneration is corruption; A13, extra despatch defined; A14, inhibition of remuneration for extra despatch acts as security against factitious delay and extortion; A15, in case of urgency, minister to apply to finance minister by remuneration draft; A16, quasi-judicial assertion to establish extra despatch; A17, quasi-judicial assertion defined; A18, extra despatch book, headings of entries; A19, entry from extra despatch book to be included in remuneration draught; A20, examples of remuneration draught, how distributed; A21, signature of finance minister to acknowledge receipt of remuneration draught; A22, if no payment by fixed date, finance minister to issue non-payment excuse and benemeritant may transmit to p.m., a non-payment complaint; A23, importance of publicity emphasized; A24, leg. to arrange for secrecy for extra despatch, where necessary as in time of war; A25, provisions for extra despatch do not apply to all extra service

DESPOTISM: II.A24, and English government; VI.20.A17, 'power without obligation' is despotism; 25.A46, undiscontinued relocability and subversion of representative democracy to despotic monarchy; 31.A22, oriental despots and abuse of power; IX.16.A69n, and English jury system; 17.Con.Inst.A1, establishment of aptitude and dethroned despots; 25.A39, secret and silent despotism v. openly and freely discussed legislation in the use of dispensing power. *See* ENGLISH PRACTICE; TYRANNY

DIAGRAM(S): IX.7.3rd.A24, limitations on use of. *See* MIMOGRAPHICAL MODE

DIGNITY AND FACTITIOUS DIGNITY: IV.A14, dignity as remuneration; VI.19.A1, dignity added to remuneration of members of leg.; VI.25.A20, dignity as matter of corruption; 27.A52, factitious dignity and House of Lords; 30.A1, acceptance of factitious dignity from foreign governments, as cause of dislocation of members of leg.; VII.3, appetite for factitious dignity and honour to be avoided by legislators; 4, dignity for nation at expense of indigent not aspect of legislation; 8, factitious dignity not to be received by legislators; VIII.12.A1, dislocation of p.m. for accepting factitious dignity from foreign governments, as security for app. apt.; IX.5.A12, factitious dignity as a form of superiority; 15.A29, factitious dignity repugnant to principles of constitution; A30, instruments for conferring factitious dignity: titles of honour and ensigns of dignity; A31-3, examples given; A34, factitious dignity unsuitable, even if judicially conferred; A35, arbitrary conferring of factitious dignity sufficient to destroy constitution; A47, factitious dignity and artificially extravasated reward; 17.A49, factor in the payment of personal service; 23.A12, factitious dignity, no exemption from suspicion of delinquency; 25.A3, dislocability of ministers for accepting factitious dignity from foreign governments, as security for app. apt. *See* HONOUR; REMUNERATION; REWARD AND PUNISHMENT

DIRECTION: IV.A2, constitutive authority not to give individual or specific direction to members of leg.; A3, legislative authority to give on occasion individual direction to chiefs of administrative and judiciary depts.; IX.5.A4, power of, necessary to subordination; A25, where necessity of direction, rank in scale of subordination has place; A26, account-giving, subordination, and need of direction; A27, examples given; A28-30, distance between functionaries, subordination, and direction; 21.A4, abuse of power of direction and oppression; 25.A32, information about inaptitude of subordinates and directive power of ministers. *See* DIRECTIVE FUNCTION

DIRECTIVE FUNCTION: VI.3.A1-2, ex. by leg. in relation to sublegs.; VIII. 2.A2, ex. by p.m. in relation to administrative authority; IX.4.A44, ex. by ministers collectively with regard to deputes or subordinates; A49, applicative v. directive f.; A54, directive and inspective fs.; 5.A4, f. ex. in scale of subordination; A5-6, where present, directive f. combined with power to ex. suspensive and temporarily suppletive fs.; A17, directive power and accountableness; 19.A2, subordinate subject to ex. of directive f. by superordinates; A29-31, ex. of directive f., military v. non-military service; 20.A4, directive f. and inspection; A10, with private institutions separation of inspective f. from directive and dislocative fs.; A14, insubordination of subordinate functionary based on non-compliance with direction of superordinate; A25, non-compliance of subordinate to direction of superordinate, powers given; 21.A35, abuse of ex. of directive f., remedies against oppression. *See* DIRECTION

DIRECTIVE MODE: VI.29.A3-4, and emendation; A3-6, IX.25.A1n, directive or corrective mode v. reeditive. *See* REEDITIVE MODE

DISLOCATIVE FUNCTION: V.2.A2, ex. by constitutive authority; A5, functionaries in relation to whom ex.; A6, functionaries in relation to whom ex. from within each district; 3.A4, how ex. by constitutive authority in relation to leg.; A5, in relation to subleg.; A6, dislocative f. and avoidance of fallacies; VI.2.A2, ex. by electors when leg. passes anti-constitutional ordinance; A8, ex. by constitutive authority where breach of faith over contracts; VIII.2.A5, ex. by p.m. in relation to ministers; IX.4.A44, ex. by ministers collectively in relation to persons; A44, A52, dislocative v. eliminative fs.; 5.A4, ex. in scale of subordination; 20.A10, with private institutions separation of inspective f. from dislocative and directive fs.; 21.A36, remedies against oppression by abuse of dislocative f.: directly applying v. indirectly applying; 25.A26, dislocative power and responsibility of ministers for subordinates; A32, dislocative power of ministers. *See* CONSTITUTIVE AUTHORITY; ELECTION CODE; LOCATION AND DISLOCATION; LOCATIVE FUNCTION

DISPUNITIVE FUNCTION: IX.15.A9, arbitrarily conferred, neither good nor evil

DISSENT: VIIn, VII.1.A3-4, provision for in legislator's inaugural declaration; A5, dissent to essence of declaration and arrangements for new election

DISTRICT(S): I.A3, territory of state divided into districts which serve as election districts; A3, one deputy to leg. from each district; A3, each district is territory of subleg.; A3, district is territory of appellate judicatory; A3, districts listed; A4, each district divided into subdistricts; IV.A9, each district has a subleg. under the leg.; A12, one seat in leg. for each district; V.2.A3, constitutive authority divided into election districts, ex. locative f.; A6, dislocative f. ex. by each district; VI.22.A2-3, distance between districts and leg. and term of service of members of leg. *See* CONSTITUTIVE AUTHORITY; SUBDISTRICT(S)

DISTRICT MINISTER(S): *See* SUBMINISTER(S)

DISTRICT PRIME MINISTER(S): *See* SUBPRIME MINISTER(S)

DISTURBANCE: VI.16, security of leg. against disturbance by members; 30.A1, disturbance of assembly as cause of dislocation of members of leg.; 31.A43, security against disturbance of legislative meetings as security for app. moral apt.; VIII.3.A9, message from p.m. v. communication through minister to secure freedom from disturbance of leg.; IX.20.A24, leg. to determine which grades to have security against disturbance by suitors, inspectees and evidence holders

DOCUMENT(S): *See* EVIDENCE; INFORMATION; MANIFOLD WRITING MODE; PUBLICATION SYSTEM; REGISTRATION SYSTEM; STATISTIC FUNCTION

DOMAIN MINISTER: IX.2.A1, serves under p.m.; 9.A7, joint visits and ex. of inspective f.; 16.A15, requisite talents for position. *See* DOMAIN SUBDEPARTMENT; MINISTER(S)

DOMAIN SUBDEPARTMENT: IX.2.A10, potentially joined with interior communication subdept.; 9.A4, offices to be visited in ex. of inspective f.; 16.A15, talent requiring situations and requisite talents, examples given. *See* DOMAIN MINISTER

DONATIVE FUNCTION: *See* ELIMINATIVE FUNCTION

DUTY AND OBLIGATION: II.A16n, reward, punishment, and obligations; V.5.A5, moral v. legal obligation for functionaries and non-functionaries to ex. statistic f.; 6.A2, better defamation than breach of official duty; A3, restrictions on publications, breach of duty; VI.1.A9, duty of deputy to constituents; A10, duty of deputy where interests of constituents conflict with national interest; A11-12, deputy's duty to public v. duty to constituents; 20.A17, power without obligation is despotism; A18-23, duty and obligation in U.S. legislative practice; 22.A1, term of service and performance of duty of legislators; 25.A20, ease v. duty in monarchy; 28.A7, duty of legislators and membership of legislation penal judicatory; VII.3, appetite for ease v. duty; 4, neglect of duties and dutiless offices, as corruption and waste; 5, publicity to laws and obligations of citizens; 10, obligation of attendance by legislators; 12, duties of members of leg., whole time occupation; VIII.4.A1, 12.A1, p.m.'s obligation to locate depute as security for app. apt.; IX.4.A7-9, obligation as fictitious entity; A7-9, obligations v. rights; 5.A17-18, obligations of subordinates to ex. statistic f.; A20, obligation to transfer money; 6.A1, A10, obligation of ministers to ex. self-suppletive f.; 7.4th.A30, entries in loss book arranged to avoid insincerity while fulfilling obligation to make entries; 11. A10-14, obligation to furnish information; 16.A12-14, location system and apt fulfilment of duties; 17.A42, locating functionary's breach of duty; 19.A22, obligation of ministers in filling vacancies to be compatible with responsibility; A23-6, minister has power but not obligation to repeat qualification examination; A27, pecuniary competition may be held, but not obligatory, in filling vacancies; 21.A13, power and obligation of judges regarding oppression; 25.A3, obligations of ministers toward deputes, as security for app. apt.; 26.A48, duty of monarchs noted. *See* RIGHT(S)

EDUCATION MINISTER: IX.2.A1, serves under p.m.; 9.A7, joint visits and ex. of inspective f. *See* EDUCATION SUBDEPARTMENT; MINISTER(S)

EDUCATION SUBDEPARTMENT: IX.2.A10, potentially joined with indigence relief subdept.; IX.9.A4, offices to be visited in ex. of inspective f.; 20.A13, private institutions which may be subject to inspection, examples given. *See* EDUCATION MINISTER

EJECTIVE FUNCTION: *See* ELIMINATIVE FUNCTION

ELECTIONS: *See* CONSTITUTIVE AUTHORITY; ELECTION CODE; ELECTION MINISTER; ELECTION SUBDEPARTMENT; IMPARTIALITY AND PARTIALITY; LEGISLATURE; PRIME MINISTER; RELOCATION; VOTING

ELECTION CLERK: VII.1.A1, notification of election by election clerk

ELECTION CODE: I.A4, each subdistrict a voting district; V.1.A2, constitutive authority and election code; 3.A1, election code and ex. of locative f. by constitutive authority in relation to leg.; A2-3, and sublegs.; VI.4-17, election code incorporated; 22.A4, and arrangements for elections; VIII.8.A2, and secret election of p.m.; 11.A6, and evil of publicity of secret vote. *See* LEGISLATURE

ELECTION DISTRICTS: *See* DISTRICTS; ELECTION CODE; LEGISLATURE

ELECTION DISTRICT OFFICE: VII.1.A1, and legislator's inaugural declaration

ELECTION MINISTER: V.3.A4, election minister and the ex. of dislocative f. by constitutive authority; A8, and ex. of punifactive f. by constitutive authority; VI.20.A5, and publication of absences of legislators at time of general election; 22.A4, and arrangements for elections; IX.2.A1, serves under p.m.; 5.A33, minister's subdept. needs, as subordinates, election clerks and vote-receiving clerks only; 9.A7, joint visits in ex. of inspective f.; 26.A17-18, as not necessarily subject to direction of p.m., no need for contiguous offices. *See* ELECTION SUBDEPARTMENT; MINISTER(S)

ELECTION SUBDEPARTMENT: IX.9.A4, offices to be visited in ex. of inspective f. *See* ELECTION MINISTER

ELECTORS: *See* CONSTITUTIVE AUTHORITY; ELECTION CODE; LEGISLATURE; VOTING

ELICITATIVE FUNCTION (EVIDENCE ELICITATIVE FUNCTION): VI.27.A3, ex. by legislation enquiry judicatory in obtaining evidence; A4, how connected to imperative f.; A5, desirable, though impractical, for both fs. to be performed by same person; A6, factors determining leg.'s undertaking ex. of elicitation f.; A11, evidence elicitative f. and procedure code; A39, elicitative f. and ex. of methodization, condensation, and application fs.; A50, importance of House of Commons v. judiciary in English practice in ex. of evidence elicitative f.; IX.21.A16, special judges applying remedies against oppression have no evidence elicitation power. *See* EVIDENCE; EXTRACTIVE FUNCTION; INFORMATION ELICITATIVE FUNCTION; LEGISLATION ENQUIRY JUDICATORY

ELIMINATION: IX.4.A53, submodes of elimination listed. *See* ELIMINATIVE FUNCTION

ELIMINATIVE FUNCTION: IX.4.A52, ex. by ministers collectively in regard to things; A44, A52, eliminative v. dislocative fs.; A53, fs. corresponding to submodes of elimination: consumption-authorizing, venditive, donative, mercede-locative, commodative, ejective; 23.A14, peculation and ex. of eliminative f. *See* ELIMINATION

EMPTIVE FUNCTION: *See* PROCURATIVE FUNCTION

ENDS AND MEANS: I.A1n, means and ends in constitutional code and remainder of Pannomion; II.A1, end in view of constitution, greatest happiness of greatest number; A2, means employed, max. apt. and min. expense; A8, evil as a means in relation to greatest happiness principle; A10, pleasure as end and means; V.5.A6, end of greatest happiness principle and amendments to code; A6, direct v. collateral ends of justice; VII.2, all-comprehensive end of government v. specific and direct ends, positive and negative; IX.1.A1, max. good and min. evil as ends in view; 1.A1, universal end, greatest happiness of greatest number; A2, main end, max. good v. collateral end, min. evil; A3, importance of collateral end; 3.A23, end, greatest happiness of greatest number v. subends (or means), max. apt., min. expense; 7.1st.A2-5, statistic f., ends in view——max. good, min. evil; 17.A47, opposite ends substituted for greatest happiness principle; 19.A10, term of service, ends in view; 21.A26, rules of deportment and ends of justice; 26.A1, ends in view and importance of architecture; A2, main ends: max. good, min. evil; A3, collateral ends—reduction of delay, vexation, and expense. *See* APTITUDE; EXPENSE; GOOD AND EVIL; HAPPINESS; MAXIMIZE AND MINIMIZE; PRINCIPLES; RULES

ENGLISH PRACTICE: I.A6(inst.diss.), 'mayor' and fs. of local headman; A6(inst.diss.), 'parish' and tri-subdistrict; A6(inst.diss.), English terminology and territorial divisions; II.A16n, in England, expense max. rather than min.; A24, moral responsibility and English government: 'monarchico-aristocratical despotism, with a spice of anarchy'; V.2.A3n, 'deputy' v. 'representative' and English practice; 4.A4, public opinion as a system of law v. English common law; VI.20.A8, in England corporal punishment or death for soldier punished as deserter; A15–16, uses of prorogation and adjournment in English practice to serve interests of monarchy and aristocracy; A17, non-attendance in House of Commons; A24, architectural arrangements and exclusion of observers from judiciary; 25.A7, elections without competition: (i) East India Company, (ii) Bank of England; A8, (iii) City of London Common Council; A11, (iv) House of Commons; A35, House of Lords, experience and apt.; A47, perpetual non-dislocability and English rump parliament; A51, liberty of press in England; 27.A11n, use of word 'examinant'; A24, 'grand inquest of the nation' used to designate House of Commons; A39, use of word 'report'; A41–56, English practice and eliciting evidence; A43–4, House of Commons, object in view and mode of enquiry; A45–8, House of Commons v. judiciary on rules of evidence; A49, good aspects of House of Commons v. judiciary; A50, impotence of House of Commons in ex. of evidence elicitation f. discussed; A51, House of Lords v. House of Commons in use of oaths; A52, enquiries initiated by House of Lords; A53, House of Commons committees v. monarch's commissions and reform and improvement; A54, powers of monarch's commission to elicit evidence deficient; A55, composition of monarch's commission discussed; A56, suppression of interrogatories and names of interrogators in reports in English practice; 31.A18, English judges acting as legislators; A29, A39–40, common law and resistance to securities for app. apt.; A29, English practice and the lawyer class in representative democracy; A30, and in England; A34–5, British India and securities for app. apt.; A36–41, mixed monarchy and securities for app. apt.; A40n, English judicial practice and Bentham's 'Indications respecting Lord Eldon'; IX.3.A11, 'board' defined; A12–13, use of boards and app. apt.; A22–38, use of boards in English executive depts. examined; A27, location and dislocation of cabinet by monarch; A27n, size of cabinet and other boards; A27n, grades of power in cabinet; A32, in English practice administration v. judiciary in location and dislocation; A34–6, self-judication principle in English practice; 4.A10, distinction between realty and personality, source of confusion; A33, 'rule' applied with confusion to transitory and permanent mandates; A33, 'order' added to 'rule'; A34–5, rules, orders and payment of fees in English practice; A36, 'mandate' not employed in English practice; 5.A37, A40, English army and navy: large number in highest grades, and max. of expense; IX.7. 2nd.A22n, Paper Office in English practice; A25n, stowage of articles sent a distance; 4th.A20n, English navy and loss of money in fabrication projects extended over many years; 6th.A5n, use of Latin abbreviations by clerk of the pell; A5n, Queen's College, Oxford bookkeeping; 10.A2, in English practice, 'information' used in administrative branch and 'evidence' in judiciary;

A22-3, no comprehensive system for furnishing information; A25, information from distant dependencies deficient; 11.A13, obligation to disclose information spontaneously in cases of high treason; 16.A24n, East India Company, method of voting; A25n, examinations at Woolwich Academy; A69n, chance v. choice in English practice, especially in jury trials; 17.A45, general opinion that price of commodities, including labour, should be min. by competition; A46, reluctance of statesmen to apply competitive principle to their own labour; A47, why at present the expense of official labour is max. and apt. min.; A48, especially where education, remuneration and location are in the hands of ruling few; A49, House of Commons and justices of the peace: pecuniary competition v. gratuitous service; A55, patronage and corruption in City of London; A56-9, arguments against economy in English practice; 17.Con.Inst.A1n, delusion and corruption rather than ignorance used to prevent change of government by subject many; 21.A4, 'non-user' in English law; A25, system of procedure v. English practice; A28, Articles of War and Mutiny Act—as codes of deportment; A29-30, military courts, v. ordinary courts and the ends of justice; 22.A5-6, extortion and fraudulence combined in English judicature; 25.A50, use of courts martial and military enquiry courts; A51, arbitrary dislocability mixed with virtual undislocability in non-military subdepartments; A52, King's Bench ineffectual; A53, judge and jury system corrupt and evidence arrangements exclude all but willing testimony; A54, p.o. trib. checks oppression in spite of law; A55-6, purchase of justice in English practice; A57, no security against oppression in English practice; A58, military procedure superior to judicial practice; 26.A20n, English practice and Panopticon plan. *See* MIXED MONARCHY; MONARCHY

ENTITIES: IX.4.A4, real and fictitious; A5, real entities comprised of persons and things; A6, fictitious entities comprised of fictitious persons and things; A7, fictitious entities called by lawyers 'things incorporeal'; A7-9, fictitious entities: obligations and rights; A10, immovables and movables; A11, movables at large and money; A12, fictitious entities as noticed: occurrences; A13, states; A14, interior and exterior; A15, important and unimportant; A16-17, relevant; A18, written instruments; A40, arrangements defined as fictitious entities; A41, institutions and establishments defined as fictitious entities

EQUALITY: VII.2, max. equality as an end of government; IX.16.A25n, modes of choice where candidates are equal; 17.A53, equality subordinate to security, or society cannot exist

ETHICS: *See* APTITUDE; DEONTOLOGY; DEPORTMENT

EVENTUALLY EMENDATIVE FUNCTION: IX.12.A4, included in the melioration-suggestive f.; A4, how ex.; 24.A5, judges' eventually emendative f. and ministers securing Pannomion from deterioration

EVIDENCE: VI.27.A1-6, legislation enquiry judicatory and the eliciting of evidence; A7, preappointed evidence defined; A8-9, examples given; A10, oral v. epistolary evidence; A11, active v. passive elicitation; A12, sources of evidence distinguished; A16, self-condemning evidence discussed; A17, limits to extraction of evidence discussed; A18, desirable properties of evidence discussed; A19-21, securities against deception by falsehood; A30-31, confrontation in gathering evidence, occasions and purposes; A31, counter-evidence defined; A41, regularly v. occasionally elicited evidence; A42-56, English practice in eliciting evidence; A44, desirable properties in evidence: appositeness, clearness, correctness, impartiality, all-comprehensiveness, non-redundance, instructiveness, and non-deceptiveness; A48, exclusionary rules of evidence in English judicial practice; A50-1, use of oath in English practice; VIII.10.A5, use of manifold writing system and evidence; IX.10.A2, A8, evidence v. information; 16.A20-1, evidence and mode of procedure in qualification judicatory; 21.A7, oppression of evidence holders; A20, securities for clearness, correctness, relative completeness in evidence as indirectly-applying remedy against oppression; A53, A58, problems of exclusion of all but willing witnesses in English practice; 26.A37, problem of false evidence. *See* LEGISLATION ENQUIRY JUDICATORY; PROCEDURE; PROCEDURE CODE; STATISTIC FUNCTION

EVIDENCE ELICITATION COMMITTEE(S): *See* LEGISLATION ENQUIRY JUDICATORY

EVIDENCE HOLDER: VI.27.A12, IX.20.A5, defined; A7, and quasi-insubordination; A22, remedy for non-compliance of evidence holder; A24, leg. to determine which grades to have security against disturbance and non-compliance by evidence holders; 21.A4, evidence holders as oppressees; A7, examples given; A20, evidence holders and use of incidental complaint book

EVIL: *See* GOOD AND EVIL

EXAMINATION(S): *See* LOCATION AND DISLOCATION

EXCLUSION (FROM OFFICE): VI.26.A1, exclusion from leg. by force, fraud, or accident; A2, legislative authority belongs to majority present at meeting; A3, effect on majority where members wrongly excluded; A4, responsibility of members involved in exclusion; A5, exclusion and dislocation by constitutive authority; VI.27.A27, participation in elicitation process and virtual exclusion from office; 31.A42, wrongful exclusion and securities for app. apt. of leg. *See* ATTENDANCE AND NON-ATTENDANCE; LEGISLATURE

EXECUTIVE: IV.A6, consists of administrative and judiciary depts.; VI.1.A5, dependence on legislative authority; A6, where non-performance or inaptitude, leg. can take over fs. of executive

EXECUTIVE FUNCTION: V.5.A3, ex. by p.o. trib.; 6.A1, all members of human species have right to ex. executive f.; VIII.2.A1, ex. by p.m.

EXEMPLAR(S): VI.27.A8, as examples of preappointed evidence; VIII.2.A15, exemplars and manifold writing system; A15n, exemplars v. copies and transcripts; 4.A8, exemplars and instruments of location of p.m.'s deputes; 10.A2-4, exemplars and manifold writing mode; A6, and security against destruction of judicial documents; IX.8.A22, and issuance of procuration mandates; 12.A5, and ex. of eventually emendative f.; 17.A10, exemplars of location instrument; A36, of deputation instrument; 21.A73-6, and record of judicatories to obviate oppression; 25.A20, exemplars of remuneration draught, how distributed

EXERTION: IX.16.A47-8, remuneration and exertion of instructors in location system; A49, extra-remuneration and motives for exertion; A61, use of chance as inducement to exertion in examination; 17.A52, unopulence as cause of exertion and apt.; A59, apt., exertion and money

EXPENSE: I.A6(inst.diss.), expense and number of divisions of territory discussed; A6(inst.diss.), expense of time wasted on long journeys to government offices; II.A2, min. of expense, means to greatest happiness; A3, included in expenditure is punishment as well as reward; A12, need to min. expenditure in reward and punishment; A16n, often max. under governments by emphasizing reward rather than punishment; A17, principles to establish app. apt. and min. of expense; VI.23.A19, A22, expense caused by election of deputy's substitute v. appointment by deputy; A21, expense caused by election of substitute at end of session; 27.A17-18, A28, delay, vexation and expense and extraction of evidence by leg.; A48, expense max. in English judicial practice; A55, expense and monarch's commissions in English practice; 31.A29, delay, vexation and expense and common law; VII.2, min. of expense as negative end of government; 4, expense and government economy; 6, expense and provision of judicial services; 8, no addition to opulence of one state at the expense of another; 8, expense of armaments is robbery; 11, power of leg., created at expense of people; VIII.10.A2-3, A5, expense and manifold writing mode; 11.A3, A9, good of publicity v. evil of expense; A5-6, evil of publicity and evil of expense; 12.A1, IX.25.A23, factor of expense in publication system a consideration in securities for app. apt.; IX.3.A14, many-seatedness and expense; 7.2nd.A24, expense min. by mimographical mode of registration; 10.A12, consideration of expense and the supply of information; A25, expense of subject many and information from dependencies; 15.A1, expense min. leading principle of const.; A3-6, min. expense as a way of max. apt.; A44, naturally extravasated remuneration, no expense to community; A46, v. artificially extravasated reward, expense to community; 16.A44-7, government v. individual expense for instruction; 17.A43, expense of the community when pecuniary competition principle sacrificed to patronage; A47, expense of official labour max. in English practice; A49, pecuniary competition v. gratuitous service; A55, pernicious expense the result of association of liberality and merit; 19.A12-13, no increase in remuneration for length of service; A14, or longevity; A24, no additional expense in repetition of qualification examination; A26, decline of those in pecuniary competition, increase in expense; A38, augmentation of emolument, increase in expense; 21.A29, wealth of lawyers at expense of community; 25.A3, min. of expense and securities for app. apt.; A43, common law and expense of time and thought; A57-8, expense of justice in English practice; 26.A20n, expense and rejection of Panopticon plan in England; A38, expense in providing living accommodation for ministers and families discussed. *See* DELAY; GOOD AND EVIL; MAXIMIZATION AND MINIMIZATION; REMUNERATION; REWARD AND PUNISHMENT; VEXATION

EXPERIENCE: VI.25.A32-5, experience v. app. apt. and reason for undiscontinued relocability; A37, experience and elections, why no perpetual nonrelocability; A53n, experience and evolution of Bentham's thoughts on relocation; 31.A42, experience and securities for app. apt. of leg.; VIII.8.A6, experience and instruction from employment of secret and open voting; IX.3.A31, experience and number in office

EXTORTION: VI.19.A1, VIII.6.A1, extortion v. corruption; VI.27.A55, extortion and English judicial practice; IX.20.A1, legislator to consider applicability of arrangements for obviation of extortion to military branch of army and navy services; 21.A2, oppression v. extortion; 22.A1, extortion defined; A2, when committed; A3, extortion and oppression may be combined; A4, applicable remedies; A5-6, extortion and fraudulence combined in English judicial practice; 23.A3, extortion as a mode of peculation; 25.A14, inhibition of remuneration for extra despatch as security against extortion. *See* CORRUPTION; ENGLISH PRACTICE; PECULATION; REMUNERATION

EXTRACTIVE FUNCTION: IX.10.A8, included in information elicitative f.; 11.A8, ex. by a number of persons at the same time; 16.A62, correspondent

f. of examiners to responses by examinees. *See* ELICITATIVE FUNCTION; INFORMATION ELICITATIVE FUNCTION

FABRICATIVE FUNCTION: *See* PROCURATIVE FUNCTION
FACTITIOUS DIGNITY: *See* DIGNITY AND FACTITIOUS DIGNITY
FACTITIOUS HONOUR: *See* HONOUR, NATURAL AND FACTITIOUS
FALLACIES: V.3.A6, ex. of dislocative f. by constitutive authority and avoidance of fallacies; VII.13, use of table of fallacies; IX.17.Con.Inst.A2, fallacies employed to prevent introduction of instruction system; A2.19.A31n, and distinction between theory and practice
FAMINE: *See* CALAMITY
FEDERATIVE OR FEDERAL GOVERNMENT: VI.3.A5, relation between leg. and sublegs. *See* LEGISLATURE; SUBLEGISLATURE(S)
FEMALE(S): V.1.A3, excluded from suffrage; 4.A2, but included in p.o. trib.
FEW AND MANY: (i) Opulent or wealthy few and unopulent or indigent many. I.A6(inst.diss.), V.6.A3, VII.4, IX.4.A34, 7.4th.A31; (ii) Ruling or influential few and subject many: II.A23, VI.31.A17-20, A41, VII.8, IX.10.A24-5, 15.A37, 17.A45-6, A48, 17.Con.Inst.A1n, 25.A43; (iii) General: VIII.11.A6, IX.19.A14, happiness of few at expense of many; 25.A49, distinguished few and comparative many
FIELDS OF SERVICE, LOGICAL AND LOCAL: (i) Logical field of service: I.A6(inst.diss.), and functionaries inferior to local headman; IV.A11, supreme leg., sublegs., administrative depts. and logical field of service; VI.1.A1, logical field of service of supreme leg.; VIII.1.A2-4, p.m.'s logical field of service; A4, minister's logical field of service; 2.A1-3, A5, A8, p.m.'s fs. within logical field of service; IX.2.A4, 'subdepartment' and 'minister' and logical field of service; (ii) Local field of service: I.A6(inst.diss.), local field of service of local headmen; IV.A11, supreme leg., sublegs., administrative depts. and local field of service; VI.1.A1, local field of service of supreme leg.; VIII.1.A1, p.m.'s local field of service coextensive with leg.; (iii) In general: VI.28.A9, leg. not to act as appellate judicatory; A10, exceptions discussed; VII.12, encroachment by leg. on fields of service of subordinate authorities; IX.19.A1, leg. to allot to subordinates in subdepts. grades with distinctive fields of service and fs. *See* FUNCTION(S)
FINANCE MINISTER: IX.2.A1, serves under p.m.; 5.A31, all functionaries accountable to, but not subordinates of; 9.A7, joint visits and ex. of inspective f.; A7, acts as a check on expenditure of other subdepts.; 15.A57, cares for indemnification of ministers for inspection visits; 16.A15, requisite talents for position; 25.A15, application to finance minister by remuneration draught for remuneration for extra despatch in cases of urgency; A20, exemplar of remuneration draught to finance minister; A21, signature of finance minister to acknowledge receipt of remuneration draught; A22, finance minister to issue non-payment excuse if he fails to pay for extra despatch by fixed date. *See* FINANCE SUBDEPARTMENT; MINISTER(S)
FINANCE SUBDEPARTMENT: IX.2.A10, potentially joined with trade subdept.; IX.9.A4, offices to be visited in ex. of inspective f.; 16.A15, talent requiring situations and requisite talents, examples given. *See* FINANCE MINISTER
FORCE (PHYSICAL): VI.26.A1-5, and exclusion from leg.; IX.20.A21, use of. *See* INDUCEMENT AND COERCION; REWARD AND PUNISHMENT
FOREIGN GOVERNMENT(S): VI.30.A1, acceptance of office or honour from

foreign government, as cause of dislocation of members of leg.; VIII.12.A1, dislocation of p.m. for accepting office, gift, honour, dignity from foreign government as security for app. apt.; IX.25.A3, dislocability of ministers upon accepting office, honour, gift from foreign government, as security for app. apt. See CONTRACT(S): DIGNITY AND FACTITIOUS DIGNITY; HONOUR, NATURAL AND FACTITIOUS; INTERNATIONAL RELATIONS

FOREIGN RELATION MINISTER: IX.2.A1, serves under p.m.; 9.A7, joint visits in ex. of inspective f.; 16.A15, requisite talents for position. See FOREIGN RELATION SUBDEPARTMENT; MINISTER(S)

FOREIGN RELATION SUBDEPARTMENT: VIII.11.A6-7, and evils of publicity; A15-17, and time limits on secrecy; IX.9.A4, offices to be visited in ex. of inspective f.; 16.A15, talent-requiring situations and requisite talents, examples given; 17.A23, A29-30, need for temporarily initiative location. See FOREIGN RELATION MINISTER

FRANCE: I.A6(inst.diss.), 'maire' and functions of local headman; A6(inst.diss.), French terminology and territorial divisions; II.A24, p.o. trib. and England v. France; VI.25.A10, chamber of deputies and election with competition; IX.26.A20n, Panopticon plan in France

FRAUD: VI.26.A1-5, and exclusion from leg.

FREEDOM (LIBERTY): V.6.A3, freedom of speech; A5, freedom of opinion; VI.25.A49, A52, relocation of members of leg. and freedom of choice; A50, liberty of the press and p.o. trib.; VIII.3.A9, freedom of legislative assembly from disturbance; IX.16.A24n, liberty of suffrage professed, but not practised in East India Company; 16.A35, liberty of interrogation regarding moral apt. of candidates for location; 17.A47, free and unrestrained competition favoured; 19.A24, liberty to take qualification examination; 26.A8, secret suffrage preserves liberty of suffrage

FRUGALITY: IV.A14, frugality not diminished by ex. of self-suppletive f.; VIII.11.A3, max. publicity and max. frugality; IX.16.A47, max. apt. and frugality of instructors; 17.A53, frugality-maximizing principle and pecuniary competition; 17.Con.Inst.A3, use of frugality as excuse to exclude foreign instructors; 23.A13, publicity limited by frugality

FUNCTION(S): V.2.A2, constitutive authority ex. locative, dislocative, and punifactive fs.; 5.A1, fs. of p.o. trib.: statistic; A2, censorial; A3, executive; A4, melioration-suggestive; VI.3.A1-4, leg. to ex. directive, corrective and arbitrative fs. over sublegs.; 27.A3, leg. to ex. evidence elicitative f.; A4, preparatory to ex. of imperative f.; A5-6, desirable though impracticable, for elicitative and imperative fs. to be performed by same person; A39, methodization, condensation, and application fs. ex. in legislation enquiry report; VIII.2.A1, p.m.'s fs.: executive; A2, directive; A3, locative; A5, dislocative; A8, imperative; 3.A3-4, p.m.'s fs. ex. in sending messages to leg.: informative; A5, indicative; A6-7, initiative; A10, statistic; 4.A1-9, p.m. ex. self-suppletive f.; IX.4.A1, fs. v. operations; A2ff., subject matter of fs., distinctions to be made; A3, fs. designated by names or more ample descriptions; A13, registrative f. concerned with 'states' and 'motions'; A13, registrative f. composed of minutative, conservative, publicative fs.; A44, fs. ex. by ministers collectively regarding persons: locative, self-suppletive, directive, dislocative, conductive, compulsorily procurative; A45-6, things: procurative, including emptive, conductive, fabricative, requisitive, transreceptive, transmissive, retroacceptive, retrotransmissive; A47, requisitive v. procurative fs.; A48, custoditive; A49, applicative; A50, reparative; A51, transformative; A52-3, eliminative, including consumption authorizing, venditive, donative, mercede locative, commodative, ejective; A54, inspective; A55, visitative; A56, persons, things, money, occurrences: statistic; A57, registrative; A58, publicative; A59, officially informative; A60-1, persons, things, money, instruments of statistication, registration, and publication, ordinances, arrangements: melioration suggestive; A65-70, fs. liable to be competitive, listed; 5.A4-6, modes of power necessary to subordination: directive f., suspensive f., dislocative f., punifactive f., suppletive f.; 10.A8, information elicitative f. and extractive f.; A16, officially informative f. and information receptive f.; 11.A8, ex. of extractive f.; 12.A1-4, included in melioration suggestive f. are: indicative, ratiocinative, eventually emendative fs.; 15.A9, arbitrary remuneration and dispunitive f.; 17.A21, 19.A16, initiative and consummative fs. ex. in location; 19.A1, leg. to allot subordinates in subdepts.——grades with fields of service and fs.; 21.A17, fs. of judges in applying direct remedies against oppression; 23.A14, malpractice in ex. of procurative, reparative, eliminative, venditive fs. with respect to land, buildings, vessels and goods more important than malpractice in ex. of receptive, custoditive, and transmissive fs. with respect to money; 24.A1, ex. by ministers in leg.: argumentative f., initiative f., and responsive f.; A2, but not votative f.; A5, judges' contested interpretation reporting f., eventually emendative f., and sistitive f. applied to ministers; A6, subordinates to minister ex. contested interpretation f. as well as melioration suggestive f.; A7, leg. to decide who ex. preinterpretative f.; A8, and sistitive f.; 25.A23, importance of access to register book for ex. of lective, inspective, commentative, and melioration suggestive fs. *See these functions* APPLICATION; APPLICATIVE; ARBITRATIVE; ARGUMENTATIVE; CENSORIAL; COMMENTATIVE; COMMODATIVE; COMPULSORILY PROCURATIVE; CONDENSATION; CONDUCTIVE; CONSERVATIVE; CONSUMPTION AUTHORIZING; CONTESTED INTERPRETATION AUTHORIZING; CORRECTIVE; CUSTODITIVE; DIRECTIVE; DISLOCATIVE; DISPUNITIVE; DONATIVE; EJECTIVE; ELICITATIVE; ELIMINATIVE; EMPTIVE; EVENTUALLY EMENDATIVE; EXECUTIVE; EXTRACTIVE; FABRICATIVE; IMPERATIVE; INDICATIVE; INFORMATION ELICITATIVE; INFORMATION RECEPTIVE; INFORMATIVE; INITIATIVE; INSPECTIVE; LECTIVE; LEGISLATION REGARDING; LOCATIVE; MELIORATION SUGGESTIVE; MERCEDE LOCATIVE; METHODIZATION; MINUTATIVE; OFFICIALLY INFORMATIVE; OPINATIVE; PREINTERPRETATIVE; PROCURATIVE; PUBLICATIVE; PUNIFACTIVE (PUNITIVE); RATIOCINATIVE; RECEPTIVE; REGISTRATIVE; REPARATIVE; REQUISITIVE; RESPONSIVE; RETROACCEPTIVE; RETROTRANSMISSIVE; SELF-SUPPLETIVE; SISTITIVE; STATISTIC; SUPPLETIVE; SUSPENSIVE; TRANSFERENTIAL; TRANSFORMATIVE; TRANSMISSIVE; TRANSRECEPTIVE; VENDITIVE; VISITATIVE; VOTATIVE. *See also* CONSTITUTIVE AUTHORITY; PUBLIC OPINION TRIBUNAL; LEGISLATURE; MINISTER(S); SUBORDINATE(S) AND SUPERORDINATE(S)

FUNCTIONARY(IES): II.A16n, functionaries prefer reward to punishment to create responsibility in themselves, but punishment to reward to create responsibility in others; A18, functionaries and power indicated; IV.A14, self-suppletive f. and provision of auxiliaries for functionaries; V.5.A5, moral v. legal obligations for functionaries and non-functionaries in ex. of statistic f.; IX.1.A2, good and evil with respect to functionaries' actions; 3.A1, number in office, one; 20.A2, securities for functionaries and non-functionaries against insubordination, oppression, extortion, and peculation; A2, non-functionaries as suitors, inspectors, and evidence holders; A3-5, defined and distinguished; 21.A4, functionaries and non-functionaries as oppressors and oppressees, examples given; A8, functionaries as oppressees, examples given; A34, remedies for oppression, functionaries as oppressees; 26.A2, affected by evils of delay, vexation and expense; A3, app. architectural arrangements reduce evils to both functionaries and suitors; A21-35, arrangements for oral communication with suitors with use of waiting boxes, public and private. *See* APTITUDE; ARCHITECTURE; FUNCTION(S); LEGISLATURE; LOCATION AND DISLOCATION; MINISTER(S); OPPRESSION; PRIME MINISTER; REMUNERATION; REWARD AND PUNISHMENT, SECURITIES; SELF-SUPPLETIVE FUNCTION; SUBORDINATE AND SUPERORDINATE

GERMANY: IX.19.A31, and origin of Russian code
GOD: IX.23.A12, anyone exempt from suspicion of delinquency is not man, but god upon earth
GOOD AND EVIL: II.A4, punishment as evil; A5, evil composed of pain and loss of pleasure; A6, reward as good; A7, good composed of pleasure and exemption from pain; A8-9, evil employed as means, as punishment; A11, in reward, good employed only as instrument of inducement; A12, evil as punishment, as opposed to reward, has larger role in government; A13, rulers employ good for themselves by instruments of inducement and evil for rulees by instruments of coercion; A16&n, expectation of evil establishes responsibility; A16n, evil as waste, depradation, and corruption; A21, evil and compensational v. punitional responsibility; A22, punishment, dislocation, and evils of inapt.; V.5.A3, good and evil and executive f.; A6, evils——delay, vexation, and expense——v. justice; A8, good and evil effects from amendments; 6.A4, criminal evil consciousness and penal code; VI.1.A9, deputy cares for good of community; A10, insincerity as evil in relations between deputy and constituents; 20.A11, evil effects of interrupted attendance of legislators; A20, good done v. good left undone and U.S. president's message to congress; 23.A10, evil and fluctuation in attendance at leg.; A14, evil and adequacy of supply of deputy's substitutes; 24.A10, evil and short life of leg.; 25.A14-17, A46, evil and undiscontinued relocability; 27.A5, evil and separation of elicitative and imperative fs.; A17, evil and limits to extraction of evidence by leg.; A48, 'evil doers' and 'evil deeds' in English judicial practice; A49-50, good and evil in House of Commons; 28.A11, evil and unredressed wrongs; 29.A6, good and bad effects indicated in emendation in reeditive mode; 31.A11-12, evil and serving private interest; A16, need to prevent evil; A17-19, evil recognized in subject many, but not in ruling few; A23, propensity to evil and need for securities; A28, evil from lawyer class in representative democracy; A42, evil and securities for app. apt.; VIIn, evil and use of legislator's inaugural declaration; 2, evil and ends of government; 6, tax on justice produces by law the evils of anarchy; 11, evil and need for secrecy; VIII.1.A5, incorrect names and resultant evil; 3.A8, evil and p.m.'s responsibility; 8.A6, good and evil of open and secret voting; 11.A3, evil of expense v. good of publicity; A4, good of publicity discussed; A5-6, A14, good and evil of publicity; A8, time limit to secrecy to min. evil; A10, no limits to good of publicity; A15, good of publicity and limits to secrecy; IX.1.A1, max. good and min. evil as ends; A2&n, good and evil defined; 3.A7, evil increased in proportion to number in office; 4.A54, good, evil, and serviceable v. disserviceable

dispositions; 7.1st.A17, A19, uses of service and loss books to max. good, min. evil; 4th.A31, evils of expenditure on needless amusements; 6th.A6, evil intention and evil consciousness, and securities against misconduct in ex. of statistic f.; 10.A24, evil in English practice where parties in office control information; 11.A10, evils and extraction of information; 13.A3, evil and length of service of minister; 15.A7, liberality as good and evil; A9, arbitrary remuneration, neither good nor evil; A44, naturally extravasated remuneration, pure good 17.A37, evil consciousness and criminal responsibility; A39, evil and invalidation of mislocatee's acts; A44, pecuniary competition principle, as applied, good without evil; A53, evil would outweigh good by rejection of examination and pecuniary competition systems; 17.Con.Inst.A4-5, for public good and to min. evil, functionaries to quit jobs or acquire instruction, when instruction system introduced; 19.A28, good and evil effects of promotion; A31, good and evil in arrangement of power, rank, and emolument of Catherine the second of Russia; 20.A20, mass of evil—delay, vexation and expense—in judicial procedure in most governments; 21.A24-5, factitious delay, vexation and expense and evil in remedy in systems of procedure; A66, evil and use of word 'transference' instead of 'degradation'; 24.A9, evil in ex. and non-ex. of sistitive f. by administrative functionaries considered; 25.A23, importance of publicity where no great evil or expense; A26, evils where minister can screen misdeeds of subordinates; A36, estimates of relative evil in functionaries' ex. of extraordinary power; A37, leg. and remedy of evils which prompted functionaries' ex. of extraordinary power; 26.A2, relative good and evil in relation to architectural arrangements; A2, evils of delay, vexation and expense; A8, good of secret suffrage; A12, architectural arrangements as means to achieve goods dependent on publicity and secrecy. *See* CORRUPTION; DELAY; EXPENSE; EXTORTION; MAXIMIZE AND MINIMIZE; OPPRESSION; PECULATION; PLEASURE AND PAIN; PUBLICITY; SECURITIES; VEXATION

GOVERNMENT (THE): IV.A6, consists of legislative and administrative depts.

GOVERNMENT ADVOCATE: IX.15.A26, and suits concerning remuneration

GOVERNMENT ADVOCATE GENERAL: V.3.A7-8, and ex. of the punifactive f. by constitutive authority; VI.2.A9, defendant in suits brought by foreign governments; IX.15.A26, and suits concerning remuneration

GRAND JURY: *See* ENGLISH PRACTICE

HAPPINESS: (i) Happiness or greatest happiness of greatest number: II.A1, V.3.A6, 6.A5, VI.2.A1, 31.A42, VII.2, IX.1.A1, 3.A23, 26.A49; (ii) Greatest happiness principle: II.A1, A8-9, A11, A12, A14, V.4.A4, 5.A6, VI.31.A3, IX.17.A43, A47, 20.A11, 25.A43; (iii) Maximize happiness: II.A13, A14, A16, A23, VI.27.A43; (iv) V.5.A3, happiness; VIII.11.A4, happiness of individuals; A6, IX.19.A14, happiness of few at expense of many; VII.9, happiness of people; IX.3.A23, greatest happiness of ruling one and subruling few; 4.A15, A16, 21.A21, sum of happiness. *See* ENDS IN VIEW; GOOD AND EVIL; PLEASURE AND PAIN

HEALTH MINISTER: IX.2.A1, serves under p.m.; 9.A7, joint visits in ex. of inspective f.; 16.A15, requisite talents for position. *See* HEALTH SUBDEPARTMENT; MINISTER(S)

HEALTH SUBDEPARTMENT: VIII.11.A6, and evils of publicity; IX.9.A4, offices to be visited in ex. of inspective f.; 16.A15, talent-requiring situations and requisite talents, examples given; 20.A13, private institutions which may be subject to inspection, examples given. *See* HEALTH MINISTER

HONOUR, NATURAL AND FACTITIOUS: VI.30.A1, acceptance of factitious honour from foreign state cause of dislocation of member of leg.; VII.3, appetite for factitious honour and dignity to be avoided by legislators; 4, honour for nation at expense of indigent not object of legislator; 8, factitious honour not to be received by legislators; VIII.12.A1, dislocation of p.m. for acceptance of factitious honour from foreign government, as security for app. apt.; IX.5.A12, factitious honour and superiority; 15.A19, natural honour defined; A18, no other honorary reward under constitution allowed; A19, rendered by p.o. trib. for extraordinary service; A20, A23, natural honour judicially augmented; A21-7, recorded in public merit register; A28, publication as arranged by leg.; A29, factitious honour repugnant to principles of constitution; A30-1, titles of honour, examples given; A34, quantum of natural honour adjusts always to quantum of merit, factitious honour does not; 25.A3, dislocability of ministers for accepting factitious honour from foreign governments. *See* DIGNITY AND FACTITIOUS DIGNITY; REMUNERATION

HOSTILITY: VII.2, security against hostility as positive end of government. *See* COMMOTION; SECURITIES; WAR

HOUSE OF COMMONS: *See* ENGLISH PRACTICE

HOUSE OF LORDS: *See* ENGLISH PRACTICE

IMMOVABLE(S) AND MOVABLE(S): VI.27.A12, immovables and movables and the sources of evidence; IX.4.A10, everything not fictitious entity referable to; A10, distinction based on Roman law; A10, preferable to distinction between realty and personalty; A11, things movable: movables at large and money; A11, fs. ex. differently for each; 23.A14, 'money's worth' in all its shapes, movable and immovable, and peculation. *See* ENTITIES, REAL AND FICTITIOUS; EVIDENCE

IMPARTIALITY AND PARTIALITY: V.3.A10, trial of member of leg. by legislation penal judicatory and avoidance of partiality; VI.27.A18, A44, impartiality, a desirable property of evidence; A54, impartiality of evidence elicited by monarch's commissions; 28.A8, impartiality and membership of legislation penal judicatory; VII.7, impartiality in elections by legislators; 8, impartiality in international relations discussed; 9, impartiality in ex. of power discussed; IX.16.A67, use of lot to exclude partiality in examination system. *See* EVIDENCE; PECULATION

IMPEACHMENT: *See* LEGISLATION PENAL JUDICATORY

IMPERATIVE FUNCTION: VI.27.A4, imperative and elicitative fs., how connected; A5, desirable, though impractical, to be performed by same person; VIII.2.A8-11, A13-16, p.m. to ex. imperative f. in relation to defensive force; IX.21.A17, judges ex. of imperative f. and undivided responsibility; A36, not to be ex. by dislocation judicatory; A39, opinative v. imperative fs.

IMPORTANT AND UNIMPORTANT: IX.4.A15, occurrences subject to registration f; A15, defined and distinguished; A19, and written instruments; A56, and statistic f.

IMPROVEMENT: *See* REFORM

INCIDENTAL COMPLAINT BOOK: IX.21.A20, used as indirectly applying remedy against oppression

INDICATIVE (OR SUGGESTIVE) FUNCTION: VIII.3.A5, ex. by p.m. in sending messages to leg.; 12.A1, responsibility of p.m. to ex. as security for app. apt.; IX.12.A2, included in melioration suggestive f.; A2, how ex.; 25.A3, responsibility of ministers to ex. as security for app. apt.

INDIGENCE: VII.4, and waste and corruption; IX.17.A56, and depredation. *See* INDIGENCE RELIEF MINISTER; INDIGENCE RELIEF SUBDEPARTMENT

INDIGENCE RELIEF MINISTER: IX.2.A1, serves under p.m.; 9.A7, joint visits and ex. of inspective f.; 16.A15, requisite talents for position. *See* INDIGENCE RELIEF SUBDEPARTMENT; MINISTER(S)

INDIGENCE RELIEF SUBDEPARTMENT: IX.2.A10, potentially joined with education subdept.; 9.A4, offices to be visited in ex. of inspective f.; 16.A15, talent-requiring situations and requisite talents, examples given; 20.A13, private institutions which may be subject to inspection, examples given. *See* INDIGENCE RELIEF MINISTER

INDUCEMENT AND COERCION: II.A9, evil as punishment employed as instrument of coercion; A11, good employed in matters of reward as an instrument of inducement; A13, necessary to employ instrument of coercion to rulers; A13, rulers tend to employ inducement to themselves and coercion to rulees. *See* REWARD AND PUNISHMENT

INFORMATION: VI.24.A8-10, information and continuation committee; 31.A44, information and securities for app. intellectual apt.; VIII.11.A4, publicity and information; A14, information and rules for limiting secrecy; 12.A2, p.m. to act on information of misconduct or inaptitude of ministers; IX.10.A1, need of information for public and private business; A2, information v. evidence; A3, direct information v. communicated information; A4, communication upon application v. spontaneous communication; A5-6, received v. elicited information; A7, neglect of information by legislators; A8, arrangements in legislative and judiciary depts.; A9, need for arrangements for information in administrative dept., in addition to registration and publication systems. *See* EVIDENCE; INFORMATION ELICITATIVE FUNCTION; INFORMATIVE FUNCTION; OFFICIALLY INFORMATIVE FUNCTION; PUBLICATION SYSTEM; PUBLICITY AND SECRECY

INFORMATION ELICITATIVE FUNCTION: IX.10.A8, alloted to leg.; A15, and officially informative f.; IX.11.A1, may be ex. by every functionary; A2, exceptions noted; A3, receptive v. extractive mode for communication between functionaries; A4, and non-functionaries; A4, spontaneous v. unwilling communicators; A4, unwilling communication and judiciary establishment; A5, unwilling communication: administrative v. judiciary depts.; A6, ministers have power to elicit information; A6, legislative to determine which subordinate functionaries to have power; A6-7, securities against abuse; A8, extractive f., ex. by number of people at same time; A9, leg. to determine power to extract information in army and navy subdepts.; A10, leg. to avoid abuse of extractive power by functionaries; A11, avoidance of information on religious opinions; A12, leg. to determine obligations to disclose information; A13, obligation to furnish information spontaneously, examples given; A14, and English practice; 16.A62, correspondent f. of examiners to exhibition of examinees; A63, modes of elicitation applicable to examination. *See* ELICITATIVE FUNCTION; INFORMATION; INFORMATIVE FUNCTION; OFFICIALLY INFORMATIVE FUNCTION

INFORMATION RECEPTIVE FUNCTION: IX.10.A16, and officially informative f. *See* OFFICIALLY INFORMATIVE FUNCTION

INFORMATIVE FUNCTION: VIII.3.A3-4, ex. by p.m. in sending messages to leg.; 12.A1, responsibility of p.m. to ex. as security for app. apt.; IX.25.A3, responsibility of p.m. to ex., as security for app. apt. *See* INFORMATION; MESSAGES; OFFICIALLY INFORMATIVE FUNCTION

INFORMER(S): IX.26.A32-7, motives of and reasons for secret meetings with ministers. *See* ARCHITECTURE

INITIATIVE FUNCTION: VIII.3.A6-7, ex. by p.m. in sending messages to leg.; A6n, U.S. practice; A7, f. may be ex. through deputy or minister; 12.A1, responsibility of p.m. to ex. as security for app. apt.; IX.17.A21, 19.A16, ex. in location; 24.A1, ex. by ministers in legislative assembly; 25.A3, responsibility of ministers to ex. as security for app. apt. *See* CONSUMMATIVE FUNCTION

INQUIRY(IES): *See* LEGISLATION ENQUIRY JUDICATORY; LEGISLATION PENAL JUDICATORY

INSANITY: VI.30.A1, as cause of dislocation of members of leg.

INSPECTION: VI.27.A55, inspection of distant dependencies by commissioners in English practice; IX.26.A20n, importance of, and Panopticon. *See* INSPECTIVE FUNCTION; INSPECTOR(S)

INSPECTIVE FUNCTION: VIII.10.A6, use of exemplars in ex. of; IX.4.A54, ex. by ministers collectively in regard to things; A54, ex. prior to ex. of directive f.; A54, includes quasi-inspective f.; A54, objects stated; A55, and visitative f.; 9.A1, inspective v. visitative fs.; A1, progresses v. circuits; A2, frequency of visits to offices in subdepts.; A2, visit by minister or depute permanent; A2, spontaneous visits v. visits directed by p.m.; A3, purposes of visitation system, examples given; A4, offices to be visited, examples given; A5, different ministers may inspect the same office, but no clash of authority; A5-6, p.m. to arrange that no visits by ministers coincide, to act as check; A6, exception where need for consultation; A7, examples given where joint inspection of ministers desirable; A8, use of chance to secure unexpected visits desirable; A9, as security, how best used; A10, special importance of inspective f. at establishments under private management; A11, advantages and disadvantages of unexpected visits; 15.A57, indemnification of ministers for inspection visits; 20.A10, separation of inspective f. from directive and dislocative fs.; A10-11, importance to constitution of public inspection of private institutions; A13, private institutions which may be subject to inspection, examples given; 25.A12, inspective f. ex. by inspectors as members of p.o. trib., and visitors' deportment rules; A23, importance of access to register books for ex. of. *See* INSPECTION; INSPECTORS; INSUBORDINATION

INSPECTOR(S) AND INSPECTEE(S): IX.20.A2, as non-functionary; A4, inspectee defined; A7, and quasi-insubordination; A21, remedies for noncompliance of inspectees; A24, leg. to determine which grades to have securities against disturbance and non-compliance of inspectees; 21.A4, inspectees as oppressees; A6, examples given; A20, inspectees and use of incidental complaint book; 25.A12, inspectors as members of p.o. trib. and visitor's deportment rules. *See* INSPECTION; INSPECTIVE FUNCTION; INSUBORDINATION; OPPRESSION

INSTRUCTIVENESS: VI.27.A18, A44, as desirable property of evidence

INSUBORDINATION: IX.20.A1, leg. to consider applicability of arrangements for obviation of insubordination to army and navy services; A2, securities for functionaries and non-functionaries regarding insubordination; A3-5, non-functionaries: suitors, inspectees, evidence-holders defined; A6, insubordination defined; A7, quasi-insubordination defined; A8, insubordination v. quasi-insubordination; A9, modes of disturbance listed; A10-11, importance to constitution of inspection of private institutions; A10, separation of inspective f. from dislocative and directive fs.; A12, secret institutions under representative democracy and tyranny; A13, private institutions which may be inspected, examples given; A14, insubordination by subordinates, when committed; A15, remedies for quasi-insubordination; A16, rules for deportment of non-functionaries to prevent disturbance; A17, called rules of good behaviour, good manners, good breeding or decorum; A18, execution of rules and moral sanction of p.o. trib.; A19, leg. to consider where legal sanctions applicable; A20, use of judicial procedure and consideration of delay, vexation, and expense; A21, remedy for non-compliance of inspectee; A22, remedy for non-compliance of evidence-holder; A23, remedies against insubordination, same as for quasi-insubordination; A24, leg. to determine which grades to have securities against disturbance and non-compliance of suitors, inspectees and evidence-holders; A25, non-compliance of subordinate, remedies given; 21.A2, insubordination v. oppression; A67, temporary transference to inferior grade as punishment for insubordination. *See* OPPRESSION; SUBORDINATE AND SUPERORDINATE

INTEREST(S): II.A16, sovereign power to those with interest in max. happiness; VI.1.A9, deputy and particular will v. universal interest; A10, aggregate of particular interests v. national interest; A11–12, deputy's duty when opposed to particular interest of constituents; 20.A12, non-attendance in mixed monarchies caused by sinister interest of rulers; 24.A12, sinister interest and interest-begotten prejudice of rulers, reason for no provision for continuation committee; 25.A23, corruptive influence and interest of district at expense of general interest of state; 27.A28, delay detrimental to public interest and elicitation committees; A32, diverse and conflicting personal interests and elicitation judicatory; A33–4, conflicts of interest and use of professional advocates; A46, House of Commons and common interest; A47, A50, rightly directed and directing interest v. sinister interest of English judiciary; A47, universal interest v. sinister interest of monarch; A52, inutility of House of Lords to every interest but its own; 29.A6, interest of the community expressed in emendative ordinances; 31.A11–12, man will advance private interest at expense of public interest; A18, English judges and allies, a community of particular and sinister interest; A42, locators have interest in happiness of greatest number; VII.5, interests of individuals and the laws; 8, international relations and opening eyes of men to true interests; 9, avoiding partiality through self-regarding interest and interest inspired by sympathy and antipathy; VIII.8.A6, seductive influence of personal interests in choice of p.m.; 11.A6, one's own interest v. general interest and secret voting; A7, hostility to interest of greatest number and publicity; IX.3.A8–9, number in an office and community of sinister interest; A32, sinister interest in English judiciary; IX.9.A7, united and antagonizing interests and inspection by two or more ministers; 10.A7, particular and sinister interest of legislators; A24, sinister interest and English leg.; 15.A44, self-regarding or sympathetic interests and naturally extravasated reward; 16.A29, instructors as quasi-jurymen, interest of reputation; 17.A43–4, aggregate pecuniary interest gains with pecuniary competition; A44, personal interest of locating superordinate; A47, interest now in max. expense of labour; A49, sinister interest of part v. interest of whole and gratuitous service; 17.Con.Inst.A1, powerful particular and sinister interests v. p.o. trib.; A1n, government favourable to interests of many prevented by delusion and corruption; 19.A10, service for life, as security against self-regarding interest; A23, interest of public and repetition of qualification examination; A31, universal interest v. particular interests; A36, particular, personal and sinister interest of monarch in Russia; A38, public interest and extra remuneration; 25.A1, pleasure and pain create motives and then interests; A47, particular and sinister interest of some classes v. universal interest; 26.A34, self-regarding or sympathetic interest and informers; A35-6, one's own v. public interest and secret information; A40, interest of monarch, sacrifice required

INTERIOR AND EXTERIOR: IX.4.A14, as occurrences referable to official establishment, defined and distinguished; A19, and written instruments; A56, and statistic f.; 7.1st.A14, and journal books. *See* OCCURRENCES; STATISTIC FUNCTION

INTERIOR COMMUNICATION MINISTER: IX.2.A1, serves under p.m.; 9.A7, joint visits and ex. of inspective f.; 16.A15, requisite talents for position. *See* INTERIOR COMMUNICATION SUBDEPARTMENT; MINISTER(S)

INTERIOR COMMUNICATION SUBDEPARTMENT: IX.2.A10, potentially joined with domain subdept.; 9.A4, offices to be visited in performance of inspective f.; 16.A15, talent-requiring situations and requisite talents, examples given. *See* INTERIOR COMMUNICATION MINISTER

INTERNATIONAL RELATIONS: VII.8, justice in international relations discussed. *See* FOREIGN GOVERNMENTS; STATE; WAR

IRELAND: I.A6(inst.diss.), and size of territorial divisions; IX.26.A20n, and Panopticon plan

JUDGEMENT: *See* APTITUDE; WILL

JUDICATORY(IES): *See* JUDICATORY, APPELLATE; JUDICATORY, IMMEDIATE; JUDICIARY AUTHORITY; LEGISLATION ENQUIRY JUDICATORY; LEGISLATION PENAL JUDICATORY; QUALIFICATION JUDICATORY

JUDICATORY, APPELLATE: I.A3, each district is territory of appellate judicatory; IV.A13, one judge in each appellate judicatory; VI.28.A9-16, leg. as appellate judicatory; VIII.10.A6, use of exemplars from immediate judicatories; IX.21.A15, power of special judge to invoke assistance of judge immediate in case of oppression; A16, reasons given; A17, fs. stated; A72, power of special judge appellate to invoke assistance of ordinary judge, leg. to determine. *See* JUDICATORY, IMMEDIATE; JUDICIARY AUTHORITY

JUDICATORY, IMMEDIATE: I.A4, each subdistrict is territory of immediate judicatory; IV.A13, one judge in each immediate judicatory; VIII.10.A6, and use of exemplars from appellate judicatories; IX.21.A12, right of appeal to judge appellate in cases where minister or judge immediate applies remedies against oppression; A72, special judge appellate to invoke assistance of ordinary judge, leg. to determine. *See* JUDICATORY, APPELLATE; JUDICIARY AUTHORITY

JUDICIAL REVIEW: *See* ANTI-CONSTITUTIONAL ORDINANCES

JUDICIARY AUTHORITY: IV.A1, judiciary, one of four authorities in state; A3, leg. to locate and dislocate chiefs of judiciary dept. and upon certain occasions give individual direction; A5, judiciary to give execution and effect to ordinances of leg. where there is litiscontestation; A6, administrative and judiciary depts. compose the executive, and the executive and judiciary depts. compose the operative; A7, use of word 'supreme' discussed; A8, for each authority, a dept.; A13, single-seated in judiciary dept.; V.2.A5, judges dislocable by constitutive authority; 4.A1, member of p.o. trib. v. member of judiciary dept.; VI.1.A5, dependence on legislative authority; A6, where non-performance or inapt., leg. can take over fs. of judiciary authority; 2.A2, and anti-constitutional ordinances; A5, judicial enforcement of contracts; A6, between government and foreign state; A7, between government and subject of foreign state; A9, judicial remedy for wrong done to foreign government; A10, and action of leg.; 20.A24, English judges and architectural arrangements to exclude observers; 25.A30, applicability of rule of minimizing contact to judiciary noted; 27.A1, legislation enquiry judicatory v. ordinary judicatory; A5, desirable, though impracticable for elicitative and inspective fs. to be performed by same person; A15-17, powers of legislation enquiry judicatory; A26, judges eligible to serve as legislation elicitors; A29, liberty of choice of building for legislation enquirers v. judicial proceedings; A36, employment of judge as legislation elicitor; A37, secrecy and size of judicatory; 28.A9-16, leg. as an appellate judicatory; 31.A1, judiciary establishment and all pervading system of securities; A42-4, judiciary and securities for app. apt. of leg.; VII.6, judiciary branch accessible to all without taxes or other obstacles; 9, impartiality and legislators as judges; 12, judiciary authority and encroachment by leg.; VIII.10.A5, use of manifold writing system by judiciary; A6, manifold writing system as security against destruction of judicial documents; A7, preservation and destruction of judicial documents; 11.A6, judiciary and evils of publicity; IX.3.A32, number in office and judiciary v. administrative in English practice; 4.A32-7, terminology of 'rules', 'orders', and 'mandates' and use in judiciary; 5.A7, judiciary superordinate to administrative authority in ex. of punitive power, but subordinate in power of direction, suspension, dislocation, transfer, suppletion; 10.A8, judiciary and elicitation of evidence; 11.A4-5, and unwilling communication of evidence; 15.A20-7, and natural honour augmented; A34, factitious honour unsuitable, even if judicially conferred; A52-3, judges to guard against fraud in extraordinary remuneration; 16.A3, judges to certify app. apt. of candidates for location; A18, judges who are members of qualification judicatory for entry on locable list enumerated; 17.A59, judges in English practice; 18.A7, minister not dislocable by sentence or decree of a judge; A8-10, reasons given; 21.A11-17, in directly-applying remedies for oppression where oppressor a functionary, oppressee to have judicatory or minister as special judge; A13, power and obligation of judge; A13-14, remedies listed; A15, judges immediate of district may be invoked; A16, reasons given; A17, fs. of judges; A18, p.m. as special judge where oppressor a minister; A19, legislation penal judicatory where p.m. is oppressor; A36, in directly-applying remedies against oppression by abuse of dislocative f., judge has no power of relocation; A20, proceedings in administrative dept. as in judiciary dept. for indirectly-applying remedies against oppression; A28-31, military judicatories v. ordinary judicatories in English practice; A37-8, dislocation judicatory, where held; A39, decrees, options open; A40, uses of decrees; A41-2, decrees, not obligatory; A43, minister may give effect to decrees; A73, arrangements for exemplars of record; 25.A42, judge made law v. leg. made law; A49, acting on precedent is anti-constitutional when by executive and judiciary in opposition to leg.; A50, use of proposed judicial procedure in the non-military subdepts. of the administrative dept., denied in English practice; A51, English judicial practice combines arbitrary dislocability mixed with virtual undislocability; A52, King's Bench ineffectual; A53, judge and jury system corrupt and evidence arrangements exclude all but willing testimony; A54, p.o. trib. in English practice checks oppression in spite of law; A55-6, purchase of justice in English practice; A57, no security against oppression in English practice; A58, military procedure superior to English practice; 26.A10, greatest publicity needed in judiciary dept.; A54, judicial offices to be separate from those of administrative dept. *See* ENGLISH PRACTICE; JUDICATORY, APPELLATE; JUDICATORY, IMMEDIATE; LEGISLATION PENAL JUDICATORY

JUSTICE AND INJUSTICE: V.5.A6, IX.20.A20, ends of justice and the procedure code; A6, delay, vexation, and expense v. justice; 6.A2, defamation of functionaries and injustice and justice; A5, injustice and suppression of truth; VI.25.A20, vengeance at expense of justice in monarchy; 27.A33, justice, conflicts of interest and use of professional advocates; A36, justice, occasionally served by secrecy in legislation enquiry judicatory; A47, justice and injustice and English judiciary; 28.A11, injustice of unredressed wrongs; VII.3, injustice and factitious honour; 6, accessibility to justice and judicial system discussed; 8, justice in international relations; IX.3.A32, 4.A34, 25.A55-6, sale of justice in English practice; 15.A34, justice, injustice and reward; A45, mislocated reward is injustice; A45, naturally present in monarchies; A45, excluded from code by exclusion of all arbitrarily conferred reward; 16.A25n, A29n, justice and injustice and modes of voting; A61, chance used to min. injustice in examinations; 21.A26, A29, A30, ends of justice and rules of deportment; 22.A6, justice denied in English judiciary; 25.A28, justice and responsibility for subordinates; 26.A21, unjust favour in audience with minister avoided; A46, need for protection against public commotion where conduct of government is just or unjust. *See* ENGLISH PRACTICE

JUSTICE MINISTER: IV.A13, one justice minister in state; V.2.A5, dislocable by constitutive authority; VI.25.A19, justice minister, corruption and undiscontinued locability; 28.A1, subject to trial by legislation penal judicatory; A8, impartial trial by legislation penal judicatory; A15, role of justice minister noted; VII.7, impartial election by leg. of justice minister; VIII.1.A2, p.m.'s logical field of service v. justice minister's; 10.A6, use of exemplars in ex. of inspective and melioration suggestive fs.; IX.15.A9, justice minister and exemption from punishment; 16.A18, justice minister or depute, presiding judge of qualification judicatory for entry on locable list; 21.A38, and dislocation judicatory; 26.A54, office remote from administrative dept. *See* JUDICIARY AUTHORITY; MINISTER(S)

JUSTICES OF THE PEACE: *See* ENGLISH PRACTICE

KNOWLEDGE: *See* APTITUDE

LABOUR & LABOURER(S): VI.20.A10, remuneration of day labourers v. high government officials; 31.A38, wealth extorted from those whose labour produces it, in mixed monarchies; IX.15.A6, competition and the price of labour; 16.A52, public remuneration of instructors not to be larger than that received for subsistence by lowest-paid class of labourers; 17.A45, price of labour, skilled and unskilled, min. by competition; A46, application of principle by rulers to their own labour resisted; A47, in England expense of official labour max.; A51, intellectual labour and timid merit; 19.A14, labour in public service and remuneration for longevity; A26, time and labour wasted in qualification examination for situations of trust; A29, power as inducement to time and labour; 25.A45, labour of thought saved in following precedents

LANGUAGE: I.A6(inst.diss.)&n, names of territorial divisions exhibit characteristics of universal language; VIIn, structure of sentences in code discussed;

IX.4.A3, names are nouns-substantive; A3, only by names are fs. designated

LAW OR MANDATE: VII.5, law to be clearly presented and readily available for use and instruction; VIII.11.A4, publicity and the force of the law; IX.4. A23, defined as written instrument from functionary to subordinate or to non-functionary; A24, transitory v. naturally permanent mandates; A25, transitory mandates defined; A26, naturally permanent mandates defined; A26, naturally permanent mandates from legislative authority called laws; A27, leg. can issue transitory mandates; A28, transitory mandates usually issued by authorities subordinate to leg.; A29, spontaneous v. elicited mandates; A30, elicited mandates produced by application instrument; A31, ordinance defined as any permanent mandate but especially from legislative authority; A31, law v. ordinance; A31, 'law' defined as species of command; A32, rules, regulations, orders—confused phraseology in common practice; A33, rule defined; A34-5, confusion and abuse in English practice; A36, 'mandate' superior term to 'rule' or 'order'; A38, mandates and written forms; A39, application to judiciary; A40, arrangement defined; A47, procurement mandate and ex. of procurement f. See AMENDMENT(S): LEGISLATURE; MOTION(S); WRITTEN INSTRUMENT(S)

LAWYER(S): VI.31.A27, lawyer class in representative democracy opposed to securities; A28, example of U.S. government given; A29, ascendancy in English practice and common law; A30, U.S. practice v. English practice; A41n, professional lawyers and English practice; IX.21.A29, max. wealth, power and reputation at expense of community; 25.A47, lawyer subclass and particular and sinister interest. See ADVOCATE(S)

LECTIVE FUNCTION: IX.25.A23, importance of access to register books for ex. of

LEGISLATION ENQUIRY JUDICATORY: VI.27.A1, defined and distinguished from ordinary judicatory; A2, leg. to ex. power to elicit evidence; A3, called elicitative f.; A4, how connected to ex. of imperative f.; A5, desirable, though impracticable, for imperative and elicitative fs. to be performed by same person; A6, factors determining leg.'s undertaking ex. of elicitative f.; A7, preappointed evidence defined; A8-9, examples given; A10, oral v. epistolary evidence; A11, active v. passive elicitator; A12, sources of evidence distinguished; A13, evidence elicitation committee v. whole leg.; A14, provision for legislation enquiry judicatory; A15, powers to secure attendance at legislation enquiry judicatory stated; A16, powers of leg. to extract information discussed; A17, limits to the extraction of evidence discussed; A18, desirable properties of evidence discussed; A19-21, securities against deception by falsehood; A22, how leg. will conduct enquiry; A23, committee for elicitation of evidence, how organized; A24, committee members termed 'legislation elicitors'; A25, eligibility for membership on committee; A26, judges eligible to serve as legislation elicitors; A27, elicitation process not to conflict with legislative duties of deputy or continuation commiteeman; A28, no limit to number of committees established by leg.; A29, max. of publicity and choice of edifice for enquiry; A30, number to be examined at once; A30-1, confrontation in examinations: occasions and purposes; A32, arrangements where diverse and conflicting interests; A33, use of professional advocates; A34, but avoiding delay where conflict between public and particular interests; A35, publicity max.; A36, employment of judge as legislation elicitor; A37, secrecy and size of judicatory; A38, securities applicable to legislation enquiry judicatory same as for leg.; A39, legislation enquiry report and ex. of methodization, condensation and application fs.; A40, best written by single hand; A41-56, English practice for eliciting evidence; 31.A44, legislation enquiry judicatory and securities for app. intellectual apt.; IX.4.A27, and temporary mandates; 10.A8, and information. *See* ENGLISH PRACTICE

LEGISLATION MINISTER: V.3.A4, legislation minister and the ex. of the dislocative f. by the constitutive authority; VI.20.A5, keeps record of and publishes absences of legislators; 21.A3, legislation minister and arrangements for secret sittings; 23.A4-6, and arrangements for ex. of self-suppletive f.; A31, and arrangements for new election in absence of excuse paper; 25.A2, and relocation of deputies; 29.A4, as attestator to amendments; A9, consulted by members of leg. proposing ordinances; 31.A44, and securities for app. intellectual apt.; VII.7, election of legislation minister to be impartial, promised by legislators; VIII.2.A15, to receive exemplars of p.m.'s actions regarding subordinates; IX.2.A1, serves under p.m.; 5.A34, no subordinates besides writing clerks may be required; A42, registrar and writing clerks as subordinates; 9.A7, joint visits in ex. of inspective f.; 26.A17, as not necessarily subject to p.m., no need for contiguous offices; A18, location of legislation minister's office best close to leg. *See* LEGISLATION SUBDEPARTMENT; MINISTER(S)

LEGISLATION PENAL JUDICATORY: V.3.A9, serves as judicatory when punifactive f. is ex. by constitutional authority; A10, arrangements to ensure impartiality when accused is member of leg.; VI.23.A32, and possible punishment for non-attendance in leg.; 26.A4, and wrongful exclusion of members of leg. by other members; 28.A1, functionaries subject to trial by legislation penal judicatory listed; A2, number of members of judicatory three or five; A3, eligibility as judges; A4, located by secret ballot; A5, leg. to appoint pursuers; A6, leg. to decide if time permits to take on legislation penal judicatory; A7, no vacancy should result in leg.; A8, impartiality in trials of p.m. and justice minister greater where judges not members of leg.; A9-16, leg. as appellate judicatory; 31.A43, legislation penal judicatory and security for app. moral apt. of legislators; VIIn, legislation penal judicatory v. p.o. trib. and conduct of legislators; VIII.12.A1, punishment by as security for app. apt. of p.m.; IX.21.A19, as special judicatory when p.m. is accused of oppression

LEGISLATION REGARDING FUNCTIONS: IX.24.A1, each minister to ex. argumentative, initiative and responsive fs. in seat in leg.; A2, but no minister may vote; A3, minister bound to attend sessions of leg. to answer questions; A4-5, minister to act to improve and secure Pannomion from deterioration through use of legislative and judicial fs.; A6, to every situation subordinate to minister belong the contested interpretation reporting f. as well as the melioration suggestive f.; A7, leg. to determine which functionaries to ex. the preinterpretative f. with reference to Pannomion; A8, also sistitive f.; A9, consideration of evil to occur with ex. and non-ex. of sistitive f.

LEGISLATION SUBDEPARTMENT: IX.9.A4, offices to be visited in ex. of inspective f. *See* LEGISLATION MINISTER

LEGISLATOR(S): *See* DEPUTY(IES); ENGLISH PRACTICE; LEGISLATURE; LEGISLATOR'S INAUGURAL DECLARATION

LEGISLATOR'S INAUGURAL DECLARATION: VI.31.A43, as security for app. moral apt. of legislators; VIIn, chief use to subject leg. to p.o. trib.; VIIn, applicable where legal sanction not effective; VIIn, penalty of moral sanction, loss of popularity; VIIn, legislator's inaugural declaration as moral code and map of field of legislation; VIIn, provision for dissent and amendment; 1.A1, where and when read by elected members of leg.; A2, arrangements for unavoidable absence; A3, arrangements for amendments and reservations; A4, reasons for dissent and amendments to be noted; A5, dissent to essence of declaration and arrangements for new election; 2, comprehensive and specific ends of government stated; 3, discussion of the avoidance of appetites which have sinister influence; 4, avoidance of waste and corruption discussed; 5, law clearly presented and readily available for use and instruction; 6, judicial branch accessible to all members of society without tax or other obstacle; 7, legislator to be impartial in election of p.m., legislation minister, justice minister; 8, justice in international relations discussed; 9, impartiality in ex. of power discussed; 10, constant attendance at leg. promised; 11, no withdrawal of legislative proceedings from public scrutiny; 12, encroachment by leg. on subordinate authorities opposed; 13, sincerity in formulating legislative ordinances and debate promised; 14, legislator but an agent of his constituents; VIII.8.A2, after legislator's inaugural declaration, leg. elects p.m. *See* CONSTITUTIVE AUTHORITY; LEGISLATURE; PUBLIC OPINION TRIBUNAL

LEGISLATURE: I.A3, leg. composed of one deputy from each district; A3, leg. to alter the districts by union and division; A4, and subdistricts; A5, and bis-subdistricts; A6, alteration must be commensurable with original plan; IV.A1, legislative authority——one of four in state; A2, constitutive authority to locate, dislocate, relocate, members of leg.; A2, not to give individual or specific direction to leg.'s measures; A2, relocation and dislocation as reward and punishment by constitutive authority; A3, leg. to locate and dislocate and give individual direction at times to chiefs of administrative and judiciary authorities and punish for non-compliance; A4, administrative dept. to give execution and effect to ordinances of leg.; A5, judiciary department to give execution and effect to ordinances of leg. where there is litiscontestation; A6, legislative and administrative depts. to form the government; A6, legislative and executive depts. form the operative; A7, use of term 'supreme' discussed; A8, for each authority, a dept.; A9, leg. has under it as many sublegs. as there are districts; A11, supreme leg. and local and logical fields of service; A12, supreme leg. many-seated, one seat for each district; V.2.A3, constitutive authority ex. locative power in sending deputies to leg.; A3n, 'deputy' v. 'representative'; A5, members dislocable by constitutive authority; 3.A3, leg. to settle details of mode of election to subleg.; A4, leg. and the ex. of dislocative f. by constitutive authority; A7-10, leg. and the ex. of punifactive f. by constitutive authority; 6.A3, prohibition or taxation of political tracts by leg. is anti-constitutional and breach of duty to constitutive authority; A4, and exception for defamation; VI.1.A1, leg. is omnicompetent; A1, local and logical fields of service; A1, unlimited power, but checks are applied by securities; A2, past legs. have no power over current one; A3, acts of earlier legs. confirmed unless action to the contrary; A4, preservation of government engagements; A5, executive and sublegs. dependent on leg.; A5, leg. dependent on constitutive authority; A6-7, leg. can, where non-performance or inaptitude, take over fs. of executive and sublegs.; A8, subjects of attention for leg. where exemplified; A9, communication between constituents and deputy; A9, duty of deputy to constituents; A10-12, duty of deputy where conflict between interest of constituents and national interest; A13, constitution variable by leg.; 2.A1, leg. to give execution and effect to the will of constitutive authority to max. greatest happiness of greatest number; A2, anti-constitutional ordinances of leg.; A3, constitutional authority alone can enforce contracts entered into by leg.; A4, observance of contracts discussed; A5, judicial enforcement of contracts between government and individuals of state; A6, between government and foreign state; A7, between government and subject of foreign state; A8, constitutive authority to ex. dislocative and punifactive fs., where breach of public faith; A9, judicial remedy for wrong done to foreign government; A10, and action of leg.; A11, and constitutive authority; 3.A1-4, leg. to ex. directive, corrective, and administrative fs. in relation to sublegs.; A5, arrangement for federative government; 4, election seats and districts; 5, electors; 6, eligibility; 7, election offices; 8, election apparatus; 9, proposal of members; 10, voters' titles; 11, election laws; 12, designation of election and voting districts; 13, vote making habitations; 14, term of service; 15, vacancies; 16, security of assembly against disturbance by members; 17, indisposition of presidents, how obviated; 18.A1-2, leg. sits every day except vacation days (every seventh day); A2, legislator is 'physician of body politic'; 19.A1, remuneration of legislators stated; 20.A1, single entrance to assembly chamber; A2, arrangements in assembly chamber for remuneration; A3, arrangements for departure from assembly chamber; A4, remuneration for days attended only, sickness not excepted; A5, absentation book and publication of record of absence of legislators; A6, arrangements for sickness; A7, suspicion of using sickness as pretence obviated; A8, withholding remuneration for non-attendance as punishment; A9, punishment of common soldier v. high government official; A10, remuneration by day discussed; A11, non-interrupted attendance v. interrupted attendance of legislators discussed; A12-13, interrupted attendance of legislators in mixed monarchies serves sinister interest of rulers; A14, use of prorogation and adjournment by monarch; A15-17, English practice; A18, U.S. practice; A19, importance of non-interrupted sittings; A20-1, U.S. practice and 'good left undone'; A22, time unemployed and wasted in legislative business; A23, resistance to accepting obligations which make business more efficient; A24, good government depends on architecture; A25, other causes of retardation and frustration of legislative business; 21.A1, sittings of leg. are public, and p.o. trib. reports to constitutive authority; A2, access of p.o. trib. to sittings max.; A3, arrangements for secret sittings; A4-5, disclosure by subsequent leg.; 22.A1, shorter the term of service for leg. the better; A2-3, exception for distance from leg.; A4, settled arrangements for elections favoured; A5, practice in monarchies; A6, U.S. practice; [23.A1-28, See SELF-SUPPLETIVE FUNCTION] A29, distinctive dress and members of continuation committee; A30, notice of non-attendance by deputy and substitute to be posted by election clerk of district; A31, in absence of excuse paper new election arranged; A32, leg. to determine the validity of excuses; [24.A1-21, See CONTINUATION COMMITTEE] [25.A1-55, See RELOCATION] [26.A1-5, See EXCLUSION] [27.A1-56, See ENGLISH PRACTICE; LEGISLATION ENQUIRY JUDICATORY] [28.A1-16, See LEGISLATION PENAL JUDICATORY] [29.A1-10, See MOTION(S)] [30.A1, See LOCATION AND DISLOCATION] [31.A1-45, See SECURITIES] VIIn, chief use of legislator's inaugural declaration to subject leg. to p.o. trib.; 1.A5, dissent to essence of declaration and arrangements for election; 7, impartiality in elections by leg.; 11, secrecy in legislative proceedings discussed; 12, encroachment by leg. on subordinate authorities opposed; 13, avoidance of fallacies in formulating ordinances and in debate; VIII.1.A1, p.m.'s local field of service coextensive with leg.; 2.A1, p.m.'s ex. of executive f. and relation with leg.; 3.A1, p.m. has no seat in legislative assembly; A1-2, communication between p.m. and leg. by message only, unless invited or ordered by leg. to appear personally; fs. ex. by p.m. in relation to leg.: (i) A3-4, informative f.; (ii) A5, indicative f.; (iii) A6-7, initiative f.; A8, p.m. responsible for neglect of fs.; A9, usual communication through minister rather than by message; (iv) A10, statistic f.; 5.A4, failure of leg. to elect p.m.; 6.A2, power of p.m. in relation to leg.; 7.A1, eligibility for location as p.m. by leg.; 8.A1, p.m. elected by leg.; A2, arrangements for election; A2-4, secret and open voting employed; A5, reaching a majority; A6, secret v. open voting discussed; 9.A1, p.m. dislocable by leg.; A2, and by constitutive authority; A3, grounds for dislocation, same as for member of leg.; 10.A7, leg. to arrange for preservation and periodic destruction of documents; 11.A15, p.m.'s report to leg. on need for secrecy; A16, committee of leg. to report, as check; A17, report discussed; A18, new members in leg. and prevention of concealment; 12.A1, registration system and leg., and security for app. apt. of p.m.; A1, dislocation by leg. as security for app. apt. of p.m.; IX.1.A3, ends to guide the legislator; 2.A9, concurrence of leg. required for separation of subdepts. once joined; 3.A21, single-seatedness not applicable to leg.; 4.A26-8, leg. and transitory v. permanent mandates; 5.A32, leg. to establish and vary number of grades within each subdept.; 6.A11, leg. can except certain subordinate grades from ex. of self-suppletive f.; 7.5th.A2, creation of subsidiary books by leg. for ex. of statistic f.; 6th.A1, use of abbreviations, determined by leg.; 8.A2, leg. alone issues procurement mandates; A3, may delegate authority to p.m. or ministers; A18, leg. provides for outset supply; A19, determines on general supply day; A20, leg. to determine use of spontaneous mandate v. requisition instrument; A21, spontaneous procurement by leg. v. spontaneous procurement based on powers conferred by leg.; A23, leg. to use results of statistic and registration systems to determine supply; A23, to draw line between ordinary and extraordinary service; A23, and determine from and to which offices requisition instruments may be transmitted; A24, considerations to guide leg.; A29, leg. to have regard for cheapest form of procurement; 10.A11, information of all occurrences furnished to leg. and p.m.; A12, exceptions made by leg.; A14, leg. makes arrangements for information sent to offices higher than immediate superordinates; 11.A6, leg. to determine which subordinate functionaries to have power to elicit information; A6-7, and to establish securities against abuse; A9, leg. to determine power to extract information by army and navy subdepts. for defence purposes; A10, leg. to avoid evil from abuse of extractive power; 13.A2-3, minister v. member of leg., terms of service; 14.A2, leg. to determine proportion of minister's time to be devoted to indoor and outdoor service; A3&n, need for continual attendance of leg. to receive reports from ministers, judiciary, and sublegs.; 15.A28, publication is arranged by leg. of matter in public merit register; 16.A8, commencement of courses of instruction, times appointed by leg.; A10, leg. to have made and published office calendar, containing list of positions; A32, leg. to choose between various modes of voting in qualification judicatory after experience of each; A34, leg. will limit topics for interrogation regarding moral apt.; A47-8, leg. to make payment for instructors dependent on number of pupils and strenuousness of exertion; A51, leg. to regulate extra remuneration of instructors; A55-6, A58, leg. to make arrangements for examination; A60, and for examination of app. moral apt.; 17.A6, leg. to arrange for pecuniary security for locatees in positions of trust, or talent and trust; A11, leg. to consider further checks against mislocation; A13, leg. may add to headings of location instrument; A15, leg. may arrange for property as pecuniary security to be inalienable by possessors; A19, leg. to consider differences in grades in subdepts. for bidding in competition system; A20, attention given to pain of humiliation, if superordinate and subordinate reverse positions; A20, distinguished from rise of one person above another functionary; A21, leg. to make exceptions as to locators; A32, leg. and p.m.'s substitution of locables; 18.A5, every minister dislocable at all times by leg.; 19.A1, leg. to allot to subordinates in subdepts. grades with distinctive fields of service and fs.; A2-3, subordinate subject to ex. of directive f. of superordinate, exceptions to be made by leg.; A4, leg. to determine which register books to be kept in each grade; A5, leg. to determine which grades have power to ex. self-suppletive f.; A6, and requisitive f.; A7, and melioration suggestive f.; A11, leg. to determine application of rules of attendance to each office; A15, leg. to determine to which subordinate positions principles of location system can be applied; 19.A32, leg. to decide permanent v. temporary functionaries for government fabrication; A42, leg. to determine when distance requires suspension by subordinate to minister pending decision by minister regarding dislocation; A43, examples given; 20.A1, leg. to consider application of arrangements regarding insubordination, oppression, and extortion to military branch; A19, leg. to consider where legal sanction applicable to rules for deportment of non-functionaries; A24, leg. to determine which grades subordinate to minister to have securities against disturbance and non-compliance by suitors, inspectees and evidence holder; 21.A20, leg. to determine whether variations in rules of deportment necessary for army and navy subdepts., as indirectly-applying remedies against oppression; A38, leg. to consider circumstances for place where dislocation judicatory is held; A44-6, leg. has power to dislocate, promote, and transfer subordinate functionaries; A72, leg. to determine when appellate judge to invoke assistance of ordinary judge in case of oppression; A77, further considerations for leg. regarding extent of territory, distances from metropolis, facility of communication, numbers of grades in subdepts.; 23.A13, leg. may vary rules for receipt and disbursement of money; A14, legislator's vigilance regarding peculation; 24.A1, each minister, subject to leg., to ex. argumentative, initiative and responsive fs. in seat of leg.; A2, but no minister, even with consent, may vote in leg.; A3, ministers bound to attend sessions of leg. to answer questions; A7-9, leg. to determine which administrative functionaries to ex. the preinterpretative and sistitive fs. with reference to the Pannomion; 25.A1n, sketch of securities applicable to members of leg.; A2, leg. to decide which securities applicable to leg. and p.m. are applicable to ministers; A3, relevant securities listed; A3, dislocability of ministers by leg. as security for app. apt.; A9, leg. to arrange for new series of convicted list when list becomes too long; A24, leg. to arrange secrecy for extra despatch when necessary, as in time of war; A33, leg. to look for and exclude illegal ex. of power by functionaries and min. expansion of power based on necessity; A34, examples given; A35, leg. not to delegate power to ministers for emergencies; A37, leg. and conditions for exemption from punishment for functionaries' extraordinary ex. of power; A49, acting on precedent is anti-constitutional when by executive and judiciary in opposition to leg. *See* CONSTITUTIVE AUTHORITY;

ENGLISH PRACTICE; MINISTER(S); PRIME MINISTER; PUBLIC OPIN-
ION TRIBUNAL

LIBERALITY: IX.15.A7, as virtue and vice in private and public spheres; 17.
A55, 'liberality' v. 'munificence'; A55, liberality and merit, connection
denied. *See* WASTE

LIBERTY: *See* FREEDOM

LITERACY AND ILLITERACY: V.1.A3, non-readers excluded from suffrage;
4.A2, but included in p.o. trib.

LOCAL HEADMAN: I.A5, each bis-subdistrict the territory of local headman;
A6(inst.diss.), number of local headmen in territory and fs. discussed; IV.A13,
in each ultimate section of territory, one headman; V.2.A5, dislocable by constitutive authority; VI.31.A1, local headmen and all pervading system of
securities; A42, local headmen and securities for app. apt. of leg.

LOCAL REGISTRAR(S): V.2.A5, dislocable by constitutive authority; VI.27.
A9, local registrars and preappointed evidence; 31.A1, and all pervading system of securities; A42, A44, and securities for app. apt. of legislators

LOCATION AND DISLOCATION: II.A17, principles for official apt.: public
examination, pecuniary competition, and responsible location; A20, dislocational responsibility discussed; A22-3, dislocation, punishment, and legal
responsibility discussed; IV.A2, constitutive authority to locate and dislocate
members of leg.; A3, leg. to locate and dislocate chiefs of administrative and
judiciary depts.; V.1.A1, constitutional authority and location and dislocation, immediately and interventionally; 2.A1, immediate v. interventional
dislocation; VI.1.A9, duty of deputy to constituents and grounds for dislocation; 23.A1, location of depute and ex. of self-suppletive f.; A3, eligibility for
location as substitute; 24.A1-2, location of continuation committee; 25.A48-
9, p.m.'s power of location and dislocation as security against corruption;
26.A4-5, dislocation and wrongful exclusion of members of leg. by other
members; 28.A1, trial by legislation penal judicatory where dislocation
deemed not sufficient punishment; A4, judges located by secret ballot; A8,
impartiality by members of legislation penal judicatory; 30.A1, causes of dislocation of members of leg. listed: (1) resignation; (2) acceptance of other
office in state; (3) acceptance of office in foreign state; (4) acceptance of
factitious honour or dignity from foreign state; (5) insanity; (6) disturbance
of legislative proceedings; (7) criminal delinquency; (8) dislocation by constituents; 31.A44, location system and security for app. intellectual apt. in leg.;
VIII.2.A3, p.m.'s ex. of locative f.; A5-7, and dislocative f.; A11, p.m. and
location and dislocation in army; A13, and navy; A14, authenticating instruments; A15, use of manifold writing system; A16, arrangements for redress;
4.A1, location and dislocation of depute; A5-6, responsibility of principal for
depute and dislocation; A7-8, arrangements for location of depute; A10,
death of principal and location of successor; A11, dislocability of depute;
5.A4, dislocation of leg. and responsibility to hold election of p.m.; 6.A2,
location and dislocation and power of p.m. in relation to leg.; 7.A1, eligibility
for location as p.m.; A2, monarchs and relations of monarchs excluded; A3,
residency requirements stated; 8.A1, p.m. located by leg.; A2, arrangements
for election; A2-4, open and secret voting employed; A5, reaching a majority;
A6, secret v. open voting discussed; 9.A1, p.m. dislocable by leg.; A2, and by
constitutive authority; A3, grounds for dislocation, same as for leg.; 12.A1,
dislocation of p.m. by leg. and by constitutive authority as security for app.
apt.; A1, dislocation of p.m. on accepting other office in state, as security for

app. apt.; A1, location system as security for p.m. through checks to arbitrary appointment; IX.3.A16-17, U.S. practice and location and dislocation of heads of executive depts.; 4.A44, submodes of location: allective and compulsive; A44, ex. of conductive and compulsorily procurative fs.; A44, bissubmodes of location listed; 5.A4, power of dislocation, necessary to subordination; 13.A2-3, term of service and arrangements for dislocation, minister v. legislator; 15.A4, opulence and avoidance of dislocation; 16.A1, location system established at public expense in all subdepts. to max. apt. and min. expense; A2, and collateral benefit of instruction; A3, leading features indicated: choice from number of proposed candidates by p.m.; moral restriction on his choice by p.o. trib.; app. apt. of candidates certified by judges; competition for public service at least expense among equals or near equals on scale of apt.; risk to reputation of p.m. if wrong choice is made; power of dislocation separate from power of location; dislocative power a check to arbitrary patronage; A4, preparation period v. consummation period; A5-6, defined; A7, courses of instruction increasing degree of app. apt.; A8, commencement of courses of instruction, times appointed by leg.; A9, those reaping benefit from courses of instruction preferred in location over those without acquired apt., as security for app. apt.; A10, leg. to have made and published office calendar, containing list of positions; A11, general headings: situations of talent, simple trust, trust and talent; A12, situations of talent defined; A13, situations of simple trust defined, examples given; A14, situations of talent and trust defined; A15, talent requiring situations and requisite talents, examples given; A16, each individual to be entered on locable list prior to admission to office; A17, qualification judicatory to determine those qualified for entry on locable list; A18, composition of judicatory; A19, suppositions of judicatory: returns made to advertisements; need for places to be filled ascertained; sufficient supply of funds determined; sufficient time for instruction elapsed; A20-1, mode of procedure of qualification judicatory; A22-32, decree of judicatory formed by secret and open modes of voting; A33, comparative apt. of instructors exhibited in ranking table; A34, leg. will limit topics for interrogation regarding moral apt.; A34, judges, quasi-jurymen, and competitors (with permission) may interrogate; A34, irregularities of sexual appetite, prohibited subject of inquiry; A35, until leg. limits topics, unlimited liberty of interrogation; A35, may be limited by majority of judges or at instance of candidate; A35, responsibility for false statements indicated; A36, results of scrutiny entered in candidate's character book; A37, app. moral apt. not subject of voting, but results available to each locator; A38, results of voting process framed, printed, and published by registrar; A38-9, opinative decree and imperative decree; A40, no candidate refused entry on locable list on grounds of intellectual apt., unless by express decree of majority of judges; A41, record of moral inaptitude printed and published by registrar; A42, advertisement for instructors; A43, questions for prospective instructors, examples given; A44, object of advertisement; A45, government's share of expense, capital v. periodic allowance; A46, government expense of capital for instruction limited; A47, legislators to make money for instructors dependent on number of pupils and strenuousness of exertion; A48, leg. to see that cost of remuneration of instructors is borne by pupils and relatives; A49-50, extra remuneration, when necessary, examples given; A51, leg. to regulate extra remuneration of instructors; A52, no public remuneration of instructors to be larger than that received for subsistence by lowest paid class of labourers;

A53, no allowance for lodging and diet of pupils; A54, disgust of opulent at sight of indigent, grounds for clothing allowance for pupils; A55-6, leg. to make arrangements for examinations; A55, examination appointing day v. examination day; A55-6, examination appointing advertisement; A57, consummation period, day of commencement; A58, and preparation period; A59, when instruction available, no one is placed on locable list without it; A59, those already in office excepted; A60, leg. to make arrangements for examination of app. moral apt.; A61, use of chance v. choice in examination system; A62, responses and exhibitions, tokens of app. apt.; A62, and ex. of correspondent fs. by examiners; A63, information needed antecedent to responses and exhibitions; A64, mode of procedure for elicitation of responses; A64, use of question books; A65-6, not all information to be tested; A67, use of lot to exclude partiality in choice of questions; A67, mode of procedure; A68, arrangements of questions; A69, drawing out of question tickets; A69n, choice v. chance in English practice, especially in jury trials; A70, procedure applicable to exhibitions; A71-8, use of lottery discussed; 17.A1, office competition process, p.m. to advertise for offers; A1-4, A54, reductional v. emptional v. compound bidding, defined and distinguished; A5, only those tried by qualification judicatory locable; A6, leg. to make arrangements for pecuniary security by locatee for positions of trust and talent and trust; A7, position of minister involves talent and trust; A8, instrument of location, required; A9, headings listed; A10, distribution of exemplars; A11, leg. to consider further checks on mislocation; A12, minister to advertise for his own subordinates; A13, and location instrument; A13, leg. may add to headings of location instrument; A14, in position of simple trust, inferior talent no bar, and preference given on bidding and pecuniary security; A14, self-seated v. extra-seated property as pecuniary security; A15, leg. may arrange for property as pecuniary security to be inalienable in hands of possessor; A16, minimum age for location; A17-18, exceptions for offices in army and navy; A19, leg. to consider differences in grades in subdepts. for bidding in competition system; A20, attention given to pain of humiliation if superordinate and subordinate reverse positions; A20, distinguished from rise of other persons above functionary; A21, initiative and confirmative locators; A21, minister, the initiative locator; A21, A31, p.m., the confirmative; A21, leg. to make exceptions; A22, distance may require temporarily initiative locator in addition to minister; A23, examples where app.; A24-6, and army subdept.; A27, and navy subdept.; A29-30, and foreign relation subdept.; A31&n, locative f., mode of ex. and avoidance of suspension; A32, p.m. to give reasons for substitution of another locable; A33-4, deputes permanent must be chosen from locable list; A35, location instrument for deputes; A36, provision for exemplars; A37, mislocation, responsibility assigned; A38, no act performed by mislocatee invalid; A39, reason given; A40, examples given; A41, all profit from wrong to be divested; 17.A42-58, contribution of the employment of the competition principle, in subordination to apt. manifestation system; A43-4, reasons given; A43, deduced from greatest happiness principle; A45, English practice, general opinion that price of commodities should be min. through competition; A46, reluctance of statesmen to apply competition principle to their own labours; A46, only will do so when energy of people is troublesome; A47, why, at present, the expense of official labour is max. and apt. min.; A48, especially where education, remuneration, and location are in hands of ruling few; A49, pecuniary competition v. gratuitous

service; A50, objections to public examination system and pecuniary competition listed and answered: (i) A51, timid merit excluded; A52, unopulence
as a cause of apt.; (ii) A53, unopulent excluded and thus equality violated;
(iii) A54, venality established; (iv) A55, liberality excluded; (v) A56-8, depredation increased by indigence of functionary; (vi) A59, apt. follows opulence;
18.A1, modified v. unmodified location; A1-3, defined and distinguished;
A2, modes of modified location, listed; A4, every minister at all times dislocable by p.m.; A5, also by leg.; A6, dislocation by constitutive authority;
A6, security against undue dislocation; A7, minister not dislocable by sentence or decree of a judge; A8-10, reasons given; 19.A10, arbitrary v. judicial
dislocation and security of functionary; A12, pecuniary competition and no
increase in remuneration while in office; A15, leg. to apply location system
to suitable subordinate positions; A16, subordinates located with initiative
f. ex. by minister and consummative f. ex. by p.m.; A17, considerations of
distance; A18, A19&n, securities in filling vacancies; A21, A23-5, A27,
repetition of qualification examination and pecuniary competition in filling
vacancies; A26, qualification examination and pecuniary competition only
applicable to situations of talent; A40, all subordinates dislocable by minister;
A40-1, exceptions and restrictions noted; A42, leg. to determine occasions
when distance requires suspension by subordinate to minister pending decision
by minister regarding dislocation; A43, examples given; 20.A8, dislocation
impossible for quasi-insubordination; A25, dislocation and non-compliance
by subordinate to direction of superordinate; 21.A4, A8, abuse of power of
dislocation and oppression; A8, dislocation through oppression; A14, oppressor subject to dislocation as directly-applying remedy; A37, dislocation judicatory, where held; A38, exceptions; A39, decrees, options open; A40, uses
of decrees: securities against oppression and opportunities to clear reputation; A41-2, functionary's ex. of fs. not impeded, as decrees are not obligatory; A43, minister to give effect to decrees or to transfer subordinate or
superordinate; A44, simple dislocation of functionaries, subordinate to minister, only by minister, p.m., leg.; A48, dislocation instrument required for
dislocation or modified dislocation as indirectly applying remedy against
oppression; A49, exceptions; A50, dislocation instrument: headings for
simple dislocation; A51, resignation in place of dislocation, not acceptable
for deficiencies in moral apt. but acceptable otherwise; A52, resignation also
applicable where no deficiency in app. apt., examples given; A53, minutes of
record of decree to be attached to dislocation instrument; A54, application
of instrument to suspension, headings of entry; A55-6, preventing suspension becoming *de facto* dislocation; A59, evidence to warrant dislocation;
A60, application of instrument to permanent transference, headings of entry;
A61, temporary transference, headings of entry; A64, permanent transference to inferior grades, headings of entry; A65, temporary transference to
inferior grades, headings of entry; A68, definitive stoppage of promotion,
headings of entry; A69, temporary stoppage of promotion, headings of entries; A70, publicity max. in all proceedings; A71, exception for secrecy in
time of war; 25.A1, power of location and dislocation and security for app.
apt.; A3, dislocation of ministers by leg. and constitutive authority, as securities for app. apt.; A3, qualification judicatory and pecuniary competition as
securities for app. apt.; A3, dislocability of ministers upon accepting another
office, or upon accepting office, honour, gift, from foreign government as
security for app. apt.; A26, A28, location and dislocation and responsibility

of ministers for subordinates; A32, dislocative power of ministers and inaptitude of functionaries; 26.A38, pecuniary competition and arrangements for living accommodation of ministers discussed. *See* DEPUTE(S); DISLOCATIVE FUNCTION; ENGLISH PRACTICE; LEGISLATOR'S INAUGURAL DECLARATION; LOCATIVE FUNCTION; LOT; PROMOTION; PUBLIC OPINION TRIBUNAL; RELOCATION; SELF-SUPPLETIVE FUNCTION; SUSPENSION; TRANSFER; VOTING

LOCATIVE FUNCTION: V.2.A2, ex. by constitutive authority; A3-4, ex. in sending deputies to leg. and members to sublegs.; 3.A1, locative f., how ex. by constitutive authority in relation to leg.; A2-3, and sublegs.; VIII.2.A3, ex. by p.m. in relation to ministers; IX.4.A44, ex. by ministers collectively in regard to persons; A44, defined; A44-5, locative v. procurative fs.; A44, submodes of location: conductive and compulsorily procurative fs.; 17.A31&n, locative f., mode of ex., and avoidance of suspension; 25.A26, and responsibility of ministers for subordinates. *See* CONSTITUTIVE AUTHORITY; DISLOCATIVE FUNCTION; ELECTION CODE; LOCATION AND DISLOCATION

LONGEVITY: IX.19.A14, no increase in remuneration for longevity. *See* SENIORITY; SUBORDINATE AND SUPERORDINATE

LOT: VIII.8.A5, use of lot to break tie in election of p.m. by leg.; IX.16.A25n, possible use where equality among candidates; 16.A61-78, use of lot as instrument of selection; A67, use of lot to exclude partiality in examination; A67, mode of procedure; A68, arrangements of questions; A69, drawing out of question-tickets; A71, other uses of lot besides in location system; A72, in distribution of benefits, examples given; A73, location of burdens, as for military and quasi-jury service; A74, where burdens not divisible; A75, in punishment; A76, chance and choice used in association; A77-8, lottery constituted: by contract of parties v. law with absence of consent; A78, government lottery v. individual lottery; 19.A36, lot preferred to choice in corrupt system of government as basis of promotion. *See* LOCATION AND DISLOCATION; VOTING

LOTTERY: *See* LOT

MAJORITY(IES): VI.26.A2, legislative authority belongs to majority present at meeting; A3, effect on majority where members wrongly excluded; VIII.8.A5, comparative v. absolute majorities in election of p.m. by leg.

MANDATE(S): *See* LAW OR MANDATE

MANIFOLD WRITING MODE: VIII.2.A15&n, use of, with exemplars; 10.A1&n, A2, use of, in registration system; A3-4, saving expense and security against falsification; A5, use by judiciary; A6, as security against destruction of judicial documents; 11.A3, manifold writing system and publicity; A12, manifold writing system v. printing press as instrument of internal publicity; IX.5.A24, min. expense in transmission of information; 7.2nd.A11, A19, use of mimographical mode of registration; 8.A35, uniformity of paper in manifold writing system; A36, v. printing for cheapness and legibility. *See* EXEMPLARS; MIMOGRAPHICAL MODE OF REGISTRATION; PUBLICITY AND SECRECY; REGISTRATION SYSTEM; STATISTIC FUNCTION

MASS(ES): IX.25.A48, governed millions as a mass

MAXIMIZATION AND MINIMIZATION: (i) Max. happiness/happiness of greatest number: II.A1, A13, A14, A16, A23, VI.2.A1, 29.A43, VII.2, (ii) Max. app. apt. and/or min. expense: II.A2, A12, A16, A17, A19, VII.2, 4,

VIII.12.A1, IX.3.A2, A23, A31, 4.A38, 5.A22, A24, A38, 7.2nd.A24, 4th.A31, 15.A1-3, A5, A6, 16.A1, A3, A42, A47, 17.A50, 19.A25, A27, 25.A3, 26.A20n, (iii) Max. good and/or min. evil: II.A13, VII.2, VIII.11.A8, IX.1.A1, A2, 4.A54, 7.1st.A3, A5, A17, A19, 21.A25, 24.A9, 26.A2, A4, A43, (iv) Other: II.A16&n, A23, IV.A14, VI.21.A2, 25.A28, 27.A5, A21, A29, A35, A38, A47, A48, 31.A2, A34, VII.2, VIII.11.A2, A3, IX.4.A17, A43, 5.A36, 7.1st.A4, 8.A24, 16.A20, A61, 17.A45, A47, A53, A54, 19.A31, 21.A29, A70, 23.A13, 25.A42, 26.A19. *See* APTITUDE; EXPENSE; GOOD AND EVIL; HAPPINESS

MELIORATION SUGGESTIVE FUNCTION: V.5.A4, ex. by p.o. trib.; 6.A1, all members of human species have right to ex. melioration suggestive f.; VI.28.A16, and redressing wrongs by judges; VIII.10.A6, use of exemplars in ex. by justice minister; A7, melioration suggestive f. not inhibited by destruction of useless documents; 12.A1, ex. by p.o. trib. as security for app. apt. of p.m.; IX.4.A61, ex. by ministers collectively; A61, purposes: reform and improvement; 12.A1, ministers to draw up melioration suggesting report and transmit to p.m.; fs. included in melioration suggestive f.: A2, indicative; A3, ratiocinative; A4, eventually emendative f.; A5, exemplars, how disposed; A6, benefits from this f. depend on ex. of other fs.; 19.A7, leg. to determine which grades to ex. melioration suggestive f.; 24.A5, ex. of melioration suggestive f. and securing the Pannomion against deterioration; A6, in every situation subordinate to minister, belongs the contested interpretation reporting f. as well as the melioration suggestive f.; 25.A3, ex. by p.o. trib. as security for app. apt. of ministers; A23, importance of access to register books for ex. *See* EVENTUALLY EMENDATIVE FUNCTION

MENDACITY AND VERACITY: VI.27.A48, mendacity max. in English practice in rules of evidence in judiciary; A50, mendacity and veracity in eliciting evidence by House of Commons; A54, veracity of evidence elicited by monarch's commissions; VIII.12.A3, problem of mendacity and secret informers of minister's misconduct or inaptitude; IX.10.A2, mendacity licence mentioned

MERCEDE-LOCATIVE FUNCTION: *See* ELIMINATIVE FUNCTION

MERCHANT(S): IX.25.A47, mercantile subclass and particular and sinister interest

MERIT: IX.15.A34, merit, natural honour, and remuneration discussed; 17.A51, timid merit and public examination system, objection answered; A51, timidity may accompany, but is not a cause of merit; A55, liberality no proof of merit; 19.A14, fallacious notion of moral merit; A37, for meritorious service, no augmentation of emolument necessary; A38, extra remuneration for meritorious service, private v. public practice; A39, extra merit only basis of extra remuneration. *See* APTITUDE; DIGNITY AND FACTITIOUS DIGNITY; HONOUR, NATURAL AND FACTITIOUS; LOCATION AND DISLOCATION; REMUNERATION

MESSAGE(S): VIII.1.A9, in U.S. practice, president communicates with congress by message; 3.A1-2, communication between p.m. and leg. by message only, unless invited or ordered by leg. to appear personally; fs. ex. by p.m. in sending messages; A3-4, informative f.; A5, indicative f.; A6-7, initiative f.; A8, p.m. responsible for neglect of fs.; A9, communication with leg. usually through minister; A10, in ex. of statistic f., p.m. to send annual messages to leg. on general condition of state

METHODIZATION FUNCTION: VI.27.A39, ex. in preparation of legislation

enquiry report. *See* LAW OR MANDATE; LEGISLATION ENQUIRY JUDI-
CATORY; WRITTEN INSTRUMENTS

METROPOLIS: VI.2.A9, foreign government to sue in judicatory in metropolis
for breach of contract; 23.A15, metropolis of state, seat of leg.; A22, many in
metropolis to serve as deputes; IX.21.A37, A77, judicatory in metropolis to
be used, but problem of distance

MIGRATION: VII.8, no barrier in state to immigration or emigration

MILITARY SERVICE: IX.16.A73, and use of lot in selection for; 19.A29-31,
distribution of power, grade and emolument non-military v. military situations. *See* ARMY MINISTER; ARMY SUBDEPARTMENT; NAVY MINI-
STER; NAVY SUBDEPARTMENT

MIMOGRAPHICAL MODE OF REGISTRATION: IX.7.2nd.A7, also named
receptacular or mimetic mode; A7, explained; A8, usefulness indicated; A9,
subdepts. where most applicable; A10, present usage; A11, and manifold system; A12, use in describing not only original amount but also changes in
quantity of articles in public store; A13, subdept. where applicable; A14,
application to store of written instruments; A15-23, applicability described;
A24, use in ex. of applicative, custoditive, and procurative fs.; 8.A11, mimographical documents indicate need for issuing requisition instruments; A12,
indicate stock in hand for entry on requisition instruments; A14, mimographical documents serve as checks on requisition. *See* EXEMPLARS; MANIFOLD
WRITING MODE; REGISTRATION SYSTEM; STATISTIC FUNCTION

MINISTER(S): IV.A13, one minister for each subdept.; V.2.A3n, deputy of
minister called minister depute; A5, ministers and deputes dislocable by constitutive authority; VI.29.A9-10, consultation with ministers over proposed
ordinances by members of leg.; 31.A1, all-pervading system of securities
applied to ministers; A42, ministers' securities for app. apt. and leg.; VIII.
1.A4, logical field of service of ministers; 2.A2, ministers and p.m.'s ex. of
directive f.; A3, ministers located by p.m.; A5, and dislocated by p.m.; 3.A7,
ministers and ex. of initiative f. by p.m. in relation to leg.; A9, usual communication by p.m. through ministers to leg.; IX.1.A1, ministers collectively,
ends aimed at; A2, app. good and correspondent evil specified; 2.A1, ministers under p.m. enumerated; A2, each minister has one or more subdepts.;
A3, ministers collectively v. individual ministers; A4, A6, minister v. subminister; A5, minister v. p.m.; A7, p.m. v. subprime minister; A8, allotment
of ministers; A9, A10, potentially united subdepts.; [3, *See* SINGLE AND
MANY SEATEDNESS] [4, *See* FUNCTIONS] [5, *See* SUBORDINATE
AND SUPERORDINATE] [6, *See* SELF SUPPLETIVE FUNCTION] [7, *See*
STATISTIC FUNCTION] [8, *See* REQUISITIVE FUNCTION] [9, *See*
INSPECTIVE FUNCTION] [10, *See* INFORMATION; OFFICIALLY IN-
FORMATIVE FUNCTION] [11, *See* INFORMATION ELICITATIVE FUNC-
TION] [12, *See* MELIORATION SUGGESTIVE FUNCTION] [13, *See*
TERM OF SERVICE] [14, *See* ATTENDANCE AND NON-ATTENDANCE]
[15, *See* REMUNERATION] [16-18, *See* LOCATION AND DISLOCA-
TION] [19, *See* SUBORDINATE AND SUPERORDINATE] [20, *See* IN-
SUBORDINATION] [21, *See* OPPRESSION] [22, *See* EXTORTION] [23,
*See* PECULATION] [24, *See* LEGISLATION REGARDING FUNCTIONS]
[25, *See* SECURITIES] [26, *See* ARCHITECTURE]. *See* ARMY; DOMAIN;
EDUCATION; ELECTION; FINANCE; FOREIGN RELATION; HEALTH;
INDIGENCE RELIEF; INTERIOR COMMUNICATION; LEGISLATION;
NAVY; PREVENTIVE SERVICE; AND TRADE MINISTERS. *See also*

CORRUPTION; EVIDENCE; MIMOGRAPHICAL MODE OF REGISTRA-
TION; REGISTRATIVE FUNCTION; REGISTRATION SYSTEM; OPPRES-
SION; VOTING

MINUTATION: IX.21.A20, as indirectly applying remedy in obviation of oppression by administrative functionaries

MINUTATIVE FUNCTION: *See* REGISTRATIVE FUNCTION

MIXED MONARCHY: VI.20.A12–17, effect of non-attendance of legislators in
mixed monarchies; 31.A15, A36–41&n, and reception to the use of securities
for app. apt.; IX.25.A38, and abuse of ex. of extraordinary power; A48,
power-holding class in democracy v. mixed monarchy. *See* ARISTOCRACY;
ENGLISH PRACTICE; MONARCHY

MONARCHY: II.A23–4, monarchy and responsibility; VI.2.A4, and coronation
oath; 22.A5, and origin of systems of representation; 24.A13, as convener of
leg.; 25.A20, and corruption; 31.A25, A31–5, pure monarchy and reception
to use of securities for app. apt.; A34–5, and reception in pure aristocracy;
VIII.5.A4, representative democracy changed to monarchy and aristocracy
where leg. fails to elect p.m.; 7.A2, exclusion of monarch and relations of
monarch from eligibility for location as p.m.; IX.3.A24, A27, arbitrary rule
of; 15.A35, monarchy and factitious dignity; A45, reward mislocated *in toto*,
natural and habitual in monarchy; 17.A56–7, monarchy, opulence, and depredation; 20.A12, absolute monarchy and secret institutions; 25.A51, in absolute monarchies, dislocation arbitrary; A53, aristocracy's dependence on
monarchy; 26.A40, representative democracy v. monarchy and expense of
moving from place to place; A48, in monarchy, all but one become slaves;
A49–52, greatest happiness requires residence of functionaries, including
monarch, located where their service can be of most use. *See* ARISTO-
CRACY; ENGLISH PRACTICE; MIXED MONARCHY

MONEY: VI.25.A20, money and money's worth as matter of corruption; VII.3,
appetite for money to be avoided by legislators; 4, money gained by false
pretences to be avoided by legislators; IX.4.A11, money and movables-at-
large; fs. regarding money: A56, statistic; A57, registrative; A58, publicative;
A59, officially informative or report making; A61, melioration suggestive;
5.A19, accountableness at large and money; 23.A13, rules for receipt and
disbursement of money listed; A14, peculation, in the ex. of the procurative,
reparative, eliminative, and venditive fs. more dangerous, because easier, than
malpractice with money. *See* CORRUPTION; EXPENSE; PECULATION;
REMUNERATION; STATISTIC FUNCTION

MORAL: (i) Moral apt. and inaptitude: II.A22, VI.24.A1, A18, 25.A19, A32,
A33, A50, 28.A8, A16, 31.A1, A24, A38, A41n, A43, VII.2, IX.3.A3,
16.A12, 25.A1, A31; (ii) Moral responsibility: II.A24, VI.23.A26, 25.A49,
IX.16.A3; (iii) Moral rights: IX.4.A9n; (iv) Moral sanction: II.A20, VIIn,
IX.20.A18, 21.A26, 25.A1, A54; (v) Moral obligation: V.5.A5; (vi) Other:
V.4.A3, subjects of dramatic entertainment of a political or moral nature;
VI.25.A26, in moral world, attraction of corruption is like attraction of
gravity; VIIn, legislator's inaugural declaration as moral code; VIIn, insincerity
as moral disease; IX.16.A3, morally binding right; 19.A14, moral merit,
fallacious notion; 21.A21, rules of deportment analysed as rules of morality;
25.A54, good manners and good morals. *See* APTITUDE; DEONTOLOGY;
DEPORTMENT; LEGISLATOR'S INAUGURAL DECLARATION; RIGHTS;
SANCTION(S); SECURITIES

MOTION(S): VI.29.A1, emendative v. non-emendative proposed ordinances;

A2, if emendative, need to declare it to protect Pannomion; A3, emendative ordinance, directive mode explained; A4, formula for amendments; A5–6, reeditive mode explained; A7, every member of leg. has right to propose motions; A7, motions discussed, when seconded; A8, remedies for ill-considered or time-wasting motions; A9, obviation of confusion from numerous motions, remedies proposed; A9–10, consultation with ministers over proposed ordinances; 31.A44, apt form of new laws and securities for app. intellectual apt.; IX.24.A1, motions made by ministers in ex. of initiative f. in legislative assembly; A4, member's motions and ministers. *See* LAW OR MANDATE; LEGISLATURE

MOTIVE(S): (i) IX.25.A1, motives as subject matter for securities for app. apt.; A1, motives create interests; (ii) VI.31.A20&n, A21, pure and impure motives; (iii) other. VI.23.A16, A25, IX.26.A33. *See* INTEREST(S); PLEASURE AND PAIN

MOVABLE(S) AND IMMOVABLE(S): *See* IMMOVABLE(S) AND MOVABLE(S)


NAMES: *See* LANGUAGE

NATURE AND NATURAL: V.5.A5, natural v. factitious reward; VII.3, inalterable nature exposes one to sinister influence; 9, natural or acquired talents and scale of comparison; IX.4.A9, natural or simple; A9, simple or natural right created by absence of obligation; 15.A18–20, natural honour and reward; A44, naturally extravasated remuneration; A44, A46, natural v. artificial extravasated remuneration; 17.A47, natural talents and natural place; 19.A29, emolument considered natural accompaniment to grade and power in military service; 21.A1, human nature and suffering wrong in administrative dept.; 22.A5, history and human nature in English practice

NAVY MINISTER: IX.2.A1, serves under p.m.; 9.A7, joint visits in ex. of inspective f.; 16.A15, requisite talents for position; 19.A41, and power of dislocation. *See* MILITARY SERVICE; MINISTER(S); NAVY SUBDEPARTMENT

NAVY SUBDEPARTMENT: VI.27.A15, functionaries in field and powers of legislation enquiry judicatory; VIII.2.A9, A13, A14–16, ex. of imperative f. by p.m. as commander-in-chief; 11.A6–7, where publicity may be harmful; A15–17, and time limits on secrecy; IX.2.A10, potentially joined with army and preventive service subdepts.; A10n, navy courts martial and judiciary; 5.A40–1, number of functionaries in highest grades, English v. U.S. practice; 9.A4, offices to be visited in ex. of inspective f.; 11.A9, extraction of information for defence purposes; 16.A15, talent-requiring situations and requisite talents, examples given; 17.A18, minimum age for service as lowest grade of officer; A23, A27, need for temporarily initiative location; 20.A1, legislator to consider applicability of arrangements for obviation of insubordination, oppression and extortion to military branch of navy services; 21.A20, leg. to determine whether variation in rules of deportment are necessary for navy subdept. as indirectly-applying remedies against oppression; A27, military codes and repression of wrongs between functionaries; A49, use of dislocation instruments. *See* MILITARY SERVICE; NAVY MINISTER

NEWSPAPER(S): *See* PRESS


OATH: VI.2.A4, monarch's oath, contracts, and oppression; 27.A50, use of oath as security for verity in eliciting evidence; A50–1, House of Lords v. House of Commons in use of oath; VIIn, legislator's inaugural declaration, not an oath

OBLIGATION: *See* DUTY AND OBLIGATION

OCCURRENCES: IX.4.A12, fictitious entities designated occurrences; A13, states and motions, names of occurrences which are subject of registrative f.; A14, interior and exterior occurrences defined; A15, important and unimportant occurrences defined; A16, relevant and irrelevant occurrences defined; A17, relevant occurrences to be max., irrelevant min.; fs. regarding occurrences: A56, statistic; A57, registrative; A58, publicative; A59, officially informative or report making. *See* FUNCTION(S); STATISTIC FUNCTION

OFFICE(S): IX.26.A7, use of publicity and secrecy varies between office and office; A16, offices defined. *See* ARCHITECTURE

OFFICE CALENDAR: IX.16.A10, made and published by leg.; A10, contains an all-comprehensive list of positions; A11, general heads: situations of talent, situations of simple trust, situations of talent and trust; A12–14, defined and distinguished; 25.A8, convicted lists to be inserted in office calendar; A9, arrangements for new series of convicted lists. *See* LOCATION AND DISLOCATION

OFFICIALLY INFORMATIVE FUNCTION: IX.4.A59, ex. by ministers collectively in regard to persons, things, money, and occurrences; A59, defined; 10.A11, information of relevant occurrences to be furnished to leg. and p.m.; A12, exceptions made by leg. with regard to encumbrance and expense; A13, subordinate functionaries to supply information to ministers; A14, arrangements to offices other than a grade superior made by leg.; A15, officially informative f. and information-elicitive f.; A16–17, and information receptive f.; A17–19, presumption of receipt of information; A20, why distinct f. needed; A20, officially informative f. v. registrative f.; A21, officially informative f. ex. in every state; A22, no comprehensive system in English practice; A23, consequences stated; A24, special need for information from distant provinces; A25, deficiencies in English practice. *See* INFORMATION; INFORMATIVE FUNCTION

OMNICOMPETENCE: VI.1.A1, supreme leg. is omnicompetent. *See* LEGISLATURE

OPERATIVE: IV.A6, consists of legislative, administrative and judicial depts.; A6, operative v. constitutive

OPINATIVE FUNCTION: IX.21.A39, opinative v. imperative fs. *See* IMPERATIVE FUNCTION

OPPRESSION: VI.2.A4, justification of oppression and use of oath by monarch; 27.A27, oppression and non-attendance of deputies due to participation in elicitation process; A37, and secrecy in legislative enquiry judicatory; A56, aristocratical oppression in English practice; 31.A31, A33, oppression and pure monarchy; A34, oppression and pure aristocracy; VII.4, waste and corruption leading to oppression; 6, oppression and tax on judicial services; 12, oppressive power and temptation of leg. to encroach on subordinate authorities; IX.9.A3, complaints regarding oppression taken during ex. of inspective f.; 15.A7, oppression and expenditure of public funds; 20.A1, legislator to consider applicability of arrangements for obviation of oppression to military branch of army and navy services; A2, A21, securities for functionaries and non-functionaries regarding oppression; 21.A1, functionaries v. non-functionaries, and functionaries as subordinates, superordinates and coordinates—

all stand exposed to wrong by human agency; A2, insubordination v. quasi-insubordination v. oppression; A2, oppression and extortion, defined and distinguished; A4, oppressors and oppressees defined and distinguished; A5, suitor as oppressee, examples given; A6, inspectee as oppressee, examples given; A7, evidence-holder, as oppressee, examples given; A8, functionary as oppressee, examples given; A9, remedies for oppression non-functionary as oppressee; A9, generally-applying remedies v. specially applying remedies; specially applying remedies: A10, directly v. indirectly applying remedies; A11–19, directly applying remedies, cases given; A11–17, where oppressor is a functionary inferior to minister, minister may be special judge; A13–14, remedies listed; A15–16, power to invoke assistance of judge immediate of subdistrict, reasons given; A17, fs. of judges; A18, where oppressor is minister, p.m. to be special judge; A19, where p.m. is oppressor, legislation penal judicatory serves as special judicatory; A20, indirectly-applying remedies, listed; A21, rules of deportment analysed as rules of ethics; A22, where penal code applicable; A23, enforceability of rules; A24, and importance of system of judicial procedure; A25, English system of procedure contrasted; A26, rules of negative-effective benevolence, not enforceable with advantage in all states where procedure system aims at injustice; A27, military codes as codes of deportment; A28–31, English practice; A32, reasons for not inserting codes of good manners into constitutional code; A33, problem of adequate penal code in most nations; A34, remedies for oppression, functionary as oppressee, same remedies as for suitor; A35, remedies for abuse of ex. of directive f.; A36, remedies for abuse of dislocative f.: directly and indirectly applying; A36, with directly applying remedies judge has no power of relocation; A37, judicatory held in metropolis, reasons given; A38, exceptions to be established by leg.; A39, decrees, options open; A40, uses of decrees: as securities against oppression and opportunities to clear reputations; A41–2, functionary's ex. of fs. not impeded, as decrees are not obligatory acts; A43, minister to give effect to decrees or to transfer subordinate or superordinate; A44, simple dislocation of functionary, only by minister, p.m. or leg.; A45, only minister, p.m., or leg. may stop promotion of functionary; A46, only minister, p.m. and leg. to effect transfer without consent of functionary; A47, suspension may be effected by immediate or any other superordinate of functionary, reasons given; A48, dislocation instrument required for dislocation and modified dislocation as indirectly applying remedy against oppression; A49, exceptions; A50, dislocation instrument: headings for simple dislocation; A51–2, dislocation and resignation; A53, minutes of record of the decree to be attached to dislocation instrument; A54, application of dislocation instrument to suspension, heads of entries; A55–6, rules for time of suspension and renewal; A57, termination of suspension, causes listed; A58, minutes of record attached to instrument; A59, when dislocation or suspension warranted; A60, permanent transfer to not inferior grade, headings of entries; A61, temporary transfer, headings of entries; A62–3, discussed; A64, permanent transfer to inferior grade, headings of entry; A65, temporary transfer to inferior grade, headings of entry; A66, word 'transference' preferred to 'degradation'; A67, temporary transference to inferior grade as punishment; A68, definitive stoppage of promotion, headings of entry; A69, temporary stoppage of promotion, headings of entry; A70, publicity max. in all proceedings; A71, exceptions for secrecy in time of war; A72, leg. to determine when special appellate judge to invoke assistance of ordinary judge;

A73-6, arrangements for exemplars of records and instruments; A77, further considerations for leg. regarding extent of territory, distances from the metropolis, facility of communication, number of grades in subdepts.; 22.A2, extortion as 'predatory oppression'; A3, how extortion and oppression may be combined; 25.A47, peerage and oppression; A54, p.o. trib. in English practice checks oppression in spite of the law; A57, law and judiciary no security against oppression in English practice. *See* CORRUPTION; DEPREDATION; ENGLISH PRACTICE; EXTORTION; PECULATION; SECURITIES

OPULENCE: II.A16n, A23, opulence and pecuniary responsibility discussed; V.6.A2, opulence and defence against defamation; VI.23.A24-6, the opulent and deputy's substitutes; A54-5, effect on opulent of pecuniary punishment; VII.4, opulent and indigent and expense of gratification of tastes; 6, effect of tax on judicial services on rich and poor; 8, legislators not to add to opulence of state; 9, opulence and impartiality by legislators; VIII.11.A6, open voting in elections favours few and rich at expense of many; IX.16.A54, disgust of opulent at sight of indigent, grounds for clothing allowance for pupils; IX.17.A52, unopulence as cause of exertion and apt., discussed; A53, unopulent excluded by pecuniary competition system, discussed; A56, opulent have greater probability of depredation than unopulent; A56-68, reasons given; A59, apt. does not increase with increase in pay and opulence; 23.A12, wealth and exemption from suspicion of delinquency, denied; 25.A44, by opulence men rendered indolent; A46, opulence and motives for mental exertion. *See* FEW AND MANY

ORDINANCE(S): *See* LAW OR MANDATE; LEGISLATURE; MOTION(S)

PACKING: VI.27.A54, packed witnesses and packed judges in English practice; IX.16.A69n, packing juries, chance, and choice

PANNOMION: Title n, defined; Title n, constitutional code, first in importance in Pannomion; VI.29.A2, Pannomion and proposed emendative ordinances; A2n, Pannomion, Greek origin of term; A3-4, Pannomion and emendation in directive mode; A5, Pannomion and emendation in reeditive mode; IX.24. A4, A5, A7-9, ministers, leg., and improving and maintaining the Pannomion; 25.A39, Pannomion and ex. of extraordinary power. *See* CONSTITUTIONAL CODE

PANOPTICON: IX.26.A20n, prison system discussed

PARTY(IES): VI.31.A37, two competing parties in mixed monarchy; IX.10. A22, party in office and control of information in English practice

PATRONAGE: VI.23.A26, patronage and deputy's substitute, no corruption in this case; 25.A20, patronage as matter of corruption; VII.8, patronage, corruption, and dominion over other states; 12, patronage and encroachment by leg. on subordinate authorities; IX.16.A3, dislocative power a check to arbitrary patronage by p.m.; 17.A43, patronage and undue benefit avoided with pecuniary competition principle in situations of simple trust; A53, patronage, opulence, and corruptive influence; A54, competition system min. patronage and the relish for money; A55, liberality, venality, and patronage; 19.A36, patronage of superordinates in corrupt governments. *See* CORRUPTION

PECULATION: IX.15.A7, liberality and peculation; 20.A2, securities for functionaries and non-functionaries regarding peculation; 23.A1, peculation defined as indirect way of trustee obtaining undue pecuniary profit; A2, trust violated: private v. political; A2, political trust: public v. semi-public;

A3, direct modes of making undue profit, examples; A4, theft v. embezzlement; A6, prevention of peculation in ex. of procurative f.; A7, arrangements
to question minister's partiality and connections in ex. of procurative f.;
A8, but quality and cheapness are main considerations with regard to contracts; A9, with publicity, procurement from friends or relatives would be
a security against peculation; A10, grounds for interdiction of such contracts;
A11, limitations on remedies; A12, exemption from suspicion of delinquency
discussed; A13, in situations of trust, rules for receipt and disbursement of
money listed; A14, peculation, in the ex. of the procurative, reparative, eliminative, and venditive fs., more dangerous because easier than malpractice with
money; A15, sinister profit by peculation, examples given; A16, importance
of recordation, publication, and interrogation powers stressed as bar to peculation. *See* CORRUPTION; EXTORTION
PENAL CODE: V.6.A2, and defamation; A3–4, and free circulation of political
tracts; A4, and criminal evil consciousness; VI.19.A1, and extortion and corruption of legislators; IX.4.A9, and natural v. sanctional rights; 7.6th.A6,
and punishment for evil consciousness and negligence, in ex. of statistic f.;
15.A9, and arbitrarily conferred remuneration; 16.A78, and use of lottery;
17.A37, A39, A41, and mislocation; 20.A9, and disturbance by vexation;
21.A9, and generally-applying remedies against oppression; A22, and rules of
ethics; A33, and punishment for delinquency; 22.A4, and remedies against
extortion; 23.A5, and remedies against peculation; A12, and delinquency
PENSION(S): *See* REMUNERATION
PEOPLE, THE: *See* CONSTITUTIVE AUTHORITY
PERSON(S): VI.27.A12, personal v. real evidence; VIII.1.A3, persons and p.m.'s
logical field of service; A14, and rules for limiting secrecy; IX.4.A5, persons
v. things; A5, real entities comprised of persons and things; A6, fictitious persons v. fictitious things; A6, all fictitious entities comprised of fictitious persons and fictitious things; fs. regarding persons: A44, locative, self-suppletive,
directive, dislocative; A56, statistic; A57, registrative; A58, publicative; A59,
officially informative or report making; A61, melioration suggestive; 20.A21,
physical force against persons; 25.A1, persons and securities for app. apt. *See*
STATISTIC FUNCTION
PLEASURE(S) AND PAIN(S): II.A5, evil defined as pain and loss of pleasure;
A8, pain and pleasure in punishment; A10, pleasure as an end and means;
A21, pain and punitional responsibility; VII.4, minimum quantity of pain for
punishment; IX.17.A20, pain of humiliation, and pain of degradation in location; 25.A1, pleasures and pains as objects of desire and aversion and motives
for giving effect to securities; 26.A51, A52, monarch in pursuit of pleasure
and residence of functionaries. *See* GOOD AND EVIL
POLITICAL ECONOMY: IX.16.A15, subject of study for ministers and subordinates; 17.Con.Inst.A5, lectures by John MacCulloch
POPULATION: IX.16.A53, allowance for lodging or diet of pupils rejected as
producing population excess
PORTUGAL: II.A24, moral responsibility and England v. Portugal; VI.25.A53n,
and Bentham's earlier ideas on leg.
POWER(S): II.16, sovereign power and subordinate power; A16n, power as
matter of reward; A18, powers as fs. of functionaries; IV.A12, many-seatedness
and fractionized power; A14, power as remuneration for auxiliaries deputed
by self-suppletive f.; V.2.A1–6, powers of constitutive authority; 4.A1, power
of p.o. trib. is judicial; A4, p.o. trib. as check to pernicious ex. of power of

government; 6.A2, he who has power and defence against defamation; VI.1.
A1, power of supreme leg. is unlimited but checked by securities; A2, past
leg. has no power over current one; 2.A2, power of constitutive authority
diminished by anti-constitutional ordinances; 19.A1, power added to remuneration and inseparable from office of leg.; 20.A17, and non-attendance
of legislators in English practice; A17, power without obligation is despotism;
A18, and U.S. practice; 23.A1, deputy has power of location of substitute;
A22, power of deputy v. substitute; 25.A5, power and responsibility in
relocation; A20, A22, power and corruption; A46, appetite for power and undiscontinued relocability; A48, power of p.m.; A49, checks to his power;
A52, power and temporary non-relocability; 27.A2, power of leg. to elicit
evidence; A14-16, powers of legislation enquiry judicatory; A27, power of
location, exclusion from office, and legislation enquiry judicatory; A37,
power afforded by secrecy obviated; A44, powers of House of Commons regarding evidence; A49, power of p.o. trib. in English practice; A50, powers of
House of Commons v. judiciary in eliciting evidence; A54, powers of monarch
in eliciting evidence; A56, abuse of power in reports; 28.A7, power to create
vacancy in leg.; A11, power to redress wrongs; 31.A1, security against abuse
of power and app. moral apt.; A3, power of functionaries and greatest happiness principle; A5, arrangements for restraint and security against abuse of
power; A13-15, limitations on power not harmful to public service or individuals; A13, ample provision of power of public functionaries in code; A22-3,
greater a man's power, greater the propensity to abuse it; A31-3, securities
against abuse of power in pure monarchies; A34-5, securities against abuse of
power in pure aristocracies; A36-41&n, securities against abuse of power in
mixed monarchies; VIIn, power of moral sanction as ex. by p.o. trib.; VIIn,
power of legal sanction v. power of p.o. trib.; 3, appetite for power considered; 6, tax on judicial services and power; 7, power of legislators; 8, power
and justice in international relations; 9, power and impartiality; 11, the
people, only legitimate source of power; 12, appetite for oppressive power
and encroachment by leg. on subordinate authorities; 14, power and influence of legislators; VIII.2.A10-11, power and grades of defensive force;
A11n, power of president of U.S. as commander-in-chief; 4.A1, p.m. has
power of self-supply; A4, power of principal and power of depute; A9, power
passing between principal and depute; 6.A2, power of p.m. in relation to leg.;
11.A6, legal power and secret suffrage; A8, tutelary power of p.o. trib.,
always needed; IX.3.A10, scale of power and delinquency; A17, absolute
power of U.S. president over subordinates; A20, arbitrary power constituted
by exemption from control; 5.A4, modes of power necessary in subordination: direction, suspension, dislocation, punition, suppletion; A4, modes of
power incidentally useful in subordination: transferential and promotion-
stopping; A4, and corresponding functions; A22, power and money as part
of reward; 11.A6-9, power of extracting information; A10, inquisitorial
abuse of power; 15.A47, fractional masses of supreme power; 16.A3, dislocative power in number of hands divested of inducement to abuse of power;
A3, location system v. arbitrary power of patronage; A3, power of corruption
min. in location system; 17.A49, power as factor in the engagement of personal service; A53, powers of office converted to instrument of depredation;
A54, abuse of powers and pecuniary competition; 17.Con.Inst.A1, arbitrary
power in location before system established; 19.A5, power corresponding to
self-suppletive f.; A10, dislocative power and term of service of ministers;

581

A20, exercise of power and location by p.m.; A22, power of minister's depute to make choice in filling vacancies rejected; A23, power without obligation to repeat qualification examination; A28, scale of directive power and promotion; A29, distribution of power in military v. non-military situations; A29, power as inducement to time and labour; A31, arbitrary power and Russian code; A35, power of unrestrained choice and app. apt.; A36, power converted to poison in corrupt government; A38, power of extra-remuneration, benefit to superordinate; 20.A25, for non-compliance of subordinate, powers of superordinate listed. 21.A2, oppression and power; A4, abuse of power, positive and negative; A13, power and obligation of judges regarding oppression; A15, power to invoke special judges; A16, evidence-elicitation power; A29, power of lawyers at expense of community; A35, abuse of directive power and oppression; A36, abuse of power in ex. of dislocative f. and oppression; A36, power of relocation not imperative; 22.A1, official power and extortion; 23.A12, abuse of power and exemption from suspicion of delinquency; 25.A1, misuse v. non-use of official powers; A26, power: self-suppletive, suppletive, locative, dislocative, and suspensive, and responsibility for subordinates; A30, subjection to the power of p.o. trib.; A32, subjection to power of legal tribunals; A33, securing responsible and excluding irresponsible ex. of power; A35, delegation of power to ministers by leg. in emergencies prohibited; A36, functionaries and ex. of extraordinary powers; A38, abuse of power in ex. of extraordinary power in mixed monarchy; A39–41, dispensing power discussed; A43, power of legislation and following precedents; A48, power-holding class in representative democracy v. aristocracy ridden monarchy; A53, support to power howsoever exercised in English practice; 26.A36, interest corresponding to love of power. *See* AUTHORITY(IES); FUNCTION(S)

PREAPPOINTED EVIDENCE: *See* EVIDENCE

PRECEDENT(S): IX.25.A43–9, evils of following precedents discussed

PREINTERPRETATIVE FUNCTION: IX.24.A7, leg. to determine which functionaries under minister to ex. the preinterpretative f. with reference to Pannomion

PRESS, THE: VI.20.A5, publication of absences of legislators in government newspaper; 25.A50, efficiency of p.o. trib. depends on liberty of the press; IX.17.A51, the press and gaining a reputation by intellectual labour; 25.A29, periodical press as medium of p.o. trib. for enquiry into lack of vigilance by superordinate for subordinate; A30, use of press to comment on apt. of functionaries. *See* PUBLIC OPINION TRIBUNAL

PREVENTIVE SERVICE MINISTER: IX.2.A1, serves under p.m.; 9.A7, joint visits and ex. of inspective f.; 26.A47, ex. of directive f. over military guard in protection of public property. *See* MINISTER(S); PREVENTIVE SERVICE SUBDEPARTMENT

PREVENTIVE SERVICE SUBDEPARTMENT: VIII.11.A6–7, and evils of publicity; IX.2.A10, potentially joined with army and navy subdepts.; 9.A4, offices to be visited in ex. of inspective f. *See* PREVENTIVE SERVICE MINISTER

PRICE(S): IX.17.A45, general opinion that prices of labour and commodities in general should be min. through competition, in English practice; A46, application by rulers of competition principle to price of their own labour

PRIME MINISTER: IV.A13, one p.m. in state; V.2.A3n, deputy of p.m. called prime minister depute; A5, p.m. dislocable by constitutive authority;

VI.25.A19, p.m., corruption and undiscontinued relocability; A48, continuity of p.m., as security against corruption; A49, and other securities; 28.A1, subject to trial by legislation penal judicatory; A8, and impartial trial by legislation penal judicatory; 31.A1, and all pervading system of securities; A42, and securities for app. apt. of leg.; VII.7, p.m. and impartial election by leg.; VIII.1.A1, local field of service of p.m. coextensive with leg.; A2, p.m.'s logical field of service v. justice minister; A3, p.m.'s logical field of service defined; A4, applied to minister; A5-10, use of term 'prime minister' justified; A7, Spanish 'gefe politico' v. 'prime minister'; A8-10, U.S. 'president' v. 'prime minister'; 2.A1, fs. of p.m.: executive f.; A2, directive f.; A3-4, locative f.; A5-7, dislocative f.; A8-15, imperative f., ex. by p.m. in relation to defensive force; A16, arrangements for redress by functionaries due to ex. of fs.; 3.A1-2, communication between p.m. and leg. by message only, unless invited or ordered by leg. to appear personally; A3-4, fs. ex. by p.m. in sending messages to leg.: informative f.; A5, indicative; A6-7, initiative f.; A8, p.m. responsible for neglect of fs.; A9, usual communication through minister rather than by message; A10, statistic f.; [4.A1-11, See SELF-SUPPLETIVE FUNCTION]; 5.A1, term of service of p.m.; A2, re-eligibility; A3, arrangements for election; A4, arrangements, if no election; 6.A1, remuneration of p.m. stated; A2, power of p.m. in relation to leg.; 7.A1, eligibility for location as p.m.; A2, monarchs or relations of monarchs excluded; A3, residency requirements; 8.A1, elected by leg.; A2, arrangements for elections; A2-4, secret and open voting employed; A5, reaching a majority; A6, secret and open voting discussed; 9.A1, p.m. dislocable by leg.; A2, and constitutive authority; A3, grounds for dislocation, same as for leg.; 10.A1&n-2, p.m. and use of manifold writing mode in registration system; A3-4, saving expense and security against falsification; A7, arrangements for preservation and periodic destruction of documents; 11.A15, p.m.'s report to leg. on need for secrecy; A16, committee of leg. to report, as check; A17, preventing unintentional disclosure; A18, new members in leg. and prevention of concealment; [12.A1-4, See SECURITIES] IX.2.A1, ministers serving under p.m. enumerated; A8, allotment of ministers to subdepts.; A9, no power without concurrence of leg. to separate subdepts. and to add additional ministers; 7.4th. A28, p.m. to secure from ministers, entries in loss books; 10.A11-12, information of all relevant occurrences furnished to leg. and p.m.; 15.A35, p.m. conferring factitious dignity could subvert constitution; 16.A3, location by single person, p.m.; A3, legal and moral responsibility for choice rests with p.m.; A18, p.m. and other ministers, judges in qualification judicatory; A42, under direction of p.m., advertisement for instructors; 17.A1, pecuniary competition process, p.m. to advertise for offers; A21, A31, p.m. as confirmative locator; A32, reasons to be given for substitution of another locable; 18.A4, every minister at all times dislocable by p.m.; 19.A16, p.m. to ex. consummative f. in location of subordinates; A18-19, securities in filling vacancies; A19, securities against dislocation by p.m.; 21.A18, p.m. may be special judge where minister is alleged oppressor; A19, provision for case where p.m. is oppressor; A38, p.m. and dislocation judicatory; A44, p.m. and simple dislocation of functionaries subordinate to ministers; A45, and promotion of functionaries; A46, and transfer of functionaries; 24.A5, p.m. and receipt of reports designed to prevent deterioration of Pannomion; 25.A1, p.m. as person to whom securities apply; A2, leg. to decide which securities applicable to p.m. are applicable to ministers; A3, relevant securities listed;

A20, p.m. to receive exemplars of remuneration draft; A22, p.m. to receive non-payment complaint if failure to pay remuneration for extra despatch; 26.A17, ministers' offices arranged in crescent shape with p.m.'s office at centre. *See* CONSTITUTIVE AUTHORITY; LEGISLATURE; MINISTER(S); PUBLICATION SYSTEM; PUBLIC OPINION TRIBUNAL; REGISTRATION SYSTEM; SECURITIES

PRINCIPLE(S): (i) Greatest Happiness Principle: II.A1, A8–9, A11, A12, A14, V.4.A4, 5.A6, VI.31.A3, IX.17.A43, A47, 20.A11, 25.A43 (ii) Other: II.A2, official apt. max. principle, expense min. principle; A17, public examination principle, pecuniary competition principle, responsible location principle; VI.31.A2, confidence min. principle, control max. principle; VIII.11.A3, principles regarding publicity; IX.3.A34, self-judication principle in English practice; 7.4th.A24, individual responsibility principle; 15.A1, leading principles of code regarding remuneration: apt. max., expense min.; A29, factitious dignity contrary to principles of constitution; 16.A9, principles of location system; 17.A39, disappointment preventing principle; A42–59, pecuniary competition principle discussed; A45, competition principle; A53, frugality-maximizing principle; 19.A11, principles of official attendance; A15, principles of location system; 26.A15, juxtaposition principle; A15n, superposition principle. *See* HAPPINESS; RULE(S)

PROCEDURE: IX.16.A20, A21, mode of procedure of qualification judicatory; 20.A20, use of judicial procedure and min. of evil; 21.A20, arbitrary v. judicially grounded procedure; A24, enforceability of rules and importance of system of judicial procedure; A25, English system contrasted; A26, rules of negative-effective benevolence, not enforceable with advantage in states where procedure system aims at injustice; 25.A50–8, arbitrary administrative procedure and English practice, preference of military model. *See* EVIDENCE; PROCEDURE CODE

PROCEDURE CODE: V.5.A6, and amendments; VI.23.A31, and excuses for non-attendance at leg.; 27.A11, A15, A17, A19–20, IX.10.A8, and evidence elicitation; IX.4.A9, and rights; 10.A2, and mendacity licence; 20.A5, A22, and evidence-holders; 21.A20, A25, and judicial procedure; A54, and future communication securing arrangements; 23.A7, and questions addressed to ministers; 25.A17, and quasi-judicial assertion; A58, and judicial and military procedure

PROCURATION MANDATE: *See* PROCUREMENT MANDATE

PROCURATIVE FUNCTION: IX.4.A45, ex. by ministers collectively in regard to things; A45, defined; A45, procurative v. locative fs.; A46, fs. corresponding to submodes of procurement: emptive, conductive, fabricative, requisitive, transreceptive, transmissive, retroacceptive, retrotransmissive; A47, preceded by ex. of requisitive f.; A53, retroacceptive and retrotransmissive fs., and mercede locative f.; 7.2nd.A24, uses of mimographical or receptacular mode of registration and ex. of procurative f.; 8.A28, modes of procurement, competing forms, examples given; 19.A32, government fabrication and use of permanent v. temporary functionaries, leg. to decide; A33, examples given; A34, fabricative f., custoditive f., and reparative f., permanent v. temporary employees; 23.A6–12, A14, prevention of peculation in ex. of procurative f. *See* PROCUREMENT MANDATE(S)

PROCUREMENT: *See* PROCURATIVE FUNCTION; PROCUREMENT MANDATE(S)

PROCUREMENT MANDATE(S): IX.4.A47, and procurative f.; 8.A1, defined and called procuration mandate; A2–3, issued by leg. alone, unless delegated to p.m. or ministers; A13, issued by requisitee when confirming requisition instrument; A15, transmitted to requisitor either directly or through finance minister; A22, where issued, exemplars to all intermediate offices. *See* PRO-CURATIVE FUNCTION; REQUISITIVE FUNCTION

PROFIT(S): (i) Sinister profit: V.6.A2, IX.10.A25, 17.A54, 23.A14–15, 25.A26–9 (ii) Oppression for profit is extortion: IX.21.A2, 22.A2 (iii) Profit from expense: VI.27.A48, IX.3.A23, 4.A70, 25.A58 (iv) Profit from wrongs or undue profit: IX.17.A41, 23.A1, A3 (v) Other: IX.17.A53, 21.A6. *See* INTEREST(S)

PROMOTION: VIII.2.A4, promotion, defined as location; A11, p.m. and promotion in army subdept.; A13, and navy subdept.; A14, authenticating instruments; A15, use of manifold writing system; A16, arrangements for redress; IX.4.A44, promotion is bis-submode of location; 18.A2, promotion as mode of modified dislocation; 19.A21, A28, promotion, not to be used in filling vacancies; 20.A25, stopping promotion and non-compliance of subordinate with direction of superordinate; 21.A45, only minister, p.m., or leg. may stop promotion of functionary; A68, application of dislocation instrument to definitive stoppage of promotion, headings of entry; A69, temporary stoppage of promotion, headings of entry; A73, A76, arrangements for exemplars of record and instruments. *See* LOCATION AND DISLOCATION; SUBORDI-NATE(S) AND SUPERORDINATE(S); SUSPENSION; TRANSFER

PRUDENCE: VII.8, false honour and dignity at expense of self-regarding prudence; IX.21.A21, A26, self-regarding prudence v. extra-regarding prudence and rules of deportment; 25.A28, ordinary prudence and presumption of culpable deficiency of ministers. *See* DEPORTMENT

PUBLIC AND PRIVATE: VI.27.A29, public and private edifices used for legislation enquiries; 31.A16, public and private evil; VII.4, public and private occupations; IX.9.A4, A10, inspective f. and public and private business; IX.20.A10–13, public inspection of private institutions; 21.A1, private and public wrong; A32, private and political deontology; 26.A21, public and private waiting-boxes. *See* PECULATION; PUBLICATION SYSTEM; PUBLI-CATIVE FUNCTION; PUBLICITY AND SECRECY; PUBLIC OPINION TRIBUNAL

PUBLICATION SYSTEM: VI.31.A44, and securities for app. intellectual apt. in leg.; VIII.11.A1, publication system defined; A2, publicity max. in all depts. and offices; A3, exception for expense; A4, value of publicity discussed; A5, exception where publicity is an evil; A6–7, examples given; A8, time limit to secrecy; A9, no limits to publicity except expense and temporary evil; A10, no limits to good of publicity; A11, internal v. external publication; A12, manifold writing v. printing press; A13, importance of registration system to internal and external publication; A14, rules for limiting secrecy; A15, limitations on time of secrecy; A15, p.m. to make annual report to leg.; A16, legislative committees to report as check; A17, preventing unintentional disclosure; A18, new members in leg. and prevention of concealment; 12.A1, publication system and security for app. apt. of p.m.; IX.9.A3, ex. of inspective f. and publication system; 25.A3, as security for app. apt. of ministers; 26.A43, as security against loss of manuscripts in treasury. *See* PUBLICATIVE FUNC-TION; PUBLICITY AND SECRECY; REGISTRATION SYSTEM

PUBLICATIVE FUNCTION: IX.4.A13, follows ex. of registrative f.; A58, ex. by ministers collectively in regard to persons, things, money, and occurrences;

A58, defined. *See* PUBLICATION SYSTEM; PUBLICITY AND SECRECY; REGISTRATION SYSTEM; REGISTRATIVE FUNCTION

PUBLICITY AND SECRECY: VI.20.A5, publication of absences of legislators; 21.A1, sittings of leg. are public, and p.o. trib. reports to constitutive authority; A3, arrangements for secret sittings; A4-5, disclosure by subsequent legs.; 27.A29, A35, max. of publicity in enquiries; A36, and employment of judge as legislational elicitor; A37, secrecy and size of judicatory; A55, secrecy and monarch's commissions in English practice; 28.A1, trial by legislation penal judicatory where dislocation with publicity not considered sufficient punishment; A4, judges appointed by secret ballot; VI.31.A42, publicity and securities for app. apt. of legislators; VII.11, secrecy in legislative proceedings discussed; VIII.11.A2, publicity max. in all depts. and offices; A3, exception for expense; A4, value of publicity discussed; A5, exception where publicity is an evil; A6-7, examples given; A8, time limit to secrecy; A9, no limits to publicity except expense and temporary evil; A10, no limits to good of publicity; A14, rules for limiting secrecy; A15, limitation on time of secrecy; A15, p.m. to make annual report to leg.; A16, legislative committee to report as check; A17, preventing unintentional disclosure; A18, new members in leg. and prevention of concealment; 12.A1, publicity and secrecy and security for app. apt. of p.m.; A3, secrecy of identity of informant of misconduct and inaptitude of ministers; IX.9.A10, light of publicity difficult to shine on establishments under private management; 16.A3, publicity and provision for moral apt. in location system; A20, publicity max. in qualification judicatory for entry on locable list; 20.A12, secret institutions in representative democracy and tyranny; 21.A10, A20, and indirectly applying remedies against oppression; A16, and directly applying remedies against oppression; A70, publicity max. in proceedings for dislocation; A71, exceptions for secrecy as in time of war; 23.A13, recordation and publicity in receipt and disbursement of money; A16, publicity and avoidance of peculation; 25.A16, recordation and publicity in quasi-judicial assertion; A23, importance of publicity in administrative dept.; A24, leg. to make arrangements for secrecy in extra despatch where necessary, as in war; A32, provision for secrecy in proceedings relating to inaptitude of functionaries; 26.A4, architectural arrangements to serve purposes of publicity and secrecy; A4, publicity of greater utility than secrecy; A5, A6, subjects for consideration in choosing publicity or secrecy; A7, varying demands for publicity and secrecy as between depts., subdepts., and offices; A8, A9, greatest use and extent of secrecy required in constitutive dept. in secret ballot; A10, greatest publicity needed in judiciary dept.; A11, administrative dept. is intermediate between constitutive and judiciary depts.; A12, uses of publicity and secrecy and architectural arrangements; A22, use of waiting-boxes to augment publicity; A32-7, secret meetings between suitors and ministers, motives and reasons. *See* ARCHITECTURE; INSPECTIVE FUNCTION; PUBLICATIVE FUNCTION; REGISTRATION SYSTEM; REGISTRATIVE FUNCTION

PUBLIC MERIT REGISTER (or EXTRAORDINARY SERVICE REGISTER): IX.15.A22, for recordation of judicially recognized extraordinary public service; A23, entry to be concluded with opinative and imperative decrees; A24, suit for entry in register, how initiated; A25, suit may be initiated for another, with or without consent; 25.A5, official merit register, as instrument of security for app. apt.

PUBLIC OPINION TRIBUNAL: II.A20, moral sanction, p.o. trib. and responsibility; A24, moral responsibility, p.o. trib. and English government; V.4.A1, p.o. trib., essential authority in constitution; A1, power basically judicial; A2, composition of p.o. trib.; A3, committees of p.o. trib., examples given; A4, p.o. trib., as a system of law v. English common law; A4, public opinion and greatest happiness principle; 5, fs. of p.o. trib.: A1, statistic f.; A2, censorial f.; A3, executive f.; A4, melioration suggestive f.; A5, moral v. legal obligation for functionaries and non-functionaries to ex. statistic f.; A6, the formulation · of amendments to law, headings given; A7, amendments and the preservation of symmetry; A8, reasons to be given for proposing amendments; A9, p.o. trib. and securities for good conduct of judiciary dept.; 6.A1, all members of human species have right to ex. statistic, executive, and melioration-suggestive fs.; A2, and censorial f.; A2, defamation discussed; A3, prohibition or taxation of political tracts by leg. is anti-constitutional and breach of trust; A4, defamation and free circulation of political tracts; A5, suppression of truth hostile to greatest number; VI.20.A17, p.o. trib. softens the rigor of despotism in English practice; 21.A1, sittings of leg. are public, and p.o. trib. reports to constitutive authority; A2, access of p.o. trib. to sittings max.; 23.A9, p.o. trib. and absentation from leg. and corruption; 25.A50, p.o. trib., moral apt. and liberty of press discussed; A53, p.o. trib. and temporary non-relocability v. undiscontinued relocability; 27.A37, p.o. trib. and securities against oppression where secrecy necessary in legislation enquiry judicatory; A38, p.o. trib. to max. efficiency of securities applicable to legislation enquiry judicatory; A49, power of p.o. trib. hatched under wings of House of Commons; A56, p.o. trib. and reports in English practice; 31.A32–3, p.o. trib. and security against abuse of power in pure monarchies; A35, in pure aristocracy; A37, power of p.o. trib. in mixed monarchies; A43, p.o. trib. and securities for app. moral apt. in leg.; VIIn, chief use of legislator's inaugural declaration to subject leg. to p.o. trib.; VIII.8.A6, influence of p.o. trib. and open voting; 11.A4, A8, p.o. trib. and the value of publicity; 12.A1, p.o. trib. ex. statistic, censorial, and melioration-suggestive fs. as security for app. apt. of p.m.; IX.3.A15, p.o. trib. as substitute for control by many-seated functionaries; A24, A27, influence diminished with many-seated system as in England; A25, single-seatedness and p.o. trib.; 7.1st.A20, statistic f. provides matter for p.o. trib.; A20, censure by p.o. trib. where legal punishment not warranted; 4th.A10, p.o. trib. and detection of fraud; A29, to judge veracity of entries in loss books; 6th.A5, use of abbreviations and comprehension by p.o. trib.; A5, use of abbreviations to elude scrutiny of p.o. trib.; IX.10.A23, absence of information and control by p.o. trib. impossible; 15.A19, A34, natural honour rendered by p.o. trib. for extraordinary service; A34, p.o. trib. cannot be corrupt; 16.A3, p.m. morally restricted by p.o. trib. in choice of candidates in location system; 17.A32, p.o. trib. and p.m.'s substitution of locables; 17.Con.Inst.A1, p.o. trib. to urge adoption of system of instruction for location system; A1, resistance to be expected from ministers to protect interests; A2, fallacies to be employed by government to prevent introduction of instruction system; A3, patriotism and frugality to be used by government to exclude foreign instructors; A4–5, for public good, functionaries must quit situations where system is introduced, or acquire instruction; 19.A14, p.o. trib. and increased remuneration for longevity; A20, importance of filling vacancies and responsibility to p.o. trib.; A25, repetition of qualification examination and influence of p.o. trib.; A36, p.o. trib. and succession in corrupt governments; 20.A18, p.o. trib. and execution of moral sanctions for compliance of non-functionaries to rules of deportment; 21.A10, p.o. trib. and indirectly applying remedies against oppression; A37, p.o. trib., where present at judicatory, best security against abuse; 25.A1, p.o. trib. and ex. of moral sanction, as security for app. apt.; A3, ex. of statistic, censorial, and melioration-suggestive fs. by p.o. trib. as security for app. apt.; A12, inspectors as members of p.o. trib. and visitor's deportment rules; A29, role of p.o. trib. where minister's vigilance of culpable deficiency of subordinate is lacking; A30-1, power of p.o. trib. over public functionaries, as security; A49, and acting on basis of precedent; A54, importance of p.o. trib. in English practice in providing security against arbitrary procedures in administrative dept.; 26.A20n, Panopticon, inspection, and p.o. trib. *See* CONSTITUTIVE AUTHORITY; PUBLICITY AND SECRECY

PUNIFACTIVE (OR PUNITIVE) FUNCTION: V.2.A2, ex. by constitutive authority; 3.A7-10, how ex. by constitutive authority; VI.2.A2, ex. by electors when leg. passes anti-constitutional ordinance; A8, ex. by constitutive authority where breach of faith over contracts; IX.5.A4, punifactive or punitive f., ex. in scale of subordination; A5, superordinate must have power to ex. to certain extent. *See* CONSTITUTIVE AUTHORITY; GOVERNMENT ADVOCATE GENERAL; LEGISLATION PENAL JUDICATORY; REWARD AND PUNISHMENT

PUNISHMENT: *See* REWARD AND PUNISHMENT
PUNITION: *See* REWARD AND PUNISHMENT
PUNITIVE FUNCTION: *See* PUNIFACTIVE FUNCTION

QUALIFICATION JUDICATORY: *See* LOCATION AND DISLOCATION
QUASI-JUDICIAL: IX.25.A16, quasi-judicial assertion to establish extra-despatch for special remuneration; A17, defined
QUASI-JURYMEN: IX.16.A18, members of qualification judicatory for entry on locable list; A28-9, voting by quasi-jurymen, secret mode only; A29, as quasi-jurymen serve as instructors, each has interest in highest rank for his pupils; A73, and use of lot in selection. *See* LOCATION AND DISLOCATION

RATIOCINATIVE FUNCTION: IX.12.A3, included in melioration suggestive f.; A3, called reason-giving f.; A3, how ex.
REAL: *See* ENTITIES; EVIDENCE
RECEPTIVE FUNCTION: IX.23.A14, peculation v. embezzlement in ex. of receptive f.
RECORDATION: *See* REGISTRATION SYSTEM; REGISTRATIVE FUNCTION
REDUNDANCY: VI.27.A18, A44, non-redundancy, desirable characteristic of evidence. *See* EVIDENCE; MANDATES; WRITTEN INSTRUMENTS
REEDITIVE MODE: VI.29.A5-6, emendation in reeditive mode explained; IX.25.A1n, corrective v. reeditive modes. *See* DIRECTIVE MODE
REELECTION: *See* RELOCATION
REFORM (IMPROVEMENT): VI.24.A9, and continuation committee; 25.A4, and relocation; 27.A43, A53, and English practice; IX.25.A49, acting on precedent as bar to reform
REGISTRAR(S): IX.5.A43, an indispensable subordinate; 11.A3, reception and communication of information, performed by one man; 16.A38-41, results of votation process published by registrar
REGISTRATION SYSTEM: VI.27.A8, and examples of preappointed evidence:

31.A44, and securities for app. intellectual apt. in leg.; VIII.10.A1&n, A2, p.m. and use of manifold mode in registration system; A3–4, saving expense and security against falsification; A5, use in judiciary authority; A6, as security against destruction of judicial documents; A7, arrangements for preservation and periodic destruction of documents; 11.A9, no limits to publicity except expense and need for secrecy and registration system; A13, importance of registration system to publication system; 12.A1, registration system as security for app. apt. of p.m.; IX.9.A3, ex. of inspective f. to secure working of registration system; 21.A21, registration and indirectly applying remedies against oppression; 23.A13, recordation and publicity in receipt and disbursement of money; A16, recordation and avoidance of peculation; 25.A3, as security for app. apt. of ministers; A16, recordation and publicity in quasi-judicial assertions; 26.A43, as security against loss of manuscripts in treasury. *See* MANIFOLD WRITING MODE; PUBLICATION SYSTEM; PUBLICITY AND SECRECY; REGISTRATIVE FUNCTION

REGISTRATIVE FUNCTION (RECORDATIVE FUNCTION): IX.4.A13, registrative f. composed of minutative, conservative fs. and, with exceptions, followed by publicative f.; A57, ex. by ministers with regard to persons, things, money, and occurrences; A57, also named recordative f.; A57, defined; A57, and statistic f. *See* PUBLICATION SYSTEM; PUBLICATIVE FUNCTION; PUBLICITY AND SECRECY; REGISTRATION SYSTEM; STATISTIC FUNCTION

RELEVANT AND IRRELEVANT: IX.4.A16, occurrences subject to registrative f.; A16, defined; A17, subdepts. to max. number and value of relevant occurrences; A17, distinction especially applicable to ex. of statistic and registrative fs.; A19, and written instruments. *See* OCCURRENCES

RELIGION: IX.11.A11, no obligation to furnish information on religion

RELOCATION: IV.A2, relocation of leg. as reward by constitutive authority; VI.25.A1, no relocation of deputies unless number of former deputies reach certain number; A2, ascertained by legislation minister; A3, relocation procedure and continuation committee; A4, competition for office is essential for improvement; A5, essential for avoiding power without responsibility; A6, examples of elections without competition: joint proprietors of funds; A7, East India Company; A7, Bank of England; A8, City of London Common Council; A9, U.S. practice; A10, French practice; A11, English House of Commons; A12–13, two candidates required for effective choice; discontinued relocability, reasons given: (i) A14, evil prevented (ii) A15, continuity provided by continuation committee (iii) A16, no disappointment for legislators; (iv) A17, prevention of inaptitude; (v) A18, prevention of inaptitude by avoiding effective possession of office for life; (vi) A19–27, prevention of moral inaptitude and corruption; A28–9, rule of min. time of contact to deal with corruption; A30, application to judiciary; A31, rule not yet applied in any country; A32, utility of experience considered; A32, A34, A35, experience v. apt.; A33, app. apt. secured through continuation committee; A36, experience of electors considered; A37, why not perpetual non-relocability; A38–9, period of non-relocability discussed; A40–41, opportunities for temporarily dislocated deputies; A42–5, app. apt. and period of founding new states discussed; A46, undiscontinued relocability a greater risk than temporarily discontinued locability; A47, example of English rump parliament considered; A48, corruption excluded by continuity of executive; A49, other securities discussed; A50, moral apt., p.o. trib., and liberty of the press discussed; A50, U.S. practice; A51, English practice; A52, objections to temporary non-relocability system discussed: lack of freedom of choice, unmerited suffering by legislators, power too slight to attract candidates; A53, temporary non-relocability system with continuation compared with undiscontinued relocability: competition, experience and new men, watchmen outside leg., supply of experienced men for sublegs. and other government offices; A54-5, relevance of securities relating to attendance and remuneration discussed; 31.A42, relocation and securities for app. apt. of legislators; VIII.2.A16, p.m., not judicatory, to determine relocation after successful appeal against dislocation; 5.A2, re-eligibility of p.m. *See* LOCATION AND DISLOCATION

REMEDY(IES): IX.21.A9, remedies for oppression, oppressee a non-functionary; A9, generally-applying v. specially applying; A10, specially applying: directly applying v. indirectly applying; A11-19, directly applying remedies, cases given; A20, indirectly-applying remedies listed; A34, remedies where oppressee a functionary; A35, remedies for abuse of directive power; A36, remedies for abuse of dislocative power; A48, dislocation instrument as indirectly applying remedy; 22.A4, remedies for extortion; 23.A5, remedies for peculation; A10-11, limitations on remedies; 26.A34, punifactive, satisfactive, suppressive, and preventive remedies. *See* JUDICIARY AUTHORITY; OPPRESSION; PENAL CODE; REWARD AND PUNISHMENT

REMUNERATION: II.A16n, remuneration no basis for responsibility; IV.A14, self-suppletive f. and remuneration; VI.19.A1, remuneration of legislators stated; 20.A2, arrangements in assembly chamber for remuneration; A4, remuneration for days attended only; A8, withholding remuneration for non-attendance as punishment; A10, remuneration by day discussed; 25.A54-5, effect of pecuniary punishment for non-attendance in leg. discussed in light of other securities; 31.A43, remuneration and securities for app. moral apt. of legislators; VII.4, official pay, waste, and corruption discussed; VIII.6.A1, remuneration of p.m. stated; IX.5.A22, superordinateness does not merit increase in pay; 9.A3, extra remuneration and ex. of inspective f.; 15.A1, leading principles of code regarding remuneration: apt. max., expense min.; A3, min. of expense, a means to max. of apt.; A3, the smaller the remuneration, the greater the relish for the office; A3, even greater, if individual pays for the office; A4, large remuneration leads to decrease in apt.; A5, min. of expense, both end and means; A6, rule for remuneration: competition by those possessing app. apt. for smallest remuneration; A7, liberality ex. by public functionaries is waste; A8-10, A45, arbitrary remuneration repugnant to constitution; A11, public service as basis of reward; A12, ordinary v. extraordinary service to public; A13, ordinary service defined; A14, extraordinary service defined; A15, pecuniary v. honorary reward; A16-17, both may be demanded from judicatory for extraordinary service; A18, reward for natural honour augmented only; A19, natural honour spontaneously renewed by p.o. trib. for extraordinary service; A20, A23, natural honour judicially augmented by opinative and imperative decrees; A21-2, recorded and published in public merit register; A24-7, suit for entry in public merit register; A28, publication as arranged by leg.; A29, factitious honour contrary to principles of constitution; A30, instruments for conferring factitious dignity: titles of honour and ensigns of dignity; A31-3, examples given; A34, factitious dignity unsuitable, even if judicially conferred; A35, arbitrary conferring of factitious dignity, sufficient to destroy constitution; A36, ultra-concomitant remuneration repugnant to constitution; A36, defined; A37, all ultra-remuneration unjustifiable; A38, modes of ultra-concomitant remuneration, examples given; A39, artificially mislocated remuneration, repugnant to constitution; A40, defined; A41-3, mislocated *in toto* v. extravasated, defined and distinguished; A44, naturally extravasated remuneration distinguished; A45, reward mislocated *in toto*, examples given; A45, excluded from code; A46, reward artificially extravasated, examples given; A47, especially repugnant when combined with factitious dignity; A48, exemplified in hereditary titles of honour; A49, extraordinary service analogous to ordinary service, remuneration given; A50, defined; A51, examples given; A53, judicially conferred; A52, judge to guard against fraud; A54, minister's pay stated; A54, standard for pecuniary competition; A55, all ministers' remuneration the same; A56, pay not increased if minister allotted to more than one subdept.; A57, indemnification of expenses for inspection visits; 16.A48, remuneration of instructors, and motives for exertion; A49-50, extra-remuneration, when necessary, examples; A49, and other motives for exertion; A51-2, leg. to regulate extra-remuneration of instructors: not to be larger than that received for subsistence by lowest-paid class of labourers; A53, no allowance for lodging and diet of pupils; A54, disgust of opulent at sight of indigent, grounds for clothing allowance; 19.A12, no increase in remuneration for continuance in office, reasons given; A13, nor for length of service in official establishment; A14, nor for longevity, reasons given; A29, A30, A31, emolument, power and grade, correspondence in military v. non-military service; A31, max. of reward can lead to max. of corruption; A35-8, augmentation of remuneration in corrupt v. ordinarily meritorious service; A39, extra-merit, only basis of extra-remuneration; 25.A13-25, remuneration for extra-despatch. *See* ARBITRARINESS; DESPATCH; LOCATION AND DISLOCATION; REWARD AND PUNISHMENT

REMUNERATION DRAFT: *See* DESPATCH

REPARATIVE FUNCTION: IX.4.A50, ex. by ministers collectively in regard to things; A50, defined; 19.A34, ex. of reparative f. by permanent v. temporary functionaries; 23.A14, peculation and ex. of reparative f.

REPRESENTATIVE: *See* DEPUTY

REPRESENTATIVE DEMOCRACY: VI.25.A46, subversion of by undiscontinued relocability; 31.A25-6, most favourable to use of securities for app. apt.; VIII.5.A4, representative democracy changed to monarchy and aristocracy where leg. fails to elect p.m.; 11.A6, democracy changed to aristocracy by publicity given to secret voting; IX.5.A15, necessary distinctions in foreign relations grades in representative democracy; 20.A12, and secret institutions; 25.A48, power-holding class in representative democracy v. aristocracy-ridden monarchy; 26.A40, representative democracy v. monarchy in expense in moving from place to place; A46-7, even a republic requires military guard to protect buildings and contents from popular commotion

REPUTATION: II.A16n, as reward; V.6.A2, and defamation; VI.25.A20, and matter of corruption; VII.9, and impartiality of legislators; IX.16.A3, of p.m. and improper choice in location; 17.A49, factor in the engagement of personal service; A51, reputation and opportunities for timid merit; 21.A40, dislocation judicatory and opportunity to clear reputation. *See* CORRUPTION; LOCATION AND DISLOCATION; REWARD AND PUNISHMENT

REQUISITIVE FUNCTION: IX.4.A47, precedes ex. of procurative f.; 8.A1, procurement mandate, necessary to ex. of f.; A2-3, leg. to issue or delegate to p.m. or ministers power to issue; A4, when requisitive f. ex. without authority, expense is equivalent to imposition of a tax; A5, requisitive f., preparatory to ex. of procurative f.; A6, requisitive f. ex. where no procurement mandate in force; A7, defined; A7, ex. by application to leg. or delegated functionary; A8, application made by requisition instrument; A8, requisitor v. requisitee; A9, requisition instrument necessary for valid procurement mandate; A9, requisition instrument is to the procuration mandate as, in law, the initiative is to the consummative; A10, requisition v. petition; A11, offices where requisition instruments are issued; A11, need indicated by mimographical documents; A12, requisition instrument—examples of headings of entries; A13, requisitee, when confirming requisition, issues procuration mandate; A14, checks on requisition in mimographical documents and other data; A15, procurement mandate transmitted to requisitor immediately or through finance minister; A16, ministers required to transmit 'appropriate and timely' requisition instruments to p.m. to meet needs of depts.; A17, ordinary v. extraordinary service; A18, arrangements at outset of code for supply; A19, renewal of supply; A19, solar v. service year; A19, general supply day; A20, spontaneous mandate v. requisition instrument; A21, spontaneous procurement: diverse forms distinguished; A22, use of exemplars; A23, use of statistic and registration system to determine supply; A23, leg. to distinguish between ordinary and extraordinary service; A23, and determine from and to what offices requisition instruments may be transmitted; A24-5, latitude of subordinates min.; A26, self-supply when possible, examples; A27-8, modes of procurement, competing forms, examples given; A29, effect of failure to choose cheapest form: a tax; A30, emphasis on clearness, conciseness, uniformity, legibility, cheapness; A31, clearness defined; A32, conciseness defined; A33, use of abbreviations; A34, rules for uniformity of expression; A35, uniformity of paper used, especially in manifold writing; A36, manifold writing v. printing for cheapness and legibility; A37, writing v. stamping; A38, application to sublegs.; 19.A6, leg. to determine which grades to ex. requisitive f. *See* LEGISLATURE; PROCUREMENT MANDATE; STATISTIC FUNCTION

RESIGNATION: VI.30.A1, as cause of dislocation of members of leg.; IX.21. A51, resignation for deficiencies of app. apt.; A51, where deficiency in moral apt. resignation not acceptable; A52, causes of resignation other than deficiencies in app. apt. listed. *See* LOCATION AND DISLOCATION

RESPONSIBILITY: II.A16, max. responsibility of those possessing subordinate power to those possessing sovereign power; A16&n, responsibility established by expectation of evil and punishment, but not by good and reward; A16n, word 'responsibility' discussed; A20, responsibility in its effects: punitional, satisfactional, and dislocational; produced by legal and moral sanctions; A21, compensational v. punitional responsibility; A22, legal responsibility discussed; A23, pecuniary responsibility discussed; A24, moral responsibility discussed; IV.A14, self-suppletive f. and responsibility of functionaries; VI.1.A13, responsibility and changes in constitution by leg.; 23.A2, responsibility of deputy for substitute (self-suppletive f.); A26, moral and pecuniary responsibility of deputy for substitute; 25.A49, moral and legal responsibility of deputies and electors; 26.A4, members of leg. involved in wrongful exclusion of others are compensationally, punitionally, and dislocationally responsible; 31.A42, responsibility and securities for app. apt. of legislators; VIII.3. A8-9, responsibility of p.m. for ex. of fs.; 4.A5-6, responsibility of p.m. for depute: punishment, compensation, dislocation; 5.A4, responsibility of leg.

for failing to hold elections of p.m.; 12.A1, responsibility of p.m. to ex. initiative, indicative, informative fs. as security for app. apt.; A1, responsibility of p.m. for his deputes and subordinates, as security for app. apt.; A1, responsibility of p.m., punitionally and compensationally, as security for app. apt.; A2-3, responsibility of informant of misconduct or inaptitude of minister; A4, p.m. responsible for ministers appointed by predecessors; IX.5.A21, subordinateness, accountableness, and responsibility; 7.4th.A21, one person responsible for loss of any article; A22, also responsible for losses of assistants and deputes; A23, responsibility of inspectors v. custodients; A24, individual responsibility: rule and principle; 15.A4, opulence does not increase responsibility; 16.A35, responsibility for false statements in qualification judicatory; 17.A37, responsibility for mislocation, compensational and punitional; 21.A17, judge's ex. of imperative f. and undivided responsibility; 25.A3, responsibility of ministers to ex. informative, indicative, and initiative fs., as security for app. apt.; A3, responsibility for apt. of depute, as security; A3, A26-7, responsibility for apt. of immediate subordinates, as security. *See* LOCATION AND DISLOCATION; REWARD AND PUNISHMENT; SECURITIES

RESPONSIVE FUNCTION: IX.24.A1, ex. by ministers in leg.; A3, ministers bound to attend sessions of leg. to answer questions

RETROACCEPTIVE FUNCTION: *See* PROCURATIVE FUNCTION

RETROTRANSMISSIVE FUNCTION: *See* PROCURATIVE FUNCTION

REVOLT: IX.19.A30, and need for correspondence of grade, power, and emolument in military service. *See* COMMOTION; MILITARY SERVICE; REVOLUTION

REVOLUTION: VI.25.A46, undiscontinued relocability and violent revolution. *See* COMMOTION; REVOLT

REWARD AND PUNISHMENT: II.A3, punishment and reward included in matter of expenditure; A4, punishment defined; A6, reward defined; A8, evil employed as means, as punishment; A9, as an instrument of coercion; A10, pleasure as means in matter of reward; A11, good employed in reward as instrument of inducement; A12, smaller proportion of reward than punishment employed in government; A16, punishment, reward, and responsibility; A16n, fear of punishment and not reward will create responsibility; A20, punitional responsibility; A21, compensational preferred to punitional responsibility; A22, dislocation and punishment and legal responsibility; A23, compensational responsibility and punition; IV.A2, relocation and dislocation as reward and punishment of legislators by constitutive authority; A3, leg. to punish chiefs of administrative and judiciary depts. for non-compliance; V.5.A3, punishment and ex. of executive f. by p.o. trib.; A5, reward for ex. of statistic f.; A5, natural v. factitious reward; VI.20.A8, corporal and capital punishment discussed and rejected; A8, withholding remuneration for non-attendance as punishment; A9, punishment of common soldier v. high government officials; 23.A9, absentation, corruption, and the avoidance of punishment; A32, punishment and insufficient excuse for non-attendance; 25.A54-5, effect of security of pecuniary punishment on members of leg. discussed; 27.A50, punishment by House of Commons v. judiciary in eliciting evidence; A51, punishment for perjury in House of Lords v. House of Commons; A55, punishment and commissions in English practice; 28.A1, trial by legislation penal judicatory where punishment by dislocation not sufficient; A8, punishment and impartiality by legislation penal judicatory; A14, punishment by leg. of wrongful accusers; 31.A17-18, attitude to punishment by rulers in relation to ruled; A19-21, attitude of rulers to themselves; A41n, punishment and English judicial practice; VIIn, legislator's inautural declaration applicable where punishment not effective; 2, reward and punishment and min. of expense in government; 4, no punishment by legislators over difference of taste, opinion, or belief; VIII.4.A5-6, punishment and responsibility of principal for depute; 5.A4, punishment and responsibility of leg. for failing to hold election of p.m.; 12.A1, punishment by legislation penal judicatory as security for app. apt. of p.m.; IX.5.A4, power of punition, necessary to subordination; A22, power being part of reward, higher rank requires no increase in pay; 7.6th.A6, punishment for negligence or intentional misconduct in ex. of statistic f.; 15.A4, 17.A56, opulence and avoidance of punishment; A9-10, arbitrary reward rejected; A11, public service as basis of reward; A15-17, pecuniary v. honorary reward; A18-28, natural honour and reward; A29-33, factitious dignity; A34, natural v. factitious reward; 16.A29n, corporal punishment and Hazelwood School; A75, use of lot in punishment; 17.A37, responsibility for mislocation and punishment; 19.A29, power, grade, and emolument, military v. non-military situations; A31, max. of reward can lead to max. of corruption; 20.A11, punishment as subtraction of reward; 21.A33, reward and punishment in absence of adequate penal code; A67, temporary transference to inferior grade as punishment; 23.A11, punishment and peculation; 25.A30, punishment and powers of p.o. trib.; A37, conditions for exemption from punishment where functionary ex. extraordinary powers; 26.A8, reward and punishment and secret suffrage; A33-7, reward for informers dicussed; A52, punishment and the absence of functionaries to deal with offenders. See DIGNITY AND FACTITIOUS DIGNITY; HONOUR, NATURAL AND FACTITIOUS; REMUNERATION; RESPONSIBILITY

RICH AND POOR: See FEW AND MANY; OPULENCE AND INDIGENCE

RIGHT(S): V.6.A1, all members of human species have right to ex. statistic, executive, melioration suggestive fs.; A2, and censorial f.; VI.24.A3, continuation committeeman has right of argumentation and initiation; A14, A17, A18, and right of voting; 25.A33, right of speech and motion but not right to vote in continuation committee; 29.A7, right of members of leg. to propose motions; IX.4.A7, rights—fictitious entities; A7-9, rights v. obligations; A9, natural rights v. sanctional rights; A9n, moral rights and confusion; A9n, moral rights v. legal rights; 5.A18, powers or rights of superordinates and obligations of subordinates; 17.A37, where mislocation no right to office; 20.A19, right of being inspecting visitor; 21.A4, abuse of power, non-exercise of and right; A12, right of appeal in cases regarding oppression

RIGHT AND WRONG: VI.28.A11, A13, A16, leg. as appellate judicatory and unredressed wrongs; VII.2, right and proper end of government; IX.16.A3, morally, but not legally binding right produced by location system; A3, favour v. right; 17.A59, right and wrong and judges; 21.A1, human nature and suffering wrong; A2, insubordination v. corruption v. extortion as wrongs to public service; 23.A12, right and wrong and abuse of power; 25.A1, right and proper use of powers

ROMAN LAW: IX.4.A10, source of distinction between immovables and movables

RULE(S): II.A1, all comprehensive and all-directing rule: max. happiness; A2, rules: max. app. official apt., min. official expense; A16, rules for max. app.

apt. listed; VI.25.A28, rule to avoid corruptive influence: min. time of contact; 27.A44-8, rules for eliciting evidence and English practice; 31.A3, rule to limit power of functionaries; A4, rule to obtain efficient security for app. apt.; A5, rule to obtain security against abuse of power; VIII.11.A3, rules regarding publicity; A14, rules for limiting secrecy; IX.3.A26, rule for establishing single seated offices; A31, expense min. rule; 5.A48, rule for establishing no intermediate grade between operating functionary and minister; 7.4th.A24, individual responsibility rule; 8.A34, rules for uniformity of expression; 15.A6, rule for remuneration; 19.A11, rules for official attendance of functionaries; 20.A16, rules for deportment of non-functionaries before functionaries; A17, styled rules of good behaviour, good manners, good breeding, or decorum; A18-20, discussed; 21.A5, rules of official deportment and oppression of suitors; A6, and inspectees; A20, rules of deportment for functionaries as remedies for oppression; A21, A22, A29, rules of deportment analysed as rules of ethics; A23, enforceability of rules; A24, and importance of system of judicial procedure; A26, rules of self-regarding prudence, positive effective benevolence, negative effective benevolence; A55-6, rules for suspension; 23.A13, rules for receipt and disbursement of money; 25.A10-12, rules of deportment as instrument of security; 26.A15, rule for placing offices in contiguity. *See* PRINCIPLE(S)

RUSSIA: II.A24, England v. Russia; IX.19.A31, Russian code of Catherine the Second

SANCTION(S): II.A20, moral and legal sanctions, source of responsibility; VIIn, moral sanction and legislator's inaugural declaration; VIIn, legal sanction and legislator's inaugural declaration; VIIn, penalty of moral sanction, loss of popularity; IX.20.A18, rules of deportment and moral or popular sanction; A19, A20, and legal sanction; 21.A22, sanctions of penal code and rules of ethics; A26, moral or popular sanction, only sanction in corrupt society; 25.A1, sanctions and security for app. apt.; A54, moral sanction of p.o. trib. *See* MORAL

SCOTLAND: I.A6(inst.diss.), and size of territorial divisions; V.2.A3n, sheriff-depute in Scottish law

SEATS (SEATEDNESS): *See* SINGLE AND MANY SEATED

SECRECY: *See* PUBLICITY AND SECRECY

SECURITIES: II.A19, securities and max. of app. apt.; A24, moral responsibility as imperfect, but important, security against misconduct; V.2.A3n, in English practice, 'representative' fictitious and fallacious security for the people against monarch; 5.A9, p.o. trib. and securities provided by judiciary dept.; VI.1.A1, power of supreme leg. is unlimited but checked by securities; A13, securities, responsibility, and changes in constitution; 20.A7, securities for non-attendance; 23.A13, deputy's substitute as security against accidental decision by leg.; 25.A48, continuity of p.m., as security in temporarily discontinued relocability system; A49, other securities discussed; A53, securities and temporary non-relocability v. undiscontinued relocability; A54-5, effect of pecuniary punishment for non-attendance in leg. discussed in light of other securities; 27.A19-21, securities against deception by falsehood; A37, securities against oppression where secrecy necessary in legislation enquiry judicatory; A38, securities applicable to legislation enquiry judicatory same as for leg.; A50, absence of securities against mendacity in ex. of evidence elicitation f. by House of Commons; 31.A1, all-pervading system of securities described; A1, security against abuse of power is one branch of security for app. moral apt.; A2, confidence min. principle, control max. principle; A3-5, corresponding rules stated; A6, basic assumptions about propensities of all human minds; A7, self-regard and sympathy present in all human minds; A8, self-regard prevalent over sympathy; A9, example given; A10, task of leg. and moralists to increase the influence of sympathy, but to assume its slight influence; A11, unless prevented, men will do evil to serve their private interests; A12, exceptions considered; A13, limitations on power not harmful to public service; A14-15, nor to individuals; A16, precautions necessary to prevent evil; A17-18, recognized by rulers in relation to the ruled; A19-21, but not in relation to themselves; A22, abuse of power in rulers, examples given; A23, propensity to evil and need for securities; A24, reception of securities, test of app. apt.; A25, different reception in different governments; A26, most favourable reception in representative democracy; A27, except by lawyer class; A28-30, examples given; A31-3, reception to securities in pure monarchy; A34-5, reception to securities in pure aristocracy; A36-41&n, reception to securities in mixed monarchy; A42, securities for all branches of app. apt. of members of leg. listed; A43, for moral apt. listed; A44, for intellectual apt. listed; A45, for active apt. listed; VII.2, max. of security as a positive end of government; 6, tax on judicial services as security-denying act; VIII.10.A4, manifold writing mode and security against falsification; A6, and security against destruction of judicial documents; 11.A4, publicity as security for app. apt.; 12.A1, securities for app. apt. of p.m. listed: (i) registration system; (ii) publication system; (iii) dislocation by leg.; (iv) dislocation by constitutive authority; (v) responsibility for ex. of informative, indicative and initiative fs.; (vi) dislocation upon accepting other office in the state; (vii) dislocation upon accepting office, gift, factitious honour, or dignity from foreign government or foreign person; (viii) obligation to keep depute; (ix) responsibility for apt. of subordinates; (x) securities applying to subordinates; (xi) checks to arbitrary location of subordinates; (xii) ex. of statistic, censorial, melioration-suggestive fs. by p.o. trib.; (xiii) dislocation, with punitional and compensational responsibility, before legislation penal judicatory; A2, p.m. to act on information of misconduct or inaptitude of ministers; A3, secrecy of informant's identity considered; A4, p.m. responsible for ministers appointed by predecessors; A5, additional securities listed; IX.7.6th.A6, securities in entries in ex. of statistic f.; 11.A6-7, leg. to establish securities against abuse in elicitation of information by subordinate functionaries; 13.A3, securities for app. apt., minister v. member of leg.; 16.A9, no one is locable without instruction, so long as any one with app. apt. is available, as security for app. apt.; 17.A6, pecuniary security for positions of simple trust and talent and trust; A14, self-seated v. extra-seated property, as pecuniary security; A15, and inalienability of security by possessor; A53, pecuniary competition system as security for app. apt.; A53, equality must be subordinate to security, or society cannot subsist; A54, securities for app. apt. more efficient in code than in any existing government; A58, systems of securities will prevent depredation; 18.A6, security against undue dislocation of ministers; 19.A10, subordinates appointed for life as security against arbitrary dislocation; A18-19, securities in filling vacancies; A20, why security for despatch in filling vacancies; 20.A2, securities for functionaries and non-functionaries against insubordination, oppression, extortion, peculation; A24, leg. to determine which grades to have securities against disturbance and non-compliance by suitors, inspectors, and evidence-holders; 21.A16, securities for app. apt. of special judges; A20, securities for clearness, correctness, relative completeness in evidence as indirectly applying remedy against oppression; A37, p.o. trib. of metropolis as best security against abuse of dislocative power; A40, security against oppression and decrees of dislocation judicatory; 23.A5, A9, securities against peculation; A23, security to be provided by those involved in receipt and disbursement of money; 25.A1, analytic sketch of subject-matter of securities, heads: (i) elements of app. apt.; (ii) motives; (iii) sanctions; (iv) persons to whom applied; (v) persons by whom applied; (vi) purposes; (vii) time factor; A2, leg. to decide which securities applicable to p.m. and leg. are applicable to ministers; A3, relevant securities listed: (i) registration system; (ii) publication system; (iii) dislocability by leg.; (iv) dislocability by constitutive authority; (v) responsibility for ex. of informative, indicative, and initiative fs.; (vi) dislocability for acceptance of other office; (vii) dislocability for acceptance of gift, office, factitious honour from foreign government; (viii) obligation to have deputes and responsibility for their apt.; (ix) responsibility for apt. of immediate subordinates; (x) securities in location system, especially in qualification judicatory; (xi) pecuniary competition system; (xii) authority of p.o. trib. in ex. of statistic, censorial, and melioration-suggestive fs.; instruments of security: (i) A4, character index; (ii) A5, official merit register; (iii) A6, official demerit register; A7, headings of entry; A8, convicted lists inserted in office calendar; A9, arrangements for new series when list becomes too great; (iv) A10, deportment rules displayed in every functionary's audience chamber; A11, inclusion of information from character index in functionary's deportment rules; A12, visitor's deportment rules for suitors and inspectors; A13, gift or remuneration for extra-despatch is corruption; A14, inhibition of remuneration for extra-despatch acts as security against extortion and factitious delay; A15, exceptions, in case of urgency, minister to apply to finance minister by remuneration draught; A16, extra-despatch to be established by quasi-judicial assertion; A17, quasi-judicial assertion defined; A18, extra-despatch book, headings of entries; A19, entry from extra-despatch book to be included in remuneration draught; A20, exemplars of remuneration draught, how distributed; A21, signature of finance minister to acknowledge receipt of remuneration draught; A22, if no payment by certain date, finance minister to issue non-payment excuse and benemeritant may transmit to p.m. a non-payment complaint; A23, importance of publicity and access to register books emphasized; A24, leg. to arrange for secrecy for extra-despatch, where necessary, as in time of war; A25, provisions for extra-despatch do not apply to all extra-service; A26-7, responsibility of ministers for subordinates defined; A28, presumption of culpable deficiency with respect to minister's vigilance, examples given; A29, role of p.o. trib. where minister's vigilance is deficient; A30-1, power of p.o. trib. over functionaries, as security; A32, minister's ex. of dislocative or directive power on information of inaptitude of subordinates; A33, leg. to look for and exclude irresponsible ex. of power of functionaries and to establish necessary powers to diminish demand for expansion of power based on necessity; A34, examples given; A35, leg. not to confer power on ministers for emergencies; A36, functionary's ex. of extraordinary power, need to estimate evils; A37, ex. of extraordinary power and conditions for exemption from punishment; A38, abuse of power in mixed monarchy in ex. of extraordinary power; A39, dispensing power as abuse of power; A40, places executive authority wrongly above legislative authority; A41, in English practice; A42, dispensing power and other abuses; A42, judge-made law v. leg.-made law; A43, evils of following precedents; A44, blindness from one generation to another; A45, lowest apt. required; A46-7, and class of persons to whom system of following precedents is well adapted; A48, representative democracy v. aristocracy-ridden monarchy and power-holding classes; A49, acting on precedent is anti-rational and anti-constitutional; A50, use of judicial procedure in non-military subdepts. denied in English practice; A51, English practice combines arbitrary dislocability with virtual undislocability; A52, King's Bench is ineffectual; A53, law and jury system fail to provide remedies; A54, importance of p.o. trib. in English practice in providing securities against oppression in administrative depts.; A55-6, purchase of justice in English practice; A57, no security against oppression in English practice; A58, military procedures superior in English practice; 26.A42-7, arrangements for security of buildings and contents against loss. *See* APTITUDE; ARCHITECTURE

SELF-REGARD AND EXTRA-REGARD (OR SYMPATHY): VI.31.A7, self-regard and sympathy present in all human minds; A8, sympathy has root in self-regard; A8, self-regard prevalent over sympathy; A9, example given; A10, task of legislator to increase the influence of sympathy but to assume its slight influence; A16, evil doing by the preference of self-regard over sympathy; VII.9, impartiality v. self-regarding interest and interests inspired by sympathy and antipathy; IX.3.A9, self-regarding interests and sympathy and community of sinister interests; 15.A44, self-regarding or sympathetic interests and naturally extravasated remuneration; 19.A10, self-regarding interest and dislocative power; A14, mis-directed sympathy and remuneration for longevity; A14, and self-regard and benevolence; 26.A34, self-regarding or sympathetic interest and secret information. *See* INTEREST(S)

SELF-SUPPLETIVE FUNCTION: IV.A14, and provision of auxiliaries for functionaries; VI.20.A7, as security against non-attendance of legislators; A25, as remedy for retardation of public business; 23.A1, every deputy to ex. self-suppletive f.; A2, deputy responsible for substitute; A3, eligibility for location as substitute; A4-6, arrangements for appointment and admission of substitute to assembly chamber; A5, permanent v. occasional substitute; reasons for provision of substitute given: (i) A7, same use as deputy; (ii) A8, secures continuous attendance; (iii) A9, prevention of corruption by absence during votes; (iv) A10, prevention of fluctuation of voting from number in attendance; (v) A11, saving time in soliciting attendance; (vi) A12, will actually expressed to equal will intended to be expressed in leg.; (vii) A13, security against accident in decisions of leg.; reasons for powers of appointment in deputy as opposed to constituents given: (i) A14, adequacy of supply better ensured; (ii) A15, apt persons in metropolis of the state; (iii) A16, substitute within call of deputy; (iv) A17, constancy of supply; (v) A18, danger of non-attendance during election when vacancy; (vi) A19, vexation and expense of elections; (vii) A20, absence of supply of substitutes during period of elections; (viii) A21, vexation and expense of elections for substitutes at the end of session; (ix) A22, public expense of elections and salary saved if deputy appoints substitute; (x) A23, person with app. apt. but not able to become deputy could serve as substitute; (xi) A24, the opulent with app. apt., but otherwise indolent, could serve as deputy's substitute; (xii) A25, opportunity for new men with promise and app. apt. but who would not be willing or likely to be chosen by electors; (xiii) A26, patronage without corruption; A27, option left to deputy as to whether deputy or substitute will attend; A28, distinctive dress of substitutes discussed; 25.A53n, origin of Bentham's ideas; 31.A42, A45, and securities for app. apt. of legislators; VIII.4.A1, location of depute by p.m. in ex. of self-suppletive f.; A2, depute defined and fs. stated; A3, occasions for assuming power listed; A4, power of principal and depute; A5–6, responsibility of principal for depute; A7, arrangements for location of depute; A8, instrument of location; A9, power passing between principal and depute; A9–10, arrangements for death of principal; A11, dislocability of depute; 12.A1, obligation of p.m. to ex. self-suppletive f. as security for app. apt.; IX.3.A14, and avoidance of vacancies without expense; 4.A44, f. ex. in regard to persons; A44, defined; A44, and procurative f.; 6.A1, power of self-supply and obligation to ex. it belongs to every minister; A1, ex. by location of depute; A2, arrangements for united subdepts.; A3, time allowed for location; A4, instrument of location; A5, exemplars, where sent; A6, arrangements for emergencies; A7, when depute is needed; A8, eligibility for location as depute; A9, depute dislocable at any time either by minister or authorities locating minister; A10, f. also ex. by subordinates to ministers; A11, exceptions noted; A12, benefits of widespread use in administrative dept. of deputes: sufficient staff and frugality secured; A13, reasons given for sufficient number of deputes being available; A13, principal is to depute as master is to apprentice; 19.A5, leg. to determine which grades need to have power to ex. self-suppletive f.; 25.A26, and responsibility of ministers for subordinates   .

SENIORITY: IX.19.A35, official v. natural age; A35, use of official age as opposed to natural age as basis of succession in corrupt governments suggested; A36, succession by seniority and corruption; A37, in ordinary service, no need for increased emolument based on age. *See* LONGEVITY; SUBORDINATE AND SUPERORDINATE

SERVICE: VII.3, service v. factitious honour and dignity; IX.7.3rd.A13, estimating value of service of functionaries; 15.A11, service to public, basis of reward; A12–14, ordinary v. extraordinary service defined and distinguished; A19, extraordinary service and natural honour; A49, for extraordinary service analogous to ordinary service, remuneration given; A50, defined; A51, examples given; A53, judicially conferred; A52, judges to guard against fraud; 17.A54, service to public, result of competition system. *See* REMUNERATION; REWARD AND PUNISHMENT

SHORTAGES OF FOOD (DEARTH): *See* CALAMITY

SILENCE: VI.27.A16, silence and self-condemning evidence; IX.23.A7, and inference of peculation; 25.A30, silence of functionaries before interrogation of p.o. trib.

SINCERITY AND INSINCERITY: VI.1.A10–11, insincerity as evil in relations between deputy and constituents; VIIn, insincerity as moral disease; 1.A3, provision for sincerity in legislator's inaugural declaration; 13, sincerity in formulating ordinances and debate; VIII.12.A3, insincerity and secrecy of identity of informant. *See* FALLACIES

SINGLE AND MANY SEATED: IV.A12, leg. and sublegs. many seated; A13, administrative and judicial depts., single seated; VI.27.A37, secrecy and size of legislation enquiry judicatory; A55, single and many seated commissions in English practice; IX.3.A1, one minister only in each office; A2, single-seated offices v. plurality, reasons given; A3, single-seated offices and moral apt.; A4, and intellectual apt.; A5, and active apt.; A6, and min. of evil; A7, evil of many seatedness increases with number of seats; A8, many seatedness and larger community of sinister interest; A9, elements of community of sinister interest; A10, the higher in scale of power, the greater the delinquency; A11-13, A22-36, English practice compared; A14, self-suppletion deals with problem of vacancy; A15, code has other means to achieve benefits of many seatedness; A16-17, U.S. practice compared; A18, limitations on power of location and dislocation; A19, many-seatedness provides opportunity for appeal to superordinate; A20, arbitrary power and absence of control; A21, single v. many seatedness, leg. v. administration

SISTITIVE FUNCTION: IX.5.A4, power of, useful to subordination; 24.A5, judge's sistitive, or execution-staying f., and minister securing Pannomion from deterioration; A8, leg. to determine which administrative functionaries to ex. sistitive f.; A9, evil to be min. which may occur either with or without the ex. of this f.

SOVEREIGNTY: II.A16, sovereign power given to those whose interest it is to max. happiness; III.A1, sovereignty in people ex. by constitutive authority; VI.31.A42, sovereignty and security for app. apt. in leg. *See* CONSTITUTIVE AUTHORITY

SPAIN: I.A6(inst.diss.), 'alcalde' and fs. of local headman; II.A24, England v. Spain; VI.27.A49, Spanish Inquisition and English judiciary; VIII.1.A7, use of 'gefe politico' v. 'prime minister'; IX.26.A20n, and Panopticon plan

STATE: I.A1, state named; A1, constitution adopted; A2, territory and boundaries delineated; A3, territory divided into districts, which serve as election districts; A4, division into subdistricts; A5, division into bis-subdistricts; A6, leg. to alter arrangements in manner commensurate with original plan; (inst.diss.), method of division discussed; (inst.diss.), tris-subdistricts, greatest division envisaged; (inst.diss.), in small states, one division only, or even none; (inst.diss.), terminology discussed; (inst.diss.), size of territorial divisions discussed; (inst.diss.), expense and number of divisions in territory discussed; IV.A1, state has four authorities: constitutive, legislative, administrative, judiciary; VII.8, relations between states discussed; VIII.7.A3, residency requirement for eligibility for location as p.m. *See* CONSTITUTIVE AUTHORITY; DISTRICT(S); LEGISLATURE; SUBDISTRICT(S)

STATE(S) AND MOTION(S): IX.4.A13, names of occurrences which are subject of registrative f. *See* OCCURRENCES

STATISTIC FUNCTION: (i) In general: V.5.A1, ex. by p.o. trib.; A5, moral v. legal obligation for functionaries to ex. statistic f.; 6.A1, all members of human species have right to ex. statistic f.; VI.31.A44, statistic f. and securities for app. intellectual apt. in leg.; VIII.3.A10, ex. by p.m. in annual message to leg.; 10.A7, use of exemplars and ex. of statistic f.; 12.A1, ex. of statistic f. by p.o. trib., as security for app. apt. of p.m.; IX.4.A17, statistic f. and relevant and irrelevant occurrences; A56, ex. by ministers collectively in regard to persons, things, money, and occurrences; A56, defined; A56, and directive f.; 5.A17, and accountableness; 7.1st.A1, original information v. reminiscences; A1, needful v. needless information, relative distinction; A2, general topics for consideration in ex. of statistic f.; A3-5, ends in view: max. good, min. evil; A4, usefulness of ex. of f. in proportion to clearness, correctness, and completeness of the results; A6, subject matter of registration; A7, periods of relative time: entrance, continuance, exit; A7-8, application to use and relative time; A9, desirable properties for entries: clearness, correctness, comprehensiveness, and symmetry; A10, symmetry explained; A11, service books v. loss books; A12, service books: outset v. journal books; A12, outset books: original v. periodical; A12, generic v. specific books; A12, specific books: personal, immovable, movable, money, occurrence books; A12, sub-specific books: entrance, continuation exit; A13, original outset book defined; A14, journal books defined; A15, periodical outset books defined; A15, solar year v. service year; A16, superbooks v. subbooks; A17-22, uses of books de-lineated; A17-18, use of service books: aggregate v. particular uses; A19-22, uses of loss books, aggregate v. particular; A23, offices defined; A23, books to be kept by all offices; A23, head office v. suboffices; A23, books v. sub-books; 5th.A1, subsidiary books: retroacceptation and retrotransmission books; A2, provision for additional books; 6th,A1, use of abbreviations in ex. of statistic f. determined by leg.; A2, arguments for and against practice; A3-5, rules for abbreviations enumerated; A5n, use of abbreviations in mathematics and application to ex. of statistic f.; A5n, Italian bookkeeping nomenclature criticized; A5n, use of Latin abbreviations in English practice; A6, securities for correct and complete entries enumerated; 9.A3, ex. of inspective f. to secure execution of statistic f.; 19.A4, leg. to determine which register books to be kept in each grade in ex. of statistic f.; 23.A5, statistic f. and indirect remedies against peculation; 25.A3, ex. by p.o. trib. as security for app. apt. of ministers; A4, character index as instrument of security; (ii) Original outset book(s): IX.7.1st.A13, defined; 2nd.A1, (a) personal stock book, headings of entries; A2, uses of entries; A3, particular importance in subdepts., with large employment of personnel; A4, (b) immovable stock book, headings of entries; A5, uses of entries; A6, (c) movable stock book, headings of entries; A7, mimographical or receptacular mode of registration; A8, uses of mimographical mode; A9, subdepts. where most applicable; A10-25, mimographical mode discussed; A26, headings under which articles be-longing to movable stock may be listed; A27-9, (d) money stock book, headings of entries; A30, entries made in suboffices to serve as checks; (iii) Journal books: IX.7.1st.A14, defined; 3rd.A1, pertains to interior occurrences subsequent to day of outset; A2, time periods to be mentioned: entrance, continuation, and exit; A3, operation performed at entrance: receipt; A4, operation performed with continuation: application to use; A5, operations performed at exit listed; A6, specific books listed: personal, movable, immov-able, and money stock books; A7, subspecific books listed: entrance, applica-tion, exit; A8, (a) personal stock book: entrance book, headings of entries; A9, application book, headings of entries; A10, exit book, headings of entries; A11, uses of books listed; A12, obligation of giving evidence; A13, estimating value of service; A14, (b) immovable stock book: entrance book: limited use; A15, application book: headings of entries; A15, application to profit v. loss; A16, exit book: headings of entries; A17, headings of entries for additions to immovable stock; A18, (c) movable stock book: entrance book, headings of entries; A19, application book, principal v. subsidiary or instrumental modes; A20, principal mode: transformative v. conjunctive modes of application; A21, headings of entries; A22, use of entries; A23, exit or issue book: headings of entries; A25, (d) money book: entrance or receipt book, headings of entries; A26, application book, none; A27-8, exit or issue book, headings of entries; A29, headings also applicable to movables; A30, (e) exterior occurrence book, subdepts. where most applicable; A31, headings of entries; A32, information to be traced to its sources; (iv) Loss books: IX.7.1st.A11, loss books v. service books; A19–22, uses listed; 4th.A1, subject matter v. efficient cause; A2, subject matter of loss: personal service, things movable, things immovable, money; A3, efficient causes of loss: purely human agency, purely natural agency, mixed agency; A4–5, (a) loss of personal service: examples given; A6, (b) loss of things immovable: examples given; A7, (c) loss of things movable: examples given; A8, dangers of fraud in selling; A9, subdepts. most exposed to danger of fraud: navy, finance; A10, p.o. trib. to watch for fraud; A11, spontaneous deterioration, efficient causes; A12, spontaneous destruction, efficient causes; A13, natural durability of things, examples given; A14, age may increase or diminish value of stock; A15, effect of age on persons; A16, effect of age on things; A17, headings of entries where effect of age relevant; A18, things, length of time in use, considered; A19, movable things subject to loss listed; A20, (d) loss of money, examples given; A21, for prevention of loss, one person responsible for each article; A22, one person responsible for loss by assistants and deputes; A23, responsibility of inspectors v. custodients; A24, individual responsibility: rule and principle; A25, A26, A30, estimated value of loss, headings of entries; A27, entries made by directing functionaries; A28, p.m. to secure entries by ministers in each subdept.; A29, p.o. trib. to judge veracity of entries; A30, entries in loss book to avoid insincerity while fulfilling obligation to make entries; A31, causes of loss by human agency, examples given; A32–3, stock-in-hand books. See EVIDENCE; MIMOGRAPHICAL MODE OF REGISTRATION; REGISTRATION SYSTEM; REGISTRATIVE FUNCTION

SUBDEPARTMENT(S): IV.A10, within administrative dept., there are 13 subdepts.; IX.2.A2, subdepts. headed by ministers; A2, number of subdepts. to ministers; A9, potentially united subdepts., examples given; 26.A7, use of publicity and secrecy varies from subdept. to subdept. See MINISTER(S); ARMY, DOMAIN, EDUCATION, ELECTION, FINANCE, FOREIGN RELATION, HEALTH, INDIGENCE RELIEF, INTERIOR COMMUNICATION, LEGISLATION, NAVY, PREVENTIVE SERVICE, TRADE SUBDEPARTMENTS

SUBDISTRICT(S): I.A4, each district is divided into subdistricts; A4, each subdistrict is a voting district; A4, sends deputy to subleg.; A4, territory of immediate judicatory; A4, subdistricts listed; A5, each subdistrict divided into bis-subdistricts, which is territory of the local headman; A5, further division named tris-subdistrict; A6(inst.diss.), tris-subdistrict furthest division envisaged; IV.A12, one seat in subleg. for each subdistrict; V.2.A4, constitutive authority in subdistricts elect members of subleg. See SUBLEGISLATURE(S)

SUBLEGISLATURE(S): I.A3, district is territory of subleg.; A4, each subdistrict as voting district sends deputy to subleg.; IV.A9, each district has a subleg. under the leg.; A11, subleg. and local and logical fields of service; A12, subleg., many seated, one seat for each subdistrict; V.2.A4, constitutive authority ex. locative f. in sending deputies to sublegs.; A5, members of sublegs., dislocable by constitutive authority; A6, officials dislocable by constitutive authority belonging to each district; 3.A2–3, locative f., how ex. by constitutive authority; A5, dislocative f., how ex. by constitutive authority; VI.1.A5, dependence of subleg. on authority of supreme leg.; A6, where non-performance or inaptitude, leg. can take over fs. of subleg.; 3.A1–4, leg. ex. directive, corrective, and arbitrative fs. in relation to sublegs.; 25.A52–3, temporary non-relocability system and supply of men for sublegs.; 31.A1,

sublegs. and all-pervading system of securities; VII.12, encroachment by leg.
on subleg. discussed; VIII.8.A6, method of choosing p.m. applicable to p.m.
of sublegs.; A6, usefulness of experimentation in sublegs.; IX.2.A6, subminister is to subleg. as minister is to leg.; A7, subprime minister is to subleg. as
p.m. is to leg.; 8.A38, ex. of statistic, recordative, publicative, and requisitive
fs. by subleg.; 10.A24, need for sublegs., due to abuses in distant provinces;
14.A3&n, sublegs. and uninterrupted sittings of leg. *See* LEGISLATURE;
SUBDISTRICT(S): SUBMINISTER(S)

SUBMINISTER(S): IV.A13, one subminister for each subdept. of district;
V.2.A6, dislocable by constitutive authority belonging to district; IX.2.A4,
A6, minister v. subminister. *See* SUBLEGISLATURE(S)

SUBORDINATE AND SUPERORDINATE: II.A17, and responsible location
principle; VII.12, encroachment by leg. on subordinate authorities; VIII.1.A6,
'prime minister' implying subordination and superordination; A7, Spanish
'gefe politico', only superordination; 2.A5-6, dislocation of subordinates by
p.m.; 12.A1, p.m. responsible for subordinates, as security for app. apt.; A1,
checks to arbitrary appointment by p.m., by location system, as security for
app. apt.; IX.3.A15, A17, subordination and superordination and number in
an office; 5.A1, scale of subordination, subordination grades necessary; A2,
subordination presupposes superordination; A2, modes of inferiority and
superiority; A3, power is efficient cause of subordination; A4, mode of power
ex. in subordination; A5-6, fs. superordinate must ex. to be responsible for
subordinate's misconduct; A7, administration v. judiciary; A8, scale of
subordination——grades enumerated; A9, highest grade taken as starting point
for scale; A9, lower grades continually vary; A10-13, superordinateness v.
superiority; subordinateness v. inferiority; A13-16, inferiority in power v.
inferiority at large; A17, A19-20, subordinateness and accountableness; A18,
obligation of subordinates v. powers and rights of superordinates; A21, subordinateness and responsibility; A22-4, superordinateness, superiority, and
remuneration; A25, where need of direction, rank in scale of subordination
required; A26-7, instances noted where subordination required due to need
of account giving, but not direction; A28-30, distance between functionaries
and need for direction; A31, to finance minister, all functionaries accountable in respect of money, but not subordinate; A32, leg. to establish initially
and vary the number of grades in each subdept.; A33-4, subdepts. with
smallest number of grades: election and legislation; A35, largest number in
army subdept.; A36-41, number of functionaries in highest grades and English v. American practice in armies and navies; A42, legislation subdept. to
have smallest number of grades; A43, degree of subordination of registrars
limited by need to record acts of superiors; A44, lowest grade of subordination, writing clerk; A45, but not lowest pay; A46-7, grades v. official situations; A48, rule as to number of grades in subdept.; 15.A45, remuneration of
superordinates for work done by subordinates, injustice; 17.A10, receipt by
superordinates of exemplars of instrument of location; A12, advertisement
for subordinates to minister, made by ministers; A20, pain of humiliation
when subordinate rises to position above superordinate; A43-4, pecuniary
competition principle its application in location, situation of simple trust,
and situation of trust and talent; 18.A7-10, dislocation of minister by judge;
19.A1, leg. to allot to subordinates in subdepts. grades with distinctive fields
of service and functions; A2, subordinate subject to directive f. ex. by superordinate; A3, exceptions to be made by leg.; A4, leg. to determine which

register books to be kept in each grade; A5, leg. to determine which grades need to ex. self-suppletive f.; A6, and requisitive f.; A7, and melioration-suggestive f.; A8, subordinate's term of service is for life; A9, exceptions stated; A10, reason given as security against arbitrary dislocation; A11, leg. to apply rules of attendance to each subordinate position; A12, no increase in remuneration for continuance in office, reasons given; A13, nor for length of service in official establishment; A14, nor for longevity, reasons given; A15, leg. to determine to which subordinate position the principles of location system can be applied; A16, subordinates located, initiative f. by minister, consummative f. by p.m.; A17, considerations of distance; A18-19, securities in filling vacancies; A19, security against dislocation by p.m.; A20, why security for despatch in filling vacancies; A21-2, minister to have choice in filling vacancies; A21-2, depute permanent not automatic choice; A21, A23-7, minister to have powers but not obliged to repeat qualification examination; A21, A27, pecuniary competition may be repeated in filling vacancies but not obligatory; A21, A28, promotion not to be used in filling vacancies; A29, distribution of power, grade, and emolument, non-military v. military service; A30, necessity to avoid dissolution, resignation or revolt dictates correspondence of power and emolument in scale of subordination in military service; A30, no necessity present in non-military service; A31, system of Catherine the Second of Russia wrongly bases non-military service on analogy with military service; A32, permanent v. temporary functionaries for government fabrication, leg. to decide; A33, examples given; A34, permanent v. temporary employees in ex. of fabricative, reparative, and custoditive fs.; A35, succession by official age in corrupt government; A36, use of lot preferred to choice in corrupt government; A37, for meritorious service no augmentation of emolument necessary; A38, private v. public practice; A39, extra-merit, only basis of extra remuneration; A40, subordinates dislocable by ministers; A41, exceptions in military service; A42, leg. to determine when distance requires suspension by subordinate to minister, pending decision by minister regarding dislocation; A43, examples given; 25.A3, responsibility of ministers for apt. of immediate subordinates as security for app. apt.; A26-7, responsibility of ministers for subordinates defined; A28, presumption of culpable deficiency with respect to minister's vigilance, examples given; A29, role of p.o. trib. where minister's vigilance is deficient. *See* INSUBORDINATION; LOCATION AND DISLOCATION; OPPRESSION

SUBPRIME MINISTER(S): IV.A13, one subprime minister for each subleg.; V.2.A6, dislocable by constitutive authority belonging to district; IX.2.A7, p.m. v. subprime minister. *See* PRIME MINISTER; SUBLEGISLATURE(S); SUBMINISTER(S)

SUBSISTENCE: VII.2, max. of national subsistence as positive end of government

SUFFRAGE: *See* CONSTITUTIVE AUTHORITY; ELECTION CODE; LEGISLATURE; LOCATION AND DISLOCATION; PUBLICITY AND SECRECY; VOTING

SUGGESTIVE FUNCTION: *See* INDICATIVE FUNCTION; MELIORATION SUGGESTIVE FUNCTION

SUITOR(S): VI.27.A47-8, tax on suitors and English judicial practice; IX.1.A2, A3, prevention of evil to suitors; A4, 20.A3, suitor defined; A7, and quasi-insubordination; A24, leg. to determine which grades to have securities against disturbance and non-compliance by suitors; 21.A4, suitors as oppressees;

A5, examples given; A20, and use of incidental complaint book; 25.A12, and visitor's deportment rules; 26.A2, affected by evils of delay, vexation, and expense; A3, app. architectural arrangements reduce evils to both functionaries and suitors; A21-35, arrangements for oral communication with functionaries with use of waiting boxes, public and private. *See* ARCHITECTURE; OPPRESSION; PUBLIC OPINION TRIBUNAL

SUPPLETION: IX.5.A4, power of, necessary to subordination. *See* SUPPLETIVE FUNCTION

SUPPLETIVE FUNCTION: IX.5.A4, ex. in scale of subordination; A5, temporarily suppletive f. must accompany directive power; A5, superordinates must have power to ex. permanently suppletive f.; 25.A26, ex. of suppletive f. and responsibility of ministers for subordinates. *See* SELF-SUPPLETIVE FUNCTION; SUPPLETION

SUPPLY AND DEMAND: IX.7.1st.A18, use of service books to estimate

SUPREME: IV.A7, use of 'supreme' authority discussed; V.2.A3, 'supreme legislature' called 'legislature'

SUSPENSION: VIII.2.A7, defined as temporary dislocation; A11, p.m. and army subdept.; A13, and navy; A14, authenticating instruments; A15, use of manifold writing system; A16, arrangements for redress; IX.4.A44, bissubmode of location, allective and compulsive; 5.A4, power of, necessary to subordination; 17.A31&n, locative f., mode of ex. and avoidance of suspension; 18.A2, suspension as mode of modified dislocation; 19.A42, suspension by subordinate to minister, leg. to decide when distance so occasions; A43, examples given; 20.A25, suspension and non-compliance by subordinate to direction of superordinate; 21.A47, suspension of functionary may be effected by either the immediate or any other superordinate of functionary, reasons given; A54, application of dislocation instrument to suspension, heads of entries; A55-6, rules for time of suspension and renewal; A57, causes of termination of suspension; A58, minutes of record attached to instrument; A59, when dislocation warranted; A74, arrangements for exemplars of record and suspension instrument; 25.A26, A28, and responsibility of ministers for subordinates. *See* LOCATION AND DISLOCATION; PROMOTION; SUBORDINATE AND SUPERORDINATE; SUSPENSIVE FUNCTION; TRANSFER

SUSPENSIVE FUNCTION: IX.5.A4, ex. in scale of subordination; A5, must accompany directive f.; A6, to make superordinate responsible for subordinate's misconduct; 25.A26, and responsibility of minister for subordinates. *See* LOCATION AND DISLOCATION; SUBORDINATE AND SUPERORDINATE; SUSPENSION

SWITZERLAND: I.A6(inst.diss.), Swiss canton and division of territory of state

SYMPATHY: *See* SELF-REGARD AND EXTRA-REGARD

TASTE(S): VII.4, legislator not to impose standard of taste on fellow-citizens

TAXATION: V.6.A3, taxation of political tracts by leg. is anti-constitutional; VII.6, no tax on judicial services; IX.17.A53, to reject pecuniary competition system is to increase taxation

TERM OF SERVICE: VI.22.A1, the shorter the term of service for leg., the better; A2-3, exceptions for distance from leg.; A4, settled arrangements for elections favoured; A5, practice in monarchies; A6, U.S. practice; 24.A10, term of leg. one year, or two years where problem of distance; 31.A42, term of service and securities for app. apt. of legislators; VIII.2.A5, term of service of principal and location of deputes; 5.A1, p.m.'s term of service——4 years suggested; A2, no relocation until choice of several available; A3, arrangements for elections; A4, leg.'s failure to hold election; 6.A2, term of service of p.m. and relation to leg.; IX.13.A1, minister's term of service, for life; A2, ministers v. legislators; A3, dislocation and securities for app. apt.: minister v. legislator; 19.A8, subordinates continue in office for life; A9, exceptions noted; A10, reasons given, as security against arbitrary dislocation. *See* LOCATION AND DISLOCATION; RELOCATION

THEORY AND PRACTICE: IX.17.A59, and English practice; 17.Con.Inst.A2, good in theory, but unsound in practice, as fallacy; 19.A31n, distinction between theory and practice examined

THINGS: VI.27.A12, things and sources of evidence; VIII.1.A3, things and p.m.'s logical field of service; IX.4.A5, things v. persons; A5, real entities comprised of things and persons; A6, fictitious things v. fictitious persons; A6, fictitious entities comprised of fictitious things and fictitious persons; A7, things incorporeal as fictitious entities; A10, immovables and movables; A13, occurrences of things named states and motions; A18, written instruments as things; A45-6, fs. regarding things: procurative; A47, and requisitive f.; A48, custoditive; A49, applicative; A50, reparative; A51, transformative; A52-3, eliminative; A54-5, inspective; A56, statistic; A57, registrative; A58, publicative; A59, officially informative or report-making; A61, melioration-suggestive; A64, things belonging to each subdept.: edifice, land, furniture, stationery, instruments for lighting, heating, and cooling; 8.A7, requisitive f. ex. in regard to things; 20.A21, physical force and things. *See* STATISTIC FUNCTION

TIME: VI.27.A6, time and leg.'s undertaking to ex. elicitative f.; A50, time factor and impotence of House of Commons in eliciting evidence; A51, in House of Lords; 28.A6, time and leg. taking on legislation penal judicatory; 31.A39, time for judicial decisions in English practice; VII.12, use of time and encroachment on subordinate authorities by member of leg.; VIII.11.A8, time limit to secrecy to min. evil; A14, time and rules for limiting secrecy; IX.25. A1, time in relation to application of securities; A1, antecedential v. concomitant v. consequential, as relative points of time. *See* DELAY; STATISTIC FUNCTION

TRADE MINISTER: IX.2.A1, serves under p.m.; 9.A7, joint visits in ex. of inspective f. *See* TRADE SUBDEPARTMENT

TRADE SUBDEPARTMENT: IX.2.A10, potentially joined with finance subdept.; 9.A4, offices to be visited in ex. of inspective f. *See* MINISTER(S); TRADE MINISTER

TRANSFER: VIII.2.A11, p.m. and army subdept.; A13, and navy; A14, authenticating instruments; A15, use of manifold writing system; A16, arrangements for redress; IX.4.A44, transfer as bis-submode of location; 18.A2, transfer as modes of modified dislocation: permanent and temporary, to the same, inferior or superior grades; 20.A25, transfer and non-compliance of subordinate to direction of superordinate; 21.A43, minister may transfer subordinate or superordinate as result of decree of dislocation judicatory; A46, only minister, p.m. and leg. to effect transfer without consent of functionary; A60, application of dislocation instrument to permanent transference to grade not inferior, heads of entry; A61, temporary transference, headings of entry; A62, transference with and without blame; A63, except where vacancy, transference involves at least two functionaries; A64, permanent transference to inferior grade, headings of entry; A65, temporary transference to inferior grade, headings of entry; A66, word 'transference' preferred to 'degradation'; A67, temporary transference to inferior grade, as punishment; A75, arrangements for exemplars of record and instruments. *See* LOCATION AND DISLOCATION; PROMOTION; SUBORDINATE AND SUPERORDINATE; SUSPENSION; TRANSFERENTIAL FUNCTION

TRANSFERENTIAL FUNCTION: IX.5.A4, power of, useful to subordination; 21.A43, minister to ex. in light of decree of dislocation judicatory. *See* SUBORDINATE AND SUPERORDINATE; TRANSFER

TRANSFORMATIVE FUNCTION: IX.4.A51, ex. by ministers collectively in regard to things; A51, defined

TRANSMISSIVE FUNCTION: IX.23.A14, peculation v. embezzlement and ex. of transmissive f. *See* PROCURATIVE FUNCTION

TRANSRECEPTIVE FUNCTION: *See* PROCURATIVE FUNCTION

TRIS-SUBDISTRICTS: *See* SUBDISTRICTS

TRUST: *See* LOCATION AND DISLOCATION; PECULATION

TYRANNY: V.6.A5, and suppression of opposite opinions; VI.25.A51, and liberty of the press in England; 27.A27, 'tyrannical dominion' and non-attendance of deputies due to participation in elicitation process; IX.10.A25, English lord ex. tyranny over distant dependencies; 16.A24n, tyranny and election of directors at India House; 20.A12, secret institutions and tyranny; 25.A43, tyranny of few over many in following precedents; A57, and English practice. *See* DESPOTISM; ENGLISH PRACTICE

UNDERSTANDING: *See* WILL

UNITED STATES OF AMERICA (ANGLO-AMERICAN UNITED STATES): VI.20.A18, and interrupted attendance of leg.; A20, president's message to congress; A21, insolvency laws; 22.A6, term of service of legislators; 25.A9, competition in election of legislators; A43, problems of app. apt. in founding new states; A50, liberty of press; 27.A49, U.S. government v. English government as least corrupt forms; 31.A28–30, lawyer class and securities for app. apt.; VIII.1.A8–10, use of 'president' v. 'prime minister' discussed; 2.A11n, power of president as commander-in-chief; A12, as commander-in-chief, U.S. president not necessarily military man; 3.A6n, U.S. practice and p.m.'s ex. of initiative f. in messages to leg.; IX.3.A16, single-seated executive depts.; A17, power of president over executive dept. heads, absolute; 5.A16, distinctions in diplomatic service; A30, distance between functionaries; A39, A41, grades in military service, expense min.; 15.A37, ultra-remuneration has no place; 26.A20n, and Panopticon plan; A53, offices of president and ministers, how arranged

UTILITY AND INUTILITY: VI.27.A52, inutility of House of Lords; IX.17.A44, intrinsic utility and reason for pecuniary competition; 19.A7, relative utility and ex. of self-suppletive f.

VACANCY IN OFFICE: *See* LOCATION AND DISLOCATION; SELF-SUPPLETIVE FUNCTION; SUBORDINATE AND SUPERORDINATE

VALUE: IX.25.A36, elements of, magnitude, propinquity, and probability

VENALITY: IX.17.A54, competition system does not introduce venality into office; A54, word misapplied to bidding system; A54, venality and corruption, both prevented; A55, virtue of liberality derived from vice of venality in city of London

VENDITIVE FUNCTION: IX.23.A14, peculation and ex. of venditive f. *See* ELIMINATIVE FUNCTION

VEXATION: VI.23.A11, prevention of vexation and deputy's substitute; A19, vexation caused by election of deputy's substitute at end of session; A21, vexation caused by election of substitutes; 27.A17-18, delay, vexation and expense and limits to extraction of evidence by leg.; A28, avoiding delay, vexation, and expense and use of elicitation committees; 31.A28, delay, vexation and expense and common law; VII.6, vexation equal to a tax; IX.20.A9, modes of vexation. *See* DELAY; EXPENSE; GOOD AND EVIL

VISITATIVE FUNCTION: *See* INSPECTIVE FUNCTION

VOTATIVE FUNCTION: IX.24.A2, ministers may not ex. votative f. in leg.

VOTING (VOTATION): VIII.8.A2-4, election of p.m. by leg. given first in secret mode and then in open mode; A5, reaching a majority; A6, secret v. open voting discussed; 11.A6, evil of publicity of secret vote; IX.16.A22, decree of qualification judicatory formed by secret and open modes of voting; A23, method of secret voting, example given; A24, mode of giving in votes; A24n, East India Company practice noted; A25, mode of scrutiny of votes; A25n, practice at Woolwich Academy noted; A25n, possible use of lot where equality; A26, open mode of voting, mode of procedure; A27, performed after secret mode, but before votes made by secret mode are examined; A28-9, votes of quasi-jurymen, secret mode only; A29, as quasi-jurymen serve as instructors, each has interest of highest rank for his pupils; A29n, size of body of candidates prohibits each to judge each other, as is practice at Glasgow University and Hazelwood School; A30, results of both modes of voting published in ranking table at same time; A31, both modes to be guides; A32, provision for experiment and choice among various modes of voting; 26.A8-9, voting and secret suffrage. *See* CONSTITUTIVE AUTHORITY; ELECTION CODE; LEGISLATURE; LOCATION AND DISLOCATION

VOTING DISTRICT(S): *See* SUBDISTRICT(S)

WAR(S): VII.8, war, when justified; IX.7.4th.A31, expenditure on needless wars; 25.A24, war, publicity, and secrecy for extra despatch

WASTE: II.A16n, waste as evil; VII.4, waste and corruption; IX.15.A7, liberality by functionary is waste; A35, and English monarchy; A48, and hereditary titles of honour; 19.A27, rule that superior grade leads to superior emolument, source of waste. *See* CORRUPTION; ENGLISH PRACTICE; GOOD AND EVIL; EXPENSE; STATISTIC FUNCTION

WEALTH: *See* OPULENCE AND INDIGENCE

WILL: VI.1.A9, will v. judgement in deputy's duty to constituents; 23.A12, will actually expressed v. will intended to be expressed in leg.; 24.A18, will, understanding, and influence

WRITTEN INSTRUMENT(S): VI.27.A39-40, legislation enquiry report as written instrument; IX.4.A18, defined; A19, distinguishable as relevant and irrelevant, important and unimportant, interior and exterior; A20, by functionary or non-functionary; A21, persons writing v. persons addressed; A22, instruments created by act of registrative f. addressed to public; A38, written forms prepared for giving expression to mandates and replies; A39, all-comprehensive formulary applicable to judiciary dept.; 7.2nd.A14, called papers; A14, and mimographical mode of registration. *See* LAW OR MANDATE

WRONG: *See* RIGHT AND WRONG

# INDEX OF NAMES

This is an index of names of persons and places appearing in the introduction, text, and notes; the last (whether Bentham's or the editors') are indicated by 'n'. Under Bentham's name only references to his other works are indexed.

Abbot, Charles, 1st Baron Colchester: 17n
Aberdeenshire: 206n
Adam: 119
Adams, John Quincy: xvi & n, xxviiin, xxxv & n
Alcalá: xxxiii
Alembert, Jean le Rond d': 441n
America: 4, 209
Ancona: xx
Anglo-American United States: *See* United States
Anhalt-Zerbst: 378n
Argenson, Marc-René-Maire de Voyer de Paulmy, marquis d': xvn
Argentina: xxxii
Athens: 453n
Augustus, Roman Emperor: 453n
Austria: 25

Barbary States: xvi
Barrington, Sir Jonah: 59n
Bavaria: xl & n
Bembridge, Charles: 359n
Bengal: xlin
Bentham, George: xxviii & n
Bentham, Jeremy
    *Analysis of the Influence of Natural Religion*: xxviii
    'Bentham on Humphreys' Property Code': xxxviiin, xl,159 n, 161n, 162
    *Bentham's Radical Reform Bill*: xix, xxv & n, xxvi, xxx, xxxiii, xliv, 33n, 48n, 58n, 163n
    *The Book of Fallacies*: xxvii & n, 34 & n, 146n
    *Chrestomathia*: xxviii
    *Codification Proposal addressed to All Nations Professing Liberal Opinions*: xii & n, xiii & n, xiv & n, xxxiii

*Declaración o Protesta de Todo individuo de cuerpo legislativo al tómar posesión de su destino*: xxxivn
'Defence of Economy against the late Mr. Burke': 308n
'Defence of Economy against the Right Hon. George Rose': 308n
*Deontology*: 396n
*Elements of the Art of Packing*: 333n
*Equity Dispatch Court Bill*: xxxvi & n, xxxixn, 5n, 38n, 67n, 96n, 99n, 250n
*Equity Dispatch Court Proposal*: xxxixn, 5n
*Extract from the Proposed Constitutional Code*: xxxix, 297n, 304n, 313n, 314n, 321n, 329n, 345n, 362n, 363n, 364n
*Indications Respecting Lord Eldon*: 129n
*An Introduction to the Principles of Morals and Legislation*: 122n
*Jeremy Bentham to his Fellow Citizens of France*: 357n
*Justice and Codification Petitions*: xxxviin
*Leading Principles of a Constitutional Code*: xviii & n, xix & n, xxxiii–xxxiv, 352n
*Lord Brougham Displayed*: xxxviin
*Nomography; or the Art of Inditing Laws*: xlin
*Not Paul but Jesus*: xxviii & n
*Official Aptitude Maximized; Expense Minimized*: xxxix, xli, xlii, 130n, 266n, 297n, 304n, 308n, 313n, 314n, 321n, 329n, 331n, 333n, 334n, 345n, 346n, 347n, 349n, 350n, 351n, 354n, 356n, 361n, 362n, 363n, 364n

Bentham, Jeremy (*cont.*)
Of Laws in General: 378n
Pannomial Fragments: xxxixn, xlin, 188n
Panopticon: 443n
Papers relative to Codification and Public Instruction: xiii & n
Parliamentary Candidate's proposed Declaration of Principles: xliii, 133n, 146n
Plan of Parliamentary Reform:53 & n
Principios que deben servir de guía en la formación de código constitucional para un estado: xxxivn
Principles of Judicial Procedure: xxviin, 38n, 96n, 99n, 250n, 283n, 384n, 389n, 405n, 413n, 424n
Principles of Penal Law: 40n
Propuesta de Código dirigida por J.B. a todas las naciones que profesan opiniones liberales: xxxiiin
Rationale of Judicial Evidence: xxvii & n, xxxvi, 38n, 94n, 99n, 105, 250n, 283n, 437n
The Rationale of Punishment: xxvii & n, 40n
The Rationale of Reward: xxvii & n, 40n
Scotch Reform: 283 & n
A Table of the Springs of Action: 122n, 419
Tactique des Assemblées Législatives: xxxii
Théorie de peines et des récompenses: xxvii & n, 40n
Three Tracts relative to Spanish and Portuguese Affairs: 90n
Traités de législation civile et pénale: xxviiin, xxxi, 40n
Tratados de legislación civil y penal: xxxin
Bentham, Sir Samuel: xv & n, xxviiin, 161n, 234n, 258n, 378n
Bentinck, Lord William Cavendish: xli & n
Berlin: 206n, 335 & n
Bingham, Peregrine, xxvii & n, 34n
Birmingham: 320n
Blackstone, Sir William: xxxviii, xxxix, 100n

Blaquière, Edward: xvi, xvii & n, xviii, xix
Bolivar, Simon: xxxii & n, xxxiii & n, xxxiv & n, xxxix & n
Bowring, Sir John: xi & n, xviii & n, xix, xxiiin
Britain, British, British Isles: 17, 83n, 84n, 126
British Empire: xli, 4, 16
Brougham, Henry Peter, 1st Baron Brougham and Vaux: xxxvi, xxxviin, xl & n
Browne, Arthur: 358n
Buckingham, James Silk: 344n
Buenos Aires: xxxii
Burdett, Sir Francis: xxxin
Burke, Edmund: 358
Byron, George Gordon, 6th Lord Byron: xix, xx & n

Caesar, Julius: 123n
Canning, George: 344n
Catherine II, Empress of Russia: 378 & n
Cavendish Bentinck: See Bentinck
Chadwick, Sir Edwin: xxviii & n
Charles I, King of Great Britain: 85n
Charles II, King of Great Britain: 357
Clarence, William, Duke of: 212 & n
Colls, John Flowerdew: xvn, xxiii, xxviii, xxixn
Colombia: xxxii
Connecticut: 59 & n
Constantine, Roman Emperor: 453n
Constantinople: 321n
Cromwell, Oliver: 85n
Cromwell, Richard: 85n

Del Valle, José: xxxii & n, xxxivn, xli, xliin
D'Ghies, Hassuna: xv & n, xvi
Doane, Richard: xi & n, xiv, xviii, xix & n, xx, xxvn, xxvii, xxix, xlii, xliii, 38n, 96n, 137n, 357n
Dublin, Trinity College: 358n
Dumeril, André Marie Constant: 16n
Dumont, Pierre Étienne Louis: xii & n, xv & n, xxvii, xxviiin, xxxi & n, xxxii, xxxixn
Dundas, Henry, 1st Viscount Melville: 186n, 436n

Edgar, King of England: 17n
Edward III, King of England: 17n
Eldon: *See* Scott
Elgin Burghs: 206n
England, English: xii, xxv, xxxi, xxxvi,
    xliv, 16, 17, 21n, 25, 30n, 36,
    48n, 51, 52, 56, 75, 80, 85, 87,
    99, 103, 104, 107, 121, 130n,
    149, 176, 179, 180, 184, 185,
    193, 194, 210, 211, 212, 213,
    229, 236n, 237n, 258n, 264n,
    283, 288, 290, 293, 305, 333n,
    348, 362n, 397, 398, 410, 411,
    431, 444n
Entzelt, Christoph: 122n
Eve: 119

Felgueiras, João Batista: xin
Forbes, Jonathan: 151n
Fox, Henry, 1st Baron Holland: 359n
France, French: xii, 14, 16, 17, 18,
    25, 444n
Frederick II, King of Prussia: 206 & n

Genoa: 266n
George III, King of Great Britain: 211n,
    212n, 357n, 359
Glasgow University: 319n, 320n
Graham, Sir James: xliin
Greece, Greek: xiii, xvi–xxxi, xxxix &
    n, 72n, 453n
Grey, Charles, 2nd Earl Grey: 182n
Grote, George: xxviii & n
Guatemala: xxxii

Hanover: 182n
Hastings: *See* Rawdon-Hastings
Hazelwood School: 320n, 321n
Herrera, Prospero de: xliin
Herries, J. C.: xln, 5n
Heward, Robert: xlii
Hume, Joseph: 53n
Humphreys, James: xxxviii & n
Huskisson, William: 364 & n

India: xix, xli & n, 126n, 319n, 344n
Ireland: 16, 17, 60n, 444n
Italy: xii, 453n

Jackson, Andrew: xvin, xxviiin, 151n
Jerusalem, New: 3

Johnson, Samuel: xvii

Karamanli, Ali: xvn
Kentucky: 83n
Koe, John Herbert: xii & n
Korais, Adamantios: xxx & n

Lambton, John George, 1st Earl of
    Durham, 344n
Latin America: xii, xxx, xxxi, xxxix,
    xl, xli, 14, 83n
Lawrence, William: 335n
Lincolnshire: 17n
Livadia: 321n
London: xvi, xix, xxviin, xxviiin, xxxiii,
    74, 206, 333n, 356, 444n, 449n
London, Greek Committee: xix
London, University College: xxviiin,
    xxxviiin, xlv
Louis XVI, King of France: 444n
Louisiana, Purchase: 83n
Louriottis, Andreas: xvii & n, xxvi &
    n, xxix
Ludwig, King of Bavaria: xl & n

MacCulloch, John Ramsay: 364 & n
Mahratta, Wars: 319n
Martens, Georg Friedrich von: 205n
Massari, family: 266n
Mavrocordato, Alexander: xvii, xviiin,
    xxvii
Meyer, Johann Jakob: xxxi & n
Mill, James: xii & n, xxvii, xxix, xli
Mill, John Stuart: xxvii & n
Missolonghi: xxn, xxxin
Mitchell, Sir Andrew: 206 & n

Nakos, Stamos: 321n
Napier, Macvey: 364n
Neal, John: xxviii & n, 55n, 515
Necker, Jacques: 358
Negris, Theodore: xxx & n
Nepean, Sir Evan: 443n
Netherlands: xl & n
Newton, Sir Isaac: 266n
North, Frederick, Lord North, 2nd
    Earl of Guilford: 182n, 183n

O'Connell, Daniel: xxxvi, xxxvii & n
Orlandos, John: xviiin, xxvi & n, xxvii,
    xxix

Oxford, Queen's College: 265n

Paccioli, Luca: 266n
Paris: xxx, 234n
Parr, Samuel: xvii & n, xxxn
Parry, William: xx & n
Peel, Sir Robert: xxxvi, xxxviin, xxxixn, xln, 130n, 333n
Peisistratus: 453 & n
Petty, William, 2nd Earl of Shelburne, 1st Marquess of Lansdowne: 182n, 183n
Pitt, William (the Younger): 126n, 436n
Place, Francis: xxviii & n, 53n
Pope, Alexander: 283n
Portugal, Portuguese: xi & n, xii & n, xiii, xvi, xxxi, 4, 25, 83n, 90n
Powell, John: 359n
Prussia: 206 & n
Puigblanch, Antoni: xxxiii, xxxiv & n

Quincy Adams: See Adams

Rallis, Eustratios: 321n
Rammohun Roy: xli & n
Rawdon-Hastings, Francis, 2nd Earl of Moira, 1st Marquess of Hastings: xix
Ricardo, David: 364n
Rickman, John: 17 & n
Rivadavia, Bernadino: xxxii & n
Robinson, Frederick John, Viscount Goderich, 1st Earl of Ripon: 364 & n
Rochford: See Zuylestein
Rockingham: See Watson-Wentworth
Rush, Richard: xxviiin
Russia: 25, 378 & n

Salas, Ramón: xxxi
Santander, Francisco de Paula: xxxii, xli
Say, Jean-Baptiste: xixn, xln
Scandalides, John: xviiin
Schwartz, Pedro: xxxivn
Scotland, Scottish: 16, 17, 18, 31n
Scott, Sir John, 1st Earl of Eldon: 130n
Shelburne: See Petty
Sisyphus: 72 & n

Smith, John Adams: xxviiin
Smith, Richard: xxvii & n, 40n
Spain, Spanish: xii, xiii, xvi, xxxi, xxxiii, 4, 14, 25, 83n, 107, 358n, 444n
Stanhope, Leicester, 5th Earl of Harrington: xix, xx & n, xxiii–xxvii, xxix & n, xxxi & n
Suetonius Tranquillus, Gaius: 123n
Switzerland: xii, 13

Tennessee: 83n
Theodore of Tarsus: 17n
Thompson, Thomas Perronet: xxviii & n
Tripoli: xv & n, xvi
Turks: xvii
Tyrell, John: xliin

United States of America: xii, xvi, xxii, xxv, xxxv, 52, 54 & n, 59, 74 & n, 83 & n, 84n, 87 & n, 107, 124, 148 & n, 149, 151 & n, 153n, 177 & n, 179, 206 & n, 209, 211, 212, 213n, 227n, 306, 444n, 456, 515

Vermont: 83n

Washington, George: 151
Watson-Wentworth, Charles, 2nd Marquess of Rockingham: 182n
Wedgwood, Ralph: 161n
Wellesley, Arthur, 1st Duke of Wellington: xl & n
Willes, Francis: 183n
William I, King of the Netherlands: xl & n
Woolwich Academy: 319n
Wyatt, Charles: 443n
Wyatt, John: 443n

York, Frederick, Duke of: 211 & n
Yorkshire: 17n
Young, James: xxviii & n, xl & n, xlin, 319n
Young, John: 319n

Zuylestein, William Henry, 4th Earl of Rochford: 183n